The Making of American Foreign and Domestic Policy

Essays from the Political Science Quarterly

Edited by **DEMETRIOS CARALEY**
and **MARY ANN EPSTEIN**

Distributed by
DABOR SOCIAL SCIENCE PUBLICATIONS
140 Gazza Blvd. Farmingdale, New York 11735

Introduction © 1978 Demetrios Caraley

Essays © 1975, 1976, 1977, 1978 Academy of Political Science

Library of Congress Cataloging in Publication Data

Main entry under title:

The Making of American foreign and domestic policy.

  Includes index.
  1. United States- -Politics and government- -1945-
Addresses, essays, lectures. 2. United States- -Foreign
relations- -1945-   - -Addresses, essays, lectures.
3. United States- -Economic policy- -1961- Addresses,
essays, lectures. 4. United States- -Social policy- -Ad-
dresses, essays, lectures. I. Caraley, Demetrios. II. Epstein.
Mary Ann. III. Political science quarterly.
JK271.M265   320.9'73'092   78-21152
ISBN 0-89561-070-1

A General Health Publishing Corporation Book

Printed in the United States of America

Acknowledgments

Our most immediate debt is to the authors of this collection of essays, for having originally published them in the *Political Science Quarterly* and for later giving permission to reprint them in this volume.[1] We also want to use this opportunity to record certain more continuing obligations that we feel as editors of *Political Science Quarterly:* to members of the journal's editorial advisory board and other anonymous referees for evaluating article manuscripts; to William V. Farr, the business manager of the Academy of Political Science—*PSQ's* publisher—, for continuing to be available with helpful counsel not only on business matters but on all aspects of the journal's operations; and to Robert H. Connery, the Academy's president, for being a continuing source of support and encouragement.

Demetrios Caraley
Mary Ann Epstein

[1]The essays have been reprinted exactly as they first appeared in the *Political Science Quarterly.* A few biographical summaries have, however, been updated to reflect the authors' current status.

CONTENTS

Introduction

DEMETRIOS CARALEY

The essays in this book focus on the making of American policy, both foreign and domestic. In selecting these essays, it was assumed that determining the content of policies, that is, policy making, is the core of the governing process. It was further assumed that policy making is a "political" process that normally takes place in a context of conflict. The conflict typically involves rival coalitions of government officeholders and private activists who support different and often contradictory policy positions and try to impress their preferences on official decisions. Once conflict develops, the content of public policy is then determined largely by the relative influence of the rival coalitions.

It should be understood that conflict in government policy making is not pathological. For policy making is not akin to some purely analytical exercise like geometry where to any stated problem there is always a single correct solution on which all persons of good will and intelligence must eventually agree. For one thing, the impact of a public policy is never neutral: some people and groups will profit by a policy and others will lose; among those who profit, some will profit more than others, and among those who lose, some will lose more than others. The kinds of gains and losses involved include access to government services and facilities, money, ideological principles, power, physical safety, and public office. Obviously, those who have interests, goals, and values that will be enhanced by a proposed policy support it, just as those who have interests, goals, and values that will be hurt by the same policy oppose it. Of course, not all conflicts over policy stem from mutually exclusive interests, goals, and values among rivals. Many conflicts arise over the choice of means thought to be most effective in promoting goals that are shared. Other conflicts result from differing priorities: even when their goals are shared, policy makers may disagree about the acceptable cost for a given policy. Given that the resources of the federal government are scarce relative to all the policies that officials, interest groups, and members of the general public wish to pursue, the adoption of one policy may mean that the opportunity to adopt some other desired policy is lost. In sum, policy makers and their allies differ in their interests, goals, and values; in their estimates of the efficacy or efficiency of particular means; and in their assignments of priorities to policies that they all may nevertheless desire. Therefore, the process of policy making on important issues is normally conflictive.

I

The conflict over policy is not a shapeless free-for-all in which the combatants can use whatever means they want. Policy-making conflicts are channeled by a constitutional and cultural framework. A central feature of our Constitution is that the legal power to make policy is distributed among many hands. First, policy-making powers are divided between the federal government and the states. Second, such powers are further divided at the federal level among the president and other executive branch officials, the two houses of Congress, and the federal court system capped by the Supreme Court. Finally, some policy-making powers, such as to restrict various civil liberties and civil rights, are reserved to the people. Such restrictions could be imposed by government officials only if the elected representatives of the people, through the constitutional amending process which requires special procedures and extraordinary majorities of approval both at the federal level and by the states, repealed the constitutional protections for civil liberties and civil rights in the Bill of Rights and the Fourteenth Amendment.

In a largely celebratory essay that first appeared during the height of the bicentennial festivities in July 1976, Alpheus Thomas Mason reviews these and other constitutional principles. He praises the Founding Fathers for fashioning government institutions that have protected us from tyranny and have provided for bringing about major policy changes through elections instead of through violent revolution. Basically, the framers believed that tyranny could be prevented by parceling out policy-making powers to separate institutions—the so-called "separation of powers"—and by giving each of those institutions prerogatives to "check and balance" the others. This device was intended to protect both the jurisdiction of the several institutions and the rights of the citizenry.

Thus, the framers established, as John Quincy Adams once put it, not "democracy the most simple"—that is, unqualified majority rule—, but "the most complicated government on the face of the globe." Since none of the original complications has been removed, we still have a set of government institutions in which it is much easier to prevent than it is to adopt new policies. There is no question that this built-in bias against change has thwarted the introduction of many unwise and potentially harmful policies, even when they perhaps enjoyed temporary majority support. And this counterthrust has protected various minorities who have feared that under those policies they would be unjustly oppressed. But by the same token, other policies that might have benefited the general populace have been blocked by minorities which were merely protecting their own special interests.

Robert Dahl is much less satisfied with the principles and values implicit in the American constitutional system and their influence on what he calls "full procedural democracy." Dahl speaks of five basic "commitments" made by the nation at different times, some of which have fostered, but others of which have impeded, the kind of democracy he espouses. Dahl, like Mason, sees the principal commitment of the Founding Fathers not to majoritarian democracy but to a "liberal" constitutional and political order that gave primacy to the protection of individual political and civil liberties. Dahl argues that a commitment to democracy—meaning at the time majority rule of adult white males—was made only at the end of the Jacksonian era, as political participation became widespread and as an agrarian economy predominantly of family farms minimized inequalities in economic resources. The impediments to democracy came from the next three commitments. By the late nineteenth century, America had switched from an economy of privately owned family farms to corporate capitalism based on the privately owned commercial, financial, or industrial corporation. This shift created much greater inequalities in wealth, income, social esteem, and thus gave the privileged groups in the society an ever-greater capacity to use the antimajoritarian policy-making system we have to resist reforms desired by the less resourceful. The fourth historic commitment, according to Dahl, was to have the national government intervene in the economic order of corporate capitalism to the extent necessary to relieve the most acute hardships and injustices it was causing, but without making radical change in the central economic role of private corporations. Yet even this kind of welfare state intervention, which became widely accepted during the Franklin Roosevelt administration's New Deal, spawned impediments to democracy: extensive federal bureaucracies to administer welfare state programs and the development and justification of vastly enhanced presidential power to direct those bureaucracies.

The fifth historical commitment, begun during the later years of the Roosevelt administration, was to a major role for the nation as a world power. The immediate emergency that precipitated that international involvement was World War II. But even after that war was over, the nation maintained what by prewar standards was a vast military establishment. Furthermore, the deployment of this military establishment came more and more under the president's control and enabled him to execute foreign and military policies, some of which did not enjoy congressional or popular support.

Dahl's prescription is to resolve the internal inconsistencies among the five commitments he outlines, primarily by giving the highest priorities to the political ends of liberty, equality, and justice and by studying ways to weaken the powers of the presidency. Still, the dilemma remains: In order to bring about greater equality, the liberty of those whose talents or inherited privileges allow them to become more than equal must be curbed. Similarly, the presidency, despite the excesses of Vietnam and Watergate, has been the chief engine for overcoming the built-in inertia and the antimajoritarian bias of the rest of the policy-making system. Diluting the power of the presidency may reduce not only its capacity to work evil, but also its capacity to promote good.

II

Part II contains essays that depict the various policy-making roles played by leading actors in the system. The president is obviously on center stage as a policy maker: The constitution itself obliges him, and hence gives him the right, to propose legislation in his annual State of the Union message and in additional special messages as he sees fit. The Budget and Accounting Act of 1921 obliges him, and hence again gives him the right, to submit to Congress his annual executive budget, which recommends the size of congressional appropriations for all departments and programs. The president has the power of veto, with which he can block legislative policy of which he disapproves, and the vetoed policy can then become law only if passed again by extraordinary two-thirds majorities in both houses of Congress. The president according to the Constitution must "take care that the laws be faithfully executed," meaning that he is in charge of directing the implementation of policies embedded in congressional legislation. And since much legislation is written in broad, general terms, which must be further defined by executive orders and departmental regulations, he has opportunities to set the details of policies within the limits of the statutory language. The president, with the consent of the Senate, appoints the secretaries, assistant secretaries, and other important, top-level executive officials and thus can place in strategic executive branch positions persons who hold a particular policy view. In addition, and again with the consent of the Senate, the president can make appointments to fill vacancies on the Supreme Court and lesser federal courts and thus place persons with his policy orientation in judicial positions.

In foreign affairs the president and his appointees monopolize all direct negotiations with foreign nations. He and his agents negotiate treaties (which, however, require approval of two-thirds of the Senate to take effect). By sending and withdrawing ambassadors, the president makes policy by determining which foreign governments the United States recognizes.

Finally, the president is by constitutional provision "commander-in-chief" of the armed forces, and thus has extensive opportunities to create situations in which his deployment of military forces will force the nation into a particular foreign policy stance.

The Constitution, nearly two-hundred years worth of Supreme Court decisions, plus provisions of congressional legislation give the president certain irreducible legal powers and also impose some fairly rigid constraints. Between what is required and what is prohibited, each president has had broad leeway to impose his unique personality on the office and to shape it in ways favorable to his particular foreign and domestic policy goals.

James David Barber's essay reviews how personality has powerfully influenced the way particular presidents have defined policy issues, what kinds of facts and views they have seen as relevant to policy decisions, and how they have reacted to crisis. His analysis of the personalities of presidential candidates leads Barber to believe that the general style in which a candidate would conduct his presidency can be predicted, and that the electorate should reject "active-negative" personalities. Barber is severely troubled that despite an abundance of evidence on the public record of Nixon's "active-negative" instability and of what some had defined as his semiparanoid view of opponents as enemies who had to be defeated and destroyed, the Republican leaders nominated him and the American people elected him to the presidency. There, with somewhat better luck and fewer self-destructive acts, Barber thinks Nixon might have turned our system of two-party democratic elections into an American "tyranny."

Doris Kearns' essay is also about the personality of a president—this time Lyndon Johnson's—and how his inner needs for power and control led to immensely constructive legislative accomplishments as a leader in the Senate and as a president who promoted large-scale policies of reform aimed at remedying the conditions of deprived minorities and the poor. Kearns also shows, however, that Johnson's skill in mobilizing congressional majorities through private persuasion, bargaining, and implicit coercion was useless and indeed self-defeating on the foreign policy issues of Vietnam. Whether—if one could have predicted the contradictory nature of Johnson's presidential performance—Johnson should have been supported or opposed is unclear.

The essays by Richard Neustadt and Harrison Wellford deal with another aspect of the presidency, namely, the organization of the Executive Office of the President including the president's immediate White House staff. The organization of presidential staffs reflects both the style and self-perceived needs of each particular president and those staff functions that have become so institutionalized through legislation or custom, that no president feels free to abolish them, such as the budgetary preparation and administrative functions of the Office of Managment and Budget. The main policy issues on staffing have traditionally concerned the size of the White House staff, whether a senior staffer should be designated "chief of staff" through whom all papers and requests for personal appointments flow to the president, and to what extent the president tries to impose his policy initiatives on the operating departments through his White House aides instead of through the cabinet heads of the departments.

According to Neustadt and Wellford, a year after President Carter took office his White House staff remained large by pre-Nixon standards, he had no chief of staff to coordinate or control it for him, he did not wish his staff to override his cabinet heads, and where there was a choice, he preferred informal "ad hoc" mechanisms to formal institutions.

As I have mentioned earlier, presidents may try to impose their policy preferences for proposed legislation or for the implementation of existing law through the heads of the cabinet departments. Traditionally, presidents have made three kinds of cabinet appointees: those who were essentially representatives of the clientele groups served or regulated by their departments and hence had independent political support; those who possessed technical expertise on the substantive policies under the jurisdiction of the department and thus were prone to resist policy demands not in conformity with the prescriptions of their professional specialities; and those who were political generalists without ties to interest groups or technical expertise and hence more likely to be receptive to presidential initiatives in the policy direction of their departments.

Political scientists have generally favored patterns of appointment that enhanced the president's policy control over the operating departments and agencies of the executive branch. Yet Nelson Polsby points out in his essay the dangers of a cabinet weighted heavily with political generalists who lack either a clientele group power base or the intellectual justification of acknowledged expertise to resist presidential policy directives that they feel are wrong. Polsby explains why political generalist cabinet appointments reflect a dangerous notion of policy legitimacy, which is that only the president has the right to set policy for the executive branch and that his election in effect nullifies the policy directives of past presidents and most especially the policy directives contained explicitly in congressional authorizing legislation or in appropriations voted for a department's programs.

Though not the main actor on center stage, Congress clearly plays a supporting role second only to the president in influence over the policy-making process. It is in the "Congress of the United States" that Article I of the Constitution vests "all legislative powers." And those include the power to make policy by law on the laying of taxes, the spending of money for "the common defense and general welfare of the United States," the regulating of commerce, the declaring of war, the raising and supporting of armies and the maintaining of a navy, as well as to make all other laws "which shall be necessary and proper" for carrying into execution the enumerated powers in Article I "and all other powers vested by [the] Constitution in the government of the United States, or in any Department or Office thereof."

In addition, Congress through its committees can conduct investigations into any area of policy it chooses and during hearings on pending legislation or appropriations has plentiful opportunities for directing informal policy "advice" to executive branch officials who are called to testify. The Senate, furthermore, has special powers to refuse consent to presidential appointments and to treaties negotiated by the president and his designees, and in extreme situations, Congress can remove from office, executive branch officials including the president through impeachment by the House and conviction by the Senate.

Although the formal powers vested in Congress potentially should permit it to be equal to the president and perhaps to be even the dominant actor in national policy making, from the 1930s to the early 1970s Congress acquiesced in playing a much less stellar role. This was especially so in foreign policy, military interventions, weapons procurement, intelligence and counterintelligence activities, and impoundments by the president of appropriated funds. In part this diminution of the congressional role in policy making was caused by emergencies such as the great depression, World War II, the emergence of nuclear weapons, and the Korean and Vietnam Wars—all of which appeared to require quick, decisive actions that Congress either did not have the capacity to make or did not want the responsibility for making. In part, however, this trend reflected the overreaching of a string of "imperial" presidents from Franklin Roosevelt to Richard Nixon who, among other things, withheld critically important information from Congress.

Since about 1973, Congress has been reasserting its right to be at least the president's equal in policy making. And indeed, as Harvey Zeidenstein's essay explains, Congress has legislated various provisions that go beyond the simple facilitation of its traditional policy-making role through the passage of general legislation and the appropriation of funds. The most congressionally "imperial" of these provisions allows Congress to use concurrent (two-house) or simple (one-house) resolutions—which do not require the president's signature and are therefore exempt from his veto—to stop the president and other executive branch officers from carrying out specific administrative acts. In the summer of 1978, President Jimmy Carter and Attorney General Griffin Bell announced that they considered most provisions for such "legislative vetoes" of administrative acts uncon-stitutional and did not feel obliged to comply with them, even though they would at times do so "in the spirit of comity." Whether there will have to be a series of presidential–congressional confrontations to settle the issue of legislative vetoes remains to be seen.

Because Congress is a collective body, a majority of the members in each chamber must agree on a policy before the institution as a whole can act. Such agreement does not come about by coincidence when some 218 representatives and 51 senators just happen to prefer the same policy. What creates working majorities is leadership cues. The House and Senate receive these cues from the various committees that consider legislation or appropriations, from the legislative party leaders, from individual members who are considered to be experts on particular issues, and from the president. If all these cues are mutually reinforcing, the voting decision for individual members is simple and agreement is reached quickly. However, when these cues are mutually contradictory, and especially when the situation is compounded by conflicting cues that come from organized interest groups, from heterogeneous constituencies, and from other special sources, the voting decision for individual members is more difficult.

Both my essay and Robert Trice's try to account for voting decisions by weighing the influence of a limited number of general factors that can be measured systematically in quantitative terms. My data show that in 1977, support in both the House and Senate for urban policies that give financial aid to large cities depended much more on a member's party affiliation—contrary to what some policy makers claim—than on the large-city or suburban or rural areas in the member's constituency or state. The data also show that in 1977 the "snowbelt" and "sunbelt" sections emerged as factors that influenced voting on urban policies, especially in the Senate where section was already about as important as party.

Robert Trice's data show that from 1970 to 1973 support in the Senate for aid to Israel was overwhelming. The data also show that whatever the differences that may have existed among the senators, they had little to do with such factors as liberal ideological views, the proportion of Jewish voters in a senator's state, or monetary support in the form of speakers' honoraria from Jewish groups.

Both Trice's data and mine show that it is risky to try to predict the policy positions of individual members of Congress from some small number of seemingly self-evident factors, like the urban nature or the percentage of Jewish voters in their constituencies. The influences that shape the policy positions of members of Congress are numerous and complex, some being conscious and some unconscious. As a result, members of Congress are more open to persuasion through the presentation of facts and logical arguments than they would be if they were closely constrained creatures of their constituencies or their fixed ideological positions.

To have an effect on the real world, most government policies embodied in presidential directives or in legislation must be carried out by career civil servants or "bureaucrats." These are the people who translate policy statements into the concrete acts of performance. And while doing so they have ample opportunities for shaping the details of policies, both in ways that are not inconsistent with the objectives of the original policy makers but also in ways that further their own policy preferences or protect their personal power, prestige, security, or convenience. In short, the career bureaucracy can reshape policies in the name of implementation and when they find policies set at higher levels extremely unpalatable, they can fail to put them into effect simply by dragging their feet. And all of this reshaping of policy can be justified by the career bureaucrats to themselves on the grounds that their years of experience in a particular department give them a much better basis for judging what correct policy should be than the "political short-timers," "birds of passage," or "in-and-outers" that temporarily fill the top policy-making positions in their department.

Hugh Heclo's essay analyzes the ways in which political executives like cabinet secretaries, undersecretaries, and assistant secretaries try to come to terms with their career bureaucrats. Heclo questions the effectiveness of the tough, order-giving approach whereby the political executive simply tries to command the bureaucracy by invoking his superior legal powers. Nor does the executive fare any better, in Heclo's view, by playing the pleasant, "nice-guy" who goes along with whatever policies his bureaucratic subordinates want. What he should do instead is to stimulate "conditionally cooperative behavior." Such conditional cooperation proceeds on the assumption that political executives and career bureaucrats can do some useful things for one another and that the astute political executive should be able to find ways to enlist or "buy" the cooperation of those bureaucrats whose actions and services determine the success or failure of the executive's policy. To the extent that career bureaucrats can resist policy direction from the political executives who are their hierarchical superiors, government policy remains largely insulated from the changing currents of opinion that are registered in presidential and congressional elections.

Robert Steamer's essay reminds us that policy is made not only in the nominally policy-making organs of the national government—the executive branch and Congress—but also in the federal court system, and most importantly in the Supreme Court. Of course Supreme Court justices have no legal powers to promulgate executive orders or legislation that embody general policy decisions but can only decide cases that arise as lawsuits or criminal prosecutions. But cases that are decided by the Supreme Court serve as precedents that alert government policy makers and private citizens to what the legal outcomes would probably be in similar circumstances and thus those precedents shape the conduct of policy-making officials and other governmental employees who want to avoid having their actions or decisions declared illegal or unconstitutional.

Precedents set by the Supreme Court while interpreting provisions of executive orders or legislation can be nullified by the authors of those instruments by changing their language to make it clear that the Court misinterpreted what they had in mind. Precedents set by the Supreme Court while interpreting constitutional provisions, however, are very much more final, since they can be overturned only by subsequent Court decision or by the passage of a constitutional amendment. In reviewing the work of the Burger Court, Steamer analyzes the policy implicit in its pattern of decisions in three important consitutional areas: the degree and kind of liberty citizens are entitled to under the First Amendment; the degree of procedural protections that must be given by the police and trial courts to persons accused of crimes; and the kinds of government classifications or criteria on the granting or denial of benefits or the imposition of regulations that are, like race or national origin, unconstitutionally discriminatory and therefore impermissible.

III

The essays in Parts I and II illuminate the process through which public policy is made at the national level of government. How that process operates is obviously of great intrinsic interest to those directly involved in it and also to students of political science with a keen interest in how influence shapes government policy. But the process does, after all, have only instrumental value since it is the substance of the policies it produces that have various impacts on some 200 million Americans as well as on hundreds of millions of other people who might be advantaged or disadvantaged by foreign policy decisions. Part III contains essays on key aspects of recent foreign policy issues and Part IV contains articles on recent domestic policy.

The dominant foreign policy issue of the postwar period has been the cold war between the United States and the Soviet Union. Broadly speaking, the American foreign policy response has been to maintain unprecedently large military forces capable of delivering nuclear attacks on the Soviet Union and of fighting smaller conventional wars. The United States has also entered into military alliances with a large number of nations that feel or used to feel threatened by the Soviet and sometimes the Chinese Communist regimes, and has actually intervened militarily—in Korea and Vietnam—when our foreign and military policy makers concluded that intervention was necessary for "containing the spread of Communism."

Bruce Russett's contribution deals with the critical foreign policy question of whether Vietnam and the coming of age of a generation that has no adult memory of World War II or the beginnings of the cold war has caused a basic shift in public attitudes away from support of American international involvements. Displaying various kinds of evidence about the attitudes of the mass public and of business elites, Russett finds sharply increased opposition to military spending and to military intervention in aid of other nations and a great erosion in the cold war sense of urgent threat to American security.

The policy implications of this shift in public attitudes are unclear: How constrained by public opinion are the high executive branch officials and legislators who actually make foreign policy and how responsive to it should they be? Will the "lesson" of Vietnam be that military intervention is unjustified when the cost is high, the probability of success slim, and the threat to vital national security interests, low? Or will it be the more unqualified one that military intervention is never justified even if the most vital interests of the nation are at stake? And will neo-isolationism in the United States, if it leads to a withdrawal from the world scene that goes beyond simple reluctance to intervene militarily, help or hinder the search for solutions to the diplomatic problems that beset the Middle East, Africa, and the increasingly tense relations between the northern hemisphere's economic "haves" and the southern hemisphere's "have nots"?

Walter LaFeber's essay reviews the roles of two prominent and powerful secretaries of state—Truman's Dean Acheson and Nixon and Ford's Henry Kissinger—in creating and seeking to maintain the cold war consensus that supported the containment of communism everywhere and at whatever cost, including the subordination of domestic needs and politics to the requirements of an anticommunist foreign policy. Ultimately, Kissinger failed to keep the consensus from eroding in the wake of the failures in Vietnam and given his inability to perceive the impossibility of cultivating congressional and public support for a foreign policy that was having tragically adverse consequences for domestic politics. One of LaFeber's prescriptions is that the post of secretary of state should go—as in the nation's earlier history—to individuals who are themselves powerful domestic political figures and thus would recognize automatically the interrelations between domestic politics and foreign policy.

Whether presidents will appoint secretaries of state who are major political figures in their own right and not mere foreign policy technicians remains an open question. And so remains the question of whether presidents and secretaries of state will be more forthcoming in sharing information about foreign policy issues with Congress and the general public even if they believe that such a wider sharing will give ammunition to opponents of the foreign policies they consider sound and necessary for the nation's security interests. Of course, with the newly legislated congressional requirements that the president or his subordinates provide Congress with various kinds of information about foreign and military policies and intelligence operations, presidents and secretaries of state may have no choice but to be forthcoming.

The essays by Robert Bresler and Robert Gray and by Philip Dyer confront classic East-West, or American plus European vs. Soviet, cold war foreign policy issues. The Bresler and Gray piece examines how the concept of the "bargaining chip" has in the past ten years become embedded in the most serious and complex issues of nuclear arms and disarmament policy. In theory, a bargaining chip is a weapons system that the United States is prepared to downgrade or abandon in exchange for a similar concession from the Soviets and thus, presumably, a bargaining chip serves as a lever for reducing armaments and increasing stability. In fact, however, some very major weapons systems, whose design and production were first announced and justified in bargaining chip terms, became permanent "building blocks" in our strategic arsenal and spurred the Soviets to match our new weapons with improved weapons of their own. Thus bargaining chip strategy served to stimulate rather than curb the arms race.

The basic dilemma is that if research and development and sometimes limited deployment of a weapons system show that it is not a very powerful addition to our arsenal, there is little incentive for the Soviet Union to give anything up in exchange for its curtailment. If, on the other hand, the weapons system is effective and threatening enough to cause the Soviets to want to negotiate for its limitation, the American military establishment, supported by its satellite constellation of weapons manufacturers, may not want to give it up in the interests of arms control and thus forego the added nuclear capacity its widespread deployment would confer.

Philip Dyer's essay deals not with strategic nuclear weapons but with tactical ones—specifically the tactical nuclear weapons deployed by the United States in western Europe for the ostensible purpose of deterring a Soviet invasion. A widespread mindset of American military and foreign policy makers assumes that the Soviets are waiting, ever-ready, for the opportune time to conquer western Europe. The justification most often cited for the deployment of tactical nuclear weapons is that without them, the Soviets could overwhelm NATO quickly and cheaply through their superior conventional forces, given that western Europe has been unwilling to commit the necessary resources to build up conventional forces of NATO to a point of rough equality with those of the Soviets.

Yet Dyer argues that from the Soviet point of view the benefits of a European conquest do not appear large enough to justify the certain costs of having to fight a large-scale conventional war plus the possible costs of a full-scale nuclear exchange with the United States. Even if despite this seemingly unfavorable cost/benefit equation, the Soviets still attempted an invasion of western Europe, would the tactical nuclear weapons help the NATO cause, given that if the United States as part of NATO initiated the use of tactical nuclear weapons, the Soviets would almost certainly use theirs? And would not the use of tactical nuclear weapons wreak as much or more destruction on our NATO allies, in whose territory they would be used, than on the Soviet invaders? Thus is it likely that the United States and NATO would in fact initiate the use of tactical nuclear weapons when faced by the near certainty of Soviet retaliation? Obviously no one knows. But ironically the fall-back argument for positioning tactical nuclear weapons in Europe is precisely the "confusion" or "uncertainty" they create: That is, since the American foreign and military policy makers don't really know whether they would ever use such weapons to repel an invasion, then neither can the Soviets know. Consequently, so the argument goes, that uncertainty in itself creates a deterrent effect.

Many foreign policy analysts would argue that although nuclear exchanges and invasions of western Europe are foreign policy scenarios that are still possible and must be prepared for, the most serious foreign policy threats to the United States in the years immediately ahead are more likely to be encountered elsewhere. The international political order has become much more complex than in the classic cold war years, with the threats more subtle and the solutions more difficult to fashion. Edward Friedland, Paul Seabury, and Aaron Wildavsky examine one of those threats—the power of the OPEC countries to unilaterally set the price of oil for the importing nations of the free world (including our own) and to threaten the destruction of their economies through an oil embargo such as the one imposed during the Yom Kippur War of 1973.

Although oil price increases and embargoes cannot, like a nuclear exchange, bring instant death to hundreds of millions, the adverse consequences are nevertheless severe: an outflow of larger and larger amounts of money from the United States and other oil consumers, rising balance of payments deficits, increased prices, a slowing of economic growth and, overall, a decline of the standard of living of Americans as a result of the upwardly spiralling cost of a raw material basic to our industrial economy. The consequences for our western European and Japanese allies, who are much more heavily dependent on oil imports because they lack our own domestic production capacity, are even more serious. Furthermore, if the United States, when faced with a crisis, wished to take a foreign policy position opposed by OPEC countries—such as in aiding Israel—policy makers would have to consider, at the least, that no western European allies would likely support such a position for fear of an embargo and that, at worst, the United States itself might find its own middle eastern supplies of oil cut off.

What is a realistic foreign policy response? Threaten the oil producing countries with nuclear destruction? Occupy the oil fields with military force? Counterembargo foodstuffs or spare parts for American-made military equipment? Seize OPEC investments in the United States? Or learn to adapt our foreign policies more and more to Arab interests so as to cultivate "reasonable" attitudes among Arab leaders on the size of oil price increases and to avoid the threat of embargoes even at the cost of abandoning our traditional democratic ally, Israel?

U.S. foreign policy toward African nations also must respond to vague, complex, and rapidly changing situations that offer no clear prescriptions for maximizing American interests. American foreign policy makers concerned about Africa seem to be guided by the following desires: to continue the flow of African raw materials to the United States, especially the rare minerals found principally in South Africa, Southeast Africa, and Rhodesia; to keep the Soviet Union from establishing military bases in Africa that might threaten the movement either of American missile-launching submarines in the Indian Ocean poised to strike at the Soviet Union or of oil tankers carrying middle east oil to the United States or its western European allies; and to maintain or enhance the general influence of the United States in various African nations vis à vis that of the Soviet Union or Soviet allies like Cuba.

William Foltz's analysis of U.S. foreign policy toward southern Africa asks how well- or ill-based such aspirations are—especially the assumption that the United States has any "vital" strategic or economic interests in that part of Africa. He also questions the ideologically based belief found among conservative governmental policy makers, businessmen, and military officers that whatever American interests there are in southern Africa would be best served by helping white-dominated governments last as long as possible.

Though many of the new and complicated foreign policy problems that confront the United States are posed by the Third World, not all of them are. For example, American foreign policy makers and the American public may still be willing to help western European nations defend themselves against a Soviet attempt to impose communist regimes upon them through invasion and military force. But what kind of policy would be supported if through the ballot box western European communist parties became partners in governing parliamentary coalitions and later, having won majority status, actually became the freely elected communist governments of, say, some of our NATO allies?

Alan Platt and Robert Leonardi examine the record of U.S. foreign policy toward the post-World War II Italian Socialist and Communist parties. They trace both the overt and covert activities engaged in by the United States to strengthen the centrist Italian parties and to keep the Italian left—both Socialist and Communist—from playing a role in the government. These efforts were not successful, however. In 1963 the Socialists became part of a center-left governing coalition, and then in 1978 so did the Communists. The question still remains open, however, of what the U.S. foreign policy response would be if the Communists became the dominant partner in the coalition and assumed control of key cabinet posts dealing with the military, foreign affairs, and police.

IV

The essays in Part IV discuss various issues in American domestic policy. The most important problems that such policy has had to deal with in the past ten to fifteen years include poverty, inadequate schools and health care, crime, racial discrimination, and urban decay and "white flight" from fiscally distressed central cities to the suburbs. The Johnson administration Great Society programs from 1964 to 1968 attempted to deal aggressively with all of these problems. During those years the rate of economic growth was high and the rate of inflation and unemployment, low, so the national government through its progressive tax system was able to generate large additional revenues each year at steady or even declining tax rates. Consequently the Great Society programs could be funded "painlessly," without damaging the purchasing power or standard of living of the great bulk of taxpayers who were not beneficiaries of those programs. Eventually, however, the Vietnam war began to require such large expenditures that the painless availability of new resources for domestic programs ended.

The 1970s have, on the whole, been a time of slow economic growth, large-scale unemployment, and rapid inflation—all of which cause expenditures for poverty and unemployment policies to climb faster than new revenues generated by a slowly growing national economy. Expenditures for policies aimed at helping the "have-nots" or the "haves-less" are therefore seen much more by the "haves-more" as coming at their direct expense, and at a time when inflation is already hurting even the "haves" by eroding their purchasing power and threatening their standard of living. There has been, consequently, strong incentive to find that social welfare programs don't really work—"you can't solve problems by throwing dollars at them"—so as to justify the reduction of efforts by the federal government to help the poor and otherwise deprived minorities.

Sar Levitan and Robert Taggart review and evaluate the Johnson administration Great Society programs. One important question the authors raise is the proper standard for judging policies and programs successful enough to warrant their continuation: If the standard requires that immense and extremely complicated social problems be solved completely—not merely reduced—and at low monetary cost with no negative "spillovers," almost every policy or program would have to be branded a failure. Yet if the standard, as Levitan and Taggart suggest, were more compassionate and assumed success unless failure were demonstrated, policy makers would almost never reduce or end a program. To prove failure means, presumably, to show that a policy or program has had no beneficial effect at all, and that becomes nearly impossible especially in such indeterminate areas as teaching children to read, ending the cycle of welfare dependency, or reducing crime rates.

Given the voters', revolt against paying larger and larger shares of their income in taxes for government programs from which they benefit marginally if at all, large-scale new resources for ambitious domestic programs are likely to remain scarce. For one thing, as Everett Ladd explains, the working and lower-middle classes no longer see themselves as the beneficiaries that they once were in New Deal days and therefore no longer give their broad-based support to "liberal," expanded government spending programs. Instead, these groups have become "conservative": they are now anxious to protect their enhanced status in society and feel that they achieved it by hard work. Since their hold on that status is still only tenuous, they are unwilling to share more of their income to benefit people they consider to be "undeserving." The black working and lower-middle classes are exceptions in still being willing to support liberal spending programs. And in another switch from New Deal days, individuals of the higher socioeconomic classes who were then antispending conservatives have now become more liberal than their lower socioeconomic cohorts. The crucial question for domestic policy makers is how, in a society in which majorities determine elections, support can be generated for expensive ameliorative programs that are almost by definition aimed to help only particular minorities?

Problems of poverty and physical decay are found everywhere in the United States. But in the past two decades, these problems have become disproportionately concentrated and thus most visible in larger and older cities, particularly those in the northeastern-mid western "snowbelt." This decline resulted in part from the vicious circle in which the cities were caught: In city after city thousands of jobs and tens of thousands of middle-and upper-income families, which had required no welfare services from city government but had substantial taxpaying ability, fled to the suburbs, thus eroding the city tax base. City governments were therefore forced to raise tax rates to meet the steadily increasing costs of providing housekeeping services, antipoverty programs, and crime protection efforts, all of which were only holding their own or, more typically, deteriorating. And because the quality of services was declining, large cities became still less attractive to middle- and upper-income families and to businesses which saw themselves paying constantly higher taxes for what they perceived to be a moribund physical, social, and economic environment. Thus the incentive was continuously strengthened for even more of this "low service-demanding" and "higher-taxpaying" part of the population and economy to move to the suburbs, causing a further erosion of the city tax base, which in turn made necessary still higher tax rates just to pay for the declining quality of services being received, and which provide still stronger incentive for exodus to the suburbs, etc., etc..

· One response of city governments was to try to shift the funding of as much of their expenditures as possible from taxes to grants from their states and the federal government, both of whose tax-gathering powers are wider-reaching and extend to the suburbs. In fiscal 1975-76, large cities with populations of 300,000 or more received, on average, 17 percent of their expenditures in the form of grants and shared taxes from their states and 18 percent from the federal government. The state grants were earmarked mostly for schools, welfare, and highways, while the federal grants extended to urban renewal and model cities, public housing, food stamps, public service jobs, countercyclical assistance, and general revenue-sharing. Until 1972 it was the policy of the national government that essentially all federal grants were "categorical," meaning that the funds granted had to be used for specific purposes or "categories" specified in the enacting legislation. As part of the New Federalism of the Nixon administration, some sets of related categorical grants were replaced by "block grants" that ostensibly gave recipient city governments greater leeway to expend funds for purposes that they considered to have the highest priority.

The essay by Richard Nathan and his Brookings Institution colleagues traces the changing patterns of beneficiaries resulting from the consolidation in 1974 of seven categorical grant programs including urban renewal, model cities, water and sewer facilities, and neighborhood facilities into a combined block grant program for "community development." The authors find that as a result of the change there were regional shifts in the amounts of funds received by city governments, shifts in influence over how to expend the funds from federal and local officials with specialized responsibilities to "generalist" city officials, and shifts within metropolitan areas in the proportion of funds going to central cities as opposed to suburban jurisdictions.

Whether to have categorical or block delivery systems for federal grants is not a matter of technical administrative detail, but has very large policy implications: Categorical grants allow federal officials, who have had over the years a better record of responsiveness to slum minorities than city governments, to target funds to those minorities regardless of the city government's priorities, since the funds cannot be used for any other purpose. Block grants, on the other hand, while allowing city officials greater freedom to impose their own priorities, also allow funds to go for projects favored by the city's more dominant groups rather than those favored by its deprived minorities. Thus the key policy question for the national government is whether it is more important to give local majorities and city officials greater say in the spending of federal grant funds under the principle of decentralization or to tie the hands of local majorities and city officials so that funds raised by the federal government will be spent for purposes and projects to which the federal government attaches the highest priorities.

One other way for city governments to straddle the gap between required expenditures and insufficient tax revenues, besides raising tax rates or getting larger grants, is to borrow. Borrowing money for the construction of capital projects like bridges and municipal buildings through the sale of bonds is a long-accepted local government practice. The rationale is that these bulky items are too expensive to pay off in a single year and that in any event, the cost should be spread over all the generations of users of the project. Selling long-term bonds and then repaying portions each year over, say, a twenty or thirty year period accomplishes this spreading of cost. City governments also borrow money through the sale of tax- and revenue-anticipation notes to cover short-term cash flow shortages caused by the fact that required expenditures by the city government are constant during the year while tax collections and grants come in only at intervals. When the anticipated taxes and other revenues come in, the short-term notes are supposed to be paid off.

The essay by the Congressional Budget Office shows how the largest city in the nation—New York—brought itself to the brink of bankruptcy:

Excessive borrowing eventually led to the refusal of the financial community in 1975 to buy any more New York City bonds or notes; thus the city could borrow no more for any purpose. Measured by various economic indicators, New York City was far from being the city with the most severe underlying fiscal problems. Fiscal crisis overtook New York because the city used various "gimmicks" to borrow on a very grand scale and for more than commonly accepted purposes. First, city officials hid in the capital budget so they could cover even those items through borrowing, items that are normally considered operating expenses to be paid out of current revenues. Second, substantial amounts of taxes and other revenues that the city "anticipated" to justify the sale of short-term notes never materialized and indeed were known not to have a realistic chance of materializing. Consequently, the short-term notes could not be paid off by incoming revenues, but had to be "rolled over," meaning that more money had to be borrowed just to pay off the short-term notes coming due. Finally, the balanced budget that New York State requires city governments to adopt was increasingly "balanced" by New York City only on paper, by overestimating revenues and underestimating expenditures; when the inevitable year-end deficit occured, it too had to be covered through short-term borrowing and without any realistic expectation of how to pay off that borrowing except through further borrowing roll-overs. By 1975 New York City had to raise some $5.3 billion in short-term notes to cover that year's and previous years' operating deficits that it had no prospect of repaying except through further borrowing.

Were New York City officials wrong to resort to so much borrowing to finance its operations? For a long time, city and state officials as well as the financial community praised the various gimmicks that were astutely thought up to spare New York City from cutting back on services. The use of the gimmicks was rationalized by predictions that the national and municipal economies would eventually improve, thus stimulating city sale and income tax receipts to bring in surpluses to pay off past debts, and that when a new Democratic national administration took office, the flow of federal grants to the city would be greatly enlarged. Neither of those predictions or, more accurately, wishes came true, yet the gimmicks staved off retrenchment for about three years. Was the trade-off implicit in New York City fiscal policy making a good one, or should fiscal solvency have been given the highest priority and services cut immediately, to bring expenditures into line with the city's reduced means? And was it sound policy for the national government to bail out New York City by extending it seasonal loans when the city could not borrow anywhere else?

The movement of families out of central cities to the suburbs has had racial overtones, namely, that the families that had the money to move to the suburbs have been disproportionately white, and the families left behind for lack of money and because of discriminatory renting and selling practices have been heavily black. This racially-skewed, principally "white flight" to suburbia coupled with large-scale black migration from the rural South to central cities where the growth rate of the black population was already high, has since the 1950s caused the populations of the older and larger cities to shift steadily to a larger and larger black proportion. The 1970 census revealed black majorities in three large cities—Washington, D. C., Newark, and Atlanta—and ten other large cities—Baltimore, Chicago, Cleveland, Detroit, Memphis, New Orleans, Philadelphia, St. Louis, Birmingham, and Oakland—where blacks constituted between 30 and 50 percent of the population.

The causes for the massive white flight from large central cities are multi-faceted and complex. In the 1950s the stimulus was primarily the pull of the availability in suburbia of roomier housing, yards with trees, and newer schools. Furthermore, widespread rising affluence coupled with the availability of government guaranteed long-term mortgages plus the almost universal ownership of private automobiles and the construction of new express highways made suburbanization feasible for large numbers. In the 1960s and 1970s these pulls were supplemented by pushes from central cities experiencing deteriorating services with rising taxes, accelerated blight, mounting crime rates, and the steady expansion of black neighborhoods into previously all-white areas. Some policy makers believe that an additional powerful push came from court-ordered or voluntarily-initiated long-distance busing of schoolchildren from their neighborhoods to other neighborhoods. The purpose of such busing was to end single-race schools that reflected single-race neighborhood housing patterns or had been caused by explicit or covert de facto segregation in the school system.

One notable student of school desegregation, James Coleman, has argued in recent years that school busing not only provides an extra push for white flight to the suburbs but that it is also counterproductive even for its explicit purpose of school desegregation, for it reduces the total number of white children that remain in central city schools below what is necessary simply in numerical terms to achieve racial balance. Yet Christine Rossell's essay, which reports data from an extensive analysis of the consequences of deseg-regation of 113 cities, finds that school desegregation had little or nothing to do with accelerating white flight. Whether school desegregation through long-distance busing hastens white flight and in very recent years even black, upper-middle-class flight is an important question for national policy makers who would foster racially mixed cities with racially mixed schools. But there is very little clear, unambiguous evidence to guide the policy makers in promoting their objectives.

It is the policy of many suburban government jurisdictions to keep out subsidized, low-rent housing and apartments and to zone exclusively for single-family houses on large lots. This policy inflates the cost of suburban housing far beyond what low-income families can afford. Some white low-income families are also excluded from the suburbs by this restrictive policy, but given that poor families are, proportionately, more often black than white, exclusionary zoning in the suburbs works most severely against blacks.

Michael Danielson's essay explains why there is so little political support within suburban jurisdictions for change in land-use policies so as to make it easier for less affluent families to move there. The poor, and especially the black poor, are seen as the cause of many of the problems that trouble central cities: crime, the burdens of welfare financing, neighborhood deterioration, and the imbalance between taxpaying inability and the need for services and other benefits. Is it plausible to expect that as long as land-use and zoning controls are in the hands of scores to hundreds of local government jurisdictions that form each suburban ring, these jurisdictions will change policies to ones they see as causing them direct economic detriment? Or is it possible only for the national government to devise a policy providing such incentives and sanctions that might, if accepted, create a society where real choices would be open to all for living in revitalized central cities or in suburbs, without regard to the color of their skin or the size of their income?

PART I

The Constitutional and
Cultural Context of
American Policy Making

America's Political Heritage: Revolution and Free Government— A Bicentennial Tribute

ALPHEUS THOMAS MASON

In 1974, two years before the bicentennial of America's birth as a nation, free government experienced a crisis comparable only to the Civil War. Thoughtful Americans gravely wondered whether there would be anything to celebrate in 1976. Confronted with unprecedented betrayals, the institutions of free government—press, Congress, and courts—responded. Without loss of a drop of blood, America ousted from the highest office in the land a rebellious conspirator to obstruct justice.[1] To rid themselves of Britain's tyrannical rule, the colonies resorted to revolution. Thanks to the Founding Fathers' constitutional handiwork that was not necessary on the eve of America's bicentennial.

No happenstance, this timely tribute to the resilience of eighteenth-century institutions was the result of careful planning. James Madison, "Father of the Constitution," boasted that the American people "accomplished a revolution which has no parallel in the annals of human society. They reared the fabrics of government which have no models on the face of the globe. They formed the de-

---

[1] There are remarkable parallels between 1776 and the constitutional crisis of 1974, striking similarities between the charges Jefferson leveled against King George III in the Declaration of Independence and the Articles of Impeachment the House Judiciary Committee voted against President Nixon. Both were charged with obstructing "the administration of justice." Jefferson portrayed King George as the rebel. On March 28, 1975, Federal District Court Judge Noel Fox labeled President Nixon a "putative rebel leader," conducting "an insurrection and rebellion against constitutional government itself . . ." [*Murphy* v. *Ford*, 390 F. Supp. (1975), 1372–1373].

ALPHEUS THOMAS MASON is McCormick Professor of Jurisprudence Emeritus at Princeton University and currently is visiting professor at Claremont Men's College. He is best known for his biographies of Supreme Court Justices Brandeis, Stone, and Taft and is also the author of *Free Government in the Making* and *The Supreme Court from Taft to Warren*.

sign of a great Confederacy which it is incumbent on their successors to improve and perpetuate."[2]

Madison's unqualified acclaim seems parochial, self-serving, even more so when one takes into account the fact that these exalted pronouncements were published in a newspaper article, circulated during the heated campaign to win support for the proposed Constitution. Ratification was uncertain; America's constitutional future was clouded in doubt. Circumstances put a high premium on hyperbole. How do Madison's lofty claims measure up in the light of nearly two centuries of history?

REVOLUTION WITHOUT PARALLEL

Nowadays few words are bandied about more freely than revolution. For most it evokes images of violence, disruption, and anarchy. Yet the right of revolution, historically and logically, has high claim as the focus of America's bicentennial. How can Americans denigrate contemporary models and celebrate 1776? In his classic formulation, Jefferson made revolution seem glorious, noble, Heaven sent.

> We hold these truths to be self-evident, that all men are created equal, that they are endowed by their Creator with certain unalienable rights. That among these are Life, Liberty and the Pursuit of Happiness. That to secure these rights, Governments are instituted among men, deriving their just powers from the consent of the governed. That whenever any Form of government becomes destructive of those ends, it is the Right of the People to alter or to abolish it, and institute a new Government, laying its foundations on such principles and organizing its powers in such form, as to them shall seem most likely to effect their safety and happiness.[3]

The Declaration of Independence is our national birth certificate. Our first state constitutions, some of them prefaced with the Declaration, denounced the doctrine of nonresistance against arbitrary power and oppression as "absurd, slavish, and destructive of the good of mankind."[4] Lincoln called the people's "*right* to rise up, and shake off the existing government, and form a new one that suits them better—a most sacred right—a right, which we hope and believe, is to liberate the world."[5] In 1953, Arthur Schlesinger, Sr., listing Amer-

---

[2] Benjamin F. Wright (ed.), *The Federalist*, (Cambridge, Mass., 1916), no. 14, pp. 154–155. Quotations are from this edition.

[3] See Julian P. Boyd, *The Declaration of Independence: The Evolution of the Text as Shown in Facsimiles of Various Drafts by Its Author, Thomas Jefferson* (Princeton, N. J., 1945); W. S. Howell, "The Declaration of Independence and Eighteenth Century Logic," *William and Mary Quarterly*, 18, no. 4 (October 1961), 463–484; Carl Becker, *The Declaration of Independence: A Study in the History of Political Ideas* (New York, 1948).

[4] Maryland constitution, Article 6. Fifteen states have, at one time or another, specifically endorsed the right of people to "alter, reform or abolish" the existing form of government. For a listing, see Justice Douglas, dissenting in *Scales v. United States*, 367 U.S. 203 (1961), 278.

[5] Roy P. Basler (ed.), *The Collected Works of Abraham Lincoln* (New Brunswick, N. J., 1953), Vol. 1, pp. 138–139.

ica's ten contributions to civilization, accorded top rank to the right of revolution.[6] At no time in our history could we reasonably or gracefully turn our backs on it. Nor can we do so in 1976.

"If there be a principle," James Madison commented in 1793, "that ought not to be queried within the United States, it is that every Nation has a right to abolish an old government and establish a new one. . . . It is the only lawful tenure by which the United States hold their existence as a Nation."[7] "It is in vain," Madison wrote in *Federalist*, No. 41, "to oppose constitutional barriers to the impulse of self-preservation. It is worse than in vain, because it plants in the constitution itself necessary usurpations of power, every precedent of which is a germ of unnecessary and multiplied repetitions." Although not always in agreement with his *Federalist* collaborator, Alexander Hamilton called revolution "an original right of self-defense, paramount to all positive government."[8]

The right of revolution has an honorable heritage. In immortalizing it, Jefferson drew ideas and phraseology from John Locke's *Two Treatises of Government*. Locke had proclaimed: "Should either the executive or the legislative, when they have got power in their hands, design, or go about to enslave or destroy them, the people have no other remedy than this, as in all other cases when they have no judge on earth, but to appeal to Heaven"[9]—apparently a euphemism for revolution.

A staunch conservative, Locke held that the "end of civil society is civil peace." Wary of its disruptive possibilities, he argued that rebellion is not likely to occur. With both ruler and ruled in mind, he suggests that "the properest way to prevent the evil is to show them the danger and injustice of it who are under the greatest temptation to run into it." Rulers would be more inclined to remain on good behavior, and the people, aware of the consequences, would be willing to suffer "slips of human frailty" until evils became insufferable. Thus, for Locke, revolution seems not so much a right to be asserted as a recipe for its avoidance.

Locke's constitutionalism is marked by the absence of any worldly authority for resolving conflicts between unabashedly tyrannical government and palpable grievances:

> Who shall be Judge whether the Legislative act contrary to their Trust? To this I reply, The People shall be Judge. . . . But this cannot mean that there is no judge

[6] Arthur M. Schlesinger, "Our Ten Contributions to Civilization," *The Atlantic*, March 1959, pp. 65–69.

[7] G. Hunt (ed.), *The Writings of James Madison* (New York, 1906), p. 164.

[8] *The Federalist*, No. 28.

[9] John Locke, *Two Treatises of Government*, Peter Laslett (ed.) (New York, 1966). This and subsequent excerpts are from the Laslett edition.

At certain points, Locke uses "rebellion" and "revolution" interchangeably; at others, these terms seem distinguishable.

The interpretation of Locke presented here owes much to N. C. Phillips, "Political Philosophy and Political Fact: The Evidence of John Locke," in *Liberty and Learning: Essays in Honor of Sir James Hight* (Christchurch, 1950).

at all. For where there is no Judicature on Earth to decide controversies amongst Men, *God* in Heaven is *Judge.*

Omission of a common power over all in Locke's system seems the more extraordinary in light of the fact that under his theory men left the state of nature and entered civil society to enjoy the advantage of such an arbiter.[10] Yet for individuals and minorities in his civil society, the "Appeal to Heaven" would seem to be an empty declamation:

> The right of resisting, even Manifest Acts of Tyranny, will not suddenly, or on slight occasion, disturb the Government. For if they reach no further than some private Mens rights, though they have a right to defend themselves, and to recover by force what by unlawful force is taken from them; yet the right to do so, will not easily engage them in a contest, wherein they are sure to perish.

Belying Locke's expectations, the American colonies rebelled. Against incalculable odds, they invoked force against force. Locke's *Second Treatise of Government* justified their Appeal to Heaven: "The use of force without authority always puts him that uses it into a State of War, as the aggressor, and renders him liable to be treated accordingly." Ironically, the rationale Locke used to uphold the supremacy of Parliament, Jefferson asserted to repudiate it.

Locke's theory had been working itself into the minds of the colonists long before 1776. The real revolution being, as John Adams said, "in the minds and hearts of the people," it was "effected before the War commenced."[11] Furthermore, as we shall see, the revolution continued after the war ended.

In the prerevolutionary controversy, lawyers and law-minded leaders played a prominent role. Arguing their case against Britain in constitutional terms, the colonists deplored denial of representation, rejected parliamentary supremacy and proclaimed a theory of higher law which, though advocated in England by the eminent Lord Coke, was never sanctioned in the mother country. In denouncing the infamous Writs of Assistance, James Otis, challenging the supremacy of Parliament, claimed for the executive courts power to declare "the act of a whole Parliament void."[12]

The constitutional argument ended ultimately in an irreconcilable impasse. Parliament asserted its supremacy; in rebuttal, the colonies asserted their own. Want of a common power over all, as in Locke's *Two Treatises*, to resolve conflicting claims, led to the most forbidding of all political monsters—*imperium in imperio*—many sovereigns in the same community.

Inspired, finally, by the vision of "a great country, populous, and mighty" (Franklin's language), even the lawyers shifted ground, deepening the base of their grievances. "To what purpose," James Otis asked, "is it, to base the col-

---

[10] "To avoid this State of War [due to want of a common power over all] is the great *reason of Mens putting themselves into society,* and quitting the State of Nature."

[11] John Adams to Hezekiah Niles, February 13, 1818. Quoted in Richard J. Hooker (ed.), *The American Revolution: The Search for Meaning* (New York, 1970), p. 9.

[12] James Otis, *The Rights of the British Colonies,* 1764. Quoted in A. T. Mason, *Free Government in the Making* (New York, 1965), p. 98.

onists' argument on the cases of Manchester and Sheffield? If those, now so considerable places are not represented, they ought to be."[13] This moral approach became the fundamental premise of the call for revolution and independence.

As formulated in the Declaration of Independence, the right of revolution, a moral rather than a legal or constitutional imperative, was both conservative and radical. Jefferson's animating purpose, like Locke's, was conservative. The colonists revolted, not so much to initiate a completely new order as to reestablish British rights and liberties on this side of the Atlantic.[14] We have taken up arms, the Continental Congress explained, July 6, 1775, "in defense of the freedom that is our birthright, and which we ever enjoyed til the late violation of it."[15]

Edmund Burke, symbol of conservatism, warmly endorsed the American revolution, and harshly denounced the French. The French began inauspiciously, he commented, "by despising everything that belonged to them."[16] The Americans, on the other hand, exhibited unswerving devotion to liberty according to British ideas and experience. Parliament, not the colonies, exercised power contrary to the British Constitution.

America never had a revolution comparable to the upheavals in France and Russia. The revolution of 1776 did not wipe the constitutional slate clean. In the modern European sense of the word, the momentous step taken in 1776 was hardly a revolution at all.[17] Tocqueville noted "the great advantage of the Americans." They arrived at a condition of liberty without rejecting their inherited principles.[18]

The Declaration of Independence is also radical. It sanctioned the belief, extreme even by present-day standards, that all men, regardless of race, color, or creed, are endowed by their Creator with certain unalienable birthrights. Endorsed is the potentially subversive doctrine that just governments can safely rest on reason and consent rather than on fear and coercion.

"Fear, the foundation of most governments," John Adams wrote in 1776, "is so sordid and brutal a passion, and renders men in whose breasts it predomi-

---

[13] Quoted in Carl Becker, *Declaration of Independence* (New York, 1933), p. 133.

[14] Carl N. Degler, "The American Past: An Unexpected Obstacle in Foreign Affairs," *American Scholar*, Spring 1963, p. 193.

[15] Ibid.

"America sought not a revolution; she yielded to it, compelled by necessity, not because she wished to extort a better condition than she had before enjoyed, but because she wished to avert a worse one prepared for her." Frederick Gentz, *The French and American Revolutions Compared*, translated by John Quincy Adams (Chicago, 1955), p. 56.

[16] Edmund Burke, *Reflections on the French Revolution* (Maynard's English Classic Series), p. 18.

[17] Daniel Boorstin, *The Genius of American Politics* (Chicago, 1953), p. 68. For various interpretations of the American Revolution and the massive scholarship relating to it, see George Athan Billias (ed.), *The American Revolution: How Revolutionary Was It?* (New York, 1965); Jack Greene, *The Reappraisal of the American Revolution in Recent Historical Literature* (Washington, D. C., 1967).

[18] Alexis de Tocqueville, *Democracy in America*, F. Bowen (ed.) Vol. 2 (1873), p. 123.

nates so stupid and miserable, Americans will not be likely to approve of any political institution which is founded on it."[19] Although "the capacity of mankind for self-government" had yet to be demonstrated, Madison singled out this "honorable determination" as the motivating force in "all our political experiments."[20]

Reason is among the most fragile, the most uncertain ingredients in the lexicon of statecraft. When rationalism was in its heyday, a contemporary of the Founding Fathers, Dr. Samuel Johnson, cautioned in *Rasselas:* "Of the uncertainties in our present state, the most dreadful and alarming is the uncertain continuance of reason." Small wonder Jefferson called the decision of 1776 "the bold and doubtful election we then made for our country."[21] "Experience must be our only guide," John Dickinson cautioned the Philadelphia Convention delegates in 1787. "Reason may mislead us."[22] Not until our own time, barring the Civil War, has this country experienced in full measure the precarious dimensions of the epochal decision of 1776.

Henry Steele Commager declares that the Declaration of Independence is more subversive than the *Communist Manifesto.*[23] Marx's apocalyptic vision precludes further revolution.[24] For Jefferson it is a continuing political phenom-

---

[19] *Thoughts on Government,* 1776. C. F. Adams (ed.), *The Works of John Adams,* Vol. 4 (Boston, 1851), pp. 193–200. Reprinted in Mason, *Free Government in the Making,* p. 144.

[20] *The Federalist,* No. 39.

[21] Jefferson to R. C. Weightman, June 16, 1826. Quoted in Mason, *Free Government in the Making,* p. 371.

[22] Max Farrand (ed.), *The Records of the Federal Convention of 1787,* Vol. 2 (New Haven, Conn., 1911), p. 278.

[23] "No other nation has had a revolutionary history so long or so comprehensive, and perhaps no other has a record that was, in the eyes of the world, so deeply subversive as ours." Henry Steele Commager, *U.S. Congress. Senate Hearings before the Committee on Foreign Relations.* 90th Cong., 1st Sess., February 20, 1967, p. 11.

Justice Holmes, recognizing free government's potentially subversive aspect, declared: "If in the long run the beliefs expressed in proletarian dictatorship are destined to be accepted by the dominant forces of the community, the only meaning of free speech is that they should be given their chance and have their way." Dissenting in *Gitlow* v. *New York,* 268 U.S. 652 (1929), 673.

[24] In a remarkable letter to Karl Marx, two years before the *Communist Manifesto* was published, the French socialist, P. J. Proudhon, pleaded unsuccessfully with Marx to make the proletarian revolution self-consistent.

Dear Mr. Marx:

> Let us seek together, if you wish, the laws of society, the manner in which these laws are realized, the process by which we shall succeed in discovering them; but, for God's sake, after having demolished all the *a priori* dogmatisms do not let us in our turn dream of indoctrinating the people; let us not fall into the same contradiction as your countrymen, Martin Luther, who after having overthrown Catholic Theology, began at once with the help of excommunications and anathemas, to found a Protestant Theology. . . . I applaud with all my heart your thought of bringing to light all opinions; let us carry on a good and loyal polemic; let us give the world the example of a learned and far-sighted tolerance but let us not, because we are at the head of a movement, make ourselves the leaders of a new intolerance, let us not pose as the Apostles of a new religion, even if it is the religion of logic

enon, as inescapable as it is desirable. With reference to Shays' rebellion in Massachusetts, he exclaimed: "God forbid we should be twenty years without such a rebellion. . . ."[25] Commager suggests that "ardent conservatives who fear revolution everywhere might logically start by banning the Declaration from schools and textbooks."

Jefferson's rationalization of revolution includes negative and positive aspects. It asserts the natural right of people to alter or abolish tyrannical government, and affirms their right to establish a new government more in keeping with their safety and happiness. Thus the Declaration of Independence and the Constitution are parts of one consistent whole.[26] For both, liberty and justice were the animating principles. The negative phase, elimination of arbitrary power, was relatively easy; establishing a free government was far more difficult. "The generation which commences a revolution," Jefferson noted, "rarely completes it."[27]

Our revolutionary fathers were dissenters; we are the descendants of dissenters. Unlike some of the modern breed, they did not proclaim the rottenness of their entire heritage, and urge its destruction, root and branch. After throwing off the British yoke, the victorious revolutionaries knew that a more difficult task lay ahead—that of building a constitutional order in which man's destructive impulses could be brought within the framework of civility, rationality, and law. If the American revolution had been merely destructive, dislodgment of lawless government, it would not have been justified. If "the precious blood of thousands" had been spilt, Madison declared, so that "the government of the individual states . . . might enjoy a certain extent of power . . . ," it would not have been worthwhile. The only justification for revolution was the replacement of Britain's tyrannical rule with a government capable of advancing "the real welfare of the great body of the people."[28]

By 1783, the revolutionaries of 1776 were triumphant. The American states had achieved independence not only from Great Britain, but also from each other. One problem was solved only to create another. In the sense of want of a common power over all, the states, after 1776, were in a Lockean state of nature. Because separation from Britain would place states, like Locke's individuals in his imaginary precivil society, in a position of independence with respect to each other, Loyalists Daniel Leonard and Samuel Seabury resisted revolution.

---

and reason. Let us gather together and encourage all protests, let us condemn all exclusiveness . . . let us never regard a question as exhausted. On this condition, I will gladly enter into your association: Otherwise, No!

Correspondence de P. J. Proudhon, Vol. 2 (Paris, 1875), pp. 198–202. Also in P. J. Proudhon, *Confessions d'un révolutionnaire* (Paris, 1929), pp. 434–435. Also in *Dissent*, Winter 1958.

[25] To W. S. Smith, November 15, 1787. Julian Boyd (ed.), *The Papers of Thomas Jefferson*, Vol. 12 (Princeton, N. J., 1955), p. 356.

[26] See B. F. Wright, *Consensus and Continuity, 1776–1787* (New York, 1958).

[27] P. L. Ford (ed.), *The Works of Thomas Jefferson* (New York and London, 1904–1905), Vol. 10, p. 269.

[28] *The Federalist*, No. 45.

"Two supreme or independent powers cannot exist in the same state," Leonard warned. "It would be what is called *imperium in imperio*, the height of political absurdity."[29] Although a forerunner of independence, John Adams, anticipating the conditions that made American political life so critical in the 1780s, declared: "Two supreme and independent authorities cannot exist in the same state any more than two supreme beings in one universe."[30]

By declaring that "each state retains its sovereignty, freedom and independence" the Articles of Confederation created precisely the political absurdity Leonard and Adams had foreseen and condemned. "They still seem to cherish with blind devotion," Hamilton commented derisively, "the political monster of an *imperium in imperio*."[31] Enforcement difficulties arose from the fact that the Articles operated on states in their corporate capacity instead of on individuals. Deploring gross inadequacies, John Quincy Adams observed:

> The work of the founders of our independence was but half done. For these United States, they had formed no *Constitution*. Instead of resorting to the source of all constituted power [the people], they had wasted their time, their talents, . . . in erecting and roofing and buttressing a frail and temporary shed when they should raise the marble palace of the people, to shelter the Nation from the storm.[32]

Yet the Articles performed invaluable service. The Confederation Congress waged war, made peace, and kept alive the idea of Union when it was at its lowest ebb. In 1783, the war was over, the Revolution unfinished.

"There is nothing more common," Dr. Benjamin Rush declared in 1787, "than to confound the terms of the *American Revolution* with those of the *late American War*. The American war is over; but this is far from being the case with the American Revolution. On the contrary, nothing but the first act of that great drama is closed. It remains yet to establish and perfect new forms of government." Underscoring his sense of urgency, Dr. Rush appealed to "Patriots of 1774, 1775, 1776—heroes of 1778, 1779, 1780. Come forward! Your country demands your services! The Revolution is not *OVER*."[33]

Dr. Rush's call was heeded. In 1787, delegates from the various states (not including Rhode Island) assembled in Independence Hall, Philadelphia, the

---

[29] Daniel Leonard, *Massachusettensis*, Letters Addressed to the Inhabitants of the Province of Massachusetts Bay, 1775. Quoted in Mason, *Free Government in the Making*, p. 119.

[30] Quoted in ibid, p. 125.
Foreshadowing America's "critical period" of the 1780s, loyalist Samuel Seabury wrote: "If we should succeed in depriving Great Britain of the power of regulating our trade, the colonies will probably be soon at variance with each other. Their commercial interests will interfere; there will be no supreme power to interpose, and discord and animosity must ensue." Ibid., p. 118.

[31] *The Federalist*, No. 15.

[32] John Quincy Adams, *The Jubilee of the Constitution* (1839), pp. 17–18.
See E. S. Corwin, "The Progress of Constitutional Theory Between the Declaration of Independence and the Meeting of the Philadelphia Convention," *American Historical Review*, 30 (1925), 511–536.

[33] H. Niles, *Principles and Acts of the Revolution* (1876), pp. 234, 236.

same place where eleven years earlier, the Declaration of Independence had been signed. In 1776 reason and consent had been solemnly proclaimed as viable foundations of government. In 1787, these supports were subjected to a severe test. Hamilton posed the crucial issue: Could political communities called states, through "reflection and choice" be transformed into "a union under one government"?[34]

The Constitution, like the Declaration of Independence, highlights the role of reason in statecraft. The Convention began auspiciously, Jefferson commented, "by assembling the wise men, instead of the armies."[35] America, he said, "set the world an example of the formulation of political institutions by reason alone without bloodshed."[36] James Wilson boasted,

> America now exhibits to the world a gentle, a peaceful, a voluntary, and deliberate transition from one constitution of government to another. In other parts of the world, the idea of revolutions in government is connected with the ideas of wars and all the calamities attendant on wars. But happy experience teaches us to view such revolutions in a very different light: to consider them as progressive steps in improving the knowledge of government, and increasing the happiness of society and mankind.[37]

A century later, John W. Burgess denounced the Constitutional Convention as counterrevolutionary, designed to turn back the democratic tide unleashed in 1776. "What they [the Convention delegates] actually did, stripped of all fiction and verbiage," Burgess wrote in 1890, "was to assume constituent powers, ordain a constitution of government and of liberty, and demand the *plebiscite* thereon, over the heads of all existing legally organized powers. Had Julius [Caesar] or Napoleon committed these acts, they would have been pronounced coup d'état."[38]

Burgess' indictment seems extreme. The Convention continued the revolution Jefferson adumbrated in 1776. It was, however, revolutionary both technically and substantively. In mandating that the document be ratified by nine rather than all the state conventions, it violated a provision in the Articles of Confederation which required unanimity. The Constitution was revolutionary, as Madison conceded, in deriving all authority not from states but from people. Confessing irregularities, Madison explained that these proceeded from "an irresistible conviction of the absurdity of subjecting the fate of twelve states to the perversion or corruption of a thirteenth." In the end, he grounded his justification in the right of revolution, in "the great principle of self-preservation," in

---

34 *The Federalist*, No. 1.

35 To David Humphreys, March 17, 1789. Ford, *Works of Thomas Jefferson*, Vol. 5, p. 470.

36 To Edward Rutledge, July 18, 1788. Boyd, *Papers of Thomas Jefferson*, Vol. 13, p. 378.

37 Jonathan Elliot (ed.), *The Debates of the Several State Constitutional Conventions on the Adoption of the Federal Constitution*, Vol. 2 (Washington, 1836), p. 406.

38 John W. Burgess, *Political Science and Comparative Constitutional Law*, Vol. 1 (Boston, 1890), p. 105.

the "transcendent and precious right of the people to abolish or alter their government as to them shall seem most likely to effect their safety and happiness."[39]

The right of revolution, a legitimatizing concept in 1776, remained so in 1787. "Supreme, absolute, and uncontrollable authority *remains* with the people," James Wilson declared on December 4, 1787. "I recollect no constitution founded on this principle: but we have witnessed the improvement, and enjoy the happiness, of seeing it carried into practice. The great and penetrating mind of *Locke* seems to be the only one that pointed towards even the theory of this great truth."[40]

FREE GOVERNMENT IN THE MAKING

Since revolution was, as Madison recognized, "the only lawful tenure by which the United States hold their existence as a Nation," it was incumbent on the Founding Fathers to institutionalize, legitimize, and domesticate it—bring it within the four corners of the Constitution—to fill the yawning hiatus in Locke's constitutional system.

Louis Hartz declares that Locke "dominates American thought as no thinker anywhere dominates the political thought of a nation."[41] Jefferson's appraisal was less categorical. For him "Locke's little book on government is perfect so far as it goes."[42] Jefferson's quarrel with Locke concerned "practice" rather than "theory." In 1787, as in 1776, *Two Treatises of Government* was an arsenal of ideas. On the institutional side, it was of limited usefulness. Apart from the basic notion that all just governments derive their power from the consent of the governed, the functioning of America's political institutions differs as fundamentally from Locke's as it does from the British system today. Locke's concern for liberty and property is reflected in his stress on natural law and natural rights. But his constitutionalism boils down to political limits on government —those imposed at election time, plus the faith that rulers and ruled alike would be guided by considerations of justice and common sense. The idea of a constitution limiting and superintending the operations of government forms no serious part of Locke's system. It has been said that Locke was "unreasonable only in his faith in reason."[43]

The artless "Appeal to Heaven" posed a challenge for our Constitution mak-

---

[39] *The Federalist*, No. 40.

[40] Elliot, *The Debates*, Vol. 2, p. 426.

[41] Louis Hartz, *The Liberal Tradition in America* (New York, 1955), p. 140.

[42] Jefferson to Thomas Mann Randolph, Jr., May 30, 1790. Boyd, *Papers of Thomas Jefferson*, Vol. 16, p. 449.

[43] Phillips, "Political Philosophy and Political Fact."

The shades of John Locke have not vanished from the councils of the judiciary. See the illuminating colloquy between Justices Douglas and Frankfurter in *Perez* v. *Brownell*, 356 U.S. 603 (1958), 622, and *Kingsley Pictures Corp.* v. *Regents of New York*, 360 U.S. 648 (1960), 699. Quoted in A. T. Mason, *The Supreme Court: Palladium of Freedom* (Ann Arbor, Mich., 1962), p. 7.

ers. Needed were terrestrial procedures and forums that would reduce the occasions for revolution to the minimum. Madison articulated the crucial question: How could "the mild and salutary *coercion* of *magistracy*" be substituted for "the destructive *coercion* of the sword"?[44]

As Madison envisaged it, the problem was twofold: to enable government to control the governed and oblige government to control itself. Dependence on the people was recognized as the "primary control," but experience demonstrated the need for "auxiliary precautions."[45]

The Constitution's framers were inspired by profound suspicion of any and all power holders. "The truth is," Madison remarked, "all men having power ought to be mistrusted." Jefferson concurred: "It would be a dangerous delusion were a confidence in the men of our choice to silence our fears for the safety of our rights: Confidence is everywhere the parent of despotism—free government is founded in jealousy, and not in confidence."[46]

Trying experience under the Articles of Confederation and the new state constitutions had brought democracy into question, including its primary tenet, majority rule. Disillusioned by the actual working of these hastily constructed institutions, the delegates convened at Philadelphia in 1787 realized that "the temple of tyranny has two doors"—monarchy and democracy. One had been bolted by proper restraints, the other left open, thus exposing society to "the effects of our own ignorance and licentiousness."[47] Both history and experience made democracy suspect. "Remember," John Adams warned, "democracy never lasts long. It soon wastes, exhausts, and murders itself. There never was a democracy yet that did not commit suicide."[48]

What the framers established was not "democracy the most simple" but "the most complicated government on the face of the globe."[49] They called their creation *free government*. More easily described than defined, it involves a complexus of controls designed to temper together into one consistent work the sometimes opposite, sometimes complementary, elements of liberty and restraint.[50] Madison stated the Founding Fathers' objective in *Federalist*, No. 37: "To combine the requisite stability and energy in government with inviolable

---

[44] *The Federalist*, No. 20.

[45] Ibid., No. 51.

[46] Quoted in Mason, *Free Government in the Making*, p. 371.

[47] Dr. Benjamin Rush, "Address to the People of the United States, 1787," in Niles, *Principles and Acts of the Revolution*, p. 234.

[48] Adams, *Works of John Adams*, Vol. 6, p. 484. See R. R. Palmer, "Notes on the Use of the Word 'Democracy,' 1789–1799," *Political Science Quarterly*, 68 (1953), 203–226.

[49] Adams, *Jubilee of the Constitution*, p. 115.

"If there be any truth . . . , it is that in proportion as a government is free, it must be complicated. Simplicity belongs to those only where one will governs all, . . . where few arrangements are required because no checks to power are allowed. . . ." Joseph Story, *Miscellaneous Writings*, W. W. Story (ed.) (Boston, 1853), p. 619.

[50] For James Wilson's definition of free government, see Elliot, *The Debates*, Vol. 2, p. 484. In his *Reflections on the French Revolution*, p. 121, Burke, with certain qualifications, underscored essential aspects of the system.

attention to liberty and the republican form." This goal could be achieved only by a constitutional arrangement setting interest against interest, ambition against ambition, power against power.

"In questions of power," Jefferson admonished, "let no more be heard of confidence in man [power holder], but bind him down from mischief by the chains of the Constitution."[51] Besides the right of revolution, these constitutional shackles include government under law, separation of powers, federalism, the Bill of Rights, and judicial review.

Government under Law

Locke's legislature, though avowedly supreme, was supposed to keep within the bounds set by natural law as well as "promulgated established law." But these limitations, like the right of revolution, were parchment barriers. The American Constitution makes the idea of higher law a truly operative principle. Madison cited "the distinction, so well understood in America, but little understood in any other country, . . . between a constitution established by the people and unalterable by government and a law established by government and alterable by government." He noted that: "Even in Britain where the principles of political and civil liberty have been most discussed, it is maintained that the authority of the parliament is transcendent and uncontrollable."[52] Not so in America.

"Superiority of the Constitution," James Wilson declared, means "control in *act*, as well as right." "To control the power, and conduct of legislatures, by an over-ruling constitution," Wilson told the Pennsylvania ratifying convention, "was an improvement in the science and practice of government reserved for the American states."[53] For Oliver Ellsworth, third chief justice of the United States, the Philadelphia Convention's signal achievement was the substitution of "coercion of law" for the "coercion of arms."

For the first time in history two levels of law were recognized and put into practical effect: the higher law of the Constitution, which the people alone could make and unmake; and statutory law, to be made and unmade within limits imposed by the Constitution. Locke had hinted at this idea, as had Lord Coke. It had been broached in the early 1760s by James Otis and others on this side of the Atlantic. But in not one state, following independence, did a constituent assembly meet and establish a new government. None of the new constitutions was an act of constituent power, in accord with the idea Jefferson adumbrated in the Declaration of Independence.

"There was never any sovereign government in America,"[54] Woodrow Wil-

---

[51] Resolutions relating to the Alien and Sedition Laws, 1798. Ford, *Works of Thomas Jefferson*, Vol. 8, p. 475.

[52] *The Federalist*, No. 53.

[53] Elliot, *The Debates*, Vol. 2, p. 406.

[54] W. Wilson, *Constitutional Government in the United States* (New York, 1907), p. 146.

son said. Government under law was not a new idea. Aristotle, universal wise man of all time, had anticipated it. Among others, he had the idea. Article 6, paragraph 2, embodies this concept. To be recognized and accepted as "the supreme law of the land," the laws of the United States and of the states must be passed "in pursuance of" the Constitution.

Separation of Powers

No man, no government official, high or low, can escape the Constitution's limitations. Written restrictions, though important, do not suffice. "You may cover whole skins of parchment with limitations," John Randolph said, "but power alone can limit power."[55]

By 1787, experience had demonstrated that the primary control—"dependence on the people," the ballot—was not enough. Noting that "the science of politics," since 1776, had "received great improvement," Hamilton listed as "wholly new discoveries the regular distribution of power into distinct departments of government, the introduction of legislative balances and checks; the institution of courts composed of judges holding their offices during good behavior, the representation of people in the legislature by deputies of their own election."[56]

A mutually checking arrangement governs the legislative branch. The Senate acts as an "impediment against improper acts of legislation" in the House of Representatives and vice versa. The president's veto provides a barrier against oppressive legislation by both Houses. Though often restrained from engaging in "unjustifiable pursuits" by "apprehension of congressional censure," the president is also subject to impeachment. Hamilton proudly pointed to this provision as a vast improvement over the British system where "the person of the King is sacred and inviolable." He is "amenable to no constitutional tribunal, no punishment without involving the crisis of a national revolution."[57] America runs no such risk. The president may be impeached and removed from office and thereafter be liable to prosecution and punishment in the ordinary courts of law. Hamilton praised the provision for impeachment (until 1974 considered more or less moribund) as substituting "the mild magistracy of the law for the terrible weapon of the sword."

In support of this realistic approach, the framers invoked Montesquieu's *Spirit of the Laws* and his key to liberty—separation of powers. "Every man invested with power," the French nobleman had written, "is apt to abuse it. . . . There can be no liberty where the legislative and executive powers are united in the same person or body of magistrates."[58] For Madison, "no principle" was of "greater intrinsic value." Subscribing to it, he wrote:

[55] W. C. Bruce, *John Randolph of Roanoke*, Vol. 2 (New York, 1922), p. 211.
[56] *The Federalist*, No. 9.
[57] Ibid., No. 69.
[58] Montesquieu, *Spirit of Laws*. Quoted in Mason, *Free Government in the Making*, p. 45.

The great security against a gradual concentration of the several powers in the same department consists in giving to those who administer each department the necessary means and personal motives to resist encroachments of the others. The provision for defense must in this, as in all other cases, be commensurate to the danger of attack. Ambition must be made to counteract ambition, . . . supplying by opposite and rival interests the defect of better motives.

Separation of powers is a misnomer. The Constitution separates organs of government; it fuses functions and powers. Montesquieu's principle, Madison explained, does not mean that various departments ought to have "no partial agency or no control over the acts of each other." The three departments must be "connected and blended." Otherwise the "degree of separation which the maxim requires, as essential to free government, can never in practice be duly maintained." This "sacred maxim of free government" is "subverted" where "the *whole* power of one department is exercised by the same hands which possess the *whole* power of another department."[59]

Montesquieu's "political truth," sanctioned with "the authority of countless patrons of liberty" (Madison's words), was incorporated in the Constitution. The idea was not new. America institutionalized it.

Federalism

Federalism, America's nearest approach to a unique creation, is another device for obliging government to control itself. It is a dual system in which two authorities, nation and states, govern the same territory and the same people, each supreme in its own sphere, neither supreme within the sphere of the other. Just as the states would naturally resent encroachments by national authority, so the central government would protect the people from the tyranny of their own state governments. Citing the provision of the Constitution which guarantees each state a republican form of government, Madison echoes a Lockean refrain: "existence of a right to intervene will generally prevent the necessity of exerting it."[60] But there is always the possibility that encroachments may be carried so far as to provoke an "Appeal to Heaven." Anticipating this eventuality, Hamilton wrote:

> The State legislatures, who will be not only vigilant but suspicious and jealous guardians of the rights of the citizens against encroachments from the federal government, will constantly have their attention awake to the conduct of the national rulers, and will be ready enough, if anything improper appears, to sound the alarm of the people, and not only to be the voice, but if necessary, the *Arm* of their discontent.[61]

Hamilton faced up to the possibility of violent conflict, but played it down,

---

[59] *The Federalist*, Nos. 47 and 48.
[60] Ibid., No. 43.
[61] Ibid., No. 26.

arguing that countervailing forces alone would suffice to preclude resort to force: "The extreme hazard of provoking the resentments of the state governments, and a conviction of the utility and necessity of local administrations for local purposes, would be a complete barrier against oppressive use of such a power."

In light of profound concern among antifederalists, Madison and Hamilton's reassurances, even then, must have seemed strained. Yet Hamilton bore down on the point: "It may safely be received as an axiom of our political system, that the State governments will, in all possible contingencies, afford complete security against invasions of public liberty by the national authority."[62] The Civil War tragically belied these confident expectations.

Bill of Rights

As the Constitution came from the hands of the framers, the powers of the national government were enumerated but not defined. Without specification or definition, other powers were reserved to the states or to the people. The Constitution was drafted, submitted to state conventions, and ratified without a Bill of Rights. While the states pondered ratification, Jefferson urged specific restraints on national authority. Arguing that "a bill of rights is what the people are entitled to against every government on earth," he insisted that natural rights "should not be refused or rest on inference."[63]

Alexander Hamilton and James Wilson demurred. Both contended that a bill of rights was unnecessary. Why make exceptions to power not granted? "In a government of enumerated powers," Wilson declared, "such a measure would not only be unnecessary, but preposterous and dangerous." For Hamilton, bills of rights "would sound much better in a treatise on ethics than in a constitution of government."[64]

Thanks to Jefferson, these arguments did not prevail. Insisting on curbs over and beyond structural checks, he advocated "binding up the several branches of the government by certain laws, which when they transgress their acts become nullities." This would "render unnecessary an appeal to the people, or in other words a rebellion on every infraction of their rights."[65] When a reluctant James Madison[66] yielded to Jefferson's plea for a bill of rights and deduced supporting reasons, Jefferson singled out the argument of "great weight" for him—the legal check it puts in the hands of the judiciary.[67]

Once again, America owed a heavy debt to the past. The idea of natural rights

[62] Ibid., No. 28.

[63] Jefferson to Madison, December 20, 1787. Quoted in Mason, *Free Government in the Making*, p. 319.

[64] *The Federalist*, No. 84. For Wilson's negative views on a bill of rights, see Elliot, *The Debates*, Vol. 2, p. 408ff.

[65] Quoted in Mason, *Free Government in the Making*, p. 168.

[66] Mason, *The Supreme Court*, p. 51.

[67] Said Jefferson: "In the arguments in favor of a declaration of rights, you omit one which

was not new. It came to America most directly from Locke. These fundamental maxims of a free society gained no greater moral sanction by incorporation in our basic law, but individuals and minorities could thereafter look to courts for their protection. Rights, formerly natural, became civil.

Judicial Review

For peaceful resolution of controversies, whether among the three branches of the national government or between the central authority and the states, Hamilton and Madison, and the Founding Fathers generally, relied on the Supreme Court. "One court of supreme and final jurisdiction," Hamilton observed, is "a proposition . . . not likely to be contested." In a flash of remarkable foresight, he suggested that discharge of its responsibilities would "have more influence upon the character of our governments than but few may imagine."[68] Madison considered judicial review helpful in warding off conditions that might lead to rebellion. "Some such tribunal is clearly essential," he declared, "to prevent an appeal to the sword, and a dissolution of the compact; and that it ought to be established under the general, rather than under the local governments is a position not likely to be combated."[69]

It was not to be supposed, Hamilton observed, "that the Constitution could intend to enable the representatives of the people to substitute their *will* to that of their constituents." Accordingly, courts "were designed to be an intermediate body between the people and the legislature, in order, among other things to keep the latter within the limits assigned to their authority."[70]

John Marshall, destined as fourth chief justice of the United States to enforce Hamilton's ideas as the law of the land, had envisioned judicial review as an alternative to revolution. "What is the service or purpose of a judiciary," he inquired in the Virginia Ratifying Convention, "but to execute the laws in a peaceful, orderly manner, without shedding blood, or creating a contest, or availing yourselves of force? . . . To what quarter will you look for protection from an infringement on the constitution, if you will not give the power to the judiciary? There is no other body that can afford such a protection."[71]

---

has great weight with me, the legal check which it puts into the hands of the Judiciary." Jefferson to Madison, March 15, 1789. Boyd, *Papers of Thomas Jefferson*, Vol. 12, p. 659.

[68] *The Federalist*, No. 81.

[69] Ibid., No. 39.

[70] Ibid., No. 78.

[71] Elliot, *The Debates*, Vol. 3, p. 503.

"A fear of popular majorities lies at the very basis of the whole system of judicial review, and indeed our entire constitutional system." E. S. Corwin, "The Supreme Court and the Fourteenth Amendment," *Michigan Law Review*, 7 (1909), 643, 670. Charles Evans Hughes expressed the same idea: "We protect the fundamental rights of minorities, in order to save democratic government from destroying itself by the excess of its own power." Hughes, *Proceedings in Commemoration of the 150th Anniversary of the First Congress*, H. R. Doc. No. 212, 76th Cong., 1st Sess. (1939), p. 32.

Judicial review is the most conspicuous weapon in the arsenal of devices for substituting "the mild magistracy of the law" for "the terrible weapon of Force." Not expressly authorized by the Constitution, an auxiliary of all other "auxiliary precautions," it was taken for granted in 1787 and for nearly a century thereafter. For the framers of the Constitution, judicial review rested "upon certain general principles [government under law, separation of powers, federalism, Bill of Rights] which in their estimation made specific provisions for it unnecessary."[72] Not until after 1890 when judicial *review* became judicial *supremacy* did the legitimacy of judicial review become a topic for scholarly research.

Distrust of government in all its branches and at all levels is free government's dominant characteristic. Courts are the only apparent exception. "No one says anything against judges," Edmund Randolph commented in the Virginia Ratifying Convention.[73] "Were I to select a power which might be given with confidence," Madison observed in the same forum, "it would be judicial power."[74] As a member of the first Congress, Madison, introducing the Bill of Rights amendments, declared that courts would be "an impenetrable bulwark against every assumption of power in the Legislative or Executive."[75] Jefferson, later Chief Justice Marshall's archcritic, initially believed that the courts, "if rendered independent . . . merit confidence for their learning and integrity."[76]

But the judiciary, like other organs of government, is limited and sometimes the target of distrust. From Justice Stone, a knowledgeable and sophisticated jurist, comes one of the most astonishing comments in the annals of the Supreme Court. In an otherwise trenchant dissenting opinion, he wrote: "While unconstitutional exercise of power by the executive and legislative branches of the government is subject to judicial restraint, the only check upon our own exercise of power is our own sense of self-restraint."[77] There are, in fact, various restraints on the judiciary, formal and informal, including impeachment and threat of court-packing. When its restraining power affects vital issues of the day as under Jefferson, Lincoln, the two Roosevelts, and Lyndon Johnson, the Supreme Court falls under criticism and control as defying the all-important element in our constitutional tradition—distrust of power as such.

On occasion, the Supreme Court as an alternative to Locke's "Appeal to Heaven" has been disappointing. In 1857, a sharply divided Court outlawed the Missouri Compromise[78] and thus helped to precipitate the Civil War. In the late 1960s and early 1970s, several unsuccessful efforts were made to test the constitutionality of the Vietnam war. Justices Douglas and Stewart protested

---

[72] E. S. Corwin, *The Doctrine of Judicial Review* (Princeton, N. J., 1914), p. 17.

[73] Elliot, *The Debates*, Vol. 3, p. 208.

[74] Ibid., p. 487.

[75] *Annals of Cong.* [1789–90], Vol. 1, pp. 432, 439.

[76] Jefferson to Madison, March 15, 1789. Quoted in Mason, *Free Government in the Making*, p. 323.

[77] Justice Stone, dissenting in *United States* v. *Butler*, 297 U.S. 1 (1936), 79.

[78] *Dred Scott* v. *Sanford*, 19 How. (1857), 393.

the Court's denial of certiorari in a case which might have dealt with the president's power to wage an undeclared war. Three soldiers had rejected duty in Vietnam, contending that the war was illegal and immoral. Said Justice Stewart: "These are large and deeply troubling questions. . . . We cannot make these problems go away simply by refusing to hear the case of three obscure Army privates. I intimate not even tentative views upon any of these matters, but I think the Court should squarely face them by granting certiorari and setting this case for argument."[79] In 1970, Massachusetts went to extraordinary lengths to obtain a judicial ruling on a war neither initially authorized nor subsequently ratified by Congress, except by the Tonkin Gulf Resolution. Proceeding as *parens patriae*, the state passed a law designed to protect its citizens from forced participation in combat or support of combat troops in Vietnam. Acting under this statute, Massachusetts sought leave to file a bill of complaint against Secretary of Defense Laird in the Supreme Court's original jurisdiction. Against the objections of Justices Douglas, Harlan, and Stewart, the Supreme Court denied the motion.[80]

Deeply disturbed, Justice Douglas expressed his concern in *Points of Rebellion*, published in 1970. No longer responsive to human needs, government had become, he argued, "a police state in which all dissent is suppressed or rapidly controlled." Drawing a dramatic parallel with 1776, Douglas concluded: "George III was the symbol against which our Founders made a revolution now considered bright and glorious. . . . We must realize that today's Establishment is the new George III. Whether it will continue to adhere to its tactics [of suppression], we do not know. If it does, the redress, honored in tradition, is also revolution."

RIGHT OF REVOLUTION INSTITUTIONALIZED

Neither the Declaration of Independence nor the Constitution was designed to end the revolutionary cycle. The "exercise of an original right of the people," "a very great exertion not frequently to be repeated" (Chief Justice Marshall called it),[81] the Constitution was "intended to endure and to be adapted to the various crises in human affairs."[82] American constitutionalism can be fairly viewed as a series of limited revolutions. Besides the doubleheader, 1776 and 1787, there is the "Revolution of 1800," so labeled by Jefferson himself. It was "not effected by the sword," he observed, "but by the rational and peaceful instrument of reform, the suffrage of the people."[83] Other revolutions followed:

[79] *Mora* v. *McNamara*, 389 U.S. 934 (1967), 935.
[80] *Massachusetts* v. *Laird*, 400 U.S. 886 (1970).
[81] *Marbury* v. *Madison*, 1 Cranch 137 (1803), 176.
[82] *McCulloch* v. *Maryland*, 4 Wheat. 316 (1819), 415.
[83] To Spencer Roane, September 16, 1819. Ford, *Works of Thomas Jefferson*, Vol. 12, p. 136. Quoted in Harris Mirkin, "Judicial Review, Jury Review and Right of Revolution against Despotism," *Polity*, 9 no. 1 (Fall 1973), 39.

the Jacksonian revolution, the constitutional revolution of the 1890s, when judicial *review* became judicial *supremacy*, the Roosevelt revolution, the Warren Court revolution.[84]

For James Iredell of North Carolina, "one of the greatest beauties of the American system was revolution by Amendment. Without it, the people would have to bring about amendments more or less by civil war."[85] Recognizing the inevitability of social and economic transformations, sometimes of revolutionary dimensions, Madison declared in *Federalist*, No. 41: "A system of government, meant for duration, ought to contemplate these revolutions, and be able to accommodate itself to them." With one exception—the Civil War—all occurred without violence, within the bounds of law.

The *Federalist*'s authors did not close their eyes to the possibility of "mortal feuds," "conflagrations through a whole nation," which "no government can either avoid or control."[86] "It is a sufficient recommendation of the federal Constitution," Madison argued, "that it diminished the risk of a calamity, for which no possible constitution can provide a cure."[87]

The Constitution demonstrates the power of reason in statecraft. The Civil War proved its limitations. By 1860, it became clear that the framers' most significant creation—federalism—carried within it an irreconcilable ambiguity. Madison had fashioned federalism's blueprint six weeks before the Philadelphia Convention assembled. Anticipating, on April 8, 1787, that "some leading propositions would be expected from Virginia," he wrote Governor Edmund Randolph:

> I hold it for a fundamental point, that an individual independence of the States is utterly irreconcilable with the idea of an aggregate sovereignty. I think, at the same time, that a consolidation of the States into one simple republic is not less unattainable than it would be inexpedient. Let it be tried, then, whether any *middle ground* can be taken, which will at once support a *due supremacy* of the national authority, and leave in force the local authorities so far as they can be *subordinately useful*.[88]

An architect would hesitate to begin construction of a house with drawings so imprecise as Madison carried to the Constitutional Convention. But the delegates were in Philadelphia not to build a house but to erect a federal system of government—union without unity. Their handiwork, though in close accord with the Madisonian model, proved inadequate.

---

[84] Functioning as a "revolutionary committee," the Court may have "saved the country from a far more dangerous and disorderly change." Adolf Berle, *The Three Faces of Power* (New York, 1967), pp. vii–viii. See also Archibald Cox, *The Warren Court: Constitutional Decision as an Instrument of Reform* (Cambridge, Mass., 1968), p. v.

[85] Elliot, *The Debates*, Vol. 4, p. 182.

[86] *The Federalist*, Nos. 16 and 43.

[87] Ibid., No. 43.

[88] Madison to Edmund Randolph, April 8, 1787. Quoted in Mason, *Free Government in the Making*, pp. 192–193. Italics added.

Just as years of debate preceding independence proved powerless to resolve the issue of sovereignty between Britain and the colonies, so decades of discussion on the political platform, in Congress, in the hustings, and the Supreme Court were unable to tame *imperium in imperio.*

AMERICA'S "APPEAL TO HEAVEN"

In *Federalist* No. 22, Hamilton had denounced as "gross heresy" the notion that "a party to a *compact* has a right to revoke that *compact.*" Nullification and secession—state sovereignty asserted in its boldest form—proclaimed the heresy Hamilton deplored. The constitutional response was the Civil War amendments, particularly the Fourteenth. Framed in the most sweeping terms by a radical Republican Congress, the latter was designed, apparently, to clip the wings of state sovereignty, once and for all. Directed explicitly to the state, that amendment declares that "no state shall make or enforce any law which shall abridge the privileges and immunities of citizens of the United States, nor shall any state deprive any person of life, liberty, or property without due process of law, nor deny to any person within its jurisdiction equal protection of the laws." The apparent intention was to make the first eight amendments binding on the states and enforceable by Congress and the federal courts.

Yet in the first case[89] involving this amendment, the Supreme Court emasculated its major provisions—"privileges and immunities," "due process," "equal protection." For a majority of six, Justice Miller's explanation borders on apology:

> The argument we admit is not always the most conclusive which is drawn from the consequences urged against the adoption of a particular construction of an instrument. But when, as in the case before us, these consequences are so serious, so far-reaching and pervading, so great a departure from the structure and spirit of our institutions; when the effect is to fetter and degrade the state governments by subjecting them to the control of Congress, in the exercise of powers heretofore universally conceded to them of the most ordinary and fundamental character; when, in fact, it radically changes the whole theory of the relations of the State and Federal governments to each other, and both of these governments to the people; the argument has a force that is irresistible, in the absence of language which expresses such a purpose too clearly to admit of doubt.[90]

Justice Miller's sensitivity to a theory of federal-state relations, presumably established in 1789, is such that despite the amendment's all-embracing injunctions against state power vis-à-vis individual rights, he shrinks from the belief that the Congress, which framed the Fourteenth Amendment, intended to alter that relationship. Any such change even by amendment, seemed suspect. In a vehement dissenting opinion, Justice Field charged that the Court's restrictive

---

[89] *Slaughter-House Cases,* 16 Wall. 36 (1873).
[90] Ibid., p. 78.

interpretation reduced the Fourteenth Amendment to "a vain and idle enactment, which accomplished nothing."[91]

When the Civil War was over, the Supreme Court was confronted with the
practical question—whether during that conflict Texas was out of the Union.
Chief Justice Chase replied in the negative, fashioning a theory of federalism
that practically restates the Madisonian formula of 1787:

> The preservation of the States, and the maintenance of their governments, are as
> much within the design and care of the Constitution as the preservation of the
> Union and the maintenance of the National government. The Constitution, in all
> its provisions, looks to an indestructible Union of indestructible States.[92]

By judicial fiat, if not by constitutional amendment, America's "Appeal to
Heaven" left federalism virtually intact. A theory of the Union which reason
could not establish was won by resort to force. What John Quincy Adams said
of the Constitution was equally applicable to the Union. It had to be "extorted
from the grinding necessities of a reluctant nation."[93] Justice Holmes, himself
a soldier in Lincoln's army, understood the subtleties involved:

> When we are dealing with words that are also a constituent act like the Constitu-
> tion of the United States, we must realize that they [the framers] have brought
> into life a being the development of which could not have been foreseen com-
> pletely by the most gifted of its begetters. It was enough for them to realize or to
> hope that they had created an organism; it has taken a century and has cost their
> successors much sweat and blood to prove that they created a nation.[94]

A FLEXIBLE CREATION FOR FALLIBLE MEN

We return to Madison's boast: revolution without parallel; fabrics of government without a model. The Father of the Constitution was right on both scores.
That twofold effort established free government. Its meaning, strength, and inescapable risk are rooted in human nature. "Man's capacity for Justice," theo-
logian Reinhold Niebuhr observed, "makes democracy possible, but man's inclination toward injustice makes it necessary."[95] Society is torn not only by
conflict between men of good will and mutual assistance, on the one hand, and
the vicious and degenerate on the other, but also by a more baffling struggle

[91] Ibid., p. 96.
In the years ahead, ironically, the Supreme Court was destined to play the role it had spurned
in 1873—"perpetual censor" of state legislation under the Fourteenth Amendment. See, in this
connection, A. T. Mason, Security Through Freedom: American Political Thought and Practice
(Ithaca, N. Y., 1955), pp. 28–41.

[92] Texas v. White, 7 Wallace 700 (1869), 725.

[93] The Jubilee of the Constitution, p. 55.

[94] Missouri v. Holland, 252 U.S. 416 (1920), 433.

[95] R. Neibuhr, The Children of Light and the Children of Darkness (New York, 1944), p. xi.
Neibuhr's thought was inspired by Paul's Epistle to the Romans, 7:18–25.

raging within each individual. "For the good that I would I do not: but the evil which I would not, that I do" (Romans, 7:19). The Constitution reflects this dualism. It grants and limits power.

The Founding Fathers did not postulate goals obtainable only if men were sinless. "If angels were to govern men," Madison commented "neither external nor internal controls on government would be necessary."[96] Hamilton warned that "the supposition of universal venality is little less an error in political reasoning than the supposition of universal rectitude."[97] The major objective was to fashion a constitutional system in which both aspects of man's nature could find expression.[98]

Not even unqualified majority rule is a safe guardian of inextricably related values, liberty and restraint.[99] Without ignoring ends, the Constitution stresses means. The framers endorsed the seemingly fatalistic view that free government "is a method of finding proximate solutions for insoluble problems."[100]

In 1787, Hamilton applauded the "great improvements" made in "the science of politics."[101] Among other things, he noted the distribution of powers among the various organs and agencies of government. But Madison cautioned that "no skill in the science of government" had been able "to discriminate or define with sufficient certainty the different provinces of government."[102]

Constitutional lines of demarcation, whether between national government and state, among president, Congress, and Court, or that most precious barrier circumscribing power at all levels vis-à-vis individual rights, are not drawn with mathematical exactness. For Madison, it was "a melancholy reflection" that liberty would "be equally exposed to danger whether the government have too

[96] The Federalist, No. 51.

[97] Ibid., No. 76. Madison concurred: "As there is a degree of depravity in mankind which requires a degree of circumspection and distrust, so there are other qualities in human nature which justify a certain portion of esteem and confidence. Republican government presupposes the existence of these qualities in a higher degree than any other form." Ibid., No. 55.

[98] Ibid., No. 37.

[99] By 1787, the injustice of state laws and other excesses had brought "more into question the fundamental principle of Republican government, that the majority who rule in such governments are the safest Guardians both of the public Good and private rights." Madison, "Vices of the Political System of the United States." Quoted in Mason, Free Government in the Making, p. 171. See also The Federalist, No. 10.

[100] Niebuhr, The Children of Light, p. 118.

[101] The Federalist, No. 1.

[102] Ibid., No. 37. For Madison the methods of science are inappropriate in politics for three reasons: "complexity of the subject," "imperfection of the organ of perception," "inadequacy of the vehicle of ideas"—words. Rousseau, concerned lest the reader accuse him of self-contradiction, cited "poverty of language" as the excuse. The Social Contract (Everyman edition New York, 1913), p. 27n.

Commenting on the mechanical approach in the context of constitutional interpretation generally, Holmes wrote: "The provisions of a constitution are not mathematical formulas having their essence in their form; they are organic living institutions transplanted from English soil. Their significance is vital, not final; it is to be gathered not simply by taking the words and a dictionary, but by considering their origin and the line of their growth." Gompers v. United States, 233 U.S. (1914), 604, 610.

much or too little power, and that the lines which divide these extremes should be so inaccurately defined by experience."[103] The imponderable nature of politics and the ever-present imperatives time and circumstance suggest that the effort to draw precise constitutional dividers would have been fruitless, even if tried. The framers knew the "dangers of a delusive exactness."

"The lines of politics," Edmund Burke declares, "are not like the lines of mathematics. They are broad and deep as well as long. They admit of exceptions; they demand modifications. No lines can be laid down for civil or political wisdom. They are a matter incapable of exact definition."[104] Distribution of powers among distinct departments and levels of government, along with the fusion of power and functions, creates tension—"vibrations of power," Hamilton called it, "the genius of our government."[105]

The enduring lesson of American history is that opposition, freedom to disagree, protest, dissent, built into the organization and structure of our constitutional system, are its lifeblood. Criticism of official conduct, Madison said, "is the duty as well as the right of intelligent and faithful citizens." Society is entitled to the advantages of such criticism, and so are would-be usurpers of power. Divergence of opinion quickens our notion of the common interest. "If there were no different interests," Rousseau commented, "the common interest would barely be felt, as it would encounter no obstacles; all would go of its own accord, and politics would cease to be an art."[106] Enemy lists, ruthless elimina-

---

[103] Madison to Jefferson, October 17, 1788. Hunt, *Writings of James Madison*, Vol. 5, p. 274.

For certain of the most liberal Supreme Court justices, the Bill of Rights does not draw constitutional lines with absolute precision. See Justice Holmes's qualifications, *Schenck* v. *United States*, 249 U.S. 47 (1919), 52; *Frohwerk* v. *United States*, 249 U.S. 204 (1919), 206. In a broader context, Holmes commented: "A word is not a crystal, transparent and unchanged, it is the skin of a living thought and may vary in color and content according to the circumstances and the time in which it is used." *Towne* v. *Eisner*, 245 U.S. 418 (1918), 425. See Justice Brandeis in *Whitney* v. *California*, 274 U.S. 357 (1927), dissenting, p. 373; Justice Douglas, dissenting in *Dennis* v. *United States*, 341 U.S. 494 (1951), 585. See also Walter Lippmann, *The Public Philosophy* (New York, 1956), p. 132.

[104] Quoted in A. T. Mason, "Politics: Science or Art?" *Southwestern Social Science Quarterly*, December 1935, p. 3.

[105] Hamilton to Rufus King, February 3, 1802. Henry Cabot Lodge (ed.), *The Works of Alexander Hamilton*, Vol. 10 (New York, 1904), p. 439.

In *The Federalist*, No. 83, Hamilton wrote: "The truth is that the general *Genius* of a government [identified as 'vibrations of power'] is all that can be substantially relied upon for permanent effects."

[106] Rousseau, *The Social Contract*, p. 25n.

"He that wrestles with us," Edmund Burke observes, "strengthens our nerves and sharpens our skill. Our antagonist is our helper. . . . Time is required to produce that union of mind which alone can produce all the good we aim at." *Reflections on the French Revolution*, pp. 105, 108.

For John C. Calhoun *The Federalist* highlighted divergence of opinion, accommodation, and compromise, convincing him that "this admirable constitution of ours . . . is superior to the wisdom of any or all of the men by whose agency it was made. The force of circumstance, and not foresight or wisdom, induced them to adopt many of its wisest provisions." R. K. Cralle (ed.), *The Works of John C. Calhoun*, Vol. 4 (New York, 1888), p. 417.

tion of opposition and dissent are less demanding than the art of bringing differing minds into constructive accord.

Justice Holmes, declaring that the best test of truth is the power of thought to get itself accepted in the competition of the market of ideas, identified this as "the theory of our Constitution."[107] Earlier he had denied that the Constitution "is intended to embody a particular *economic* theory, whether of paternalism and the organic relation of the citizen to the state or of *laissez faire*." Anticipating the *political* theory enunciated many years later, he declared: "It is made for people of fundamentally differing views, and the accident of our finding certain opinions natural and familiar, or novel, and even shocking, ought not to conclude our judgment upon the question whether statutes embodying them conflict with the Constitution of the United States."[108] It may be, as Holmes said, that "the ultimate kingship"[109] belongs to the man who initiates fundamental ideas, but even these need to be tested by contact with others, especially by those inclined to disagree with them.

Like all ideals, political truth—justice—is unattainable. Consensus cannot be ranked as an ultimate. Truth and justice are goals to be striven for with the tacit understanding that they may not be reached.[110] "Sometimes new truth," Niebuhr remarked, "rides into history upon the back of an error."[111]

Essential to the successful operation of free government are mutual respect, accommodation, tolerance. The "healing balm of our Constitution," Jefferson warned, is that "each party should shrink from all approach to the line of demarcation, instead of rashly over-leaping it, or throwing grapples ahead to haul to hereafter."[112] With rare exceptions, Jefferson's recipe for avoiding an impasse between nation and state, among the various organs of our tripartite system, and between government at all levels and individual rights—has been followed. Confrontations, as in the Civil War and 1974, are the exception rather than the rule.[113]

---

[107] *Abrams* v. *U.S.*, 250 U.S. 616 (1919), 630.

[108] Dissenting in *Lochner* v. *New York*, 198 U.S. 45 (1905), 75–76.

[109] Mark DeWolfe Howe (ed.), *Holmes-Laski Letters*, Vol. 1 (New York, 1953), pp. 310–311.

[110] "Justice is the end of government," Madison wrote. "It is the end of civil society. It ever has been and ever will be pursued until it be obtained, or until liberty is lost in the pursuit." *The Federalist*, No. 51.

[111] Niebuhr, *The Children of Light*, p. 75.

[112] Jefferson to Judge Roane, June 27, 1821. Ford, *Works of Thomas Jefferson*, Vol. 12, p. 203.

[113] Besides the Civil War, notable exceptions are the deadlock between the judiciary and the political branches of government in the 1930s, and the Nixon administration's betrayals. In 1935–1936, the Supreme Court, often by vote of five to four or six to three, transcending the undefined line set by the separation-of-powers principle, became a super-legislature. President Franklin D. Roosevelt, impervious to Jefferson's warning against "rashly overleaping" lines of demarcation, counterattacked with his Court-packing threat. Happily, the outcome was ambiguous. Both sides won; both lost. Roosevelt achieved judicial endorsement of his legislative program. Congress defeated Court-packing. If either had scored outright victory, the separation-of-powers principles would have been, by Madison's test, "subverted." The beneficiaries of this give-and-take outcome were the American people and free government.

Constitution, structural checks, bill of rights—none of these safeguards nor all combined will render free government secure. In the Virginia Ratifying Convention of 1788, Madison warned: "To suppose that any form of government will secure liberty or happiness without virtue in the people is a chimerical idea."[114] In various ways and on many occasions, Jefferson pointed to its ultimate reliance—character and spirit of the people.*

[114] Elliot, *The Debates*, Vol. 3, p. 489.

* This article is an expansion of the introductory lecture in the Merrill Bicentennial Series, delivered October 29, 1975, at Utah State University.

On Removing Certain Impediments to Democracy in the United States

ROBERT A. DAHL

What this nation can become will be influenced, though not fully determined, by the ways in which we think about ourselves as a people. With a people as with a person, it is a sign of wisdom and maturity to understand and accept limits that are imposed by nature's laws and the scarcity of resources, whether physical, human, or political. In this sense we Americans may at last be entering into our maturity. But to accept as real, limits that are imposed only by our own minds, is not wisdom but self-inflicted blindness.

Out of our past we have inherited ways of thinking about ourselves that condemn us to try too much and accomplish too little. We fail not so much because our aspirations are too high but because they conflict; and within ourselves, too, we are conflicted in ways we do not fully recognize. In this sense our consciousness, both individual and collective, distorts our understanding of ourselves and our possibilities.

An important part of this distortion comes out of a series of historical commitments this country has made. It might free up our consciousness for greater political creativity if we were to see those commitments more clearly, to understand better how they conflict with one another, and to choose self-consciously rather than blindly among our possible futures.

The expression "historical commitment" may carry misleading connotations. An historical commitment in the context of this article is nothing neat, tidy, wholly self-conscious, broadly understood, much less agreed to by all, nor a well-shaped historical drama with a clear beginning, a middle, and an end.

ROBERT A. DAHL is Sterling Professor of Political Science at Yale University. He is the author of *A Preface to Democratic Theory, Who Governs?, After the Revolution?,* and other works. He is now working on two books on democratic theory.

Rather, it pertains to periods in our history in which some alternative possibilities seemed open to the principal historical actors, who, however, were in conflict over the relative desirability of the alternatives they perceived. The conflict among them became overt, bitter, sometimes prolonged, and in one way or another finally came to involve a substantial number of citizens. In time, however, one set of advocates won out. Thereafter the issues so fiercely contested ceased to be salient in American political life. What had recently been a sharply contested possibility thus came to be accepted as pretty much an undebatable aspect of the status quo by the major parties, political leaders, writers and publicists, and (so far as these things can be discerned) the voters themselves. If dissenters continued to fight rearguard actions, they were few in number and on the margins of American politics, public attention, and political acceptability. Thus the historic commitments soon came to possess all the extraordinary advantages of things as they are and, after a generation or so, as they seem always to have been. This article will focus on five historical commitments this country has made to goals that are in some respects incompatible and will condemn us to a confused sense of national purpose unless and until we recognize these conflicts and decide on our priorities.

FIVE AMERICAN COMMITMENTS

The first commitment was the one this country made to a liberal political and constitutional order that gave primacy to the protection of certain political and civil rights among its citizens. Although the whole colonial period was crucial to the development of sentiment favoring that commitment, the most active stage might be conveniently if rather arbitrarily placed somewhere between 1776 and 1800 or thereabouts. Sometime not long after 1800, conflict over the validity of the existing constitution pretty much recedes and soon hardly an American voice is heard in opposition to it. So profound is its acceptance, in fact, that the great constitutional quarrels to follow were not so much over the validity of the Constitution as over its meaning, assuming its unquestioned validity.

The second historical commitment, consolidated somewhere between 1800 and 1836 or thereabouts, was to the belief that the only proper constitutional and political system for Americans is a democracy. Although democracy mainly meant adhering to democratic procedures in the operation of the government, it also carried with it notions of a larger society within which social and economic conditions would favor the high degree of political, social, and economic equality necessary to democracy. By extraordinary luck, such a social order already existed in the United States. This was an agrarian society where, in an economy predominantly of family farms, the adult white male citizens lived with fewer social, economic, and political inequalities than any larger number of persons in history had existed up to that time, and very likely since. Tocqueville was not the first observer nor would he be the last, though he may have been the most gifted, to see how marvelously the agrarian society fostered a condition of equality among the citizens, or rather among the white males.

Yet that agrarian order was not only an historical rarity, but it had no future. During the harsh struggles over the new socioeconomic order that was to replace it, Americans who wished to retain the old order were the most numerous, persistent, and politically successful opponents of the new. But even with the whole weight of tradition on their side, they and their occasional allies were unable to prevent the displacement of the old agrarian order by a new order based on commercial and industrial capitalism, in which the ideal engine of economic production and growth was no longer to be the privately owned family farm but the privately owned commercial, financial, or industrial corporation. The contest that eventuated in the triumph of the new order over the old dominated American political life through the last three decades of the nineteenth century. During this time a number of alternatives to the new order—agrarianism, anarchism, socialism, individually owned consumers' and producers' cooperatives, selective government ownership and operation, economic regulation, limits on corporate size, monetary schemes, enforced competition, and many others— were thrust forward, debated, and finally pretty much defeated. The election of 1896 might be taken as the turning point in the victory of the new order over its rivals. Thereafter, the national commitment to the socioeconomic order of corporate capitalism swelled into a current so powerful that opponents could make no headway against it and were swept out of the mainstream of American life. Even socialists, who in Britain and Europe gained greater support as industrial capitalism expanded, remained a small and largely uninfluential minority in the United States.

If by 1900 or so this country was committed to corporate capitalism, aspects of the new order nonetheless remained at issue. Widespread hardships were engendered by an economy with as little public control as the dominant political coalition demanded. These hardships were real enough to ensure a following for a politician who advocated reform—at any rate so long as he did not attack the basic commitment to private ownership, whereupon his following would shrink into the futilities of minor party politics. Thus if socialism was unpopular, reform was not. As a result, from time to time regulatory laws won out in particular states and occasionally, as with Wilson's New Freedom, even in the federal government. But the country's commitment to only a modest interference by government in the conduct of corporate capitalism was more accurately reflected by the administrations of McKinley, Taft, Harding, Coolidge, and Hoover and by Theodore Roosevelt's bombastic style and ineffectual policies— speak loudly but carry a small stick—than by the brief interlude of reform during Wilson's first term. As we all know, it took the trauma of the Great Depression finally to convert a hitherto oppositional minority into a majority coalition. The product of this coalition was the fourth historic commitment which was, of course, to the idea and institutions of a welfare state. The prior commitment to private ownership and control of economic enterprises, and thus to corporate capitalism, was mainly upheld. Yet some of the most acute hardships and injustices generated in the socioeconomic order were to be removed or alleviated by government actions—mainly by the federal government. Orthodox as this commitment now seems, one who did not live through that period may find it difficult to recapture how intense, bitter, and at times violent was the conflict over the inauguration of a welfare state by Franklin Roosevelt and the New Deal. However, as with the preceding commitments, the main elements of this one soon gained such wide acceptability that opposition to the commitment itself, as distinguished from criticism of specific means, came to be an exercise in political futility.

Even before the main battles of the New Deal were finished, conflict had begun over what was to be the fifth historic commitment. This was the commitment to play an international role as a world power. Again, it may be hard to recapture how bitterly divided Americans were over this issue in the late 1930s. Yet the advocates of an American role as an active world power were riding an overpowering current of events that swept along most of their opponents and swamped the rest or left the few survivors stranded far behind the main body of American opinion.

All five of these historic commitments remain strong. Even after the shame and disaster of Vietnam, there is not really much likelihood of our renouncing our position as a world power, though the way we use our position and power cannot possibly be to everyone's liking or, alas, to everyone's benefit, and could easily be as harmful to ourselves and others once again as it has been in the recent past. Within limits, the strength of each of the five commitments seems to wax and wane; one is eroded here and another grows firmer there. But the commitments still dominate the way we think about ourselves and our future. And that is a source of difficulty, for the commitments are in some ways incompatible.

IMPEDIMENTS TO DEMOCRACY

In particular, certain impediments to the realization of democracy in the United States have resulted from the other historic commitments. We can begin with the Constitution itself, the political system it helped to form, and the political ideas and beliefs embedded in and strengthened by the constitutional and political system. As we have seen, this country's commitment to democracy came after and not before the formation and adoption of the Constitution. Even as late as the Constitutional Convention, the desirability of a representative democracy was a debatable issue. Consequently, the framers could not and did not agree to establish a representative democracy. They could and did agree to establish a representative republic with a framework of government that would, as they believed, rest on popular consent and yet ensure as best they knew how the preservation of certain basic rights to life, liberty, and property that they held to be morally inalienable. In this sense, the framers were liberals and republicans though they were not democrats; they intended to establish a liberal framework of government, though it could be, and later was, democratized to a degree that, for a time, would astonish the world.

The political system the framers helped bring into existence was in at least two major respects defective by democratic criteria. First, in spite of the eloquent universality of the language used in the Declaration of Independence and common at the time, in actuality the framers gave much narrower scope to the principles of consent and political equality. Without seriously qualifying, much less abandoning their universal norms, they nonetheless created a government that would demand obedience to its laws from a majority of adults—women, nonwhites, and some white males—who were excluded from active participation in making those laws, whether directly or through their elected representatives. The majority of adults were thus provided with as little opportunity to give their active consent to the laws which they were bound to obey as their colonial predecessors had enjoyed under laws enacted by the English Parliament.

Second, in order to achieve their goal of preserving a set of inalienable rights superior to the majority principle—a goal many of us would surely share—the framers deliberately created a framework of government that was carefully designed to impede and even prevent the operation of majority rule. Thus when the country committed itself to their framework of government, two different arguments became confounded in the national consciousness, and they remain confounded to this day. There is the liberal argument that certain rights are so fundamental to the attainment of human goals, needs, interests, and fulfillment that governments must never be allowed to derogate from them. But in addition there is the American constitutional argument that the highly specific, indeed unique, set of political arrangements embodied in our constitutional and political practices is necessary to preserve these rights. While the writer accepts the liberal argument, the American constitutional argument seems seriously defective.

Now the matter of what ought to constitute inalienable rights beyond the reach of any government, and the proper relationship between such rights and democratic procedures, are questions far too complex to examine here. Certainly the solutions are not easy to come by, either theoretically or practically. Moreover, we might agree on the need to preserve fundamental rights against government without necessarily agreeing on what these rights should be. The point is, however, that the elaborate system of checks and balances, separation of powers, constitutional federalism, and other institutional arrangements influenced by these structures and the constitutional views they reflect, are both adverse to the majority principle, and in that sense to democracy, and yet arbitrary and unfair in the protection they give to rights. However laudable their ends, in their means the framers were guilty of overkill. As only one example, the presidential veto has generally been used, and quite recently, for purposes no loftier than simply to prevent the adoption of policies disliked by the president and the political coalition whose interests he seeks to advance. It is not as if a president uses the veto only when a majority coalition threatens the inalienable rights of a minority. What is typically at stake is purely a disagreement about policy. Insofar as all policies have costs and gains and thus influence the distribution of advantages and disadvantages, the policies of a majority (like those of a minority) are likely to be adverse to the interests of some persons; but we can hardly say—nor can the framers have intended to say—that every privilege that happens to exist does so by inalienable right.

Yet there is this strong bias against majorities in the political system the framers helped to create. Because they succeeded in designing a system that makes it easier for privileged minorities to prevent changes they dislike than for majorities to bring about the changes they want, it is strongly tilted in favor of the status quo and against reform. In their effort to protect basic rights, what the framers did in effect was to hand out extra chips in the game of politics to people who are already advantaged, while they handicapped the disadvantaged who would like to change the status quo. From a moral perspective, the consequences seem arbitrary and quite lacking in a principled justification.

We ought to be able to design a way of preserving fundamental rights that is not so biased in favor of existing privilege and against reform. A number of other countries that place fewer barriers in the way of majority rule than exist under our political system manage to preserve at least as high a standard of political liberty, with less procedural unfairness. But of course to bring about such changes meets precisely the obstacle to change just mentioned, the antimajoritarian bias of the constitutional and political system.

This brings us to another consequence of the framer's antimajoritarian design that is unsatisfactory both as a protection for morally inalienable rights and as a device for procedural democracy. It may not be going too far to say that although the framers were unable to prevent the democratization of the constitutional system, they created a potentially lethal instrument for that democratization in the presidency. When the democratic commitment referred to earlier was undertaken, the antimajoritarian constitutional design was not merely preserved but identified with democratic government itself, a confusion that remains all but universal among Americans, as visitors from other democratic countries and teachers of political science to American undergraduates repeatedly discover. However, democratizing the Constitution required a transformation that some of the framers had feared and had sought to prevent. The claim was now made that the president was the sole authentic spokesman for and representative of national majorities. Indeed, the constitutional framework hardly provided any other possibility. Given the nature of the Senate and even of the House, the claim on behalf of the presidency was plausible, and one that the defenders of Congress found hard to rebut. In the long run, as we know, Congress failed to uphold its claim and the claims made on behalf of the presidency pretty much won out. Endowed with legitimacy deriving both from constitutional interpretation and democratic ideology, the presidency became the institutional center from which a majority coalition, if there was to be one at all, would be mobilized, organized, and given voice. Thus one consequence of the framers' institutional design was to channel the process of democratizing the Constitution into transforming the presidency, a process that was not to end, if it has yet ended, before that office became what lately has been variously called an elective monarchy, an imperial presidency, a plebiscitary chief executive, and other epithets still harsher.

The irony is, then, that the first and second historic commitments taken in their entirety endow us with a political system in which any majority coalition supporting changes adverse to existing privileges is likely to succeed only if the presidency has access to a concentration of political resources great enough to make the office a standing danger to majority rule and procedural democracy itself. Thus the justifiable effort to strengthen the majority principle in a constitutional system that was designed to impede it has led not to democratization of the Constitution but rather to the pseudo-democratization of the presidency.

Under the agrarian economic order, the pseudo-democratization of the presidency did not matter very much nor would it have gone very far. The white males who comprised the demos enjoyed an astounding degree of autonomy in relation to one another and to all governments. Their political resources, and the opportunities and incentives for using them should the need arise, were vast in comparison with the weak coercive means available to any of the American governments. Hence, the potentiality of widespread governmental coercion of the demos or any substantial part of it was perhaps as minimal as it had ever been anywhere among a numerous body of people. As for the members of the excluded majority, their very exclusion from political rights meant that they could not successfully appeal to the government to prevent private or public coercion, unless they happened to have the support of a majority of white males, and not necessarily even then if a substantial minority in the demos opposed the change sought by or in behalf of the disfranchised. In practice, then, the excluded groups had little protection against oppression.

The third historic commitment was to change the distribution of resources so favorable to the demos. An agrarian order that historically speaking was extraordinarily congenial to democracy was now displaced by a new socioeconomic order of corporate capitalism that was much less compatible. The basis of the new order was a fundamentally different kind of economic enterprise. The small family owned and operated farm that was modal if not universal in the agrarian order was now displaced by one of the most radical innovations that mankind has ever invented for economic organization, control, and growth. This was the privately owned and operated business corporation. Through a highly successful case of ideological transfer, the Lockean defense of private property, which in the agrarian order made good sense morally and politically, was shifted over intact to corporate enterprise. This ideological triumph successfully warded off attacks not only from nascent socialist movements opposed to private property in the means of production but also from the historical rear guard defending the old agrarian order, which had at hand no convincing way of distinguishing private ownership and control of one kind of enterprise, the farm, from private ownership and control of a radically different kind, the business corporation. Thus by an extraordinary ideological sleight of hand, the corporation took on the legitimacy of the farmer's home, tools, and land, and what he produced out of his land, labor, ingenuity, anguish, planning, forbearance, sacrifice, risk, and hope. The upshot was that the quite exceptional degree of autonomy the farmer members of the demos had enjoyed under the old order, an autonomy vis-à-vis both government and one another, was now granted to the corporation.

Two consequences of this new order were particularly adverse to democracy. First, the new order generated much greater differences than the old in political resources, skills, and incentives within the demos itself. The degree of social and economic differentiation that had already been foreshadowed in the cities of the eastern seaboard was no longer marginal, as it had been when the socio-economic order was overwhelmingly agrarian, but central to the new order. Great differences in wealth, income, social esteem, education, occupational skills, and ethnic status now differentiated wage earners and pieceworkers in industry, ship, mine, and forest—a rising proportion of whom were immigrants —from the middling strata of white-collar and professional people, who for some time to come were predominantly Anglo-American in origins, and these in turn from the opulent few. Because differences like these are readily convert-ible into political resources, the wide, if by no means perfectly equal dispersion of political resources among the demos in the agrarian order was now consider-ably more concentrated. Inequalities in political resources added further to the handicaps of any majority coalition that sought changes in the allocation of privileges and disadvantages.

Second, because the internal government of the corporation was not itself democratic but hierarchical and often despotic, the rapid expansion of this revo-lutionary form of economic enterprise meant that an increasing proportion of the demos would live out their working lives, and most of their daily existence, not within a democratic system but instead within a hierarchical structure of subordination. To this extent, democracy was necessarily marginal to the actual political system in which the members of the demos lived their daily lives. Thus the transfer of the Lockean view to the corporation was a double triumph. By making ownership the only, or at least primary, source of legitimate control over corporate decisions, the new order not only excluded democratic controls in the internal government of the enterprise but placed powerful ideological barriers against the imposition of external controls by a government which, for all its deficiencies, was much more democratic than were the governments of business firms.

The fourth and fifth commitments extended the domain of hierarchy even further. To be sure, from the New Deal onward the commitment to a welfare state helped to reduce the autonomy of economic enterprises. By protecting the rights of workers to join unions and bargain collectively with employers, the New Deal helped to democratize some aspect of some enterprises for some employees. By regulatory devices of various kinds it also reduced the autonomy and thus the arbitrary and sometimes despotic power of the rulers of economic enterprises. However, if the commitment to a welfare state has altered it has not profoundly reduced the two adverse consequences of the corporate capitalist order mentioned a moment ago. The evidence seems to show that what appear to be great changes in levels of taxation and transfer payments have not much reduced the inequalities in the distribution of wealth and income and thus the relative political advantage or disadvantage associated, at least loosely, with access to these resources. And except for the limited effects of trade unions among a minority segment of the labor force, the American commitment to a welfare state has not done much to alter the hierarchical structures of corporate government under which so many Americans live.

In fact, the commitment to a welfare state has added even more burdens to democracy. For one thing, the reforms undertaken in behalf of the commitment could not be carried through without the leadership of an energetic president, who could increase, organize, and exploit all the political resources of the office. If we want to find the recent rather than the Jacksonian origins of the imperial presidency, as good a place as anywhere to begin is the presidency of Franklin Roosevelt. Among other things, what his presidency did was to disarm most intellectuals and academics, not least political scientists, who, being mostly in favor of reform, enthusiastically came forward with whatever was needed in the way of a justification for enhanced presidential power. Moreover, in order to achieve its gains, the welfare state needed extensive governmental bureaucracies. Even if these are never fully controlled by official hierarchies, or for that matter, by anyone else, they do provide an ambitious president with very considerable political resources—far beyond anything the framers ever dreamed of—for persuasion, inducement, manipulation, and coercion. By now this proposition needs no documentation beyond what Watergate has furnished us. Finally, like the governments of corporate enterprise, the bureaucracies in the government of the state are also hierarchical in structure. Far from diminishing hierarchy, therefore, even in the course of regulating economic enterprise the welfare state has multiplied the number, domain, and scope of hierarchies in American life.

The fifth commitment, of course, compounded these consequences adverse to democracy. As an active world power, the country had need—at first quite suddenly—of a large military establishment, thus still another hierarchy, even more rigidly hierarchical than the rest, one perhaps even more difficult to control, yet available to the president for executing foreign and military policies that could be, as events were to show, the arbitrary and personal expressions of a chief executive whose decisions on these matters were for all practical purposes beyond the control of Congress, the courts, or the demos. In a further irony, constitutional language and interpretation had left a substantial gap in the framers' imposing array of checks and balances. Successive presidents plunged through and widened this gap. By action and inaction, the Congress, the courts, and the demos—cheered on, it has to be said, by political scientists, historians, lawyers, and other intellectual spokesmen who should have known better—all gave their blessing to the emerging imperial presidency. It took national shame, disaster, scandal, and prolonged investigation to make us realize what sort of an institution the presidency had become.

To understand these changes in the presidency it is important to keep in mind that for the better part of two generations this country was involved in war, near-war, war crisis, or cold war. Three decades of war would be enough, one might think, to undermine a weaker republic. Perhaps we should consider ourselves lucky that our first two commitments held as well as they did. Even so, as a world power things were done and widely thought to be justified that surely would have been condemned as unjustifiable in less paranoidal circumstances. An obsession with national security and loyalty fostered secrecy in government, the enormous expansion of domestic spying, the harassment of radicals, and other excrescences. And even if some important reforms were carried out, mainly with respect to civil rights, these decades were on the whole unfavorable to reform, and certainly to any changes that might seem to question the validity of our historic commitments.

THE DOCTRINE OF PROCEDURAL DEMOCRACY

If we were now to search for a perspective on our potentialities as a people that would not be distorted either by self-glorification or self-hatred, that recognized our capacities for great evil, great good, and plain mediocrity, and discerned in the conflicting commitments of our past that weigh heavily on our present some criteria of excellence against which to measure our achievements in the future, where would we begin?

We might begin near the beginning, with our first two commitments. Ignoring for a moment the contradictions described earlier, these may be interpreted as an aspiration toward a society with a political system in which liberty, equality, and justice would jointly prosper, a society therefore requiring also a socioeconomic system that would foster these ends by supporting the kind of policy necessary to them. Thus interpreted, these two commitments would give priority to political ends over economic ends, to liberty, equality, and justice over efficiency, prosperity, and growth, a priority that the commitment to corporate capitalism reversed both in ideology and in practice, and which has remained reversed down to our own day.

The guiding criteria against which to measure political performance implied by this interpretation are, in the author's view, the criteria of procedural democracy, which, together with their most crucial assumptions, constitute what one might call the doctrine of procedural democracy. What follows is a very brief and incomplete account of that doctrine.

To become fully operative with respect to any association, the doctrine of procedural democracy presupposes a judgment that at least two conditions exist among some set of persons who constitute or intend to constitute an association.

First, there is a *need for collective decisions* binding on the members of the association. That is, this set of persons is confronted by a matter which they think it would be disadvantageous to leave entirely to individual action or to choices made exclusively through a market, and comparatively advantageous to make collectively and enforce on the members.

Second, among the persons obligated to abide by collective decisions on this matter, there is a subset, the *demos*, whose members are *roughly equally qualified, taken all around*. That is, no member of this qualified subset, or demos, believes that any other member of the association or any subset of persons different from the demos is significantly more qualified than the demos to arrive at a correct choice with respect to matters requiring collective decisions. Under the *maximal* interpretation, the members believe that the demos includes all qualified members of the association and all members of the demos are in all relevant characteristics equally qualified with respect to matters requiring collective decisions. Under the *minimal* interpretation, no members of the association are in any relevant characteristic so clearly more qualified as to justify their making the decision for all the others on the matter at hand.

A government of any association in which these conditions are judged to exist is, on these matters, a *putatively democratic government in relation to its demos.* Thus a judgment that these conditions exist implies a rejection of claims that might be advanced on behalf of a government over the demos on these matters by a putative aristocracy, meritocracy, or governing elite.

The doctrine of procedural democracy holds that for any putatively democratic government, collective decision making by the demos should satisfy at least three criteria:

1. The criterion of *political equality*. The decision rule for determining outcomes must equally take into account the preferences of each member of the demos as to the outcome. To reject this criterion is to deny the condition of roughly equal qualification, taken all around. This criterion implies that the procedures and performance of any putatively democratic government ought to be evaluated according to the extent to which the preferences of every member of the demos are given weight in collective decisions, particularly on matters members think are important to them.

2. The criterion of *effective participation*. In order for the preferences of each member of the demos to be equally taken into account, every member must have equal opportunities for expressing preferences, and the grounds for them, throughout the process of collective decision making. This criterion implies, then, that any putatively democratic government ought to be evaluated according to the opportunities it provides for, or the costs it imposes on, expression and participation by the demos.

3. The criterion of *enlightened understanding*. In order to express preferences accurately, each member of the demos ought to have adequate and equal opportunities for discovering and validating, in the time available, what his or her

preferences are on the matter to be decided. This criterion thus implies that any putatively democratic government ought to be evaluated according to the opportunities it furnishes for the acquisition of knowledge of ends and means, of oneself and other selves, by the demos.

Any government that satisfies these criteria, and only such a government, is *procedurally democratic in relation to its demos.*

As the doctrine is interpreted here, the demos defines itself. This is one of the most tricky and difficult aspects of democratic theory and practice. Because the demos defines itself, it need not include all the members of the association who are obliged to obey its rules. Whenever this is so, some members of the association, who are excluded from the demos, will also be excluded from the rights, opportunities, and protections of procedural democracy. Probably no association that has ever attempted to constitute a government for a state has admitted children into the demos. Now if children are excluded from the demos because they are judged to be unqualified, and yet are subject to the laws, then of course they are governed without their consent. Yet few of us would argue that the interests of children, inadequately as they are often protected, would be served better if they were made full voting members of the demos. To protect the rights, needs, and interests of children, we must rely not on procedural democracy but on the strength of adult feelings toward children of love, nurturance, pity, joy, compassion, and hope, and on laws and practices that these feelings may foster.

It is a very different matter with adults, among whom these feelings are ordinarily much too weak to ensure adequate protection for those who may be excluded from the demos. Consequently, we need to make explicit in the doctrine a proposition that has often been omitted or obscured. To do so requires a fourth criterion, that of *inclusiveness.* The demos includes all adults who are obliged to obey the rules of the association. Because the demos is inclusive, the criteria of procedural democracy apply to all the adults. Any government that satisfies all four criteria might be called a *full procedural democracy.*

One further point: probably no one who believes that full procedural democracy is a relevant aspiration thinks that it must hold for all matters, including judgments on highly technical, judicial, and administrative matters of every kind. Rhetorical assertions that seem to make procedural democracy the only proper method of making decisions have again and again been shown to be illusory and self-defeating. Yet as with the problem of inclusion, there is an exceptionally tricky problem here, one that can be dealt with only summarily in this article by stipulating a fifth criterion, that of *final control by the demos* ("popular sovereignty"). That is, the scope, domain, and procedures for making decisions other than by full procedural democracy are subject to decisions made by full procedural democracy. An association that satisfies all five criteria might thus be called a *fully democratic association in the procedural sense.*

Before turning to the implications of this doctrine for the United States, let us consider several objections. It is often said that procedural justice, and thus procedural democracy, does not guarantee substantive justice. This is true. It is said further, however, that as a consequence substantive justice should take priority over procedural justice and therefore over procedural democracy. This is partly right but mainly wrong. It is partly right because procedures should be judged by the ends they serve. Procedures that do not tend toward good ends cannot be judged good procedures. But the criticism is mainly wrong in implying that other solutions, particularly solutions that accept the claims of a putative governing elite, are more likely to lead to substantive justice. This is rarely a better short-run solution and practically always worse in the longer run. Finally, it is said that procedural democracy is in any case too anemic in its standards to compel us toward the robust aspirations of our nobler selves, for it speaks only to process and thus says nothing about the content of a good society. This criticism is only partly right in its premise and thoroughly wrong in its conclusion. It is obvious that all societies, including our own, fall very far short of satisfying the criteria of procedural democracy. If we in this country are to reduce the gap between criteria and performance in a large way, we shall have to make changes of great moment. What is more, these changes will have the effect of satisfying many of the claims for substantive justice as well. Such claims as could remain would constitute the very essence of healthy controversy —controversies that are properly adjudicated by means of procedural democracy and not by yielding to the claims of a putative governing elite or allowing a minority to impose its views on a majority.

NEEDS AND PROSPECTS

Suppose we were to interpret our first two historic commitments, taken together and after eliminating the inconsistencies, as a commitment to procedural democracy. Suppose further that we were to test our commitments against the requirements of this doctrine. Suppose, finally, that we resolved to move toward procedural democracy by reducing obstacles to it, at any rate up to some limit at which the trade-offs in other values became excessive. Given these suppositions, what changes would we make? Of course, not everyone accepts these suppositions; and even if they did, we might disagree about the answers. We might disagree both because the location of the limit at which trade-offs become excessive cannot be satisfactorily described in a precise way, and also because different persons will evaluate the trade-offs differently and thus reach different judgments about the location of the limit.

Nonetheless, it is possible to specify some directions in which changes are needed. At the outset these require changes in the way we think about ourselves and our institutions.

Consider the liberal thrust of the first historic commitment, to the preservation of morally inalienable rights. Such rights are assumed to be beyond the reach of government, and superior to any claims to other rights that conflict with them. But it has never been clear what rights are to be understood as inalienable or primary, and what rights are secondary and alienable, and hence must yield when they conflict with primary rights. The difficulty is that the grounds are not at all clear on which the distinction between primary and secondary, or inalienable and alienable rights, is to be made and justified.

Yet the conditions and criteria contained in the doctrine of procedural democracy are very rich in their implications for rights. For example, any judgment that the conditions for a putatively democratic government exist among some set of persons asserts a right to a government that satisfies the criteria of procedural democracy. Obviously, an assertion never establishes the validity of a claim. As with other rights, there is no automatic, self-enforcing determination of the validity of a claim. Judgments have to be made, and among a large number of people such judgments will rarely be unanimous. Claims may be rejected, justly or unjustly. Rights asserted usually have to be fought for.

Consider claims advanced on behalf of adults excluded from the demos that they are qualified to participate in American political life. The whole burden of American experience demonstrates not only that any group of adults excluded from the demos will be lethally weakened in its own defense, but also that those who govern will fail to protect the rights, needs, and interests of the excluded group. There is no convincing evidence in American history for the existence of one group of adults qualified to rule over adults who are excluded from full citizenship in the demos.

Yet for 200 years after the lovely universalistic phrases of the Declaration, the wellsprings of American national life were poisoned by the denial of claims to full citizenship, and by the injustice and oppression this denial entailed. To reject these claims, as American policy and practice did, was in effect to deny that full procedural democracy ought to exist in the United States. If we are now on, or past the threshold at which these claims are finally accepted as valid, then we are also obliged to accept the criteria of procedural democracy as valid measures of our national performance.

These criteria imply the existence of a body of primary rights, the rights necessary, though not sufficient, if a people is to govern itself. It could be readily shown that this body of primary rights must include most, though not all, of the rights and liberties the Supreme Court has held to be protected by the Constitution. As long as the primary rights necessary to procedural democracy exist, then all the political rights exist that are necessary if a people is to govern itself. Surely no narrower definition of inalienable rights ought to be acceptable to us. At the same time, however, any broader definition that includes rights inconsistent with these primary rights ought not to be acceptable to us. For to claim a right inconsistent with the primary rights necessary to procedural democracy is to deny the validity of procedural democracy and thus the capacity and right of a people to govern itself. If doctrine and practice were to treat these primary rights as inalienable, then all claims to rights inconsistent with these primary rights would be subject to final determination by the ordinary processes of collective decision making, and thus by voters, representatives, and legislators. To hold otherwise would be to deny that, taken all around, citizens are roughly equally qualified to make judgments on matters involving secondary rights. But since practically any public policy will infringe upon someone's existing privileges and thus give rise to a claim that a right has been diminished, if citizens are held to be incompetent on all matters involving secondary rights, what matters are they qualified to decide?

Viewed in this light, the commitment to corporate capitalism needs to be reconsidered. Earlier, when the framers had discussed their fears about majorities that might invade the rights of minorities, more often than not they mentioned rights to property. Their reasoned justification of a right to property, if they held one, would no doubt have been Lockean. Yet the Lockean justification of property makes no sense, it was suggested earlier, when it is applied to the large modern business corporation. It is absurd to regard as inalienable one's right to buy and thereafter own shares in ITT, and it approaches the ridiculous to argue that because one owns shares in ITT one possesses an inalienable and exclusive, if in practice quite useless, right to choose the directors of the firm, and that the primary legal obligation of the directors and management is, by a legal extension of the original doctrine, to protect the interests of owners above those of any other claimants.

If we abandon the absurdities in extending Locke on private property to ownership or control of the modern business corporation, then the rights of owners must be seen as secondary in relation to the primary rights that are necessary to self-government.

If ownership and control of corporate enterprise are matters of secondary not primary right, then the mere assertion of a right to private property does not provide a rational justification for private ownership of a large economic enterprise. If privately owned enterprise can be justified at all, it must be on the grounds of comparative social effectiveness: that is, of all the possible alternatives, this form provides the greatest social advantage with least social disadvantage. The only question we need to ask, then, is whether a privately owned corporation is more effective in achieving our social purposes, including procedural democracy, than all the possible alternatives to it.

In this perspective, any large economic enterprise is in principle a public enterprise. It exists not by private right but only to meet social goals. Questions about these social goals, and the comparative advantages and disadvantages of different forms, are properly in the public domain, matters for public discussion, choice, and decision, to be determined collectively by processes that satisfy the criteria of procedural democracy.

To be sure, none of this implies a direct answer to the question of how a large enterprise should be organized, controlled, or owned. To arrive at a correct answer depends as much on technical as on philosophical or ideological judgments, and perhaps a good deal more. Although this assertion contradicts a nearly universal dogma held on all sides, it is readily demonstrable by even the briefest consideration of the range of alternatives. If we were to take into account only the most obvious possibilities with respect to the internal government of enterprises, external controls, markets, prices, and the locus of ownership together with the rights and obligations of owners, we would quickly arrive at a very large array of theoretically possible combinations. Few of these can be dismissed a priori as unsuitable. Probably none can be shown to be superior to all the others in all circumstances. Consequently what has already become standard practice in advanced countries in this century will, one hopes, be taken for granted by citizens in advanced societies in the twenty-first century: a complex society cannot protect the rights, needs, and interests of its people with one single, prevailing form of economic organization but requires instead a network of enterprises organized in many different combinations of internal government, external controls, and ownership.

However, in choosing among the large number of possible combinations available in any particular instance, citizens of a country committed to procedural democracy would obviously want to avoid consequences adverse to procedural democracy. Earlier it was suggested that this country's commitment to corporate capitalism resulted in at least two such adverse consequences. As to those resulting from the unequal distribution of political resources, a country committed to procedural democracy must either place effective limits on the extent to which economic resources can be converted into political resources, or else ensure that economic resources are much more equally distributed than they are in the United States at present. So far we have tried only the first; that approach has largely failed. Perhaps it may prove possible by regulation to reduce the direct and indirect impact on political equality, effective participation, and political understanding of vast differences in income and wealth, but the record so far is dispiriting. It is time—long past time—to consider the other approach. Moreover, considerations of substantive distributive justice would seem to require a considerable reduction in inequalities in wealth and incomes. At the very least, the question of distribution of wealth and income ought to be high on the agenda of national politics.

As to the second of the adverse consequences of corporate capitalism, the enormous expansion of hierarchical systems of control, we need to be open to new ideas about governing economic enterprises and to a rapidly growing body of experience and experiments in this country and abroad. The author believes that the requisites of procedural democracy hold among the people who work for economic enterprises, and that the criteria of procedural democracy ought therefore to be applied to the government of firms. But a reasonable claim can be made for each of many other possibilities. Moreover, it seems obvious, though often ignored, that forms of control are not fully determined by forms of ownership. Government ownership is as consistent as private ownership with despotic control of enterprises. The form of control should be treated as a problem that is prior to the question of the form of ownership. What is a desirable form of ownership ought to be viewed, at least in part, as subordinate to and dependent on a judgment as to what is a desirable form of control. In any case, the range of alternatives this country ought to consider and experiment with is really quite broad and needs a great deal of systematic study.

Let us now turn back to the fourth and fifth historic commitments of the United States mentioned earlier. It is not an excessively harsh judgment to say that over three decades the presidency was transformed into a kind of plebiscitary principate with despotic tendencies toward arbitrary, ruthless, and self-aggrandizing exploitation of power. What is more, the other major political actors, including the Congress, the Supreme Court, the parties, the electorate, and the most active and attentive political strata all collaborated in that transformation. Only with the utmost reluctance and in the final hour was the Congress compelled to rediscover in the impeachment process a constitutional means for firing a president guilty of criminal acts. Now that impeachment has been used successfully and shown to be effective and salubrious, it is not too much to hope that the machinery will be kept oiled and ready for use. No president should ever again forget that he or she is anything other than the chief executive officer of a democratic republic.

If one part of the Constitution has proved to be workable, the fact that there was a need for impeachment proved how badly the constitutional system had been working. Yet nothing has changed in the fundamental institutional structure itself to reduce the pressures toward the pseudo-democratization of the presidency. For it still remains true that without a strong concentration of political resources in the presidential office, the policies preferred by a majority of citizens and their elected representatives stand a good chance of defeat by a well-entrenched opposition. Not only is this arrangement inconsistent with procedural democracy but it is arbitrary and unfair in its substantive results. Moreover, taken over any considerable period of time the evidence does not show that these minority vetoes constitute a defense of primary rights; rather, they tend to ensure the triumph of secondary rights or privileges over primary rights.

Taking all these problems into account, political scientists need to begin a serious and systematic reexamination of the constitutional system much beyond anything done up to now. They need to give serious and systematic attention to possibilities that may initially seem unrealistic, such as abolishing the presidential veto; creating a collegial chief executive; institutionalizing adversary processes in policy decisions; establishing an office of advocacy to represent interests not otherwise adequately represented in or before Congress and the administrative agencies, including future generations; creating randomly selected citizen assemblies parallel with the major standing committees of the Congress to analyze policy and make recommendations; creating a unicameral Congress; inaugurating proportional representation and a multiparty system in congressional elections; and many other possibilities. Unfortunately, designing a constitution is very far from an exact science. It is questionable whether the best political scientists, or for that matter citizens drawn from any source, have the knowledge and skills to excel the performance of the framers. Probably we do not even know how best to proceed toward the cultivation of the knowledge and skills of constitution making that we or our successors may one day be expected to provide.

The difficulty of arriving at knowledge of this kind points directly to the most challenging of the criteria of procedural democracy, the criterion of enlightened understanding. The criteria of political equality and effective participation are intended to ensure that citizens have a final say as to the goals that effectively determine the ends of public policy, and whenever they wish, a final say as to the means as well. But if a people were to meet these criteria perfectly and yet meet the criterion of enlightened understanding badly, the democratic process would be irrelevant to their preferences, needs, and interests. For if people regularly choose means that impede rather than facilitate attaining their goals, or if they invariably choose goals that damage their deeper needs, then of how much value is the process?

The criterion of enlightened understanding is not only the most difficult to meet but the most resistant to precise statement. Every key word in the criterion as it was presented earlier is ambiguous, and the concepts the words are intended to signify are difficult and complex. However, even if it might well be impossible to define the criterion so rigorously as to specify quite precisely what we would regard as a condition of satisfactory fulfillment, it is a much less difficult task to judge when the criterion is *not* satisfactorily met and what some of the obstacles are. Surely it is far from being satisfactorily attained in this country and elsewhere.

In a loose and general way, it is obvious that if people are to know their preferences, they need knowledge both of means and ends. Adequate knowledge of means and ends requires an understanding not only of the external world but also of the inner world of the self.

It seems obvious too that if citizens are to understand the external world, they must have access to experts. It may have been realistic for Rousseau or Jefferson or the framers but it would be profoundly unrealistic today to expect citizens, even highly educated ones, to have enough technical knowledge. Think of the complexities of current policy decisions: breeder reactor, B-1, Trident, Middle East, catalytic converter, inflation-unemployment trade-offs, rate of increase in the money supply, costs and administrative problems of alternative health care arrangements, SST, Amtrak, limitations on artificial losses, outer continental shelf. . . . Most of the time all of us are ordinary citizens without a great deal of technical knowledge about matters like these. Consequently, whatever may have been the situation in previous centuries, in our own and surely in the next, it is foolish to think that the demos can achieve its purposes without experts.

Yet even in the best of circumstances experts are hard to control. Decisions as to means can also determine ends. Democracy only for general ends and meritocracy for means will soon become meritocracy for both means *and* ends. Thus if the demos is to retain final control over ends, citizens will also need responsible and responsive intermediaries—quasi-experts—to help them hold experts accountable, and to gain an adequate understanding of their own basic rights, needs, and interests, and of the policies best designed to satisfy these needs. Even if all our elected officials were to perform this intermediary role well—and many do not—they would not be enough. We need quasi-expert intermediaries spread among the whole body of citizens, so that every citizen has ready access to technical understanding. While it is surely asking too much to expect that most citizens can be experts on many of the issues of national politics, it is not foolish to hope that one day almost every citizen might be sufficiently informed about some of the issues so that a less informed citizen could readily turn to a more informed fellow citizen, a quasi-expert, for a responsible clarification of the matter at hand.

When we turn toward the inner self and ask what we need in order to understand the needs and interests of the self, including those crucial aspects of oneself that are inextricably bound up with and require a sympathetic understanding of other selves, we confront a question to which the answer is inescapably open-ended. The answer must be open-ended because at any given moment human consciousness is necessarily limited by itself, that is, by its own condition. It seems not wildly unrealistic to hope that in the epoch ahead, human consciousness will change profoundly, and that what we might now consider as enlightened understanding, and the best ways to reach it, will be seen by our successors in a vastly different perspective. If mankind is spared as much time as separates us from Socrates, or even as brief an interval as separates us from the historical situation that necessarily limited the understanding of Mill, Lincoln, Freud, and Marx, we cannot say what vast transformations human consciousness may undergo. The criterion of enlightened understanding beckons us forward but it cannot tell us what we shall discover.

It goes without saying, of course, that the world is full of the most acute dangers to human progress and even to human survival. More perhaps than at any time in some millions of years, the prospects of humankind depend on the outcome of a perilous race in which the growth of an enlightened understanding of ourselves and our universe is pitted against the consequences of actions taken out of ignorance or misunderstanding of our most fundamental needs and interests.

No matter what it does, this country alone cannot ensure a successful outcome to that race, though we can by our own unaided mistakes cause a fatal outcome. Some Americans may be tempted to conclude that in a world so hazardous, our salvation and that of the world require us to bring the rest of humanity rapidly around to our way of thinking. But experience suggests that when Americans, or anyone else for that matter, begin to talk about a national mission to save the world, it is time for everyone to run for cover. Instead, one might propose a very different approach. If we want to move a bit closer toward the best standards to which we are already committed by our national experience, a good way to start is not so much by trying to change others as by changing ourselves.*

* In this article I have drawn freely from a lecture, "Liberal Democracy in the United States," delivered at the University of Texas, February 25, 1976, to be published in William Livingston (ed.), *The Prospects for Liberal Democracy*.

PART II
Actors in the Policy-Making Process

The Nixon Brush with Tyranny

JAMES DAVID BARBER

The Presidency is a peculiar office. The Founding Fathers left it extraordinarily loose in definition, partly because they trusted George Washington to invent a tradition as he went along. It is an institution made a piece at a time by successive men in the White House. Jefferson reached out to Congress to put together the beginnings of political parties; Jackson's dramatic force extended electoral partisanship to its mass base; Lincoln vastly expanded the administrative reach of the office, Wilson and the Roosevelts showed its rhetorical possibilities—in fact every President's mind and demeanor has left its mark on a heritage still in lively development.

But the Presidency is much more than an institution. It is a focus of feelings. In general, popular feelings about politics are low-key, shallow, casual. For example, the vast majority of Americans knows virtually nothing of what Congress is doing and cares less. The Presidency is different. The Presidency is the focus for the most intense and persistent emotions in the American polity. The President is a symbolic leader, the one figure who draws together the people's hopes and fears for the political future. On top of all his routine duties, he has to carry that off—or fail.

Our emotional attachment to Presidents shows up when one dies in office. People were not just disappointed or worried when President Kennedy was killed;

JAMES DAVID BARBER is James B. Duke Professor of Political Science at Duke University. This article is adapted from the recently published second edition of his book, *The Presidential Character*. Except for minor editorial changes, the predictive analysis of the Nixon Presidency that appears at the beginning of the article remains unchanged from when it was originally written in 1971 for the first edition of *The Presidential Character*. Professor Barber is now at work on a study of the relation between the mass media and presidential policies.

people wept at the loss of a man most had never even met. Kennedy was young and charismatic—but history shows that whenever a President dies in office, heroic Lincoln or debased Harding, McKinley or Garfield, the same wave of deep emotion sweeps across the country. On the other hand, the death of an ex-President brings forth no such intense emotional reaction.

The President is the first political figure children are aware of (later they add Congress, the Court, and others, as "helpers" of the President). With some exceptions among children in deprived circumstances, the President is seen as a "benevolent leader," one who nurtures, sustains, and inspires the citizenry. Presidents regularly show up among "most admired" contemporaries and forebears, and the President is the "best known" (in the sense of sheer name recognition) person in the country. At inauguration time, even Presidents elected by close margins are supported by much larger majorities than the election returns show, for people rally round as he actually assumes office. There is a similar reaction when the people see their President threatened by crisis: if he takes action, there is a favorable spurt in the Gallup poll whether he succeeds or fails.

Obviously the President gets more attention in schoolbooks, press, and television than any other politician. He is one of very few who can make news by doing good things. *His* emotional state is a matter of continual public commentary, as is the manner in which his personal and official families conduct themselves. The media bring across the President not as some neutral administrator or corporate executive to be assessed by his production, but as a special being with mysterious dimensions.

We have no king. The sentiments English children—and adults—direct to the Queen have no place to go in our system but to the President. Whatever his talents—Coolidge-type or Roosevelt-type—the President is the only available object for such national-religious-monarchical sentiments as Americans possess.

The President helps people make sense of politics. Congress is a tangle of committees, the bureaucracy is a maze of agencies. The President is one man trying to do a job—a picture much more understandable to the mass of people who find themselves in the same boat. Furthermore, he is the top man. He ought to know what is going on and set it right. So when the economy goes sour, or war drags on, or domestic violence erupts, the President is available to take the blame. Then when things go right, it seems the President must have had a hand in it. Indeed, the flow of political life is marked off by Presidents: the "Eisenhower Era," the "Kennedy Years."

What all this means is that the President's *main* responsibilities reach far beyond administering the Executive Branch or commanding the armed forces. The White House is first and foremost a place of public leadership. That inevitably brings to bear on the President intense moral, sentimental, and quasi-religious pressures which can, if he lets them, distort his own thinking and feeling. If there is such a thing as extraordinary sanity, it is needed nowhere so much as in the White House.

Who the President is at a given time can make a profound difference in the whole thrust and direction of national politics. Since we have only one President at a time, we can never prove this by comparison, but even the most superficial speculation confirms the commonsense view that the man himself weighs heavily among other historical factors. A Wilson re-elected in 1920, a Hoover in 1932, a John F. Kennedy in 1964 would, it seems very likely, have guided the body politic along rather different paths from those their actual successors chose. Or try to imagine a Theodore Roosevelt ensconced behind today's "bully pulpit" of a Presidency, or Lyndon Johnson as President in the age of McKinley. Only someone mesmerized by the lures of historical inevitability can suppose that it would have made little or no difference to government policy had Alf Landon replaced FDR in 1936, had Dewey beaten Truman in 1948, or Adlai Stevenson reigned through the 1950s. Not only would these alternative Presidents have advocated different policies—they would have approached the office from very different psychological angles. It stretches credibility to think that Eugene McCarthy would have run the institution the way Lyndon Johnson did.

I am not about to argue that once you know a President's personality you know everything. But the degree and quality of a President's emotional involvement in an issue are powerful influences on how he defines the issue itself, how much attention he pays to it, which facts and persons he sees as relevant to its resolution, and, finally, what principles and purposes he associates with the issue. Every story of Presidential decision-making is really two stories: an outer one in which a rational man calculates and an inner one in which an emotional man feels. The two are forever connected. Any real President is one whole man and his deeds reflect his wholeness.

As for personality, it is a matter of tendencies. It is not that one President "has" some basic characteristic that another President does not "have." That old way of treating a trait as a possession, like a rock in a basket, ignores the universality of aggressiveness, compliancy, detachment, and other human drives. We all have all of them, but in different amounts and in different combinations.

PREDICTING PRESIDENTS

The best way to predict a President's personality—character, world view, and style—is to see how he constructed it in the first place. Especially in the early stages, life is experimental; consciously or not, a person tries out various ways of defining and maintaining and raising self-esteem. He looks to his environment for clues as to who he is and how well he is doing. These lessons of life slowly sink in: certain self-images and evaluations, certain ways of looking at the world, certain styles of action get confirmed by his experience and he gradually adopts them as his own. If we can see that process of development, we can understand the product. The features to note are those bearing on Presidential performance.

Experimental development continues all the way to death; we will not blind ourselves to midlife changes, particularly in the full-scale prediction case, that of Richard Nixon. But it is often much easier to see the basic patterns in early life histories. Later on a whole host of distractions—especially the image-making all politicians learn to practice—clouds the picture.

In general, character has its *main* development in childhood, world view in adolescence, style in early adulthood. The stance toward life I call character grows out of the child's experiments in relating to parents, brothers and sisters, and peers at play and in school, as well as to his own body and the objects around it. Slowly the child defines an orientation toward experience; once established, that tends to last despite much subsequent contradiction. By adolescence, the child has been hearing and seeing how people make their worlds meaningful, and now he is moved to relate himself—his own meanings—to those around him. His focus of attention shifts toward the future; he senses that decisions about his fate are coming and he looks into the premises for those decisions. Thoughts about the way the world works and how one might work in it, about what people are like and how one might be like them or not, and about the values people share and how one might share in them too—these are typical concerns for the post-child, pre-adult mind of the adolescent.

These themes come together strongly in early adulthood, when the person moves from contemplation to responsible action and adopts a style. In most biographical accounts this period stands out in stark clarity—the time of emergence, the time the young man found himself. I call it his first independent political success. It was then he moved beyond the detailed guidance of his family; then his self-esteem was dramatically boosted; then he came forth as a person to be reckoned with by other people. The *way* he did that is profoundly important to him. Typically he grasps that style and hangs onto it. Much later, coming into the Presidency, something in him remembers this earlier victory and reemphasizes the style that made it happen.

Character provides the main thrust and broad direction—but it does not *determine*, in any fixed sense, world view and style. The story of development does not end with the end of childhood. Thereafter, the culture one grows in and the ways that culture is translated by parents and peers shapes the meanings one makes of his character. The going world view gets learned and that learning helps channel character forces. Thus it will not necessarily be true that compulsive characters have reactionary beliefs, or that compliant characters believe in compromise. Similarly for style: historical accidents play a large part in furnishing special opportunities for action—and in blocking off alternatives. For example, however much anger a young man may feel, that anger will not be expressed in rhetoric unless and until his life situation provides a platform and an audience. Style thus has a stature and independence of its own. Those who would reduce all explanation to character neglect these highly significant later channelings. For beyond the root is the branch, above the foundation the superstructure, and starts do not prescribe finishes.

FOUR TYPES OF PRESIDENTIAL CHARACTER

The five concepts—character, world view, style, power situation, and climate of expectations—cluster the Presidents since Theodore Roosevelt into four types. This is the fundamental scheme of my analysis. It offers a way to move past the complexities to the main contrasts and comparisons.

The first baseline in defining Presidential types is *activity-passivity*. How much energy does the man invest in his Presidency? Lyndon Johnson went at his day like a human cyclone, coming to rest long after the sun went down. Calvin Coolidge often slept eleven hours a night and still needed a nap in the middle of the day. In between the Presidents array themselves on the high or low side of the activity line.

The second baseline is *positive-negative affect* toward one's activity—that is, how he feels about what he does. Relatively speaking, does he seem to experience his political life as happy or sad, enjoyable or discouraging, positive or negative in its main effect. The feeling I am after here is not grim satisfaction in a job well done, not some philosophical conclusion. The idea is this: is he someone who, on the surfaces we can see, gives forth the feeling that he has *fun* in political life? Franklin Roosevelt's Secretary of War, Henry L. Stimson wrote that the Roosevelts "not only understood the *use* of power, they knew the *enjoyment* of power, too. . . . Whether a man is burdened by power or enjoys power; whether he is trapped by responsibility or made free by it; whether he is moved by other people and outer forces or moves them—that is the essence of leadership."

The positive-negative baseline, then, is a general symptom of the fit between the man and his experience, a kind of register of *felt* satisfaction.

Why might we expect these two simple dimensions to outline the main character types? Because they stand for two central features of anyone's orientation toward life. In nearly every study of personality, some form of the active-passive contrast is critical; the general tendency to act or be acted upon is evident in such concepts as dominance-submission, extraversion-introversion, aggression-timidity, attack-defense, fight-flight, engagement-withdrawal, approach-avoidance. In everyday life we sense quickly the general energy output of the people we deal with. Similarly we catch on fairly quickly to the affect dimension—whether the person seems to be optimistic or pessimistic, hopeful or skeptical, happy or sad. The two baselines are clear and they are also independent of one another: all of us know people who are very active but seem discouraged, others who are quite passive but seem happy, and so forth. The activity baseline refers to what one does, the affect baseline to how one feels about what he does.

Both are crude clues to character. They are leads into four basic character patterns long familiar in psychological research. In summary form, these are the main configurations:

Active-positive. There is a congruence, a consistency, between much activity and the enjoyment of it, indicating relatively high self-esteem and relative success in relating to the environment. The man shows an orientation toward productiveness as a value and an ability to use his styles flexibly, adaptively, suiting the dance to the music. He sees himself as developing over time toward relatively well defined personal goals—growing toward his image of himself as he might yet be. There is an emphasis on rational mastery on using the brain to move the feet. This may get him into trouble; he may fail to take account of the irrational in politics. Not everyone he deals with sees things his way and he may find it hard to understand why.

Active-negative. The contradiction here is between relatively intense effort and relatively low emotional reward for that effort. The activity has a compulsive quality, as if the man were trying to make up for something or to escape from anxiety into hard work. He seems ambitious, striving upward, power-seeking. His stance toward the environment is aggressive and he has a persistent problem in managing his aggressive feelings. His self-image is vague and discontinuous. Life is a hard struggle to achieve and hold power, hampered by the condemnations of a perfectionistic conscience. Active-negative types pour energy into the political system, but it is an energy distorted from within.

Passive-positive. This is the receptive, compliant, other-directed character whose life is a search for affection as a reward for being agreeable and cooperative rather than personally assertive. The contradiction is between low self-esteem (on grounds of being unlovable, unattractive) and a superficial optimism. A hopeful attitude helps dispel doubt and elicits encouragement from others. Passive-positive types help soften the harsh edge of politics. But their dependence and the fragility of their hopes and enjoyments make disappointment in politics likely.

Passive-negative. The factors are consistent—but how are we to account for the man's *political* role-taking? Why is someone who does little in politics and enjoys it less there at all? The answer lies in the passive-negative character-rooted orientation toward doing dutiful service; this compensates for low self-esteem based on a sense of uselessness. Passive-negative types are in politics because they think they ought to be. They may be well adapted to certain nonpolitical roles, but they lack the experience and flexibility to perform effectively as political leaders. Their tendency is to withdraw, to escape from the conflct and uncertainty of politics by emphasizing vague principles (especially prohibitions) and procedural arrangements. They become guardians of the right and proper way, above the sordid politicking of lesser men.

Active-positive Presidents want most to achieve results. Active-negatives aim to get and keep power. Passive-positives are after love. Passive-negatives emphasize their civic virtue. The relation of activity to enjoyment in a President thus tends to outline a cluster of characteristics, to set apart the adapted from the compulsive, compliant, and withdrawn types.

PREDICTING NIXON, SPRING 1972

One could hardly be wrong about Nixon's overall placement in the active-negative category. Particularly in campaigning, Nixon on the way up was famous for his grueling schedule of speeches, not only on his own behalf, but also for innumerable Republican candidates in off-year elections. From 1950 through his defeat for the Presidency a decade later, Richard Nixon was to be found rustling the hustings, flat-out, day after day, night after night, short on sleep, often exhausted, but never too tired for just one more speech. In office his pace slowed only slightly: Nixon-watchers were continually discovering him "exhausted," "almost grey with fatigue," cutting vacations short because he "simply could not stand the idleness." He traveled 160,000 miles as Eisenhower's emissary, wrote almost all his own speeches, and campaigned in 36 states in six weeks for Goldwater in 1964. Out of office in 1961, Nixon became the "pacesetter" for his Wall Street law firm. The main thing he liked about working in New York was that he found it "a place where you can't slow down—a fast track. Any person tends to vegetate unless he is moving on a fast track."

In the 1968 campaign, Nixon was persuaded to slow down his normally fractic schedule and to intersperse periods of rest and relaxation. He took it easier, learned to pace himself. Was this an exception or a new rule? Even if he had always worked as he did in the 1968 campaign, Nixon would have to be scored on the active side. And the overwhelming evidence from the rest of his pre-Presidential life confirmed that.

The evidence on Nixon's affect toward his experience is similarly clear. Through his political years, he has presented himself as a man intensely engaged in action he find emotionally punishing. On numerous occasions Nixon saw himself as *about to quit*:

—In 1952, after his dramatic speech about the Nixon fund, he was "ready to chuck the whole thing," according to his manager.

—In 1954, "Nixon confided to a few intimates the only consolation was that it would be his last campaign," and "He and his wife discussed their future from all angles, and the Vice-President agreed to retire from politics after his term ended in 1957. At Mrs. Nixon's request he noted the date and the decision on a piece of paper that he tucked in his wallet."

—In 1956, when Eisenhower intimated Nixon could have a Cabinet post instead of another term as Vice-President, "Nixon planned to quit public life in disgust, then resolved to run again. . . ."

—In 1961, he spoke to the Senate of his 14 years of government service, "as I complete that period."

—In 1962, after his defeat for the California governorship, he told the press, "You won't have Nixon to kick around any more, because, gentlemen, this is my last press conference."

But there were also in the Nixon record as of January 1969 many more direct indications of his feeling that *the price of success has been suffering*, indications of depression, anxiety, and sadness in his political experience that contrast sharply with the sentiments positive types express.

—In 1947, as a new Congressman, Nixon "had the same lost feeling I had had when I went into military service." Then, after the Hiss case was broken, he said that no one could fight Communism without "expecting to pay the penalty for the rest of his life." Having won out over Hiss, "I should have been elated. . . . However, I experienced a sense of letdown which is difficult to explain or even to understand. . . . There was also a sense of shock and sadness that a man like Hiss could have fallen so low."

—In 1950, running for the Senate, Nixon was "a sad but earnest underdog."

—In 1952 the "Nixon Fund" episode left him "gloomy and angry"; in particular, Eisenhower's hesitation about retaining him on the ticket made him look "like someone had smashed him" and he "forced a disbelieving smile and muttered something to himself." Mrs. Nixon said, "Why should we keep taking this?" Leaving his hotel to deliver the "Checkers" speech "seemed like the last mile," Nixon recalled. After the speech he said, "I loused it up, and I am sorry. . . . It was a flop." He "turned away from his friends—and let loose the tears he had been holding back." (In fact, the speech was a great success.)

—From 1953 on, as Vice-President, "the first year was a disappointment. But the second—1954—was far worse; the worst of Nixon's twelve years in politics." In 1954 he told a friend, "I am tired, bone tired. My heart's not in it." He was "disappointed with much that had happened" and "disappointed also in the caliber of many Republicans and the Party's organization generally."

—In 1955, when Eisenhower had the first of his heart attacks, "Only a few friends were aware how acutely uneasy Nixon was about his capacity to meet the challenge. He aged the equivalent of quite a few years during those three months—in his own estimation, as well as that of those with whom he worked." "His voice was hoarse and charged with emotion. 'It's terrible, it's terrible!' he said over and over. . . . [H]e was trying to keep his composure, but he was in semi-shock. His eyes were red and his face drawn and pale."

—In 1956, Ike's hesitation about keeping him on the ticket was "an emotional ordeal for Nixon, one of the greatest hurts of his career." A friend said at the time, "He is a pessimist, and was running scared."

—In 1960, after his first debate with Kennedy, "The Nixon camp became grim and nervous and could talk only of 'recouping.' "

—In 1962 came his despondent diatribe after being defeated for the governorship.

Clearly Nixon was one for whom the burdens outweighed the enjoyments, the responsibilities outweighed the pleasures. His political life—which was nearly his whole life—was a punishing one. At most he derived from it a grim satisfaction in endurance, but there was not much of the spontaneous, easy enjoyment a fundamentally self-loving person feels from time to time as he goes about his chosen round. Nixon exerted extraordinary energies in a life which brought him back extraordinary hardships.

Nixon's is a special variant of the active-negative character. With his remarkable flexibility regarding issues and ideologies, Nixon can be "defeated" any number of times on specific questions of policy without feeling personally threatened. His investment is not in values, not in standing fast for some principle—although, if he were to stand fast, his doing so would certainly be rationalized in terms of principle. His investment is in himself, and Nixon's self is taken up with its management. As Margaret Mead has noted, "The President thrives on opposition. It is a form of stimulation for him." Thus he will court the strains of political resistance, finding in them yet another confirmation of his virtue.

But let the issue reach his central concern, the concern of self-management, and the fat may go into the fire. Threats to his independence in particular—the sense that he is being controlled from without because he cannot be trusted, because he is weak or stupid or unstable—will call forth a strong inner response. For Nixon, the prime form of the active-negative command "I must," is this: "*I must make my own way.*" Only when a crisis gathers around him, one he cannot escape by moving on to some alternative crisis, and he experiences a sense of entrapment is he likely to move toward the classic form of rigidification.

The key variable here is time. "Time running out," the President wrote on his pad before Cambodia. As the clock ticks forward, Nixon confronts his future in two stages. First is 1972. As the election approaches, Nixon's Presidential fate will clarify itself. If the uncertainties fade in the light of the polls, and the probability of a defeat for Nixon rises sharply, this President will be sorely tempted to do what he feels he must do before it is too late. The loss of power to forces beyond his control would constitute a severe threat. That would be a time to go down, if go down one must, in flames.[1]

THE NIXON PERFORMANCE, SPRING 1976

How quickly the fog of history settles over the brutal terrain of the past! Wars become romantic adventures, depressions provide material for folksy fables, the pestilence is made into an antique amusement. Thus with "Watergate." The President who came after Nixon told us it had been just a nightmare and it was all over. "The system" took care of such problems (and surely would again, if need be). There was nothing fundamental to worry about, so we should put all that nastiness behind us and move on to make a better future.

Of course, that is the Nixonian way of looking at it. He always did have a

---

[1] For an expanded discussion of this point see James David Barber, *The Presidential Character: Predicting Performance in the White House* (Englewood Cliffs, N.J.: Prentice-Hall, Inc., 1972), p. 442.

knack for diverting the public mind, whenever it began to focus too strongly on him. Like a television camera, Nixon moved from scene to scene, quickly, lest understanding set in. He knew, too, how to cooperate with the empiricism of history, by drowning the truth in the facts; today the obsessed Watergate buff can find a lifetime occupation tracing out just where, say, Ulasewicz was when he called Kalmbach on such and such an evening—much as the assassination buffs used to do. The flood of fact-packed books on the subject swells across the bookshelf.

I think Nixon was neither an accidental nightmare nor an automaton whose rise and fall were inherent in "the system." He will be back, in his essentials, the next time the public elects an active-negative President. He very nearly got away with establishing a Presidential tyranny in the United States. He was caught by a mistake he could easily have avoided—whatever the system. Because it is so important to the future of the Presidency to keep it out of the hands of future Nixons, his case is worth examining in detail.

Chapters 10 through 12 of my book *The Presidential Character*, written in late 1971 and published in the pre-Watergate spring of 1972, predicted what would happen with second-term President Nixon—not an astrological prediction of details, but an analytical forecast of the main themes. This brief essay does not untangle the whole complex story of Nixon and Watergate—that would take another book—but it points to the key evidence on the theory's critical points. Even in this truncated form, though, it is the story of our nearest brush yet with an American tyranny.[2]

THE NIXON TYRANNY

The Nixonians at the top of the Presidency took their cues and views from the President. Under his direction, and often encouraged by personal enthusiasm, they succeeded in a wide range of tyrannous achievements:

—They made secret war.
—They made secret agreements to sell immense quantities of deadly weapons to nervous nations.

[2] At the end of the Nixon regime there was a coup: the Presidency was run by a general who, by the luck of the draw, had a passion for reason, if also a certain lack of moral imagination. The general, who more than a year previously had ripped out Nixon's taping systems without permission, in the summer of 1974 entered into negotiation with the Vice President regarding the conditions under which he could come to power—the general again acting on his own. Another military leader, the Secretary of Defense, established a system by which he could veto the Commander-in-Chief's orders to the armed forces. A Presidential order conveyed to the Secretary of State elicited the reply, "Tell the President to . . . himself." (Bob Woodward and Carl Bernstein, The Final Days [New York, Simon and Schuster, 1976], p. 199). No tanks in the streets. No bearded madman gesticulating from a balcony. Just some quiet little rearrangements to keep things going—without the interference of the People's Choice. Fortunately it was one of the Nixon administration's few Horatios, rather than one of its many Iagos, who grabbed power. A system that has to depend on that kind of fortune is dangerous.

—They supported foreign governments which ruled by terror and they helped overthrow progressive governments.

—They received bribes and sold high offices.

—They recruited and operated a secret White House police force and ordered them to break the law, continually and casually.

—They abrogated Congress's power of the purse by impounding huge sums.

—They subverted important segments of the electoral system, the judicial system, the law enforcement system, the tax system, and the free speech system.

—They purposefully and systematically lied to the public, the Congress, foreign heads of state and diplomats, and the loyal leadership of their own party and administration about matters of high political significance.

The important point here is not that Nixon was a bad man (he was), or that he was mentally unbalanced (he may well have been, toward the end), or even that he was guilty of any crimes for which he could have been convicted in a court of law (we will never know). Had Nixon never been President, none of that would have mattered much. It is his *political* significance that lends immense significance to his tawdry triumph over our Constitution.

Nixon demonstrated the vulnerability of the American political system. Throughout his career, his repeated victories after disastrous defeats show with dramatic clarity how the process of evaluating potential Presidents failed miserably to predict and guard us from the machinations of an expert flim-flam man. The American people had every opportunity to know what they were getting. They elected Nixon despite the most abundant evidence ever available regarding the character of any Presidential candidate.

Similarly with checks and balances. Nixon had no need to march on the Capitol at the head of his White House guard or to throw barbed wire around the Justice Department. He simply set up his own little government on top of the Constitutional one and dared the world to say him nay. It took four and a half years for Congress to begin to suppose that his impeachment should be suggested, and they took this move only after they had evidence hard and massive enough to choke Caligula's horse. Through nearly all his Presidency, Nixon had but to assert his authority to enhance his power, be it the power to bomb or tap, to impound or burgle, to broadcast or blackmail and bribe.

For those who take it as a sign of the system's stability that he was ultimately driven from office, it is sobering to remember that his downfall was nearly accidental. At point after point he could have been rescued by other accidents or by easy efforts of his own, as I hope to show in a few pages.

Perhaps there is some way the electoral machinery and the system of checks and balances can be readjusted, to prevent such enormous political risks. Or perhaps there is some way, without major procedural reform, to help the existing institutions acquire the vision and the will to see to it that we get quality Presidents. I see the most promising development along this line in the steady improvement of data and theory by which present-day decision-makers can predict, if not the "great" Presidents, at least the disastrous ones.

Drawing on the work of many scholars, journalists, and biographers, I was able to see some parts of Nixon's pattern before he became President. On the eve of his first inauguration, January 19, 1969, I wrote that, "The primary danger of the Nixon administration, then, will be that the President will grasp some line of policy or method of operation and pursue it in spite of its failure." I wondered that night,

> How will Nixon respond to challenges to the morality of his regime, to charges of scandal and/or corruption? First such charges strike a raw nerve, not only from the Checkers business, but also from deep within the personality in which the demands of the superego are so harsh and hard. (For every President, this kind of thing comes up.) The first defense is pleading innocent: I didn't know, it didn't affect me. The guilty party (Walter Jenkins, Bobby Baker) is not my boy, I am not involved. The ordinary processes of justice must take their course. There will not be as in Harry Truman's case a sense of loyalty to the Pendergasts no matter what the charge, or Ike's readiness as in Dixon-Yates to make all the facts public, while withdrawing a bit. The first impulse (before the above) will be to hush it up, to conceal it, bring down the blinds. If it breaks open and Nixon cannot avoid commenting on it, there is a real setup here for another crisis, a dramatic appearance in which he is vindicated.[3]

In the early Spring of 1969, I followed up with a speech at Stanford asking, "Will there be a 'Tragedy of Richard Nixon?' " In this speech I suggested that Nixon was likely to follow the pattern of rigidification that had earlier been seen in Woodrow Wilson, Herbert Hoover, Andrew Johnson, and Lyndon Johnson. Other papers followed, leading up to the publication of *The Presidential Character* in early 1972.[4] The book was filled with retrospective "predictions": we *could* have known in advance what past Presidents would do (in the main) by noticing key biographical characteristics and combining them with the main situational elements. But, with one exception, all those "predictions" concerned events that had already happened. The Nixon case was the best test so far for my theory because there it was possible to make real predictions: given certain situations, Nixon's character, style, and world view would produce certain lines of action.

Unless we are willing to lapse again into the political sleep that brought us Johnson and Nixon—that gave us a decade of disaster in the White House—we need some way to improve radically on our predictions. In that spirit, I will first check the main Nixon characteristics against his history as it followed after the predictions, then trace the course of his rigidification, and finally speculate on the possible meanings, for our political future, of Nixon's peculiar obsession with appearance.

[3] James David Barber, "A Summary of Predictions of Richard M. Nixon as President," a paper distributed to colleagues at the Center for Advanced Study in the Behavioral Sciences, Stanford, Calif., January 19, 1969, pp. 6, 18.
[4] See also "Some Strategies for Understanding Politicians," *American Journal of Political Science*, Spring 1974.

OLD RELIABLE NIXON

Strangely, no one seems to have suggested that Watergate (by which I mean the whole wash of woe that flooded forth after that gate was opened in June 1972) gave us a "new Nixon." Through so many even-numbered years in the past, the discovery of new Nixons seemed to have become a national pastime as observers hoped against hope that he was not what he had been. In the event, though, old reliable Nixon came through.

The clearest continuity was Nixon's active-negative character. As he had before 1972, he poured on energy, night and day, at home and away. His Presidential activities came to take up nearly all his waking hours and, more and more frequently as his end approached, he woke and worked at night. "As long as I am physically able," he pledged in November 1973, "I am going to continue to work sixteen to eighteen hours a day. . . ."[5] He was a man in motion, restlessly flying off to Camp David, Key Biscayne, or San Clemente, where he often plagued his Secret Service guards to "drive somewhere, anywhere." As of the end of November 1973, the President had stayed in the White House only four of the forty-four weekends of his second term; in his last six weeks in office he spent only six days there.[6]

Reliable Nixon continued also in his stance as a suffering martyr in the Presidency. Even the version of the White House tapes he himself released to the public has him in continual complaint: "This damn case!" "I've been working very hard as you can imagine with everything." "I was up so late last night."[7] He told visiting Congressmen has had been through "seven months of pure hell."[8] He refers again and again to his troubled life, in all sorts of circumstances: he wants the truth "even if it hurts me," he says, and he has "broken my ass to try to get the facts of this case." Even after his enormous victory in the 1972 election, Nixon conveyed a "joyless, brooding quality," one of his Cabinet members remembered, and talked of how all Presidents had gone down hill in their second terms.[9] Even when he sat at ease in Washington while his bombers smashed out the lives of Vietnamese peasants, his sense of proportion and comparison deserted him: the Vietnam bombing became "my terrible personal ordeal."[10]

Nixon the manager of himself, "RN" the stage director or producer of the

---

[5] Elizabeth Drew, *Washington Journal: The Events of 1973-1974* (New York, Vintage Books, 1976), p. 108.

[6] Theodore H. White, *Breach of Faith: The Fall of Richard Nixon* (New York, Atheneum Publishers, Reader's Digest Press, 1975), p. 292; Drew, *Washington Journal*, p. 138; White, *Breach of Faith*, p. 306.

[7] *Submission of Recorded Presidential Conversations to the Committee on the Judiciary of the House Representatives by President Richard Nixon* (Washington, D.C., Government Printing Office, 1974), pp. 580, 696, 836.

[8] J. Anthony Lukas, *Nightmare: The Underside of the Nixon Years* (New York, Viking Press, 1976), p. 450.

[9] White, *Breach of Faith*, pp. 218, 171.

[10] *Submission of Recorded Presidential Conversations . . . by President Richard Nixon*, p. 1304.

Nixon project—that is the place, I argued in 1972, to look for Nixon's strongest emotional investment. The typical compulsiveness of the active-negative person, which usually takes the form "I must," with Nixon invariably became "I must do it my way." Into his second term Nixon continued to insist on just that. The Watergate saga—particularly the cover-up—took its shape from Nixon's old sense that nothing would be right unless he controlled the way of it. His fear of being dead though living, of having no feelings, contributed heavily, I think, to his need to feel he had to do what he had to do—and in just the right way.[11] In the Autumn of 1973, Nixon said, "What matters most, in this critical hour, is our ability to act—and to act in a way that enables us to control events, not to be paralyzed and overwhelmed by them."[12] His Watergate vocabulary is full of the language of compulsion: "We've just got to ride it through." "I've got to get [it] out and I've got to get it out today! . . . The White House has got to move . . . we have to get out in front in some way."[13] The "way" was infinitely important. Safire pointed out to Nixon that his three favorite words were "in a way."[14] Nixon never seems to have judged the rightness of the "way" by any external criteria of ethics, morality, or even expediency. What mattered most was that things be done in a way that he could feel was *his* way—that is, a way that reflected his own dramatic sense of himself.

THE POWER DISEASE

Jonathan Schell finds "the fear of impotence" a recurrent theme in Nixon's public statements, as when he worried about moves to "tie the hands of the President" or "cut off the President's legs," or when he feared that America might become "a pitiful helpless giant."[15] One need not be so psychoanalytic, for the ambiguities inherent in the concept of "impotence" could detract from the important political truth that Nixon was a President in perpetual anxiety about holding and advancing his power. In the end, he lost not only power but authority, not only sanction but office, and along the way his aides learned to discount his more ridiculous orders, such as not to serve soup because some spilled one day, or "No more landing at airports!" after a foul-up at the end of a flight.[16] Nixon's fear of losing power undoubtedly is tied to his fluctuating sense of power, which he expressed precisely when he said to his press secretary: "That's an order, Ron—no discussion. Unless, of course, you disagree."[17] Given these fears

---

[11] Safire, *Before the Fall*, p. 534.

[12] Drew, *Washington Journal*, p. 49.

[13] *Submission of Recorded Presidential Conversations . . . by President Richard Nixon*, p. 711; Lukas, *Nightmare*, p. 326.

[14] Safire, *Before the Fall*, p. 482.

[15] Schell, *The Time of Illusion*, p. 372.

[16] William Safire, *Before the Fall: An Inside View of the Pre-Watergate White House* (Garden City, N.Y.: Doubleday & Company, Inc., 1975), p. 287.

[17] *Ibid.*, p. 286.

and uncertainties, it is no wonder he turned to a man of the type Charles Colson used to be, a hit man ready to obey whatever the President told him to do. "Break all the china in the White House if you have to," Nixon ordered.[18] That was the kind of man he needed. "Colson—he'll do anything. He'll walk right through doors," Nixon bragged.[19] What balm it must have been to his bruised power sense to hear his CIA Director say, "There is only one President at a time. I work only for you," or to learn that his White House general-in-residence informed a Deputy Attorney General of the United States: "Your commander-in-chief has given an order. You have no alternative."[20] At least once, Nixon in a fury undertook to rein in Kissinger. Colson reports the President's reaction to an apparent Kissinger press leak:

> He exploded, ordering me to call Kissinger at once. (It was then 6:30 A.M. in California.) "I will not tolerate insubordination," he barked into the telephone. "You tell Henry he's to talk to no one period! I mean no one. And tell him not to call me, I will accept no calls from him." With that he slammed the receiver in my ear.[21]

Of course, Nixon did tolerate insubordination—or at least he experienced plenty of it at the end, when he could not find much subordination anywhere. But he was forever railing against it at the same time as he struggled to control his own aggressive impulses. Like Lyndon Johnson, Nixon could take the pettiest ways to demonstrate his powerfulness, such as demanding, on a sudden whim, to be taken to a concert at the Kennedy Center, despite all the inconvenience and disruption an unscheduled Presidential appearance would cause.[22] This was a President who wanted to believe about himself that he was powerful—indeed, a "sovereign" who had his "subordinates" "on a short leash."[23] In a thinly disguised account of a diatribe by "President Monckton," novelist John Erhlichman portrays his boss's power feelings:

> . . . this government is shot through with miserable little people who do not love this country. Ideologues. They would pull down our institutions if they could; they have no real concern for the well-being of America. The only thing that motivates them is their desire for the realization of their left-wing goals, in education or health or welfare or whatever their narrow little field is. And they hate me, because they know I will try to stop them . . . Oh, I don't mind their hate. I understand it. I am the first President in this country who really threatens them, and they know it. They fear me and so they hate me. And they should fear me; I intend to root them out. I don't care that they are disloyal to me personally. . . . But the Federal bureaucracy must not be disloyal to the Presidency—or

18 Ibid., p. 559.
19 Charles W. Colson, Born Again (Old Tappan, N.J., Chosen Books, 1976), p. 72.
20 Lukas, Nightmare, pp. 85, 438.
21 Colson, Born Again, p. 79.
22 Ibid., Chapter Four, "The President's Night Out."
23 Submissions of Recorded Presidential Conversations . . . by President Richard Nixon, p. 641.

the country. I have concluded that their disloyalty has reached such a magnitude that it seriously threatens our constitutional system, and even the nation. The goddamn traitors. . . .[24]

Yet this character is a fictionalized version of the same President who had to ask his aides for permission to enter their conversation—"Can I spend a minute?"—sometimes repeatedly in the same conversational sequence, as his own version of his tapes reveals.[25]

Nixon's confused inner feelings about power would have had little political importance had not the President acted politically on them. He did, with a vengeance, and with apparent indifference to the Constitution. Almost as soon as he came into office in 1969, he had contingency plans drawn up to handle a possible national uprising. As early as that first November, in preparation for the Vietnam Moratorium demonstrations, the President—who was very closely involved in the situation, despite his disclaimers—took extreme measures. The Washington police department set up a joint command with the CIA to collect "intelligence" about the demonstrators. This system was revived for the 1971 May Day demonstrations, when approximately 10,000 citizens were arrested without charges and detained. When the courts finally got around to disposing of these cases, only one defendant out of the first two thousand was found guilty.[26]

The Presidential subversion of the CIA, the National Security Agency, the Secret Service, the Post Office, and so on proceeded apace. The beginnings were unknown or only hinted at when *The Presidential Character* was published in 1972, but there was already some evidence of the President's power moves. His early attempts to control the bureaucracy by infiltrating it with political operatives, were in fact little more than exaggerated versions of what other Presidents had tried, but in 1970 one White House aide found an additional justification that throws more light on the mind-set then operative at 1600 Pennsylvania Avenue: "It works in the Vatican. It works in the Mafia. It ought to work here."[27]

Nineteen-seventy was also the year that produced a temporary but widespread implementation of the secret "Huston Plan," dubbed for the twenty-nine-year-old White House staffer to whom the plan gave the responsibility for "domestic intelligence and internal security affairs" by means of mail-peeking, sneak-thievery, and the like. The one guideline under which Huston worked was the fact that there were no guidelines: "All restraints which limit this coverage are to be removed."[28] The President approved this plan, then withdrew his approval only when J. Edgar Hoover, armed with his own secret files, threatened

---

[24] John Ehrlichman, *The Company: A Novel*, p. 275 ©1976 by Simon & Schuster. Reprinted by permission.

[25] *Submission of Recorded Presidential Conversations . . . by President Richard Nixon*, pp. 476, 349.

[26] Schell, *The Time of Illusion*, pp. 30, 71, 150-51.

[27] Drew, *Washington Journal*, p. 168.

[28] White, *Breach of Faith*, p. 135.

the President. Although the plan was supposedly scrapped—Huston claimed it was never formally rescinded—some of its elements were later put into effect, in such totalitarian "capers" as the Ellsberg break-in, the wiretaps on newsmen and on Nixon's own brother Donald, and the varities of threats and acts against Americans on Nixon's steadily expanding "enemies list."[29] It was these domestic measures, in conjunction with the Presidential subversion of the armed forces, that were most significant, for they bought to bear, in illegal and harmful ways, the state's monopoly of force.

I think Nixon needed secrecy and surprise to feel powerful. Was there not in him a certain pleasure, a thrill of danger and escape, when he would look Senator Scott in the eye and say, "Hugh, I have nothing to hide. The White House has nothing to hide. I repeat we have nothing to hide, and you are authorized to make that statement in my name"? Or as he spoke with such a frank air to Elliot Richardson: "I'm innocent. You've got to believe I'm innocent"?[30] What even more transcendent gratification did he experience as he lied, again and again, to Special Prosecutor Leon Jaworski—who, *as Nixon knew*, knew he was lying? He had long made it a practice to divert attention from his misdeeds by preaching against them—damning lawbreaking as he broke the law, condemning chiselers as he chiseled away, advertising his straightforwardness while he coached his aides in perjury. Perhaps the technique worked, for the casual political audience could easily mix up the prosecution with the defense in such circumstances. But I also think (though it cannot be proved) that a Nixon hungry for crisis and fearful of the "vegetable life" might be specially needful of the kind of triumph one experiences when one has hoodwinked the enemy. This is the triumph that is especially delicious to the man filled with resentment.

RIGIDIFICATION ROAD

Watergate was Nixon's rigidification, his political nemesis and tragedy. The theory and data in my book, published the season before the burglary, could in no way have predicted that a certain specific event—the June 17 break-in—would trigger the tragedy of Richard Nixon. Such forecasting is the business of astrology. Rather, *The Presidential Character* predicted contingently: given specified conditions, and given an active-negative character like Nixon's, a predictable process of rigidification was likely.

As predicted, that process was set off by "a serious threat to his power and his moral confidence."[31] Nixon moved into his crisis pattern and tried repeatedly to escape by means of his usual get-on-with-it diversion. When that didn't work, he froze up and ruined himself, along the way sapping the spirit of a political generation.

[29] Staff of the New York Times, *The End of a Presidency* (New York, Bantam Books, 1974), p. 218.
[30] Schell, *The Time of Illusion*, p. 320; Woodward and Bernstein, *The Final Days*, p. 61.
[31] *Ibid.*

The full story of Nixon's political demise has yet to be told. There have been numerous books (and Nixon's own is yet to come), but none of them has made clear the most interesting and important biographic aspect of the story: the interplay between the private Nixon (as revealed in the tapes and the recollections of his aides) and the public Nixon (as revealed in the speeches and press conferences and summit shows). Certainly that story is too long and detailed for telling here, even if it could be done. Rather I must proceed by summary, inviting all the while the serious critic to dredge up competing evidence.

For a character like Nixon, disaster is always just around the corner, no matter how well things are going. Indeed, the better things are going the sooner you can expect disasters. In the spring of 1972, despite all sorts of good signs, Nixon was running scared. There were plenty of reasonable causes for his anxiety, for a wary fear that the election might suddenly demote him to citizen. From his perspective, he had lost, almost lost, or barely won too many times to take comfort in early poll leads. How much more distressing it must have been when the Harris poll in February had Muskie over Nixon at 43 to 40 percent, in March 44 to 39, in May 47 to 39.[32]

In his Watergate testimony, John Dean retrieved from his tape recorder memory the fact that within a few days of the break-in he warned two chieftains at the Justice Department that "I did not know what would happen if the investigation led into the White House, but that I suspected the chances of re-electing the President would be severely damaged. . . . I did not think the White House could withstand a wide-open investigation."[33]

The way to cut this risk to the President's power was to keep the whole affair as quiet as possible until after the election. At first the prognosis did not seem bad, for the break-in was initially reported on page 30 of the *New York Times*. There were some subsequent Watergate reports, a good deal of suggestive information on campaign "dirty tricks," and opponent McGovern's eloquent warning:

> We are confronted, in short, with both a moral and a Constitutional crisis of unprecedented dimensions. Ambitious men come and go, but a free society might never recover from a sustained assault on its most basic institutions. And one can only ask, if this has happened in four years, to what lengths would the same leadership go in another four years, once freed of the restraints of facing the people for reelection?[34]

In general, though, Watergate was kept almost as far from the headlines as the White House would have wanted. A poll in October, just before the election, showed only about half the public had even heard of the Watergate break-in. Nixon was endorsed by 753 daily newspapers, compared to 56 for McGovern,

---

[32] Lukas, *Nightmare*, p. 8.

[33] *Ibid.*, p. 246.

[34] Frank Mankiewicz, *Perfectly Clear: Nixon from Whittier to Watergate* (New York, Popular Library, 1973), p. 262.

and won the election by an enormous margin, 61 to 38 percent. Not until the following February would the Senate decide on an investigation.[35]

From Nixon's perspective, then, the gamble had paid off. Close attention—before the election—to the White House iceberg underlying the Watergate tip, whether by the press or Congress, constituted a very severe threat to his power because of the very real danger of his losing the election. On the other hand, the risk of covering-up seemed minimal: they had done it many times before and the whole issue appeared to be fading away.

THE FEAR OF SCANDAL

The second essential reinforcement for Nixon's rigidification was the fact that Watergate threatened to reveal the President as an immoral and unvirtuous person. Indeed, the eventual revelation of the tapes elicited just the condemning reaction Nixon feared. Even in their Presidentially sanitized version, the tapes showed a Nixon he would just as soon had remained private. As Representative Mann of South Carolina put it, "The more that people know about him, it seems the more trouble he's in." Even Senator Hugh Scott, a loyalist if ever there was one, dolefully concluded that the tapes showed "a shabby, disgusting, immoral performance by all those involved." This reaction was general among Congressmen, newspapers which previously had supported Nixon, and the public as revealed in the polls. Leading churchmen were reminded of "a felon's lair" and of conversations that "reek with the stench of moral decay." Columnist Joseph Alsop reacted with "sheer flesh-crawling repulsion." The Oval Office had become "the back room of a second-rate advertising agency in a suburb of hell." To William Randolph Hearst, Jr., Nixon emerged as "a man totally immersed in the cheapest and sleaziest kind of conniving." The President not only had broken the law, his oath, and his word, but also had shattered the public's trust that their President was at least as straight as they were. Even Nixon's old standby the Chicago *Tribune* had to admit that the tape transcripts and the scandal about Nixon's tax returns "stripped the man to his essential character, and that character could not stand that kind of scrutiny."[36]

Rigidification is a process, a slow freeze. Nixon's rigidification developed as one piece after another of the threatening pattern fell into place. At some point in the autumn of 1973 one Republican Senator perceived a key transition: the affair had "got to the ridicule stage . . . even among serious people." Nixon himself—who kept saying he wanted to be considered "un homme sérieux" like de Gaulle—predicted, as he released his doctored tape transcripts, that "they will embarrass me . . . and . . . they will become the subject of speculation and even ridicule. . . ."[37] One of them was played at a Washington cocktail party.

---

[35] Schell, *The Time of Illusion*, pp. 220, 291; Lukas, *Nightmare*, p. 277.
[36] Drew, *Washington Journal*, pp. 256, 262, 271.
[37] *Ibid.*, p. 133; Safire, *Before the Fall*, p. 689; Drew, *Washington Journal*, p. 247.

There was speculation that the tapes would eventually become a commercial item for disc jockeys and teenagers to chuckle over. To the active-negative mentality, ridicule is not funny. It is too close to the truth. It helps freeze a man.

STEPS IN NIXON'S RIGIDIFICATION

Certainly all the main elements of the active-negative rigidification process, as exemplified in the stories of Wilson, Hoover, and Johnson, were present in Nixon's slow-motion fall from the heady altitudes of his 1972 election victory. Plain to see are: the sense that one must resist the temptation to "give in"; the feeling that salvation lies in effort; the perception of oneself as engaged in a lone struggle; the appeal to faith; the sense of oneself as surrounded by lurking enemies.

The Fight Against "Giving In." Like his active-negative predecessors, Nixon moralizes his preferred line in such a way as to define the alternatives as temptations. Thus resisting becomes a virtue. His "but-that-would-be-the-easy-way" habit continued: "The easiest course would be for me to blame those to whom I delegated the responsibility to run the campaign. But that would be a cowardly thing to do," he said in a television address. As soon as the cameras were off, he told the crew; "It wasn't easy." As the end approached, he said he would not resign because, "From a personal standpoint, resignation is an easy cop-out." To Senator Buckley's suggestion that he resign, Nixon replied sarcastically that, "While it might take an act of courage to run away from a job that you were elected to do, it also takes courage to stand and fight for what you believe is right, and that's what I intend to do." He told the Cabinet that he could not resign because that would change the Constitution, and so "I will go through this with my head high—right up to the end, if it comes." The temptation was always toward weakness, relaxation, collapse: "All these people have come in here crying. I ought to be the one crying. I don't want anyone crying." He wanted others to know that "I sometimes feel like I'd like to resign. Let Agnew be President for a while. He'd love it." And earlier, when discussing the cover-up with Ehrlichman, Nixon equates "being forthcoming" with "caving [in]."[38]

The point is clear: although Nixon eventually does all the things he is "tempted" to do in these passages, he does them long after they would have done him any good. Along the way, the temptations—to cry or quit or talk—must be resisted with all his moral force and fervor.

The Answer in Effort. On the other side of the temptation coin is the exhausted face of the gladiator straining upward, lost in his quest, experiencing the sufferer's confirmation that he cannot possibly be doing this from any selfish mo-

---

[38] Lukas, *Nightmare*, p. 338; Drew, *Washington Journal*, p. 198; White, *Breach of Faith*, p. 294; Woodward and Bernstein, *The Final Days*, pp. 386-87, 435; *Submission of Recorded Presidential Conversations . . . by President Richard Nixon*, pp. 1270, pp. 468-470.

tive. We have seen the suffering-and-striving Nixon already: working to all hours, exhausted, constantly complaining and reaching for sympathy, all the while denying that he needs any of that. The tapes are full of Presidential metaphors of masochism: having to "bite the Dean bullet today," to "prick the boil and take the heat," "to get beat on the head and shoulders," "to be nibbled to death by a thousand hurts," not to mention numerous variants of Nixon's "scab-flicking" simile. But far from passive acquiescence, Nixon would do unto others as he expected they would try to do unto him, by sharp, disciplined struggle, however "painful." As the "crisis" deepened in the fall of 1973, Julie Nixon wrote on her calendar, "Fight. Fight. Fight."[39]

The Lone Struggle. As far back as January 1971, Nixon realized he had an image problem regarding isolation and tried to correct it by proclaiming "Open Door Hours." Statistics were to be gathered on how many people saw the President, and aides were to "build on the theme that he's the most 'Open Door' President in history."[40] It did not work and could not last, because Nixon simply was not an Open Door person. As Watergate deepened, this famous loner of a President got loner and loner. His contacts with the press, which already had been in steep decline, became even rarer.[41] Not only did his Cabinet members have trouble seeing him; even his own lawyers were sometimes ut out. St. Clair confessed that he had not heard the crucial tapes, and Garment complained at the end, "We had no access to our client."[42] Nixon spent hours alone in the Lincoln room, which is furnished for one, the air conditioning on high, the fire ablaze at his hearth, pondering his fate to the strains of "Victory at Sea." Cynics said that when he wanted to be alone, he brought along Bebe Rebozo, and the tow of them would sit together for long stretches without talking.[43] Your average politicians would rather talk than eat, argue than sleep, but by Christmas 1973 Nixon "didn't want to see anyone"—a problem that would have been more severe if the converse hadn't also been true: "and no one really wants to see the President."[44]

The fact of Nixon's isolation is evident. What it meant to him is summed up in his comment to John Dean, on March 13, 1974: "Bullshit: Nobody is a friend of ours."[45] By April of that year, J. Anthony Lukas reports, "Nobody trusted anybody in the Nixon camp. Haldeman, Ehrlichman, and Dean were routinely taping their conversations with each other and any other potential witness." At

---

[39] *Ibid.*, pp. 457, 509, 611, 1161; Safire, *Before the Fall,* p. 370; Drew, *Washington Journal,* p. 99.

[40] Jeb Stuart Magruder, *An American Life* (New York, Atheneum, 1974), p. 140.

[41] Safire, *Before the Fall,* p. 349.

[42] White, *Breach of Faith,* p. 271.

[43] Rebozo's 1973 Christmas card bore a startlingly cynical Yuletide greeting: "Neither material wealth, fame, power, nor admiration necessarily brings happiness." Drew, *Washington Journal,* p. 151.

[44] Lukas, *Nightmare,* p. 467.

[45] *Ibid.,* p. 307.

the end of April, Nixon at last fired these brittle and prideful counselors and took on a new crew. But the new aides, as Theodore White noted, "were loyal only to the public policies of Richard Nixon, his proclaimed purposes, the record that had won him the largest popular election margin in American history. He could trust such men to serve such public purposes, but not to protect him personally. He was alone—all alone against . . . 'the system.' "[46]

The Appeal to Faith. I will spare readers an extensive account of Nixon's litany of self-justifying idealisms called forth in order to protect himself from the prying eyes of reporters, courts and special prosecutors. On the one hand, Watergate was one of those "petty, little, indecent things that seem to obsess us," one of "the murky, small, unimportant, vicious little things" that contrasted so sharply with the high risk of "building a better world."[47] On the other hand, throughout his exhortations, Watergate threatened the Presidency itself, the fundamental Constitutional order, and the very peace of the world. Nothing is more familiar, to those who lived attentively through those days, than Nixon's extraordinary capacity to link his pettiest acts with his proudest purposes. The public could not be allowed to hear him plotting to fool them because "the President of the United States, under our Constitution, has a responsibility to this office to maintain the separation of power and also maintain the ability of not only this President but future Presidents to conduct the office in the interests of the people."[48] The active-negative's enormous capacity for moralistic self-justification shone brightly through the Watergate miasmas.

The Emergent Enemy. "As you know, we're up against ruthless people," Nixon reminded Alexander Haig as the crisis persisted. Nixon was used to that. He lived in what he saw and felt as a *generally* dangerous world, and always had. He could sense the lurking ambushers: "I guess the Kennedy crowd is just laying in the bushes waiting to make their move," he told John Dean. His aide Safire thought he was the first political paranoid with a majority.[49]

In an interesting exhortation in February 1973, Nixon told his Cabinet what he had learned from another sovereign:

> I was talking to King Hussein of Jordan. When he was sixteen years old, an assassin shot his grandfather, and he ran after the assassin and got shot himself. He made the point—if people throw rocks at you in a parade, you cannot sit down and look for protection. *The moment a leader shows timidity he encourages people to go after him.* People can sense when a leader is timid and they automatically attack. Remember, you are a member of the President's Cabinet.

---

[46] *Ibid.;* White, *Breach of Faith,* p. 221.

[47] *Ibid.,* p. 398.

[48] Congressional Quarterly, *Watergate Chronology of a Crisis,* Vol. 2 (Washington, D.C., Congressional Quarterly, 1974), p. 170A.

[49] Woodward and Bernstein, *The Final Days,* p. 45; Safire, *Before the Fall,* p. 275.

Try to be conciliatory when others are conciliatory toward you, but when the other side doesn't want to heal wounds, fight 'em—you bet more respect.[50]

In a world of piranhas, one had better be a shark.

As the Watergate crisis failed to vanish in the wake of the grand tours, his list of enemies, so perceived, multiplied. There were the "Harvards," the Kennedys, the "upper intellectual types," the "establishment," the Jews, the Italians.[51] The famous "enemies lists' ran the gamut from James Reston to Robert Sherrill, and included such dangerous folk as Carol Channing, Steven McQueen, Barbara Streisand, Gregory Peck, Bill Crosby, Tony Randall and Joe Namath.[52] Former friends, such as Dean, Magruder, and Mitchell, and former henchmen, such as Hunt, Liddy, Barker, and the other burglars, become objects of disdain and derision, to be "stroked" or "nailed."

Choice or Necessity?

If Nixon's response to the Watergate accusations was simply that of a realist to reality, an inexorable ride down the slippery slope of tragedy, then his character would have little to do with it, once the process was begun. One could conceive of the story that way, just as any other historical sequence can be etched retrospectively into inevitability. What happened happened. That Nixon was ridiculed or challenged or whatever could be seen as having little to do with the case, once the case became a case. The alternative is to believe, as our own personal experience teaches us, that there are indeed choices to be made, forks in the road of life, and that how and why those choices are made can have fateful consequences.

We know now that Nixon was deeply into the Watergate affair almost immediately after the break-in, if not before. The break-in occurred on June 17, 1972. Nixon aide Haldeman's notes show the President and his top team talked it over on June 20th, but the tape of the conversation was later obliterated—probably by Nixon himself, if his secretary's testimony that he ran the thing back and forth indicates anything. The June 23 tape—the one Nixon held out to the end, the one that turned his most ardent loyalists against him—makes it abundantly clear that he was deep into what he, at least, thought of as choices about the exact way to handle the details of the cover-up. Despite all his subsequent claims that he was too busy making world peace to attend to such trivia, that all the relevant facts were out, that he and his were innocent and had nothing to hide, or that, at various points in time, he had only just recently learned what

---

[50] *Ibid.*, p. 685.

[51] White, *Breach of Faith*, p. 254; *Submission of Recorded Presidential Conversations . . . by President Richard Nixon*, p. 101; Woodward and Bernstein, *The Final Days*, p. 169; *Time*, May 12, 1975, p. 74.

[52] Marvin Miller, compiler, *The Breaking of a President*, Vol. I (Therapy Productions, 1974), p. 85.

was going on, the June 23rd tape made it unmistakably clear that he had been in up to his eyeballs from the very start. In that tape Nixon told Haldeman to stop the investigation by pretending that it threatened CIA work. A haberdasher like Harry Truman, a soldier like Eisenhower would have understood that that was not the thing to do; a lawyer like Nixon must have known that it was an "obstruction of justice." The nation's chief lawman had cut the FBI off at the pass to save his own skin. " 'Don't go any further into this case, period!' " Nixon ordered Haldeman to tell the FBI.[53]

That was a choice. He could have chosen otherwise. He could have destroyed the tapes. He could have gone on television and made a clean breast of the whole affair, admitting his indirect culpability and dismissing those directly responsible. Even after the Ervin Committee investigation began, he could have brought that inquiry to a quick halt by testifying—his word as President of the United States of America against that of a young lawyer assistant who admitted his own perfidy. "If the President had come to testify in the early days of the hearings, he could have bowled the legs out from under us," thought Terry Lenzner of the Ervin Committee staff.[54] He could have promptly complied with the early subpoenas for tapes; it was at least possible that would have ended it. And at nearly any point before the last, he could have made a public confession of complicity, and a promise to reform, and a plea for forgiveness. In retrospect it seems that any one of these moves would have left him in the Presidency, especially considering how loath the Congress was to impeach him.

Instead, Nixon concentrated on rhetoric. In speech after speech, he urged the public to forget this Watergate nonsense and march on into the future. This was a trick that had worked so well in the past that it had become Nixon's habitual way to wind up a crisis before plunging into a new one. All the way back to the Checkers speech, Nixon had succeeded not by giving us new facts but by giving us new explanations, not by acting but by redefining the meanings of acts. I believe there were two reasons that this strategy did not work with Watergate. First, once the courts got into it, television flim-flam became ineffective. A court proceeding is a social invention for focusing attention, strongly and continuously, on a set of specific experiences. It does not always work to that end, but in this case the judge, John Sirica, was one of those rare birds who will not let go until he has pulled out the whole worm. The series of judicial proceedings, culminating in the 8-0 Supreme Court decision requiring Nixon to turn over the tapes, was the least promising stage upon which Nixon could hope to play St. Richard in order to hide King Richard.

A second and I think stronger reason why Nixon failed in his rhetorical escape efforts was the fact that in the final analysis he did not really want to escape. Like Presidents Wilson, Hoover, and Lyndon Johnson before him, something in his character attracted him to the path of grim perseveration, to the long, hard, lacerating march to a tragic denouement. Of course he was ambiv-

---

[53] Woodward and Bernstein, *The Final Days*, p. 271.
[54] White, *Breach of Faith*, p. 232.

alent on this score; part of him wanted to escape. But another part seemed to be caught up in the same personal tragic tale, the same predestined plot arranged by the man himself for his own political destruction.

In the end, the most significant of all the many "lessons" of Nixon and Watergate was this: our political system did not protect us from an enormous and long-lasting Presidential confidence game. Nixon the rhetorician was a smashing success, over the years, especially considering what he had to sell. His history demonstrates a democratic vulnerability, a weakness in the nation's political fabric, through which the most loathsome deeds—disguised as bravery—can seep. He was finally pushed out of office only because of an accident. At the end of a long-afternoon, some investigators for a Congressional committee stayed just a little longer, asked just one more question, and uncovered the tape system. Otherwise Nixon would have got off scot free and the rest of us might well be in danger of our democratic lives.

Lyndon Johnson's Political Personality

DORIS KEARNS

Lyndon Johnson's life took him through a succession of public institutions: the House of Representatives, the Senate, the vice-presidency, and the presidency. He first came to Washington when Herbert Hoover was still president; his public career spanned the depression, the New Deal, World War II, Korea, postwar economic expansion, the cold war, the Eisenhower years, the New Frontier, the Great Society, and Vietnam. He was a candidate for office from a fairly liberal congressional district with a populist tradition, then from a conservative state dominated by powerful economic interests, and, finally, his constituency was the entire nation.

This staggering diversity of historical circumstances and public institutions which constituted the changing environments of Lyndon Johnson's public life provides an unusual opportunity for understanding the interplay between personality and institutions in America. Lyndon Johnson's character, his favorite methods of acquiring power and of using that power, his personal strengths and weaknesses, can all be viewed in different contexts, thus providing an invaluable look at both the changeless dynamics of power and the changing structure of the American political system in the past forty years.

This article first examines Johnson's characteristic ways of dealing with the world, formed through his various experiences within his family and cultural setting. The study will then turn to a comparative examination of two of the major institutions Johnson encountered—the Senate and the presidency—in an attempt to assess the impact of personality on successful leadership in different settings.

DORIS KEARNS is a professor in the Department of Government at Harvard University. She has recently published the book, *Lyndon Johnson and the American Dream*.

PERSONALITY DEVELOPMENT

The picture of Johnson's early life suggests a childhood torn between the irreconcilable demands of his mother—who hoped to find in his intellectual and cultural achievement a recompense of her dead father, unhappy marriage, and thwarted ambition—and those of his father, who considered intellect and culture unmanly pursuits. This may not, of course, be a wholly accurate or complete description, but the evidence we have—Johnson's recollections, his early letters to his parents, and his later behavior—supports this conclusion. His parents, most significantly his mother, seemed to bestow or withdraw approval on the basis of his behavior at home and, later, his accomplishments at school. All her expressions of satisfaction and love were related to something her son had done, just as his implied appeals for approval were accompanied by descriptions of all the good deeds he had accomplished.

Thus as Johnson grew up, he identified the success of his performance as the source of love. He could not allow himself to doubt that his mother loved him or that her praise was evidence and expression of her love. Unfortunately, however, words of admiration, praise, satisfaction, joy, even of love, which seemed a response to Johnson's activities in the many worlds through which he moved, could never truly fulfill his need for love. For the "love" whose experience, denial, or withdrawal is basic to the configuration of a given psychic structure must be, psychoanalysts tell us, perceived as a response to one's own being, unqualified by success or failure, by mental or physical defects, or by relationships to the external world. When this fundamental love is denied, or, as in Johnson's case, attached to external performance, then no recognition of personal qualities and gifts, such as integrity, warmth, energy, and talent, can suffice to satisfy inward needs. Performance alone can prevent the sense of failure and that performance must be continually displayed since past effectiveness is swiftly erased and soon counts for nothing at all. Thus continual motion and limitless ambitions become the necessities of daily life.

Lyndon Johnson found the source of his achievement in the acquisition of power and control. Yet control is not the only road to success, even in public life. For Johnson, however, control fulfilled another need as well: mastery of the outer world was necessary to mastery of the self; controlling his home environment was the only means for reconciling the profound inward tensions imposed by the contradiction between his mother's demand for intellectual achievement and his father's notions of manly pride. And control of the external world was also the only way of containing the powerful mixture of hate, rage, and love he experienced at various times toward his mother, his father, and himself. Mastery of the outer world was necessary to mastery of the self. And the drive for control was a surrogate for his urgent childhood desires to control the earliest of his environments and change his position within his parental family, thus enabling him to compel love and prevent conditions that created inner conflicts, dangers, and fears.

This understanding of the inward forces that contributed to Johnson's pursuit of power should not diminish respect for his extraordinary achievements; on the contrary, it should increase our regard for the masterful way in which—most of the time—he was able to harness and direct his personal needs toward constructive, social ends. Why some men cope and others do not remains a mystery. While we are able to suggest a number of possible bases for Johnson's strength —his grandfather's reliability, his mother's early devotion, his father's interest and attention—we have no theory to connect these observations in a coherent pattern. The psychoanalytic literature is able to analyze sources of weakness better than sources of strength.

It is also important to recognize that, while the demands of psychic structure led Johnson to pursue power, they did not determine that politics would be the avenue for that pursuit. The larger social setting provided content for Johnson's ambitions. Had his father and his father's friends been engaged in business or finance, one can imagine Johnson pursuing a very different career. But the options for a poor boy from a poor place in central Texas were limited—practically, if not theoretically. Politics was the one profession that seemed to offer both a reasonable chance of entry and a limitless future. In short, the same drives set in a different society or in another age might have led to very different pursuits.

And one thing is certain: his childhood relationships, the manner in which he sought, out of necessity, to resolve conflicts, protect his identity, and find personal fulfillment, may have shaped and energized his ambitions, but they did not, and could not, ensure their realization.

Johnson's success and achievements—his performance—were made possible, to a very large extent, by his unusual capacities, his intellect, energy, talent, and insight into men and the nature of institutions, through which he developed techniques of incredible and intricate subtlety. To his knowledge and skill he applied an innovative genius to construct a large variety of instruments which increased the coercive powers that enabled him to impose his will. And that very success only strengthened and increased his ambition.

On the foundations of the basic elements of his psychic structure, Johnson constructed characteristic forms of behavior and conduct which he repeated constantly throughout the various stages of his career. Every time he entered an institution whose structure made such a relationship possible and productive, Johnson apprenticed himself to a man with superior power—Cecil Evans, the president of his college, Richard Russell, Senate leader of the southern bloc, even President John F. Kennedy; he became the invaluable helper, the deferential subordinate willing and able to perform a dazzling range of services for his master, until, step by step, the apprentice accumulated the resources that enabled him to secure the master's role.

But Johnson was not alone in playing the role of apprentice, a role marvelously suited to a political system marked at important institutional levels by seniority and gradual ascent. What distinguished his behavior from others' was the skill with which he managed to avoid remaining a completely loyal subordinate (a position that halted the ambitions of others), yet, even while changing his role, to retain his master's support. The skills he evidenced here resonated of ones he had shown much earlier in his life as he walked the even more treacherous path between his parents conflicting demands. The boy's earliest relationship with his mother was shaped by the idea that she needed him, and the confidence that he was capable of fulfilling that need. But with his mother, more than with anyone else, the role of apprentice required a distance; nothing less than survival of the self was at stake. So Johnson instinctively reached for the only other base of power he knew: identification with his father provided the independence he needed to separate from his mother.

In the exercise of his power, Johnson used a related technique drawn from an old tradition: he obligated his followers by providing them with services or benefits which they desired or needed. But the line between obligation and coercion was often thin. In return for his gifts, Johnson demanded a high measure of gratitude, which could only be acceptably demonstrated by the willingness to follow his lead. Though with some colleagues (those not central to his pursuit of power) he was able to grant the leeway and independence he himself had demanded, his more typical pattern required a continuing proof of loyalty so extreme that their autonomy was endangered. These demands for submission invariably worked against him, insulating him from the give and take of an adversary proceeding. He seemed to fear that any relaxation of control, even in front of his closest colleagues, would open the door to unknown enemies.

Of course, this kind of behavior cannot be attributed solely to Johnson's inner needs. It was also a response to the nature of the political world. When every situation is translated into one of power lost or gained, all relationships, including friendships, are reduced to a series of shifting, undependable alliances. In such a world it is easy to succumb to the belief that even one's closest "friend" must be watched for signs of treason.

But the vicissitudes of the political career account for neither the urgency beneath Johnson's demands for submission nor the passions he projected onto his critics. These emotions can be understood only by recognizing the fears of illegitimacy and loss that plagued Johnson from his earliest experience with power (his position in his mother's home), where he knew that all the power he commanded, while momentarily great, was subject to instant removal the moment his father returned. And these fears of illegitimacy and loss were undoubtedly reinforced by the circumstances of a political career that depended over and over on death (in 1937, Congressman Buchanan's sudden death opened up the seat in the Tenth Congressional District; in 1948, Senator Morris Sheppard's death opened the second senatorship from Texas, and of course, in 1963, John Kennedy's assassination opened up the presidency) and political defeat (Lucas and McFarland, successive Senate Democratic leaders before Johnson, were defeated in the 1950 and 1952 elections). Nor was his sense of the precariousness of his power relieved by the narrow victory that launched his Senate career (eighty-seven votes).

Throughout his career, Johnson exhibited an unmatched capacity to persuade individuals in one-on-one or small private settings, coupled with a crippling incapacity to present himself effectively before large public audiences. This juxtaposition of traits has long served as a puzzle for Johnson watchers. Countless descriptions have been offered of his uncommon skill in personal encounters, his brilliant blend of calculation and instinct, his unmatched richness of language and tone. One can safely assert that no American political leader has ever equaled Lyndon Johnson in the capacity to know the motives, desires, and weaknesses of those with whom he dealt. He seemed to possess a wholly intuitive ability to perceive a man's nature so accurately and profoundly as almost to be unnatural. Yet this same man, forced to speak before a large public audience, invariably stiffened up, his words delivered in monotone voice, his smile frozen, his hands tightly gripping the lectern.

This contrast is partially accounted for by the recognition that formal settings were less suitable to Johnson's particular talents—crude and colorful metaphors are less appropriate in formal speeches, and the power of physical touch is obviously reduced when the speaker stands before an audience of ten thousand or sits alone in a bare television studio. And part of the explanation for the problem in his later years can be found in the concept of the president as a statesman above the fray, a concept that Johnson shared with many others.

Yet many of the skills involved in the one were applicable to the other, as Johnson's own successes showed. His best speeches were those in which he departed from the text, and by far his most effective television appearance as judged by a poll of viewers was a long, informal conversation with three reporters during which he alternately sat in his chair, roamed around the room, or stood beside his desk, raising and lowering his voice at will. After this appearance, the opinions of his advisers were unanimous: he must adapt his informal style to his public appearances. Johnson refused with a stubborn persistence that can only be understood by searching back in his past, to the contrast already mentioned between the rich and natural mode of talk he adopted from his father and his mother's very different standards of acceptability, which produced in him a measure of shame and a determination, at least in public, to meet his mother's ideal. Yet the son of the woman who taught elocution and debate was dismissed from his lessons in public speaking for mumbling too much—suggesting perhaps an unconscious impulse to take revenge on his mother—and he never conquered his terror of speaking before an audience.

Johnson's career was marked by a continuing effort to avoid confrontation and choice, to prevent passionate and emotional divisions over issues. This inclination can be understood as a response to his particular family situation. From his earliest days he had learned that if he chose his father, he might jeopardize the love and respect of his mother; if he chose his mother, his identity as a man would be in danger. The challenge then, as always, was to find a method of satisfying both—to shape an intermediate path, to find consensus. But Johnson's drive for consensus was not simply a product of inner need; its roots can be seen in the traditions and historical experience of his cultural environment, in the prevailing attitudes and ideals that comprised his view of the world.

The political heritage of Johnson's hill country was that of populism. There Johnson absorbed the established concept that government existed to help the ordinary citizen, and that the ordinary people's basic wants were essentially the same. He built his first campaign for the Congress on the promise that he alone could bring the benefits of the New Deal to the people of his district. And once elected he kept his promise: he brought water and electric power to the Tenth District; he developed a slum-clearance project for the poor; he focused on the problems of the Mexican-Americans. But the populism that influenced Johnson did not include a theory of class conflict. Johnson's family was poor, but it did not identify with the poor, choosing instead to identify with the great majority of Americans, who believed in the possibility of progress and quelled their resentments of the rich by the conviction that someday they, too, would be rich.

Over time, as Johnson stretched his ambition from the Tenth District to the state of Texas, he stretched his conception of "the people" to include the oil and gas men, the big ranchers, the big builders, and the cotton growers. Needing the support and the money of these powerful men, Johnson revised his definition of governmental responsibility to include help for the few as well as services for the many. He became a specialist in defense, a friendly agent ready to deliver any number of government contracts in return for campaign contributions and political support. He moved up in the world, but he never forgot the place where he had been born; he simply added new constituents to the ones he had originally served. Separate packages separately designed for separate groups—this was the winning strategy as Johnson defined it. Thus Johnson built his career on a series of disparate layers; he added one incompatible constituency on top of another; he juxtaposed contradictory ideas without choosing between them. This was a source of his personal strength in rising to power, but it also reflected the nature of a political system that rewards those capable of appealing to a variety of interests.

Johnson wanted many things, but among them, without doubt, that **every** American should have enough nourishing food, warm clothing, decent shelter, and a chance to educate his children; and later, as the presidency extended his reach, he wanted to restore nature, rebuild cities, even build a Great Society. He wanted to out-Roosevelt Roosevelt and, at the same time, thought that what he wanted, everyone wanted, or would want if only he could explain it to them.

So as president he took the course that was most congenial to his character, and probably the only course possible in 1963. He would persuade everyone— businessmen, union chiefs, bankers, politicians—that his goals were in their interest, an interest that he thought, perhaps naïvely, was buried somewhere in every man—the desire to contribute, to leave behind a mark of which he could be proud. This drive to avoid conflict was a source of his greatest achievements in using his power: his success in bringing the Senate to its peak of effectiveness in the 1950s and in forging a consensus on the Great Society that went beyond the splitting of differences. Yet the drive was also a source of weakness. The American political system, superb in developing the technique of consensus, proved less capable of providing direction. Where positive goals were lacking, consensus could not supply them. Where hard choices had to be made (between constituents and ideas), Johnson could not choose. He could not choose between the Great Society and Vietnam; not only when—as in 1965—that choice seemed unnecessary because of an expanding economy and a faith in technology, but, more revealingly, when the failure to choose was obviously destroying the Great Society, the prospects of the war, and Lyndon Johnson himself. Still refusing to face even the necessity of choice, Johnson evolved an elaborate and illusory system (statistics on the continuing progress of the Great Society, statistics on Vietnam proving that the war was indeed being won), which distorted his vision and limited his real options. But practical necessity could not shift his course; the fear of choice had its roots too deep in his character and experience.

PERSONALITY AND INSTITUTIONS

Experience would strengthen Johnson's capacities, modify and supplement his modes of behavior. Man's identity, as Erikson has pointed out, is not fixed; it continually evolves through different phases of life. Some experiences induce growth in character, others provoke regression or even mental disintegration. Johnson's life history shows that he could adapt his conduct to the requirements of different political settings, that his priorities and commitments could change with the circumstances of the time. But that adaptation was possible only within limits. Some of his techniques and his ways of dealing with the world were so deeply rooted in his character and his nature that alteration proved impossible, even when those techniques proved no longer effective.

Having examined these characteristic techniques, let us consider here two of the many institutions Johnson encountered—the Senate and the presidency—in order to assess the impact of personality in varying settings. In the present state of knowledge, it is not possible to describe the interaction of men and institutions in full and accurate detail. Institutions like individuals change over time; history moves on. The process itself cannot be frozen for inspection. The requisites for success in the same institution are different at different periods of time. This does not, however, make it impossible to analyze the interaction of men and events at a specific period of time and to draw conclusions, which I shall now attempt to do by examining the Senate first and then the presidency.

The Senate

When Lyndon Johnson became a senator, he entered an institution extremely well suited to his capacities, and at a time in the history of both Senate and country that made it possible for him to exert those capacities with great effect. No matter how great his abilities, Johnson's rise to power would not have been possible if the institutional conditions of the Senate had, like those of the House, not been favorable.

First, power in the Senate was less institutionalized than it was in the House. It was, for the most part, exercised by an informal group known as the "inner club"—the chairmen of important committees, mostly southerners and predominantly conservative—whose acknowledged leader was Richard Russell. The hierarchy was not rigid, nor did it attempt to extend control over all the details of Senate activity. The formal leadership positions had little actual authority, and were not sought by ambitious men who had invested years of service in anticipation of being selected; their occupancy was seen more as a duty than as a base of power. Moreover, as Truman's administration neared its close the Democratic party was in disarray, the president himself preoccupied with the Korean War, his influence dwindling. Thus there was no external party influence either on the current leadership or on the process of selection, as there might have been under a strong Democratic president and a united Democratic party.

All these factors contributed to a situation where Johnson was able by skillfully cultivating one man—Russell—to provide an entry for himself into the power structure without infringing on the authority and prerogatives of others. There was no need to displace existing leadership—happenstance opened the posts— or to fight the organized candidacies of others. He had simply to make himself both desirable to Russell and the inner club and at least acceptable to the northerners. And meeting the requirement, he played a skillful game: he apprenticed himself to Russell, performing all manner of tangible and psychic services, yet he avoided being placed in an ideological category that would have made him totally unacceptable to the other senators. Thus he was prepared for the leadership opportunity when it came—through the successive vacancies of the officers of party whip and minority leader.

Once he became minority whip and leader, Johnson was able to accumulate power by exploiting institutional vulnerabilities—some the very ones that had made his selection possible—and the changing conditions of national and political life. Slack in the system was perhaps the most important condition. The inner club exercised its power only over those matters it considered important or of special interest. In other areas there was no real authority, nor was there any leadership concerned with the interest of the Senate as a whole. Moreover, the inner club tended to exercise its power along ideological lines, enforcing interests and attitudes that were generally conservative and southern. Its members were not concerned with the inevitable resentments of other senators who did not share their convictions, because their power was based not on majority vote but on control over committees and tacit acknowledgment of their right to authority. Nor did the inner club try to placate the inevitable resentment of an increasing number of new senators who felt that the established customs, leadership, and procedures barred them from a significant role in the legislative process, diminishing their opportunity to perform as they wanted and as their constituents expected.

Yet, if resentments smoldered and needs went unmet, there was no organized or coherent effort on the part of any group to displace the present leadership with a majority leadership of its own. The formal discipline that would have been required for such a revolt was hard to find in a body characterized by independent bases of power for each of its members. Each senator had interests distinct from those of every other—derived primarily from the necessities of his own political career. While a senator's concern for the effective functioning of the Senate as a whole was not absent, it was not generally a priority concern compared to his relationship with his constituents. Thus the alternatives history provided—strong, elective party leaders with party caucuses to bind votes and men —seemed even less appealing than a disorderly, uninstitutionalized Senate.

The situation was ripe for a personal leadership style: one that could lessen the tensions resulting from the southerners' tight control, concern itself with the smoother operation of the Senate, gather central resources to help individuals, but always remember that a senator's relationship with his constituency was the primary concern.

So upon taking over, Johnson assumed some burdens of leadership that had not previously been exercised—allotment of office space, scheduling of legislation, appointments to committee delegations. Able to comprehend the current structure of the Senate as a whole, he formed a mental picture of a different structure and moved toward it with such skill that he managed to bring everyone along with his changes, even those who would potentially lose power under the new system. He began by persuading the inner club to relax seniority just a little, to provide more seats on important committees to new members as a token means of quelling incipient resentment and as a way of making the Senate function more effectively. By this move, however, he obligated the freshmen senators to him; he established the appearance that his authority was the source of their ability to do their work effectively. At the same time, the small size of the Senate allowed him to gather information about every senator: what he was going to do, was likely to do, or might be persuaded to do. Over time, Johnson became the only source of authoritative information on the Senate as a whole. Thus he became useful, and often indispensable, to other senators who were forced to rely upon his judgment about, for example, the chances of passing legislation in which they were interested, or what form of compromise could bring agreement, or when they could take a trip without missing a crucial vote. In addition, he made it impossible for others to separate the appearance of power from its reality. If, for example, he told a senator that he would make sure of a favorable vote on his bill and the bill passed, one could not know whether Johnson had exerted his authority or whether he had already known what the result would be. In this way he secured obligations not only by rendering real services and rewards but by seeming to produce results that were not, in fact, of his doing.

The insulation of the cloakroom, where much of the Senate's business occurred, allowed Johnson to impose his will separately on each senator and in such a way as to reduce awareness of the coercive nature of his leadership. Had there been collective forums of decision in which he had forced individuals to go his way, the coercive nature of his tactics would have been all too clear. And, in fact, Johnson drained the collective organs, the caucus and the conference, transforming most of the Senate's business to his own office, where his relations were seen as bargaining. And, true, his capacity to bargain and persuade was undoubtedly an important element in his leadership. Yet the process was essentially coercive; over time, Johnson's power became increasingly necessary to the capacity of others to sustain and exercise their own authority. Every time he bargained there was always the implicit threat—never voiced, but inherent in the very disproportion of power and rewards—that failure to go along might have damaging consequences. And in most cases the senators yielded, except, of course, on matters of fundamental concern to their constituencies—a limit Johnson understood and respected. When he anticipated failure, he didn't try to persuade—a fact that only enhanced his reputation as a leader who accomplished what he set out to do.

The disguise was essential. For no senator could afford to let others know he was being compelled to act by another, that he was submitting to Lyndon Johnson's will. The nature of the Senate required unanimous acceptance of the mask —continual recognition of the majority leader's skills, his brilliance in argument, his effectiveness in conducting the business of the Senate, his genius at compromise—but not of his power to enforce his will. It is true that Johnson disliked, even feared, direct and open confrontation. But he was essentially a coercive personality, working in a situation in which bargaining and persuasion were the necessary forms for the acquisition of power and the exercise of control. Such forms were also more congenial to his personal qualities, reducing the possibility of failure, since one could not be defeated in a discussion or defied and overcome by another's inability to understand the wisdom of one's advice and arguments.

If institutional process and structure made the most important contribution to Johnson's power and the manner of its use, he was also helped by historical conditions and political circumstances, which—and partly because they were so congenial to his own character—in turn, influenced his conduct in the Senate. It is, for example, difficult to imagine Johnson's achieving a similar concentration of power in the Senate of Daniel Webster or John Calhoun. He came to Senate leadership during a time of relative quietism. The economy was doing well, and occasional recessions seemed nothing more than transient interruptions in the steady growth of personal affluence. There were no passionate issues of the kind that led to deep and irreconcilable divisions along lines of fundamental interest or ideology.

And the political circumstances were also congenial: a president uninterested in social reform, whose popularity restrained most Democrats from too open or strong opposition, permitted Johnson to avoid disruptive debates whose outcome he could not control. And that same president, because he was a Republican, made it unnecessary for Johnson to subordinate his conduct to the White House as he might have had to do with a strong Democratic leader.

Let us now turn to the influence of his power on the structure of the institution and on national events. Clearly, he had achieved more power as leader than any other leader in decades. And he had built that power from the qualities and structure of the institution. But he had not created institutionalized power. His powers had not, with a few exceptions, been incorporated into the formal authority of the majority leader. He had transformed a position of limited significance into one of great power. But he had used the majority leadership and not transformed it. His system depended on his capacities, knowledge, and command over a variety of procedures which he enforced but did not establish. As a result, when he left, the Senate had no centralized structure of leadership—unless it could find another Lyndon Johnson, which seemed unlikely, since it had waited two centuries for the first one.

Despite the failure to institutionalize his power, we must conclude that Johnson did bring the Senate during his reign to unprecedented heights of effective function. Legislation was moved from introduction to committee to floor and then enacted smoothly and with dispatch. Conflicts were reduced and respect for the Senate increased. Johnson's leadership is also responsible for speeding up the process through which the powers of the conservative southern coalition were redistributed to the Senate as a whole, a process made inevitable by population shifts and the loss of a one-party South, and for reducing some of the inequalities resulting from the seniority system. The old system had rested on accepted traditions and procedure, informal alliances based both on common outlook and mutual interest and on established procedure—seniority—for the acquisition of authority. Once that system had changed, then the belief that the way things were was the only way they could be was shattered. Nor was it likely that any new group of senators would now deliberately grant authority to a group of committee chairmen dominated by southern authority.

Yet the powers once held by the inner club were not, after Johnson, lodged in a new leader; they were simply fragmented to the benefit of individual senators. These senators have since developed a stake in the existing system of leadership. Any change now would entail a transfer of power, a probability that familiar modes of conduct would be changed; the ultimate consequences are uncertain and thus appear as risk. This is precisely why structures of power in the Senate are not codified, but, instead, continually evolve over a long period of time with changes in the nature of the Senate membership. Johnson's rise was exceptional in this regard. The Senate would never have voted to give him the powers of leadership that they so often praised. Nor are they likely to bestow the same powers on any other majority leader or on the position itself. That would require a sense of devotion to the Senate as a whole, which would only be possible in an instiution that was a collective body—that is, in a different institution.

Johnson's system of power and leadership influenced not only the Senate as an institution but national conditions and events. For one thing, he inhibited the development of effective and coherent opposition on domestic issues. There were serious national problems—persisting poverty, inadequate health care, recurrent recession, and unemployment—along with questions of defense policy and foreign affairs. There was debate on this issues, both in the country and, later, during the 1960 presidential campaign. But the Senate was potentially the most important forum for the expression of opposition. It could influence the national dialogue, many of its members were themselves significant political figures, and with a Democratic majority could force a confrontation. Historically, it had often taken this role (congressional opposition during the later New Deal, the great and partly decisive debate over the Marshall Plan, etc.). This does not mean that the Senate could have substituted its policies for those of Eisenhower, but it abdicated the possibility even of stimulating national debate; of influencing, if not decisively changing, the course of events and those administration policies that needed senatorial acquiescence. Yet the days of the Senate's involvement with legislation had been steadily waning even before Johnson, and on the other side of the ledger is the fact that Johnson's leadership was vital to the passage of the first civil rights act since 1867, and in forcing the government to initiate a large-scale space program. And there were other accomplishments. Nevertheless, we must conclude that while Johnson's leadership style—his avoidance of issues and his fear of confrontation—may have increased his power over the Senate, it lessened the influence of the Senate on the country.

Under Johnson's reign, floor debate was substantially reduced in importance, and with it, the role of the Senate in foreign policy. Again we must acknowledge an institutional evolution toward increased executive authority in foreign policy. Yet in the decades before, Congress had felt free to debate—often along partisan lines—to oppose, and occasionally to act against the president's foreign policy. Since then, the felt requisites of unity in the difficult period of the cold war had worked to reduce open debate. But Johnson led in a time of peace, in a time when the Senate might have—as Senator Joseph Clark repeatedly suggested—moved to increase its supply of information without threatening executive authority. But Johnson refused, preferring always to resolve issues by private compromise followed by public agreement, and thus contributed to the general weakening of the Senate's role.

And once the traditional responsibilities were abandoned, there was little move to reclaim them. Because Senate constituencies had little interest in most matters of foreign policy, the most important incentive to action was missing. And the irony was that Johnson's own performance in the presidency would itself be seriously influenced by this weakening of the Senate—by reducing an important check that might well have constrained his decisions on Vietnam in ways helpful to him as well as to his country.

The Presidency

In 1963 Johnson entered an arena vastly different from the Senate. Yet for the first twelve months the circumstances of the transition period and the election allowed him to conduct his presidency in a manner consistent with his previous efforts to acquire and exercise power.

Upon his succession to the presidency, Johnson confronted a dual problem: he had to guide the country through a traumatic and uncertain moment and work to ensure his nomination at the Democratic Convention, which was only eight months away.

The course he chose to meet the first objective—the theme of continuity—was natural to his character and to the need of his time. Moreover, he was helped in this endeavor by the institutionalized process of succession—established by constitutional and historical precedent—which immediately placed in his hands all the powers, institutional authority, symbolic functions, and impressive trappings of the American chief of state—a transfer that was more than a transfer, but rather a replacement thought so necessary and appropriate that not a single dissenting voice marred the population's unquestioning acknowledgment of its legitimacy.

The circumstances of the public mood even allowed Johnson while in the presidency to assume his accustomed role of the faithful follower—this time of the memory of a dead president. Now, unlike the vice-presidency, where he had nothing to give, he could, as he had done with Russell, provide a significant service (the enactment of the dead man's program) and then reap the rewards that would enable him to consolidate his power.

This was possible because he had come into the legislative cycle at the ideal moment for his particular talents. Kennedy had already articulated the goals—most of the issues on Kennedy's agenda were suspended between formulation and approval—leaving the new president the familiar task of mobilizing congressional support.

Moreover, 1964 was a year of relative tranquillity in foreign policy, while the country itself experienced relative economic stability, and there were no serious or turbulent manifestations of domestic distress. Serious and visible crises would have required him to devote attention to unaccustomed responsibilities. In their absence, the enormous resources and elaborate machinery of the modern presidential institution—bureaucracies, established hierarchies of authority and decision, experts, a White House staff large and specialized enough to exercise some form of White House jurisdiction over every activity of importance and make decisions in his name—could ensure that the activities of government were continued, decisions made, foreign leaders placated, etc., without compelling him to divert his attention to unfamiliar matters or to consider and resolve problems unrelated to his immediate objectives: legislative achievement and election.

In the election, too, the circumstances created an ideal situation for Johnson. He had always sought to avoid campaigns based on divisions over issues, trying instead to focus attention on his performance. Now his performance would be the main issue—a transition performance whose circumstances allowed him to combine a deferential dignity with a dazzling display of effectiveness, which brought first relief, then approval and even admiration from the press and the general public. Indeed, his display of large abilities and presidential stature was so significant that he could, even though he had been in office for only a few months, run on the record; and the shortness of his incumbency enabled him to define that record as a demonstration of stature and performance rather than of the substance and directions of his policies, which would obviously be more divisive.

To these conspicuous and influential circumstances was added the nomination of Goldwater, reflecting the culmination of an evolution—a shift part ideological, part geographical—of power within the Republican party. Goldwater's candidacy —his insistence that he was truly ideological, the nature of some of his support for the nomination, and some of his speeches—gave the impression that he wanted to eliminate many of the programs and institutions established in the decades since Roosevelt took office, which had come to be viewed by moderates and many conservatives not as liberal experiments or intrusions but as part of the established order. The same interests who had opposed Social Security and government regulation of business activity had no desire to tear apart a structure they were now accustomed to, had conformed their activities to, and under which, moreover, they were doing better than before.

One can hypothesize a moderate to liberal Republican candidate who could have made a serious issue of Johnson's already expressed intentions and their implication of greatly increased federal activity and spending, who might have accused him of dangerous incapacities in foreign policy, or have debated the Democrtaic party's intention—already manifested by the actions of Kennedy and Johnson—to reverse Eisenhower's refusal to intervene militarily in Indochina; a debate that would have permitted the Republicans to exploit the public's recollection of Truman and Korea and the vague identification of the Democratic party as the party of war. Instead, however, the Republicans nominated a candidate whose campaign imposed upon his candidacy the most serious traditional vulnerabilities of both parties.

This made possible the kind of campaign most congenial to Johnson's own temperament. His election was in everybody's interest: to the conservative, complacent, or fearful, he was the protector of the system; to a people whose enthusiastic response to the Test Ban Treaty had surprised even Kennedy, he was the man of peace who would meet crises with restraint; to the poor and the blacks, he offered not only understanding but a demonstrated capacity for effective action; to the middle class, he could appear as both a guarantor of increasing affluence and, without seeming inconsistent, as one who understood and would try to alleviate many of the sources of middle-class discontent—the state of the environment, pollution, the conditions of urban life. He was under no compulsion to set forth a coherent program, which might have revealed the difficulties of fulfilling such diverse and often conflicting expectations, whose content and potential consequences would have increased opposition. The unusual conditions of political life in 1964 allowed him to rely, instead, on general statements of purpose, principle, and intention. His opponent not only did not challenge him from the middle, but made *himself* and not Johnson's policies the issue (McGovern was to perform a similar service for Nixon in 1972). Johnson was, therefore, in the fortunate circumstance of being able to combine elements of the kind that contributed to the disparate appeal of both Eisenhower and Roosevelt.

So everywhere he went huge crowds assembled to greet his arrival, attend his movements through the streets. Millions of people he hadn't met, didn't know, whose motives and interests he had not calculated in order to decide how best to impose his will, cheered, almost screaming, often jumping excitedly, in their enthusiasm at his presence. No advance men or organization could have produced such multitudes or intensities. He had accomplished some significant things, but less than several other presidents, far less than he intended, yet he was hailed as if he were a national conqueror. And even if he didn't understand and only half-trusted it, he couldn't get enough of it, traveling from place to place, descending into every crowd, touching the few he could reach as if to reassure himself it was really happening, and more obviously out of an uncontrollable and understandable exuberance. And who could blame him? It was the closest he could come to feeling loved, and who would not express—in his own manner and to the extent he could—exultance at the unexpected approach toward satisfaction of this universal longing?

The election of 1964, both the victory and its size, changed the nature of Johnson's political constituency. The Democratic party itself was no longer a factor in the exercise of power or its renewal. His election left the party apparatus in his hands, and he would soon move to eliminate any remnants of independent authority or access to resources that the Kennedy White House had left intact. As an incumbent, his renomination, if he wanted it, was assured—or so he had every right to assume, and must have assumed. It was, therefore, no longer necessary to direct efforts or policies to cultivate the support of groups because of their potential influence on the party. Their importance to Johnson now depended on their potential influence on the outcome of a national election, and—of more immediate and pressing significance—on the extent to which they could help or obstruct the achievement of his objectives, mostly the passage of legislation.

After the 1964 election, Johnson found himself in command of an institution very different from the institutional and political settings in which he had spent virtually his entire life, and through which he had pursued his ambitions with enormous, if not uninterrupted, success. He had great powers whose acquisition he could now regard as the consequence of his own abilities and that could, therefore, be exercised for his own purposes. However, it is unlikely that he fully understood the extent of the differences in function and structure between the presidency and the earlier settings for his activity and ambition, nor the extent to which presidential powers were not only greater but of a different nature.

In the presidency, unlike in the Senate, the standards of achievement had to be established in relation to accomplishments external to the presidential institution. Here Johnson's own skill and natural inclination, reinforced by the experience of the transition, led him to establish standards of achievement based on his success in designing and enacting a program of domestic reform. Moreover, institutional relationships between the president and Congress required that he must also determine the substance of that program—the general policies and the content of the legislation he would propose. Here Johnson could benefit from the ideas of a liberal tradition institutionalized in his agencies and the Bureau of the Budget, which for twenty years had been proposing legislation that had never passed; now their time had come and they had a ready agenda.

However, neither Johnson's own ambitions and convictions nor the ready agenda would have prevailed under adverse conditions. But in 1965 conditions could not have been more auspicious for domestic reform. Sustained economic growth combined with a relative stability of prices had strengthened a conviction that affluence was inevitable. Moreover, there was still a general desire for the reestablishment of some form of shared national purpose: a sentiment that had formed the theme of Kennedy's successful 1960 campaign. The absence of paramount domestic divisions made it unnecessary for him to take positions that would have aroused the kind of opposition that would have extended beyond the issues themselves to him and his administration. Economic conditions and, even more, established economic expectations made it possible to convince people that the poor and disadvantaged could be helped and that national problems—conditions of urban life, disintegration of the natural environment, transportation facilities, etc.—could be resolved without requiring any group to sacrifice income or significant interests.

Finally, there was the influence of Johnson's own leadership—his natural capacities and unequaled knowledge of Congress, which enabled him to confound the traditional relationship between president and Congress, mixing the two so that both branches were involved in the acts of proposing and disposing. Moreover, the familiar resources of the presidential institution enabled him to provide a great variety of benefits and services tthat would create obligation and various degrees of dependency. Most importantly, as president Johnson could now bargain directly with leaders of powerful interest groups—business executives, leaders of financial communities, union chiefs, the acknowledged spokesmen for minority groups, etc. As president, he could virtually command their presence, allowing him to exert his formidable personal powers. Even more significantly, every important group in the society was affected by the activities of the federal government, especially by the executive branch Johnson commanded. Thus every encounter also involved an awareness—rarely, if ever, expressed—of mutual interest more direct and specific than their shared patriotism and belief in the American dream. Thus Johnson was able to enlist support, or, at the least, mute potential opposition, from those interest groups whose views could influence the decisions of Congress. They were important, not just because of their wealth or numbers, but because there was no member of Congress whose political base was not subject to the influence of one or more of them. As president, Johnson could thus do what he could not do in the Senate—extend his reach to the foundation and source of office.

Of course, without general public support this would have been to no avail.

But the aspect of consensus politics that made effective performance possible was a consensus among a limited number of special groups, whose leaders could be identified, making possible the personal contact that was the medium through which Johnson could make the most effective use of his personal powers and tangible resources—to persuade, convince, bargain, obligate, or coerce. As long as the objective was congressional action—the passage of legislation—the presidential institution enormously increased the effectiveness of behavior that had been successful in other contexts.

In particular, in the area of civil rights Johnson's legacy is clear: his position on racial issues was more advanced than that of any other American president; had he done nothing else in his entire life, his contributions to civil rights would have earned him a lasting place in the annals of history.

But if the modern presidency permitted Johnson an unparalleled authority in domestic affairs for the successful exercise of his qualities and abilities, modes of conduct and methods of exercising power, it also permitted an equally unparalleled failure when those same qualities and patterns of behavior were applied where all Johnson's talents and skills were not merely inadequate but irrelevant and, even more, counterproductive.

Lyndon Johnson did not create the framework within which his country defined its commitment to South Vietnam. That framework, developed in the space of more than twenty years by three previous presidents and their many advisers, rested on a series of assumptions derived from historical experience: the experience of World War II and the events that precipitated it; the initial confrontations between the Soviet Union and the United States; the fear of making concessions to adversary powers; the identification of the potentially dangerous power—the Soviet Union—with the ideology of communism, an identification which required that any political leader or insurgent chief who called himself a Communist was simply an extension of Soviet power.

Of course, experience was not all so one-sided. We had resigned ourselves to the "loss" of Eastern Europe and China, accepted stalemate in Korea, refused to intervene in Indochina; in other words, had shown that our policies, the underlying convictions, and their sometimes violent expression by leaders such as John Foster Dulles had not destroyed our ability to assess realities, and to accept limits imposed by the calculation of practical possibilities.

But the institutional structure Johnson inherited in 1963–1964 narrowed access to the information and perceptions that might have placed Vietnam in one of the above categories. All Johnson's principal advisers agreed on the critical nature of the goal of a non-Communist Vietnam, on the interpretation of the internal struggle as a struggle against communism, and on the possibility of achieving that goal with gradual escalation short of large-scale war.

Clearly, Johnson's own qualities influenced his initial decision to escalate. In domestic affairs, particularly in the passage of legislation, he was used to grasping practical realities first and then adapting his goals to those realities. But his lack of intimate knowledge about foreign policy and Vietnam led him to rely, instead, on the goals and principles themselves, losing sight of the question of available means. The failure to ask "Will it work?" was reinforced by a pristine concept of foreign policy as an arena of choice that should be removed from ordinary political consideration. Therefore his means were subordinated to his ends; his ends *became* his means. Lack of experience and confidence also produced in Johnson an unquestioning acceptance of the "experts' " advice, something he would never have accorded to anyone in domestic affairs. Moreover, Johnson's adversary in Vietnam—unlike nearly all his opponents at home—was unwilling to bargain. Even if Johnson had been able to sit down with Ho Chi Minh, there was nothing to talk about so long as the goals of the two countries remained irreconcilable. So, faced with a situation he could not control and an adversary who was unwilling to bargain, Johnson would force him to bargain. And since he could not compel in his usual way—the denial of rewards or necessities—he was forced to act more directly, in this case with the only instrument of compulsion he had: military force. And, given his character, that force would be exercised in graduated degrees (thus avoiding the even more uncontrollable situation of all-out war).

To say Johnson's qualities were expressed in the decision to escalate is not, however, to say that his character caused that decision. On the contrary, in late 1964 and early 1965, as we have seen, all the relevant elements of the governing process moved in the same direction, making it impossible to filter out the particular weight of personality. Indeed, given the momentum, the necessity of choice—since at this point not choosing would have meant turning South Vietnam over to the Communists—and the consistency of advice from almost every corner, it is easy to imagine many other presidents, acting under very different internal compulsions, making the same decision.

The influence of Johnson's personality on the decision making in Vietnam is easier to observe in his conduct of the war—in the decision to conceal its nature and extent from the American people. Here the advice was not unanimous; indeed, most of Johnson's principal advisers recommended a different course from the one Johnson chose, urging him to go to the Congress, declare a state of emergency, and put the economy on a wartime footing. Johnson refused, opting instead to hide the costs of the war in the Defense Department budget, keeping the pretense of a peacetime economy, and letting the public know as little as possible about the nature and extent of the war—all of which he assumed would allow the Great Society to continue on course.

This decision was Lyndon Johnson's decision. It is easy to imagine another president, less concerned with domestic reform, more capable of choosing between goals, less confident of his ability to move in contradictory directions at the same time, less experienced in the arts of secrecy, deciding differently. Indeed, this decision seems almost to sum up the character of the man. The very qualities and experiences that had led to his political and legislative success were precisely those that now operated to destroy him. His tendency to resolve conflict instead of accepting it—responsible for his rise to power and his success in the

Senate—now led him to manipulate and orchestrate the political process in order to shape a formula that could accommodate both the Great Society and Vietnam. Years of experience in gaining and exercising power had taught Johnson that the leader could move in contradictory directions at the same time so long as he compartmentalized everything he did and kept his dealings with one group secret from those with the next. Finally, the bipartisan tradition in foreign policy, responsible for producing consensus behind World War II and the Marshall Plan, now led to the conclusion that complicated decisions of foreign policy should be left in the hands of the leaders; the people would only be hurt by knowing too much.

As it turned out, however, the people were not hurt by knowing too much; Lyndon Johnson was hurt by knowing too little. The loss of public debate on the war lessened the possibilities of judgment, depriving Johnson of the chance to test various responses to different policies and of the opportunity to dispel misconceptions. Nor, in the absence of any clear understanding of the goals in Vietnam, could he expect to sustain the public's support.

He had hoped that a middle course at home and abroad would secure his place in history as a leader of war and a leader of peace. Instead, halfway measures on both fronts produced a condition of half-war and half-peace which satisfied no one and created resentments on all sides.

Moreover, the failure to increase taxes produced inflation, which produced, in turn, a squeeze on moneys for the Great Society instead of the steadily expanding supply of resources Johnson had originally promised. (At this stage of the Great Society, the difficulties Johnson experienced on questions of implementation were similar in nature to those that plagued him on Vietnam. Here, too, because he was so sure of the ends and because the persons involved in implementing the means were so far away, he underestimated the problems of making his programs work.) Furthermore, diversion from the Great Society was not only a question of economic resources; the war drained time, energy, and attention as well.

As the Great Society crumbled and the war continued with no end in sight, Johnson's popularity began to drop. The effective performer was no longer performing effectively, and once that measure of favorable judgment was gone, there was nothing else on which to base his relations with the people—except all those qualities he had never trusted: public advocacy, personal integrity, credibility.

Gradually, and for almost the first time, Johnson now found himself amid events and men he could not master: Vietnam and the Kennedys, and, later, the press, Congress, and even the public whose approval was all he could experience of love. One could have anticipated the result. As his defenses weakened, long-suppressed instincts broke through to assault the carefully developed skills and judgment of a lifetime. The attack was not completely successful. The man was too strong for that. Most of Johnson—the outer man, the spheres of conscious thought and action—remained intact, for most of the time. But in some ways, increasingly obvious to his close associates, he began to crumble; the suspicions congenital to his nature became delusions; calculated deceit became self-deception, and then matters of unquestioned belief.

Moreover, Johnson, was aided—or, more accurately, hurt—in this process of deception by the nature of the institutional relationships around him. The White House itself—as opposed to the Senate—was not manned by individuals with independent political bases and formal authority. Here Johnson was in command, and, expectedly, the coercive aspects of his nature manifested themselves. He could impose his will much more directly upon colleagues—members of his staff and of his cabinet—whose positions and power within the government rested primarily on him. Of course, he, in turn, depended on the abilities of these men, but that meant that the only hold they had was the right to resign. And it was not much of a hold. For Johnson knew that few men easily relinquished their high positions in government. Both Johnson and his subordinates knew that resignation involved forfeiting recognized status and power in return only for escape. Under these conditions, the independence of the cabinet members and of those in charge of the most important White House functions was gradually reduced. The president's will, once expressed, was not challenged. Advisers began to anticipate his reactions before they said or did anything; self-deceptions multiplied in this hall of distorting mirrors. The more Johnson's energies turned to his critics, the more obsessed he became with the need to discredit his opponents, the less anyone tried to stop him.

Nor did the president have to listen to the Congress so long as it continued, out of tradition, habit, and deference, to appropriate funds for the war, and so long as it refused to take a single vote on the war itself. Nor—for three years— did any other external force break through. Surrounded by the White House staff, cocooned in an institutional framework protecting him from the outside world (his schedule, secretaries, planes, and cars), Johnson effectively insulated himself from information he did not want to hear.

But there was a limit to Johnson's insulation and his self-defeating belief in the possibility of turning the corner in Vietnam. The Tet offensive and the presidential primaries changed the framework within which Johnson had to work. Finally, the checks and balances of the political system came back into play.

Forced to confront a precipitous drop in his public standing, a sharp shift in editorial reaction, and the loss of support from key interest-group leaders, Johnson finally accepted the fact that he was in a situation he could no longer control and that further escalation would produce only more uncontrollability. Faced at the same time with loss of love and gratitude on what seemed an irretrievable scale, Johnson had no choice but to withdraw. Nor did he have any choice but to believe, since he had to believe it in order to survive, that eventually his withdrawal would make possible even more control over and more love from history —the only constituency that really mattered in the end.

CONCLUSIONS

Lyndon Johnson's public career, with the exception of a single election defeat, was one of uninterrupted and unparalleled success in the accumulation of power and—although with less consistency—in the use of power to achieve practical results. This implies that varied repositories of public authority share common elements of structure, which are, moreover, relatively resistant to rapid historical change. Our examination of Johnson's leadership proved to be a study not only of particular institutions but of attributes and vulnerabilities which are common to several institutions, and which, therefore, probably derive from the more comprehensive institutional processes of politics and government.

I offer these general observations more by way of suggestion than conclusion, but useful, perhaps, in framing questions that might enable us to understand better the relationship between leaders and the qualities of leadership, events and historical circumstances, and institutional structure. I offer these as only a few possibilities. The reader hopefully will see many more.

First: Different institutions reward different qualities—although what constitutes "reward" depends not only on the institution but upon the nature of the individual leader's ambitions. Neither John Kennedy nor Richard Nixon wanted to become a great Senate leader; to them the Senate was a useful platform, though not the only one possible, to advance their careers. Of equal importance, the abilities and characteristic modes of conduct of both men kept them from attempting to become powerful Senate leaders, and would have kept them from accomplishing such an objective.

Johnson, on the other hand, in psychic nature, modes of conduct, and natural abilities, possessed all the qualifications required by the structure in the Senate as it existed at a particular moment for becoming an enormously powerful leader. The institution rewarded his qualities, and that reward was the object of his ambitions. Of course, he, too, had higher aspirations. But his qualities, forms of conduct, the demands and fears that were an aspect of his nature seemed to foreclose other routes. He had to depend, as he always had, upon effective performance—which meant controlling his institutional environment. He was further restrained by the fact that this performance not only was his means of advancing his ambition but was also an end in itself, and he was not capable of risking it for actions that might seem to enhance his chances for more significant power in another institution.

In fact, the qualities the Senate rewarded were not adapted to the institutional process of presidential nomination nor, probably, to that of presidential election, for it was unlikely that Johnson could have moved from majority leader to election as president on his own.

Not only do institutions reward different qualities, but their demands are often contradictory. The same qualities and capacities that make success probable in one setting may be inconsistent with success in another setting. Johnson was fortunate that conditions in 1964 and 1965 permitted him to use many of the abilities and qualities with which he had mastered the legislative process to conduct his presidency with some success. However, when circumstances changed, these capacities proved ill-suited to the presidency, which was a vastly different institution. He could not lead or inspire the nation by secret deals; he did not understand foreign policy; he could not deal with conflicts taking place in a setting where he could not establish personal detailed knowledge of the problems and the participants; and the same search for control that gave such force and direction to his legislative career caused him now to move toward coercive action and to transform the executive branch into a personal instrument, and a weapon for concealing facts and policies from other branches of government and the people.

Of course, Johnson was unique, as was his career. However, that career suggests that many of the qualities that make for success in the legislative branch—compromise, avoidance of conflict, secrecy, the effort to submerge personal responsibility for success or failure in a collective body, the vision of law as the end of the process, etc.—may be contradictory to those required for effective national leadership: indeed, that a career in the legislative process may inculcate modes of behavior or strengthen existing qualities inconsistent with the nature of the presidential institution. This conjecture, which I believe to be true, is of special importance at a time when the Congress has become a significant platform for presidential candidates.

However, it demonstrates the fact that talent for public life is not a unity, but that there are distinct, often contradictory, talents, which are relevant to success in one area of public life and not in another. This is important in assessing not only whether a leader is likely to achieve his ambitions in a particular setting, but—more significantly—whether his leadership is likely to benefit or damage the country.

Second: Johnson demonstrated hitherto unsuspected powers in the executive branch. There was, as many have observed, a growing evolution toward concentration of power in that branch. However, Johnson did not merely continue this evolution. He gave it a new dimension. Previous evolution had rested on changing circumstances, e.g., federal intervention in economic policy and problems of public welfare, the growing significance of foreign policy, the size of the defense establishment, involvement in war, etc. For the most part, this expanding power was exercised with the knowledge and acquiescence of Congress and the informed public. Johnson discovered that the resources of the presidency allowed him to conceal much of the exercise of power; that presidential authority could be exerted on the basis of undisclosed information and the private interpretation of information; indeed, that in many cases even presidential actions and decisions could be concealed. Of course, the effect of many such decisions would eventually become visible, thus revealing the decision itself. But not all. Moreover, concealment of the decision-making process shut out the opportunity for public discussion that is an essential part of the institutional process in our representative democracy. Johnson's actions became known because they were directed toward public goals, their objectives were of a public nature, and, hence, their effects would inevitably be revealed. Nixon illustrated how this power of concealment could be used for other kinds of objectives so that the probability of continuing concealment was increased. The development or discovery of a capacity to exercise substantial executive power in secret is not simply an increase in the power of the presidency; it represents a change in the relationship of institutions within the constitutional framework, a change which, in some part, has the potential of moving the presidential institution outside the framework itself.

Third: This aspect of institutional change, developed under Johnson, and reinforced by the fate of the Nixon administration, suggests that the most effective checks on presidential power are not the institutions that form the constitutional system of "checks and balances." They are the media and public opinion, catalyzed, in Johnson's case, by the presidential primaries. In both administrations these nongovernmental institutions were more effective restraints on presidential actions and usurpations than established governmental institutions.

Fourth: Johnson's career also helps to reaffirm the significance, probably the necessity, of consensus politics to effective presidential leadership. Historically, the only exceptions have been under special conditions—depression under Roosevelt, shifts and growth of population under Jackson—which produced large popular majorities whose interests were opposed to those protected by the dominant structure of economic and political power. Jefferson, after all, moved to placate the Federalists, even at the cost of disappointing some of his Republican followers, while Theodore Roosevelt took steps to placate his business supporters even while establishing a reputation as a trust buster. Johnson, however, showed that consensus could be a foundation for an extensive program of domestic reform even at a time when there were no serious class hostilities nor any economic crisis. That accomplishment requires a modification of what is meant by "consensus," or, rather, a recognition that the term is susceptible to different definitions. Eisenhower's consensus consisted of the fact that a large popular majority was satisfied with his policies, and no substantial proportion of the population was urging him in another direction. Under Johnson as well, there was no significant movement for domestic reform (with the exception, for a time, of the civil rights movement). He himself was the initiating force. Admittedly, the absence of serious division, and favorable economic conditions, made it possible for him to initiate such a program. However, he also saw that consensus did not require him to marshall public enthusiasm and support. He would achieve consensus among groups of special interests and concerns, usually organized and with identifiable leaders, who could influence congressional action directly. And each program required a different kind of appeal to different kinds of groups. By persuading religious and educational associations, he could remove obstacles to a program for aiding education. Certain programs of public welfare required union support and the willingness of business groups to, at least, withdraw opposition. Thus, in a manner similar to the way in which he imposed his will in the Senate, he constructed a consensus from an assembly of particular groups and interests, most of them led by individuals with whom he could deal directly. He created an interlocking web of services and obligations. Finally, many were willing to support particular programs about which they had reservations because they believed that, on the whole, Johnson's program was good for them and for the country. It was a pluralistic consensus, an agreement among groups of limited, often contradictory interests. This consensus, Johnson knew, would shape the actions of Congress. Popular support, that other form of consensus, would be a consequence of achievement, not its source.

We cannot determine, however, the extent to which Johnson had developed a method for public action that can be applied in other situations, and how much its effectiveness depended upon his unique qualities and capacities. And of course, events during the last years of his administration showed that even a consensus built on majority support and the desire for action cannot survive serious public divisions.

Fifth: Johnson's career also provides further evidence that the basic qualities of a leader do not change when he assumes new and larger responsibilities. It is more a metaphor than an accurate description to say, for example, that a man "grows" in office. Of course, individuals do learn from experience—some better than others, and some become more skillful. But basic abilities, ambitions grounded on inner needs, modes of conduct, and inclinations of behavior are deeply and permanently embedded. It may be that these qualities cannot be displayed in a particular setting, or are not suited to achievement within a particular institutional framework and/or under certain historical conditions; yet in another place they can be the basis of accomplishments and actions that others would not have anticipated. One thinks of Truman. Or it may be that the widened constituency of the presidency allows a broadening of goals. Yet, while Johnson's landslide victory did stretch his aspirations, it did not change the essential elements of his behavior. Even his possession of the most powerful office in the country did not diminish his need to extend control or increase his capacity to deal with certain kinds of conflict or resistance. All his newly acquired ability to command did not reduce his drive to coerce. And under the right conditions, these qualities, which many had seen in him previously, were bound to emerge. And just as great office could magnify, if not change, his strength, so it could disastrously extend the consequences of his flaws. So, too, we discovered that the new Nixon was the old Nixon with much more power.

Therefore the best evidence of what can be expected of a candidate for high office—especially the presidency—can better be found in an examination of his pattern of activity at other stages of his public life than in his statements or goals, and particularly in situations of stress, when he was confronted with difficult decisions that were bound to affect his ambitions, his leadership, and his concept of himself.

Sixth: The dilemma of the modern presidency is not as simple as the contemporary talk of the imperial president suggests. Admittedly, the presidential institution has widened in power, as has the capacity of the president to concentrate that power in his own hands—a consequence less of tyranny than of the steady weakening of the various institutions designed to check the president—the cabinet, the Congress, and the party. But the same centralization of resources that allows an almost unconstrained initiation of policies in some areas (the making of war and peace) and the exercise of almost unilateral authority in others (the dropping of bombs) incapacitates implementation of both domestic and foreign programs and eventually weakens the president's ability to lead. With a weakened cabinet, the president has less chance of controlling his vast bureaucracy; with a shattered party and diminished Congress, he is unable to command that restrained public support essential for the continued viability of both his policies and his leadership. Thus the concentration of resources is at once enabling and constricting; the analytical problem is to understand not only where the president is too strong but also where he is too weak; to delineate what is meant by strong and weak and to describe the curious relationship between the two.

Seventh: The president's ability to focus national attention upon his every word and deed—which is made possible, and almost inescapable, by the nature of the national media—is a source of both power and illusion. And the same can be said of the enlarged White House staff and the use of a technological apparatus unparalleled in history. For five years, between 1963 and 1968, Lyndon Johnson dominated public life in Washington to such an extent that the cabinet was *his* cabinet, the Great Society *his* program, the Congress *his* instrument. With every technological innovation at his disposal, he could tape his own television shows, tell his pilots ten thousand miles away where and when to bomb, talk with the Soviet premier on a moment's notice, and fly around the world in less than two days. But the man in the center when things are good remains in the center when things go bad, and the resources technology provides are often illusory, substituting the sense of control for real control. Thus the war in Vietnam became Lyndon Johnson's war; he personally was dropping the bombs, disrupting the economy, making prices rise, setting back the progress of black and poor. Obviously, neither image—villain or hero—is valid; historical circumstances and institutional conditions were vital to both success in the Great Society and failure in Vietnam. And this understanding is of more than intellectual interest, for exaggeration of the president's personal powers (both self-induced and media propelled) is an inevitable source of frustration as the president's actions invariably fall short of expectations, producing a destructive cycle for the man, the office, and the nation.*

---

* This article is based primarily on extended conversations I held with Lyndon Johnson about his childhood and his political career and on Johnson's personal papers.

Staffing the Presidency: Premature Notes on the New Administration

RICHARD E. NEUSTADT

In December 1976, with an August 1977 deadline, I was asked to do something very hard—to give fellow president-watchers useful information that would "up-date our lecture notes" on the institutional presidency, carrying forward from Ford to Carter, from Republicans to Democrats, an outline of Executive Office organization, White House included.

What made this task hard was the qualification *useful*. The ostensible staffing pattern of a new regime in its seventh month (when this analysis was due) is an uncertain guide for the years to follow, especially when viewed from the outside. The Truman pattern of late 1945—more crazy-quilt than pattern—gave no hint to outsiders (or insiders for that matter) of the stabilized relationships to come, built up by personalities not yet in place, among others, Clark Clifford and James Webb. The Nixon pattern of mid-1969 had seeming "openness," even competitiveness in domestic policy. Daniel Patrick Moynihan balanced Arthur Burns, while Henry Kissinger struggled for acceptance by the Nixon loyalists, a struggle then in doubt. At that point Bryce Harlow, the congressional liaison man from Eisenhower's time, had far higher status in the new regime than, say, John Ehrlichman. But six months later Haldeman and Ehrlichman were "in," Kissinger entrenched, the others gone or going. Therefore in August 1977 one cannot write with confidence of Hamilton Jordan and company, to say nothing of Bertram Lance!

RICHARD E. NEUSTADT, author of *Presidential Power* and *Alliance Politics*, is professor of government at Harvard University and was an advisor to presidents Truman, Kennedy, and Johnson. He has also served as a consultant to Carter's Reorganization Project. This article is adapted from comments prepared for the September 1977 Meeting of the American Political Science Association.

However, 1977 yields one special feature which may lend current arrangements rather more weight than usual: Reorganization Plan No. 1 of 1977, and more importantly the study that preceded it. The study gave President Carter and his chief aides more instruction on and understanding of Executive Office institutions generally, and of their own performances to date—buttressed by quite dispassionate case studies—than previous presidents have ever had so early in the game. Carter made conscious choices, after study, only last July. We can assume, therefore, that for some time to come he will stick with those choices to the maximum extent allowed by unexpected losses of key people or by unforeseen defects in key procedures. No doubt there will be some of both. Barring a flood of them, however, I think we can anticipate, this year and probably next as well, that Carter's Executive Office, White House included, will resemble what we see in his first Reorganization Plan and its accompanying statements.[1]

Personalities along with strains that history can put upon procedures—especially in economics and in national security—may wreck this prediction. I accept that. But at least we start now, seven months into Carter's term, with relatively stabilized relationships and conscious choices made by light of some experience. Thus Nixon's case *may* not apply. A lot depends on personalities, of course, and how they grow, or don't.

Let me introduce those Carter choices by asking where the Executive Office now stands in relation to what went before: How has the Carter administration dealt with its inheritance of structures and procedures from previous presidents?

In the institutional development of the Executive Office since 1939, innovative structures and procedures that survive a change of administration from one party to the other seem firmly rooted thereafter, altering their inner character perhaps, with the passage of time, but not their external form or ostensible functions: for example, legislative clearance in the then Budget Bureau after 1952; or congressional liaison à la Harlow after 1960; or a special staff for trade negotiations, like the Kennedy Round, after 1968; or a substantive staff for the president in foreign policy à la Bundy (nominally under NSC), expanded after 1968 with Kissinger as super-Bundy. Or take the Council of Economic Advisers launched in 1946, which very nearly did *not* survive Truman. Eisenhower left it up to Arthur Burns, and Burns's CEA was carried on by Kennedy, then Johnson, Nixon, Ford, and so to Carter.

What seem to be the counterparts today? What innovations from the Nixon years and Ford's now seem built in, part of the long-term presidency because—so far—they have survived under Carter? Let me list ten at random.

[1] For a full statement of Executive Office reorganization as envisaged in July 1977 see Reorganization Plan No. 1 of 1977, with a "Statement by the President," July 15, 1977, a "Fact Sheet" dated the same day, and the transcript of an OMB press conference. These are available from OMB in a document entitled "Reorganization Plan No. 1, July 1977."

OFFICE OF MANAGEMENT AND BUDGET

The Rooseveltian Budget Bureau keeps the awful title Nixon's people fastened on it in 1970, "Office of Management and Budget" (OMB), with all its historic functions intact, except for those of Roosevelt's Central Statistical Board (never effectively integrated, increasingly downgraded, and now transferred with some hope of upgrading to Commerce). Internally, OMB keeps the administrative layer of so-called PADs (Program Associate Directors) inserted in Nixon's time between front office and career staff. PADs are political executives presumably attuned both to the White House and to Capitol Hill. Their presence testifies to doubts in Carter's time, no less than in Ford's or Nixon's, about leaving careerists on their own while budget directors may be otherwise engaged (for example, George Shultz, Bert Lance) and while congressional dealings multiply along with congressional staffs. OMB also continues to stress the M in its title, encountering as always a dilemma: how to avoid being swallowed by the B, or being swamped by services for second-string officials whose needs are remote from the president's. The answer of the moment is to focus in the main upon a temporary task, the President's Reorganization Project, and secondarily on intergovernmental issues, so as to backstop the White House. One thing OMB will not keep is the statutory Federal Property Council and staff, mostly devolved to GSA, while OMB retains, as it should, a watching brief.[2]

TWO LESSER AGENCIES: COWPS AND CEQ

COWPS, the Council on Wage and Price Stability, a cabinet committee with staff, is a statutory relic of Nixonian controls.[3] It survives for much the reason it came into being on the heels of decontrol: there has to be some symbol of the government's concern and some staff capability to monitor key sectors. The new regime, indeed, is buttressing that staff while subordinating it at the same time to the chairman of the Council of Economic Advisers. Charles Schultze now wears two hats. Thereby the CEA retains the character that it assumed in Burns's time, a largely academic staff on short-term leaves, a link between the profession and the president, a source of personal advice to him on matters mainly *macro*-economic. Sectoral issues seem to be a sphere for COWPS staff under Schultze's other hat. Perhaps this makes a nice division of

---

[2] The Federal Property Council, with a staff of about forty, is being transferred for the most part to the General Services Administration, but the OMB retains residual responsibility for review and coordination in the sphere of property management (as in most other spheres of executive operation).

[3] The Nixon administration, using discretionary authority, established mandatory price and wage controls in 1971 and gradually removed them during 1972 and 1973, following which the United States experienced the sharpest inflation ever. In the process the discretionary authority lapsed and was not renewed by Congress. COWPS was then established (1974).

labor; it is too soon to say. At any rate the new institution, like the old, survives, and they are joined as not before.

CEQ, the Council on Environmental Quality, is another Nixon creation and like CEA a staff group, not a cabinet council.[4] It passes the test of survival, although now reduced in size, after pressure tactics previous presidents would have resented fiercely. How Carter feels I do not know. Probably there are more reorganizations coming of environmental functions generally, including this one.

Office of Science and Technology Policy

OSTP, the Office of Science and Technology Policy, is a revival of OST, the Science Adviser's office, started under Eisenhower, institutionalized under Kennedy, abolished under Nixon.[5] OST had let itself become spokesman *to* the president for the second-string concerns of half-a-dozen federal scientific agencies: not his concerns, theirs. And its advisory bodies had included outspoken opponents of the Vietnam War. Abolition under Nixon seemed natural. Revived in 1976 by act of Congess, OSTP was only just beginning to organize when Ford left office. The new administration drew on an almost clean slate with Frank Press as Director. Press reportedly was quick to distinguish between helping the White House frame policy options and helping all others press claims on the White House. Reorganization Plan No. 1 envisages devolving from OSTP all statutory duties which would make it prone, like OST, to serve as routine spokesman for those others. Press is said to be enthusiastic about devolution, a good augury for OSTP's usefulness. The survival test, however, cannot be applied full-scale until the next Republican administration.

Domestic Policy Staff

Nixon's most ambitious institutional innovation was the Domestic Council, a statutory cabinet committee with staff created in 1970 on the model, it was said, of NSC. The "council" feature never became real: intended for a small number of superdepartments, it failed to function when they failed to come into existence, having been blocked by Congress. A council of existing departments, being no improvement on the cabinet, was not used. The staff, however, had reality from the start, although a checquered career thereafter. It began as John Ehrlichman's instrument for policy planning and ad hoc coordination, and it dominated many agencies. After Ehrlichman's fall, and partly because of it, the Domestic Council staff sank almost out of sight and under Ford had

---

[4] The CEQ, a statutory agency, modelled roughly on CEA, was established in 1970, predating the EPA which came into existence by Reorganization Plan at the end of that year.

[5] The OST (now replaced by OSTP) was created by Congress in 1962 at Kennedy's instance, formalizing the science advisory bodies established at the White House under Eisenhower after "Sputnik" in 1957.

an uncertain evolution, often kept at arm's length from the day to day flow of presidential business. But Carter's aides, who needed slots for Stuart Eizenstat's campaign issues coordinators, emptied the Domestic Council of Ford's people and installed their own, although in lesser numbers. Since January 1977 a Domestic Council staff of eighteen or twenty professionals has worked for Eizenstat, the president's Assistant for Domestic Affairs and Policy, in very much the way that Joseph Califano and his staff of five or six served Lyndon Johnson: as substantive assistants in development of legislative programs for a new administration, while helping to track presidential interests or frame presidential options, day by day. The staff thus plays as key a role as it ever did under Ehrlichman, although it is decidedly a Democratic variant which lacks Ehrlichman's reach for control, and is mindful of Carter's professed interest in "cabinet government."

Reorganization Plan No. 1 acknowledges this evolution by relabelling the Council a "Domestic Policy Staff," with Eizenstat wearing two hats, one inside the White House, one out, precisely paralleling Carter's NSC Assistant, Zbigniew Brzezinski.[6] Like the National Security Council staff (there "Council" remains in the title), this Domestic Policy Staff is only a very small step "outside" the White House. The step is small but perhaps consequential: White House aides are automatically presumed to be on Carter's business; aides from NSC or DPS are merely on Brzezinski's or Eizenstat's business, until they show otherwise. The main thing to note is that both staffs not only survive but flourish, smaller in numbers but larger, by all accounts, in effect on policy than they were under Ford.

THREE WHITE HOUSE OFFICES

In the White House itself many traces of Ford's arrangements remain. These in turn owed much to Nixon's, something even to Eisenhower's. Most important, the traditional post of Appointments Secretary, known to every Democrat from FDR through LBJ as a key place for politics, now has the grander title of Assistant to the President and is buttressed by associates, effectively subordinate, each one of whom does part of what old-style Appointments Secretaries were supposed to do. There are special assistants for scheduling, for personnel, for White House management, and a Staff Secretary for the paper flow, each with a deputy or two and help from White House careerists who were once almost the sole recourse for an Appointments Secretary. That officer, retitled now and freed from total immersion in minute detail, can put his mind on whatever the president wants.

Nixon, who pioneered this arrangement, came to want a choke-point, in effect a deputy, sometimes a coconspirator: H.R. Haldeman. Ford wanted not a

---

[6] Brzezinski's formal title is Assistant to the President for National Security Affairs, and as such he directs the staff of the National Security Council. Eizenstat is Assistant to the President for Domestic Affairs and Policy, and Director of the Domestic Policy Staff.

deputy but a priority-setter and strong facilitator: Donald Rumsfeld, later Richard Cheney. Carter evidently wants political strategy and perspective: Hamilton Jordan—who, wisely refusing to be called a "chief of staff," sits where those others sat while doing his own thing.

Another trace of Ford, and through him of Nixon, can be found in Carter's White House aides for public liaison, under Midge Costanza, also an Assistant to the President. Her staff is somewhat smaller but addresses the same purposes as it did under the Republicans (shaded for differences in party style and emphasis): it affords status symbols and a set of open doors to groups not otherwise well connected, at least in their own estimation (for example, ethnic minorities). "Public liaison" seems here to stay. This is a sobering thought for those of us who favor a lean White House, but it is justified, perhaps, by history, demography, and the collapse of parties.

Still another trace of Ford—which improves on Nixon—is found in Carter's Special Counsel to the President, Robert Lipshutz. He is *not*, as in the old days of a Rosenman, a Clifford, or a Sorensen, domestic policy adviser and speechwriter combined. Nor is he the one but not so much the other as in Johnson's time, when Califano and Harry McPherson divided those functions (or as Eizenstat now divides them with a Special Assistant for speechwriting, James Fallows). Lipshutz, rather, is the direct heir of Ford's Counsel, Philip Buchan, a legal adviser per se on propriety, conduct, and conflict of interest in a president's staff *after* Watergate.

ECONOMIC POLICY GROUP

A further trace of Ford, or anyway a glimmering, attaches to the Steering Committee of Carter's Economic Policy Group, an adaptation of the Executive Committee in Ford's Economic Policy Board. The EPB was Ford's foremost institutional innovation. Its executive committee was chaired by the Secretary of the Treasury but with a secretariat consisting of a senior White House aide—William Siedman—and an able junior, Roger Porter. Those two coordinated, processed, and scheduled preparatory efforts and follow-up on virtually every economic issue, micro as well as macro, legislative as well as operational, or informational, which Ford personally dealt with in 1975 and 1976.[7] EPB's committee thus combined the reach (though not the authority) of Nixon's economic czar, George Shultz—who was both Treasury Secretary and White House Assistant—with the ostensible terrain of the Council on International Economic Policy, and the macro role of Kennedy's "troika": Treasury, Budget, CEA.

The EPG Steering Committee now starting to function for Carter as an outgrowth of reorganization, may or may not turn into an equivalent or an improvement. There is reason for hope, but it is much too soon to tell. The

---

[7] A major study of the Economic Policy Board as it functioned in Ford's time is now underway at Harvard, directed by Roger Porter, Special Assistant to President Ford (1974-76).

Committee is Kennedy's threesome expanded to four: Messrs. Blumenthal, Lance, and Charles Schultze, plus the Under Secretary of State for Economic Affairs, Richard Cooper. (Commerce and Labor, there in Ford's time, are now gone.) Treasury chairs and also furnishes the executive secretary—a striking shift from EPB—but a fifth and a sixth member, both *"ex officio,"* are the president's two policy assistants, Brzezinski and Eizenstat. How they and their functions relate to this Steering Committee and vice versa, and what Blumenthal makes of his chairmanship, and where his able aid, the Committee's Secretary, Curt Hessler, comes to rest, we perhaps will know in six months time, after budget season and the annual messages of 1978. This may turn out in retrospect a legacy from Ford, a Carter innovation, or a passing phase.

WHITE HOUSE TITLES

A final legacy from Ford and Nixon is the five-way spread of current White House titles (up from four in LBJ's time, three in Truman's). Nixon put "Assistants to the President" in senior places previously held by "Special Assistants." It followed as night from day—and still does—that there then would be "Deputy Assistants to the President," "Special Assistants to the President," and "Deputy Special Assistants to the President" (maybe even some 'Administrative Assistants to the President," the old Rooseveltian title), as well as a still lower, fifth level of assistantships without those magic last three words.

Carter, to be sure, has cut the White House staff. Professional-level personnel (distinct from clerical and service staffs) employed in the White House proper drops from some 250 to about 180, as I understand the new reorganization. No one will be surprised that I applaud it and am heartened by it. Combined with Rumsfeld's cuts in 1975, these reverse Nixon's indiscriminate expansion of the White House Office—when the comparable figure rose above 300—and go far to restore its status as a personal staff (not far enough to suit *me*, but as far as I suppose we are likely to get from now on).

But that five-way spread of titles has wreaked havoc with one Democratic precedent, namely, that those three words "to the President" were meant to signify a close, continuing relationship with *him*, and serious engagement on *his* work from day to day. Roosevelt, Truman, Kennedy, and even Johnson gave out those words sparingly. Nixon, and only less so Ford, now Carter, cast them wide. By way of compensation, Carter's people draw a sharp distinction—as did Ford—between "senior staff" and all others. Seven Assistants to the President, together with the presidential Counsel (all equal but some more equal than others) rank everybody else in the White House Office save the Vice President, a special case. This now becomes familiar to the Washington community and nobody but me seems bothered in the least by more than thirty aides entitled something-to-the-President.

So much for innovations since the Johnson years adapted now and carried on by Carter. There are also some things that he now chooses to discard. Four units first established under Nixon have *not* passed the survival test. The Energy

Resources Council goes to the new department. The Council on International Economic Policy, long moribund, is abolished. So is the Office of Tele- communications Policy, its functions split between the president's Domestic Policy Staff and a new Assistant Secretary of Commerce. The Office of Drug Abuse Policy is being replaced by a White House Special Assistant. An Eisen- hower innovation modified by Kennedy and later Ford has also been abolished (made redundant by new oversight committees on the Hill): the Foreign Intelli- gence Advisory Board. A Nixon unit abandoned by Ford remains dead: the so- called Director of Communications. Carter's press secretary, Jody Powell, still another "Assistant to the President," does all that this regime intends to do by way of White House-media relations, with half the staff of Nixon's although four times that of Truman's—a tribute to the size of the accredited press corps, *and* to TV.

At the same time, Carter has made innovations of his own, especially inside the White House. One of these is embodied in Jack Watson's double role as Cabinet Secretary and Assistant to the President for Intergovernmental Re- lations: an interesting conception, hard to bring to life. Another—just now being installed—is a set of interdepartmental procedures for policy develop- ment meant to make Eizenstat a process manager on the lines of Brzezinski, or the early Henry Kissinger, in NSC. Still another innovation, yet to be com- pleted, is a Central Administrative Unit which consolidates some services for the Executive Office as a whole.

But these and other changes of the same sort are dwarfed by Carter's quite unprecedented use of the Vice Presidency and this, combined with what he seems to want from Jordan, has enormous influence on his general staffing pattern, especially the fostering of separate staffs for foreign and domestic policy.

In 1977, after all we should have learned since World War II about the risks of separating foreign from domestic staff-work for a president—shades of Korean War aims, or the Bay of Pigs, or soybeans for that matter, let alone Vietnam— it may appear extraordinary at first glance that DPS and NSC staff are in wholly separate boxes on the Carter chart. The fine print discloses that Eizenstat is a nonstatutory member of the NSC, which helps some. It also shows, I under- stand at second-hand, that Jordan has access at will to any papers moving through those boxes, either one. And so does the Vice President who is sup- posed to actively participate in everything, and evidently does, and has his own staff to backstop him. By all accounts the president treats Mondale as a "work- ing partner," and—remarkably—their staffs respect the relationship.[8] If so, with these arrangements, Carter has more chance for integrative staff-work linking foreign with domestic policy and politics than we have known before. Those

[8] "Working partner" is a term coined by the *New York Times*. A circumstantial account of the Carter-Mondale relationship can be found in that newspaper, signed by Marjorie Hunter, July 20 1977. Her account squares with what I have been told by OMB and White House aides.

boxes we can hope are far less separate than they seem. Carter's use of Jordan is in part the reason. And so is Mondale, the man with separate staff.

The reorganization study contemplates formalizing Mondale's role, in this respect and others, by making him the chairman of a staff group at the White House, tentatively titled an "Executive Committee." They and their chairman would watch and adjust substance in the president's agenda, set and review priorities among the issues headed toward him (or those needing staff attention but not getting it) throughout the Executive Office, NSC, DPS, OMB, and the cabinet besides—and EPG presumably, although that remains to be seen. The president's seven Assistants, Jordan, Powell, Eizenstat, Brzezinski, Watson, Costanza, and Moore (the Congressional Liaison), the president's Counsel, Lipshutz, the Budget Director, Lance, and perhaps one or two others, thus become collectively, under Mondale's chairmanship, a sort of super-Rumsfeld. If this is implemented as intended it will crown the procedures now envisaged by the new regime for staffing out substantive issues, foreign and domestic, presumably including economic, at presidential level—a remarkable development.

But do not count on it yet! Whether a committee of ten or more crowns anything, except *pro forma*, is open to doubt. Or more precisely, everything depends then on its chairman's standing with the rest—and with the president.

Procedures are no substitute for judgment, of course, nor are they meaningful apart from operating styles, and styles fuel judgment in the sense that they determine when and how and with what coloration issues get presented to a president. What matters is the *interlock* of operating styles between him and his aides and among them. In early months when he and his associates are still adjusting to the new conditions of their lives, both work methods and human interactions are uncertain and are subject to considerable change. Later, sometimes much later, stabilized relationships emerge, which outsiders can discern and characterize with some precision. So far as I can tell, Carter's White House has not reached that stage. Nor is it likely to for quite a while, especially if Lance should step aside, leaving the others to adjust afresh.

Presidential transitions are not short-term affairs. This one is far from over. Carter, I am told, still exhibits some of Truman's early tendencies to grab and make decisions out of hand. Brzezinski's "process" may now be the envy of domestic aides, but his command of it and management are said to leave a lot to be desired. The early Frank Moore plainly had his troubles. So it goes. These details will alter. Others not now visible are certain to emerge. The likelihood is that a year from now the staffing pattern set so consciously last summer will remain in outline although changed in some particulars. But in the cycle of a presidential term, the seventh month is too soon to be altogether sure of anything: these notes are premature. They may suffice for lectures in the fall of 1977; the word a year hence should be, "check before using."

Staffing the Presidency: An Insider's Comments

HARRISON WELLFORD

Dick Neustadt asked me to think about what the reorganization of the Executive Office meant to the president in terms of an insider's understanding of his style and preferences. The first guideline we received from the president was that he wanted the units of the Executive Office to serve his major decision processes. He wanted the Executive Office staff to look to the president and to provide information and options for his major decisions from his point of view, and not represent outside interests to the president. As we talked about the pros and cons of abolishing a particular unit, the president would frequently look back on the first six months of his presidency and ask how many times had he met with the people in the unit, how aware was he of the things they were doing. He was testing their usefulness by his own experience. That principle of trying to mold the Executive Office staff to serve the president from his perspective guided our study throughout, but there are exceptions. Though we felt on the whole that the Council on Environmental Quality (CEQ) could perform its functions adequately outside the Executive Office, it was nevertheless decided, after a lot of discussion and some political negotiations, to continue CEQ in the Executive Office.

A second point was the president's concern that the Executive Office staff and the White House personal staff be organized so as to make cabinet government a reality. Virtually every modern president has come into office in January saying that he wanted cabinet government. We all know that six months later that ideal goes aglimmering. In this administration I think cabinet government has, in fact, characterized our process, mainly because the president insists on governing the process to make it work. In the reorganization work that my staff does we are often in potential conflict with cabinet members because we are in the uneasy role of telling a department head that he may lose part of his

HARRISON WELLFORD, a lawyer, is Executive Associate Director for Reorganization and Management in the Office of Management and Budget. His most recent book is *Sowing the Wind: Food Safety and Chemical Harvest*.

domain or that he may have to reorganize the units within his department. It could easily develop into a situation in which we became a kind of super-staff making a great many decisions for the cabinet in areas that they would feel were peculiarly their own. But because of the president's concern for cabinet government, we have taken great pains to develop a cooperative arrangement with the major agencies and departments that we're reorganizing and we are acting with them to a significant extent as partners in a common effort. Sometimes we give a little bit, sometimes the cabinet member gives a little bit. But the reason we take such pains is that the president really does want the primary initiation of policy including reorganization to come from his major cabinet officers.

A third point I would make is that the president stated all along that he had a preference for "ad hocery" over formal institutions. And as a result, we made a number of recommendations which tried to get away from creating permanent institutionalized staffs in the Executive Office. In the Executive Office, particularly, we need flexible institutions to respond to the shifting needs of the presidency. The Economic Policy Group is probably the best example of that. It was tending to become a formal institution with an independent staff in the early part of this administration. But the reorganization plan turned that around and the EPG at least for now is much more flexible in the way it's working. It does not have an independent staff but draws staff from principals as problems arise. Mr. Eizenstat's staff, the Domestic Policy Staff, by the way, is much more involved in economic issues than its predecessors were.

Contrary to press reports, we did not recommend that the president designate a chief of staff. A.D. Frazier and I did go to Hamilton Jordan to discuss problems in the White House policy process but did not suggest that Ham assume the mantle of chief of staff. We pointed out a number of coordination problems that beset the present White House policy system and suggested that we needed to develop a remedy for these problems. We did not recommend a chief of staff because the president had made it clear in all of our meetings with him that he did not want a chief of staff—that is, somebody at the top of the pyramid through whom everything else was channeled. Hamilton is in many respects first among equals and gets involved in both domestic and foreign policy when he thinks it's of importance to the president to do so. But he is not sitting at the top with all papers and decisions flowing through him.

The president acts as his own chief of staff. He is a prodigious reader. The memos we send in sometimes come back with more comments than original text. I don't know how long he can keep this up but he has a passion for getting involved in the details of a lot of these decisions—even decisions that less hardworking presidents probably felt could have been handled below the Oval Office.

One remedy we proposed is a central planning and tasking mechanism for both domestic and national security policy. Pursuant to our recommendation, the Vice President is now chairing an executive committee of senior staff which has responsibility for planning the president's agenda for 1978 and beyond. We're in the process now of trying to develop the guidelines for this system.

Finally, we have reduced the professional staff at the White House quite substantially, thus reversing the long-term trend toward steady increases.

A January 1978 Postscript

RICHARD E. NEUSTADT

A few weeks after my original words were written Lance did step aside, leaving all relationships, all human interactions, operating styles to adjust afresh. As presidential confidant, authentic Georgian, and Budget Director, with commensurate weight in the EPG, Lance was a key member of the inmost inner circle. Those in outer circles were fast stabilizing their relationships with one another—and indeed with the president—around and through Lance. His departure slammed the White House entourage back almost to square one, and forced them to relive the uncertainties of February in October.

The Lance affair, moreover, with its slow-motion dénouement and Carter's evident dislike for what he had to do, gave the Washington press corps a field day, fleshing out an otherwise lean season.[1]

The president's honeymoon with the press ended then and there. With it went a share of his professional reputation. And when, immediately after, Senate moves against his energy proposals prompted no effective counter-measures from the White House, criticism in the press and in Washington generally reached quite remarkable proportions: remarkable because so fre-

---

[1] The acute phase of the Lance affair ran from August 18, 1977, with Carter's reaffirmation of faith in Lance after the Comptroller of the Currency Report, to September 21, 1977, with Carter's reluctant announcement of Lance's resignation despite vigor in his own defense at Senate hearings. For the Pesident's statements and accompanying news accounts see the *New York Times*, August 19, p. A19, and September 22, p. 33.

quently addressed to managerial detail—like Jordan's failure to assume the staff coordinative tasks assigned Ford's "chief of staff."[2]

That the absence of a White House "chief of staff" should cause complaint in Washington within months of a Democrat's inauguration is in itself remarkable, worth notice, and deserving of thought. Since presidential staffing in a serious sense started under FDR, no Democratic president has tolerated in the White House anyone with Rumsfeld's relative authority over most other aides, to say nothing of Haldeman's in Nixon's time or Sherman Adams's under Eisenhower: authority, that is to say (always in all regimes with some exceptions), to superintend the flow of people and of papers into the Oval Office, while simultaneously chairing staff meetings, handing out assignments, vetting performance, vetoing initiatives, all in the president's name, and generally policing his priorities (if not, indeed, contriving them). Roosevelt, Truman, Kennedy, and Johnson all preferred and usually tried to do such things themselves. Yet in the fall of 1977, journalists with Democratic leanings, Congressmen of liberal persuasion, Washingtonians-at-large had at Carter for weeks, belaboring him for his failure to turn Jordan into Rumsfeld or to replace him.

There may be diverse reasons for this phenomenon. Perhaps because Rumsfeld and Cheney worked for Ford, a president who liked to deal with detail and to hear from all and sundry, their retrospective reputations are benign, contrasting well with Haldeman's whose image now has faded. Perhaps because Republican administrations, relative to Democratic ones, have pressed less controversial social legislation on reluctant Congresses, White House "coordination" seems a relatively simple thing, a matter more of process than of substance. A Rumsfeld would not square well with an Eizenstat—or with a Clifford, a Califano, or a Sorensen—but under the Republicans there was less need for one (unless like Ehrlichman he was the staff-chief's chum and deputy). Perhaps because the Johnson White House, pre-Vietnam, is a decade or more behind us, too long for most journalistic memories, unknown to most Congressmen and Senators elected since (a larger group than usual), what startles and seems novel is reversion to a "prewar" pattern, while the Cheney-Rumsfeld-even-Haldeman precedents are taken for "modern times."

Besides, if Carter is to be considered his own chief of staff, he seems to lack an attribute of his Democratic predecessors: wide accessibility. Truman chaired daily staff meetings; Kennedy had functional equivalents; Johnson noticed; all reached out. And all presided over White House groups far smaller than Carter's: no counsel (in the current sense), little "public liaison," few deputies, no staff or cabinet secretaries, an embryonic domestic policy staff, a modest National Security staff, and no fifth layer (in Truman's case no fourth). Carter is the first Democrat to work in a Republican-sized White House. Republicans who tried it quickly got themselves staff-chiefs. Carter so far has not. Yet he regularly visits face-to-face with relatively few of his aides; reading what

---

[2] For one example of many see Charles Mohr, "Carter's First Nine Months: Charges of Ineptitude ise," *New York Times*, October 22, Sec. 1, p. 36.

they write does not have a commensurate effect upon the loyalty and cohesion of the rest. This, rather than lack of memory, may account for some of the concern expressed in Washington last fall.

On the other hand Carter has at least two things the Republicans lacked. For one he has the old Domestic Council harnessed to a policy aide in the best Democratic tradition. Eizenstat by all accounts is turning out to be a proper heir to Clifford and the like. He even seems to be achieving the degree of "process management" envisaged by last summer's reorganization. Carter also has Mondale, the first vice president to disappear from sight not because he is cold-shouldered at the White House but because he is so busy there. I write in December 1977. Thus far, Mondale has shown no signs of taking on himself, or on his nominal committee, operational coordination of his colleagues day by day. But what he seems to be engaged in is coordination of their views about priorities and timing for initiatives ahead, the stuff of Carter's own agenda. This too is in the spirit of July's Reorganization Plan.

Every new administration, in the fall of its first year, discovers afresh that preparation for its January messages to Congress is the nearest thing it can expect (however far from perfect) by way of opportunity for comprehensive program planning. Thereupon each new regime works up procedures whereby it can take advantage of the opportunity. To play a part in those procedures is to get at the heart of the president's key peacetime role in government, the clerk-ship from which, in my view, all leadership must emanate: the taking of initiatives for other parts of government—and interest-groups—to chew on. As of December, Mondale by all accounts plays such a part. That does not make him chief-of-staff. But along with yeoman work by Eizenstat it helps explain why, at this time of year, Carter can carry on without either a Rumsfeld or a long-term replacement for Lance.

Presidential Cabinet Making: Lessons for the Political System

NELSON W. POLSBY

When a new president picks his cabinet, he gives observers the first set of solid clues about the kind of president he intends to be. Like the campaign rhetoric that preceded the election, a cabinet can be read in a variety of ways. And it affords only fragmentary evidence about how the president plans to run the government. But fragmentary though it is, it is hard to ignore, for unlike campaign promises, cabinet members do not disappear into thin air. Rather they take office, and, to a greater or lesser extent, actually administer the affairs of the nation. President Eisenhower's appointment of "nine millionaires and a plumber" gave quite a good forecast of the sort of presidency General Eisenhower wanted to have. When John Kennedy became president he struck a dominant theme of self-consciously moving beyond his own range of personal acquaintance to form a governing coalition. Likewise, his appointment of his brother as attorney general telegraphed a strong desire to keep close control of the civil rights issue.

It is possible to see in Richard Nixon's cabinet appointments a mirror of his emerging view of the role of the president vis-à-vis the rest of the government (Table 1).[1] After beginning with a politically diverse and reasonably visible group of

[1] For much of my discussion of President Nixon I draw on Nelson W. Polsby, *Congress and the Presidency*, 3rd ed. (Englewood Cliffs, N.J.: Prentice Hall, 1976), pp. 48–61. An account of President Nixon's administrative goals and activities early in his presidency is contained in Rowland Evans and Robert Novak, *Nixon in the White House: The Frustration of Power* (New York: Random House, 1971). It is useful to contrast Richard Nathan's *The Plot That Failed: Nixon and The Administrative Presidency* (New York: John Wiley & Sons, 1975), written from the perspective of later events.

NELSON W. POLSBY is professor of political science at the University of California, Berkeley. He is the author of numerous books about American politics, including *Congress and the Presidency*.

Political Science Quarterly   Volume 93   Number 1   Spring 1978   115

TABLE 1

Decline in Prior Political Experience of Nixon Cabinet

	President Nixon's First Cabinet	President Nixon's Last Cabinet
Prior political experience extensive (includes office-holding)	William Rogers, State Melvin Laird, Defense Walter Hickel, Interior Maurice Stans, Commerce Robert Finch, HEW George Romney, HUD John Volpe, DOT	Rogers C.B. Morton, Interior Earl Butz, Agriculture
Prior political experience moderate (active in state party, etc.)	Winton Blount, Post Office	Frederick Dent, Commerce Peter Brennan, Labor Caspar Weinberger, HEW
Prior political experience slight	David Kennedy, Treasury John Mitchell, Attorney General Clifford Hardin, Agriculture George Shultz, Labor	Henry Kissinger, State William Simon, Treasury James Schlesinger, Defense Robert Bork, Acting Attorney General James Lynn, HUD Claude Brinegar, DOT

cabinet appointees, Nixon increasingly appointed people of no independent public standing, and with no constituencies of their own. In this shift we can read a distinctive change in the fundamental political goals and strategies of the Nixon administration, from early concerns with constituency-building to a later preoccupation, once Mr. Nixon's reelection was assured, with centralizing power in the White House.

His first Secretary of Labor, George Shultz, though unknown to begin with, became an early star of the Nixon cabinet owing to his intelligence and quick grasp of problems. The first major reorganization of the Nixon presidency shuffled Mr. Shultz into the White House. He was replaced by an efficient but unprepossessing figure, who in turn gave way to a maverick union official who was not even on speaking terms with the head of the AFL-CIO. This was not the only example of a movement away from clientele concerns in cabinet-building, and toward the accretion of managerial capacity within the White House. Seemingly by design the access of large and significant interest groups to the president was greatly hampered. Labor, education, the scientific community, conservationists, and others felt not merely that Richard Nixon was a president whose goals differed from their own, but also that their voices were being choked off, that they were shut out from the White House, and that their case was being rejected before it was heard.

If Mr. Nixon's administrative appointments were designed to be increasingly weak in their capacity to carry messages from interest groups to policy makers, they were far stronger in executing orders, in providing a conduit from the various arms of the White House executive apparatus—the Domestic Council, the Office of Management and Budget, the National Security Advisor—to the levels of policy execution.

Centralization of policy making was only half of the latter-day Nixon administrative program. The other half consisted in systematic attempts to place functionaries who can only be described as political commissars in the bureaus and departments, agents whose job it was to report to the White House on the political fidelity of the executive branch.[2]

Presidents and their political appointees have frequently puzzled over the problem of making the enormous apparatus of the executive branch responsive to their will. The legitimacy of this claim is based upon the results of the last election; presumably a president is elected and makes appointments, at least in part, to carry out his promises with respect to the future conduct of public policy, and the necessary instruments of that conduct reside in the unelected agencies of the executive branch.

Executive agencies, however, are seldom merely passive receptacles awaiting the expression of a president's preferences. Rather, they embody a number of persistent characteristics that from time to time may serve as bases for conflict with presidential directives. Expertise, for example, a body of doctrine about the right way to do things, may well thwart responsiveness to presidential demands. So may alliances between agency executives and the congressional committees that have program and budgetary oversight over them. So may strong ties between agencies and the client groups they serve.

The case of a conservative president facing an executive agency doing what he believes is liberal work is especially poignant. The very existence of a bureaucratic apparatus attests to the mobilization, at some time in the past, of a majority of sufficient strength to pass a law and put an agency to work. So long as the law is on the books, and Congress appropriates funds for it, the agency presumably has some sort of legitimate standing. Yet it was precisely the existence of all too many of these federal activities, all staffed with people devoted to the execution of their programs, that Mr. Nixon wished to question. In one famous instance—the case of the Office of Economic Opportunity— President Nixon attempted prematurely to put an agency out of business altogether.

In each of Mr. Nixon's attempts to organize and reorganize the executive branch an observer can note efforts to cope with a hostile administrative environment. Revenue sharing, of course, had the effect of removing responsibilities altogether from federal agencies. Nixon vastly strengthened the White House National Security Office and invented a domestic counterpart in the Domestic Council, politicized and reincarnated the Bureau of the Budget as the

[2] Additional discussion of the Nixon administration's public administration problems, together with documentation, is contained in Subcommittee on Manpower and Civil Service, *Final Report on Violations and Abuses of Merit Principles in Federal Employment* (Washington, D.C.: U.S. House of Representatives Committee on Post Office and Civil Service, December 30, 1976).

Office of Management and Budget, and drastically increased the number of employees in the Executive Office of the President. Just as the storm of Watergate was breaking over his head he proposed a reorganization plan that would have officially denied cabinet officers direct access to the president by shifting supervisory power to four "supercabinet" officers who were supposed to act as special presidential assistants.

It would be wrong to suggest that these devices for limiting the power of government departments, agencies, and bureaus were in some sense illicit. For the most part they were not, yet they reflect a distinctive view of executive branch legitimacy, and its monopoly in the presidential office. Mr. Nixon's view, it became clear, was that his reelection by a landslide not only provided him with a special entitlement to pursue his vision of public policy, but it had, in addition, delegitimized all other possible actors in the system.[3]

The last pre-Watergate months of the Nixon presidency saw neither the first, nor necessarily the last manifestation of the view that the president is the source of all the legitimacy on which the entire government runs. Indeed, even today the theory is widely held that because the president is the only elected official in the executive branch, political choice by the executive branch is legitimized only insofar as it can be plausibly seen to have been radiated down from a presidential choice or order or preference.

Sustenance for this view comes from a conception of the American political system in which legitimacy arises chiefly, if not exclusively, from the electoral process. If the direct results of elections are the only source of political legitimacy, then it follows that the legitimacy of the entire executive branch rests, like a gigantic inverted pyramid, on the quadrennial election of the single member of that branch who is elected, the president. Given this view of the situation, there can be no grounds upon which hierarchical subordinates of the president might legitimately act to thwart, undermine, modify or attenuate the will of the president in public policy, once it is expressed.

This is not, to be sure, the only view of political legitimacy in the executive branch. Another view is that while the electoral process does provide a very significant measure of legitimacy for the acts of government, this process by itself is neither adequate to the task of providing accountability, nor the only process actually provided for in the constitutional design and in the pattern of American politics that has since evolved in harmony with the spirit of the constitution. In contrast with this hierarchical, pyramidal, or plebiscitary view of legitimacy there is the check-and-balance, or multiprocess view favored, for example, by the authors of The Federalist, in which the rightful power to govern is spread about in the government, and even, in a more modern version, extended to interest groups and other mobilizers and organizers of popular desires, needs, and sentiments.

[3] This evidently included even the Congress that had been elected at the same time, as contemporary accounts suggest. See, e.g., Elizabeth Drew, Washington Journal (New York: Random House, 1975). A more thorough elaboration of this theme is contained in Nelson W. Polsby, Political Promises (New York: Oxford University Press, 1974), pp. 6–14.

Patterns of Cabinet Building

It is interesting to contemplate the extent to which a presidency-centered view of the proper relations between the presidency and the bureaucracy has survived intact through Watergate, and indeed through the fashionable disparagement of the Imperial Presidency. This is reflected in President Carter's address to the problem of cabinet building and what appears, consequently, to be his initial perspective on the permanent government.

There are at least three alternative ways to build a cabinet. First alternative: Each of the great departments of government serves clientele in the population at large. Each has custody over a range of policies that tend to affect some Americans more sharply than others. Thus one strategy for building a cabinet is to enter into a coalition with the client groups of departments by finding appointees who already have extensive relationships or political alliances with relevant client groups. A cabinet in which this alternative is dominant is one heavy with former political office holders. Characteristic pathologies of this mode of cabinet building are those associated with complaints from interest groups whose competitors have succeeded where they have not. So, for example, conservationist groups may feel exceedingly well served by the appointment of one sort of secretary of interior. Grazers, miners, and loggers may feel quite differently about the matter. The impossibility of accommodating all the groups into which Americans may legally divide themselves for the purpose of pursuing a common interest is, no doubt, one of the facts of life that give vitality to a competitive two-party system at the presidential level. The fact that ungratified client groups can form alliances with the out-party helps to legitimize the inevitable choices that presidents must make among contending interests, since a mechanism is thereby provided for limiting the extent to which any incumbent may ignore the strongly held preferences of large numbers of citizens, without suffering electoral defeat.

Second alternative: A president may choose a cabinet of substantive specialists. Specialists possess technical mastery, knowledge of programmatic alternatives, and understanding of particular governmental agencies and their impact on the world. Where the client-oriented cabinet member seeks to do his job to the satisfaction of the customers, the specialist cabinet member's internal definition of success depends on satisfying the norms of performance that the agency itself (and its associated professions) generate. The characteristic pathology of this sort of leadership is given constant publicity in the folklore of government: domination by arbitrary, insensitive, "faceless" bureaucrats, the proliferation of meaningless paperwork, the manufacture of red tape, the triumph of custodial convenience over sensitivity to clientele or to political realities.

The basis for the political legitimacy of specialist leadership is far less thoroughly understood. It is, I think, fundamentally historical. At some point in the past, after all, someone had to pass a valid law for a bureaucracy to exist at all. Presumably, government agencies are administering programs because once upon a time a law-making majority, a winning coalition of president and Congress, produced a mandate for them to do so. In the absence of some equally valid set of more recent instructions, government agencies have a right to presume that what they are doing is proper and legitimate. Specialist leadership rests its legitimacy heavily upon the notion that effective, knowledgeable pursuit of an agency's mission constitutes a continuing renewal of its historic mandate.

Those cabinet members who are connected neither to clientele nor to agencies suggest a third alternative: the generalist executive. The generalist may be responsive primarily to the siren song of his own career and thus be connected to, and ultimately reachable by, nothing at all. Or he may respond with particular alertness to presidential priorities, plans and orders, to be, in fact, the president's ambassador both to the agency and to its client groups. I have already given the familiar rationale for a cabinet dominated by executives of this stripe. In such executives the presumption is strongest that the president, being the most recently elected chief executive, is entitled by his electoral mandate to command the resources of the executive branch, and to shape its programs according to his desires. The careers of generalist executives are tied not to interest groups or to agencies but to the president personally or, alternatively, to law firms, public relations firms, universities, or other organizations that provide technical skills and services to a variety of clients not closely clustered around some narrow set of policies.

Until the beginnings of President Nixon's second term, I think it is fair to say that observers were not excessively attentive to the possibility of pathology in the execution of this alternative. Yet presidents, it now appears, can ask members of the executive branch to do illegal and immoral acts, acts not contemplated and in some cases prohibited by the charters of the agencies involved. A president or his agent can seek to close down activities provided for by law, or can repudiate political alliances with devastating future effects for himself, his party and/or his successors. Generalist executives, without expertise or independent standing with interest groups, are presumably best situated to further, and least well situated to resist, these tendencies when they appear.

THE CARTER STRATEGY

No president, to my knowledge, has in modern times pursued a pure strategy of cabinet building. In all cases of which I am aware the strategy has been mixed. Yet the character of the mixture at any given time has been instructive about the claims to legitimacy made by each incumbent administration. So it is, also, with President Carter, as a consideration of the seventeen cabinet-level appointments of his administration will illustrate (Table 2).

In matters of foreign and defense policy, with the very important exception of Ambassador Andrew Young, Mr. Carter has sought subject-matter experts. Cyrus Vance, Zbigniew Brzezinski, Michael Blumenthal, and Harold Brown have all put in substantial time working for the government on problems associated with the departments they now head.

TABLE 2

President Carter's Cabinet, 1977

	Specialists	Client-Oriented	Generalists
State	Vance[a]		
Treasury	Blumenthal[b]		
Defense	Brown[b]		
Justice			Bell[a]
Interior		Andrus	
Argiculture		Bergland	
Commerce			Kreps[b]
Labor	Marshall?	Marshall (?)[b]	
Hew			Califano[a]
HUD			Harris[a]
Transportation			Adams[a]
Energy			Schlesinger[b]?
CIA			Turner
Natl. Sec. Council	Brzezinski[b]		
OMB			Lance
Council Econ. Ad.	Schultze[b]		
UN Ambassador			Young

[a] Lawyers
[b] Ph.D.'s

In two, arguably three, instances, Mr. Carter has picked cabinet members who can be considered ambassadors from interest group constituencies. One, Bob Bergland, supervises the interest group constituency closest to Mr. Carter's own in private life, agriculture. The second is Cecil Andrus, who brings to the Interior Department close ties with environmentalist groups. I am less certain that Ray Marshall of the Labor Department belongs to this category, rather than to that of the specialists.

Nine of the remaining ten appointees are, I believe, best understood as generalists. An academic labor economist serves as the chief link between the business community and the administration. Three lawyers—all Washington D.C. careerists in one way or another who might well have been interchanged—head the main urban departments. There are, as many people have observed, three Georgians, presumably presidential ambassadors par excellence, among the top seventeen, seven Ph.D.'s, five in economics, one each in physics and political science, and five lawyers.

It is not their high level of education, however, that observers have fastened upon in noting the odd resemblance between this Democratic cabinet and the Republican cabinets that immediately preceded it. Rather it is the curious neutrality of the Carter cabinet toward the vast stew of interest groups, both within and outside the government, that make up the traditional Democratic coalition.

Of Carter's top seventeen appointees, how many reach into the constituencies suggested by the old New Deal voting coalition? Where are the representatives of the Irish, the Polish, the Jews, the Italians? The cities? The labor unions? Where, indeed, are the long-time active members of the Democratic party? Not wholly absent, to be sure. But hard to find.

CAUSES OF THE CARTER STRATEGY

I have observed that in his second term Richard Nixon chose generalists for his cabinet because of his abiding hostility to the central purposes of the permanent government, as he saw them. Although he ran as an outsider to Washington politics, there is no reason to suppose that Mr. Carter shares Mr. Nixon's deep and clear-cut doctrinal disagreement with so many of the routine purposes of government. And so rather than seek the key to Mr. Carter's leadership of the government in programmatic antagonism, I believe we must look elsewhere for clues.

A first, and extremely interesting, examination of the problem has been made by Jack Knott and Aaron Wildavsky in a close analysis of President Carter as a theorist of public administration.[4] They observe, quite correctly, that President Carter has repeatedly expressed strong views about the proper procedures for making public policy. Very much in a tradition of political engineering that stretches back through Herbert Hoover to Woodrow Wilson, Mr. Carter has emphasized the importance of design considerations in the making and the presentation of public policy, and has deemphasized the content of those policies.

The goals President Carter has stressed are essentially administrative in character: simplification, reduction of duplication, and the establishment of uniformity, predictability and long-range goals. He is a believer in comprehensive reform, in finding once-and-for-all solutions to problems.

Theoretical commitment on the part of President Carter to general and far-reaching purposes, and a desire to separate himself from the piecemeal accommodations of bureaucrats and the narrowly focused desires of interest groups is thus surely part of the answer. But this answer poses a still more fundamental problem: how is it that President Carter finds it possible to gratify this theoretical preference in the harsh arena of national politics?

The answer to this, I believe, can be found in the political conditions which made Jimmy Carter's nomination and election possible. Mr. Carter is the latest in a lengthening line of political leaders—of which Mr. Nixon was also an example—who have made the claim that their electoral victories conferred on them a legitimacy direct from the people, unmediated by special interest groups, or by parochial considerations.

For a Democratic politician, the basis of this claim must rest in large measure on the transformation of the rules for nominating presidents that has occurred

---

[4] Jack Knott and Aaron Wildavsky, "Jimmy Carter's Theory of Governing" *The Wilson Quarterly* I (Winter, 1977): 49–67.

over the past decade.[5] Finance through mass mailings and through the public purse has replaced the mobilization of well-heeled backers and the seeking of alliances with interest groups. The stimulation of coverage by the mass media and the building of a state-by-state personal organization have replaced the cultivation of party regulars and state and local leaders. Primary elections, not party wheelhorses, select the vast preponderance of convention delegates.

So the idea of a party as a coalition of interests bound together by the hope of electing a president is becoming an anachronism. Party is increasingly a label for masses of individual voters who pick among alternate candidates as they would among any alternatives marketed by the mass media.

The mass news media in America, though highly professional and in many respects unideological, are nevertheless far from random in their behavior. Thus while interest groups that are mobilized in traditional ways, around the economic interests or the communal ties of their members, have diminished in their political influence, the fortunes of other interest groups have been greatly enhanced because the managers of the mass media have decided to smile upon them. Prominent among these are groups embodying what the media recognize as disinterested rectitude, such as Common Cause and the Ralph Nader organizations, and those speaking for interests widely perceived as disadvantaged, such as black, Hispanic-American, and militant women's groups.

This is not the place to argue about the realities behind the palpable gains and losses that have befallen these groups in national politics. Black leaders, like labor leaders, surely mobilize large numbers of Democratic voters, and so might have fared equally as well under the old dispensation as under the new, whereas militant women are far less successful in demonstrating that they deliver the votes even of most voting women. What is significant for our purposes is the fact that in a straight fight between leaders of militant women's groups and black groups on the one hand and, on the other, the leadership of the dominant faction of the U.S. labor movement over who was to become secretary of labor, as we all know it was labor that lost.[6] This, it seems to me, is an emblematic as anything could possibly be of the disestablishment of one sort of interest group in the Democratic party and the establishment of another.

CONSEQUENCES FOR PUBLIC ADMINISTRATION

The consequences of this change in the actual workings of government are difficult to fathom. Two, at least, are worth considering, and both suggest an increase in certain sorts of stress in the political system.

[5] A review of some of these in the context of electoral strategies rather than, as here, in relation to their consequences for public administration, can be found in Nelson W. Polsby and Aaron Wildavsky, *Presidential Elections* 4th ed. (New York: Scribner's, 1976).

[6] See, e.g. Robert G. Kaiser, "Women Lobby for Role in Carter Camp," *Washington Post*, December 5, 1976; "Dunlop Backers Call him Victim of Unfair Action," *New York Times*, January 26, 1977.

The forces that have revolutionized the presidential nominating process have been far slower to affect the thousand-odd nominating processes that supply us with candidates for Congress and the Senate. Congress is a greatly changed place from the way it was even a decade ago. The previously moribund Democratic caucus is now available as an instrument of majority will, when that will exists. But the mobilization of that will is by no means the unchallenged prerogative of the president. If anything, Congress is today better equipped than ever to find its own way into the intricacies of policy and to arrive at its own balancing of forces and priorities.

So long as elections in America are of the staggered, prescheduled, nonreferendum type, and so long as nominations to Congress are decentralized, it will be difficult if not impossible for presidents to attempt to persuade Congress by going over its head to the people. This is no substitute for the hard, frustrating, and frequently unavailing work of doing business directly with Congress. Because of the divergence that currently exists in the ways in which presidents and Congress mobilize their electorates and arrive in office, we may be entering an era in which tensions and misunderstandings between president and Congress increase—even when both are controlled by what is labeled the same party.

Another possible consequence of the modern trend in cabinet building is a decrease in the reliance of political executives on the accumulated expertise of the permanent government. When the top of the government was dominated by client-oriented political executives, bureaucrats supplied technical information, policy analysis, know-how and knowledge of programs. Some specialist cabinet officers are going to ignore the agencies they head altogether; others, specialist and generalist alike, will undertake policy evaluation and analysis in competition with their own agencies. Much of this activity, no doubt, will result in vastly improved understanding of policy alternatives at the top of government. Moreover, it can create over the long term a corps of people outside the government who can contribute to the analysis and understanding of policy.

But as the comparative advantage of being inside a bureaucracy begins to diminish, the caliber of the agency begins to slip. As agencies begin to view their nominal superiors as competitors in the supply of what they supply best, expertise, the incentives to firm up other sorts of alliances—with clientele, with Congress—increase. Thus over the long run, without strenuous effort and much good will on both sides, the cure can aggravate symptoms of the disease.

Two Models of Legitimacy

I have suggested that there are currently two models available through which the claims of the executive branch to be properly vested with power can be validated. One model, the presidential model, sees the conferring of legitimacy in our political system as having the following four features. It is episodic, in that it relies heavily upon the results of the last presidential election, which for present purposes is treated as conferring a sweeping mandate. It is concentrated, in that only the winner of the last election receives the endorsement that is claimed to be at the root of the government's entitlement to act. It is direct, in that it is claimed that permission to act is conferred by voters not on the basis of their interest group or other affiliations but through their individual, atomized responses to a particular candidate and his presentation of self during the campaign. Finally, it reflects the present or the recent past, in that only the results of the most recent presidential election are taken into account in determining the right of an official to claim the acquiescence of citizens in public policy.

A view of legitimacy in our political system alternative to the presidential model is contained in what readers will recognize as a Federalist model since it draws upon the thoughts of the earliest expositors of the logic underlying the original design of the U.S. Constitution. In this view, legitimacy is conferred not episodically, as in elections, but continuously. It is conferred both through elections and through continuous interaction among decision makers. Legitimacy is not concentrated, but dispersed, to elected officials, to appointed officials, to career bureaucrats. It is based not on election alone, but on organizational norms such as seniority, or selection by congressional caucus, or neutral competence or expertise. In the Federalist view, legitimacy is conferred not just directly, but also indirectly; for example, by the workings of the congressional committee system. Finally, not the present alone, but the more distant past as well is invoked by the Federalist model, which explicitly recognizes the legitimacy of law-making majorities of the earlier eras that produced programs that persist to this day and are embodied in the agencies of government.

The ascendancy of the presidential model has evidently survived the discredited presidency of Richard Nixon, who militantly espoused it. This has come about because of sweeping changes in the politics of presidential nomination that have fundamentally affected the ways in which interest groups must be mobilized and attended to by a Democratic presidential nominee, although it is less certain that the same vector of forces applies to a Democratic president. Nevertheless, the record of this new approach can be read in President Carter's cabinet choices.

The Reassertion of Congressional
Power: New Curbs on the President

HARVEY G. ZEIDENSTEIN

The confrontations in the 1970s between the Nixon-Ford administration and the Democratic-controlled Congress have left a legacy of restrictions on various kinds of presidential activities that are now operating on President Carter but which did not exist to limit "imperial" presidents in the era from Franklin Roosevelt to Lyndon Johnson. These restrictions came as a reaction to what became recognized as a gradual erosion of congressional checks and balances against presidents since the 1930s. They represented Congress's attempt to resurrect its disused legal powers to participate in policy making—especially in the areas of declaration and termination of national emergencies, war-making, foreign policy, intelligence operations, budget policy, and impoundments of appropriated funds.

Our concern is with executive-congressional relations in legitimate and routine policy activities. Criminal or other impeachable offenses by presidents are neither legitimate nor (we assume) routine. Consequently, restrictions unique to Watergate or to the attempted impeachment of former President Richard Nixon fall outside the scope of this study. Nonetheless, we are left with a lengthy catalog of restrictions on the president.

VARIETIES OF RESTRICTIONS ON PRESIDENTIAL ACTIONS

Through a variety of measures, Congress has increased its ability to restrict presidential actions and to hold the president and the executive branch more accountable to itself by allowing for formal congressional disapproval in some

HARVEY G. ZEIDENSTEIN is professor of political science at Illinois State University. He is the author of *Direct Election of the President* and articles on the presidency, nominations, and elections.

instances, requiring to be provided with critical information in others, and mandating that certain presidential initiatives cease automatically in other cases in the absence of congressional action to affirmatively approve those initiatives.

TERMINATION OR CONTINUATION OF EMERGENCY AUTHORITY

In 1973 a Senate special committee found some 470 provisions of federal law that could be triggered during a "time of war" or a "national emergency" declared by Congress or the president.[1] Many were as innocuous as those providing for the presentation of soldiers' medals during conflict and assistance for current school expenditures in cases of certain disasters.[2] Other laws—such as those allowing the president to order private plants to manufacture necessary products "in time of war or when war is imminent," and to maintain lists of plants capable of war production—were potentially more sweeping in granting authority to the executive.[3]

Presidents have been far more willing to declare emergencies than to end them, so emergency periods, and the laws operative in them, typically have lasted many years beyond the end of the original emergency. This motivated passage of the National Emergencies Act in September 1976.[4] The act leaves most of the 470 wartime and emergency laws intact, but creates a system for declaring and terminating national emergencies.

Declaration is by the president. Of the three methods of termination, one (discussed later) is up to Congress and two leave the initiative to the president. As in the past, an emergency can be ended by presidential proclamation. A new wrinkle is that an emergency will terminate automatically in one year unless the president informs Congress within ninety days before the end of the year that the emergency is to continue.[5] As both methods are subject to presidential discretion, their purely legal restriction on his authority is minimal to nonexistent. But their effect may be important politically. A president who does not end an emergency, or who continues it, is subject to questions. Not the least of which is why an emergency still exists a year after his administration presumably has been working on it.

CONSULTATION WITH CONGRESS BEFORE MILITARY OPERATIONS

In November 1973 Congress overrode a Nixon veto and enacted the War Powers

---

[1] U.S., Congress, Senate, Committee on Government Operations and the Special Committee on National Emergencies and Delegated Emergency Powers, *The National Emergencies Act (Public Law 94-412), Source Book: Legislative History, Texts, and Other Documents*, Committee Print, 94th Cong., 2d sess., Nov. 1976, p. 5.

[2] 10 *USC* 3750 and 20 *USC* 241-1.

[3] 10 *USC* 4501, 4502, 9501, and 9502.

[4] PL 94-412, 90 *Stat.* 1255; 50 *USC* 1601.

[5] 90 *Stat.* 1257, sec. 201 (5) (d).

Resolution.[6] The Resolution's avowed purpose is to "insure that the collective judgment of both the Congress and the President will apply" to sending American armed forces into hostilities or into situations where immediate involvement in hostilities is likely, and to the continued use of armed forces in hostilities or threatening situations.

Among other things, the Resolution requires the president "in every possible instance" to "consult with Congress" before he introduces armed forces into hostilities or into situations leading to hostilities. He also must consult regularly with Congress until the forces have been withdrawn from combat or the threatening situation.[7]

The extent of consultation before the president commits forces to hostilities is open to varying interpretation. In reporting the War Powers Resolution, the House International Relations (then Foreign Affairs) Committee stated that it expected the president himself to seek congressional advice and opinion while his decision is still pending. The committee flatly rejected the notion that consultation occurs when a president informs Congress of decisions already made.[8]

But in the May 1975 rescue of the American merchant ship *Mayaguez*, what the administration called "consultation" was the White House informing about twenty congressional leaders after President Ford had ordered U.S. Navy jets and Marines to engage Cambodian forces. In the few hours between Ford's order and the first shots of combat, the leaders were able to submit their views to the president. But their opportunity to "advise" came after the military operations approved by the president had begun.[9]

Except for the grumblings of a few ultradoves, Congress winked at Ford's minimal consultation, largely because the rescue was considered a success. As the then Senate Majority Whip Robert Byrd told the president, he "might have been in a lot better position, had this operation not been successful," if he had actually sought advice from Congress.[10] But this observation would be nearly as trenchant had there been no legal requirement to consult, as President Truman learned when the Korean conflict went sour.

In a purely legal sense, then, the consultation provision adds no new curbs on the president's freedom to act. Even if he followed the intent of the law by seeking congressional advice before making up his mind, the president is not bound to accept it. On the other hand, future presidents may follow Ford's precedent of defining after-the-fact briefings as consultation. The lesson of *Mayaguez* seems to be that in the future, as in the past, consultation—or lack of it—will be viewed in the context of existing political circumstances rather

[6] PL 93–148, 87 *Stat.* 555; 50 *USC* Supp. V (1975) 1541.

[7] Ibid., at sec. 3; ibid., sec. 1543.

[8] U.S., Congress, House, Committee on Foreign Affairs, *War Powers Resolution of 1973*, House Report No. 93–287, 93d Cong., 1st sess., June 15, 1963 [sic] [1973], pp. 6–7.

[9] Harvey G. Zeidenstein and Hibbert R. Roberts, 'The War Powers Resolution, Institutionalized Checks and Balances, and Public Policy," a paper presented at the Southern Political Science Association Convention, Nashville, Tenn., Nov. 6–8, 1975, pp. 103–105.

[10] *New York Times*, May 16, 1975, p. 15.

than according to a consistent legal definition. If the president embarks on a military venture opposed by Congress, or one that foments opposition because it fails, then lack of consultation will be a convenient legal springboard for criticism.

SENATE CONFIRMATION OF OMB HEADS

In 1970 President Nixon through a reorganization plan enlarged the old Bureau of the Budget into the more powerful Office of Management and Budget (OMB), which became a potent force for executing presidential policies. Among the more controversial policies was gutting domestic programs by impoundment— ordering the bureaucracy not to spend money appropriated by a liberal Democratic Congress.

Although the director and deputy director of OMB exerted far more authority than cabinet officers, they were appointed by the president without the advice and consent of the Senate. This changed in March 1974, when President Nixon approved an amendment to the Budget and Accounting Act of 1921. The new measure exempted the incumbents, but required that future directors and deputy directors of OMB receive Senate confirmation.[11]

The Senate's role is probably a minor foray into the executive's domain. Although confirmation hearings can be used to quiz prospective OMB heads on their views toward facets of fiscal policy, prospective appointees with enough political skill for the job probably will evade or finesse the more pointed questions. Also, traditionally, the Senate is strongly inclined to confirm whomever the president chooses for his administration. Bert Lance is a case in point. In its eagerness to recommend Lance's confirmation, the Senate Governmental Affairs Committee was ignorant of or indifferent to his personal financial ethics.

For the near future, the Lance affair probably will make the president and the Senate more sensitive to personal ethics as grounds for withholding confirmation. For serious questions about the ethics of a potential presidential appointee would be of mutual concern to the president and the Senate. Both could be criticized in the media, as they were several months after Lance's confirmation. To avoid this, we expect the executive to rigorously screen an appointee's personal affairs before his name is submitted to the Senate. The Senate confirmation process will become a fail-safe device to backstop the executive's investigation. If this reading is correct, confirmation gives the Senate not a new check, but an added responsibility.

On the other hand, Congress may have gained an increased expectation that OMB directors will testify candidly before its committees. Many on Capitol Hill believe that administration officials confirmed by the Senate are less protected by executive privilege than officials appointed exclusively by the president.

[11] PL 93-250, 88 *Stat.* 11; 31 *USC* 16.

Three recent laws obligate the president to inform Congress about his current or anticipated activities with respect to executive agreements, national emergencies, and deploying U.S. armed forces abroad.

Stung by revelations that the Johnson and Nixon administrations had made secret executive agreements with foreign governments, in 1972 Congress reacted by requiring the secretary of state to send it the text of any international agreement, other than a treaty, within sixty days after the agreement became effective. However, if the president judged that public disclosure would injure national security, the text would be submitted only to the Senate Foreign Relations Committee and the House International Relations Committee "under the appropriate injunction of secrecy to be removed only upon due notice from the President."[12] In effect, the president would inform Congress, or at his discretion only two of its committees, of faits accomplis. And short of a leak, they would be kept secret from the public as long as the president wished.

Still, Congress gained a significant inroad. It can modify or hamstring executive agreements by refusing the funds to implement them. Even secret agreements known only to the two foreign policy committees are not immune. These committees could register strong displeasure, even threats, with the administration. For example, without public disclosure of the secret details of an agreement, either committee could sponsor legislation which, in general language, nullifies its purpose. Such measures could be debated by Congress in secret sessions.

When the president declares a national emergency, the National Emergencies Act forbids him from exercising any statutory authority available during emergencies unless and until he informs Congress of the specific laws under which he proposes to act.[13] This alerts Congress to the president's probable future activities. To help Congress monitor the executive's ongoing activities during an emergency or declared war, all of the president's significant orders and all executive agency rules and regulations are to be filed, indexed, and promptly sent to Congress, by means to insure their confidentiality where appropriate. Finally, every six months during an emergency or declared war, and within three months after it has ended, the president must inform Congress of the total expenditures directly attributed to the emergency or war.[14]

When Congress has not declared war, the War Powers Resolution requires the president to inform Congress in writing within forty-eight hours after he has introduced U.S. armed forces into any of three situations: hostilities or circumstances where immediate involvement in hostilities is likely; the territory, air, or waters of a foreign nation while equipped for combat, except for such

[12] PL 92–403, 86 *Stat.* 619; 1 *USC* Supp. V (1975) 112b.
[13] PL 94–412, 90 *Stat.* 1257, at sec. 301; 50 *USC* 1631.
[14] Ibid., at sec. 401; ibid., sec. 1641.

deployments which are nonhostile; or a substantial increase in the number of, combat-equipped forces already stationed in a foreign country.[15]

The president's report must specify the reasons he introduced armed forces, the legal authority justifying their introduction, and the estimated scope and duration of the hostilities or involvement. The president must also give Congress any additional information it requests, and report every six months while American forces are involved in any of the three situations requiring his original report.[16]

The War Powers reports, as such, are not a severe encroachment on the president's authority. But the information given (or omitted) can be a basis for significantly influencing Congress's decision to support or throttle the president's military initiatives.

CIA REPORTS TO CONGRESSIONAL COMMITTEES

As a civilian agency, the CIA is outside the jurisdiction of the War Powers Resolution. Consequently, the Resolution does not require the president to inform Congress of covert CIA operations, such as the secret war in Laos in the 1960s and a variety of other CIA military and political activities intended to establish or protect friendly regimes abroad.

This gap was plugged by other measures compelling CIA accountability to selected congressional committees. First came an amendment to the Foreign Assistance Act of 1961, sponsored by Senator Harold Hughes and Representative Leo Ryan, which took effect on December 30, 1974.[17] Except for gathering "necessary intelligence," the Hughes-Ryan amendment prohibits the spending of money by or for the CIA for operations in foreign countries, "unless and until" the president finds each operation is important to national security, and the president reports, "in a timely fashion," a description and scope of each operation to the "appropriate committees" of Congress, including the Senate Foreign Relations Committee and the House International Relations Committee. Presidential approval and reports of covert operations are not required during military operations resulting from a declared war or from the president acting under the War Powers Resolution. The Hughes-Ryan amendment does not require written reports.[18] Acting as the president's delegate, the director of the CIA gives oral briefings to "appropriate" committees.[19] There are currently

---

[15] PL 93–148, 87 *Stat.* 555, at sec. 4; 50 *USC* Supp. V (1975) 1544.

[16] Ibid., at sec. 4; ibid., sec. 1544.

[17] PL 93–559, 88 *Stat.* 1804; 22 *USC* 2422.

[18] U.S., Congress, Senate, Senator Harold Hughes interpreting the intent of his amendment, 93d Cong., 2d sess., Oct. 2, 1974, vol. 120 *Congressional Record*, part 25, p. 33490.

[19] Mitchell Rogovin, Special Counsel to the Director of CIA, to A. Searle Field, Staff Director of the House Select Committee on Intelligence, Jan. 6, 1976, in U.S., Congress, House, *Intelligence Agencies and Activities: Risks and Control of Foreign Intelligence, Hearings before the Select Committee on Intelligence*, Part 5, 94th Cong., 1st sess., Nov. and Dec. 1975, p. 2020. This committee, chaired by Representative Otis Pike, investigated the CIA.

eight of them: the Senate and House Armed Services Committees, the Senate Foreign Relations and the House International Relations Committees, the Senate and House Appropriations Subcommittees on Defense, and Senate and House Select Committees on Intelligence, which have oversight and legislative jurisdiction over the entire intelligence community. The Senate Select Intelligence Committee was created in May 1976, its House counterpart fourteen months later. Both succeeded temporary committees in each house—one chaired by Senator Frank Church, the other by Representative Otis Pike—which investigated the CIA in 1975 and disbanded in 1976.

A Hughes-Ryan report is not a prerequisite for a covert operation, so the committees may be briefed after the operation has begun.[20] However, as former CIA Director William Colby testified to the Senate Government Operations Committee early in 1976, on the day the CIA is informed that the president has signed a finding approving an operation, the CIA calls the committees' staffs to notify them that there is a finding to report at the committees' convenience. "We make a point of getting that notice out immediately."[21] Colby said he has reported as early as the next morning with some committees and some weeks later with others, depending on the committee.[22]

Because of the Hughes-Ryan amendment no president or his apologists will be able to disclaim responsibility for any CIA operations in peacetime and as a result, the president is given stronger incentive to closely monitor the CIA and prevent it from undertaking operations without his authority (the so-called "rogue elephant").

Although the Hughes-Ryan amendment does not legally require reports until after covert operations have begun, the Senate has used the power of the purse to persuade the CIA and other intelligence agencies to give the Senate Select Committee on Intelligence advance notice of future covert activities also. The committee was established in May 1976 by Senate Resolution 400.[23] One section of the resolution expresses the "sense of the Senate" that executive agencies should keep the Select Committee informed of their intelligence activities, "including any significant anticipated activities," although prior notification is not a precondition to implementing the activity.[24]

No "sense of the Senate" resolution has legal force outside that chamber. But the Senate gave its Select Intelligence Committee exclusive jurisdiction over all authorization bills for the CIA, and shared jurisdiction with other committees

[20] Rogovin to Field, ibid., p. 2016.

[21] U.S., Congress, Senate, Committee on Government Operations, *Oversight of U.S. Government Intelligence Functions, Hearings before the Senate Committee on Government Operations,* 94th Cong., 2d sess., Jan. and Feb. 1976, p. 130. Hereafter cited as Senate hearings, *Oversight of Intelligence.*

[22] Ibid.

[23] U.S., Congress, Senate, 94th Cong., 2d sess., vol. 122 *Congressional Record,* No. 74, S 7563-S 7565 (daily ed., May 19, 1976). Hereafter cited as Senate Res. 400 with appropriate section number.

[24] Senate Res. 400, sec. 11 (a).

over authorizations for the intelligence activities of other agencies in the intelligence community.[25] With its hand on the money authorizing spigot, it is not surprising that the committee has been fully briefed on covert operations prior to their implementation. The committee has even voted on every proposed covert operation.

In addition to its control over authorizations, the Select Intelligence Committee may make intelligence information available to any other committee or member of the Senate. With the approval of the full Senate, the committee may inform the public of information the president wants to keep classified.[26] These powers give the committee a strong bargaining position with the executive. After being briefed on a proposed covert operation, the committee reaction, if any, can include the following:

—Comment to the executive branch;
—Referral of information to other committees, if appropriate;
—Public disclosure, if supported by a closed session vote of the Senate; and
—Funding restrictions.[27]

When the House created its own Select Intelligence Committee by passing House Resolution 658 in July 1977, it used language that was, in most parts, identical to that in Senate Resolution 400.[28] But in a notable departure from the Senate resolution, the House measure does not express the "sense of the House" that intelligence agencies should alert the House Intelligence Committee to anticipated activities. Without this mandate, it is too soon to tell whether the House Intelligence Committee will expect to receive prior notification of covert activities, although it is equal to its Senate counterpart in controlling authorizations, and equivalent to it is sharing classified information with other lawmakers and the public.

MANDATE FOR COMMITTEE DISCLOSURE OF CLASSIFIED INFORMATION

By providing a mechanism for public disclosure of classified information, the resolutions creating the Senate and House Select Intelligence Committees give these bodies a check against the president far stronger than what the other six committees have from the Hughes-Ryan amendment alone.

Each Intelligence Committee may vote to disclose any information it receives from the executive branch. After informing the president of its decision, a committee can release the information in five days unless the president objects

---

[25] Senate Res. 400, sec. 3 (a) and (b).

[26] Senate Res. 400, sec. 8.

[27] U.S., Congress, Senate, *Annual Report to the Senate of the Select Committee on Intelligence, United States Senate,* Senate Report No. 95–217, 95th Cong., 1st sess., May 18, 1977, p. 18.

[28] U.S., Congress, House, 95th Cong.; 1st sess., vol. 123 *Congressional Record,* No. 119 H, 7104–H 7106 (daily ed., July 14, 1977). Hereafter cited as House Res. 658, with appropriate section number. Note that this resolution amended the *Rules of the House of Representatives* by adding "Rule XLVII. Permanent Select Committee on Intelligence."

personally, in writing, states the reasons for his objection, and certifies that the threat to the national interest of disclosure outweighs any public interest in the information. If the committee still favors disclosure, it can vote to refer the matter to its parent body, the Senate or the House, as the case may be. Within four days of the referral, the parent body goes into closed session (required in the Senate, only if voted upon in the House). The Senate has a maximum of nine days to vote for one of three actions: to approve or disapprove disclosure of all or part of the information, or to refer all or any part of the information back to its Intelligence Committee, in which case the committee makes the final decision whether to go public.[29] The House procedure allows two hours of debate (rather than nine days), then requires a vote on whether to approve the recommendation for disclosure made by its Select Intelligence Committee. If the House votes against the recommendation, it is sent back to the Committee for further recommendation.[30] In both houses, the final vote is taken in open session without debate and without divulging the classified information at issue.[31]

The provision for public disclosure approved through these procedures is meant to inhibit the president from illegal or highly unpopular intelligence operations.

CENTRALIZING OR "DE-FRAGMENTING" COMMITTEE OVERSIGHT

Friendly critics have argued that Congress's decentralized committee system leaves it impotent in any face-off with the executive, and incapable of adopting a coherent policy of its own. Fractionalized legislative and budgetary authority by numerous, sometimes competing, committees and subcommittees has led to desultory oversight of executive agencies, to some committees sitting on information that should be shared with their parent chambers, and to ineffective coordination by each house over the total legislative and fiscal output of its committees. In sum, Congress has been constipated by an inefficient decision-making structure and process. While this condition has often hurt the president by delaying his legislative agenda and hobbling executive programs, in other circumstances it has left him or executive agencies immune from congressional checks and balances.

Oversight of Intelligence. As a case in point, both the executive and Congress were unhappy with what passed for oversight of intelligence and counterintelligence activities. After experience with the Hughes-Ryan amendment, the executive implored the House of Representatives, in the words of Speaker Tip O'Neill, "to establish a process that could provide valid oversight of all intelligence activities . . . and at the same time reduce the possibilities of leaks that might occur from the Hill."[32] O'Neill was urging his colleagues to create the

[29] Senate Res. 400, sec. 8 (b).
[30] House Res. 658, sec. 7 (b) (7).
[31] Ibid., and Senate Res. 400, sec. 8 (b).
[32] U.S., Congress, House, 95th Cong., 1st sess., vol. 123 *Congressional Record*, No. 119 H, 7115 (daily ed., July 14, 1977).

Permanent Select Committee on Intelligence fourteen months after the Senate Select Intelligence Committee was established. The anticipated benefits to the House were expressed by Representative Edward Boland, Democrat of Massachusetts. Noting that seven committees had some form of jurisdiction over various agencies in the intelligence community, Boland observed:

> All of them can secure access to the most vital secrets of our Nation, but none of them currently [July 1977] views the activities of the community as a composite.
>
> None of them, in practice, have developed a critical overview of the functioning and work-product of the entire community.
>
> [These committees] would . . . agree, I believe, that because of the lack of a strong, unified vehicle in this House—and previously in the other body—abuses occurred in the operations of some intelligence agencies, most notably the CIA.[33]

Traditionally, legislative jurisdiction over the FBI was held by the Senate and House Judiciary Committees. The Armed Services Subcommittees on Intelligence had comparable authority for the CIA and Defense Department intelligence agencies. Despite the contribution of the CIA in the formation and implementation of foreign policy, there was no role for the Senate Foreign Relations and the House International Relations Committees. Appropriations for intelligence activities were, and still are, processed by Appropriations subcommittees. But no total sum was available to Congress, for intelligence funding has been scattered throughout the budgets of several agencies.

This disjointed structure was rebuilt by establishing the Senate and House Select Intelligence Committees. Each combines unified oversight of all intelligence agencies with a mandate to share information with other committees and members of Congress. To insure liaison among other committees with jurisdiction in the field, the membership of both Intelligence Committees must include representatives from each of four committees in their respective houses: Appropriations, Armed Services, Judiciary, and Senate Foreign Relations or House International Relations.

To reduce the chance that the Intelligence Committees will fall into a protective relationship with the agencies they are supposed to monitor, no member may serve more than eight years on the Senate committee or six years on the House committee, and a third of the members of each committee is to be replaced every two years.

Congressional Budget Policy. Nothing has the universal impact on all policy areas as the federal budget and the fiscal policy it represents: levels and incidence of taxation, spending, and debt. Yet until the mid-'70s, congressional budgetary decisions were clumsily arrived at and muddled in intent. Consider these historic problems:

—Congress lacked sufficient information and expertise to effectively evaluate the president's annual budget. Most information and analytical skills rested principally in the president's Office of Management and Budget (OMB), and in the executive

---

[33] Ibid., H 7119.

departments which compiled the budget and were therefore able to defend it in Congress. Congress had no institutional staff agency comparable to the OMB.

—Congress could not coordinate revenues and expenditures. One set of committees wrote the tax laws (Ways and Means in the House, Finance in the Senate), another set the spending bills (Appropriations Committees in each house). This decentralized jurisdiction, coupled with Congress' proclivity to spend money and reluctance to raise taxes, contributed, said the critics, to chronic budget deficits and inflation.

—There was little or no coordination of expenditures. Each house's Appropriations Committee was (and is) fractured into some thirteen specialized subcommittees, each autonomous in the amount of appropriations it recommended. Total spending was the sum of whatever their recommendations happened to be, as modified and adopted by Congress on a piecemeal basis during the legislative session. There was no disciplined look at total spending or its effect on inflation, budget deficits, the national debt, and federal borrowing to pay interest on the debt.

—More importantly, perhaps, Congress had no mechanism for incorporating its own clear priorities for its spending, no coherent policy which dictated hard choices about where to spend a limited amount of money, because there was no predetermined limit. Since the president's budget reflected his priorities and hard choices, he was in a stronger position to argue with Congress when they disagreed, and to receive public support when he vetoed spending bills on the grounds of dampening inflation.

These chronic problems were addressed by the decision structure and process created by the Congressional Budget Act of 1974, which became fully effective in 1976.[34] Without getting into their fine points, the cardinal provisions of the Budget Act can be summarized as follows:

—It establishes a new fiscal year beginning October 1. Since the president sends Congress his annual budget in mid or late January, this gives Congress more than eight months to work on it, instead of the less than six months available under the old fiscal year beginning July 1.

—To match the technical knowledge and expertise of the president's OMB, the Act creates the Congressional Budget Office (CBO), empowered to secure information from executive agencies. The act also establishes Budget Committees in each house of Congress which, utilizing the staff studies of the CBO and staff studies of their own, recommend coordinated levels of revenues and expenditures and priorities for spending. In effect, these three new bodies were created to help Congress establish its own budget ceilings (targets) which, under the Budget Act, may not be exceeded.

—The Budget Committees' recommendations are embodied in concurrent budget resolutions reported to their respective houses. A first resolution sets tentative or "target" ceilings for appropriations and actual expenditures (outlays) in each functional category, as well as ceilings for total appropriations and outlays, revenues, a budget surplus or deficit, and the national debt, and is due by April 15.

—By May 15, standing committees must report new authorization bills, and Congress must adopt a first concurrent budget resolution. (As a concurrent resolution, it is not submitted to the president for approval or veto.) This resolution guides, but does not bind, subsequent congressional budgetary decisions. However, the CBO and the Budget Committees keep score on how close spending and revenue bills come to the first

[34] PL 93–344, 88 *Stat.* 297; 31 *USC* 1301.

resolution's ceilings. And in the Senate, at least, Budget Committee Chairman Edmund Muskie is not above jawboning his colleagues into fiscal restraint.

—By September 15 Congress must adopt a second, binding, concurrent budget resolution, which either affirms or revises the first resolution passed on May 15. If the money bills passed in the preceding four months do not conform to the ceilings in the second resolution, it can dictate changes in the amounts of appropriations, revenues, and the public debt. These changes are called reconciliations. Congress must then adopt a reconciliation measure to implement the second, binding, concurrent resolution and may not adjourn until this is done.

Despite some shakedown problems, the new budgetary process puts Congress on a level at least approaching the presidency in making—and taking responsibility for—policy decisions on spending and revenue raising. To the Carter administration, pledged to seek a balanced budget, the Budget Act can make Congress a competent ally. But should Congress break with the president, it would be a formidable adversary.

STOPPING THE PRESIDENT BY CONCURRENT RESOLUTION

Some of the laws defining the president's authority in selected policy areas have permitted Congress to remove his authority by adopting a concurrent resolution. Although they require a majority vote in each house, concurrent resolutions are not sent to the president, so they cannot be vetoed. Three recent laws provide for veto-proof concurrent resolutions.

The National Emergencies Act requires future national emergencies to end on the date specified in a presidential proclamation or in a concurrent resolution, whichever date comes first. No later than every six months after the emergency is declared, Congress must consider whether to end it by concurrent resolution. When the emergency ends, so do the president's special powers granted him by numerous statutes triggered by the emergency.[35]

The War Powers Resolution states that "at any time" U.S. armed forces are engaged in hostilities abroad without a declaration of war or specific statutory approval from Congress, such forces shall be removed by the president if Congress so directs by concurrent resolution.[36] Because of another provision of the War Powers Resolution discussed below, such a concurrent resolution would be practical only during the first sixty days of a conflict.

The National Emergencies Act and the War Powers Resolution contain similar rules for giving concurrent resolutions fast consideration in Congress. Unless waived by a majority vote in either house, these rules protect concurrent resolutions from committee pigeonholes in both houses and filibusters in the Senate.[37]

[35] PL 94–412, 90 *Stat.* 1255; 50 *USC* 1621.
[36] PL 93–148, 87 *Stat.* 555 at sec. 5(c); 50 *USC* Supp. V (1975) 1545 (c).
[37] PL 94–412, 90 *Stat.* 1255; 50 *USC* 1622 for National Emergencies Act. PL 93–148, 87 *Stat.* 555 at sec. 7; 50 *USC* Supp. V (1975) 1547 for War Powers Resolution.

In 1974, Congress amended Section 36 of the Foreign Military Sales Act to require the president to give Congress advance notice of any offer to sell arms or services valued at $25 million or more. By the mid-1970s, the United States had become one of the leading exporters of armaments, but Congress had had little to say about what weapons were sold to which countries. Congress had twenty days to reject any offer to sell arms by concurrent resolution, unless the president stated that an emergency required the sale in the national security interests of the United States.[38] (The quick transfer of weapons to Israel during the 1973 Yom Kippur war is an example of the kind of emergency Congress had in mind.)

After some experience with this law, Congress determined that twenty days gave it insufficient time to investigate an arms sale, and that the $25 million floor allowed a series of smaller arms sales to escape its scrutiny.[39] So in 1976 Congress further amended section 36 by giving itself up to thirty days to pass a concurrent resolution disapproving the sale of major defense equipment valued at $7 million or more, as well as any arms or services of $25 million or more.

In practice, at least some members of Congress have considerably more than thirty days to decide whether they want to support a concurrent resolution. First, by informal agreement with the executive, the Senate Foreign Relations Committee and the House International Relations Committee receive "pre-notification" of proposed sales twenty days in advance of formal notification to Congress. Formal notification initiates the thirty-day disapproval period.

Second, members of Congress may be able to buy time by threatening to pass a resolution of disapproval before the end of thirty days. The president can prevent this by withdrawing formal notification before Congress kills the sale. The president may resubmit notification later, but that begins a new, full thirty-day period. In the indefinite interim between withdrawal and resubmission of the proposed sale, Congress has ample time to influence the president and foreign governments to accept congressionally imposed compromises on foreign arms sales.

This has already occurred: in the 1975 sale of Hawk ground-to-air missiles to Jordan, and in the 1977 sale to Iran of Airborne Warning and Control System (AWACS) aircraft.[40] A third instance of compromise occurred in May 1978, when President Carter promised an additional twenty planes for Israel as part of his package sale of jet fighters to Saudi Arabia, Egypt, and Israel.

STOPPING PRESIDENTIAL ACTIONS BY SIMPLE RESOLUTION

A one house veto of a presidential recommendation by passage of a simple resolution is authorized in the Impoundment Control Act of 1974 (which appears

---

[38] PL 93–559, 88 *Stat.* 1814; 22 *USC* 2776.

[39] *Congressional Quarterly Almanac 1975* (Washington, D.C.: Congressional Quarterly, Inc.), p. 353.

[40] *Congressional Quarterly Almanac 1975* (Washington, D.C.: Congressional Quarterly, Inc.), pp. 358–359, and *Congressional Quarterly Weekly Report*, vol. 35, Sept. 3, 1977, pp. 1857–1863.

as Title X of the Congressional Budget Act of 1974).[41] In a special message to Congress, the president may propose that he defer spending specified amounts of money for certain purposes until a later time in the current fiscal year (he may not propose deferrals beyond the end of the year). But the funds must be available for expenditure if either house passes a resolution disapproving the proposed deferral. Both houses have procedures for discharging a resolution from a committee, for treating motions to consider a resolution as privileged, and for limiting debate before the final floor vote.[42]

STOPPING THE PRESIDENT AUTOMATICALLY BY INACTION

Sponsors of concurrent or simple resolutions cannot stop the president without convincing a majority of their colleagues to vote against him. Assembling a majority on any policy issue is hard enough; constructing one in opposition to the president's policy is even harder.

This problem is leapfrogged if Congress wants to stop the president from fighting an undeclared war or from permanently impounding appropriations. In both cases, the president must stop automatically by a specific deadline, unless majorities in both houses of Congress vote to approve his action. The problem of achieving a majority is faced by the president's supporters, not his opponents.

Recall that in the absence of a declaration of war, the War Powers Resolution directs the president to report to Congress within forty-eight hours after he introduces U.S. armed forces into hostilities or situations where hostilities are likely. The teeth of the Resolution are in its provision that within sixty days after the report is due, the president shall terminate American involvement in hostilities or hostile situations, unless Congress has declared war or enacted a specific authorization for the fighting, has extended by law the sixty-day deadline, or is physically unable to meet because of an armed attack against the United States.[43] Priority procedures provide that any measure supporting the president, that is, legislation authorizing the war or extending the deadline, shall be voted upon before the sixty days have elapsed. However, this is not guaranteed, for the procedures may be waived by majority vote in either house.[44]

The sixty-day deadline could be extended up to thirty additional days if the president determines that "unavoidable military necessity" requires the extra time for the safe removal of U.S. forces. The president would have to certify this need to Congress in writing.[45] (As mentioned above, Congress could force the president to disengage from hostilities at any time by passing a concurrent resolution.)

A shorter deadline is written into the Impoundment Control Act. The presi-

---

[41] PL 93–344, 88 *Stat.* 332; 31 *USC* 1400.
[42] Ibid., at 337 in the *Statutes* and 1407 in the *U.S. Code.*
[43] PL 93–148, 87 *Stat.* 555 at sec. 5 (b); 50 *USC* Supp. V (1975) 1545(b).
[44] Ibid., at sec. 6 in the *Statutes* and 1546 in the *U.S. Code.*
[45] Ibid., at sec. 5 in the *Statutes* and 1545 in the *U.S. Code.*

dent must propose permanent impoundments, called "rescissions," to Congress. However, the appropriations proposed to be rescinded have to be available for expenditure unless, within forty-five days of the president's request, Congress acts affirmatively and passes a rescission bill[46] approving the president's request. If passed, the rescission measure would repeal or amend the amounts authorized in previous appropriations acts. Both houses have provisions for expediting floor action on rescission bills.

ABOLISHING PREVIOUS PRESIDENTIAL AUTHORITY

The National Emergencies Act was signed into law on September 14, 1976. Two years from that date, all powers and authority held by the president and any other federal officer or employee as a result of past national emergencies will have terminated.[47] In effect, on September 14, 1978, the Act will have ended four emergencies: those declared by presidents Roosevelt, in March 1933 to deal with the Depression, Truman, in December 1950 after the outbreak of the Korean War, and Nixon, in March 1970 in response to a postal strike, and in August 1971 to implement currency restrictions following an international monetary crisis.[48]

The two-year grace period was to give the executive time to seek enactment of new laws to continue programs operating under statutes triggered by past emergencies. Also, of the some 470 so-called "emergency" laws, eight grant the executive authority considered essential for normal government activities. These eight provisions are exempt from termination under the National Emergencies Act, although they were subject to congressional review and possible change within nine months after the Act became law.[49] So, while the Act strips the president of most past emergency authority, it leaves him with enough for normal operations and grants him time to try to gain more. And, of course, the president may declare new emergencies in the future.

President and Congress: Three Scenarios for the Future

A combination of the Great Depression, World War II and the Cold War, and the early years of the Vietnam War left the presidency with vastly expanded responsibilities and authority. Is the final legacy of Vietnam and of presidents Johnson and Nixon to be a weakened presidency? An ascendant Congress? More generally, in what way may the new restrictions shape the future relationship of presidents and Congress?

[46] PL 93-344, 88 *Stat.* 332; 31 *USC* 1402.
[47] PL 94-412, 90 *Stat.* 1255; 50 *USC* 1601.
[48] *Congressional Quarterly Almanac 1976* (Washington, D.C.: Congressional Quarterly, Inc.), p. 522.
[49] PL 94-412, 90 *Stat.* 1258; 50 *USC* 1651.

While the definitive answer will be provided by future events, we can consider three scenarios, in order of their probability for the near future.

Scenario 1: A More Balanced Partnership.   Assuming no major changes in the existing political environment, the next few years should see a more balanced partnership between president and Congress in the adoption of public policy. Congress will insure this by exerting many of the new restrictions as checks on the president. But while there will be some retrenchment of the president's influence, there will not be a period of congressional dominance reminiscent of the nineteenth century. The president has too many responsibilities, legal and political, for that. Rather, the president will continue to propose, but Congress will more often—and more effectively—dispose. This relationship should be institutional. That is, the growth in congressional checks will be mostly (but not completely) independent of changes in specific issues or in the partisan makeup of the White House and Capitol Hill. Several factors contribute to this conclusion.

The new restrictions make it easier for Congress to offset the president. Executive actions kept secret in the past now must be reported routinely, giving Congress substantive knowledge on which to act. Previously, Congress's ultimate weapon was the power of the purse—restricting the use of future appropriations or repealing past spending authority. Both techniques were subject to delay in the legislative process and a possible presidential veto. Now the president faces veto-proof simple and concurrent resolutions, protected against committee pigeonholes and filibusters, and automatic deadlines written into existing law.

Other things being equal, the more opportunities Congress has to impose restrictions, the more likely it will. Restrictions giving Congress the most opportunities are those permanently built into routine congressional activity. One example is the annual budgetary process, with its budget committees and timetable of deadlines for spending priorities and target ceilings. The routine workload of the Intelligence Committees includes drafting annual authorization bills and receiving annual, or more frequent, reports of executive branch intelligence activities. Finally, presidential impoundment requests, and their review by Congress, have become virtually routine.

In the aftermath of Vietnam and Watergate, Congress appears to have developed a more confident self-image, a greater willingness to assert its institutional prerogatives. Consequently, Congress seems more inclined to oppose a president perceived as demeaning its dignity and downgrading its importance in the constitutional scheme of things.

With the possible exception of Lyndon Johnson, presidents since Franklin Roosevelt have not had consistently strong political bases from which they could win a serious confrontation with a determined Congress. Republican presidents Eisenhower and Nixon won huge popular pluralities in 1956 and 1972, respectively, but faced sizable Democratic majorities in Congress. Democratic presidents—Truman in 1948, Kennedy in 1960, Carter in 1976—won very close elections and ran well behind their congressional party in popular votes. There is no evidence that this phenomenon—presidents of both parties without coat-tails—will reverse itself in the immediate future.

Scenario 2: Constitutional Confrontation.   Given the necessary circumstances—president and Congress at loggerheads, with neither willing to back down or compromise—there could be a confrontation if the president challenges the constitutionality of some of the restrictions.

For example, a case can be made that Congress cannot stop the president with a veto-proof concurrent resolution. Article 1, section 7 of the Constitution states that "Every Order, Resolution, or Vote" to which both houses must agree (with the exception of a resolution to adjourn) shall not take effect until after it has been signed by the president or passed over his veto "according to the Rules and Limitations prescribed in the Case of a Bill." Consequently, one can argue that any resolution ending an emergency or a war, or preventing a foreign arms sale, must be sent to the president for his approval or veto. The rebuttal is that veto-proof concurrent resolutions comply with the requirements of Article 1, section 7, because they are authorized in statutes which have been signed by the president or passed over his veto. This constitutional argument has not been resolved by the Supreme Court.

A president might also refuse to continue reporting CIA activities, especially if they were compromised by leaks, by asserting executive primacy in the con-duct of foreign policy and national security. Congress could retaliate by citing its legislative authority for oversight and investigation.

The Supreme Court would have to be willing to resolve such issues. If it were not, either the president would eviscerate any restrictions he chose to ignore, or Congress would enforce them by other means—not excluding impeachment.

Scenario 3: Reassertion of the Dominant Presidency.   Unlikely in the near term, but not in the more distant future, is the reassertion of presidential primacy on a footing equivalent to what it was from 1932 to 1972. The present restric-tions (or most of them) might remain in the statutes, but they would be unused as politically unfeasible. The conditions for this scenario would include one or more of the following: the dimming of Vietnam and Watergate in Congress's institutional memory; a desire in Congress to escape the political heat that accompanies leadership in policy making, with a consequent deferring to the president's initiatives; and some severe crisis or emergency (a prolonged energy crunch or world famine come to mind) comparable to the Depression or World War II, in which Congress and the public give the president virtual carte blanche.

Congressional Politics and Urban Aid: A 1978 Postscript

The explanation often given for the modest nature of the Carter administration's urban policy announced in the spring of 1978 was that a more aggressive and expensive one would have been unsupportable in Congress. HEW Secretary Joseph Califano reportedly argued to President Carter while the administration's urban policy statement was being formulated that since most members of Congress did not come from large cities, a policy that focused on those cities would "[fly] in the face of political reality" and meet with congressional rejection.[1]

The Califano argument and, in so far as it is based on it, the Carter urban policy reflect a major fallacy: that members of Congress are compelled to vote their constituencies' characteristics—such as whether those constituencies are predominantly "large" or "central" city or suburban or rural—and that presumably only those members from large cities or central cities can support strong urban programs. In point of fact numerous political science studies over the years have shown that the party affiliation of a member of Congress has been almost always more predictive of his or her vote than the nature of that member's constituency.[2] Specifically with respect to congressional voting on

---

[1] *New York Times*, Jan. 25, 1978.

[2] See, for example, Julius Turner, *Party and Constituency* (Baltimore: Johns Hopkins University Press, 1951) and the revised edition edited by Edward V. Schneier, Jr. (Balitmore: Johns Hopkins University Press, 1970); David B. Truman, *The Congressional Party* (New York: John Wiley & Sons, 1959); David B. Mayhew, *Party Loyalty Among Congressmen* (Cambridge, Mass.: Harvard University Press, 1966); W. Wayne Shannon, *Party, Constituency and Congressional Voting* (Baton

DEMETRIOS CARALEY, the editor of *Political Science Quarterly*, is professor of political science in Barnard College and the Graduate School of Arts and Sciences, Columbia University. He has published books and articles on urban, congressional, and party politics. His latest book is *City Governments and Urban Problems*.

Political Science Quarterly   Volume 93   Number 3   Fall 1978   143

urban aid programs, I have earlier shown in these pages that from 1945 to 1975 Democratic members (and especially nonsouthern Democratic members) of Congress supported urban programs strongly, regardless of the central city, suburban, or rural character of their constituencies, and Republican members did not, again regardless of the type of constituency they were representing.[3]

As part of a larger, ongoing study of congressional voting behavior, I recently completed an analysis of urban voting in the 1977 session of the 95th Congress to see, among other things, whether the patterns found for the earlier period had changed. Thirty-five House and twenty-four Senate recorded votes were examined that had been taken on various aspects of eight urban-oriented assistance programs: public works jobs, public service jobs, countercyclical assistance, community development grants, subsidized housing, youth jobs, food stamps, and community legal services. From these were generated "urban support scores" for each representative and senator based on the percentage of his votes on which he took the "pro-urban" position.[4] Finally each representative and senator was categorized according to various constituency characteristics and to the region of the country in which his district or state was located.

PARTY VS. CONSTITUENCY

Analysis of the 1977 urban votes shows that regardless of the central city, suburban, or rural nature of their constituencies, Democratic members of Congress continued to support urban programs strongly and Republican members continued not to do so. The following is a breakdown of the average urban support scores of House members according to party and type of constituency:[5]

Rouge: Louisiana University Press, 1968); and Aage R. Clausen, *How Congressmen Decide* (New York: St. Martin's Press, 1973).

[3] Demetrios Caraley, "Congressional Politics and Urban Aid," *Political Science Quarterly* 91 (Spring 1976):19–45.

[4] The "pro-urban position" was considered to be (1) on the question of having or not having an urban program, to have the program; (2) on the question of having higher or lower funding or having longer-term or shorter-term authorization, to have the higher funding or the longer-term authorization; and (3) on the question of different allocation formulas, to have the formula that would tend more to "target" funds to so-called "hardship cities"—those larger and older cities primarily in the East and Midwest with the most serious social and economic problems—rather than to "spread" those funds among local governments more generally. The 1977 recorded votes on which the urban support scores were based are by Congressional Quarterly (CQ) number: in the House, 19, 20, 22, 23, 24, 35, 51, 53, 54, 60, 61, 62, 63, 148, 165, 171, 199, 201, 203, 211, 212, 218, 219, 352, 353, 355, 358, 409, 433, 434, 438, 441, 442, 577, 694; and in the Senate, 38, 43, 46, 47, 48, 126, 127, 129, 130, 132, 133, 135, 137, 163, 165, 167, 170, 171, 174, 175, 177, 512, 555, 560. See *Congressional Roll Call 1977* (Washington, D.C.: Congressional Quarterly Inc., 1978).

[5] In the House a constituency was classified as "central city," "suburban," or "rural" according to whether a majority of its population lived in a central city of a standard metropolitan statistical area, the "outside central city" portion of such a metropoliton area, or outside such a metropolitan area. Constituencies where there was neither a central city, suburban, nor rural majority were

House

68%

	central city	*suburban*	*rural*	*chamber*
Democrats	86% (84)	83% (85)	70% (73)	80% (291)
Republicans	40% (19)	46% (53)	40% (48)	44% (144)

As can be seen, for every kind of constituency the score for the Democrats is about twice as high as for the Republicans. Moreover, the differences within each party between the most urban (that is, the central city) and least urban (that is, the rural) constituencies was only about one-third to one-half the difference between the Democrats and Republicans from the same kind of constituency. One further way to appreciate the predominant impact of party is to note that the score for *rural* Democrats (including rural *southern* Democrats) was almost twice as high as for *urban* Republicans!

When House urban support scores for central city representatives are further broken down by size of the central city, we have the following array:

Central City Districts

78%

city size	*Democrats*	*Republicans*
50,000–99,999	85% (4)	56% (1)
100,000–249,999	81% (3)	35% (3)
250,000–499,999	81% (22)	40% (5)
500,000–999,999	82% (19)	39% (5)
1,000,000 and over	92% (36)	30% (3)

The scores show that for Republican House members size of city was, if anything, negatively correlated with urban support and that for the Democrats, those members representing cities of 1 million in population or larger had somewhat higher scores than those who represented smaller cities. The dramatic differences were thus not between representatives from different size cities but once again between parties: for cities of any population size Democrats had two to three times higher urban support scores than did Republicans. Furthermore, Democrats even from the smallest central cities of 50,000 to 99,999 had support scores almost three times as high as Republicans from the largest central cities of over 1 million.

In the Senate as in the House, a breakdown of urban support scores by party and type of constituency[6] shows the predominant impact of party:

---

classified as "mixed" and excluded from further analysis with respect to the impact of constituency on urban voting.

[6] Senate constituencies could not be classified in the same way as in the House since in only one state, New York, did a majority of the population live in central cities. The urban character of statewide constituencies was therefore classified as "more urban" if the state contained a city whose population was 250,000 or larger and "less urban" if it did not. No other population cut-off for the

Senate

68%

	more urban states (largest city 250,000 or over)	less urban states (largest city under 250,000)	all states
Democrats	76% (34)	77% (28)	77% (62)
Republicans	66% (18)	43% (20)	54% (38)

First, Democratic senators had essentially the same score regardless of the size of their state's largest city and, second, this score was higher than that of the Republican senators from either category of states. Thus, in a pattern similar to that found in the House, even Democratic senators from the "less urban" states had a higher score than Republican senators from the "more urban" states. Among the Republicans, however, senators from the "more urban" states did have an average urban support score 23 points higher than those from the "less urban" states—a very substantial point spread, as large as that between all Democratic and all Republican senators.[7]

The major political lesson from this analysis should be clear: at present it is not the number of central city or large city constituencies or the number of "more urban" states in Congress, but the number of Democratic members that is crucial to passing urban programs. Over the past four decades Congress has been seriously responsive to the needs of urban areas only in those few years of the Roosevelt and Johnson administrations (1933-37, 1965-66) when a Democratic president was serving with a Congress that had heavy Democratic majorities. The "heavy" Democratic majorities were needed so that there would be enough Democrats to constitute floor majorities for urban programs even in the face of substantial southern Democratic defections.

---

size of a state's largest city was found to be statistically significant in accounting for differences in the urban support scores of senators.

The urban character of each state was also classified according to the percentage of its population living in central cities as follows: 0 to 20 percent, "low urban"; 21 to 40 percent, "midurban"; and 41 to 60 percent, "high urban"; but there was no statistically significant difference in the urban support scores of senators when their states were classified in this fashion.

[7] Those readers interested in statistics should know that an analysis of variance and a multiple classification analysis (MCA) confirmed the conclusions of what may be the more intuitively meaningful analysis in the text based on point spreads. An MCA of party and constituency produced for the House adjusted beta weights of 0.64 for party and 0.16 for constituency and for the Senate, adjusted betas of 0.41 for party and 0.19 for constituency, thus reflecting the much heavier impact of party over type of constituency in both chambers.

An analysis of variance in the House testing for the impact of the size of the central city showed that for central city Republicans, size of the city was not statistically significant in accounting for differences in urban support. For the Democrats, size of the central city just barely passed the test for statistical significance at the 0.05 level (actual significance=0.0493) in accounting for difference in urban support and produced an eta of 0.3350, thus signifying that city size accounted statistically for about 11 percent (eta^2 =0.1122) in the variation among the urban support scores of central city Democrats. For a description of all these statistical tests, see Norman H. Nie et al., *Statistical Package for the Social Science*, 2d ed. (New York: McGraw-Hill, 1975), chs. 17 and 22.

The roughly two-to-one Democratic majorities of the 95th Congress were heavy enough to constitute strong potential support for important urban initiatives,[8] and these Democratic majorities were serving with a Democratic president in the White House. But in order to galvanize those potential pro-urban majorities into actual ones, strong leadership was necessary from a forceful and energetic president who was willing to dramatize the special problems of hardship cities and was not reluctant to spend money on efforts to deal with them.[9]

There is no reason to believe, incidentally, that continued high levels of support for urban programs from Democratic members of Congress regardless of the urban character of their districts or states can be taken for granted. If Democrats who do not represent central city districts or "more urban" states hear too often Califano-type arguments to the effect that they cannot afford politically to support urban programs, these nonurban or less urban Democrats may well begin to believe such arguments and make Califano's prediction a self-fulfilling one.[10]

SECTION VS. PARTY: AN EMERGING SNOWBELT-SUNBELT SPLIT?

The 1977 urban support scores also allowed analysis of whether a new sectional politics, splitting a purportedly bipartisan, pro-urban "snowbelt" against a bipartisan, anti-urban "sunbelt" is superimposing itself upon and overriding the traditional voting cleavages in Congress. If such a snowbelt vs. sunbelt sectional cleavage were to become dominant, combined majorities of Democrats and Republicans from the East and Midwest[11] would presumably be oppos-

---

[8] Some strong evidence for this proposition is that on the various pieces of the Carter administration's 1977, or implicit, urban legislative package on which this study is based, the pro-urban position prevailed on 30 of 35 votes in the House and on 21 of 24 votes in the Senate.

[9] And, indeed, on the 1978 votes for loan guarantees to New York City—which were supported energetically by the Carter administration—the margins of victory for the pro-urban position on the two crucial House votes were overwhelming ones of 291 to 109 (Democrats 236 to 25; Republicans 55 to 84) and of 247 to 155 (Democrats 203 to 59; Republicans 44 to 96). See CQ House votes 370 and 371 of 1978, *Congressional Quarterly Weekly Report,* June 10, 1978, pp. 1510–11.

The pro-urban margins in the Senate were similarly overwhelming ones of about 2 or 3 to 1 on defeating anti-urban amendments and of almost exactly 2 to 1 on final passage (final passage 53 to 27: Republicans 18 to 15; Democrats 35 to 12). See CQ Senate votes 193–197 of 1978, *Congressional Quarterly Weekly Report,* July 1, 1978, p. 1709.

[10] For a discussion of further reasons for the possible long-term vulnerability of this kind of political support from congressional Democrats, see Demetrios Caraley, "The Carter Congress and Urban Programs: First Soundings," in Walter Dean Burnham and Martha Wagner Weinberg, eds., *American Politics and Public Policy* (Cambridge, Mass.: MIT Press, 1978), pp. 213–218; and Demetrios Caraley, *City Governments and Urban Problems* (Englewood Cliffs, N.J.: Prentice-Hall Inc., 1977), chs. 6 and 20.

[11] Following the Congressional Quarterly Service, the eastern states were considered to be Connecticut, Delaware, Maine, Maryland, Massachusetts, New Hampshire, New Jersey, New York, Pennsylvania, Rhode Island, Vermont, and West Virginia; and the midwestern states, Illinois, Indiana, Iowa, Kansas, Michigan, Minnesota, Missouri, Nebraska, North Dakota, Ohio, South Dakota, and Wisconsin.

ing combined majorities of Democrats and Republicans from the South and West.[12] And they would be doing so more consistently than Democrats would be opposing Republicans or than Republicans and southern Democrats would be opposing northern Democrats—these being the traditional party and "conservative coalition" voting splits. Considerable discussion of the possible emergence of sectionalism took place in 1977 both on the floor of Congress and in the media, especially after a dramatic House urban vote pitted an almost completely unified snowbelt coalition of eastern and midwestern representatives against a less completely unified but still highly cohesive sunbelt coalition of westerners and southerners.[13]

A breakdown of the scores of House and Senate members according to the snowbelt or sunbelt location of their districts and states but without regard to party shows that in both chambers, the snowbelt did give higher support to urban programs than did the sunbelt:

	House	Senate
Chamber	68% (435)	68% (100)
All Snowbelt	74% (238)	81% (48)
All Sunbelt	61% (197)	56% (52)

This in itself, however, proves only that the snowbelt and the sunbelt differed significantly on urban voting, especially in the Senate, but not that they had become more salient as voting groups than the parties. One test of this last point is whether the difference between the average support scores of the two sectional groupings was larger than between the parties. Following are the breakdown of scores according to party:

	House	Senate
Democrats	80% (291)	77% (62)
Republicans	44% (144)	54% (38)

It turns out that in the House, the difference between all Democrats and all Republicans (a point spread of 36) was almost three times as large as between the snowbelt

---

[12] The southern states were considered to be Alabama, Arkansas, Florida, Georgia, Kentucky, Louisiana, Mississippi, North Carolina, Oklahoma, South Carolina, Tennessee, Texas, and Virginia; and the western states, Alaska, Arizona, California, Colorado, Hawaii, Idaho, Montana, Nevada, New Mexico, Oregon, Utah, and Washington.

[13] The House vote (CQ # 199 of 1977) was on an amendment to delete from the bill extending the Housing and Community Development Act of 1974 a new, alternate formula for the distribution of community development grants. The original formula enacted in 1974 was based on the size of a city's population, its amount of overcrowded housing, and its percentage of poor (this last factor counted twice). By 1977 it became widely recognized that this formula favored the newer and still-growing cities of the western and southern sunbelt at the expense of the older cities of the East and Midwest whose populations were declining and whose fiscal problems were the most acute.

The new, alternate formula was based on the amount of older, pre-1940 housing (weighted 50 percent), poverty (weighted 30 percent), and population growth lag, that is, the degree to which a city's population growth between 1960 and 1973 was less than the average population growth for all central cities of metropolitan areas (weighted 20 percent). The amendment to strike this formula, which

and sunbelt sectional groupings (a point spread of 13). In the Senate, on the other hand, the difference between all snowbelt and all sunbelt senators was slightly *larger* than between all Democratic and all Republican senators (a point spread of 25 vs. 23).[14]

A second test of the relative impact of party and section is whether the snow-belt coalition has replaced the Democratic membership as the most pro-urban grouping in Congress and whether the sunbelt coalition has replaced the Republicans as the least pro-urban. Once again the results between the two chambers differ. In the House the Democrats had a higher urban support score than the snowbelters (80% vs. 74%) and the Republicans had a lower score than the sunbelt coalition (44% vs. 61%). In the Senate, while the snowbelt senators did have a slightly higher score than the Democrats (81% vs. 77%), the sunbelt senators did not have a lower score than the Republicans (56% vs. 54%).

A third test of the impact of party and section is to compare the average cleavage (that is, the percent voting pro-urban in one grouping minus the per-cent voting pro-urban in the other grouping) between the Democratic and Republican party memberships and between the snowbelt and sunbelt coalitions. As measured over 35 House and 24 Senate votes, the average cleavages were:

	House	Senate
Average party cleavage	38%	24%
Average sectional cleavage	15%	26%

For a third time the chambers differ, with the party cleavage being two-and-one-half times the sectional cleavage in the House, but the sectional cleavage being slightly larger than the party one in the Senate.

As measured by these three tests then, party remained clearly more important than snowbelt vs. sunbelt sectionalism in the House. In the Senate, however, this kind of sectional cleavage came out to be at least as important as the party one and some differences suggest that sectionalism might actually have been slightly more important than party but these are too small to be conclusive.

When one separates the average support scores of the party groupings within each section, the impression of sectionalism having a heavier impact in the Senate than in the House is confirmed:

	House 68%		Senate 68%	
	Democrats	*Republicans*	*Democrats*	*Republicans*
Snowbelt	88% (149)	49% (89)	87% (30)	71% (18)
Sunbelt	70% (142)	37% (55)	67% (32)	39% (20)

clearly would benefit the snowbelt, failed in a vote of 149 to 261: in the twelve eastern states the vote was 110 to 1 and in the twelve midwestern states, 108 to 7 against the motion to strike; in the twenty-six southern and western states the vote was 141 to 43 in favor of deleting the alternate formula.

[14] The conclusions of the point-spread analysis in the text is again confirmed by statistical analysis

As can be seen, in the House the sunbelt Democrats have a higher urban support score than the snowbelt Republicans, indicating once again the predominant influence of party. In the Senate, on the other hand, sunbelt Democrats had a slightly lower score than snowbelt Republicans, thus showing a very heavy pro-urban sectional impact on the snowbelt Republicans.

A further breakdown of average urban support scores by party and region reveals the underlying building blocks for whatever snowbelt vs. sunbelt sectionalism is evolving:

	House		Senate	
	Democrats	Republicans	Democrats	Republicans
Easterners	91% (82)	60% (35)	88% (14)	81% (10)
Southerners	64% (91)	32% (30)	60% (19)	33% (7)
Midwesterners	85% (67)	42% (54)	86% (16)	59% (8)
Westerners	81% (51)	42% (25)	76% (13)	42% (13)

Three highly significant patterns stand out: (1) Both in the House and Senate, southern Democrats are significantly less pro-urban than the other, or "northern," Democrats; (2) Both in the House and Senate, eastern Republicans are significantly more pro-urban than noneastern Republicans; and (3) The southern Democrats' deviance from their party colleagues toward an anti-urban position and the eastern Republicans' deviance from their party toward a pro-urban position are very much stronger in the Senate than in the House. Specifically on this last point, while the southern Democrats in the House were only slightly closer to the Republicans than to the northern Democrats, in the Senate they were *four times closer*. Similarly, the eastern Republicans in the House had an average score about midpoint between the Democrats and the noneastern Republicans, but *in the Senate the eastern Republicans were actually somewhat more pro-urban than the Democratic senators as a whole and only slightly less pro-urban than the average of all the northern Democratic senators.* One final way of pointing up the extreme deviance of the eastern Republicans is by noting that they were 37 points more pro-urban than the average of the non-eastern Republican senators—a point spread larger than any other we have identified and one that is one-and-one-half times as large as the point spread between southern and northern Democratic senators and between all Democratic senators and all Republican senators.

The total implications of these findings are that there was some reality to a snowbelt vs. sunbelt sectionalism on urban voting in 1977, though it far from overshadowed traditional party cleavages and was less powerful in the House than in the Senate. In the House at best only five of the eight party-regional elements needed for a full snowbelt vs. sunbelt realignment were in place. The

---

of variance and multiple classification analysis. For the House an MCA of party and section produced adjusted betas of 0.64 for party and 0.26 for section, thus showing the much heavier impact of party. For the Senate, the MCA adjusted betas were 0.41 for party but 0.52 for section, showing that unlike in the House, section had a slightly heavier impact than party.

eastern and midwestern Democrats were, as snowbelters presumably should be, more pro-urban than the chamber as a whole, while the southern and western Republicans and the southern Democrats were, as sunbelters, more anti-urban. The eastern and especially the midwestern Republican House members were, however, still voting more as anti-urban Republicans than as pro-urban snowbelters, and the western Democrats were still voting more as pro-urban Democrats than as anti-urban members of the sunbelt. It should also be recognized that although the southern Democrats in the House were voting less pro-urban than the chamber as a whole, they were nevertheless more pro-urban than the snowbelt's eastern and midwestern Republicans, thus raising a question of whether even the southern Democrats should be considered already in place as part of a House anti-urban, sunbelt sectional coalition.

In the Senate six of the necessary eight elements for a snowbelt vs. sunbelt coalition were firmly in place in 1977, largely reflecting the fact that southern Democrats were much more deviantly anti-urban, and eastern Republicans much more deviantly pro-urban in the Senate than in the House. Thus the eastern and midwestern Democrats and the eastern Republicans were, as snowbelters presumably should be, more pro-urban than the chamber as a whole. And the southern and western Republicans and the southern Democrats were, as sunbelters, more anti-urban. The western Democrats and the midwestern Republicans were still out of place, each grouping being closer to its party than to its sectional cohorts, though even this was less so in the Senate than in the House.

One political lesson from this part of the analysis is that if snowbelt Democrats in coalition with eastern and potentially with midwestern Republicans engage too strongly in what has been called "aggressive regionalism," they may cause a serious anti-urban backlash among western Democrats.[15] Western Democrats in 1977 voted almost as pro-urban as eastern and midwestern ones. But overly aggressive regionalism by the snowbelt may cause western Democrats to start perceiving themselves not as allies, but as targets of their pro-urban Democratic colleagues from the snowbelt. And these western Democrats might then begin to vote more as sunbelters in protection of real or hypothetical, anti-urban sectional interests and less as traditionally pro-urban northern Democrats.*

[15] See the remarks of Texas Senator Lloyd Bentsen during debate on the Housing and Community Development Act, *Congressional Record*, June 7, 1977, pp. S9061–S9062.

In 1977 House western Democrats, had they all voted on every occasion, would have provided 1418 pro-urban votes on the issues examined in this study while House midwestern Republicans provided only 735. Similarly, Senate western Democrats would have delivered 237 pro-urban votes, and Senate midwestern Republicans, only 113. If the price of winning over the midwestern Republicans to become part of a bipartisan, pro-urban, snowbelt coalition were to be the loss of the western Democrats from the Democratic membership's northern, pro-urban wing, the trade would be a highly imprudent one for any pro-urban politicians to want to make.

* I thank my friends and colleagues Mary Ann Epstein, Gerald Finch, Charles Hamilton, Robert McCaughey, and Ralph Nunes for helpful advice on this article; Ralph Nunes for research assistance; the Barnard College Faculty Research Fund for a grant to help defray the costs of research assistance; and Columbia University's new Center for the Social Sciences for computing facilities and services of consultants.

Congress and the Arab-Israeli Conflict: Support for Israel in the U.S. Senate, 1970-1973

ROBERT H. TRICE

Congressional behavior in the late Vietnam and early post-Vietnam period has called into serious question the long-standing conclusion that Congress has neither the inclination nor the institutional capacity to play an active and meaningful foreign policy role.[1] However, even before Congress' recent "resurgence"[2] one set of foreign policy issues that consistently aroused widespread attention on Capitol Hill concerned American diplomatic, military, and economic support of the state of Israel. The apparent preoccupation of Congress

---

[1] See, for example, Robert Dahl, *Congress and Foreign Policy* (New York, 1950); James A. Robinson, *Congress and Foreign Policy Making*, rev. ed. (Homewood, Ill., 1967); Holbert N. Carrol, *The House of Representatives and Foreign Affairs*, rev. ed. (Boston, 1966); Holbert N. Carrol, "The Congress and National Security Policy," in David Truman (ed.), *The Congress and America's Future*, rev. ed. (Englewood Cliffs, N.J., 1973), pp. 150–175; Roger Hilsman, *The Politics of Policy-Making in Defense and Foreign Affairs* (New York, 1971); Michael K. O'Leary, *The Politics of American Foreign Aid* (New York, 1967).

[2] Analyses of this "phenomenon" and its effects on governmental policy include: John Manley, "The Rise of Congress in Foreign Policy-Making," *The Annals*, 397 (September 1971), 60–70; Leslie Gelb and Anthony Lake, "Congress: Politics and Bad Policy," *Foreign Policy*, no. 2 (Fall 1975), 232–238; Robert A. Pastor, "Congress' Impact on Latin America: Is There a Madness in the Method?" *Commission on the Organization of the Government for the Conduct of Foreign Policy, Appendices*, Vol. 3 (Washington, D.C., June 1975), pp. 259–272; Arthur S. Miller, "Congress and Foreign Policy," in Andrew M. Scott and Earle Wallace (eds.), *Politics, U.S.A.: Cases on the American Democratic Process*, 4th ed. (New York, 1974), pp. 516–523; Aage Clausen, *How Congressmen Decide: A Policy Focus* (New York, 1973). In addition, there are several analysts who maintain that Congress' role in the foreign policy pro-

---

ROBERT H. TRICE is assistant professor of political science and program advisor for Near and Middle East Studies at The Ohio State University. He is the author of *Interest Groups and the Foreign Policy Process*.

with legislation that affected Israel's interests was treated by many scholars[3] as the exception which proved the general rule of congressional passivity in matters of foreign affairs. It was generally argued that congressional interest in Israel was somehow "different"; that it reflected more the reality of the domestic political environment within which foreign policy is made than other sets of issues. Congress was seen as "pro-Israeli" for a variety of intuitively satisfying but empirically unexplored reasons, and the issue was generally closed at that point. The Arab-Israeli conflict, however, is no longer the unique case of congressional interest in foreign policy. A series of major congressional initiatives—beginning with the Cooper-Church amendment and the War Powers Act, and extending through the recent Senate investigations of the activities of multinational corporations and American intelligence agencies —clearly demonstrate that Congress has staked out for itself a major role in the foreign policy process.

With some important exceptions,[4] congressional behavior on foreign policy issues still remains largely uninvestigated. The paucity of systematic research has resulted in considerable speculation—and much confusion—concerning the nature and sources of congressional foreign policy behavior. Such misunderstanding is certainly the case with regard to congressional actions pertaining to the Arab-Israeli conflict. This study seeks to increase our understanding of congressional involvement in foreign policy by analyzing in some detail the vot-

---

cess has been consistently underestimated. See Cecil V. Crabb, Jr., *American Foreign Policy in the Nuclear Age* (New York, 1965); Ronald C. Moe and Steven C. Teel, "Congress as Policy Maker: A Necessary Reappraisal," *Political Science Quarterly*, 85 (September 1970), 463–467; and Stan A. Taylor, "Congressional Resurgence," in Martin B. Hickman (ed.), *Problems of American Foreign Policy*, 2d ed. (Beverly Hills, Calif., 1975), pp. 106–118.

[3] See, for example, Charles Peters, "Lobbies and Their Influence on Government," in Charles Peters and James Fallows (eds.), *The System: The Five Branches of American Government* (New York, 1976), pp. 137–179; Bernard C. Cohen, *The Impact of Non-Governmental Groups on Foreign Policy* (Boston, 1959); Dahl, *Congress*, p. 42; William R. Polk, *The United States and the Arab World*, rev. ed. (Cambridge, Mass., 1969), p. 264; Francis O. Wilcox, *Congress, the Executive and Foreign Policy* (New York, 1971), pp. 137–141.

[4] Some of the major exceptions are Aage R. Clausen and Carl E. Van Horn, "Policy Trends in Congress and Partisan Realignment," paper presented at the September 1974 Annual Meeting of the American Political Science Association, Chicago; Herbert B. Asher and Herbert F. Weisberg, "Congressional Voting Change: A Longitudinal Study of Voting on Selected Issues," paper presented at the Seminar on Mathematical Models of Congress, Aspen, Colorado, June 1974; Mark Kesselman, "Presidential Leadership in Congress on Foreign Policy," *Midwest Journal of Political Science*, 5 (August 1961), 284–289; Mark Kesselman, "Presidential Leadership in Congress on Foreign Policy: A Replication of a Hypothesis," *Midwest Journal of Political Science*, 9 (May 1965), 401–406; Charles M. Tidmarch and Charles M. Sabatt, "Presidential Leadership Change and Foreign Policy Roll-Call Voting in the U.S. Senate," *Western Political Quarterly*, 25 (December 1972), 613–625; Stephen Cobb, "The Impact of Defense Spending on Senatorial Voting Behavior," in Patrick McGowan (ed.), *Sage Yearbook of Foreign Policy Studies*, Vol. I (Beverly Hills, Calif., 1973), pp. 135–159; and David Garnham, "The Politics of U.S. Middle East Policy Making," *Jerusalem Journal of International Relations*, 2 (forthcoming, 1977).

ing behavior of the dominant house of Congress in foreign affairs—the U. S. Senate—on a set of highly volatile issues directly related to the Arab-Israeli conflict during the 1970–1973 period. Seven roll-call votes relevant to Israel's interests are analyzed. Each of the 127 senators who served during at least a portion of the period are assigned a "support for Israel" score on the basis of their voting records on relevant bills. The results of this first analysis are that the Senate was consistently and overwhelmingly supportive of Israeli interests during the period, and that Democrats and Republicans were equally supportive. Analysis of the potential effects of turnover show that the base of support for Israel remained largely intact during the period, although there was some erosion of support among a sizable minority of incoming senators.

The seventy-five senators who were in office for the entire period were found to be slightly more supportive than the fifty-two senators who served during only a portion of the time. Regional comparisons supported the long-standing notions that the bases of pro-Israel support are strongest in the heavily industrialized, urbanized states of the Northeast, and weaker in the South and less populous heartland of the country.

Congressmen can play at least three different roles in the policy-making process, all of which help determine the potential impact of domestic political forces on foreign policy. First, congressmen frequently formulate and express opinions on foreign affairs without any specific guidance or consultation with constituents or interest groups. In such instances, they present their preferences as individual members of the articulate public, and therefore play a more or less independent public opinion role.[5] Their second role is the more traditional and representative one as conduits for the opinions of their constituents. Third, chairmen and senior members of relevant committees, such as Foreign Relations, Armed Services, and Government Operations, represent the institutional interests of Congress in the foreign policy arena. In all these cases, congressmen provide a channel for injecting nongovernmental concerns and interests into foreign policy debates. On some issues, particularly those involving the expenditure of funds, Congress can exert a major, direct influence on foreign policy decisions. However, on other issues, such as those concerned with establishing broad foreign policy objectives or with resolving more narrowly defined diplomatic questions, Congress must gain access to and support from executive branch officials if it is to affect policy. As Congress' ability to have a direct impact on foreign policy varies from issue to issue, so will the effectiveness of nongovernmental actors who depend on congressmen as the media for translating their policy preferences into governmental decisions.

Any organized segment of society may seek support for its position on a foreign policy issue from a variety of government officials. However, the most common and most accessible allies that domestic groups can garner are members of Congress. The relationship between congressional behavior, on the one hand,

---

[5] Bernard C. Cohen, *The Public's Impact on Foreign Policy* (Boston, 1973), p. 114.

and public opinion and domestic interest group activities, on the other, is circular. Congressional support is important because of its legitimizing and sanctioning effects for interest-group activities, and the direct access to the media and to executive branch officials enjoyed by congressmen. An unreceptive Congress creates severe handicaps for domestic groups seeking to affect foreign policy. If an interest group is forced to rely solely on its own political resources, it will rarely be able to marshal the support from the mass and articulate publics necessary to play an effective policy-making role. But the ability to successfully petition Congress for support is likely to be closely tied to an ability to obtain widespread support from the articulate public. One generally does not come without the other. Foreign policy interest groups are dependent on Congress, as they are dependent on the mass media, for amplifying and disseminating their policy preferences in a manner that is beyond the group's own capabilities. If Congress is receptive to the arguments of domestic actors, the legitimacy of those arguments in the eyes of both the mass public and executive branch officials is likely to be enhanced. However, if Congress fails to provide its amplifying and legitimizing services, a domestic group is likely to find itself isolated in a political environment that is either apathetic or hostile toward its policy objectives. In this study we will be interested in determining the nature and sources of congressional behavior with regard to those domestic forces that favor strong American support for the state of Israel.

SENATE SUPPORT: AN OVERVIEW

The first task is to describe the votes to be analyzed and to provide an overview of the voting patterns of all 127 senators who served during at least a part of the time between 1970 and the end of 1973. We will then shift our focus to the seventy-five senators who served for the entire period. We can thus determine the general strength of senatorial support for Israel over time, examine the effects of turnover on senatorial voting patterns, and make interparty and interregional comparisons of support. Two primary criteria guided the selection of votes: (1) that each bill, amendment, or motion address itself to an identifiable issue directly relevant to the Arab-Israeli conflict; (2) that the bill be clear and specific enough to allow us to impute support or nonsupport for Israel's interests to senators on the basis of their votes. The frequent practice of tying different issues together in one bill eliminated many roll-call votes from consideration. Seven votes were ultimately selected from those listed in the *Congressional Quarterly Almanac* for the years 1969 through 1974. The selected votes extend over the period from June 1970 through December 1973, with at least two votes taken from each of the ninety-first, ninety-second, and ninety-third Congresses. A brief description of the substance, and the votes on the seven bills are presented in Table 1.

Two findings can be drawn from the vote totals presented in Table 1. The first is that by any reasonable standard the U. S. Senate must be judged to have been consistently and overwhelmingly supportive of Israeli interests during the period from 1970 through 1973. Of the 551 total votes cast on the seven roll calls, 463 (84 percent) could be considered supportive of Israel, while only 88 (16 percent) could be considered unsupportive. The second finding is that there was no difference between Democrats and Republicans in the degree of active support shown for Israel. Democrats cast 258 (84 percent) of 306 total votes in support of Israel. The Republican vote distribution was identical, with 205 (84 percent) of 245 total votes supporting Israeli interests. Thus, not only was the **Senate as a whole strongly** "pro-Israel" during the 1970–1973 period, but the base of this support was equally strong among both Democrats and Republicans, if we look only at votes cast and ignore absences and abstentions.

An index of support for Israel was calculated for the 127 senators who voted on one or more of the bills.[6] Individual support scores range from a low of 1.00, indicating no support for Israeli positions, to a high of 3.00 representing total support for Israeli interests on all votes during a given senator's tenure. The mean score is a very high 2.58 out of a possible 3.00. Of the 127 senators, 41 (32 percent) had the highest possible support score, while only 3—Williams (R-Del.), Abourezk (D-S.D.), and Scott (R-Va.)—had the lowest possible score.

There were twenty-seven seat changes in the Senate between June 1970 and the end of 1973. During that period, eleven (41 percent) of the twenty-seven new occupants tended to be less supportive of Israel than the men they replaced, ten (37 percent) tended to be more supportive, and six (22 percent) had support scores identical with those of the previous occupants. The implication of this finding is that the base of support for Israel remained largely intact during the 1970–1973 period, although there did appear to be some erosion of support among a sizable minority of incoming senators.

These characterizations are important in understanding the breadth of senatorial support of Israel, and in examining the general stability of senatorial sentiments from a longitudinal perspective. However, the relatively high rate of turnover in the Senate results in a small number of votes for many senators, thereby creating the possibility that some of the individual support scores do not necessarily reflect "true" policy preferences but are rather artifacts of a small sample of votes.

In order to test the validity of the characterizations derived in this overview, and to examine the behavior of the individuals who consistently fought for or against pro-Israel legislation, we shall now shift our focus to that subset of seventy-five senators who were in office during the entire 1970–1973 period. It

[6] This simple index was constructed by assigning a value of 3.0 to each vote which was considered openly supportive of Israel, a value of 2.0 for abstentions or absences, and a value of 1.0 for votes which were nonsupportive of Israel. The vote scores were summed for each senator and then divided by the number of votes that occurred during each senator's tenure. Division of the total score was necessary to make the individual scores comparable in light of the fact that different senators voted on varying numbers of bills.

is this group which is of primary interest here. Each individual had the same opportunities to express his policy preferences on at least seven different roll-call votes. Thus, the voting records of all of the senators in this group are directly comparable, and are more likely to reflect genuine opinions on Middle East issues than the scores for senators who only served during a portion of the three-and-a-half-year period. In this section we shall briefly describe the individual, party, and regional patterns of support for Israel among these seventy-five senators.

The depth of active support for Israel in the U. S. Senate is apparent from Table 2, which ranks each of the seventy-five senators on the 1.00 through 3.00 scale. The mean score for the group of seventy-five (2.59) is very close to the mean for the fifty-two senators who served during only a portion of the 1970–1973 period (2.56). The senators have been clustered into five groupings that reflect relative degrees of voting support for Israel. More than a quarter ($N = 19$) of the senators received the highest possible score and were placed in the "most supportive" group, while 44 percent ($N = 33$) had scores at or above the mean and were categorized as "very supportive." That almost 70 percent of the senators in office from the ninety-first through ninety-third Congress were such loyal supporters of Israel reflects an apparent consensus and consistency over time that is stronger than the similar trends found in voting analyses of other foreign policy issues.[7] Included in the "moderately supportive" group are eleven (14.7 percent) senators with scores that are above the "neutral" score of 2.00 yet below the senatorial average. The scores for the moderately supportive group, which range between 2.14 and 2.43, indicate that while these individuals were generally supportive, each "defected" from a pro-Israel stance to either a neutral or hostile position on at least two of the seven votes.

The eight (10.7 percent) senators in the "neutral/occasionally supportive"

[7] John Kingdon, *Congressmen's Voting Decisions* (New York, 1973); Asher and Weisberg, "Congressional Voting Change."

TABLE 1

Total Senate and Party Support for Israel on Selected Votes, 1970–1973

	Total Senate		Democrats		Republicans	
	Support-ive N	Non-Support-ive N	Support-ive N	Non-Support-ive N	Support-ive N	Non-Support-ive N
VOTE 1 H. R. 15628, June 1970. Williams (R.-Del.) amendment jeopardizing sale of Phantom jets to Israel.	59	1	36	0	23	1

TABLE 1 (*continued*)

	Total Senate		Democrats		Republicans	
	Support-ive N	Non-Support-ive N	Support-ive N	Non-Support-ive N	Support-ive N	Non-Support-ive N
VOTE 2 H. R. 1911, December 1970. Church (D.-Idaho) motion to table Williams (R.-Del.) amendment prohibiting use of foreign assistance funds for ground combat troops in Israel.	60	20	40	7	20	13
VOTE 3 H. R. 1173, November 1971. Jackson (D.-Wash.) amendment making $500 million in credit available to Israel for weapons purchases.	82	14	45	8	37	6
VOTE 4 H. R. 15495, September 1972. Defense Procurement Authoriz- ation extending president's author- ity to send aircraft and equipment to Israel.	73	5	42	5	31	0
VOTE 5 H. R. 11771, December 1973. Fong (R.-Hawaii) amendment adding $36.5 million for assistance to Soviet refugees, pri- marily Jewish immigrants to Israel.	62	25	31	16	31	9
VOTE 6 H. R. 11088A, December 1973. Humphrey (D.-Minn.) motion to table an amendment by Helms (R.-N.C.) requiring all aid to Israel to be in the form of loans rather than grants.	61	14	43	6	18	8
VOTE 7 H. R. 11088, December 1973. Israeli Emergency Assistance bill authorizing $2.2 billion for American security assistance to Israel.	66	9	21	6	45	3
TOTALS	463 84%	88 16%	258 84%	48 16%	205 84%	40 16%

category are all well below the mean for the Senate as a whole, with scores clustering around the neutral score of 2.00 or slightly below. The scores for people in this group tend to indicate either frequent absence during relevant votes, as was the case for Senators Cotton (R-N.H.) and Bellmon (R-Okla.), or a very mixed record of either active support or active nonsupport depending on the political substance of the vote. This issue-specific pattern of support or lack of support for the Israeli position characterized the voting behavior of Senators Burdick (D-N.D.), Metcalf (D-Mont.), Fannin (R-Ariz.), and Hansen (R-Wyo). On balance, however, these senators voted against pro-Israel policy preferences

TABLE 2

Individual Rankings of Support for Israel Among U. S. Senators,
1970-1973 (N = 75)

	Senator	Party	State	
Most Supportive N = 19 25.3%	Allan	D	Ala.	Score 3.00
	Bayh	D	Ind.	
	Case	R	N. J.	
	Eagleton	D	Mo.	
	Jackson	D	Wash.	
	Javits	R	N. Y.	
	Magnuson	D	Wash.	
	Nelson	D	Wis.	
	Packwood	R	Oreg.	
	Pastore	D	R. I.	
	Percy	R	Ill.	
	Proxmire	D	Wis.	
	Ribicoff	D	Conn.	
	Schweiker	R	Penn.	
	Scott	R	Penn.	
	Stevens	D	Alaska	
	Thurmond	R	S. C.	
	Tower	R	Tex.	
	Williams	D	N. J.	
Strongly Supportive N = 34 45.3%	Bible	D	Nev.	Score 2.86
	Byrd	D	W. Va.	
	Cannon	D	Nev.	
	Cook	R	Ky.	
	Dominick	R	Colo.	
	Fong	R	Hawaii	
	Hartke	D	Ind.	
	Kennedy	D	Mass.	
	Mathias	R	Md.	
	McGee	D	Wyo.	
	Mondale	D	Minn.	
	Muskie	D	Me.	
	Pell	D	R. I.	
	Sparkman	D	Ala.	
	Symington	D	Mo.	

TABLE 2 *(continued)*

	Senator	Party	State	
Strongly Supportive *(continued)*	Baker	R	Tenn.	
	Brooke	R	Mass.	
	Byrd	Ind (D)	Va.	
	Dole	R	Kan.	
	Griffin	R	Mich.	
	Gurney	R	Fla.	
	Hart	D	Mich.	Score 2.71
	Inouye	D	Hawaii	
	McGovern	D	S. D.	
	McIntyre	D	N. H.	
	Montoya	D	N. M.	
	Moss	R	Utah	
	Pearson	R	Kan.	
	Randolph	D	W. Va.	
	Church	D	Idaho	
	Cranston	D	Calif.	Score 2.57
	Hollings	D	S. C.	
	Long	D	La.	
	Talmadge	D	Ga.	
Moderately Supportive	Curtis	R	Nebr.	
	Eastland	D	Miss.	Score 2.43
	Hruska	R	Nebr.	
	Stennis	D	Miss.	
	Young	R	N. D.	
N = 11 14.7%	Bennett	R	Utah	Score 2.29
	Hughes	D	Iowa	
	Aiken	R	Ver.	
	Ervin	D	N. C.	Score 2.14
	Goldwater	R	Ariz.	
	McClellen	D	Ark.	
Neutral/ Occasionally Supportive	Cotton	R	N. H.	
	Bellmon	R	Okla.	Score 2.00
	Gravel	D	Alaska	
	Saxbe	R	Ohio	
N = 8 10.7%	Burdick	D	N. D.	Score 1.86
	Metcalf	D	Mont.	
	Fannin	R	Ariz.	Score 1.71
	Hansen	R	Wyo.	
Unsupportive *N* = 3 4.0%	Hatfield	R	Oreg.	Score 1.29
	Mansfield	D	Mont.	
	Fulbright	D	Ark.	Score 1.14

more often than they voted in favor of Israeli interests. Only three senators (4 percent) were in the "unsupportive" category, which is the lowest support score group. It should be noted, however, that none of the senators who served during the entire 1970–1973 period voted against Israeli interests on all seven votes.

Senators Hatfield (R-Oreg.) and Mansfield (D-Mont.) voted contrary to the pro-Israeli position on all occasions except the Defense Procurement Authorization bill, when they voted with the majority. Senator Fulbright (D-Ark.) did not vote on that same bill and took an unsupportive voting stance on all the others.[8]

If we are looking for the bedrock of senatorial support for Israel in the U.S. Senate we will find it among the group of fifty-two senators listed in the most supportive and strongly supportive categories in Table 2. Differences in political commitment to Israel among most senators are only matters of degree on the pro-Israel side of the continuum running from unwavering support through neutrality to open antipathy. Only eleven senators can be placed on the neutral-to-unsupportive end of that continuum. Such a top-heavy clustering of supporters among the nucleus of the Senate raises questions concerning the likely success of efforts to uncover the primary sources of congressional support for Israel. However, before testing a number of the more frequently advanced propositions used to explain why senators vote as they do on Israel-related issues, let us briefly examine interparty and interregional differences in support.

Our earlier conclusion that both parties were equally supportive of Israel for the most part applies to the smaller group as well. However, on the average, Democrats who served during the entire 1970–1973 period were slightly more supportive (mean score = 2.93) than their Republican counterparts (2.55).[9] Table 3 groups senators by state and region, and permits interregional comparisons of support to be made. The mean support score for all senators in a given region indicates how the "average" senator from that region voted, and can be compared with the mean score of 2.59 for all seventy-five senators. Two points can be drawn from Table 3. First, in an absolute sense, support for Israel is very strong among senators from most regions. All average scores are above the value of 2.00 which represents the "neutral" position between no support and all-out support for Israel. Second, in relative terms, however, there are meaningful differences among regions. The rankings in Table 3 conform closely to the long-standing notions that the bases of pro-Israel support are strongest in the heavily industrialized, urbanized states of the Northeast, and weaker in the South and the less populous heartland of the country. Particularly striking is the weak sup-

---

[8] The fact that the three senators who showed the least support for Israel on all other issues either voted for or did not vote on the Defense Procurement Authorization bill raises questions concerning the "purity" of the vote for the purposes of imputing support or nonsupport for Israel. The bill was retained in the analysis because the section pertaining to extension of the president's authority to send military equipment to Israel dominated floor discussion and provoked considerable controversy among senators, both on and off the floor.

[9] One reason for the slippage between the appearance of equal support from Democrats and Republicans for the Senate as a whole, and the small but noticeable difference among the group of seventy-five, is that for the latter group absences and abstentions are assigned a "neutral" value of 2.0 in the calculation of individual support scores. For the larger group only recorded votes of support or nonsupport were used to calculate party support. As a group, Republicans had a higher rate of absenteeism on legislation relevant to Israel than their Democratic colleagues.

TABLE 3

Average Support Scores for Israel by Region, 1970–1973 (N = 75)

Rank	Region*	N States	N Senators	Average Support Score
1	Middle Atlantic	4	5	3.00
2	East North Central	5	8	2.80
3	New England	6	9	2.69
4	Border States	4	5	2.66
5	External States	2	4	2.64
6	Pacific States	3	5	2.57
6	West North Central	7	11	2.57
8	Solid South	11	15	2.53
9	Mountain States	8	13	2.01
Totals		50	75	2.59

*All states are grouped using ICPR conventions except Tennessee, which I have included in the Solid South rather than among the Border states.

port for Israel shown by senators from the Rocky Mountain states relative to all other regions.

SOURCES OF SUPPORT FOR ISRAEL: SOME COMMON VIEWS

Thus far the empirical evidence has supported the opinion of most Congress watchers that support for Israel in the Senate is both widespread and strong. A number of arguments are commonly used to explain why some senators are more likely to vote in favor of Israel's interests than others. Our goal is to uncover whatever it is about Israel-related issues that consistently produces such a strong voting coalition among such a disparate group as the U.S. Senate, and why some members tend to join this coalition and others do not. We have already seen that while Democrats on the average were marginally more sympathetic to Israel, party differences offer little help in explaining variations in levels of support. Regional differences, however, were more apparent. But, regional differences tell us little in and of themselves, and beg the more interesting question: *Why* are senators from the Rocky Mountain states less likely to support Israel than those, say, from the Northeast?

We shall explore three factors commonly assumed to affect the voting behavior of congressmen on Israel-related issues: (1) ideological differences; (2) the Jewish vote; and (3) Jewish monetary support for selected senators.[10] We

[10] Other possible explanations, such as presidential leadership and presidential loyalty, are not explored here owing to the fact that there was no change of administration during the 1970–1973 period, and because President Nixon took a policy stand on only three of the seven votes analyzed. Furthermore, because of the small differences in support between parties, it is likely that the explanatory utility of these two models would be severely limited.

will begin by using cross-tabulation and Pearson product-moment correlation techniques to examine the association of each of these variables with the voting records of the seventy-five senators who held office during the entire 1970–1973 period. Then we shall employ step-wise regression analysis to test the collective explanatory ability of the three factors. In all of the analyses, the dependent variable is the "Individual Support for Israel" index score computed for each senator.

Ideological Differences

Two antithetical propositions can be derived from the general argument that basic ideological differences among senators are related to differences in their voting records on Israel-related issues. A common theme in journalistic analyses is that the greatest degree of commitment to Israel is found among domestic liberals in Congress.[11] It is argued that liberals tend to support Israel for one or more of the following reasons: because they are more likely to agree and empathize with the characterization of Israel as the "underdog" in the Arab-Israeli conflict; because they are more likely to carry feelings of Western guilt for the holocaust of World War II; or because they are more likely to come from heavily industrialized, urbanized states where there are significant concentrations of Jews who make their policy preferences clearly known to their representatives in Congress.

The argument is sometimes made that domestic conservatives provide the heart of congressional support for Israel.[12] It is assumed that conservatives favor Israeli interests for one or more of several reasons: because they are more likely to view Israel as an "outpost of democracy" among the "autocratic" Arab states in the Middle East; because they are more likely to see continuing support of Israel as a benchmark of American resolve to meet political and military commitments to allies and friendly states; or because they are more likely to see a militarily strong Israel as an effective check to Soviet expansion into the Middle East and the Indian Ocean.

Two propositions emerge from these contending perspectives:

> Proposition 1. The more liberal a given senator's voting record on other issues, the more supportive he will be of Israel's interests.
> Proposition 2. The more conservative a given senator's voting record on other issues, the more supportive he will be of Israel's interests.

Our measures of the variables "liberal" and "conservative" are the averages of the annual ratings given each senator during the period from 1970–1973 by

---

[11] See, for example, Gil Carl Alroy, "Patterns in Hostility," in Alroy (ed.), *Attitudes Toward Jewish Statehood in the Arab World* (New York, 1971), p. 3; Polk, *United States and the Arab World*, p. 264.

[12] See Mary Barberis, "The Arab-Israeli Battle on Capitol Hill," *The Virginia Quarterly Review*, 52 (Spring 1976), 206 ff.

the AFL-CIO's Committee on Political Education (COPE) and the Americans for Constitutional Action (ACA), respectively.[13] Proposition 1 is supported by the evidence while Proposition 2 is not so supported.[14] There is a weak to moderate positive relationship ($r = .31$) between the ratings assigned to senators by the liberal interest group, COPE, and their support for Israel scores. Thus, senators with more liberal voting records show a tendency to support Israel more than those with less liberal voting records. There is, however, a weak negative relationship ($r = -.18$) between ratings on the conservative ACA's scale and pro-Israel voting records. That is, senators with high marks from the ACA show a slight tendency to be less supportive of Israel's interests than those with lower ratings.

Thus, the correlation analyses provide evidence to show that one important source of many senators' pro-Israeli policy preferences may derive from a more general—and liberal—political philosophy. The results, however, also show that caution must be exercised in imputing meaning to the relationship between liberal voting records in general and pro-Israel voting in particular. First, the strength of association between the two sets of variables is at best moderate, in the case of COPE, and is weak when the ACA ratings are used. The clear implication is that these crude ratings of general political inclinations provide only a partial guide to understanding why some senators are more likely than others to support Israel. The relatively weak correlation coefficients indicate that there are some conservative senators for which the generalization simply does not hold. Second, there is the potential problem that liberal senators may vote for pro-Israeli legislation, not out of any strong personal conviction, but because they are more likely to come from industrialized, urbanized states where there are significant concentrations of politically aware and organized Jews. Following this logic, these senators may be responding to direct demands from

[13] The average annual ratings given each senator by four different groups were calculated. Three of the groups that monitor congressional voting consider themselves advocates of a liberal political philosophy: Americans for Democratic Action (ADA); the AFL-CIO's Committee on Political Education (COPE); and the National Farmers Union (NFU). The Americans for Constitutional Action (ACA) supports conservative political ideals. The ADA, COPE, and NFU ratings were very consistent with one another, with correlation coefficients of .9 or better among all three, while there was a very strong negative relationship ($r = -.95$ or higher) between the ACA ratings and the ratings given by other groups. Therefore we can be confident that the measures of liberalism and conservatism tap very different political values, and that senators with high scores on one scale are unlikely to have high scores on the other.

[14] We will assign the strength of association between selected variables in terms of product-moment correlation coefficients as follows:

$r = .0 -.10$ no relationship
$r = .11-.25$ weak relationship
$r = .26-.50$ moderate relationship
$r = .51-1.00$ strong relationship

significant at .05 level or better.

influential sets of constituents, and may vote in favor of Israel's interests irrespective of their own individual policy preferences. In order to explore this possibility we shall now consider the relationship between the population distribution of Jews across states and senatorial voting behavior.

The Jewish Vote

One of the most common explanations of the pro-Israel slant in congressional voting patterns found in the popular literature is the impact of the "Jewish vote."[15] According to the standard argument, Jews offset their numerical weakness as a voting group because they, more than any other ethnic minority, tend to vote as a bloc. It is contended that legislation that in any way affects Israel is of high salience to American Jews, and they are quick to articulate their policy preferences to their representatives in Congress. Because congressmen seek to garner and maintain the support of their Jewish constituents they will tend to vote in accordance with the policy demands of Jewish community leaders. Over time, congressmen come to anticipate the reactions of organized Jewry to their position on relevant legislation. As congressmen become more sensitive to the predictable responses of Jewish constituents, direct pressures by Jewish voters become less necessary, and the support of congressmen from states with sizable Jewish populations for pro-Israeli legislation becomes more automatic.

Previous studies of Jewish voting patterns in presidential elections have found that Jews do tend to vote as a bloc, but party differences rather than the policy stands of the candidates appear to be the most important factors in determining the Jewish vote.[16] At least at the national level, a Democratic candidate is almost always sure to do better than a Republican among Jewish voters. This finding held even for the 1972 landslide victory of Richard Nixon, who is generally considered to have been one of the strongest supporters of Israel ever to hold office. In this section we want to see whether or not the number of Jewish voters in a given state appears to constrain the voting behavior of its senators. If the assumptions of the "Jewish vote" argument are valid we would expect senators from states with sizable Jewish populations to be more sensitive to the policy preferences of Jewish lobby groups than those with relatively few Jewish constituents. We will examine the following proposition:

---

[15] See, for example, Saad Ibrahim, "American Domestic Forces and the October War," *Journal of Palestine Studies*, IV (Autumn 1974), 60, 63; an advertisement in the *Wall Street Journal*, March 14, 1974, entitled "Do Arms for Israel Mean No Gasoline for Americans?" placed by Alfred Lilienthal; Barberis, "Arab-Israeli Battle," p. 209; Odeh Abu Rudeneh, "The Jewish Factor in U. S. Politics," *Journal of Palestine Studies*, I (Summer 1972), 96 ff. For more systematic analyses of the Jewish vote, see Mark R. Levy and Michael S. Kramer, "The Ethnic Vote," in Thomas A. Reilly and Michael W. Sigall (eds.), *New Patterns in American Politics* (New York, 1975), pp. 111–140; and Milton Himmelfarb, "The Jewish Vote (Again)," *Commentary*, 55 (June 1973), 81–85.

[16] Levy and Kramer, "The Ethnic Vote."

TABLE 4

Estimated Jewish Population in the United States,
by Selected States, 1971

State	Estimated Jewish Population	Total Population	Estimated Jewish Percent of Total
New York	2,535,870	18,391,000	13.79
California	721,045	20,223,000	3.56
Pennsylvania	471,930	11,879,000	3.97
New Jersey	412,465	7,300,000	5.65
Illinois	284,285	11,196,000	2.54
Massachusetts	267,440	5,758,000	4.64
Florida	260,000	7,041,000	3.69
Maryland	187,110	4,000,000	4.68
Ohio	158,560	10,778,000	1.47
Connecticut	105,000	3,081,000	3.41
Michigan	93,530	8,997,000	1.04
Missouri	84,325	4,749,000	1.78

SOURCE: Morris Fine and Milton Himmelfarb, *American Jewish Yearbook, 1972* (New York, 1972), pp. 386–387.

Proposition 3. The larger the Jewish constituency for a given senator, the more supportive he will be of Israel's interests.

Table 4 lists the states with the largest absolute numbers of Jewish residents, and also shows the relative size of the Jewish population for these states. The two most obvious facts reflected in Table 4 are, first, that the bulk of American Jewry is concentrated in a relatively small number of states, and, second, that even in these states Jews generally comprise a relatively small percentage of the total population. Roughly 93 percent of the total estimated Jewish population of 6,060,000 in the United States in 1971 resided in the twelve states listed in Table 4. The question is whether or not higher voting turnout rates among Jews relative to other ethnic minorities, and a generally higher level of political involvement,[17] have succeeded in making their senatorial representatives more responsive to their foreign policy preferences than senators with fewer Jewish constituents.

There is a moderate positive relationship ($r = .30$) between the relative size of a senator's Jewish constituency and his support score. Thus, senators that come from states with relatively larger percentages of Jewish voters are, on the whole, more likely to vote in favor of Israel's interests than are those with smaller Jewish constituencies. What is remarkable about the apparent impact of Jewish voters on their elected representatives is that, with the exception of New York, the size of even the largest Jewish populations do not exceed 6 percent of the

[17] Charles R. Wright and Herbert Hyman, "Voluntary Memberships of American Adults: Evidence from National Sample Surveys," *American Sociological Review*, XXIII (June 1958), 287.

total population of any state. Of the seventy-five senators who served during the entire 1970–1973 period, sixteen came from states where Jews comprised more than 1.7 percent of the total population. Every one of these sixteen senators was in either the strongly supportive or most supportive group listed in Table 2. The implicaton is that very small Jewish populations—in some cases as small as 2 percent or less of a state's total population—were capable of generating and maintaining consistent support for their policy preferences from their respective senators. However, while senators that come from states with Jewish populations of 1.6 percent or less are distributed more evenly across the support categories than those with more than 1.6 percent Jewish constituents, many strong supporters can be found among senators with virtually no Jewish constituents. Almost 80 percent ($N = 27$) of the senators in the strongly supportive category, and more than 50 percent ($N = 10$) in the most supportive group came from states where Jews make up 1.6 percent or less of the population.

All the senators in the unsupportive, neutral and occasionally supportive, and moderately supportive categories had Jewish constituences representing 1.6 percent or less of the state's population. However, as was the case with the finding that liberals tended to support Israel more than conservatives, the "Jewish vote" provides an explanation for the voting behavior of only a limited number of senators. The size of the Jewish constituency does not account for the many senators—such as Allan of Alabama (estimated percent Jewish population .26 percent), Packwood of Oregon (.41 percent), Stevens of Alaska (.10 percent) or Jackson and Magnuson of Washington (.44 percent)—who displayed unwavering support for Israel despite the fact that they had virtually no Jewish voters to satisfy.

Jewish Financial Support

Critics of pro-Israel interest group activities frequently charge that American Jews extend their political leverage well beyond the limits of their voting strength by means of their willingess to give generous financial assistance to congressmen who are sympathetic to their policy preferences.[18] There is some

[18] For example, see the advertisement "Is America's Foreign Policy For Sale?" placed by the American Palestine Committee in the *Washington Post*, June 13, 1975; the *National Observer*, June 21, 1975; and the *Christian Science Monitor*, June 19, 1975. The advertisement reads in part as follows: "We regard this Zionist payment of money to American Legislators as a deliberate bribe to influence American foreign policy. It is a scandal that dwarfs Watergate. It involves the voting of billions of dollars of the taxpayers' money to a foreign government, with no strings attached. . . .

Whether called a free "study trip to Israel" or a campaign contribution, or an honorarium for speaking at an Israel Bond rally, it is still a bribe to the legislator for using his influence on behalf of a foreign power—and a bribe by any other name is still a bribe!"

A number of scholars have discussed Jewish campaign contributions in less passionate and critical terms. See, for example, Barberis, "Arab-Israeli Battle," p. 209, and William Quandt, "United States Policy in the Middle East," in Paul Hammond and Sidney Alexander (eds.), *Political Dynamics in the Middle East* (New York, 1972), p. 516.

TABLE 5

Reported Honoraria to Selected Senators from Jewish Organizations, 1970–1973

Senator	Reported Honoraria
Jackson (D-Wash.)	$29,250
McGee (D-Wyo.)	17,125
Bayh (D-Ind.)	15,900
Ribicoff (D-Conn.)	10,900
Muskie (D-Me.)	10,500
Gravel (D-Alaska)	8,525
Baker (R-Tenn.)	7,350
Proxmire (D-Wis.)	6,425
Packwood (R-Oreg.)	3,550
Javits (R-N. Y.)	3,500
Pastore (D-R. I.)	3,000
Saxbe (R-Ohio)	3,000
Scott (R-Pa.)	2,000

evidence to support the contention that Jews as a group do contribute heavily to congressional and presidential campaigns.[19] However, it is not possible to determine accurately the size or the recipients of these campaign contributions. There is, however, another common form of financial assistance that is measureable, and that may serve as a surrogate for campaign contributions. It is an accepted practice for domestic interest groups to assist supporters in Congress by inviting the congressmen to speak to their conventions or working groups, and to pay these speakers honoraria for their remarks. Over time these honoraria, which generally range from $500 to $1500 per engagement, can add up to reasonably large sums of money. These open payments are matters of public record.

Table 5 lists some of the senators who received sizable sums during the 1970–1973 period. The question is whether such financial assistance affects the voting behavior of the recipients. There is, of course, a "chicken and egg" problem in imputing substantive meaning to the results of any correlation analysis, and this analysis is no exception. Critics of the pro-Israel lobby may argue that giving senators honoraria amounts to little more than an attempt to buy support for Israel. Supporters of pro-Israel group efforts, however, may argue that the honoraria represent a perfectly legitimate and widely used means of giving financial backing to those incumbents who have already demonstrated their willingness to vote in favor of Israel's interest. Our purpose here is not to resolve the broader, more important issue of why particular senators receive honoraria, but rather to examine the following proposition:

Proposition 4. There will be a positive association between the total amount of honoraria received by a given senator and his support for Israel score.

[19] Rudeneh, "The Jewish Factor," pp. 98–104; David Nes, "Israel and the American Election," *Middle East International*, October 1972, p. 10; *National Report*, IV (January 8, 1972), 62.

All of the publicly reported honoraria received by each senator from Jewish groups during the 1970–1973 period were totaled, and correlated with the senator's individual support score. The proposition is supported by the evidence. There is a moderate positive association ($r = .28$) between the amount of money received by senators for speaking to Jewish groups and their voting records on Israel-related issues. Those senators who received more total money from honoraria showed a moderate tendency to be more supportive of Israel than those who received less.

However, like the other possible sources of support for Israel we have examined, the "money" argument is applicable to only a subset of the senators who held office during the 1970–1973 period, and therefore can serve as only a partial explanation for the widespread support for Israel shown by the Senate as a whole. More than 65 percent ($N = 49$) of the senators reported no honoraria from Jewish groups, including 42 percent ($N = 8$) and 65 percent ($N = 22$) of those in the most supportive and strongly supportive categories, respectively. While it was generally the case that senators in the unsupportive and neutral and occasionally supportive groups were not invited to address Jewish groups, there were two notable exceptions. Senator Mike Gravel (D.-Alaska), who reported more than $8500 in honoraria over the three-and-a-half year period, and Senator William Saxbe (R.-Ohio), who received $3000, were among the eight senators in the neutral and occasionally supportive group. The other sixteen senators who received more than $1500 in honoraria all fell into the most supportive and strongly supportive categories. Thus, while it is correct to conclude from the data that a substantial majority of senators who received the largest sums from Jewish groups were very strong supporters of Israel, one must also note that the bulk of the senators in the strongly supportive and most supportive categories received little or no money from Jewish groups.

A Multivariate Explanation

Most of the common arguments used to explain congressional support for Israel appear to have at least some factual basis. Senators who were either more liberal on domestic issues, or who had relatively larger Jewish constituencies, or who received larger sums in honoraria from Jewish groups showed some tendency to be more supportive of Israel than their colleagues. The only popular notion which was not supported by the evidence was that domestic conservatives were more likely to be stronger supporters of Israel than liberals. However, each of the explanations we examined was found to provide only part of the answer as to why some senators were more likely to vote in favor of Israel's interests than others. The strength of association between the explanatory variables and the support scores was generally in the weak to moderate range, and we could see from both the correlation and cross-tabulation analyses that single explanations did not account for the voting patterns of many senators.

As a final systematic effort to explain individual differences in support

TABLE 6

Multiple Regression of Selected Independent Variables
on Individual Support Scores

Independent Variable	Beta	Simple r
Percent Jewish population	.25	.34
COPE rating	.20	.32
Honoraria	.17	.29

Multiple $r = .44$ $F = 5.82$ with 3 DF
$r^2 = .20$
Adjusted $r^2 = .16$

among senators, we will combine the separate independent variables considered in the correlation analyses into a multiple regression model.[20] Our purpose is to see how much of the variance in voting styles can be explained by the factors we have previously identified. The results should also provide us with an idea of the "explanatory overlap"—the degree to which the different arguments explain the voting behavior of the same subset of senators—among the single-cause arguments found in the literature. Table 6 presents the results of the regression. The three variables in the equation—percent of Jewish population, COPE rating, and total honoraria received from Jewish groups—can account for only about 16 percent of the variance in individual senators' support scores, when adjusted for error. We can see from the standardized regression coefficients (betas) that in relative terms the percent of Jewish population appears to be the most important factor determining any given senator's voting record. However, in absolute terms, none of the three variables is particularly powerful, and the equation as a whole can explain relatively little variance in senatorial support for Israel.

CONCLUSIONS

In this study we have described the strength of senatorial support for Israel during the 1970–1973 period,[21] and examined in detail a few of the factors most commonly cited to explain why some senators are more supportive than others. Our

[20] Because the COPE ratings and ACA ratings were so highly correlated (−.95), inclusion of both variables would have distorted both the variance explained by the equation, and the standardized regression coefficients of the two "independent" variables. Consequently, only the COPE rating has been used in the model presented in Table 6.

[21] Additional roll-call votes indicate that the basic patterns of senatorial support established during the 1970–1973 period were not affected by the October war and its political aftermath. Support for Israel has remained reasonably constant in the post-October war period. For example, the Mondale amendment to the 1975 Continuing Appropriations bill (H. J. Res. 1131) to increase security supporting assistance to Israel by $200 million and increase military assistance to Israel by $100 million was adopted by a vote of sixty-five to twenty-six;

conclusion is that while most of these popular notions shed some light on the phenomenon, their relationship to actual voting patterns is much weaker than might have been anticipated. More interesting than the differences in support accounted for by these frequently advanced ideas is the amount of variation that remains unexplained when we rely on these factors alone. Thus, while the results of the regression analysis point toward a multicausal explanation, it is obvious that we have not considered all the relevant explanatory variables. Unfortunately, some of the factors that are likely to have a significant impact on the nature and strength of congressional support for Israel defy quantitative measurement and may not even be amenable to systematic qualitative analysis. As a result, we can do little more than note their presence and the reasons why they are likely to be important, realizing full well that we cannot accurately gauge their effects on senatorial voting decisions.

One important factor is the direct lobbying efforts of domestic interest groups. While it is not possible to measure precisely the relative influence of pro-Israel and pro-Arab groups, there is little doubt that the greater organizational strength and activity level of domestic pro-Israel groups has resulted in considerable political payoffs in terms of congressional receptivity and willingness to make public statements in support of Israeli positions.[22]

Another relevant factor that probably affects the way senators vote is the policy preferences of their key staff aides. Senators are very busy people, and many tend to rely heavily on the judgments of their staff members concerning specific issues. Some analysts[23] argue that a major source of strength for the pro-Israel movement is the network of congressional aides who are openly supportive of Israel's interests and who work hard to convince their bosses and their bosses' colleagues to support Israel. In the absence of any strong countervailing pressures from pro-Arab groups we might expect those senators with only a marginal interest in the dispute to follow the path of least political resistance and vote as their staffs and colleagues suggest.

For some senators, however, the Arab-Israeli conflict is likely to be a very salient issue. Congressmen with presidential aspirations are likely to be sensitive to the fact that as they become more nationally prominent their voting records on Israel-relevant issues will be closely and publicly scrutinized by pro-Israel groups. A mixed record of support for Israel in the past may be sufficient for some Jewish groups to question a congressman's willingness to sup-

---

the Jackson amendment to the 1975 Defense Department Procurement Authorization bill to authorize unlimited loan credits for Israel to purchase American military equipment through 1977 was adopted by a vote of sixty-eight to twenty-two; and the 1975 Sinai Accords were approved by the Senate by a vote of seventy to eighteen.

[22] See Robert H. Trice, "Interest Groups Since October 1973," in J. C. Hurewitz (ed.), *Oil, the Arab-Israel Dispute and the Industrial World: Horizons of Crisis* (Boulder, Colo., 1976); and Robert H. Trice, *Interest Groups and the Foreign Policy Process: U. S. Policy in the Middle East* (Beverly Hills, Calif., 1977).

[23] For example, see Stephen D. Isaacs, *Jews and American Politics* (New York, 1974), p. 205 ff.

port Israel if elected president. Such doubts could result in the withholding of Jewish financial and electoral support. The actual strength of domestic pro-Israel forces is not nearly as relevant as the political constraints that potential presidential candidates may perceive. Few men with either immediate or long-term visions of national office are likely to want to run the risks associated with openly challenging the political muscle of pro-Israel groups. The lack of any readily observable political benefits for assuming an anti-Israel stance, coupled with the prospect that such a position would be likely to alienate an identifiable bloc of American voters, may explain the support for Israel displayed by some senators.

Beyond these identifiable and separable sources of support looms the entire domestic political environment that surrounds the governmental policy-making system. The ability of pro-Israel groups to marshal and maintain the support of the mass media, mass public opinion, and broad cross-sections of associational life in this country such as organized labor and non-Jewish interest groups, have enabled them to amplify and disseminate their policy preferences far beyond the limits of their own organizational structures. Overlaying the specific sources of support that we have examined here is the general factor that for whatever reasons a particular congressman supports Israel, he is likely to be well in the mainstream of opinion in his home district or state. For many Americans, congressional backing for Israel has come to be generally expected, irrespective of the ethnic or religious makeup of the district. The pro-Israel sentiments of major, non-Jewish segments of the articulate public are probably at least as important in determining congressional support as the electoral and financial strength of the Jewish community in the United States.

Although it is a major if not impossible task, we must first fully understand the complex reasons that underlie the apparent affinities of diverse segments of American society for the state of Israel if we are ever to fully understand congressional support for Israel. For to the extent that congressmen are the primary media through which most domestic forces make their imprint on foreign policy, we should expect congressmen to reflect and be sensitive to broader and deeper currents of opinion within the general population. As the nature of these broader forces in the domestic environment change over time, so should the behavior of congressional policymakers. And only by expanding the scope of our analyses to include the nongovernmental processes that determine the direction and strength of domestic pressures on foreign policy issues will we be able to understand how and why Congress participates in the foreign policy process.*

* I would like to express special thanks to Martin D. Saperstein for his valuable assistance on this project. I would also like to thank John Thompson, the staff of the Polimetrics Laboratory of the Department of Political Science, and the staff of Instruction and Research Computing Center at the Ohio State University for their contributions to this effort. In addition, I would like to thank Lawrence Baum, Herbert Asher and Charles Hermann for their helpful comments on an earlier version of this article.

Political Executives and the Washington Bureaucracy

HUGH HECLO

With every new administration, hundreds of new presidential appointees arrive in Washington to "take control of the bureaucracy." Only a few ever appear to succeed, if by success we mean changing government activity in some desired direction. Why do certain political executives do better than others in leading the bureaucracy?

Of course there are many reasons. During the past several years I have attempted to distill those reasons having to do with how public executives themselves choose to act—their statecraft. In a government peopled at the top by hundreds of short-term appointees, there is clearly wide scope for variation in how political executives will choose to act. The consequences of these choices are another matter. Forces inherent in our system of executive politics go far in determining, not how appointees will choose, but whether their choices prove prudent or foolish in coping with other people in government.

Here it is necessary to summarize only the five most important conditions that shape the content of political statecraft in the bureaucracy.

—The distinction in roles between political and higher bureaucratic executives is muddled in Washington, both formally and informally. For inexperienced participants in executive politics it is extraordinarily difficult to know who's who.

—Would-be leaders among political executives are in a peculiarly weak political position in relation to each other and to career bureaucrats.

HUGH HECLO is professor of government at Harvard University. He is the author of *Modern Social Politics in Britain and Sweden, Comparative Public Policy: The Politics of Social Choice in Europe and America* (with Arnold J. Heidenheimer and Carolyn Teich Adams), and the recently published *A Government of Strangers: Executive Politics in Washington.*

—The power of the bureaucracy is mainly passive, not active. It consists in the capacity to withhold needed services rather than in the capacity to oppose political superiors directly.

—Therefore political executives' first necessity is to help themselves. They do this by extending their networks and relationships throughout Washington so as to gain confidence about the nature of the surrounding political forces.

—But it also follows that self-help is not enough. The political leaders central problem in the bureaucracy is to gain the changes he wants without losing the bureaucratic services he needs.

Given these conditions, the essence of political statecraft in the bureaucracy is strategy—maneuvering with limited resources so as to create relative advantage. In talking with almost 200 appointees and bureaucrats representing all of the postwar administrations, one hears a number of recurring themes. There is no simple set of rules guaranteeing success but there are some regularities in the scars left by past mistakes.[1]

THEORY Z: CONDITIONAL COOPERATION

Experts writing about private organizations have described two different orientations toward management control. Under so-called Theory X it is assumed that an average subordinate avoids work if he can, loathes responsibility, covets security, and must be directed and threatened with punishment in order to put forth sufficient effort to achieve managerial goals. Theory Y emphasizes a worker's need for identity and personal growth through work, rewards rather than punishment as a means of motivation, and the cooperation toward objectives that can be gained by commitments to mutually agreed upon goals rather than by strict supervision from above.[2]

What matters is not so much the academic models of "nice guy" or "tough guy" management but that public executives constantly come to Washington

---

[1] For a fuller discussion see Hugh Heclo, *A Government of Strangers* (Washington, D.C.: The Brookings Institution, 1977). Research for this book was conducted from 1973 through 1976 and draws upon more than 200 interviews with political and career executives. All postwar administrations are represented in this sample.

[2] The arguments are reviewed and set out in much greater detail in Douglas McGregor, *The Professional Manager* (New York: McGraw-Hill, 1967); Frederick Herzberg, *Work and the Nature of Man* (Cleveland: Cleveland World Publishers, 1966); and William K. Graham and Karlene H. Roberts, eds., *Comparative Studies in Organizational Behavior* (New York: Holt, Rinehart and Winston, 1972). One of the few relevant studies of civil servants is Fremont James Lyden, "Motivation and Civil Service Employees," *Public Administration Review*, 30 (May-June 1970). For a discussion of the generally lower level of commitment in government executives, see Bruce Buchanan, "Government Managers, Business Executives, and Disorganizational Commitment," *Public Administration Review*, 34 (July-August 1974), 339–47.

acting as if they subscribe to one or the other of these views. Consider one of the most extreme examples in recent years of hostility between political appointees and bureaucrats: the social service program of the Department of Health Education and Welfare during the Nixon administration.[3]

After several years on the job two of Nixon's leading appointees in these agencies pondered their different routes to ineffectiveness. Here is how one, a self-acknowledged muscleman, looked back on his approach to subordinates:

In the short run it probably helped me to be known as a monster. It established me as a force to be reckoned with. A lot of people were afraid to join battle with me. But in the long run it hurt a lot because it put people on the defensive. You'll get some reaction if people think you're mean enough or are going to be around a while or have enough powerful allies, but it can't last long enough to have much impact. You're not likely to know when you're getting real cooperation and when they're just acting out of fear. If I had to do it again, I'd spend more time getting to know the people under me and their programs. I'd keep asking why do we do it this way, Why that? It is not really effective trying to browbeat people and win every little battle.

The other political executive (in the same agency) avoided all the mistakes of his tough colleague, but reflected on the futility of his wholly compassionate approach:

I made the decisions but they [bureaucratic subordinates] just continued to argue. The delays went on until I left office. . . . The biggest problems were the procedures and paper work and special pleading by office heads under me. I was overburdened because I couldn't count on delegating it and have things turn out the way I wanted . . . I think they figured I would be an easy mark. . . . I made the same mistake the secretary did. He was too nice to knock heads and let people know he meant what he said. [A successor] came in and got things going. He let people know he expected orders to be followed in a timely fashion and when they weren't, heads got knocked, people transferred; there were early retirements.

Lessons can be drawn from these and similar experiences, but frequently only the bureaucrats are around long enough to do so and to learn from such failures. According to a high bureaucrat who watched both appointees:

They did all the wrong things. I don't think they ever understood that governing is about making a lot of different forces coalesce. The feudal bureaus, interest groups, congressional politics—these are all things to be used. There are pretty firm limits on your control and how far you can persuade people to change, but there is some room for progress by pulling these things together. . . . The smarter guys choose a manageable number of things they care about and promote key people already here who can help still the rebels. They try and bring around those opposing them. It

[3] For detailed evidence on this particular disaster area during the Nixon years, see Joel D. Aberbach and Bert A. Rockman, "Clashing Beliefs within the Executive Branch," *American Political Science Review*, 70 (June 1976); and Martha Derthick, *Uncontrollable Spending for Social Services Grants* (Washington, D.C.: The Brookings Institution, 1975).

can take three to four years and will never work if you start off by telling bureaucrats they're crap. . . .
   You don't let people buck you and run behind your back. If you catch them at
it, you can isolate them and get rid of them. . . . But you also don't get far by
coming in and setting up separate people, programs, and ideas to the exclusion of
existing ones. If it's going to stick, what you want has got to be associated with
what's going to be here after you're gone. An appointee has got to make other
people feel a part of the credit line.

Of course this bureaucrat is only one of the many people involved in executive
politics who are constantly judging and ranking each other in numerous different ways. Though in Washington anecdotes of this kind are commonplace
(and many of them naturally self-serving), there is a core of agreement about
what has constituted the statecraft of effective political executives.
   The basic point is that experience reveals the shortcomings of both Theory X
and Theory Y and suggests the value of a third approach to working relations
between political executives and ranking bureaucrats. It is what might be
termed conditionally cooperative behavior. Any premise of compassionate cooperation and participatory management overlooks the bureaucracy's divided
loyalties, its needs for self-protection, and its multiple sources of resistance.
Unconditionally negative approaches fail to recognize the enduring character
of bureaucratic power and a political leader's need to elicit the bureaucracy's
help in governing.
   "Conditional cooperation" emerges between these extremes. It implies a
kind of cooperation that is conditional on the mutual performance of the political appointees and the civil servants. It emphasizes the need of executives and
bureaucrats to work at relationships that depend on the contingencies of one
another's actions, not on preconceived ideas of strict supervision or harmoni-
ous goodwill. Conditional cooperation rejects any final choice between suspicion and trust, between trying to force obedience and passively hoping for
compliance. By making their reactions conditional on the performance of subordinates, political appointees create latitude for choice—possibilities for various types of exchanges with different bureaucrats. The basis for the executives'
leadership becomes strategic rather than "take ot or leave it."
   As opposed to a set formula that assures success, conditional cooperation is a
strategy that suggests a variety of resources and methods for trading services.
It increases the likelihood that some political executives will do better than others
in getting what they need from Washington's bureaucracies. Superficially, conditional cooperation might seem to be simply a matter of exchanging favors
with the bureaucracy on a quid pro quo basis. The reality of executive leadership is more subtle. It involves bringing others to appreciate not so much what
they have gotten as what they might get. Would-be executive leaders, remember,
are like poor credit risks in a well-established credit market; they have had little
chance to acquire a favorable standing or reputation in the eyes of other participants who are used to dealing with each other. The new political strangers have

to work at building credit in the bureaucracy precisely because they have not had—and will only briefly enjoy—a chance to put anyone in their debt. Even so, memories are short and debts are often not repaid in Washington. The real basis of conditional cooperation lies in making bureaucrats creditors rather than debtors to the political executive; that is, giving them a stake in his future performance. Any past exchange of favors between appointees and careerists is far less influential than the general hope of grasping future returns. It is the grasping rather than the gratitude that drives executive politics.

Using Strategic Resources

Strategic resources are important because they provide the possibility of exchanges with the bureaucracy that can create commitments to mutual performance. In theory, of course, it is conceivable that trust could be based on unconditional cooperation—a kind of gift relationship in which political and bureaucratic leaders expect little in return from each other. In practice, exchange is a way of life cultivated by those in the ambiguous executive roles of Washington. Political appointees cannot expect to stand—much less move—on the basis of their formal authority as appointed political leaders; neither can high careerists expect to be automatically accepted as carriers of the internal norms of civil service responsiveness. Even the institutionalist bureaucrat, the clearest example of a "model" civil servant, expects that his cooperation will be repaid with some degree of political respect for the integrity of government institutions. A distinguished academic "in-and-outer" colorfully described the public executives' strategic situation:

> I spent the first days up with [the secretary], and it was marvelous all the plans we were making—the executive suites, limousines, and all that. Then I went down into the catacombs and there were all these gray men, you know—GS 15s, 16s, and I understood what they were saying to me. "Here we are. You may try to run around us. You may even run over us and pick a few of our boys off, but we'll stay and you won't. Now, what's in it for us, sonny boy." And they were right there was nothing in it for them. The next time I got a presidential appointment, I made sure there was something I could do for them and they could do for me. We sat down together and did business.

Strategic resources in Washington are means by which executives and bureaucrats try to show "what's in it" for each other. These resources can be grouped into a few serviceable categories: goals and opportunities, procedures for building support, and ways of using people. But to many observers the most immediately obvious resource is an executive's political power. Paradoxically, a closer examination shows that political power may be one of the clearest but also one of the most limited assets for purposes of political leadership in the bureaucracy.

Political Clout

Appointees with political clout—those who are willing and able to use many different means of self-help—not only extend their circles of confidence for dealing with outsiders but also create resources for dealing with civil servants inside. One such resource is a political executive's potential access to higher political levels. Career officials recognize that political contacts can mean the difference between the views of their agency being heard versus being merely tolerated or even ignored in the secretary's office or the White House. A careerist recalled longingly:

> Our last assistant secretary had terrific relations with [the secretary and two high appointees in the White House and the OMB]. He could call up, tell them our problems, and get them to listen and see if they could help. It improved our odds. Not everything, but an awful lot in Washington is done on the strength of these one-to-one relationships. Now we can't even get in the ball game.

Information carried back from higher political levels also aids top civil servants if their political executives convey it. It helps to know, for example, "whether it's just an ad hoc decision or something implying a policy," or "what's of interest and worrying the political people; maybe it's just some prior notice the President is giving a speech on a certain subject." Without such information higher civil servants know less in advance and worry more. "You spend your time on papers that no one really cares about . . . you have no idea of how the other political people are likely to react. . . . You don't know whether it really is a topside decision by the President or secretary or a call by some young political aid three times removed."

Thus the more adept a political appointee becomes in building his circles of confidence and in protecting his prerogatives, the more the value of his advocacy appreciates in the eyes of the bureaucrats below. In every department in every recent administration, one of the chief ways political executives gained support in the bureaucracy was by being, or at least appearing to be, their agency's vigorous spokesman. "Fighting your counterparts in other departments creates confidence and support beneath you," one acknowledged. In reference to a strong advocate in his department, a civil servant said: "He was well regarded on the Hill and dealt from strength with [the interest group]. A lot of White House people were afraid of him. You could get more of what was wanted approved and through Congress." Less politically effective executives may be personally admired by civil servants but have little to offer in return for bureaucratic support. As one such cabinet secretary was described by a bureau chief: "He had charisma, a really fine and open man who a lot of civil servants around here liked. But he never got a grip on the department. He didn't really fight for what was needed and if he made a decision it was because he got maneuvered into it by the staff." Experienced bureaucrats recognize that such appointees leave their agencies and programs vulnerable to more politically aggressive competitors elsewhere. In this sense, career officials will typically prefer a strong if unpleasant advocate to an amiable weakling.

A politically effective appointee is involved in speaking out, making claims, attacking other people. Openly exercising political muscle in this way involves a high degree of public risk-taking, which civil servants themselves are likely to shun. The very fact that a political executive not only is expendable but certain to be expended can paradoxically provide a strategic resource of sorts. Since any large bureaucracy is rarely of one piece, some civil servants consider a new face that is willing and able to expose itself politically to be an opportunity for support that had better be used while it is available. After serving under a string of cabinet secretaries, a bureaucrat observed:

> One thing I've eventually learned is that new people coming in can often get things done that others around a long time can't. People in the bureaucracy are telling them it's impossible, but they don't know that something can't be done and they do it. Like some Republicans have come in with no real obligations to the unions after an election, and that can be a big advantage. On the other hand, sometimes the unions will take things from a guy they regard as "one of them" that they'd never take from anybody else. It cuts both ways, and when you get a new guy who's tough and knowledgeable, you better make hay while the sun shines.

Thus a political appointee who shows himself able to take political risks can evoke responses that belie the stereotype of bureaucrats waiting to outlast political appointees.

Generally all these resources—political access, information, advocacy, and risk-taking—are by-products of any appointee's efforts to build credibility amid the maze of strangers in the government community. Political executives who can help themselves (like those already advantaged politically by the selection process) gain compound interest in dealing with the bureaucracy. For other executives, nothing fails like failure; political weakness in dealing with outsiders exacerbates all their problems of coping with bureaucratic insiders. To those who have, more is given, and those with scant political support are likely to have even that taken away by government infighting.

The resources derived from political clout, however, are also severely limited for would-be political leaders in government agencies. Risk-taking, advocacy, and so on, all point outward and are only very indirectly related to changing the behavior of officialdom itself. If political executives do not already agree with, or are unwilling to adopt, the bulk of the careerists' own agenda, then other resources for dealing with the bureaucracy are required. A politically powerful undersecretary explained: "We got along very well in the department because we wanted to and helped the bureaucrats do what they wanted to do." But the need for political leadership often goes further than bureaucratic advocacy. The same undersecretary's deputy recalled:

> We got a lot of loyalty and backup from the civil servants in return for his confidence in them. But the result too was that we got sucked in a number of times—I mean

accepting and defending their advice that something couldn't be done. Then when the heat turned on in Congress or the press, you found out you could do these things after all. . . . What we didn't get was a lot of critical, innovative thought, because going along with the careerists in the accepted ways wasn't the way to get that. You also have to double-check, push bureaucrats, get mad sometimes.

The paradoxical fact is that the political clout of the appointees can help bureaucrats get more of what they want, but it offers little assurance that appointees can get what they want from the bureaucracy, especially if this implies changes in policy. If mere appeals to outside political power could compel changes among officials inside, the executives' lives would be easy; indeed their leadership would be unnecessary in the executive branch. But life is not so simple. As government leaders, the executives' problem is to gain the changes they want while acquiring the services they need from the bureaucracy. For that, they have to unite managerial brainwork and sensitivity to whatever political muscle they may have.

Goals and Opportunities

The pressure of time and circumstances forces political executives to confront many choices they would rather overlook. It also forces them to overlook many things they might like to consider.

In a general sense this need to focus attention is a constraint on leadership, yet in a strategic sense it can also be an asset. Experienced political executives have found that the process of goal-setting can be an important source of strength in dealing with the bureaucracy.

The underlying logic seems obvious, but it is often lost from view in the press of events and crises. A political executive who does not know what he wants to accomplish is in no position to assess the bureaucracy's performance in helping him do it. Likewise, an executive whose aims bear little relation to the chances for accomplishment is in an equally weak position to stimulate help from officials below. By trying to select goals in relation to available opportunities, political appointees create a strategic resource for leadership in the bureaucracy.

The operational word is selectivity. By the time they are leaving office, political appointees commonly regret the waste involved both in trying to do everything at once and in trying to do anything that is unrelated to the available chances for success. Here is how appointees from three different departments described what they had learned.

An assistant secretary:

"We didn't figure out what could and could not be moved in the department, with OMB, with the appropriations committee. . . . We bloodied our noses on things that couldn't really be changed.

An undersecretary:

Deciding what you can win is important because then you don't use resources needlessly. For example, here are six decision memoranda on decentralization. I had no idea there'd be such a strong congressional backlash. Next time I wouldn't try and get some general authority through. I'd decentralize only a small bit of programs at first. It's a matter of what you can and cannot win and how you can or cannot win.

An assistant secretary, after eighteen months on the job, describing a standard situation:

There's a budget cycle, a personnel cycle, a planning cycle—for what it's worth—and lots of other smaller recurrences in the department's business. It can take a year for these to unfold so you understand about them and see it is a matter of which cycles you leave for civil servants to keep running and which you try and make work for you. Doing it again, I'd spend less time trying to deal with 60 percent of everything and drop to 30 percent on some things and 90 percent on others I care about.

Obviously such comments have much in common with the bureaucratic dispositions mentioned earlier—gradualism, indirection, and so on. This does not necessarily mean that appointees have been captured by the bureaucracy, but it does suggest an accommodation to the need for fitting ends and means in the exercise of leadership. Such discrimination can be found alike in appointees who seek to expand or cut government programs and in those who see their aims as stemming from their own agenda or (as in the cases quoted above) from overall White House desires.

How do political appointees try to link choices on goals with available opportunities and thereby strengthen the incentives for bureaucratic cooperation? Specific circumstances obviously vary, but they have some common features.

Preemptive Strikes. The early days in office—particularly with a new administration—constitute a particularly rich set of opportunities for any objectives aimed at major change. "After the first year the magic is gone, the weaknesses start to show, and you get bogged down with criticisms about what's gone wrong since you came in," one appointee remarked. A top appointee in another administration related how

setting out major policy lines quickly means you're at an advantage because things are still loose and flexible in government. Later, people get more locked into positions; it's easier to get out-maneuvered. If people under you are confused in the first year about what's wanted and control is lost, then it is hard ever to get it back.

The advantages to be gained from scheduling major changes early, however, are extraordinarily difficult to realize in Washington. Most appointees cannot expect to enter office at the very beginning of a new administration. Even if they do, the incoming presidential party will rarely arrive with an operational plan for what it wants to accomplish in specific agencies. Moreover, the advantages of prompt action fit poorly with the needs of new political appointees to learn about their jobs and establish a network of relationships in the nation's capital. The exception to the normal situation was cited by one executive who had reorganized his agency, cut the work force by one-fifth, and won legislation to substantially redirect the major objectives of its programs:

> The only reason we could do it was because we knew what we wanted and moved between February and May, right after the inauguration and my confirmation. People in other agencies weren't quite sure what was happening and anybody getting upset didn't know where to go. Later in the year, without the honeymoon feeling and confusion, I'd have been stymied.

Areas of Relative Indifference. As political executives learn more about the particular views that seem to be locked into congressional committees, interest groups, and subordinate officials, they often seek advantages by choosing to act in areas of relative disinterest to other participants. They try, as one appointee said, "to charge down the corridors of indifference." Thus in many agencies the temporary executives generally find that they create less antagonism by concentrating on overall administration and organization rather than on detailed program delivery, on money grants rather than people services, on planning rather than implementation, and on squeezing rather than eliminating a program.

These strategic choices obviously reinforce inertia and marginal change in government. Such incentives can mean that many political appointees find it in their interest to deal with the easiest, not necessarily the most important, issues. But even (indeed especially) those appointees who recognize their leadership responsibility to cope with important controversial issues learn the value of selecting proximate goals that at least do not arouse a maximum of opposition initially. An executive trying to deal with programs in the Department of Agriculture described the details of a common situation:

> This is not what you'd call a common sense environment. You can't just go after things. With the Agricultural Extension Service, state and local governments pay the majority of their salaries. The state directors of FHA [Farmers Home Administration] are appointed by state political groups. The county office heads of ASCS [Agricultural Soil and Conservation Service] are appointed by elected county committees, but it handles farm programs at the core of this department's operations. We can't end the pilot school milk program, even though we now have the school lunch program, because of the school lunch lobby, equipment manufacturers, milk lobby, and our own Nutrition Service. Each program also has a certain congressman's stamp on it. Eliminate it and it's an affront to him, the clients, and the bureaucrats delivering it to them. There are just a lot of people around who can tell you to go to hell when you go after program delivery. We decided to leave this alone and not get into how they sit down with clients.

Management Missions. Even if political executives are unable to take advantage of early opportunities or areas of indifference, they can acquire advantages in dealing with the bureaucracy on the basis of objectives that are what some science administrators call "project-like." Such goals identify a given point to be reached with a particular set of resources and within a particular time.

Expectations between political appointees and civil servants become more firmly based; the mutual performance that each expects of the other becomes clearer. Everyone, as one official said, "knows the mission. You have a schedule, costs, and a group of interlocking activities that have to be performed in order to get from here to there."

Some potential executives fear the disadvantages of such engineering analogies in government (among other problems, outsiders can more easily assess the executives' own performance); others feel they make the job easier. "You've got a better idea of where you stand, who's producing it, how to motivate officials to pull together," one said. The space program of the National Aeronautics and Space Administration (NASA) is the example most frequently given, but other executives may point to a major building program, a new accounting system, a given reduction rate in subsidies, and similar "missions."

A number of efforts have been and are being made to systematize the treatment of objectives in the executive branch, and no doubt further improvements can be made. Indeed the ability to provide clear, measurable objectives is often taken as the sine qua non of rational programs and political leadership in government. There is no need to review the ample literature on attempts to analyze (the planning, programming, and budgeting system), monitor (management by objectives) and reevaluate (the current program evaluation movement) agency objectives. Here it is enough to emphasize that as a practical matter the ability of most political executives to use project-type objectives in their working relationships with the bureaucracy are often severely limited. Businessmen experienced in government usually cite the lack of measurability compared with the situation in private enterprise. "In the private sector you know the name of the game—to get a percentage return, a certain productivity increase. Here there're no profit guidelines. Dollars aren't the measure of your performance." One explained that in government since "dollars aren't the bottom line, you get proxies for performance, input measure related to doing the work, providing a service, not producing an output." Knowing when a businsss has increased its market penetration from 40 percent to 42 percent is not like knowing when people have decent housing or proper health care.

Even beyond the problem of measurability, however, there are other powerful constraints on the political executives' use of mission-like objectives. One of these limitations is that what can be measured is often unrelated to the effectiveness that is judged and rewarded. "If I sweated fat out of my organization and increased productivity by 5 percent," said an executive, "I'd be a big man in my company. Here I could do that and be out of step with the secretary or a senator and get zinged every time. Or I may be a boob and with a politically favored program still get my funds increased in a way unrelated to how I'm doing as a manager."

Another inherent limitation is that since an executive's mission in Washington usually depends on contributing actions by a number of semi-independent outside participants, it can become extremely difficult to judge who is responsible for poor performance when objectives are missed. "At NASA we were lucky because there weren't six other agencies . . . involved in trying to put a man on the moon. If our people blew it, they couldn't pass the buck as easily as they can in most places." Political appointees will probably have to accept the legitimacy of much of the outside participation in their missions, even if this blurs accountability.

Still another constraint on mission-like political objectives lies in the temporary executives difficulty in learning enough about their organizations to assess the normal gamesmanship familiar in all organizational objective-setting. As one management analyst in government observed: "Objectives set unrealistically low just make people look good when they surpass the goals. Set very high they may just frustrate people into finding ways around them. The only way to get a sense of realism is to have good substantive knowledge and experience with the programs themselves." As noted, not many political appointees can be counted on for that kind of in-depth bureaucratic knowledge.

A final and most important constraint on the public executives' use of objectives is that political leadership commonly involves changing goals, not just hitting targets. An asistant secretary in one of the few agencies where measurable objectives were established by congressional statute acknowledged: "I was there just to get the program in place and running. There wasn't the time or opportunity to look back to ask if these are still the goals we should want to accomplish. It'll have to be someone else's job to worry about redirecting the agenda." Redirection may come from a new "man with a mission," but it is more likely to evolve slowly as new men cope with the circumstances. Goals are changed, not simply because political leaders renege on promises, but also because people who are affected complain about the old goals; or because some objectives (particularly in social programs that are oversold) cannot be achieved or achievement does not have the desired effect; or because people and organizations interested in self-preservation realize that having only one finite aim can be a terminal occupation—in short because of the normal course of self-interested interaction called politics.

Climatic Pressures. Since discrete missions normally are difficult to use as a management tool, political executives improve their ability to deal with their organizations by treating goals, not as givens, but as part of an ongoing political process. "Climate" is a term frequently used to describe a variety of factors involved in adapting goals to prevailing circumstances. Sometimes a scandal may provide the impetus: "Billie Sol Estes was the best thing that ever happened to our plans for creating a post of inspector general [in the Agriculture Department]." Less drastic outside criticism can also help.

> Our secretary used to complain that the GAO [General Accounting Office] should get off his back. I was there when [the secretary of defense] told him he ought to get smart and do like he did: take advantage of every GAO report to get changes he wanted. With these reports he'd go to people in the interest groups and bureaucracy

saying, "Look, these guys are breathing down our necks. Here's what we have to do." Sometimes he even did what GAO recommended.

Frequently less tangible "ideas in good currency" surround the bureaucracy and provide some of the best opportunities for realistic goal selection. Political executives who link their aims to ideas in good currency can gain a broader base to deal with even the most entrenched bureaucracy. One experienced official watched a succession of appointees gradually change a government agency that had once been considered to be in an impregnable alliance with its powerful clientele:

> You can't really trace it to any one administration or appointee, but over time the bureau's budget was squeezed, some things taken away, nothing new added. A series of people coming in reflected the feeling in the air that there were broader policy issues that mattered more than the particular prerogatives of this bureau.

The continuity to accomplish such long-haul change exists in points of view rather than in particular people. This gradualism, of course, may not provide very much gratification for political executives interested in big payoffs within their relatively short terms of office.

Hence, as a strategic resource, the selective intermixture of goals and opportunities is important. It helps a political executive specify how his exercise of political clout on the bureaucracy's behalf is conditional on the bureaucrats' performance. It sensitizes executives to the fact that working relations with the bureaucracy depend not only on winning fights but also on selecting, transferring, bypassing, and often running away from some fights in favor of others. Yet there are also considerable limitations. Political appointees in Washington may not be able to act early or to find areas of indifference. Neither can they count on acquiring clear missions against which to measure and climatic opportunities with which to spur bureaucratic performance. And as the next section shows, however well an appointee manages to point people in a particular direction, he will discover that his job in the bureaucracy is one of selling, not pointing.

Building Support

Since few political executives have the clear missions or massive public and political backing with which to generate spontaneous cooperation, they must usually work at procedures for building support in the bureaucracy. Changing words, plans, and pieces of paper is easy. Changing behavior, especially while not losing the constructive services of officials, is much more difficult.

Efforts to build support may embrace a specific policy objective or something as vague as improvising goals through the everyday interactions of government. Whatever an executive's aims, the inertia he faces in any agency is generally a compound of at least four elements. First are the Opponents, who see vital interests harmed by change and who are unalterably opposed to the efforts of political executives. Second are what might be called "Reluctants," people who may be opposed to change but who are not immune to persuasion that there are some hitherto unrecognized advantages: they will at least listen. Third, are the Critics—civil servants who feel they have views to contribute and are willing to be supportive as long as what they have to say is seriously considered. Finally, the Forgotten are those whose failure to support political executives stems from their failure to hear what is wanted or to hear correctly.

These four bureaucratic types can no doubt be found in any organization, but they are particularly important in the public agencies of the U.S. executive branch, where a gulf of mistrust and many differences can separate the temporary leaders from those who spend their lives in government. Inexperienced appointees often visualize only the Opponents and respond with indiscriminate suspicions and withdrawal from the bureaucracy. Political executives more accustomed to the Washington environment make more efforts to cultivate the different sources of potential support, lest their reactions to Opponents prejudice possibilities of help from the others. Here I describe these efforts in terms of communications to deal with the Forgotten, fair hearings for the Critics, and consultation for the Reluctants. Outright Opponents fit more naturally into the discussion of bureaucratic sabotage and space limitations prevent dealing with this group here.

Communication. Veteran bureaucrats usually cite failures of communication as the greatest weakness in the political appointees' relations with the bureaucracy. A typical comment: "Being so suspicious, political people are hard to talk to. They and bureaucrats aren't able to get their views through to each other. What you really need is better communications." Standing in isolation, this view is difficult to assess because the same official later noted that "when you do give out information it can leak all over the place, cutting off confidence and strengthening the opposition." Political information is a strategic resource that should not be dissipated. Like the warnings, orientations, and so on that bureaucrats can offer to new executives, information held by appointees is not a free good. Hence selectivity is obviously as important for communication—in the sense of passing strategically important information—as in goal-setting.

Communication in the sense of "getting the word out," however, is another matter. It seems difficult to have too much of this kind of communication. Executives cannot tap into potential bureaucratic support if large groups of people do not know what is wanted or, even worse, if they are only vaguely aware that an appointee exists. In the musical chairs at the top, political appointees typically begin communicating by at least trying to establish a personal "presence" in their agency, although how they do so varies with personal style. Some like to "press the flesh," to make the rounds of everybody in every office. Others are more comfortable with large meetings, and still others do better to avoid personal contact if it only betrays an insincere gesture.[4] Of course, a mere presence is unlikely to change anything, but it is a beginning.

---

[4] New department heads are especially prone to ritualistic mass handshaking sessions. As

In a larger sense, political executives often fail to recognize that they are always communicating—by example, by innuendo, even by a refusal to talk with people. The real need in building support is to communicate what is intended, for both intended and unintended signals are picked up in the bureaucracy.[5] For example:

   —The agency was supposed to be preparing a tight budget, and here he was big-dealing it by flying all around the country with a huge staff contingent.
   —We read [the appointee's] address to [an outside conference] pledging to meet the needs of these people. Then when we loosened up the program and it grew, word came down complaining that things were out of control. Everyone here was dumbstruck. It showed his ignorance about what he himself was doing.

As noted earlier, even an apparent refusal to communicate provides its own signals to civil servants. "Suddenly, you're not asked things or talked to, just told what must be done. You are supposed to be just a tool—not a professional."

Particularly in the Washington environment, communication cannot consist of simply saying something once in the bureaucracy. Persistence and follow-through lie at the heart of efforts to convey accurate messages. In part this is because the immense federal organizations find it difficult to transmit any messages through their many layers. Moreover, the executives' statements often produce little detailed guidance and leave much room for competing interpretations. There is another, less obvious reason why follow-through is probably the most important aspect of the political appointees' communication. The complex Washington environment makes it extremely difficult to separate the players' real moves from symbolic ones. Those on the receiving end of messages from political executives are accustomed to applying a heavy discount factor to mere proclamations. A supergrade explained that "over the years you see that a lot of the instructions aren't intended to be carried out. It takes extra effort to make it clear to people down the line that something is meant, not just another statement for the record or some speechwriter's inspiration."

Hence for political executives to say something once is a statement of intention; to show others what is meant and that it cannot be forgotten becomes a strategic resource. These extra efforts may take the form of reporting procedures, instructions committed to writing, informal reminders, complex management information systems, and a host of other techniques. But again, none of these techniques are substitutes for personalized networks and discussions. For

---

one bureaucrat said: "Everyone had to be lined up, one by one, to get the glad hand. It was like an internee camp. Besides, he was so dumb that he did it when everyone wanted to go to lunch."

[5] Such indirect influence from the top is illustrated in Robert Sullivan, "The Role of the Presidency in Shaping Lower Level Policy-Making Processes," *Polity*, 3 (Winter 1970), 202–21. Similarly, the history of corruption investigations in Washington is replete with officials' claim that their actions were not intended to influence pending cases or decisions, even though others caught the significance of small signals, including a raised eyebrow. See Bernard Schwartz, *The Professor and the Commission* (New York: Knopf, 1959), p. 234.

purposes of communication follow-through, these networks need to include people at the operating levels of the bureaucracy. After describing the sophisticated reporting requirements he had helped create, an agency manager concluded by recognizing that "all these statistics and reports do is throw up some signals that things aren't happening at the point of impact. Our best techniques give only the signals, not the story. That's why you need personal contacts down there." There is therefore little point in advising political executives to concentrate on broad policy decisions rather than waste time on details. General decisions or guidelines may communicate little to subordinates without specific interventions and "casework" to demonstrate what is wanted in particular types of circumstances. But it is a waste of time and a source of confusion to impart details that are irrelevant to the executives' major purposes.

Follow-through often requires more persistence than appointees have time or inclination for, but there are few surrogates for the extra effort at communication required from political executives. Higher civil servants may help, but in Washington there are few generalist career officials with the responsibilities and stature that would permit them to oversee any broad-scale follow-through for a department or policy. "Try that," said one civil servant who did, "and you have political appointees jumping up against you all over the place saying that that isn't the way they understand administration policy."

Due Process Again. Efforts to get the word out imply the reciprocal: listening to those who feel they have something to say. Political executives who are unwilling to provide a fair hearing to people in the bureaucracy generally find they have forced two otherwise distinct groups into the same camp. Working relations deteriorate not only with diehard bureaucratic Opponents but also with Critics who did not feel they had to win as long as they could gain access for their views.

For many civil servants, the complexity of many policy issues can reasonably justify a range of decisions by political appointees. For these bureaucrats a specific outcome may be less important than the kind of due process noted for relations among political appointees themselves. As one career supergrade said:

> The options aren't all that different regardless of which party is in power. Most of the [decisions] are in gray areas and could go either way. You're not facing a lot of moments of truth as long as you have a chance to have a serious input. What many career people do care about is that their sorting out of the alternatives comes into play, that however they [political executives] decide, there is evidence they've paid attention and at least had to wrestle with the issues worrying us.

Political appointees denied due process (at least those interested in self-help) can be counted on to raise a ruckus with each other; bureaucrats usually shop quietly among the many alternative listening posts in Washington and find other ways of getting their views heard. At any given time the consequences can be observed in a number of agencies. A GS 16 described a familiar set of choices and his own decision on what he regarded as an important issue:

I think a lot of people feel they aren't being taken into account and are just expected to rationalize decisions from on high. It's when you are denied a voice that life becomes tough. You've got to decide if you can live with this and yourself or if you want to try and outlast it, or move. Or do what I'm doing now—find an ally elsewhere with more power than you to help make the case.

In another large agency a prominent bureaucrat described the slide into demoralization:

> The feeling has grown in both the Johnson and Nixon administrations that the bosses didn't really want to hear what the career people had to say. You're not part of anything, just stuck out in an office somewhere, doing God knows what, that has an impact who knows where. I've seen the discontent filter through the whole structure. Productivity is falling, leaks are increasing, people are playing safer than ever before.

Obviously, listening to the bureaucrats' views on every issue may be unduly costly and time-consuming for a political executive. The value of working to establish a reputation as a leader who listens is cumulative, not immediate. Such a reputation is a strategic resource because it contributes to the trust that will undoubtedly be needed as specific pressures require forbearance from those below. Moreover, whatever the substantive value of the information communicated from lower-level officials (and it may be considerable), fair hearings can create a competition among perspectives that strengthens an executive's hand.

Consultation. With the Reluctants in the bureaucracy, political executives face the choice of seeking out or avoiding more active consultation. Such consultation may involve anything from the initial selection of goals to discussions about implementation. A great deal has been written about the pros and cons of so-called participatory, or democratic, management. The argument in brief is that "significant changes in human behavior can be brought about rapidly only if the persons who are expected to change participate in deciding what the change shall be and how it shall be made."[6] A number of case studies of public agencies suggest that the degree of participatory management is unrelated to effectiveness in accomplishing the intended goals of reorganization but does improve the employees' support and reduce resistance to change.[7]

These studies, however, also suggest a more important point: that the arguments for or against active consultation with subordinates are highly dependent on the particular situation and context. For purposes of political leadership in the bureaucracy, participatory management (trying to create a sense that "we

---

[6] Herbert A. Simon, "Recent Advances in Organization Theory," in Stephen K. Bailey and others, *Research Frontiers in Politics and Government* (Washington, D.C.: The Brookings Institution, 1955), pp. 28–29. For a more recent review of this subject, see Philip Sadler, "Leadership Style, Confidence in Management and Job Satisfaction," *Journal of Applied Behavioral Science*, 6 (January-March 1970), 3–19.

[7] Frederick C. Mosher, *Government Reorganizations: Cases and Commentary* (New York: Bobbs-Merrill, 1967). See especially pp. 526 ff.

are all in it together") seems largely irrelevant if it is followed simply as a maxim or proverb of good management. Only in an abstract sense are political appointees and civil servants in anything together, other than their agency. Consultation becomes relevant as a strategic resource when it is offered or withheld
so as to serve the purpose of executive leadership. When and for what do experienced political executives feel a need to consult in detail with those bureaucrats who, far from being helpful, may actually resist the exercise of political
leadership in "their" agency?

The answers from many different agencies and administrations seem clear.
In-depth consultation (which is *not* the same thing as indiscriminate informa-
tion-passing) makes sense when bureaucratic resistance may be susceptible to
persuasion, either through intensified argument or by involving Reluctants
in processes that lead toward largely unavoidable conclusions.[8] Consultation
for what? To find what might be called the points of mutual self-interest. Since
there is never enough agreement to go around, political executives generally do
better by trying to search for these possible points of shared advantage rather
than by assuming from the outset that initial resistance is immutable. Even if
complete agreement between political and bureaucratic executives is impossible,
consultation may reveal a partial overlap of interests that suffices for the purposes at hand. "You're looking for places where you can support him so he can
support you," as one official put it. A former strong man in the Nixon administration learned to respect bureaucratic power in the agencies "because they could
push as hard as I could push them." He concluded: "You can't mandate change
there. It's a question of sitting down with people and showing how things can
be of use to them."

Mutual advantage produces institutionalized change. As the desires of a
political executive become connected with the interests of at least some of the
officials who will remain behind, the chances of an enduring impact grow.
Here, for instance, is how one fifteen-year veteran in the bureaucracy compared the results of the tenure of two assistant secretaries:

> The government is used to absorbing tigers. Thomas was bright and tough, but if
> you asked him what actually got done, what around here actually operates differently
> since he came and left, he couldn't point to anything. . . . It was all put in on top
> and like a big spring, things went back to normal when the topside pressure left. . . .
> Williams, I think, got people believing it was their own ideas. You still see some of
> the changes he got through because people [in various bureaus] were working out
> and adapting the system so it became their own way of doing business. To get rid
> of this after he left you'd have to change operating procedures and nobody likes to
> do that.

---

[8] An official known for his wide-ranging use of interoffice consultations said: "This does
not mean you bring the bureau chief into the secretary or undersecretary's office and lay out
all the sensitive information that he can then use against you with [the interest groups] and
Congress."

The particular bargaining tactics used to arrive at a sense of mutual advantage are far too numerous to discuss here. They range from the creation of formal task forces and joint decision documents, to quid pro quo side payments, to indirect leverage through third-party pressures. Again, some of the essential flavor can be conveyed by a compendium of experiences, in this case from a political appointee who cited methods used to produce a variety of changes over the course of seven years.

> When we wanted a reporting system on things of interest to minorities, the statistics section said there weren't any data. I had them publish the table headings with empty columns. That got egg on their face, and they figured they'd better get some data on minority services before they were published again. . . .
>
> Quietly we started letting it be known about how the delays were hurting a lot of people in the agency. People started getting upset and asking how improvements could be made. "Well," we said, "here are some ideas that might work. . . . " The task forces helped show who was interested and where the pockets of resistance were. There's always somebody over in the weeds, and fifteen people sitting around a table can help bring that out and gang up on him a little bit. . . .
>
> We involved at least one person from each program division. The important thing was that with them working together, when it came out, you'd have some allies among the program people. . . . You could appeal to them by saying, "Look, why are you using all this manpower for things that aren't really connected to your bureau's objectives? With this plan you can use some of the cuts and reallocate them to things you really care about. . . . " Eventually they had to come up with suggestions themselves. The subsidies clearly were not working, and you could show that continuing in the same way meant at some point down the road we couldn't afford it; people would be hurt and there'd be a big hue and cry. Middle-level people fought like hell, but ultimately the division heads couldn't argue against the logic of the situation. . . .
>
> You know when you write the procedures you're the big gun in that field and anyone trying to change them is a threat to the foundation of your authority. The real back of the opposition was broken when we won over the dean of the budget officers, who'd built his power by letting the agencies go their own way on these things. Finally, through persuasion and a lot of argument, he was won over, and I remember as clear as day the meeting where he publicly capitulated. He said that if he'd known years ago what he now knew he'd have tried to put this through then.

As with other strategic resources, there are severe constraints on the political appointees' ability to consult and bargain toward mutual advantages with reluctant bureaucratic supporters. These processes require time, which temporary executives can often ill afford. Not everyone in large bureaucracies can be brought into discussions, and so a good deal of in-depth knowledge of the organization is likely to be required to identify at least proximate sources of resistance. Another obvious but often forgotten constraint is that any executive proposal needs to make substantive sense. There is little point in trying to persuade tenured officials with a case for change that does not have the merits to stand up against strenuous argument from those affected; often this requires more substantive knowledge than political appointees can muster. A related difficulty is that active consultation downward can strain a political executive's relations with his own political superiors, particularly if they are unwilling to tolerate compromises inherent in the give and take of any serious consultation. Without some leeway in what could constitute an acceptable outcome, consultation becomes perceived as a cynical attempt at cooptation and destroys rather than builds trust.

The various procedures described above for building support do not require that political executives avoid major fights with the bureaucracy, or accept whatever bureaucrats say, or cower behind the lowest common denominator of joint decisions. They do mean that some delicacy is required if appointees are to move among the natives in the bureaucratic villages without being captured. Experienced political executives do not necessarily make efforts to build support in the bureaucracy so that they can avoid the confrontations required by political leadership. They do it so that the fights, when they do come, are not one against all and to the death.

Many things—including personality, partisan politics, and intolerant political superiors—cause some political appointees to shun such delicacy in governing people. But the price of weak communications, restricted access for lower officials, and disregard for the self-interests of subordinates is the alienation of potential support in the bureaucracy. Many of the temporary executives in Washington choose to pay this price, and thus their initial suspicions about bureaucratic inertia and sabotage become self-fulfilling. What they cannot prudently do is to pretend that their actions exact no cost at all. The following comment by a Nixon appointee, who was surprised by the lack of bureaucratic cooperation he received, is an object lesson in the lack of statecraft:

> We began by going after the big issues and pretty much ignored the bureaucrats and opposition in Congress. The idea was to create some major points to rally Republican troops for the years ahead.... After a number of defeats in the first years it was decided to drop the legislative route and work through rules and regulations in the executive branch. The bureaucrats were very uncooperative toward this administrative strategy.

In this case the imprudence consisted, not of seeking partisan advantages, but of thinking that any "administrative strategy" could easily be built on bureaucratic relations that had already been cast aside in previous years.

Using People

So far strategic resources have been discussed in terms of political power, the selection of goals and opportunities, and methods of building internal bureaucratic support. People are also a resource that needs to be used for executive leadership. Political appointees often are unable to manage simply by motivating and bargaining with incumbent bureaucrats; in many cases changes in personnel are required in order to build a team that is in agreement about what needs to be done.

The idea of using people comes easily in Washington—too easily. Political executives naturally feel a need to have people around them who can be trusted from the outset and need not be won over. Given their own limited knowledge of people in government, inexperienced appointees are unlikely to believe they can count on this loyalty from below. More to the point, the civil service system—far from offering a basis for reassurance—often exacerbates doubts that good working relationships with career personnel can be expected. The labyrinthine civil service procedures and job-specific protections, the informal personnel practices and blurry intermixture of political and career jobs, the past attempts at politicizing the bureaucracy, the organizationally ingrown civil service careers, the standoffishness of civil servants who recognize the political vulnerability and career dangers that come in working closely with political appointees—all these offer public executives ample reason to doubt the people in government they inherit. Even if new executives harbor no ill will toward the Washington bureaucracy, they have to question whether this is a civil service system they can count on for help in exercising their legitimate leadership functions.

Thus the personnel system they walk into encourages the inclination of new appointees to think that their primary strategic resource and means of control lies in filling all key jobs with an outside retinue of personal loyalists. Unfortunately those who have watched the migrations of political appointees over the years generally seem to agree on one thing: importing a large number of outside lieutenants is usually an ineffective strategy for high political executives.

By now the reasons should be clear. The new subordinates can multiply all the difficulties of the executive's inexperience by bringing with them their own problems of self-help, short tenures, mistrust, needs for orientation, and so on. Not only do their personal loyalties fail to substitute for the institutional services the executive needs, but their intermediation can further separate the executive from bureaucratic services and vitiate opportunities for building support through communication, access, and consultation. Moreover, the proliferation and general bureaucratization of political appointees readily generates a false sense of security, a feeling that enduring changes in the behavior of government officials, and thus policies, are somehow being created just because more appointees are talking to each other.

One of the more aggressive assistant secretaries in recent years acknowledged his early admiration for "Machiavelli's advice: when you capture a town, bump off the top ten people, put in your own guys, and the rest of the population will settle down." Later he thought differently. "But you've got to realize this is a lousy communication system you're setting up. . . . There's nothing wrong with being tough, but doing it again I'd be more sensitive. I was having to work fourteen hours a day just to keep the place running myself until I got a good career deputy who knew how to get things done." The deputy described how this executive "had intimidated people so much that some were withholding bad news from him and others were beginning to play around with the statistics just to get results that would please him. . . . All the schedule C types had become a filter between him and the bureaucracy, calling their own shots and creating resentment. They were costing him more than he gained."

In the end a strategy of governing through outside placements also fails because it is normally an organizational impossibility. Without a massive reversion to spoils politics in government hiring, no top political executive can begin to place enough personal loyalists in all the important positions of his organization, i.e., in positions down to the level where discretionary guidance over the work of others shades into substantial routinization. "In this agency," said a top administrator, "we have six political slots; if you tripled that you'd still have less than two dozen of your guys in an organization of 62,000, and how long will it take for those 18 to figure out what's going on?"

Again, the more productive route lies in selectivity. Experienced political executives everywhere try to build strategy resources by selectively managing the various types of career personnel. In practice this means taking personnel actions to acquire officials already in the bureaucracy who show they can be of help, and if necessary bringing in outsiders to replace the unsuitable. Every cabinet secretary will want (though by no means will always get) his own lieutenants in top executive positions at the undersecretary and assistant secretary level. But below those levels the distinctions between civil servants and political appointees blur rapidly. It is here that political executives can gain a strategic advantage by using people in the bureaucracy.

The consensus of informed opinion on this point is impressive, among both bureaucrats and appointees and in Republican and Democratic administrations alike. Asked what advice they would give to new political appointees, most high civil servants would probably echo the one who said that "a smart guy should spend a while finding out who's productive, build on the ones who will help you do things, move them, use them to get other good people, and ride them as far as you can." Political executives with service in a variety of agencies report their experience in similar terms. For example, a Democratic assistant secretary with an expanding program said: "You can't motivate everybody. Some of these divisions are disaster areas with their leaks, but if you look, there are competent people around. I moved a regional director in to work in my office, replaced him with another good man I had watched. Then I took [a GS 15], consolidated some functions under him, and raised his status." In an agency where cutbacks were the executive's aim, a Republican undersecretary learned: "You didn't need to bring in a lot of new people because there was already an undercurrent of some who wanted changes; they could be found, encouraged, and promoted so you had a hard core of bureaucrats in key positions to ride herd on things."

The reason there is such consensus about using careerists goes back to all the bureaucratic services summarized best by the self-styled Machiavellian assistant secretary quoted earlier:

> I could have, and almost did, run around [an office director], and he could have beaten my brains out. But that isn't the point. The point is that no one understanding his function should want to run around him. I'm supposed to be smart enough to know what a guy like that is worth and realize that I should use him. [He] was a great civil servant, not because he did what you told him to, but because he would tell you how to solve the problems, what you could and couldn't do and why. With him I could get the changes through in one year instead of dragging on until I'm out of the picture.

To use bureaucratic personnel as a resource does not necessarily imply a political appointee's acceptance of the status quo. Sometimes political executives can create more flexible, innovative arrangements of officials and become less dependent on the established bureaucratic routines. The practical needs of decision-making, not management theory, lead experienced political executives to use bureaucrats in crosscutting and self-monitoring ways. These arrangements take many different forms. Career personnel may be used in policy analysis shops to foster competing analyses with program units; in an executive secretariat to make sure that views are canvassed, work processed, and decisions followed up; in mobile evaluation teams to report on activities further down the line. The reckless appointee may set everybody on edge by creating "my special strike force to go into the program divisions and report back only to me." The cooler agency head may get further with "a low-key special operations group that lives with the program people, gets in on things every step of the way, and plays it straight, letting those people know when and why they are reporting disagreements to me." By making these and other flexible uses of career people, government executives can provide a constructive service to both themselves and the bureaucracy. Such efforts show that if government officialdom is ingrown and cannot see new ways of doing things—as is often the case—there is an alternative to letting the career service go to seed and pushing political appointees ever lower in the bureaucracy.

If they are to use bureaucratic officials, even the toughest political executives need sufficient sensitivity to discriminate among the different capabilities of civil servants and match them to the appropriate jobs. Noticing that a civil servant is weak in one area, new appointees frequently overlook the needed help that could be given in other areas. "I almost made a mistake and dumped Williams because he couldn't negotiate with the other agencies," one said, "but he was superb in running the procedures. Starting a program, it's a two-fisted guy you want to bridge the torrent, but to keep things running smoothly you look for a diplomat who can still the tempest."

If political executives do not isolate themselves, they have ample opportunity to make these deeper assessments and go beyond the initial hearsay and apprehensions about Washington bureaucrats. These executives will watch meetings, responses to circulating papers, and special assignments. They will see that some "make serious efforts and are actively interested in finding ways of doing things" while others offer only "rote responses, reasons for not doing anything." An experienced political executive also looks for evidence of officials who avoid withholding information that puts him at a disadvantage. Some officials rarely create attention because they are anticipating and heading off problems; others may gain prominence by solving problems that are often of their own making, and still others may only look good because they leave the problems for someone else to solve. All of this requires more than superficial observation by political appointees interested in using civil service personnel actions as a strategic resource.

The real difficulty for executives in Washington does not lie in making these assessments but in finding the *constructive* flexibility in the civil service personnel system to do something about them. Contrary to popular beliefs, firing civil servants is not impossible, but it often requires experienced personnel experts to help work through the complicated procedures. There are such officials. As one said: "If you come up through the system you get to know procedures political appointees can't begin to cope with. I've fired civil servants who are incompetent or undercutting the leadership. The section in the book on firing is twice as long as the one on hiring, and it's dog-eared in my book." But what experienced officials will know and will usually encourage political executives to realize is that outright firings are extremely costly, not in dollars but strategic resources.

> Sometimes appointees seem to want to test you and ask "How do I fire a federal employee?" I tell him to give me the names and I'll have the employees out of the job in a month or two. But think of the implications, and you'll see there's a better, more indirect way of getting rid of a person you don't want on that job.

Given the nature of the civil service system, it is far easier and therefore much more common to use the indirect means available: quiet talks, early retirements, and exchanges (such as a favorable send-off in return for a graceful exit). Or as a former Civil Service commissioner said, "There are smart ways and dumb ways of getting rid of civil servants, ways that increase or decrease tension." Personnel advisers also recognize that the more hostile and unresponsive the civil servant, the more difficult removal becomes because of the likelihood of his using outside political connections. The general practice is to try to move unwanted officials to less troublesome positions. One career executive gave an accurate assessment of the options for anyone managing government personnel:

> What are you going to do with the guy who isn't doing you any good? You can make it known he isn't wanted, but some people don't get that signal. A confrontation can simply disrupt things and tie you up in procedures. You can try and make his job disappear [through a reorganization and reduction in force], but that's likely to backfire because he probably has got seniority and can bump young people below him who are better than he is. A transfer out of town is possible, but then he can use the

grievance procedure that this is an adverse action. The normal thing is to move him to where he can do the least harm.

The difficulty for the public in these strategic moves is obvious: the other areas of the public's business used as dumping grounds are likely to suffer and the payroll costs and inefficiency of government employment are likely to grow.

But the problem of utilizing bureaucrats an executive does want, and of doing so without prostituting the concept of a career civil service, is a more important one than the oft-publicized inability to get rid of civil servants. The agency career ladders, the officials' vulnerability to political reprisals, the haphazard arrangements for broader executive development in the public service—these and more barriers obstruct efforts to utilize career personnel in a way that is both flexible for political managers and constructive for the civil service system. Good working relationships with political appointees are more apt to prejudice than to aid the bureaucrats' status and advancement as career public servants. Constructively using and moving permanent officials is a "hard sell" because bureaucrats recognize that, as one said, their "power base and career is a function of a particular job, or bosses, or relations and support from outside groups."

None of this means that experienced political executives fail to use career personnel as a strategic resource in support of their leadership. Quite the contrary. It is often precisely because institutional means are lacking that top government political executives can commonly go very far in using careerists. The point is that political appointees generally are not interested in the implications of their personal actions for the civil servants' careers, much less for the civil service as an enduring system. In fact there is every incentive for an appointee to "milk" civil servants for his own short-term advantages.

The selective efforts of political executives to use various bureaucrats readily shade into the development of personalized and politicized corteges. Rather than import a mass of outside loyalists or simply manage the capabilities of existing personnel, political appointees frequently nurture their own bureaucratic families of protégés. An assistant secretary described this common approach as follows:

People you yourself hire are going to be more supportive than anyone else. They can be career guys, but they should be your guys and have primary loyalty to you. For example, Roberts is an excellent career man. I expected little but gave him some things to do and he performed wonderfully after plodding along in [the bureau] for eight years. I got him a promotion from a GS 14 to a 15 and took him with me to [a different agency] and made him a project director. Now he's an office head. That's the kind of person you have to attract and hold with you.

An undersecretary described how inexperienced people in the White House

were stupidly checking into the party registration of career people. You can sense who in the agency is with you, working late, referring with approval to what you say. These are the guys who you move up rapidly, a GS 15 to a 16 and maybe an

18 in later years. These career guys tie their job prospects to the political appointee above them and so can succeed or fail spectacularly.

The costs of the tendency for career personnel management to merge into the development of personalized and politized bureaucratic protégés are not felt directly by political appointees, who typically move on to their own private careers. The price is paid by public officials who, although ambitious to move into challenging jobs, wish to retain some identity as career civil servants. Individual careerists can find they have indeed been used—"working your butt off for the guy and ending up as some executive assistant to a political appointee with no career development to show for it." A longtime participant in government described how those associated with a particular political executive can be "exposed, used up, and then become the holdovers and obstructionists for the next appointee to jump on." Of course, some careerists in this system will simply decide for very good reasons to cease being civil servants and to take political appointments. Others will have little choice. As one bright supergrade said: "Since he [the undersecretary] left government and [the assistant secretary] moved to HUD [Housing and Urban Development], I've got no clients for my work."

In a larger sense the real costs of the appointees' haphazard creation of bureaucratic families lie in the denigration of the concept of a career civil service. A well-known political executive went to the heart of the matter in describing the personal cortege that had moved with him between government agencies and the Executive Office of the President:

> In my experience these supergrade types in government compare favorably with almost any group I've seen in the private sector. A guy in his mid-thirties and a GS 15 has got to have a lot of political savvy and good moves. I've carried five of them with me in every job. They're my personal supporters and I look after them. . . . Civil servants identifying with people pose a real problem for the bureaucracy, but it doesn't bother me. It helps me as a political appointee because I can really deal with them. The whole civil service thing is so automated, promotions come automatically, grade-step increases, and pay changes. The only way for these guys to break through this automated system is through personal identification. What should happen if it were operating right is that the system should be throwing upwards and promoting the good, bright guys, not depending on personal identifications with patrons.

There is no need to idealize bureaucrats as "the" public service. Civil service systems are created to institutionalize a limited but important set of values in government. Among these are not simply nonpartisanship and obedience but also (and especially at higher levels) a continuous capacity to offer honest advice and uphold the integrity of government operations. Perhaps an obscure GS 15 said it best: "As the distinction blurs between an institutional career role and personalized loyalty, people start hedging. They hedge their best independent judgments, either so as not to be put into jeopardy of political identification or because once jeopardized they're trying to ingratiate themselves." Using career people as a strategic resource may help particular appointees, but it is no real help in establishing the civil service as an instrument of reliable government performance.

IMPLICATIONS

My argument has been that political executives can usually do better by evoking conditional cooperation rather than by invoking their authority. Perceptive appointees from both the Theory X and Theory Y schools of management eventually see that the political executive's real job lies between the extremes of giving orders and of taking cooperation for granted.[9] They learn that political leadership in the Washington bureaucracy is not a task for martinets or presiding officers. For those both tough and sensitive enough, it is a job of managing a pluralistic, changing consensus with limited strategic resources.

In other words, there are no magical management systems or organizational changes for "getting control of the bureaucracy." Reorganization plans or techniques like management by objectives and zero-base budgeting are all executive proclamations that presume rather than create changes in subordinates' behavior. Instituting new management techniques and making them part of the bureaucracy's standard operating procedure lie at the end of statecraft not at the beginning.

In the preceding discussion I have also emphasized selectivity and calculation in dealing with the political resources, opportunities, people, and procedures for building support. This suggests that while would-be political leaders in the executive branch *can* be agents for changing what government is doing, convulsive root and branch changes fall outside the range of everyday statecraft. If political policy calls for revamping most of the major assumptions behind what an agency is doing, there is little point in a political executive appearing on that scene in the guise of a selective strategist who uses a variety of resources for encouraging bureaucrats to terminate their way of life. An entirely new organization will in all likelihood be required. Also needed will be a genuine, widely perceived sense of crisis—an economic disaster, an unambiguous foreign threat, an acknowledged need to "war" on some domestic problem—in order to galvanize the many disparate competitors for attention and agreement in Washington. Without that general sense of alarm, trying to shake up the bureaucracy by appealing to the American people for support simply misses the point.

A desire to capitalize on such opportunities for Big Change can therefore create one of the limits on mutual support between political leaders and bureaucrats. Fortunately for the stability of government institutions, such overwhelm-

---

[9] It is revealing that the opening quotations in this article, taken from office-holders in a domestic department, compare almost exactly with the lessons drawn by a leading political executive in an organization as different as the State Department. See the extensive quotations and discussion in Donald P. Warwick, *A Theory of Public Bureaucracy* (Cambridge, Mass.: Harvard University Press, 1975), p. 209.

ing crises seem relatively rare and are short-lived when they do occur. Moreover, once the bright new organization has been created, the familiar imperatives for statecraft reappear with time. These facts, along with the dispersed veto power and shortage of agreement that permeates most of everyday life in Washington, means that no political executive need apologize for working at relationships that are usually based on conditional cooperation with the bureaucracy.

Occasions for Big Change suggest a situation in which the political leaders' demand for performance is more than the bureaucracy can supply. Limits are also set on mutual support when bureaucrats demand more performance than political appointees can supply. Civil servants have their own expectations about what is due from political leaders in their agency. The tenure of officials who wish to remain civil servants but who also allow themselves to be used by political executives is conditional on the executives' own behavior. Appointees need to reduce the risk of added exposure and insecurity for such officials. When trouble develops—something upsets a political superior, the Office of Management and Budget attacks the agency's goals, a congressional committee takes offense—a political appointee who attempts to shift blame to subordinates quickly experiences an evanescence of bureaucrats, protégés or otherwise. As one observed, "The self-preservation instinct blossoms." Careerists involved in executive hearings and consultations expect to be serious participants dealing with issues of substantive importance, not "hacks rationalizing some piece of political propaganda." Officials helping a political executive will expect as their due some clear guidance in advance rather than to have to hope for support later. Since all strategic resources are limited, conditional cooperation breaks down when—for whatever reason—bureaucrats expect more in exchange for their cooperation than political executives are able or willing to provide.

Hence demands from either side can outrun the supply of mutual performance. But conditional cooperation involves more than bureaucrats and executives in their agencies. There are third, fourth, indeed nth parties implicated in the exchanges of executive politics and they too set limits on the degree of cooperation between the appointee and the bureaucrats. A political executive's primary constraint rests in his links to other appointees and political figures. An oft-quoted opinion of a former secretary of state is that "the real organization of government" at higher levels "is how confidence flows down from the President."[10] A similar but broader principle of confidence is at work throughout and across the levels of government. Depending on the political executives' specific allegiances and accidents of selection, their ability to deal with the civil servants below them is limited by their need for live political connections up to political superiors and out to the many sources of external power.

From this perspective it becomes clear why there is much more to the politics of executive branch leadership than simple-minded assertions about a natural

---

[10] Dean Rusk, quoted in Morton H. Halperin, *Bureaucratic Politics and Foreign Policy* (Washington, D.C.: The Brookings Institution, 1974), p. 219.

animosity between presidents who long to control their administrations and parochial cabinet officers who love to be captured as departmental advocates. The fact is that requirements for statecraft in the agencies do not fit well with political prudence as seen from behind the White House gates. A president marshaling his power stakes expects to advance when there is credit to be had and withdraw as losses grow. When unpopular actions have to be taken in a government agency, his political appointees there should be hustling into the trenches of frontline support, not picking and choosing their advantages. After all, does not the President's generalship consist of using the strength of others and conserving his own? Bureaucratic politics contemplates quiet, behind-the-scenes workmanship, strategic reversals, caution, contentment with results for which everyone can share some of the credit. Presidential politics mobilizes its vital resources with the public by taking all the credit for dramatic, readily intelligible actions: big cuts, major new programs, flashy changes. Why, when the President has staked his reputation on getting something done in government, are his political executives reaching for the rapier instead of the bludgeon?

Executives in the agencies may argue that their achievements with the bureaucracy reflect favorably on the President, but to those in the White House reflected glory may not be enough. Why not? Because a political executive's selection of goals and areas of indifference may not be what the President wants or would want if he could know what goes on throughout government; because to build support in the bureaucracy invites more delay and compromise; and because the people an executive uses may become his people but not necessarily presidential supporters. In these and many other ways an unconstrained use of his strategic resources may help a political executive with the bureaucracy but leave him vulnerable to the President's "true" supporters in the White House. Yet the more detached, broadly presidential view an executive takes of his agency, the more difficult it becomes to acquire support from its officials below and clients outside.

Hence the tensions of political leadership in its presidential and executive department guises are inherent. Being unavoidable, they suggest their own lesson for presidents: prudence for any president interested in the problem of controlling the bureaucracy consists in trying to use the inevitable tensions with his executives constructively, not in trying to eliminate or drive these tensions underground with simplistic notions of cabinet government and unified executive teamwork.

However, the implications of the preceding analysis go much further than the presidency. People in government can and do manage without conditional cooperation at the political-bureaucratic interface. When political appointees have little sense of direction or statecraft, the failure to establish a constructive working relationship with higher civil servants may be inconsequential, except that the bureaucracy is left freer to pursue its own agenda. Experienced bureaucrats become quite expert at helping themselves in the Washington scramble.

Similarly, some political managers may feel no great loss if the careerists with whom they fail to build working relations have few analytic or administrative capabilities to offer or withhold; they become adept at creating their own personal teams in place of career civil servants. Appointees and bureaucrats can and do try to compensate for each other's inadequacies.

As each side maximizes its own convenience in this way, the overall quality of American democratic institutions is likely to decline. It is no consolation that appointees and top bureaucrats can compensate for having little that is worth exchanging with each other. If officialdom and professional specialists can get along very well despite an absence of political leadership above them, that should not reassure citizens who expect government bureaucracies to be guided by publicly accountable and removable political representatives. Likewise, political executives may manage without the institutionalized knowledge, continuity, and impartiality that government civil services are created to supply. That, too, is little consolation since the real strength of government machinery in a democracy is its ability to serve effectively, not just one particular set of political leaders, but any succession of leaders with a legitimate popular mandate. If democratic government did not require bureaucrats and political leaders to need each other, it might not matter so much when in practice they discover they do not.

Contemporary Supreme Court Directions in Civil Liberties

ROBERT J. STEAMER

During the past five years scores of lawyers, political scientists, and news reporters have tried their hands at analysis of what we call, for want of a more accurate term, the Burger Court. More frequently than not, what comes through is an angry and apocalyptic tone. For many of the commentators, no news from the Burger Court is good news.[1] Judicial decision making, for the contemporary critics, is akin to sailing in a boundless and bottomless sea; there is neither harbor for shelter nor floor for anchorage, neither starting place nor appointed destination.[2] Essentially, current literature is concerned with measuring the degree of erosion that the new cases inflict upon the edifice erected in the Warren years, as if the Warren construct were the ideal and should not be sullied by the tainted hands of Burger, Blackmun, Rehnquist, and Powell—and a Stevens come lately. We now have about 700 full opinions to view since Earl Warren retired, and although the professional and popular journals run to more than a million words on the subject, one can still take refuge in the advice of Justice Holmes who said that "we frequently need better understanding of the obvious rather than further investigation of the obscure."

First, the Burger Court is more like than unlike the Warren Court; second,

---

[1] Francis A. Allen, "Supreme Court Review (1975)," *Journal of Criminal Law,* 66 (1975), 391. A notable exception to the hostile critics is Alpheus Thomas Mason, "The Burger Court in Historical Perspective," *Political Science Quarterly,* 89, no. 1 (March 1974), 27.

[2] This is a transposition of Michael Oakshott who used the phrase to apply to political activity generally, but for many observers the words fit the current judiciary.

ROBERT J. STEAMER is Vice Chancellor for Academic Affairs and Provost at the University of Massachusetts/Boston. He is the author of *The Supreme Court in Crisis: A History of Conflict* and *The Supreme Court: Constitutional Revision and the New Strict Constructionism.*

the Court has tended under both Chief Justices Warren and Burger to override legislative judgments rather casually and with a minimum of constitutional proof; third, where the two Courts differ in decision, the present Court has, as often as not, taken a sensible position; and finally, in those areas of individual liberty which we rightly hold crucial to a democratic society, the Court has sometimes sounded more like a Tower of Babel than an articulate and consistent guiding force.

But before looking at some of the substantive areas of current judicial attention, we need to deal with the question of "access to the courts," that catch phrase which suggests to many of the Court's critics that it is presently more difficult for citizens to enter the federal courts than it is for the proverbial rich man to enter the kingdom of heaven. The suggestion has some basis in fact, but courts must, as they always have, use discretion in deciding which cases deserve a full hearing. The hostile critics take their cue, first from the public pronouncements of the chief justice himself, and second from some recent decisions which have in some instances turned a deaf ear to alleged violations of rights.

ACCESS TO THE SUPREME COURT

On January 3, 1976 Chief Justice Burger issued his annual report in which he pointed out that the Supreme Court faces a caseload almost four times as heavy as that which confronted the Court in the 1920s and 1930s, and that as recently as 1953–1955, the first three years of Chief Justice Warren's tenure, the Court averaged 91 full opinions a year. In the past three years the annual average has been 134. He suggested that Congress take two steps which would indeed, cut down access: (1) abolish the remaining category of three-judge federal district courts, thus eliminating direct appeals from them to the Supreme Court;[3] and (2) transfer all diversity of citizenship cases to the states, thus cutting 20 percent of the caseload of the federal trial judges. Although the chief justice is ostensibly saying that the Supreme Court cannot handle the press of litigation, his remarks in other respects indicate an attitude which organizations like the American Civil Liberties Union deplore. He said, for example, that most of the

---

[3] The Ninety-third Congress enacted two pieces of legislation which discontinued the use of the three-judge federal court machinery in specified areas. One abolished the right of the Attorney General to convene a three-judge court under the old Expediting Act of 1903 (Antitrust Procedures and Penalties Act, 88 Stat. 1706, P.L. 93–528, December 21, 1974). The second amended the Judical Review Act of 1950, the effect of which is to place the bulk of Interstate Commerce Commission litigation in the courts of appeals rather than in three-judge district courts (88 Stat. 1917, P.L. 93–584). The Ninety-fourth Congress repealed Sections 2281 and 2282 of Title 28 of the U. S. Code which had respectively required a three-judge court in cases involving injunctions against enforcement of state and federal statutes, but the law amended Section 2284 to permit three-judge courts in suits challenging the constitutionality of apportionment of congressional or state legislative districts (P.L. 94–381, 94th Cong., S537).

19,000 petitions from prisoners could be handled effectively and fairly within the prison system. "Federal judges," Burger declared, "should not be dealing with prisoner complaints which ... are so minor that any well-run institution should be able to resolve them fairly without resort to federal judges."[4] The chief justice has also been a strong supporter of the Hruska Commission Report, now U. S. Senate Bill S2762, introduced by Senator Roman Hruska on December 10, 1975, which would create a National Court of Appeals with two types of appellate jurisdiction. It would decide appeals referred to it by the Supreme Court and appeals transferred to it by the regional courts of appeals. The issue of this novel addition to the federal judiciary has been hotly debated, and those who oppose it, including former Chief Justice Earl Warren,[5] maintain that the scheme is another means of denying access to the Supreme Court.

One can cite several instances of this past term in which individuals who were denied relief might, according to the Court's critics, have obtained it during those open Warren years. In *Rizzo* v. *Goode*[6] the Court reversed a district judge who, on the basis of citizens' complaints against the police department, had ordered city officials to come up with a comprehensive plan for dealing with the problem. The majority argued that a pervasive pattern of intimidation had not been established, nor was there a strong enough link between the city officials who were the defendants and the police officers who had allegedly violated citizens' rights. Perhaps a more telling argument was the majority's emphasis on keeping the insulation between the states and the federal government. Said Justice Rehnquist: "Federal courts must be constantly mindful of the special delicacy of the adjustments to be preserved between Federal equitable power and state administration of its own law."

Coming under the rubric of "denial of access" were several other cases during the 1975–1976 term which support the thesis that it is not as easy to obtain relief in the Supreme Court as it used to be. Charles Edward Davis III was told that he had no grounds for a federal suit against the police after they had included his name and picture on a list of "active shoplifters" to be distributed to merchants. Davis had once been arrested for shoplifting but had not been prosecuted. Reputation, said the Court, is not included in life, liberty, or property and, therefore, deprivation of same without due process is not a constitutional violation.[7] In a similar vein the Court ruled unanimously that state prosecutors have

---

[4] "Chief Justice Burger Issues Yearend Report," *American Bar Association Journal*, 62 (1976), 190.

[5] See Earl Warren, "A Response to Recent Proposals to Dilute the Jurisdiction of the Supreme Court," *Loyola Law Review*, 20 (1974), 221. See also Luther M. Swygert, "The Proposed National Court of Appeals: A Threat to Judicial Symmetry," *Indiana Law Journal* 51, (1976), 327; Jack B. Owens, "The Hruska Commission's Proposed National Court of Appeals," *UCLA Law Review*, 23 (1976), 580; and Nathaniel L. Nathanson, "Proposals for an Administrative Appellate Court," *Administrative Law Review*, 25 (1973), 85.

[6] 423 U.S. 362 (1976).

[7] *Paul v. Davis*, 424 U.S. 693 (1976).

absolute immunity against civil rights suits based on a prosecutor's knowing use of perjured testimony.[8]

The present Court is also determined to narrow collateral attacks on prior convictions through the *habeas corpus* jurisdiction, an avenue to the Supreme Court that was wide open during the Warren years. In 1973 Justice Powell, concurring in *Schneckloth* v. *Bustamonte*[9] suggested that search and seizure claims under collateral review should be carefully circumscribed. During the 1975 term the Court followed Justice Powell's dictum and concluded that where the state has provided an opportunity for full and fair litigation of a Fourth Amendment claim, a state prisoner may not be granted federal *habeas corpus* relief on the ground that evidence obtained in an unconstitutional search or seizure was introduced at his trial.[10] Another reduction in the *habeas corpus* jursidiction came last year when the majority held that a state prisoner who failed to make a timely challenge to the composition of his indicting grand jury could not raise the exclusionary rule after conviction through the *habeas corpus* route.[11] Now the Court had extended to the states what it had earlier held applicable to federal criminal proceedings.[12] It should be noted that the Court did not overrule *Fay* v. *Noia*,[13] a landmark of the Warren era, and thus did not foreclose all postconviction challenges on *habeas corpus* to unfair treatment at the state level.

Certainly other examples of the current attempt to limit access are available on a detailed examination of the reports,[14] and undoubtedly there is a concerted effort on the part of Chief Justice Burger and the majority who agree with him, to cut down the litigation that eventually reaches the Court's docket. It seems doubtful, however, that the actual number of cases the Supreme Court decides each year will drop significantly below the current output. The issue, therefore, is a substantive one of letting some people in while keeping others out, and what the old Warren supporters appear to deplore is that the wrong people are being let in while the right people are being kicked out. One might suggest facetiously that it is all a matter of likes and dislikes. The Warren Court liked criminals, minorities, and people who wear sweatshirts with four-letter words on them. It did not like the police, prosecuting attorneys, or draft card burners. The Burger Court likes the police (although not enough to permit them to wear long hair), welfare people, Indians, women, and drug stores. The Burger Court also likes wild jackasses, prefers them in fact to people, on the basis of its ruling upholding the Wild Free-Roaming Horses and Burros Act against all

[8] *Imbler* v. *Pachtman*, 424 U.S. 409 (1976).

[9] 412 U.S. 218 (1973).

[10] *Stone* v. *Powell*, 96 S. Ct. 3037 (1976).

[11] *Francis* v. *Henderson*, 425 U.S. 536 (1976).

[12] *Davis* v. *United States*, 411 U.S. 233 (1974).

[13] 372 U.S. 391 (1963).

[14] See, for example, *Butler* v. *Dexter*, 425 U.S. 262 (1976); *Bellotti* v. *Baird*, 96 S. Ct. 2857 (1976); *New York Civil Service Commission* v. *Snead*, 425 U.S. 457 (1976).

human attacks. The Burger Court dislikes prisoners, shoplifters, pushcart dealers, homosexuals, and human fetuses during the first three months of gestation.

Undoubtedly the Burger Court is changing the composition of its clientele, but the change is relatively slight. It is moving away from a few areas, but moving into others, and its stand on access warrants two observations. First, the Burger majority is attempting to find a way to restrict certain litigation to the state level or to contain it in the federal courts of appeals. There is nothing pernicious about this so long as the highest tribunal is open to those cases where the alleged violation of a constitutional right is real and substantial and not technical. Second, the Court is attempting to separate the significant from the trivial. In effect, it is saying it should not be spending precious time in deciding whether a policeman has a right to wear a mustache. The Constitution says nothing about it, and a good case can be made for the Court's not entering disputes of such a low constitutional threshold. It is difficult to understand how we ever got into this condition in which every personal desire is turned into a right, but perhaps it is time the Court called a halt. Those who fail of access to the Supreme Court can take heart in the words of Dumbey in Lady Windemere's Fan, "In this world there are only two tragedies. One is not getting what one wants and the other is getting it."

SUBSTANTIVE AREAS

Our purpose here is not to analyze all possible issues of public law, but to highlight those areas of primary significance. Although there are some hairline cracks in the structures built on the great Warren legacies of *Brown*[15] and *Baker v. Carr*,[16] they are primarily in the superstructure and not in the foundation. Certainly the Burger Court has gone the last mile in school desegregation with a series of decisions beginning with *Swann*,[17] and in the 1976 case of *Hills* v. *Gautreaux*[18] it has creatively reaffirmed *Jones* v. *Alfred Mayer Co.*[19] The early reapportionment cases have been subject to some modification, but there has been no repudiation of the fundamental principle involved. We should concentrate, therefore, on three areas, the first of which, criminal procedure, exemplifies the most clearly identifiable departure from the immediate past. The other two, freedom of speech and substantive equal protection, are more or less extensions of prior doctrines into new areas.

Criminal Procedure

What was referred to during the Warren years as a revolution in criminal justice was essentially the gradual nationalization of procedural guarantees within the

---

[15] *Brown v. Board of Education,* 347 U.S. 483 (1954).

[16] 369 U.S. 186 (1962).

[17] *Swann v. Charlotte-Mecklenburg Board of Education,* 402 U.S. 1 (1971).

[18] 425 U.S. 284 (1976).

[19] 392 U.S. 409 (1968).

Bill of Rights. While never attaining unanimity on the Warren Court, the principle of applying the first eight amendments of the Constitution to the states through the due process clause of the Fourteenth Amendment (with minor exception) is so solidly imbedded in American public law that no future Supreme Court will alter that concept. Beyond that, however, were two additional doctrines of the 1960s, exemplified in the *Miranda*[20] and *Mapp*[21] cases. The *Miranda* rule has been modified although not overturned, and the *Mapp* decision, which applied the old evidentiary exclusionary rule of *Weeks* v. *U. S.*[22] to the states, has been taking a beating. Although *Miranda* was qualified in *Harris* v. *New York*, [23] *Michigan* v. *Tucker*,[24] *Oregon* v. *Hass*,[25] and *Michigan* v. *Mosley*,[26] it still retained considerable vitality in 1976 as is evidenced by the Court's overturning convictions in *Brown* v. *Illinois*, [27] *U. S.* v. *Hale*,[28] and *Doyle* v. *Ohio*.[29] In *Brown* the defendant had been arrested unlawfully, and although given his *Miranda* rights, subsequently made incriminating statements to the police. Justice Blackmun, speaking for the Court, declared that the Illinois courts were in error in assuming that the *Miranda* warnings, by themselves, always purge the taint of an illegal arrest. The *Hale* and *Doyle* cases taken together held that a state prosecutor may not seek to impeach a defendant's exculpatory story, told for the first time at trial, by cross-examining the defendant about failure to have told the story immediately after receiving *Miranda* warnings. Yet the Court held just a few months ago that a witness before a grand jury, though possibly engaged in some criminal enterprise, is not entitled to *Miranda* warnings.[30] He can, of course, invoke the privilege of self-incrimination. Given the

[20] 384 U.S. 436 (1966).

[21] *Mapp* v. *Ohio*, 367 U.S. 643 (1961).

[22] *Weeks* v. *United States*, 232 U.S. 383 (1914).

[23] 401 U.S. 222. In *Harris* the Court upheld the admission of evidence at trial, taken without Miranda warnings solely to impeach the defendant's credibility.

[24] 417 U.S. 433. In *Tucker* the Court upheld the admission of testimony given by a witness who had made incriminating statements about defendant Tucker. Tucker had given the police the name of the witness prior to having been told of his right to have counsel provided by the state if he could not afford one. In all other respects Tucker had been informed of his rights prior to interrogation.

[25] 420 U.S. 714 (1975). In *Hass* the Court approved the admission of evidence for impeachment purposes of a suspect who had been given full Miranda warnings while on the way to the police station, was told he could not see a lawyer until he reached the station, and then made the inculpatory statements prior to consulting with an attorney.

[26] 423 U.S. 96 (1975). The Court held admissible incriminating statements made by the suspect who, after having been given Miranda warnings, elected to remain silent, but then, after having been told of his rights two hours later by a second detective, made the inculpatory statement.

[27] 422 U.S. 590 (1975).

[28] 422 U.S. 171 (1975).

[29] *Doyle* v. *Ohio*, 96 S. Ct. 2240 (1976).

[30] *United States* v. *Mandujano*, 425 U.S. 564 (1976). The rule of this case was that Miranda rulings need not be given to a grand jury witness who was called to testify about criminal activities in which he might have been personally involved, and consequently his false state-

fact that Justices Stewart and White were in vigorous dissent in the original *Miranda* case, it is amazing that the rule retains as much vitality in 1976 as it does. True, it has been qualified; but it has definitely not been repudiated. The law of searches and seizures, however, is another matter.

On the Burger Court it was Justice Black who first criticized the exclusionary rule in his dissent in *Whiteley* v. *Warden*[31] in 1971 when he suggested that the Fourth Amendment "does not expressly command that the evidence obtained by its infraction should always be excluded from proof." In the same year Justice White in his plurality opinion in *U. S.* v. *White*[32] echoed a similar sentiment, but the first major assault on the principle came in *Bivens* v. *Six Unknown Federal Agents*[33] by the chief justice. While excoriating the exclusionary rule as "inflexible," "rigid" and "an anomalous and ineffective mechanism," the chief justice nevertheless did not advocate the overruling of *Weeks* and *Mapp*, but instead, endorsed a statutory remedy analogous to the Federal Tort Claims Act, as a substitute for excluding illegally seized evidence in a criminal trial. While not abandoning the exclusionary rule totally, a majority led by Burger has, since 1973, made it clear that the rule has passed its highwater mark. The rule does not apply to evidence submitted to a grand jury,[34] nor does it forbid the use in a federal civil proceeding of evidence obtained illegally by state or local police and vice versa;[35] nor may *habeas corpus* relief be granted on the ground that a state submitted illegally seized evidence at a defendant's trial.[36] Moreover, the Burger Court has held that the validity of voluntary consent to a search must be determined from the totality of the circumstances, the *Miranda* principle of a knowing and intelligent waiver not being applicable.[37] The Court has also ruled that a person's papers may be seized even when they contain self-incriminating material.[38] Although this is a sharp departure from the Warren years, it is not out of phase with past search and seizure doctrine. In fact, some of the cases have the familiar ring of the Vinson years.[39] The Fourth Amendment is one of the most ambiguous clauses in the Constitution, and its application over a century and a half has been one of vacillation between tightening and loosening restraints on the police. The Burger majority believes that the exclusionary rule does not effectively deter the police, but

---

ments made to a grand jury did not have to be suppressed in a perjury prosecution based on such statements.

[31] 401 U.S. 560 (1971).

[32] 401 U.S. 745 (1971).

[33] 403 U.S. 388 (1971).

[34] *United States* v. *Calandra*, 414 U.S. 338 (1974).

[35] *United States* v. *Janis*, 96 S. Ct. 3021 (1976).

[36] *Stone* v. *Powell*, 96 S. Ct. 3037 (1976).

[37] *Schneckloth* v. *Bustamonte*, 412 U.S. 218 (1973).

[38] *Andresen* v. *Maryland*, 96 S. Ct. 2737 (1976).

[39] See for example: *Harris* v. *United States*, 331 U.S. 145 (1947); *United States* v. *Rabinowitz*, 339 U.S. 56 (1950); *Davis* v. *United States*, 328 U.S. 582 (1946); and *Zap* v. *United States*, 328 U.S. 624 (1946).

simply permits the guilty to go free on a technicality. The rule will no longer be applied automatically unless the police have engaged in either willful or negligent wrongdoing, and it may not be unreasonable to permit a good faith defense against the exclusionary rule where police conduct is only a technical violation of the Fourth Amendment. The justices are not favorably disposed toward prophylactic rules but will look at each case to determine whether there is an injustice. In the immediate future one would expect a diminishing of requirements of probable cause for arrest and search, a more widespread use of the doctrine of harmless error, a greater emphasis on reliable evidence, and a curtailment of collateral attacks in Fourth Amendment cases.

Even with this antilibertarian stance in Fourth Amendment cases, however, the Supreme Court under Burger has upheld a substantial number of claims by criminal defendants.[40] It is this Court, moreover, that has required stringent rules surrounding the death penalty,[41] has extended the right to counsel to all infractions of the law, not simply felonies,[42] and has required a hearing before a parolee may have his parole revoked.[43] In sum, the Burger Court has subjected some of the great Warren decisions to severe restrictions, has refused to extend others, but has overruled none outright. It is wise to recall, however, that the Warren opinions in criminal procedure were bitterly criticized by a vocal minority of four in his own Court, and they were, thus, the most fragile of all his judicial creations.

Equal Protection and Due Process

We need not make any invidious comparisons between the Burger Court and its immediate predecessors when we discuss the broad clauses of the Fourteenth Amendment, for in these areas the chief justice and his flock have made changes only in degree but not in kind. The equal protection and due process clauses are potentially the most unrestrictive and indeterminate in the Constitution, and the present Court has extended the line of cases in both areas to embrace every point of contact between the individual and his government. What

---

[40] *Faretta* v. *California*, 422 U.S. 806 (1975), the right to self-representation at trial; *Mullaney* v. *Wilbur*, 421 U.S. 684 (1975), once the prosecution establishes the fact of an intentional killing, proof that no malice aforethought existed may not be required of the defense; *Gerstein* v. *Pugh*, 420 U.S. 103 (1975), the Fourth Amendment is violated when the defense is denied a probable cause hearing following a warrantless arrest; *United States* v. *Ortiz*, 422 U.S. 891 (1975), immigration officials may not search automobiles at checkpoints without probable cause; *Breed* v. *Jones*, 421 U.S. 519 (1975), the double-jeopardy clause is fully applicable to juvenile court proceedings; *Geders* v. *United States*, 425 U.S. 80 (1976), the government's prohibiting the accused from consulting with his lawyer during a recess between direct and cross-examination violates the guarantee of the right to counsel.

[41] *Furman* v. *Georgia*, 408 U.S. 238 (1972); *Gregg* v. *Georgia*, 425 U.S. 80 (1976); *Proffitt* v. *Florida*, 96 S. Ct. 2960 (1976); *Jurek* v. *Texas*, 96 S. Ct. 2950 (1976); *Roberts* v. *Louisiana*, 96 S. Ct. 3001 (1976); and *Woodson* v. *North Carolina*, 96 S. Ct. 2978 (1976).

[42] *Argersinger* v. *Hamlin*, 407 U.S. 25 (1972).

[43] *Morrissey* v. *Brewer*, 408 U.S. 471 (1972).

the Court has created is a suborder of liberties which have no ascertainable reference points, a state of affairs that provokes the question: "To what extent can the Supreme Court insist upon adherence to constitutionally inspired, but not compelled rules without considering whether the state has provided a minimally satisfactory alternative?"[44] To paraphrase Justice Cardozo, this is constitutional implementation run riot.

The equal protection clause does not describe what interest is protected, and although historically Court rhetoric suggests that the clause protects equality through the application of "equal laws," it cannot guarantee that every law shall apply equally to every person since all law classifies persons for the purpose of bestowing burdens or benefits. At a minimum, equal protection demands that the law provide adequate, and at a maximum identical, treatment of all persons, but in practice the limits of equal protection lie somewhere in between. Today the Court moves uncomfortably among three analytically separate limitations which have become a part of the equal protection gloss. First, the Court has characterized some legislative classifications as "suspect" and, therefore, subjects them to a "strict scrutiny" test. Within this framework the Court has held that legislative classifications which burden constitutionally protected rights are invalid unless it can be shown that the restriction advances a "compelling" state interest and that a less burdensome classification would not adequately serve the governmental purpose. Second, the Court has held that legislation may be invalid when a classification contained therein is not rationally related to a valid state purpose. Here the Court is returning to the old 1930s postulate that a law may not classify persons in an unreasonable, arbitrary, or capricious manner, all of these being subjective value words to be defined by the Supreme Court. A third test which the Court has used with little predictability to nullify legislative classifications or to invalidate laws under the due process clause for want of fair procedures is the "irrebuttable presumption" doctrine. The idea here is to find a requirement stated without exceptions, as in the case of *Cleveland Board of Education* v. *LaFleur*[45] in which the Court invalidated a law providing that all pregnant school teachers must quit teaching before the beginning of the fifth month of pregnancy. Since not *all* teachers in the fifth month of pregnancy are subject to the evil aimed at by the law—diminished capacity to teach causing discontinuity of instruction—to impose the rule without a hearing creates an irrebuttable presumption. Adding to the confusion in standards for equal protection is Justice Marshall's approach which is a flexible balancing of interests test, used in his dissent in *Dandridge* v. *Williams* in 1970.[46] The balancing test achieved majority status for a short period in 1972 in *Weber* v. *Aetna Casualty & Surety Co.*,[47] in which Justice Powell

---

[44] Henry P. Monaghan, "The Supreme Court—1974 Term, Forward: Constitutional Common Law," *Harvard Law Review*, 89 (1975), 9.
[45] 411 U.S. 632 (1974).
[46] 397 U.S. 471 (1970).
[47] 406 U.S. 164 (1972).

authored the Court's opinion, and in *Dunn* v. *Blumstein*[48] in which Justice Marshall was the majority's spokesman.

The specific rationale used by the justice who writes the opinion in any given equal protection case usually determines the outcome in advance. The "strict scrutiny" standard has been so rigorous that virtually no legislation could pass muster. On the other hand the "rational basis for a valid state purpose" comports with a judicial propensity to justify the law in question. Among those classifications which the Court labels "suspect" and therefore an interference with fundamental rights are race,[49] national origin,[50] alienage,[51] and illegitimacy.[52] Among those rights which have been held "fundamental" are the right to travel,[53] to procreate,[54] and the right to marital privacy including a qualified right to abortion.[55] Held not fundamental are rights to welfare,[56] housing,[57] a discharge in bankruptcy,[58] wealth and education.[59] In holding that education was not a fundamental right, Mr. Justice Powell declared that fundamental interests were limited to "rights explicitly or implicitly guaranteed by the Constitution." One presumes that by explicit rights Justice Powell meant such categorical imperatives as freedom of speech and press, the right to counsel or the right against self-incrimination. They are explicit in language, although much can be and has been inferred from those ringing guarantees. "Due process" and "equal protection" however, are open textured in the extreme

---

[48] 405 U.S. 370 (1972).

[49] The principle applies to whites as well as blacks and other racial minorities. See *McDonald* v. *Santa Fe Transportation Co.*, 96 S. Ct. 2574 (1976). The Court has not yet dealt with the trickier question of affirmative action, or temporary preferential treatment to make up for a history of invidious discrimination. Straws in the wind may be the rulings in *Pasadena City Board of Education* v. *Spangler*, 96 S. Ct. 2697 (1976) which held that once a federal district court approves a plan designed to acquire racial neutrality in school attendance, it need not order the school district to rearrange its attendance zones each year in order to attain a racial mix in perpetuity; and *Washington* v. *Davis*, 96 S. Ct. 2040 (1976) which upheld a verbal test for applicants for the police force even though it excluded a disproportionate number of blacks.

[50] *Korematsu* v. *United States*, 323 U.S. 214 (1944).

[51] *Graham* v. *Richardson*, 403 U.S. 365 (1971).

[52] *Jimenez* v. *Weinberger*, 417 U.S. 628 (1974); *New Jersey Welfare Rights Organization* v. *Cahill*, 411 U.S. 619 (1973); *Gomez* v. *Perez*, 409 U.S. 535 (1973); *Weber* v. *Aetna Casualty & Surety Co.*, 406 U.S. 164 (1972); *Levy* v. *Louisiana*, 391 U.S. 68 (1968); *Glona* v. *American Guarantee & Liability Insurance Co.*, 391 U.S. 73 (1968). In *Labine* v. *Vincent*, 401 U.S. 532 (1971) and *Mathews* v. *Lucas*, 96 S. Ct. 2755 (1976) the Court upheld some restrictions on illegitimate children in the Social Security regulations.

[53] *Dunn* v. *Blumstein*, 405 U.S. 330 (1972); *Shapiro* v. *Thompson*, 394 U.S. 68 (1969).

[54] *Skinner* v. *Oklahoma*, 316 U.S. 535 (1942).

[55] *Griswold* v. *Connecticut*, 381 U.S. 479 (1965); *Roe* v. *Wade*, 410 U.S. 113 (1973).

[56] *Dandridge* v. *Williams*, 397 U.S. 471 (1970).

[57] *Lindsey* v. *Normet*, 405 U.S. 56 (1972).

[58] *United States* v. *Kras*, 409 U.S. 434 (1973).

[59] *San Antonio Independent School District* v. *Rodriguez*, 411 U.S. 1 (1973).

and the extent to which these clauses are used to create rights depends upon the majority's view of its role in the American system.

The current attempt to articulate a satisfactory rationale for the result reached in cases alleging sex discrimination exemplifies the lack of any coherent judicial doctrine. Is sex a suspect classification? Yes and no. Since the decision in *Reed* v. *Reed*[60] in 1971 the Burger Court has moved with little sense of direction from one position to another. In *Reed* when the Court invalidated a law giving preference to males over females as administrators of estates intestate, it appeared to treat female sex as a suspect classification, and two years later in *Frontiero* v. *Richardson*,[61] in striking down the federal statute which automatically qualified male servicemen for certain benefits, but excluded females, the Court relied upon *Reed* in holding the classification to the "strict scrutiny" doctrine. But since 1973 the Court has waffled as it upheld some sex classifications but struck down others.[62] It is not an easy area because of natural differences.

If we analyze judicial voting behavior in the equal protection area we see Justices Brennan and Marshall, occasionally joined by White, adhering to "strict scrutiny." Chief Justice Burger and Justices Powell, Stewart, and Blackmun fairly consistently adhere to the "rational relationship" principle, and in those instances in which the government can make a strong case, they will vote to uphold the law and will be joined by Rehnquist who tends to give minimal support to equal protection claims generally. Just a few months ago the Court was urged to treat "age" as a suspect classification but declined to do so when it used the "rational basis" standard to uphold a Massachusetts law providing for mandatory retirement of state police officers at the age of fifty.[63]

Whither the Burger Court on equal protection? It is axiomatic that the Fourteenth Amendment was intended to prohibit all legislation that placed special burdens on the black race, and any laws which fall into that category are automatically suspect by the present Court. In fact the Burger Court has just em-

---

[60] 404 U.S. 71 (1971).

[61] 411 U.S. 677 (1973).

[62] The differing views among the justices were apparent in the various opinions in *Frontiero*. Then came *Kahn* v. *Shevin*, 416 U.S. 351 (1974), upholding a Florida law giving widows but not widowers a property tax exemption (rational distinction); *Geduldig* v. *Aiello*, 417 U.S. 484 (1974) upholding a California law providing disability benefits to employees not covered by Workmen's Compensation, but excluding pregnancy along with other disabilities (rational distinction); *Schlesinger* v. *Ballard*, 419 U.S. 498 (1975) upholding a federal statute giving women twice passed over for promotion a guarantee of thirteen years of service while providing mandatory discharge for men (rational distinction); *Weinberger* v. *Wiesenfeld*, 420 U.S. 636 (1975), striking down section of Social Security Act granting survivors' benefits to widows and children but not to widowers (no compelling governmental interest); *Stanton* v. *Stanton*, 421 U.S. 7 (1975), striking down a Utah law which cuts off parental support payment to girls at age 18 but to boys at 21 (irrational distinction).

[63] *Massachusetts Retirement Board* v. *Murgia*, 96 S. Ct. 2562 (1976).

phatically extended the concept of state action and the frontiers of constitutional rights for blacks beyond previous limits by interpreting Section 1981 of the U. S. Code as outlawing racial segregation in private commercially operated, nonsectarian schools.[64] Extending protection against arbitrary legislation to nationality appears to be a natural and acceptable reach of the Fourteenth Amendment, and the Court's position is indisputably firm in having done so. In all other areas of equal protection, however, there is a total lack of consistency. And "inconsistency in judicial decision is a sign that a legal standard is either deficient or absent, and that a court, acting creatively, is embarked upon a policy formation process without the aid of the legislative mechanism."[65] The fact is that the Burger Court, like its immediate predecessor, has attempted to create rights under the aegis of equal protection and due process, and it has not been able to anchor them with reasoning which makes sense to the intelligent body politic. The chief justice's maxim that if it does not make sense, it is not good law, needs sharper application to the Fourteenth Amendment cases.

Freedom of Speech and Press

Tinsley Yarbrough in his superb, thoroughgoing analysis of the Burger Court and freedom of expression concludes that a majority has given the "fighting-words" exception to free speech a narrow construction, has required a showing of "substantial" overbreadth in cases involving facial review of statutes regulating communicative conduct rather than pure speech alone, has attempted to tighten up the obscenity standard, and has narrowed the concept of the public forum advanced by the Warren Court.[66] Professor Yarbrough wrote the article prior to the appointment of Justice Stevens and before the 1975 term, but he suggested that the appointment of one more "strict constructionist" to the Court might produce a virtual moratorium on facial review and a more expansive application of the *Chaplinsky* exceptions to free speech in scurrilous language cases.[67] Although not yet crystal clear, the Stevens appointment appears to be in the "strict constructionist" mold, and the Yarbrough predictions may be validated. In the single majority opinion which Justice Stevens wrote in a free speech context, *Young* v. *American Mini Theatres*,[68] he indicated that: "the sovereign's agreement or disagreement with the content of what a speaker has to say may not affect the regulation of the time, place, or manner of presenting the speech." Yet, Stevens continued, whether or not speech is protected depends on its content if it incites to crime or violence. He then wrote the opinion upholding

---

[64] *Runyon* v. *McCrary*, 96 S. Ct. 2586 (1976).

[65] Robert G. Dixon, "The 'New' Substantive Due Process and the Democratic Ethic: A Prolegomenon," *Brigham Young University Law Review* (1976), 71.

[66] Tinsley E. Yarbrough, "The Burger Court and Freedom of Expression," *Washington and Lee Law Review*, 33 (1976), 37.

[67] Ibid., p. 90.

[68] 96 S. Ct. 2440 (1976).

Detroit's ordinance regulating the location of adult theatres and book stores, declaring that a state may not totally suppress these materials, but may legitimately use their content as a means of regulation. A telling phrase in Stevens' opinion was this: "But few of us would march our sons and daughters off to war to preserve the citizen's right to see 'Specified Sexual Activities' exhibited in theaters of our choice." This opinion suggests that Justice Stevens may well join the judicial conservatives in making up a majority of five in cases involving scurrilous language, symbolic speech, and "speech plus." In this instance Justice Blackmun joined with Justices Marshall and Brennan to support Justice Stewart's dissent which characterized the Detroit ordinance as prior restraint.

Probably the 1976 case most supportive of the Yarbrough analysis is *Hudgens* v. *N.L.R.B.*[69] which overruled *Logan Valley*[70] and knocked out a prop (admittedly a shaky one from the beginning) of the Warren construct. Since there were only two dissenters, for the foreseeable future the law is settled that a person does not have a First Amendment right to enter a privately owned shopping center for the purpose of distributing handbills or advertising a strike, and the public forum has indeed been narrowed. Another forum was virtually foreclosed when the Court held that a person has no generalized constitutional right to make political speeches or to distribute leaflets on a military reservation.[71] And although *Buckley* v. *Valeo*[72] should be the subject of an article in itself, the question of restraining the *quantity* of speech is a major one since it cannot be completely divorced from limitations on quality, and quantity was restricted by *Buckley* when it sustained the ceiling on campaign contributions.

But if there were several anti-First Amendment decisions, they were counterbalanced by a proportionate number of pros. Violative of freedom of speech are political patronage dismissals[73] and prohibitions against drug advertising[74] (both constitutional firsts). In 1975 the Court held that the state of Virginia could not prohibit a newspaper from taking ads that disseminated information about obtaining abortions,[75] nor could a state coerce a newspaper into granting equal space to a candidate for public office who had been subject to a critical attack by the paper.[76] And in the *Erznoznik* case[77] the majority held invalid a

---

[69] 424 U.S. 507 (1976).

[70] *Amalgamated Food Employees Union Local 590* v. *Logan Valley Plaza, Inc.*, 391 U.S. 308 (1968).

[71] *Greer* v. *Spock*, 424 U.S. 828 (1976).

[72] 424 U.S. 1 (1976).

[73] *Elrod* v. *Burns*, 96 S. Ct. 2673 (1976).

[74] *Virginia State Board of Pharmacy* v. *Virginia Citizens Consumer Council*, 425 U.S. 746 (1976).

[75] *Bigelow* v. *Virginia*, 421 U.S. 809 (1975).

[76] *Miami Herald Publishing Co.* v. *Tornillo*, 418 U.S. 241 (1974).

[77] *Erznoznik* v. *City of Jacksonville*, 422 U.S. 205 (1975). Professor Yarbrough maintains that in *Broadrick* v. *Oklahoma*, 413 U.S. 601 (1973) the Court adopted the "substantial" overbreadth standard for facial review of statutes regulating communicative conduct rather than

city ordinance that made it a punishable offense to exhibit any motion picture containing nudity where the screen is visible from a public street. In *Erznoznik* and two earlier cases involving symbolic speech (wearing the American flag on the seat of one's pants and hanging the flag upside down with a peace symbol attached)[78] the Burger Court sounded very much like the Warren Court, trotting out "overbreadth," "void for vagueness," and "no compelling state interest."

The ties to the past are manifest in free speech decisions, for at its libertarian best the Court under Warren or Stone or Hughes, and not inconceivably under Vinson, could have authored the decisions involving prior restraint such as the *Pentagon Papers Case*,[79] *Erznoznik*,[80] *Miami Herald Publishing Co. v. Tornillo*,[81] *Bigelow v. Virginia*,[82] the *Drug Advertising Case*,[83] the *Nebraska Press Case*,[84] and *Hynes v. Mayor of Oradell*.[85] The Warren Court would probably have struggled with *Buckley v. Valeo*[86] in about the same manner as did the current Court, and it would not have been discomfited by the recent symbolic speech cases or the scurrilous language cases of the early Burger years. From 1971 to 1973 the Burger Court overturned no less than six convictions, generally on the overbreadth-vagueness principle, in which people had been arrested for using foul language in public.[87] Justice Stevens may help to form a majority, including Justice Powell who, though often supporting the speaker in the past, has expressed strong concern over the "disquieting deterioration in standards of taste and civility in speech."[88] As we know, the obscenity standard has been qualified and it probably will be modified further.[89] Neither the Warren Court nor the present one has been able to deal effectively with the obscenity question, in part because of persistent disagreement among the justices. Only Justices

---

"pure speech" alone. But *Erznoznik* concerned a statute deterring the exhibition of movies in a certain place with particular consequences. Justice Powell, for the majority in *Erznoznik* thought the statute "substantially" overbroad, but the chief justice along with Justices Rehnquist and White thought it "absurd to suggest that the ordinance operates to suppress expression of *ideas*." Is there really any constitutional distinction between "substantial overbreadth" and "overbreadth"?

[78] *Smith v. Goguen*, 415 U.S. 566 (1974); *Spence v. Washington*, 418 U.S. 405 (1974).
[79] *New York Times v. United States*, 403 U.S. 205 (1975).
[80] 422 U.S. 205 (1975).
[81] 418 U.S. 241 (1974).
[82] 421 U.S. 809 (1975).
[83] 425 U.S. 748 (1976).
[84] 96 S. Ct. 2791 (1976).
[85] 425 U.S. 610 (1976).
[86] 424 U.S. 1 (1976).
[87] *Gooding v. Wilson*, 405 U.S. 518 (1972); *Rosenfeld v. New Jersey*, 408 U.S. 901 (1972); *Lewis v. City of New Orleans*, 408 U.S. 913 (1972); *Brown v. Oklahoma*, 408 U.S. 914 (1972); *Plummer v. City of Columbus*, 414 U.S. 105 (1973); *Hess v. Indiana*, 414 U.S. 105 (1973).
[88] Dissent in *Rosenfeld v. New Jersey*, Id. at 909.
[89] See *Miller v. California*, 413 U.S. 15 (1973).

Brennan, Marshall, and Stewart continue to adhere to the position that the government may regulate obscenity for only two reasons: the protection of children and the prevention of obtrusive material being thrust upon unwilling recipients.[90] There is a good chance that a solid majority of six may be willing to sustain more stringent state and local regulatory legislation.

The Burger Court, like its predecessors, has not been able to articulate any consistent theory of First Amendment rights because it has not come to grips with the real issues. The Supreme Court helped to create one of the major problems when it gradually came to accept the idea that the First Amendment guarantees freedom of "expression," a term that at first glance appears to be a logical extension of "speech" and "press." Expression, however, has a broad outreach that goes far beyond verbal and written communication to embrace conduct, and when "expression" is deemed both a fundamental right and a preferred freedom, what forms of expression become constitutionally impermissible? Beginning with *Cohen* v. *California*[91] the Court has spent valuable time each term with cases involving scurrilous language and generally has not permitted local governments to punish people for calling public officials that crude epithet beginning with M, ending with R, and with an F in between. Certainly young Cohen would not have dramatically made his point if the words on his sweatshirt had said "Copulate the Draft," nor would Patrick Henry have made his if he had said, "Give me a fair trial and freedom from unreasonable searches or life won't be worth living," but the distinction between Patrick Henry and Paul Cohen is obvious. Archibald Cox has stated that extending First Amendment protection to sheer vulgarity gives it "an imprimatur which contributes to the lowering of public discourse."[92]

But protected expression has gone far beyond the verbal to include symbolism which has no apparent limit. A year ago a federal court found a violation of freedom of expression in an anti-topless dancing ordinance.[93] Although the Supreme Court has not met the nude dancing issue frontally, or contrapuntally, it has suggested that it might be entitled to First Amendment protection.[94] It is not clear what message the nude dancer is attempting to promulgate, but, then, perhaps in McLuhan's phrase, the medium is the message, or in the old adage, some things speak for themselves.[95]

Indications are that the Burger Court may move away from granting constitutional protection to extreme forms of expression, and may formulate a

---

[90] *Paris Adult Theater* v. *Slaton*, 413 U.S. 49 (1973). See Robert Rosenblum, "The Judicial Politics of Obscenity," *Pepperdine Law Review*, 3 (1975), 1, for a careful discussion of the issues.

[91] 403 U.S. 15 (1971).

[92] Archibald Cox, *The Role of the Supreme Court in American Government* (New York, 1976), pp. 47–48.

[93] *Salem Inn, Inc.* v. *Frank*, 552 F. 2d 1045 (2d Cir. 1975).

[94] *Doran* v. *Salem Inn, Inc.*, 442 U.S. 922 (1975).

[95] See Dixon, "The 'New' Substantive Due Process," pp. 61–65, to whom I am indebted for some of the graphic language.

doctrine for obscenity regulation which would permit broad artistic creativity while excluding the pornographic, but it is not clear whether the justices are willing to produce a model which would adhere to the Jeffersonian/Madisonian concept of protecting rational discourse but permitting the representatives of the people to fix, within reason, standards of public morality.

CONCLUSIONS

Although this has been a discursive and selective treatment of current directions of the present Supreme Court, we can say in sum that the Court is skewed toward a conservative-restraint position, and yet has not broken out of old Warren pathways. All of the legal doctrine fashioned in earlier years—"fundamental rights," "vagueness," "facial overbreadth," "irrebuttable presumption," "compelling state interest," and "preferred freedoms"—remain in the arsenal of weapons with which the Court may nullify legislative discretion. With notable exceptions the Court suffers from the same malady as Courts of the past —a propensity to find derivative rights in the Fourteenth Amendment, a lack of ability to fashion creative, common sense standards for the First Amendment, an inclination to constitutionalize minor points of regulation,[96] and a tendency toward constitutional dogmatism. All of this does violence to the principle of representative democracy which holds that legislative assemblies compromise political deadlocks and broker social wants. At the same time there are indications that the Court is moving away, at least in some areas,[97] from the concept of expanded judicial review, and this gives credence to the view that judges cannot become administrators or budget makers without eroding "their own immunity from political accountability."[98] First and foremost, judicial review in the American system must be accountable to the Constitution and it must be perceived as legitimate by the people. It can be both of these only when the grounds for decision contain an inner logic of such overwhelming substance that even those who disagree with it can accept it as a proper limitation on majority rule.[99] Thus the Supreme Court cannot be simply another political agency that consciously builds a coalition of interest groups. It must be above the political battle. It must be disinterested. In contradistinction to the critics of the right who condemn the Burger Court for its judicial activism in *Roe* and *Doe* and those of the left who excoriate it for its "harmless error" atti-

---

[96] See for example, *Goss* v. *Lopez*, 419 U.S. 565 (1975), public school suspensions; *Wood* v. *Strickland*, 420 U.S. 308 (1975), liability of public school officials for student suspensions; *Cleveland Board of Education* v. *LaFleur*, 414 U.S. 632 (1974), teacher pregnancy in public schools.

[97] *Washington* v. *Davis*, 96 S. Ct. 2040 (1976), police applicant examination; *Sosna* v. *Iowa*, 419 U.S. 393 (1975), divorce residency; *McCarthy* v. *Civil Service Commission*, 424 U.S. 645 (1976), requirement that city employees be residents of the city.

[98] Dixon, "The 'New' Substantive Due Process," p. 83.

[99] Robert J. Steamer, "Judicial Accountability," *The Human Life Review*, 2 (1976), 23.

tude in criminal procedure, one might argue that it has, in fact, yet to break out of the Warren mold. It can retain the best of the Warren years, and there is much worth retaining, but it can eschew the old pitfalls. It can do so by avoiding facial nullification where "invalid as applied" will vindicate an individual's rights. It can limit adjudication to substantial constitutional issues and avoid the use of vague doctrinal rules which tend to make the legislation suspect at the very threshold of judicial review.[100] In the long run it is the legislature that must deal with reasonable political alternatives since the judiciary is not well suited for the task. The Burger Court has given some indications, but only some, that it recognizes the limits of its power.

POSTSCRIPT

This manuscript was completed in the summer of 1976 after the Court had recessed at the end of the 1975 term, but little of judicial significance occurred during the subsequent term ending July 1, 1977 that would alter the general theme of the article. Although the term saw a more restrictive posture with respect to the rights of persons accused of a crime, the Court nevertheless refused to overrule *Miranda*, even when asked to do so by twenty-two states (*Brewer* v. *Williams*), and the justices rejected a request to limit the requirement that police obtain warrants before conducting searches (*U.S.* v. *Chadwick*). Although access to the Supreme Court was denied to some, it was made easier for others, including prison inmates who now have the constitutional right of technical assistance in preparing and filing legal papers (*Bounds* v. *Smith*).

In the area of freedom of speech the Court's position on obscenity continued to be restrictive, but it extended protection to new aspects of commercial speech. It upheld the principle of lawyer advertising (*Bates* v. *Arizona*) and struck down an ordinance banning the use of "for sale" signs in front of houses, even though the aim of the law was to prevent the flight of white homeowners for racial reasons (*Linmark Associates Inc.* v. *Willingboro*). It also held violative of the First Amendment the New Hampshire requirement that noncommercial vehicle license tags bear the motto, "Live Free or Die" (*Wooley* v. *Maynard*).

The Court continued to use "equal protection" in some instances to overturn the legislative judgment, much to the annoyance of Justice Rehnquist. In *Craig* v. *Boren*, Justice Brennan writing for the majority, struck down an Oklahoma law that prohibited the sale of 3.2 percent beer to males under twenty-one and to females under eighteen, declaring that: "To withstand constitutional challenges previous cases establish that classifications by gender must serve important governmental objectives and must be substantially related to achievement of those objectives." Justice Rehnquist suggested that Brennan's phrase "comes out of thin air" and that "none of our previous cases adopt that standard." The chief

---

[100] See William D. Valente, "On Eccentric Constitutional Jurisprudence," *Catholic Lawyer*, 21 (1975), 235, for a succinct critique of the Burger Court.

justice agreed with him. And in *Trimble* v. *Gordon* when Justice Powell, speaking for the majority, deemed a violation of equal protection an Illinois law that allowed illegitimate children to inherit by intestate succession only from their mothers while legitimate children are allowed to inherit by intestate from both parents, Justice Rehnquist, once again in dissent, countered that except for "classifications based on race or on national origin . . . the Court's decisions can fairly be described as an endless tinkering with legislative judgments, a series of conclusions unsupported by any guiding principle." Other examples of judicial disagreement with the legislative judgment are manifested in the striking down of Louisiana's mandatory death penalty for murdering a policeman (*Roberts* v. *La.*), of the New York law limiting access to contraceptives (*Carey* v. *Population Services International*), and of the New York statute that bars resident aliens from state financial assistance for higher education unless they have applied for, or plan to apply for U.S. citizenship (*Nyquest* v. *Mauclet*).

Neither time nor space permits a thoroughgoing analysis of the Court's work this past term, but this sampling clearly indicates that in spite of the hand-wringing of the civil rights activists, the contrast between the Burger and Warren Courts is not as sharp as they allege. Distinctions do not stand out in bold relief but appear only as subtle shadings as the activist flavor of the Warren era remains in vogue.

PART III
Foreign Policy Issues

The Americans' Retreat
from World Power

BRUCE RUSSETT

When Vice-President Lyndon Johnson returned from the first meeting of the Kennedy cabinet in January 1961, he was deeply impressed by the intellectual capacity of that group of men drawn from the worlds of government, business, finance, and academia. After he exclaimed about these qualities to Speaker of the House Sam Rayburn, "Mr. Sam" replied skeptically, "Well Lyndon, you may be right and they may be every bit as intelligent as you say, but I'd feel a whole lot better about them if just one of them had run for sheriff once."[1]

Too many recommendations for United States foreign policy read as though they had been written by someone who had never even "run for sheriff once." Concerned with the "balance of power," or "America's responsibilities in the world," or meeting alleged threats to "vital interests," they seem to imagine that all the important variables affecting the country's foreign policy emanate from the international system itself. When pressed, of course, most commentators will acknowledge the limitations of such a view, but still may not take sufficient account of the constraints imposed by domestic politics.

This article will show that a very major shift in foreign policy beliefs and preferences has occurred among the American public—a marked

[1] Quoted in David Halberstam, *The Best and the Brightest* (London, 1972), p. 41.

BRUCE RUSSETT is professor of political science at Yale University, editor of the *Journal of Conflict Resolution,* and Co-Director of the Roper Center, Inc. His most recent books are *Interest and Ideology: The Foreign Policy Beliefs of American Businessmen* (with Elizabeth Hanson) and *Progress in Arms Control?* (with Bruce Blair).

shift away from acceptance of the political "responsibilities of world power." In this sense it is a shift in the direction of political "isolationism," though not nearly as severe as the kind of viewpoint historically connoted by the term, and it does not constitute any change from an expectation of continued and growing economic interdependence in the world. Furthermore, it is not a short-term phenomenon in reaction against the Vietnam disaster; rather it appears likely to be prevalent for a long period, probably more than a decade, and to be manifest in the very same influential circles of the American populace which formally supported the "internationalist," "globalist," "interventionist" (choose the word that suits your evaluation) American foreign policy of the cold war years.

This assessment is not a popular one among those Americans who would like to reassure the nation's allies about continued American support or who wish to retain an appearance of determination in the world. An American indifference to foreign affairs surely will make little contribution toward solving the many serious problems which face the nations of the world. But if the assessment presented here is correct, a change in policy will be manifest soon enough, and it is best to recognize openly what really are the new domestic conditions. A great deal of information can be brought forward to document this new mood. Several such pieces will be discussed, but it should be clear that they are only a few among many, merely illustrative of a great number of signs waiting to be read.

OPPOSITION TO MILITARY SPENDING

There is, first, an indication of a drastic transformation in attitudes toward defense spending and the proper size of the American military establishment. Since 1937, almost at the beginning of scientific public opinion polling in the United States, nationwide surveys have regularly asked respondents whether they thought the country was spending too much, too little, or about the right amount on defense. The wording of the question has varied somewhat, but not enough to interfere with a clear interpretation.[2]

During almost the entire period those preferring lower levels of defense expenditure were in a small minority. Even in the "isolationist" 1930s, the figure began in 1937 at 20 percent and quickly fell to below

[2] The following data and discussion are drawn from Bruce M. Russett, "The Revolt of the Masses: Public Opinion on Military Expenditures," in John P. Lovell and Philip S. Kronenberg (eds.), New Civil-Military Relations: The Agonies of Adjustment to Post-Vietnam Realities (New Brunswick, N. J., 1974).

FIGURE 1

Percentage of Population Favoring Less
Defense Spending, 1937–1974

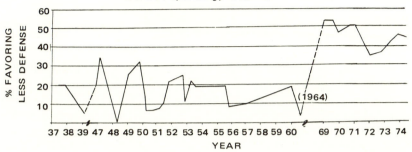

10 percent. Following World War II opinion fluctuated for a while, but those favoring less defense spending always numbered under 35 percent of the population (and the only two surveys showing more than 30 percent in this category in fact used questions biased toward producing an antidefense response). By the early 1950s the oscillations had damped down, showing a steady figure of less than 20 percent of the population thinking military spending was too high. By contrast, the number favoring more defense was always higher than 20 percent, and often very much higher. (The remainder were satisfied with the existing level, or had no opinion.) Furthermore, those favoring cuts in defense spending were drawn disproportionately from low-income, low-status groups—those least likely to be politically influential. This situation remained in effect until the mid 1960s, at which point several years passed without the question appearing in a national survey, thus breaking the time-series.

When use of the question was resumed in December 1968, however, it became evident that a great change had occurred. Beginning with that date, ten different surveys have found the number favoring a cut in defense spending to be near, and sometimes even above, the 50 percent mark, with the number favoring heavier defense spending only about 10 percent. Eliminating the "don't know" responses, a clear majority with opinions therefore wanted a smaller military budget. And while the anti-military sentiment of several years ago may have been expressing opposition to the Vietnam war, it is remarkable that the latest survey, showing 44 percent in favor of a smaller arms budget, was taken in September 1974 after direct American participation in the war had ended. These results are shown in Figure 1.[3]

[3] Figure 1 is taken from ibid., p. 67, but updated with information from a survey by the Roper Organization, Inc., in October 1971 and surveys by the American Institute

Just as striking is the turnaround in the kinds of people expressing such sentiments. Since 1968, those who want to see the defense budget cut are not those of low status, but rather are found disproportionately among professional groups, and those of high income and education. In other words, *antimilitary-spending attitudes are concentrated precisely among those most likely to take an interest in international affairs, to vote, to make campaign contributions, and otherwise to be politically active.* The same pattern shows up in surveys concerned with attitudes toward the military in general and, since 1968, in disapproval of the Vietnam war. Special surveys of elite groups also find these attitudes to be particularly strong.[4]

Professor Alan Barton and his associates at Columbia University interviewed over 500 top business executives, labor leaders, senior civil servants and political figures, leaders of major interest groups, and top media personnel: 64 percent of them, when asked the question about military spending, responded that the defense budget should be cut.[5] And in the author's own sample survey of almost 600 vice-presidents of the largest industrial and financial corporations in America—a group generally considered to be relatively conservative, at least among elites—51 percent gave the same answer.[6]

It is worth noting, too, that this tide of opinion against military spending has occurred simultaneously with a very significant decline in the proportion of national income that is in fact devoted to military purposes. Defense spending accounted for only 6.6 percent of American gross national product in 1973, the lowest percentage since 1950 and almost a full percentage point below the pre-Vietnam (1965) floor.[7] By many criteria defense spending may still be too high, and high by long-term pre-World War II standards. But the current opposition to it arises precisely at a time when the proportionate military burden nevertheless is low by cold war standards.

A great deal of similar material is available to document attitudes of this sort. Again from our survey of corporate vice-presidents in 1973, we

---

for Public Opinion in August 1972, February 1973, September 1973, and September 1974.

[4] Ibid., p. 78.

[5] Allen Barton, "The Limits of Consensus Among American Leaders," mimeo. (New York, 1972).

[6] Bruce M. Russett and Betty C. Hanson, *Interest and Ideology: The Foreign Policy Beliefs of American Businessmen* (San Francisco, forthcoming) presents in detail the evidence concerning the following material on attitudes among businessmen and military officers.

[7] Russett, "Revolt of the Masses," supplemented by material from *Survey of Current Business.*

asked whether they favored an increase, a decrease, or maintenance at the present level for both foreign economic assistance and military aid. Fully 54 percent declared that they wanted a decrease in economic aid, and 71 percent desired a cut in military aid. There once was a time when military aid for foreign countries was a more popular item among Americans than was foreign economic assistance, and when the largely "internationalist" corporate elite tended to favor both. That time is gone. Moreover, 91 percent now want to see a cut of some sort in the number of United States troops in Europe. Most—59 percent—prefer to make that cut contingent on a Mutual Balanced Force Reduction accord with the Soviet Union, but as many as 12 percent choose "total withdrawal" as the option which best describes their views.

VIETNAM AND MILITARY INTERVENTION

If there was ever any enthusiasm for the Vietnam war among the business executives surveyed, it is hard to find it now. When we asked, "Do you personally think it was correct for the United States to send ground combat troops to Vietnam?" only 37 percent replied "yes," while 53 percent said "no," and another 10 percent still could not decide. Of those who said it was not correct, only 40 percent indicated that they had held the same view since the beginning of the war. As many as 22 percent remembered themselves as having changed their opinion in 1967 or 1968. This confirms other evidence we have about when sentiment in the business and financial community shifted decisively against the war. We found that share prices on the New York Stock Exchange reacted essentially randomly to Vietnam war events before 1967, but from that time on fell into a predictable pattern of a rise in stock prices in response to peace moves by either side.[8]

The great majority of executives, whether on balance they approve or disapprove of American participation in the war, agree that it was very costly to the United States. No less than 86 percent believed that the war was "bad" for American social and political institutions, and 77 percent made a similar evaluation of the war's effects on the economy. Furthermore, over half of those think they would have retained that negative evaluation even "if inflation had been controlled."

Having been burned once, they are not anxious to undertake another war which might have similar consequences. That is evident from re-

---

[8] Betty C. Hanson and Bruce M. Russett, "Testing Some Economic Interpretations of American Intervention: Korea, Indochina, and the Stock Market," in Steven Rosen (ed.), *Testing the Theory of the Military-Industrial Complex* (Lexington, Mass., 1973).

sponses to questions about American intervention on behalf of other governments. We posed this problem:

In the event that one of the following nations is attacked by foreign communist forces and requests U. S. help, there are three courses of action the U. S. might take:

    1. Use military force to extend all needed help.
    2. Provide help, but short of U. S. military involvement.
    3. Stay out.

Please indicate the course of action you think the U. S. should take for each nation.

We then listed seven countries: Brazil, India, Japan, Mexico, Thailand, West Germany, and Yugoslavia. For only two of these states, Mexico and West Germany, were a majority—and only a bare majority in the case of Germany—prepared to recommend United States military action. As for India and Yugoslavia, a majority checked the "stay out" option, sometimes with comments like, "Are you kidding?" A national survey of the entire American public in 1970 showed an even more extreme situation—a majority were ready to use American military forces in *none* of these cases.

This skepticism about military action on behalf of allies and neutrals becomes even greater when we substitute, in place of attack by foreign communist forces, "a serious insurgency problem led by an indigenous communist movement." Then there is no longer a majority of businessmen prepared to use military force on behalf of the governments of *any* of these countries; moreover Thailand joins India and Yugoslavia as nations where a clear majority of the executives would stay out entirely. All this despite the fact that we deliberately labeled the attacking or insurgent forces as "communist."

The same questions were put to a similar sample of senior military officers—more than 600 colonel and lieutenant-colonel level officers of all services attending the war colleges, usually en route to highly responsible staff and command positions. A majority of them were ready to add Brazil, Japan, and Thailand to the list of countries they would defend by force from communist invasion. But still they would use American military forces against communist insurgents only in Mexico.

Now of course these are highly abstract, hypothetical situations, and the choice among the three options is hardly more than a parody of the enormously complex set of options that would in fact be at the disposal of a policy maker in a real world situation. Faced with the reality of an attack or insurgency against an important United States ally the respondents might be much more prepared to approve the use of force. Their statements in the abstract ought not to be used as though they were predictive. Nevertheless, the apparent reluctance to be drawn into an overseas war is striking. All these results, but especially those for the business executives, seem very strange coming from a formerly "internationalist" elite. Nor do they fit very well with neo-Marxist theories about imperialism.

Even those business executives who do not advocate substantial cuts in the defense budget seem unconvinced that such reductions really would have important deleterious effects on the United States. We offered several options as to possible increases or decreases in defense spending: only 15 percent chose the rather extreme "25 percent or more" cut option. But when we asked "Do you think a 25 percent reduction in defense spending would have an adverse effect on American security vis-à-vis other nations?" only 52 percent answered "yes" (as compared with 85 percent who favored smaller cuts, or none). Just 33 percent thought such a large cut "would have an adverse effect upon the American economy," and only 38 percent thought "a retrenchment of U. S. foreign policy commitments would have a negative effect on U. S. economic expansion abroad."

This last response is terribly important to a balanced understanding of what has been happening in the minds of American corporate executives. Certainly there is evidence of a massive decline of enthusiasm for American *political* and *military* commitments abroad. But their interest in, and expectation of, expanding *economic* activities in foreign countries remains. We asked three questions about expectations for American business expansion overseas in the next decade. In response to these questions 83 percent anticipated an increase in American involvement in foreign markets and foreign investment; 98 percent expected American business transactions with Russia and China to increase substantially; and 62 percent thought that American sales and investments in the less developed countries would increase relative to similar activities in developed countries. Expectations were a little more tempered when we substituted "your own firm" for "American business transactions" generally; the numbers then fell off to 85 percent, 60 percent, and 54 percent respectively for executives from the "Fortune 500" industrial corporations—not really a substantial drop.

Just as vital to understanding this world view is the executives' image of trade as contributing to peaceful political relations. We asked them to choose, from a fairly long list of possibilities (including, among others, strengthening international institutions, military superiority, a balance of power, and arms control) what they considered to be "the most important approach to world peace." Almost 62 percent chose the category "trade, technical cooperation, economic interdependence." Conversely, only 19 percent chose, as the most important cause of *war*,

the category "economics (scarcity, drive for profits, technical dynamism)." Many executives were especially enthusiastic about the broader
international implications of greatly expanded commerce with Russia,
Eastern Europe, and China. They see the globe as economically interde-
pendent, ultimately with beneficial political effects. This is a retreat from
power, but no simple "isolationist" turning away from the world.

THE SENSE OF THREAT: PAST AND PRESENT

What is apparent here is that Americans in general, and elites in particular, see international affairs as less threatening than they once did.
When asked, "Do you think the external threat of communism to U. S.
security has increased, decreased, or remained the same over the last decade?" only 15 percent of the businessmen perceived an increase, and 58
percent saw a decline. Almost half thought American involvement in
war during the next decade was "improbable" or "highly improbable,"
and just 30 percent put the odds at 50–50. Only 19 percent regarded it
as "probable" or "highly probable." Less than 10 percent thought that
any war that might arise would involve use of nuclear weapons.

Finally, we asked them to choose from a list of "major problems facing the United States today." The percentage naming each of the five as
"the most serious" follows:

Domestic order and stability	37%
Social and racial disparities within the United States	20
World ecological problems: Pollution and population pressures	18
National and socialist movements in less developed countries	15
Military and technological advances of China and Russia	9

"Traditional" cold war concerns came in last. The highest ranking international issue was the new set of environmental problems, and even it
ranked behind domestic problems of order and justice. And the particular content of a person's foreign-policy preferences makes little difference to this ranking. Those who remain hawks, as well as those who are
doves, agree in rating foreign policy problems as the least important.

The cold war sense of urgent threat is gone from most Americans'
political consciousness. One may or may not be surprised, given the sear-
ing effects of Vietnam on American politics. In some ways it is surprising that the change of mood was so long delayed. In 1950 Gabriel Al-
mond published his perceptive book, *The American People and Foreign
Policy*.[9] He argued that Americans' interest in foreign policy was highly
susceptible to changes of mood, that a sense of threat might be rapidly

[9] Rev. ed. (New York, 1960).

followed by a sense of complacency, and that these fluctuations in public opinion severely endangered efforts to build a stable foreign policy upon a realistic assessment of long-term risks to the nation's security. He, and many other academics as well as government officials, felt that this tendency to instability demanded a substantial effort to educate the American public about the complexity of international affairs and the abiding nature of America's problems. In light of experience during the "isolationist" 1920s and 1930s this was an altogether understandable assessment. It was reasoning like this that led Senator Vandenberg, in declaring that he supported Harry Truman's 1947 proposals for aid to Greece and Turkey, to urge the president to "go and scare hell out of the country." Only by determined efforts could a stable political base for an internationalist foreign policy be secured.

In fact that base was secured, as the data on approval of defense spending in Figure 1 illustrate. Subsequent research on Americans' foreign policy attitudes led to the conclusion that mood swings were not large during the cold war period.[10] The oscillations were soon damped, and stability was the rule. Quite the opposite of violent mood swings, many analysts of the period conclude that the "educational" campaign to awaken Americans to their external responsibilities and dangers succeeded all too well. This is evident, for example, in several interpretations of the Vietnam discussions as revealed in the Pentagon papers.

According to this view, American policy makers became imprisoned by popular anticommunism even though, in most cases, the policy makers themselves were too sophisticated really to share the popular perspective. The "loss" of China to the communists in 1948 was exploited heavily by the Republicans for political purposes. In the wake of anticommunist sentiment deliberately set in motion by political leaders of both parties, McCarthyite hysteria began to take hold in wide sectors of the populace, and to be felt especially keenly by politicians. Almost every political figure with any kind of liberal background or inclinations felt vulnerable to witch-hunting accusations that he was "soft on communism," or worse. In the words of former Senator Sam Ervin as he recalled the days of Joseph McCarthy, "You can't believe the terror that man spread among politicians."[11]

Thus politicians feared to loose still further a popular anticommunism which would punish them for foreign policy defeats, and became constrained by anticommunism even when they did not accept its premises. Believing that the people would not tolerate the "loss" of Vietnam, senior

[10] William R. Caspary, "The Mood Theory: A Study of Public Opinion and Foreign Policy," *American Political Science Review*, 64, no. 2 (June 1970), 536–547.
[11] Seminar at Yale University, February 13, 1974.

elected and appointed officials in Washington therefore resolved that Vietnam would not be lost—at least during their own terms in office. They would hang on, and escalate where necessary to avoid defeat, even though they knew the long-term prospects for holding the country were poor. They could hope to postpone the day of reckoning to a time when they themselves would not be held responsible, and perhaps to a time when the mood of the country would change so that the defeat would not be turned into a major threat to free institutions in America. Meanwhile they could hope, against the evidence available to them, that events might break favorably so that the ultimate outcome would not be disastrous. By some interpretations this kind of thinking can be found in every administration from Truman to Nixon.[12]

If this view is correct—and it rings true to many observers as at least a partial explanation of why American foreign policy went wrong, if not as *the* explanation—the new fact is simply that the situation has now changed enormously. The great backlog of popular anticommunism and determination to fight just no longer exists. Some hawks of course remain, but many are gone (dead, retired, or converted) and those who are left speak less often and less vigorously. The point is not whether their assessment of the external dangers to America in the 1950s was correct, or whether the current assessment of greatly diminished (or never serious) dangers is correct. Rather it is that people's beliefs are very different now, and that the constraints on policy makers are thus different. Many observers have held further that the sense of external threat during the cold war years became a force delaying reforms in American domestic society. Often foreign policy hawks and domestic policy conservatives were the same, or at least in alliance. When external events seemed to strengthen the political position of the hawks, the conservatives also waxed. In an atmosphere of external danger, questioning about whether American institutions really were serving fundamental American values was suppressed. It was not a time to encourage domestic experimentation, and in any case resources seemed too scarce. Priority went to military expenditures, often drawn directly from funds that would otherwise have gone to investment or to public civil programs for health, education, or urban development.[13] It may now become possible to try once again to meet some of these needs.

---

[12] This seems basically to be the interpretation of Daniel Ellsberg, "The Quagmire Myth and the Stalemate Machine," *Public Policy*, 19, no. 2 (Spring 1972), 217–274. See also Leslie Gelb, "Vietnam: The System Worked," *Foreign Policy*, no. 3 (Summer 1971), and Halberstam, *The Best and the Brightest.*

[13] Evidence for this is in Bruce M. Russett, *What Price Vigilance? The Burdens of National Defense* (New Haven, Conn., 1970), chap. 5.

A PASSING GENERATION

The end of cold war ideology in American life can be attributed to a combination of change of minds and change of bodies. For the latter, we now have in the electorate a whole generation of voters with no adult memory of American participation in World War II or even of the beginnings of the cold war. For those who took part in it, World War II was a glorious crusade against a force of undoubted evil. Its success set some mental precedents for American acts on the world stage under circumstances where the danger was more ambiguous and the prospects for success less certain. Nevertheless these attitudes did carry over into the cold war period for the containment of communism, and again were reinforced by the substantial success of these policies in the early years. Thus a whole generation was imprinted with beliefs about the power and responsibilities of the United States in the world arena. Now we have a new cohort of voters who not only do not share this imprinting, but instead are imprinted by the Vietnam tragedy and its entirely opposite "lessons." This new cohort is far less ready to accept the standard arguments for an interventionist foreign policy or the need for large armed forces.

Some data may illustrate what has happened. In the September 1970 survey about military spending, 60 percent of voters under thirty wanted to reduce military spending, whereas only 46 percent of those thirty and over gave such an answer. Similarly, an analysis of behavior in Congress has shown that representatives born after 1920 (which made them relatively young in the Congress of 1970) or first elected *after* the McCarthy years are markedly more dovish and more skeptical of military spending than are their older colleagues.[14] Many of these younger, more dovish, congressmen are relatively new to the Capitol; others have changed their views from a hawkish position while in Congress. As many of the older members die, retire from office, or are defeated for reelection the shift in the center of gravity of foreign policy position in Congress is almost certain to continue. Certainly not all old congressmen are hawks nor are all young ones doves—some of the exceptions, like former Senator Fulbright, are prominent enough—but this characterization holds in general.

Generational attitudinal changes are well-known phenomena in social science, and there is good evidence for their persistence long after the immediate stimuli have passed.[15] An explanation based on generational

---

[14] H. Wayne Moyer, "House Voting on Defense: An Ideological Explanation," in Bruce M. Russett and Alfred Stepan (eds.), *Military Force and American Society* (New York, 1973).

[15] See Davis Bobrow and Neal E. Cutler, "Time-Oriented Explanation of Na-

effects helps to make sense of the now quite famous data presented by Frank Klingberg, and which have been updated here to 1974.[16] Figure 2 shows the percentage of annual presidential messages, since 1790, devoted to foreign affairs. The annual data have been smoothed out into ten-year averages (except for the most recent, shorter period) so as to clarify the main characteristics. What is evident is a roughly forty-year cycle from trough to trough, with the cycle for the latter half of the nineteenth century somewhat foreshortened and the following one lengthened accordingly. Certainly these data should not be treated mechanically for an exercise in curve-fitting; the time-span is much too short to allow us to be very confident in any cyclical interpretation or prediction. But the other evidence available on generational changes provides a theoretically plausible interpretation for the Klingberg data.

However, it is not *only* a generational phenomenon that has occurred. In the September 1970 survey discussed above, we noted that even of those more than thirty years old, 46 percent wanted to see the military budget cut. In addition to the imprinting or conversion of the young, many of the not-so-young have changed their minds—and it is important to know what kinds of people the latter are. For the most part, it is typically the liberal on domestic policy, especially on matters of income distribution, civil rights, and civil liberties. In the 1950s there was little association of domestic liberalism with the point of view we would now term dovish. A large number of liberals in fact took pride in being identified as liberal internationalists or globalists, a posture which in its foreign policy component included foreign aid, alliance commitments for the defense of other states in the Free World, and high levels of military preparedness. Samuel Huntington reports that in Congress, northern Democrats were as likely to support higher defense expenditures as were either Republicans or southern Democrats.[17] John Kennedy could in 1960 campaign both as a liberal and against failures of the Republican

---

tional Security Beliefs: Cohort, Life Stage, and Situation," *Peace Research Society (International) Papers*, 8 (1967), 31–37, and Neal E. Cutler, "Generational Succession as a Source of Foreign Policy Attitudes," *Journal of Peace Research*, 1 (1970), 33–47. The classic paper is Karl Manheim, "The Problem of Generation," in his *Essays on the Sociology of Knowledge* (London, 1959). An excellent review of work is to be found in Alan B. Spitzer, "The Historical Problem of Generations," *American Historical Review*, 755 (December 1973), 1353–1385.

[16] Frank Klingberg, "The Historical Alternation of Moods in American Foreign Policy," *World Politics*, 4, no. 2 (January 1952), 252–253. See also the excellent article by Michael Roskin, "From Pearl Harbor to Vietnam: Shifting Generational Paradigms," *Political Science Quarterly*, 89, no. 3 (Fall 1974), 563–588. Note that the Klingberg data as presented here coincide almost perfectly with the alternating periods Roskin describes: 1890s–1919 intervention, 1920s and 1930s isolation, etc.

[17] Samuel P. Huntington, *The Common Defense* (New York, 1961), pp. 254–259.

FIGURE 2

*Percentage of President's Annual Messages Devoted to
Foreign Affairs, Ten-Year Averages, 1790–1974*

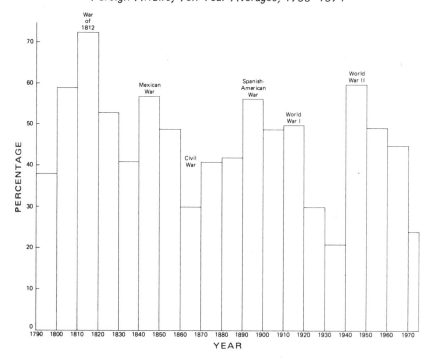

administration to keep up the nation's military guard and to prevent emergence of the alleged (and illusory) "missile gap." Many liberals today recall in rather embarrassed silence the "internationalist" rhetoric of Kennedy's inaugural address.

Liberals nevertheless saw themselves, and in large degree rightly so, as moderates on these foreign policy issues, desirous of an active American role in making the world safer, richer, and more democratic while avoiding what they termed hysterical anticommunism and military "pactomania" on the one hand and isolationist withdrawal on the other. Liberals were prominent in the arms control movement, "realistically" dismissing the "utopian" hopes of general disarmament but working arduously for limited measures to tame and stabilize the balance of terror through negotiation with the Soviet Union and lesser reliance on nuclear weapons, especially the threat of massive retaliation, to deter all kinds of attacks everywhere. This is the context in which the enthusiasm for built-up capabilities for conventional and counterinsurgency wars should be seen. In the same vein Andre Modigliani found, rather than an isolationist-internationalist dimension, that foreign policy attitudes during the Korean war could better be characterized as in one of three quite distinct directions: supporters of the administration's limited war policy; those who wanted more vigorous military effort to bring victory, à la Douglas MacArthur; and those who wanted the United States to withdraw rapidly without much regard for the consequences.[18] The first generally fit the image of liberal internationalists, the second and the third were different kinds of "conservatives."

This middle-of-the-road international image of the liberals fits with most of the quantitative evidence available for the period. For example, Leroy Rieselbach, and others before him, found essentially no systematic relations between congressmen's voting on domestic and foreign policy issues.[19] As for members of the public at large, Norman Nie found really no correlation (actually an average of −.05) between foreign policy attitudes and a liberal position on several domestic policy items ("integration," "black welfare," and "social welfare" issues).[20]

As we all know, however, that situation has by now changed dramatically. A basic divergence of beliefs on ends as well as on the means of American foreign policy has emerged, and divergences on this matter frequently coincide with divergences on domestic policy. In Nie's examination of the major public opinion surveys, the correlation between liberal attitudes on various domestic issues and "dovish" ones on cold war international issues jumped to .25 in 1964—before Vietnam—and remained at essentially that level in the 1968 and 1971 surveys. The same kind of change occurred among elites, though possibly it took place a bit later. For example, the present author found in the ninetieth Congress (1967–1968) quite a substantial correlation between Senate voting on defense and foreign policy issues on the one hand, and civil rights and urban affairs on the other. This is a new finding, not present in the analysis made of the Eighty-seventh Congress (1961–1962) or in those made by previous scholars. More relevant still are Moyer's data on the House of Representatives.[21] He found a strong (.82) correlation

[18] Andre Modigliani, "Hawks and Doves, Isolationism and Political Distrust: An Analysis of Public Opinion on Military Policy," American Political Science Review, LXVI, no. 3 (September 1972), 960–978.

[19] Leroy N. Rieselbach, The Roots of Isolationism (Indianapolis, Ind., 1966), and Duncan MacRae, Dimensions of Congressional Voting (Berkeley and Los Angeles, 1958).

[20] Norman Nie, "Mass Belief Systems Revisited: Political Change and Attitude Structure," Journal of Politics, XXXVI, no. 3 (August 1974), 540–591.

[21] Russett, What Price Vigilance? chap. 2, and Moyer, "House Voting on Defense." See also Robert A. Bernstein and William W. Anthony, "The ABM Issue in the Senate, 1967–1970: The Importance of Ideology," American Political Science Review, LXVIII, no. 3 (September 1974), 1198–1206.

in 1967–1968 between dovish votes on cold war foreign policy issues and a liberal position on civil liberties, as well as weaker correlations between a cold war scale and favorable attitudes toward government spending and also a generally liberal position on domestic politics. In the Ninety-first Congress (1969–1970) voting on a defense or "preparedness" scale also correlated very highly (.87) with scales for urban and race affairs, government spending, and domestic liberalism in general. Thus by 1969 and 1970 congressmen saw all these issues as closely interrelated, in a way that they had not only a few years before. The reason seems obvious enough. Liberals saw the heavy costs, in terms of their preferred domestic policies, being imposed by an activist foreign policy in general and by the Vietnam experience in particular: alienation, police repression, and especially demotion of spending priorities for health, urban affairs, and education because of military commitments. By the 1970s there are few liberal hawks showing the kind of "liberal messianism" associated with some members of the Kennedy administration.

Similar evidence emerges from our survey of business executives, confirming this view that foreign policy issues were brought into line with domestic policy preferences. Of the businessmen who thought it had been a mistake to get into the Vietnam war, 38 percent gave damage to American social and political institutions as the reason—more citing this than any other single reason and far more (7 percent) than those citing damage to the American economy. We asked the businessmen whether they considered themselves better or worse off as a result of the war and why. Of those who said "worse" and indicated a reason, economic reasons were cited frequently (by 42 percent), but the number listing some version of damage to American political institutions or diversion of resources away from social priorities was still greater (over 46 percent). A few quotations illustrate how executives linked these issues in their minds. Among the war's opponents:

> The most important ill effect of the Vietnam War on the United States has been on the level of morality, the becoming inured to "kill ratios," mass killing of civilians along with military disregard for human life. These have been accompanied by erosion of individual rights and privacy in the United States.

> It brought out the worst kind of actions on the part of our government officials—using any means, such as lying to the people and to Congress, that they thought justified by the end: trickery, sacrificing great virtue in our system.

Still another lamented "the pain of conscience, the shame and guilt of a racist war, the setback to social and economic progress." Among the entire samples of businessmen and military officers, by far the best "predictor" of hawk-dove *foreign* policy preference was conservative-liberal position on *domestic* issues, which was much better than information on life experience or economic interests.

The pervasiveness and the relative recency of this particular consistency of domestic and foreign policy beliefs may surprise us, but the fact that people often impose some such consistency should not. The literature on ideology, how people order their thoughts and information so as to interpret new facts, is massive. Ole Holsti states the general view well when he calls a "belief system"

> . . . a set of lenses through which information concerning the physical and social environment is received. It orients the individual to his environment, defining it for him and identifying for him its salient characteristics. . . . In addition to organizing perceptions into a meaningful guide for behavior, the belief system has the function of the establishment of goals and the ordering of preferences.[22]

More recently, social scientists have turned with great interest to theories of "cognitive processing," stressing the deductive elements of an ideology, the "decision calculus" whereby new items are interpreted, usually in a way that makes sense of the new without importantly modifying the old beliefs. Analogizing from the past, as well as overt deduction, also is a common mechanism. Thus one may equally evoke the memory of Munich as a "guide" to negotiation with an adversary as deduce an orderly set of propositions leading from general rules to the specific situation. All the literature on cognitive dissonance, and its resolution, is in some degree also relevant here.

We know that basic policy attitudes do not change drastically in response to single events, even dramatic ones. Any way one looks at the matter, it takes repeated, and deep, shocks to the effectiveness of old beliefs before they shift markedly. The first reaction is typically to deny that a new piece of information is really accurate, or to deny its importance if accurate. Or old views may be shifted temporarily, but reassert themselves when the new piece of information is no longer salient. But repeated prominent events, all supplying stimuli in the same direction, do have the ability to change attitudes in a substantial part of the population.[23] The Vietnam war, composed actually of many traumatic political events spread over almost a ten-year period and supplemented by

---

[22] Ole R. Holsti, "The Belief System and National Images: A Case Study," *Journal of Conflict Resolution*, VI, no. 3 (September 1967), 245.

[23] See Karl W. Deutsch and Richard L. Merritt, "Effects of Events on National and International Images," in Herbert Kelman (ed.), *International Behavior: A Social-Psychological Analysis* (New York, 1965).

detente, the American rapprochement with China, and other such developments, could produce such changes. Even after Vietnam is no longer prominent in conscious memory, the effects of the past decade will remain in people's minds, carrying through most of their remaining political lives. In this way it affects many people of all ages, not only those of a young and impressionable political generation. Together, this imprinting of a new generation and the conversion of many in the older one give us good reason to believe that a *long-term* change in American foreign policy interest and attitudes has occurred, and that it will be some *years before it is effectively reversed.*

To the extent that this interpretation is correct, the current and recent American debates over detente should be seen in a new light. Since the Yom Kippur war and renewed difficulties in negotiating strategic arms agreements with the Soviet Union, detente seems to have lost some of its thrust, further efforts to cut the defense budget have failed, and trade agreements with the Soviet Union have languished. Some of the old hawks have been joined, in partial coalition, by people who are uneasy about the consequences of a new tilt to American policy in the Middle East. Further progress in East-West relations has been slow. Yet if the above thesis is accepted, then these recent resistances should be seen primarily as minor fluctuations, akin to quite small year-to-year variations in economic activity over the longer and much more pronounced ups and downs of the long-term business cycle. Popular desires for a retreat from world power will remain strong for quite a while, and those dependent on American foreign policy might as well come to grips with the implications of those desires.

It is important, while recognizing the likelihood that generational phenomena are relevant, not to exaggerate the similarities between the 1970s and the years between the two great wars. A full return to the isolationism of that period is unimaginable. American economic and political involvement in the world is too great to permit it, popular attitudes have not gone that far, and responsible political leaders surely would not allow it. Nor are we seeing a revolution in attitudes like that which, in reverse, produced the outward thrust of internationalism in the 1940s. To make such an extreme argument would merely be to parody the view expressed here.

By the same token, only a Nostradamus could predict specific policy changes to follow from the attitudinal change. Surely it will become progressively harder to maintain the full American troop presence in Western Europe, to keep up what remains of the credibility of the deterrent umbrella for America's allies, and to sustain the level of military spending at even the current share of gross national product. Former President Nixon tried to do all these things, probably with greater determination and greater success than his successor is likely to do. Even "Scoop" Jackson as president would be constrained by this new public mood. A round of belligerence by the major Communist states would make a difference, but would probably have to be both dramatic and sustained to make a very great difference.

WHY PUBLIC OPINION MATTERS

We should recognize too that we have been discussing material about public opinion, or rather the opinion of various publics—mass, attentive, and elites—and not the beliefs and attitudes at the very top of the foreign policy decision-making system. More than in domestic policy, foreign policy makers do have some latitude to act independently of public opinion. Despite the constraints, they may persist for a while even if general opinion lags behind, and they may work to educate the public and bring it along to accept the policies the decision makers believe are right. We have good evidence of the decision latitude for a long time available to American presidents on Vietnam, when there was a potential majority available to be mobilized either for moderate escalation or moderate withdrawal, according to the direction in which the president chose to lead.[24] Also, the "rally 'round the flag" phenomenon of crisis behavior is well known.[25]

The effects of flag rallying are nevertheless short-term ones, and the period of its relevance becomes ever shorter the more frequently it is invoked. And many kinds of foreign policy behavior are not suitable for rallying the populace as in a crisis. The year-in, year-out maintenance of troop levels and weapons capabilities requires congressional approval under circumstances where the tradeoffs in terms of domestic welfare can become vividly apparent. A credible plan for any military action short of all-out nuclear war demands a public prepared to make sacrifices for a sustained military effort. It is one thing for a commander-in-chief to be able to order troops into a conflict without seeking prior approval; it is quite another to keep those troops there for months. or years in light of the new assertion of congressional prerogatives in this area.

It also has been said that it is not public opinion that matters, but what decision makers *think* is public opinion. By this reasoning, policy makers will implement the new mood only if they perceive it in its depth and breadth. To the extent they are isolated from it they will go on as before. Such a belief assumes, however, that decision makers are not subject

[24] Sidney Verba et al., "Public Opinion and the War in Vietnam," *American Political Science Review*, 61, no. 2 (June 1967), 317–333.

[25] See John Mueller, *War, Presidents, and Public Opinion* (New York, 1973).

to effective sanctions when they seriously misperceive public opinion over long periods. Whatever may be the case in some political systems, I doubt that is true in the American democracy. Politicians have very effective ways, certainly not limited to public opinion polling, to discover what their constituents want and how strongly they want it. The penalties for consistent misperception are simple enough—loss of office. Two former presidents could readily enough testify to those penalties. Then, too, we have been discussing the climate of opinion in which policy makers themselves form their own ideas; no man is an intellectual island, and surely no politician is. Top policy makers typically are somewhat older than the average of their countrymen, members of an earlier generation and in any case are subject to the particular formative experiences of their political roles. Therefore they by no means simply reflect their countrymen like a perfect mirror. But the differences can easily be exaggerated. Moreover, the people in powerful positions immediately below the chief, placing upon him the dual constraints constituted by intelligence sources and policy executers in any hierarchy, are rapidly being infiltrated by the new generation. Already the generation that knows Vietnam but not World War II is forty years old.[26]

AMERICA'S REAL INTERESTS IN THE WORLD

Finally, we should say some small thing about the implications of this basic attitude change for the pursuit of a foreign policy compatible with "real" American "interests." Obviously there are myriad "national interests," with as many assessments as assessors. Any such evaluation is bound to be subjective, reflecting the writer's own prejudices. If we were to limit the discussion to East-West superpower relations, I think I would find myself not very disturbed, and might even be heartened, by the new attitudes. It seems to me that cold war anticommunism has long outlived whatever usefulness it had. Renewed efforts for detente are essential and to be welcomed, and the shift in mood makes them easier and perhaps even imperative for American leaders. This does indeed imply some relaxed assessments about the degree to which the Communist powers are able, or rather unable, to mount really serious threats to really serious American interests in the next decade or two. If one is more pessimistic about those threats over a longer period, then one can take con-

[26] Even Bernard Cohen, at the end of a book highly critical (and appropriately so) of many assertions about the importance of public opinion as an actual constraint on decision makers, concludes with "the paradox that a policy making system which has mastered all the modes of resistance to outside opinion nevertheless seems, from a long-run perspective, to accommodate to it." *The Public's Impact on Foreign Policy* (Boston, 1973), p. 205.

solation from the possible upturn in "internationalism" with the next turn of the foreign policy cycle as the current generation too passes by around 2000 A.D.

But a focus merely on great power relations is myopic. It seems to me that the truly grave problems of international politics concern not relations among the "haves"—America, the Soviet Union, Europe, Japan, and even in some respects China—but rather relations between the rich and the poor. We live in a world of rising frustration as development efforts falter while images of rich people living well in their Northern Hemisphere citadels are diffused ever more widely across the globe. Modern communications have come to the poor world not in sufficient force to bring substantial economic development, but enough to bring information about how well a rich minority is managing. With the crumbling of traditional religious beliefs and acknowledgment of authority, these rising frustrations are accompanied by a falling threshold of tolerance for frustration. The weapons of destruction come increasingly into the hands of those ready to use them. Sometimes those hands control governments, more often now they control nongovernmental or transnational organizations quite prepared to take actions for which they cannot effectively be held responsible. The IRA, the Palestinian guerrillas, the Tupamaros are portents of things to come, with grievances deeply felt and often widely acknowledged as just. Many transnational actors, and even some governments of poor states, may be quite ready to go out with a nuclear bang if their frustrations cannot be assuaged. At the moment the world political anarchy is hardly prepared to cope either with the violent symptoms or with the basic human needs which underlie them.[27] Nor are standard military procedures likely to be effective.

An America turning away from the world, in a political if not an economic sense, will hardly make a sufficient contribution to meeting these problems. The current disillusionment with foreign aid is illustrative. By wide agreement the foreign economic assistance program failed to achieve either the goals it set itself or the goals which it should have set itself. As a result its political backing—always tenuous at best—has evaporated, and economic aid as a proportion of gross national product has fallen from a peak of 1.6 percent in the Marshall Plan years, or even .5 percent in 1962, to less than .2 percent now.[28] Perhaps that in itself is just as well, perhaps it was a misguided effort which could not treat the true causes of international poverty and inequality. But the tragedy is that nothing very much is coming up to replace it.

[27] These problems are discussed in Bruce Russett, *Power and Community in World Politics* (San Francisco, 1974), chap. 9.
[28] U. S. Bureau of the Census, *Statistical Abstract of the United States, 1973* (Washington, D.C., 1973), p. 775.

An American retreat from world action will do little to solve these basic problems. In some respects it may be better that the United States do nothing rather than continue some of the wrong things it has been doing, but that cessation alone would constitute a pretty minimal achievement. It is doubtful that the world's peoples will wait patiently for Americans to come naturally to their next period of looking outward.

Kissinger and Acheson:
The Secretary of State
and the Cold War

WALTER LAFEBER

Since World War II, the secretary of state's central concerns, if diagramed, resemble a wishbone. Projecting from a common center, one side extends toward areas which before 1945 were of little concern to the United States: the eastern Mediterranean, Korea, Indochina, and now Africa. The other side points toward the secretary of state's need to create and maintain a public consensus at home to support these new policies. The latter task has not been easy during many of the postwar years. Support has been hard to retain for involvements in out-of-the-way corners of the globe; or, as in the case of Indochina, it has been difficult to hide that involvement from the public and then, when it is discovered, to explain it away. The obligations overseas and those at home have consequently often been at cross-purposes. The tension has grown during the 1970s until the wishbone has nearly snapped, forcing the secretary of state into quick shuttle diplomacy, vague agreements that promise more than they can deliver, and subtle manipulation of the media. Such devices, however, have only temporarily relieved the tension.

If Dean Acheson was "present at the creation" of the secretary of state's bifurcated responsibility, Henry Kissinger was present when Acheson's creation nearly came apart. Acheson did not act alone in creating the postwar global order, and Kissinger, contrary to the carefully cultivated "lone cowboy" image, did not single-handedly attempt to hold up that sagging order. But each man brought a world view and a personality to his task that were of historical importance. David McClellan's lengthy biography, *Dean Acheson*, Bruce Mazlish's

WALTER LAFEBER is professor of history at Cornell University. He is the author of *The New Empire: America, Russia and the Cold War*, whose third edition just appeared; and a forthcoming work on the United States and Panama.

Kissinger, and John G. Stoessinger's *Henry Kissinger* explore the opening and closing of an era in world history.[1]

These volumes raise two particularly disturbing questions: first, whether even an intelligent and powerful secretary of state's conceptualization of world order (a conceptualization whose foresight and coherence enable him to guide and dominate others), is necessarily so limited, perhaps anachronistic, in regard to non-Western areas that his diplomacy is inadequate from the start; and second, whether in order to keep the wishbone connected a secretary of state must manipulate American society rather than keep it accurately informed.

The primary importance of Acheson and Kissinger is their attempt to translate personal world views into a new global order.[2] McClellan does not coherently explore Acheson's conceptual framework, although the secretary personally considered such a framework of central importance. Arguing in 1954 that "Governmental policy is an integer," and that diplomatic, military, economic, and fiscal policy is "all one," Acheson asked: "Do we cut the pattern according to the cloth or do we cut the cloth according to the pattern?" He answered, "The first requirement is that there must be a pattern."[3] Six years later, Acheson approvingly quoted Roger Hilsman: "It is almost traditional in America to view foreign affairs as a problem in public administration," but "few of our true failures are attributable to bad administration in carrying policy out. Our true failures probably lie more often in failing to recognize emerging problems in time."[4] Although he placed a high priority on a smoothly running department, Acheson apparently did not share the view of many scholars who believed American foreign policy suffered more from bureaucratic inefficiency than from a dearth of good ideas. McClellan notes, for example, that Acheson neglected the Policy Planning Staff not for organizational reasons, but because differences between the secretary of state and George Kennan, the staff's director, were "also philosophic and substantive."[5]

Acheson's most important concept, McClellan writes, "involved the twofold process of exploiting the [Soviet] threat in order to overcome the threat and to reconstitute the chaotic and demoralized Western state system."[6] His passion for order at least equaled Kissinger's. McClellan argues that Acheson, contrary to many in his "social class," had "a remarkable ability to accept social change

---

[1] David S. McLellan, *Dean Acheson: The State Department Years* (New York, 1976); Bruce Mazlish, *Kissinger: The European Mind in American Diplomacy* (New York, 1976); John G. Stoessinger, *Henry Kissinger: The Anguish of Power* (New York, 1976).

[2] On the absence of conceptual planning in American foreign policy, a provocative essay is

[3] Dean Acheson, "The Responsibility for Decision in Foreign Policy," *Yale Review,* XLIV Zbigniew Brzezinski, "Purpose and Planning in Foreign Policy," *Public Interest,* XIV (Winter 1969), 52–73.

(Autumn 1954), 1–12.

[4] Don K. Price (ed.), *The Secretary of State* (Englewood Cliffs, N. J., 1960), pp. 36, 47–48.

[5] McLellan, *Acheson,* p. 172.

[6] Ibid., p. 380.

with equanimity." The evidence in the book indicates otherwise, for Acheson quit the New Deal in 1933 because of Roosevelt's desire for rapid change, and as secretary of state he refused to recognize the need for radical reform in Asia and Latin America. His reluctance to work for social change was particularly remarkable since he had served as a law clerk with Louis Brandeis (in whose office, McClellan writes, "Acheson became acutely aware of many of the brutal social conditions of the era").[7] His quest for global order led him into areas new to American diplomacy, in order to oppose revolutionary movements in those and other areas, and, in such vital places as Greece and China, to confuse national movements with Russian expansionism.

Kissinger's policies also emerged from a world view that assumed the need for order. As might be expected, Mazlish sometimes uses psychohistory to explain that need, but his major contribution is in utilizing a wide knowledge of nineteenth- and twentieth-century Europe to write an intellectual history that judges Kissinger on his own terms, and pronounces him a failure. For although Kissinger wanted to temper American innocence and optimism with a European sense of tragedy, "he never succeeded in fusing the two traditions."[8]

In tracing Kissinger's important distinction between a desirable "legitimate" and an undesirable "revolutionary" state, Stoessinger recalls a conversation when he and Kissinger were graduate students at Harvard:

> What, I asked, would be his view if the leader of a legitimate state pursued unjust ends while the revolutionary had justice on his side? Then, the statesman must choose, Kissinger replied without hesitation. How, I wondered. Kissinger replied with a quotation from Goethe: "If I had to choose between justice and disorder, on the one hand," he said, "and injustice and order, on the other, I would always choose the latter."[9]

The most striking aspect of such an idea is not that its roots are in a particular nineteenth-century European order, or that it emanated out of a rebellion against the disorder that created Nazi and Communist power. Most striking is the similarity of Kissinger's world view to that of Acheson. The Jewish emigré and the son of an Episcopalian minister from Connecticut came to see the globe in much the same way. The two statesmen differed from the rest of their countrymen only in being able to make that view more coherent, historically rooted, and politically effective.

The differences between the two men are so minor as to be enlightening. Kissinger wrote extensively about Metternich and Bismarck, but his hero was England's Castlereagh. Acheson picked up the story at that point. During the 1930s, McClellan observes, Acheson "acquired a great admiration . . . for the Victorian period" of British history, especially London's ability to use its capital as a cornerstone of "world peace and stability. The role that Britain had played would

---

[7] Ibid., pp. 14–17.
[8] Mazlish, *Kissinger*, pp. 297–298.
[9] Stoessinger, *Henry Kissinger*, pp. 12–14.

be at the forefront of Acheson's mind in 1945 when America faced the choice between exercising a constructive role in the world or returning to isolationism."[10]

Despite similar grounding in nineteenth-century Europe, however (and here the irony is particularly revealing), both men shared with many Americans a mistrust of Western European initiatives. Acheson's determination to create the Marshall Plan and NATO emerged from fundamental American, not European, needs, and McClellan offers an interesting thesis that Acheson was distinctly cool toward European integration, particularly the European Defense Community. The main American objective was German rearmament, and Acheson tolerated unification policies in order to obtain the rearmament. Stoessinger is more blunt about Kissinger: "Europe brought out the darker side of his personal diplomacy." His "Year of Europe" speech "reminded one European diplomat of an unfaithful husband's decision to declare a 'year of the wife,' " nor did it help when he blurted out that he "didn't care what happened to NATO," and delivered lectures to Portugal that deeply angered Western Europeans.[11] Such thoughts from two secretaries of state who were supposedly "European" in viewpoint makes more understandable the reciprocal mistrust between Dulles and Kennedy, on the one hand, and France and Great Britain, on the other. One begins to wonder whether the Atlantic community's interests are as common as the Trilateral Commission and other Atlanticists believe.

Thus although both men dealt with European problems, their most important legacy might well become their policies toward non-Western, revolutionary areas. Acheson and Kissinger are sometimes considered "conservative," but the term is useful only if it means they were antirevolutionary. Neither man possessed the sense of proportion and limit associated with classical conservatives. As Mazlish notes, in both his senior thesis and later interviews, Kissinger urged "an active recognition of limits," but the Cambodian operations of 1969–1971, the Christmas bombing of Vietnam, and the wiretapping of his associates did not demonstrate that Kissinger acted on his own advice. Similarly, Acheson placed more confidence in American power than in the wisdom of recognizing national limits when he shaped the rhetoric of the Truman Doctrine and allowed MacArthur to go to the Yalu.

The two secretaries did part company over economic policy. McClellan summarizes its importance to Acheson. To "revisionists," he writes,

> Acheson was nothing more than a mouthpiece for big business. To be sure, a capitalist economy functions best in the context of a multilateral trading world, and the American economy, being the most powerful, could benefit disproportionately from such a context. But, paradoxically, Acheson's arguments were an attempt to convince the representatives of the capitalist system . . . that America had a stake in restoring the conditions of a multilateral trading world.[12]

---

[10] McLellan, *Acheson*, pp. 30–31.
[11] Stoessinger, *Henry Kissinger*, p. 219.
[12] McLellan, *Acheson*, p. 93.

(The book is marred by McClellan's beside-the-point comments about revisionist history. He apparently did not realize that in this instance, among others, most revisionists would not disagree with his own assessment of Acheson.)

If Acheson's policies rested on a comprehensive analysis of capitalist needs, including an orderly world in which business leaders could project long-term plans, Kissinger's world view was fundamentally, perhaps fatally, flawed by a neglect of economics. In this he only reflected the denigration and ignorance of economic factors found in many of the international relations works and "consensus" histories that misshaped American intellectual life during the 1950s and early 1960s. Mazlish observes that Kissinger's assumption "that the existence and expansion of Hitler's power was abetted by foolish men of goodwill" who knew nothing of power "focuses on short-range factors and neglects the deeper causes going back [to the economic settlement in] the Treaty of Versailles."[13] Kissinger's world view, while rooted in history, was so narrow and skewed when he came to power that it crippled him when he had to deal with the problems of the southern hemispheres.

For his part, Acheson fared little better in understanding those Third World affairs. From 1945 until late 1950 he was often confused about Asian problems. McClellan shrewdly argues that MacArthur did not march to the Yalu and go to war with China because, as Richard Neustadt and others would have it, the bureaucracy malfunctioned. It was a problem of perception: "The explanation seems to lie in the pervasive American tendency . . . to believe that somehow the canons of international politics are suspended when it comes to China." Acheson viewed the Peking regime as "a docile puppet of Moscow without a will of its own."[14] He paid little attention to Latin America and Africa, while his Indochina policy proved disastrous.

Acheson's policies in these areas did much to shape events in the 1950s and 1960s, and again Kissinger was a product of the times. By carefully planting the colorful "lone cowboy" image, Kissinger has successfully flummoxed a wide range of journalists and critics. By helping him build this image these observers have prevented us from coming to terms with conceptual failures that go far beyond a single actor. Kissinger, of course, seldom had to act alone. He enjoyed Fritz Kraemer's fatherly protection in the army, Carl Friedrich's and William Y. Elliott's powerful support at Harvard, Richard Nixon's alloyed blessings in Washington, and Nelson Rockefeller's influence and bankroll everywhere else. With support like that, Kissinger more resembled a cowboy riding along with the Third Army than a loner riding apart from the wagon train.

In 1968 Kissinger left Harvard to perform on the world stage, but in Mazlish's words, "It is clear that on most issues, at least till Watergate, Nixon called the tune."[15] Stoessinger's evidence, although not his thesis, substantiates that assessment, as does the testimony of some Kissinger aides who were with him during

[13] Mazlish, Kissinger, p. 292.
[14] McLellan, Acheson, p. 294.
[15] Mazlish, Kissinger, p. 217.

the yeasty 1969 to 1971 years. Nixon originated many of the initiatives, but of at least equal importance, he provided the all-important political consensus required for the success of those initiatives. That he maintained that consensus until late 1973, long after it should have been destroyed by Vietnam, and that he did it in large part through lying and criminal acts, are also remarkable.

Equally noteworthy was Kissinger's insensitivity to the delicacy of that consensus, or, indeed, even to the need for devoting attention to the maintenance of a public consensus in American foreign policy. That insensitivity is exemplified in two well-known essays written before his move to Washington.[16] When the consensus finally disintegrated in 1973–1974, Kissinger was caught intellectually naked. The story goes that during a 1974 news conference he fended off criticisms by claiming that the great American "heartland" was with him. A reporter asked him how many times he had been to the "heartland" lately. Out of an inability to answer that question satisfactorily came Kissinger's plan to deliver a series of major addresses in the Midwest and South.

By that time, however, it was too late. The consensus which Truman and Acheson had carefully created with the Truman Doctrine had collapsed. A fundamental change began in the relationships between foreign and domestic policy, a change linking the two through pocketbook issues that created new constituencies at home with which the State Department had to deal. That change required, and continues to require, someone as secretary of state who is more than merely a technician, an experienced international negotiator, or a skilled administrator.

Throughout the first century of American government, the ablest secretaries of state (Jefferson, Madison, John Quincy Adams, Seward) were, not coincidentally, also powerful domestic political figures.[17] Since the central foreign policy issues involved commercial interests or expansion into foreign-held territory that abutted the American frontier, these men necessarily equated successful foreign policy with successful politics at home.

The relationship between foreign and domestic policy changed as the United States embarked upon its overseas expansion in the 1890s. Foreign policy became more particularistic and separated from most domestic concerns. The State Department, John Hay wrote during his tenure as secretary (1898–1905), was "remote from the public gaze and indifferent to it."[18] Hay characteristically exaggerated, but in 1909 *The Nation* remarked that an experienced congressman had told a new member "to avoid service upon a fancy committee like that of Foreign Affairs if he wished to make himself popular with his constituents, as they cared nothing about international questions."[19] That also turned out to be an exaggera-

---

[16] "Domestic Structure and Foreign Policy," and "Central Issues of American Foreign Policy," in Henry Kissinger, *American Foreign Policy. Expanded edition* (New York, 1974).

[17] A good discussion of this point can be found in Alexander DeConde, *The American Secretary of State, An Interpretation* (New York, 1962).

[18] Quoted in Peter F. Krogh, "The State Department at Home," *The Annals*, CCCLXXX (November 1968), 121.

[19] *The Nation*, September 30, 1909, pp. 294–295.

tion, for in 1919 Woodrow Wilson failed the test of reconciling the public to his plans for a League of Nations.

During the 1920s, however, policy makers such as Charles Evans Hughes, aided by new groups as the Council on Foreign Relations, shrewdly created a fresh national consensus to support foreign policy. Another type of public involvement occurred in 1934 when the Reciprocal Trade Agreements Act suddenly created a tie between the State Department and domestic producers whose overseas interests were multiplying. By the eve of World War II, the department's number of economic personnel would equal its number of political officers. Such experienced observers as John Dickey, William Y. Elliott, and Don Price have agreed, in Price's words, that after the 1934 acts "no one could ever suppose again that our domestic and foreign affairs were separable."[20]

But Henry Kissinger, who learned much from Elliott on other matters, did make such a supposition. Or more accurately, he apparently believed that while they might be inseparable at points, foreign policies would not be ultimately governed by domestic affairs. His illusion probably resulted from Acheson's handiwork. More than any other official, Acheson performed a vital service for a generation of foreign policy makers by devising in the Truman Doctrine a Manichean world view that, when firmly fixed in the American mind, gave those policy makers a freedom of action that nineteenth-century secretaries of state would have found unbelievable. Acheson created this consensus, and the next four administrations worked hard to maintain it, partly out of a fear that a freewheeling public opinion would undermine foreign policy, and also out of a certain disdain for the right of Congress and the larger public to shape policy. Acheson resembled Kissinger, not Seward, Madison, or Hughes, in calling a presidential nominating convention "a mad and not a little degrading spectacle," in terming his job as State Department liaison with Congress "a low life but a merry one," and in causing one congressman to complain that when testifying before a Capitol Hill committee Acheson often looked "as if a bit of fish had got stuck in his mustache."[21]

McClellan shares many of Acheson's views, consequently overlooking evidence, including public opinion polls which circulated in the State Department during 1947, that revealed a remarkably sophisticated public which at least intuited the dangers of global military involvement far better than did Acheson or his successors. But McClellan candidly admits that Acheson and Truman "certainly contributed a stick or two" to the "fires" that reduced American perception of world affairs to a burned-out Manicheanism. The secretary of state, McClellan concludes, blurred "strategic distinctions between vital and peripheral interests. . . . Thus his efforts to explain limited politics in limited terms did not succeed."[22] In other words, he became the captive of his own supposed success.

[20] Price, *The Secretary of State*, pp. 144, 168.
[21] McClellan, *Acheson*, pp. 20–23; *Harper's*, CCXI (November 1955), 20.
[22] McClellan, *Acheson*, pp. 133–134, 404.

Kissinger apparently understood little of this, or perhaps saw no need to question it since he agreed with both of Acheson's priorities: containment of communism everywhere at all costs, and the subordination of domestic needs and politics to the containment policy. Mazlish perceptively notes that Kissinger "postulates and assumes a conservative domestic policy as a sort of given, a necessary correlate to a conservative foreign policy."[23] When the status quo crumbled under the attacks of civil rights forces and the antiwar movement, Kissinger urged a new consensus which would once again bring foreign policy debate to a halt considerably short of the water's edge. Others argued that Congress' role had to change (and, by implication, the secretary of state's role as a political leader had to be rethought) because of the decay in the two-party system. In Joseph Califano's words, "Partisan politics have thus had little relevance to the conduct of foreign policy for more than thirty years."[24]

That apparent historical fact, however, will not excuse secretaries of state from acting, as nineteenth-century secretaries acted, as political partisans. For partisanship means more than competition between the two major parties. In many of the most momentous foreign policy debates during the past seventy years, partisan divisions were intraparty: the Roosevelt-Taft division over arbitration treaties and Asian policy, the Hoover-Borah split over approaches to Japan and the Soviet Union, the Hull-Morgenthau argument over policy toward Japan and Germany, the Truman-Wallace fight over containment, the Eisenhower-Taft struggle over foreign commitments, the Johnson-Fulbright (or McCarthy or McGovern) falling-out over Vietnam, and the Kissinger-Reagan clash over détente and Panama. The "party may be over," but the politics linger on. That is why William Y. Elliott was right when he noted in 1960 that "The idea of having a Cabinet Secretary (of any department) who is 'nonpartisan' contradicts the logic of Presidential government."[25]

That is also why one of the best recent essays on the secretary of state's role focused on its political responsibilities. Since 1945, Howard Furnas observed, "foreign policy programs have been largely argued for and justified solely in foreign policy terms." In the future such arguments would be "clearly incomplete," if not "irrelevant," because they must increasingly take domestic priorities into account. A Foreign Service officer since 1947, Furnas understood that "The nation does not, after all, exist in order to conduct foreign affairs. It is not, after all, a bad thing for the American government to reflect the sense of priorities felt by the American people." At pivotal points in their careers, Acheson and Kissinger would have disagreed with that statement. It is a measure of the change that has occurred, however, that few would disagree with Furnas' assertion that henceforth the secretary of state would have to compete with domestic needs for national resources. Furnas consequently urged that future secretaries

23 Mazlish, Kissinger, pp. 154–155.
24 Joseph A. Califano, Jr., A Presidential Nation (New York, 1975), p. 154.
25 Price, The Secretary of State, p. 116.

should be of presidential caliber since such a figure could more easily gain support from the public, and "most important of all, he would in his bones understand and know how to meet the President's need for a foreign policy more closely related to the broader national scene."[26]

Bayless Manning, president of the Council on Foreign Relations, has also emphasized that decision making must occur at the intersection of domestic and foreign policies, or when, in his word, these policies become "intermestic." Instead of following Furnas' suggestion, however, Manning proposed institutional changes, including an International and Domestic Affairs Council, comprised of various cabinet members, which would resemble the National Security Council and have a new presidential special assistant acting as chairman when the president and vice-president were absent. Policy integration would occur at this point.[27]

Any such change should be considered carefully. Manning's proposal is one of the council's several initiatives that have sought to streamline bureaucratic decision making at the possible expense of political values. The executive does not need another presidential special assistant who would, among other objectionable actions, take decision making further into the bowels of the White House and out of the hands of a secretary of state who at least must give some accounting before congressional committees. The State Department, moreover, is the agency which can most effectively mobilize the information and cosmopolitan views necessary to discipline and subordinate particularistic interests, a process which Manning deems essential. Solving "intermestic" problems will be better accomplished, as Furnas suggested, by a secretary of state who can conceptualize those problems and is politically sensitive to public and congressional concern, not by another hidden White House authority.

The heart of the matter will be the secretary of state's ability to obtain congressional and broad public support for his policies, particularly those relating to explosive Third World areas. Appointing a secretary of state who has no political constituency and acts mostly as a diplomatic troubleshooter may make politics simpler for the White House, but it was not the way Washington, Jefferson, Monroe, Lincoln, Franklin D. Roosevelt, or even Warren G. Harding ran the government. Nor can it be the way now, for the wishbone has nearly pulled apart: Acheson's consensus has deteriorated, Kissinger has failed to rebuild it, and little-known but increasingly powerful parts of the world are demanding a different distribution of American wealth.

[26] Howard Furnas, "The President: A Changing Role?" *The Annals*, CCCLXXX (November 1968), 9–15.

[27] Bayless Manning, "The Congress, the Executive and Intermestic Affairs: Three Proposals," *Foreign Affairs*, LV (January 1977), 306–324.

The Bargaining Chip and SALT

ROBERT J. BRESLER
ROBERT C. GRAY

The bargaining chip, like the domino theory of the 1950s and 1960s, has become one of the most voguish ideas in the field of weapons development. Yet the concept is perhaps as old as arms competition itself—certainly as old as nuclear arms competition. Decisions to build major weapons systems have frequently been justified by their promise of some future diplomatic advantage. In April 1945 James Byrnes purportedly told President Truman that the atomic bomb would put the United States "in a position to dictate our own terms at the end of the war."[1] While there is little evidence the United States actually put forward the atomic bomb as a bargaining chip—offering to exchange its secrets for Soviet political concessions—Truman and Secretary of War Stimson did at least *consider* offering the Soviet Union partnership in an international control commission in exchange for "settlement of the Polish, Rumanian, Yugoslavian, and Manchurian problems."[2] The idea came to naught. Atomic weapons continued to be stockpiled and their promised postwar political advantage awaited fulfillment. An early study of arms control and disarmament negotiations in the late 1940s and 1950s concluded that the talks had become "one form of the arms race itself, the aim of each nation being an increase in its relative power position."[3]

[1] Harry S. Truman, *Year of Decisions* (Garden City, N. Y., 1955), p. 87.
[2] Stimson Diary, June 6, 1945, cited in Thomas T. Hammond, "Atomic Diplomacy Revisited," *Orbis*, XIX (Winter 1976), 1427.
[3] John W. Spanier and Joseph L. Nogee, *The Politics of Disarmament: A Study in Soviet-American Gamesmanship* (New York, 1962), p. 15.

ROBERT J. BRESLER is associate professor of political science at Pennsylvania State University-Capitol Campus. ROBERT C. GRAY is assistant professor of government at Franklin and Marshall College.

The purpose of this article is to evaluate the bargaining chip concept effectively, and to do this we need to understand its precise function in the strategic dialogue since SALT I.[4] The following are the kinds of questions we seek to answer: Have bargaining chip policies helped or hindered United States efforts to achieve a satisfactory agreement with the Soviets? If some bargaining chip policies do help, which ones are they and why? What role did Safeguard play in securing the ABM treaty and Interim Agreement limiting Soviet SS-9 heavy missiles? Is there agreement among defenders of the concept as to what constitutes a bargaining chip? Are bargaining chip arguments the same for all strategic weapons systems or do they vary with particular weapons? Must a weapon go into production in order to be a bargaining chip? What distinguishes a bargaining chip which stimulates an agreement from one which simply stimulates further competition? To what extent does the bargaining chip argument serve a domestic political function, i.e., as a smokescreen behind which controversial weapons are shepherded through Congress? And finally, is the bargaining chip a ploy by which SALT is converted into a mechanism for rationalizing and institutionalizing the arms race?

JUSTIFICATION FOR BARGAINING CHIP STRATEGIES

The term "bargaining chip" came into prominence with the onset of the SALT talks. A recent Library of Congress study defines the bargaining chip as "any military force, weapons system or other resource, present or projected, which a country expresses willingness to downgrade or discard in return for a concession by a particular rival."[5] The bargaining chip first gained credence in 1968 when both Senator Henry Jackson (D-Wash.) and then Congressman Melvin Laird (R-Wis.) argued that it was more than coincidence that the Soviet Union agreed to begin the SALT talks soon after the Senate approved the Sentinel ABM System.[6]

The bargaining chip concept reached broad acceptance with the signing of the SALT I agreements. President Nixon and Defense Secretary Laird argued that those agreements were a direct result of our decision to go forward with Safeguard ABM, Poseidon submarine, and Minuteman III missiles. They pointed to our decision to continue in 1969 with the construction of Safeguard as essential in persuading the Soviets to accept limits on their weapons activities, specifically

---

[4] For an interesting theoretical approach to the bargaining chip which we have found valuable, see Thomas C. Schelling, "A Framework for the Evaluation of Arms-Control Proposals," in Franklin A. Long and George W. Rathjens (eds.), *Arms, Defense Policy, and Arms Control* (New York, 1976), pp. 194–200.

[5] U. S. Senate, Committee on Armed Services, *United States/Soviet Military Balance: A Frame of Reference for Congress* (prepared by the Library of Congress), 94th Cong., 2d sess., 1976, p. 58.

[6] Alton Frye, "U. S. Decision Making for SALT," in Mason Willrich and John B. Rhinelander (eds.), *SALT: The Moscow Agreements and Beyond* (New York, 1974), p. 74.

in agreeing to limit to 313 their SS-9 missiles. Henry Kissinger told a delegation from Congress soon after the SALT I agreements were signed that the connection between ABM and SS-9 was quite clear. "We could not have negotiated the limitations on offensive weapons if it had not been linked to the limitations on defensive weapons and to their [the Soviet's] desire of stopping the deployment of [our] ABM System."[7]

Consequently, Nixon and Laird insisted that our future or success in SALT II depended on whether the Congress would approve a new set of bargaining chips such as the Trident submarine, the B-1 bomber, and the cruise missile.[8] The breadth of support this idea could command was underscored in June 1972, when Senator Mike Mansfield (D-Mont.), often a Nixon administration critic, cosponsored Senate Resolution 242 committing Congress to the proposition that the SALT agreements "were made possible by maintenance in the United States of a strategic defensive posture second to none."[9]

Since 1972, however, the concept has been questioned with greater frequency and has become a central issue in our strategic policy debates. The former chief of the SALT I delegation and director of the Arms Control and Disarmament Agency (ACDA), Gerard C. Smith, has criticized bargaining chips and bargaining chip theories as "unproductive" and "bankrupt."[10] Averell Harriman has declared that "the bargaining chip theory should be abandoned. It is utterly discredited."[11] The debate over the bargaining chip has raised some of the most serious and complex issues of strategic arms policy.

KINDS OF BARGAINING CHIPS

In order to evaluate how important the bargaining chip strategy was in bringing about the SALT I agreement, it is necessary to rigorously analyze the bargaining chip argument. One way to begin is by constructing a number of analytical categories within which to assess the dynamics of the bargaining chip and arms

[7] U. S. Senate, Committee on Foreign Relations, *Strategic Arms Limitation Agreements: Hearings on S.J. Res. 241 and S.J. Res. 242*, 92d Cong., 2d sess., 1972, p. 410 (hereafter cited as Senate, *SALT Agreements*). That this is still a fashionable argument is illustrated by the recent Senate debate on the FY1977 Military Procurement Authorizations. In seeking to restore funds that the Senate Armed Services Committee had cut from the naval cruise missile program, Senator Robert Griffin (R-Mich.) stated: "Any indication that the Congress is likely to unilaterally curtail the cruise missile program could undercut the President's negotiating position at SALT II," *Congressional Record*, May 26, 1976, p. S 8044.

[8] Luther J. Carter, "Strategic Arms Limitation (II): Leveling Up to Symmetry," *Science*, February 21, 1975, p. 629; also see text of President Nixon's June 22, 1972, news conference in *Congressional Quarterly*, July 1, 1972, pp. 1582–1583.

[9] I. F. Stone, "McGovern vs. Nixon on the Arms Race," *New York Review of Books*, July 20, 1972, p. 11.

[10] Quoted by Senator Edward Brooke (R-Mass.) in *Congressional Record*, June 10, 1974, p. S 10202.

[11] Statement by Averell Harriman in U. S. Senate, Committee on Foreign Relations, *Detente: Hearings*, 93d Cong., 2d sess., 1974, p. 8.

control. Thus it is helpful to conceive of several types of bargaining chips. The typology offered here is not rigid, however, for various weapons systems may fall into more than one category. What starts out as one type of bargaining chip may acquire the characteristics of another. (MIRV, for example, well exemplifies this phenomenon.) The assignment of a weapons system to a particular category, then, reflects a judgment on the *dominant* rationale at a given point in time.

The Contingency Bargaining Chip

One bargaining chip is a weapons program which may be requested of Congress in the event the administration decides that the arms talks are lagging or may fail. The contingency chip can be interpreted as an implicit threat which often takes the form of a public signal. Experience indicates that the military feels more comfortable if such weapons are readily available in the event they are needed. Contingency chips often involve increased production and procurement of a weapons system already in the arsenal or soon scheduled to be. Dr. John Foster, former director of Defense Research and Engineering (DDR&E), has characterized such programs as those "we would need relatively soon if agreement is not reached, recognizing that we can stop or modify these programs if agreement is reached."[12] There are numerous specific examples: in June 1972, the Nixon administration insisted it would have asked Congress for a $15 billion a year crash program in the event the Moscow talks had failed.[13] Included would have been the deployment of additional numbers of Minuteman III missiles, an expanded site defense system, added launchers to Poseidon submarines, accelerated procurement of Trident, and development of submarine-launched cruise missiles (SLCM). In the absence of any hard evidence that this contingency program was communicated to the Soviet Union prior to the signing of SALT I, documentation of the precise use of this chip is difficult. First public disclosure of this contingency plan was made in remarks by President Nixon on June 29, 1972. (Much of this contingency plan has found its way into the military budget in the past several years. As noted earlier, what begins as one type of bargaining chip soon evolves into another.)

Recent uses of the contingency chip have been more frequent and less ambiguous. President Ford on August 19, 1975, publicly warned that unless an agreement was achieved in SALT II, he would ask Congress for an additional $2–3 billion for strategic weapons programs.[14] Similarly, the present director of

---

[12] U. S. Senate, Committee on Foreign Relations, *ABM, MIRV, SALT, and the Nuclear Arms Race: Hearings before the Subcommittee on Arms Control, International Law and Organization,* 91st Cong., 2d sess., 1970, p. 425. For an alternative conceptualization of a "contingency chip," see Schelling, "A Framework," pp. 195–196.

[13] Arms Control and Disarmament Agency, *Documents on Disarmament, 1972,* pp. 437 and 514.

[14] Speech to American Legion, August 19, 1975, *Weekly Compilation of Presidential Docu-*

DDR&E, Dr. Malcolm Currie, indicated that the acceleration of the new mobile land-based missile (MX) and the Trident II program were contingencies applied to SALT II. Currie told the Senate Armed Services Committee on February 5, 1976: "if we knew right now that there was no chance for a SALT agreement that Congress and the Executive could agree to, then right now, for example, we would have to accelerate MX and the Trident II programs."[15] Experience indicates the contingency chip is not a weapons system brought to the bargaining table but rather a threat to accelerate development or production of a system about which there appears little intention to negotiate. In a revealing comment in *Foreign Affairs*, Jan Lodal, director of program analysis in the NSC from 1973–1975, indicated that the United States is reluctant to accept a Soviet offer for an outright ban on mobile ICBM's, "because of Pentagon pressure to keep the option for a land-based mobile system open."[16]

The contingency chip also serves an important domestic political function. It can be invoked to convince skeptics of the SALT process that in the absence of an agreement the rate of arms spending will be considerably higher.

The Specific Bargaining Chip

Another bargaining chip is a weapon designed, in part, to persuade the Soviets to do something quite explicit. Unlike the contingency chip, these specific chips are to be brought to the negotiating table for the explicit purpose of being traded away. Safeguard ABM was considered to be a trade-off for the Soviet SS-9; MIRV was at one point proposed by Dr. Foster as a trade-off for the Soviet ABM.

This type of chip raises a number of disturbing questions. The only weapons system actually traded away at SALT was the full Safeguard program. Was this testimony to its viability as a bargaining chip or to the fact that both sides saw it as a superfluous and technologically ineffective weapon system? Whatever became of MIRV as a bargaining chip? Dr. Foster testified in 1971 that an ABM ban would eliminate the need for MIRV. Yet, after the ABM treaty was signed, MIRV production continued unabated.[17] What is to prevent weapons systems which are first presented as specific chips from becoming building blocks

---

ments, August 25, 1975, p. 871; see also "Ford Warns USSR on Nuclear Weapons Talks," *Congressional Quarterly*, August 23, 1975, p. 1854.

15 U. S. Senate, Committee on Armed Services, *Fiscal Year 1977 Authorization for Military Procurement, Research and Development, and Active Duty, Selected Reserve and Civilian Personnel Strengths: Hearings on S. 2965, Part 4, Research and Development*, 94th Cong., 2d sess., 1976, p. 2398 (hereafter cited as Senate, *Fiscal Year 1977*).

16 Jan M. Lodal, "Assuring Strategic Stability: An Alternative View," *Foreign Affairs*, 54 (April 1976), 476.

17 Cited in Graham T. Allison and Frederic A. Morris, "Armaments and Arms Control: Exploring the Determinants of Military Weapons," in Franklin A. Long and George W. Rathjens, (eds.), *Arms, Defense Policy, and Arms Control* (New York, 1976), p. 121.

due to constituency pressures, bureaucratic politics, and/or technological momentum?

The Psychological Bargaining Chip

A third bargaining chip is not designed to extract any particular concession from the Soviets nor is it, for that matter, brought to the negotiating table. The psychological chip is, rather, conceived as a means of enabling the president to "negotiate from strength," and hence may include virtually every ongong or proposed weapons system. While proponents of such chips argue that they have a direct relationship to the SALT talks, rarely do they appear to be the subject of negotiation. After the SALT I agreements were signed, the psychological chip was pressed into service in behalf of the Trident submarine and the B-1 bomber. If the Vladivostok Agreement is any indication, there is little hope that SALT II will restrain their development.

The Domestic Bargaining Chip

The fourth chip has only a remote relationship to the actual negotiating process. It is given to the military in exchange for their support for a particular arms control agreement. In the case of SALT I it was made unabashedly clear. Representative Price (D-Ill.), while defending the $110 million supplemental appropriation requested by the Nixon administration in 1972, put it thusly: "The SALT agreement is supported by the members of the Joint Chiefs of Staff on the basis that additional effort will be made in research and development on these systems or programs mentioned."[18]

Each one of the following weapons systems has served an implicit or explicit bargaining chip function according to the four categories above. Some fit several categories, others only one or two. An evaluation of the bargaining chip concept can be made more effectively as one sees how the bargaining chip argument weaves in and out of the history of these weapons systems.

ABM—THE BARGAINING CHIP THAT WORKED?

On returning from Moscow after SALT I, Henry Kissinger joined President Nixon and Secretary Laird in publicly proclaiming the importance of Safeguard ABM as an effective bargaining chip in securing the agreement. "Our experience," Kissinger insisted in June 1972, "has been that an ongoing program is no obstacle to an agreement and, on the contrary may accelerate it. That was certainly the case with respect to Safeguard."[19] Yet in its early presentation of

---

[18] *Congressional Record*, June 27, 1972, p. 22528.
[19] Senate, *SALT Agreements*, p. 403.

the Safeguard system, the Nixon administration did not emphasize its bargaining chip role. Quite the contrary, Secretary Laird in response to a question from Senator George Aiken (R-Vt.) in March 1969, regarding Safeguard's importance as a bargaining chip insisted: "I believe that this system stands on its own feet, on its merits."[20] Only after the system ran into opposition in the Senate did the administration emphasize the bargaining chip claim. On the eve of a Senate debate on ABM in 1970 Gerard Smith sent a telegram to the Senate emphasizing the importance of Safeguard to the SALT talks.[21] Henry Kissinger, in meeting with congressional leaders on July 23, 1970, insisted that Safeguard was essential as a bargaining chip for gaining Soviet agreement to limit their SS-9 program.[22]

According to Alton Frye, who served at that time as an aide to Senator Brooke (R-Mass.), "the power of the President's appeal to senators not to rob him of diplomatic leverage was best measured by the Senate's willingness to disregard the virtually decisive technological critique."[23] A declassified Department of Defense study uncovered by Senator Fulbright (D-Ark.) indicated that Safeguard was ineffective in defending the Minutemen sites.[24] Yet the claims of the bargaining chip pushed what Frye called this "technological bombshell" into the background and overrode any objections to the system. As Lawrence Weiler, former counselor of ACDA and a member of the SALT delegation, recently remarked, after the Safeguard program "had produced enough opposition to deployment—based on technical, emotional, strategic and arms control grounds ... only the bargaining chip argument could keep the program alive."[25]

Since SALT I did result in limiting SS-9s to 313 and ABM sites to 2, there seems to be a prima facie case that, in this instance, the bargaining chip worked. While no one can simply rebut that claim, serious doubts have been raised. How could a system that had been exposed as having serious technological deficiencies be presented to the Soviet Union as a credible bargaining chip? Frye sees Safeguard as a stumbling block rather than a bargaining chip in SALT inasmuch as

[20] U. S. Senate, Committee on Foreign Relations, *Strategic and Foreign Policy Implications of ABM Systems: Hearings before the Subcommittee on International Organization and Disarmament Affairs, Part I*, 91st Cong., 1st sess., 1969, p. 178.

[21] *Congressional Quarterly*, August 14, 1970, p. 2037.

[22] John Newhouse, *Cold Dawn: The Story of SALT* (New York, 1973), p. 188.

[23] Alton Frye, *A Responsible Congress: The Politics of National Security* (New York, 1975), p. 43.

[24] Ibid. Other observers have reached similar conclusions about the bargaining chip argument and the 1970 ABM debate. "There can be little doubt that some Senators by 1970 had serious doubts about the technical and military effectiveness of the system, but supported continued deployment primarily because they belived the Administration's argument that it [ABM] was needed to secure a satisfactory SALT outcome." G. W. Rathjens, Abram Chayes, and J. P. Ruina, *Nuclear Arms Control Agreements: Process and Impact* (Washington, D. C., 1974), p. 18.

[25] Lawrence D. Weiler, *The Arms Race, Secret Negotiations and the Congress*, Occasional Paper No. 12 (Muscatine, Iowa, 1976), p. 17.

"the right to install the first elements of Safeguard" became an objective of the United States delegation in the SALT talks.[26]

John Newhouse, in his semiofficial account of the SALT talks, recognizes Safeguard's technological deficiencies as a bargaining chip but argues, nevertheless, that the system may have persuaded the Soviets due to its growth potential.[27] But one can turn that argument around. It is equally plausible that congressional action in 1970 blocking administration plans for a full twelve-site ABM, known as phase II, prevented constituent pressures from building up around an elaborate ABM infrastructure. As Jerome Slater has put it: "Faced with effective Congressional opposition to all but the most minimal ABM system, the Nixon Administration was compelled to seek a negotiated abolition or strict limitation on ABM during round one of SALT."[28] In other words, congressional opposition to Safeguard phase II forced the Nixon administration to settle for only two sites, precluding the need for a Soviet SS-9 force beyond 313. The Soviets had in fact halted the construction of new SS-9 sites at 313 almost a year before the SALT I agreements were signed.[29]

Either way, the case for the ABM is difficult to prove. The showcase of the bargaining chips remains a murky example at best. Restraint on ABM, imposed by the Congress, may have been more important to gaining the agreement than building the weapons system itself.

Trident—The Bargaining Chip for All Seasons

Reversing a previous recommendation by Deputy Defense Secretary David Packard in September 1971 to fund the Trident program (then known as ULMS) at a level of $418 million for FY73, Secretary Laird in January 1972 requested that the Trident program be accelerated, stepping up deployment from 1981 to 1978, and that funding be increased for FY73 to $926.4 million. Shortly after the January request Laird insisted that Trident "should not be looked at as a bargaining chip as far as SALT is concerned. That is not what it is all about."[30] Dr. Foster reiterated the same argument in March 1972, when he told Senator Symington (D-Mo.); "I prefer the ULMS, for a very simple reason. . . . It has nothing to do with bargaining chips. . . . It relates to the problem of ASW [antisubmarine warfare]."[31]

But after SALT these disclaimers were forgotten. Trident was now publicly

---

[26] Frye, *A Responsible Congress*, p. 86.
[27] Newhouse, *Cold Dawn*, p. 156.
[28] Jerome Slater, "The Case for Reviving the ABM," *The New Leader*, July 7, 1975. p. 10.
[29] Newhouse, *Cold Dawn*, p. 224.
[30] Quoted in *Congressional Record*, July 27, 1972, p. 25664.
[31] U. S. Senate, Committee on Armed Services, *Fiscal Year 1973 Authorization for Military Procurement, Research and Development, Construction Authorization for the Safeguard ABM, and Active Duty and Selected Reserve Strengths: Hearings on S. 3108, Part 3, Authorizations,* 92d Cong., 2d sess., 1972, p. 1890.

touted both as a psychological chip for the upcoming SALT II negotiations and as a contingency against their failure. Laird told the Senate Armed Services Committee: "Just as the Moscow Agreements were made possible by our successful action in such programs as Safeguard, Poseidon, and Minuteman III, these future negotiations to which we are pledged can only succeed if we are equally successful in implementing such programs as the Trident system. . . ."[32] Kissinger used a similar argument in 1972 to persuade Senator John Stennis (D-Miss.) to drop his opposition to Trident.[33] Laird and Kissinger, it appears, were only telling a portion of the story. For Trident was, according to John Newhouse, a domestic bargaining chip that Kissinger had granted the chairman of the Joint Chiefs, Admiral Moorer, in exchange for his support of the Interim Agreement on Strategic Offensive Arms.[34] This understanding was made quite explicit in the congressional hearing following SALT I. Laird, speaking for himself and Admiral Moorer, told Senator Strom Thurmond (R-S.C.) that their support for SALT I was "predicated upon" congressional approval of the accelerated Trident program (as well as other programs including the B-1 bomber).[35]

In the September 1973 Senate debates on the acceleration of Trident, numerous senators, including Henry Jackson (D-Wash.), John Pastore (D-R. I.), and Abraham Ribicoff (D-Conn.), supported the administration bargaining chip claims. The emphasis was largely on Trident as a contingency chip. The administration argued that if Trident were not underway until 1981, there would be a four-year gap between the expiration of SALT I and the development of a new strategic system.[36] On close examination it appears that Trident, whatever its bargaining chip function—as a contingency or a psychological chip—was never meant to be brought to the bargaining table. In a revealing letter to their Senate colleagues, four senators with close ties to the Pentagon (Senators Fannin, Tower, Ervin, and Thurmond) saw little chance of our ever giving up Trident. "If further limitations are put upon submarine systems," the letter suggests, "it is more likely that it will be the older system, Polaris/Poseidon, that would be bargained away. We couldn't do so if we have nothing else."[37] The Vladivostok Agreement allowed the United States to do just that with Trident—use it to replace old and un-MIRVed Polaris submarines. The 1320 ceiling on MIRV launchers permits the United States to have 264 Trident missiles (11 boats),

[32] U. S. Senate, Committee on Armed Services, *Military Implications of the Treaty on the Limitations of Anti-Ballistic Missile Systems and the Interim Agreement on Limitation of Strategic Offensive Arms: Hearings*, 92d Cong., 2d sess., 1972, p. 4.

[33] Herbert Scoville, Jr., "Tinkering with the Balance of Terror, *The New York Times*, July 22, 1973.

[34] Newhouse, *Cold Dawn*, p. 246.

[35] U. S. Senate, Committee on Armed Services, *Fiscal Year 1973 Authorization for Military Procurement, Research and Development . . . Hearings on S. 3108, Addendum No. 1, Amended Military Authorization Request Related to Strategic Arms Limitation Agreement*, 92d Cong., 2d sess., 1972, p. 4219.

[36] *Congressional Record*, September 26, 1973, pp. 17679 and 17681

[37] Ibid., July 27, 1972, p. 25661.

496 Poseidon missiles (31 boats), and 550 Minuteman III's As with MIRV, the Trident bargaining chip has apparently become a permanent part of the arsenal. This should be no surprise, for Trident was first approved as a domestic bargaining chip in exchange for military acquiescence in SALT. Such a chip, while often used for psychological purposes, cannot easily be offered as a specific chip to be brought to the table, for that would violate the original terms of its formation. Once a chip plays a domestic function, it soon becomes a building block.

MIRV—The Counterfeit Bargaining Chip

Explaining the origins of MIRV merely as response to the Soviet ABM program is, as numerous authorities have cautioned us, a serious oversimplification.[38] One cannot discount the importance of bureaucratic politics and technological imperatives in the development of MIRV. Yet even in the pre-SALT environment when there was little use of the term "bargaining chip," Secretary of Defense Robert McNamara and others did at least perceive an implicit bargaining chip dimension in MIRV. McNamara, in the later years of his tenure in the Pentagon, had moved to the doctrinal perspective of assured destruction and had deepened his concern with arms control objectives. To McNamara, MIRV served in part a domestic bargaining chip function vis-à-vis the Air Force. In addition to being a cost-effective hedge against a Soviet ABM, MIRV enabled McNamara to blunt Air Force demands for more ICBM's (they wanted somewhere between 2000–10,000 Minuteman launchers).[39] By going forward with MIRV, McNamara could freeze Minuteman deployment at 1000 launchers and then tacitly allow the Soviets to expand their missile force to be roughly equivalent to ours—hoping that such equivalency could set the stage for an eventual arms control agreement. MIRV may well have been, in McNamara's view, a domestic bargaining chip granted the Air Force in order to enable him to pursue his arms control objectives. Yet, retrospectively, McNamara's objectives seem quite obscure. For, given the development of MIRV, it appears shortsighted to believe that a ceiling on Minuteman launchers would in itself be a stabilizing force in arms control. Ironically, the American arsenal by the early

---

[38] See, for example Allison and Morris, "Armaments and Arms Control," pp. 99–129; Ted Greenwood, *Making the MIRV: A Study of Defense Decision Making* (Cambridge, Mass., 1975); Jerome H. Kahan, *Security in the Nuclear Age: Developing U. S. Strategic Arms Policy* (Washington, D. C., 1975), pp. 99–109; Ronald L. Tammen, *MIRV and the Arms Race: An Interpretation of Defense Strategy* (New York, 1973); Herbert York, "Multiple Warhead Missiles," *Scientific American*, 229 (November 1973), 17–27. Greenwood's is the most current and comprehensive study.

[39] James A. Nathan and James K. Oliver, *United States Policy and World Order* (Boston, 1976), p. 302, and Herbert F. York, *Race to Oblivion: A Participant's View of the Arms Race* (New York, 1971), p. 152.

1980s, rather than having the 10,000 launchers the Air Force desired, may well have 10,000 warheads.

Secretary of Defense Clark Clifford, no less than his predecessor, had a confused perception of the relationship of MIRV development to arms control, particularly as it concerned MIRV testing. Clifford approved the start of Minuteman III and Poseidon flight tests, believing that "an ongoing MIRV test series would provide added leverage for those [SALT] talks."[40] The implications of this psychological bargaining chip strategy do not appear to be well thought out, because Clifford did not alter his decision to test MIRV even after the SALT talks were delayed by the Soviet invasion of Czechoslovakia. He thereby allowed the tests to move to a much more advanced stage when the talks actually convened in November 1969—an oversight Clifford later came to regret.[41] For, MIRV, once tested, demonstrated an American superiority which the Soviets were unlikely to accept without moving forward with their own multiple warhead program.

As MIRV development progressed, it was no longer presented, as Clifford had done, as a psychological chip, but rather as a specific bargaining chip for the Soviet ABM. Dr. Foster made numerous public references linking MIRV and ABM. As he put it in 1969, "an effective limitation on Soviet ABMs should be a prerequisite to a ban on further MIRV testing." Later, in order to diminish support for congressional resolutions calling for a moratorium on MIRV testing, Foster made the specific bargaining chip argument even more explicit: "if a ban were placed on the ABM . . . there would be no need for the United States to deploy a MIRV."[42]

Senator Brooke's point that "the prospect of MIRV may well encourage diplomacy, the fact of MIRV development may well defeat it,"[43] appeared lost on the Pentagon. As their supporters in Congress were to repeat time and time again, the military does not consider research and development an effective bargaining chip. A number of years later, Senator Moss (D-Utah), speaking in another context, put the matter quite forthrightly: "Experience in the SALT talks has shown us that research alone is not overly threatening to the other side. What really matters is testing hardware in an operationally deployed system."[44] Despite Senate passage of a resolution calling for a MIRV moratorium in April

[40] Frye, *A Responsible Congress*, p. 51.

[41] Kahan, *Security in the Nuclear Age*, pp. 127–128; Frye, *A Responsible Congress*, p. 52.

[42] U. S. House of Representatives, Committee on Foreign Affairs, *Diplomatic and Strategic Impact of Multiple Warhead Missiles: Hearings before the Subcommittee on National Security Policy and Scientific Developments*, 91st Cong., 1st sess., 1969, p. 247; U. S. Senate, Committee on Armed Services, *Fiscal Year 1972 Authorization for Military Procurement, Research and Development, Construction and Real Estate Acquisition for the Safeguard ABM, and Reserve Strengths: Hearings on S. 939, Part 2, Authorizations*, 92d Cong., 1st sess., 1971, p. 1497.

[43] Quoted in Frye, *A Responsible Congress*, p. 72.

[44] *Congressional Record*, June 4, 1975, p. S 9627.

1970 by an overwhelming vote of seventy-two to six, MIRV testing went forward. By June 1970, deployment of MIRV began on Minuteman III and Poseidon deployment was soon to follow.[45]

What happened during the actual SALT negotiations seems to underscore the disingenuous nature of the Nixon administration's bargaining chip rationale. In the second round of SALT (Spring 1970) the administration coupled a proposal linking a ban on the testing and deployment of MIRV with an on-site inspection clause (added over the objections of State and ACDA), a feature known to be abhorrent to the Soviets.[46] But on-site inspection notwithstanding, an agreement on MIRV was improbable at this point. For once the United States had begun testing MIRV, it was unlikely, as Marvin and Bernard Kalb point out, that the Soviets would deprive "themselves of the chance to catch up with the United States in MIRV technology."[47]

The reluctance of the Nixon administration to bring MIRV to the bargaining table can be traced to the military's own unwillingness to acquiesce in MIRV control. This point is emphasized by Ted Greenwood. "By 1968 the military commitment to MIRV was exceedingly strong. The programs were too far advanced, deployment schedules of Poseidon and Minuteman III were too integrated with maintenance and modernization of existing systems, and too many other programs had been given up along the way for the military to forego or delay the new MIRVed missiles willingly."[48]

MIRV stands out as an example of a weapons system granted to the military as a domestic bargaining chip for what appears to be insufficiently thought-out arms control objectives. It subsequently acquired such momentum that it was virtually impossible to dislodge it from our strategic forces. The use that Foster made of the specific bargaining chip argument appears particularly misleading. For he, of all people, must have known the extent to which the military's force posture for the 1970s and beyond was based on MIRV. Yet he persisted in suggesting that with ABM control, MIRV would be unnecessary, an illusion shattered by the terms of SALT I. It can be reasonably inferred that the specific bargaining chip argument advanced by Foster was a smoke screen to protect MIRV from the skepticism of the Senate. The Air Force, anxious for a damage limitation capability, knew full well why it wanted MIRV. This is a striking contrast with the shallowness of both McNamara and Clifford's thinking on the weapon's bargaining chip potential. In the process a revolutionary weapon, first conceived as a domestic chip, evolved into a psychological chip, briefly was presented by Foster as a specific chip, and eventually became a building block —a permanent part of the arsenal, legitimized by the Vladivostok Agreement. As MARV's replace MIRV's, the destabilizing effects of multiple warheads will become even clearer, a subject to which we will return.

---

[45] Frye, "U. S. Decision Making for SALT," p. 87.
[46] Newhouse, *Cold Dawn*, pp. 179–181.
[47] Marvin Kalb and Bernard Kalb, *Kissinger* (New York, 1975), p. 140.
[48] Greenwood, *Making the MIRV*, p. 127.

CRUISE MISSILES—BARGAINING CHIPS ON THEIR WAY TO BECOMING
BUILDING BLOCKS

In the aftermath of SALT I, Secretary of State Kissinger decided it would be useful to acquire additional bargaining chips for SALT II. One area of technology not limited by SALT I and not highly developed in the United States was the strategic cruise missile—a relatively cheap weapon which, unlike a ballistic missile, flies slowly at low altitudes and is, in essence, a highly accurate pilotless jet plane.[49] The United States had early versions of the cruise in the 1950s and largely abandoned them as inefficient. Secretary Laird, nevertheless, seemed quite enthusiastic about reviving the weapon and included a request for the submarine-launched cruise missile (SLCM) in the supplemental appropriation sought immediately after SALT I. Laird did not publicly justify the request on grounds of a bargaining chip. Rather, Laird stressed that cruise missiles were not limited by SALT; that they could be added to the first ten Polaris submarines in the fleet; and that they would, as an addition to our nuclear retaliatory force, place more stress on Soviet defenses.[50]

As the cruise missile program developed, it was divided between the Navy and the Air Force. The Navy was charged with developing SLCM, which could conceivably be launched from submarines, surface vessels, or planes, and the Air Force was assigned the air-launched cruise missile (ALCM) to be launched from manned bombers.[51] The bargaining chip rationale was ever present in face of evidence that the services were not initially enthusiastic about renewed attention to the cruise missile. In 1973 congressional testimony, Peter Waterman, a Navy Research and Development (R&D) official, indicated that the idea to proceed with a strategic cruise missile prior to perfecting a tactical cruise came from the secretary of defense, who apparently had bargaining chip motives in mind. "We have been asked," admitted Waterman, "by the Secretary of Defense to provide a demonstration of capabilities of all the elements of the strategic cruise missile in time relationship to the SALT negotiations."[52]

Whatever reluctance was initially felt by the military has largely dissipated.

---

[49] John W. Finney, "Cruise Missiles Provoke Conflict Within the Military," *The New York Times*, January 21, 1976; Clarence A. Robinson, Jr., "Single Cruise Missile Set for Varied Use," *Aviation Week and Space Technology*, February 24, 1975, p. 19. For an excellent introductory article that covers most of the basic issues, see Kosta Tsipis, "The Long Range Cruise Missile," *Bulletin of the Atomic Scientists*, April 1975, pp. 15–26.

[50] U. S. Senate, Committee on Armed Services, *Amended Military Authorization Request Related to Strategic Arms Limitation Agreement: Hearings Addendum 1*, 92d Cong., 2d sess., 1972, p. 4244.

[51] Michael L. Yaffee, "Cruise Missile Engine Design Pushed," *Aviation Week and Space Technology*, July 7, 1975, p. 41; J. Philip Geddes, "The Sea Launched Cruise Missile," *Interavia*, 31 (March 1976), 260–263.

[52] U. S. Senate, Committee on Armed Services, *Fiscal Year 1974 Authorization for Military Procurement, Research and Development, Construction Authorization for the Safeguard ABM, and Active Duty and Selected Reserve Strengths: Hearings on S. 1263, Part 5, Research and Development*, 93d Cong., 1st sess., 1973, p. 3274.

In the words of the director of the Stockholm International Peace Research Institute, "when the potentialities of the weapon became clear, considerable pressures built for the fastest possible development."[53] According to Rear Admiral G. E. Synhorst, assistant deputy chief of naval operations, SLCM will be put "on every submarine," necessitating some 1000 missiles. As for ALCM, military estimates suggest between 2000–3000.[54]

Thus, what Henry Kissinger viewed as an additional psychological bargaining chip for SALT II has created a constituency for development and deployment. "How was I to know," Kissinger has lamented, "the military would come to love it?"[55] This is a lesson Kissinger could have learned long ago, but with the love affair begun, he has had to bargain on cruise with both the Soviets and the Pentagon.

The Navy's Cruise Missile Project manager, Captain W. M. Locke, is convinced that the bargaining chip argument for cruise makes little sense if it lingers in the research stage. "The Soviet Union," Locke told a Senate committee in 1975, "will be interested in seriously negotiating a reasonable ban on cruise missiles when we have a believable capability."[56] This view, disdainful of R&D programs as bargaining chips, is shared by the civilian leadership of the Pentagon as well. According to Admiral Synhorst, in 1974 the secretary of defense told the Navy to push cruise development enthusiastically because "you cannot fool anybody by having it on paper. You must start developing it or no one will believe you."[57]

Yet having cruise anywhere else but on paper may severely complicate the arms control process. For cruise, once tested and deployed, becomes quite difficult to verify by national technical means. Thus, as in the case of MIRV, there

[53] Frank Barnaby, "Will the Cruise Missile Torpedo SALT?" New Scientist, 18 (December 1975), 681.

[54] Deborah Shapley, "Cruise Missiles: Air Force, Navy Poses New Arms Issues," Science, February 7, 1975, p. 418. John Finney has reported much higher potential deployment: " . . . Mr. Kissinger says that with no restrictions, the United States could potentially deploy 11,000 cruise missiles on existing bombers and transport planes and 10,000 others on nuclear submarines, all capable of reaching targets in the Soviet Union." "The Soviet Backfire Bomber and the U. S. Cruise Missile," The New York Times, December 3, 1975. Presumably these incredibly high estimates represent a maximum effort by Secretary Kissinger to use what he has viewed as a bargaining chip.

[55] Leslie Gelb, "Another U. S. Compromise Position Is Reported on Strategic Arms," The New York Times, February 17, 1976.

[56] U. S. Senate, Committee on Armed Services, Fiscal Year 1976 and July–September 1976 Transition Period Authorization for Military Procurement, Research and Development, and Active Duty, Selected Reserve, and Civilian Personnel Strengths: Hearings on S. 920, Part 10, Research and Development, 94th Cong., 1st sess., 1975, p. 5155 (hereafter cited as Senate, Fiscal Year 1976 and July–September 1976).

[57] U. S. Senate, Committee on Armed Services, Fiscal Year 1975 Authorization for Military Procurement, Research and Development, and Active Duty, Selected Reserve and Civilian Personnel Strengths: Hearings on S. 3000, Part 7, Research and Development, 93d Cong., 2d sess., 1974, p. 3629 (hereafter cited as Senate, Fiscal Year 1975).

have been congressional attempts to enact a testing moratorium. In February of 1976, Senator Kennedy introduced a resolution calling upon the president to "offer to the Soviet Union an immediate mutual moratorium on flight testing of all strategic-range cruise missiles."[58] He defended the resolution with a succinct description of the verification problems posed by cruise.

> Because of the nature of the cruise missile it will be impossible to tell by looking at them whether a particular missile can travel a few hundred miles or a few thousand; whether it has a conventional or a nuclear warhead; whether it is a tactical weapon or a strategic weapon that can destroy missile sites and cities.
> When flight testing is finished and deployment begins, verification of cruise missiles may become impossible and it will be increasingly difficult to make firm judgments about the number of nuclear weapons on each side.[59]

There are few examples more graphic than cruise of how bargaining chips can so swiftly become building blocks. Once a bargaining chip is developed to the point at which people, in the words of Admiral Synhorst, "will believe you," serious new problems arise. Constituencies exist which are most difficult to overrule. Within a period of a few short years Admiral Synhorst himself had forgotten cruise was ever a bargaining chip. In response to a question from Senator McIntyre, the admiral forthrightly insisted that "the SLCM is not a SALT bargaining chip."[60] Yet the bargaining chip is still available when needed. In May of 1976 Senator Robert Griffin (R-Mich.), speaking in defense of cruise when $77.95 million was cut in committee from the SLCM program, resurrected the bargaining chip rationale, stating that "the Soviet Union clearly wants to restrict U. S. development of [cruise missiles] and might be prepared to make significant concessions to obtain some sort of agreement."[61]

MORE MISSILES, BIGGER WARHEADS, AND IMPROVED ACCURACY— BARGAINING CHIPS OR BUILDING BLOCKS?

In early 1974 Secretary of Defense James Schlesinger launched a debate on American nuclear strategy by advocating a more flexible targeting doctrine. He argued that flexibility (in the form of selective strikes on Soviet military and industrial installations) could be attained without "any increase in forces."[62]

---

[58] *Congressional Record*, February 25, 1976, p. S 2289.

[59] Ibid. See the amendment to the Procurement Authorization Bill offered by Senator McGovern (D-S. D.) on April 13, 1976, that would eliminate funding for ALCM's and SLCM's "unless the President certifies to Congress" the absence of a Soviet-American agreement covering them *and* the presence of a "national security interest to continue development of such missiles," *Congressional Record*, April 13, 1976, p. S 5615.

[60] Senate, *Fiscal Year 1975, Part 7*, p. 3660.

[61] *Congressional Record*, May 26, 1976, p. S 8044.

[62] U. S. Senate, Committee on Foreign Relations, *U. S.-USSR Strategic Policies: Hearings on U. S. and Soviet Strategic Doctrine and Military Policies*, 93d Cong., 2d sess., 1974, p. 2.

He nonetheless requested funds for increased accuracy of American weapons, justifying this request by reference to the Soviet research and development program which might yield a "potential net throw weight for a major counterforce capability."[63]

Since 1974 a number of changes have been proposed in the nuclear arsenal which seem designed to give the *United States* a counterforce capability. What is important here are these changes in the arsenal—changes which have frequently been justified with the rhetoric of the bargaining chip. Three programs are of special concern: increased production of Minuteman III missiles, the development and procurement of a higher yield warhead for Minuteman (Mark 12-A), and the development of a maneuverable reentry vehicle (MARV).

In addressing the counterforce improvements sought by Secretary Schlesinger, Barry Carter has succinctly expressed the basic dynamic by which weapons justified as bargaining chips end up in the arsenal:

> If the U. S. counterforce programs are allowed to continue beyond the rhetoric of announcing them, these programs would operate to undercut any progress at SALT. Of course, if announcing these programs is just a short-term ploy designed to strengthen the U. S. bargaining position for the impending SALT II agreements, then little real harm will result . . . [but] new weapons programs tend to gain a momentum of their own once they are announced. High-level officials become publicly committed to rationales for them, rationales that include more than the systems' just being "bargaining chips."[64]

It would be an understatement to say that these programs have gone "beyond the rhetoric of announcing them." They are well on their way to becoming building blocks.

Minuteman III

In the summer of 1975 America's land-based missiles were scheduled to stabilize at 54 Titan II's, 450 Minuteman II's, and 550 Minuteman III's. With no follow-on missile anywhere near production, the Utah production line was to be closed.[65] Secretary Schlesinger then requested fifty additional Minuteman missiles. The rationale was as follows: the production line should be kept open "as a hedge against the breakdown of SALT II negotiations"; the additional missiles would be used for test purposes from 1984 to 1988; and, in the words of Utah's Senator Moss: "keeping our assembly line intact should provide some incentive to the Soviet Union to reach a final agreement on this new SALT accord as soon as

---

[63] Ibid., p. 18.

[64] Barry Carter, "Nuclear Strategy and Nuclear Weapons," *Scientific American*, 230 (May 1974), 28–29.

[65] As Senator Kennedy put it in May 1976: "Each year since 1972 we have been assured that the production line is going to close when the 550 [Minuteman III] are finally purchased." *Congressional Record*, May 26, 1976, p. S 8050.

possible."[66] Senator Kennedy's amendment to delete the $203.1 million for the fifty additional missiles was defeated twenty-seven to fifty-six.[67]

In 1976 the issue surfaced again, with an April 27 supplemental administration request for $260.7 million for sixty additional Minuteman missiles. Once again Senator Kennedy sought to delete the procurement funds, arguing that his amendment "simply seeks to prevent a bargaining chip, which already has cost the American taxpayer some $800 million, from passing the $1 billion mark."[68] Although his amendment lost thirty-five to forty-nine, the debate is instructive.

Having argued in 1975 that the fifty additional missiles were for testing, it was difficult for the administration to make a "testing argument" in 1976.[69] However, the "keep the production line open" argument was still employed, and the bargaining chip was still discernible. There was also a new twist. Whereas in 1975 there was little or no mention of *deploying* the additional missiles, this *was* discussed in 1976. Robert F. Ellsworth, deputy secretary of defense, stressed that Defense was "asking for authority to protect the option of producing 60 additional MMIIIs which could be used, depending upon the outcome of SALT negotiations, for *deployment*, testing, or upgrading of MMII." Ellsworth also stated that the United States "could achieve a Minuteman III force of 700 by mid-calendar year 1979."[70]

Thus, continued production of Minuteman III has been justified both as a psychological bargaining chip and as a contingency chip against failure in SALT II. Indeed, this is a contingency chip in the sense that the administration each year seems to want to produce more Minuteman missiles if the "pace" of SALT is too slow.

Mark 12-A

Mark 12-A is an improved warhead system for Minuteman III with potential use on the follow-on ICBM (MX) and Trident II as well. Whereas the current MMIII reentry vehicle has three warheads of about 170–200 kilotons and a circular error probable (CEP)[71] of 400–500 meters, the Mark 12-A will have three war-

---

[66] *Congressional Record*, June 5, 1975, pp. S 9857–9859. Also see Clarence A. Robinson, Jr., "Continued Minuteman 3 Output Asked," *Aviation Week and Space Technology*, April 28, 1975, p. 99.

[67] *Congressional Record*, June 5, 1976, pp. S 9861–9862.

[68] Ibid., May 26, 1976, p. S 8049.

[69] As Senator Kennedy said: "We already have purchased 187 missiles beyond the 550 needed to be deployed; 17 are used for spares. . . . Another 61 have been tested and 126 remain available for testing. At the testing rate, which last year was defined as seven a year, we actually could have 18 years of testing without buying a single new missile." *Congressional Record*, May 26, 1976, p. S 8050.

[70] Letter to Senator Stennis, ibid., pp. S 8056 and 8053. Italics added.

[71] CEP equals the radius of a circle within which a warhead has a 50 percent probability of landing.

heads of about 400 kilotons and a CEP of about 250 meters. As Clarence Robinson has put it: "With guidance improvements to go along with other MK-12A improvements, the Minuteman will have been improved to its maximum growth potential."[72]

The April 1976 supplemental request for sixty additional Minuteman III missiles was accompanied by a request for $56.3 million to move up the date for procurement of the MK-12A warhead to be fitted on those missiles.[73] Senator Cranston (D-Calif.) expressed his judgment on these two programs as follows: "The production of Minuteman III's would be a waste—but the production of Mark 12-A's could be a threat—not only to the Soviet Union but, because of how their production is perceived, to our own national security as well."[74] Senator Cranston's reasoning was that with the higher yield of MK-12A and the improved accuracy of the Minuteman III (because of guidance improvements), the Soviets may perceive this new weapon as a threat to their land-based missile force. Indeed, John Finney described the MK-12A as a warhead " specifically designed as a 'counterforce' weapon for attacking military targets in the Soviet Union such as missile sites."[75]

To the extent that the United States (or the USSR) acquires true counterforce weapons, that would be destabilizing, for it would encourage the other side to adopt a "launch on warning" doctrine. That is, if one's land-based missiles cannot absorb a first strike, there is an incentive to empty the silos at the first, perhaps accidental or erroneous indication of an enemy attack. If *both* sides had such counterforce weapons, we would be at the maximum point of instability.

Perhaps the most significant question about MK-12A is whether it is in any sense a bargaining chip or whether it is an integral part of the counterforce program of the United States. Probably the most explicit administration statement suggesting a bargaining chip rationale is the Air Force justification for the April 1976, supplemental request for sixty Minuteman III's *and* accelerated pro-

---

[72] Clarence A. Robinson, Jr., "Minuteman Production Defended," *Aviation Week and Space Technology,* January 19, 1976, p. 14.

[73] Like so many weapons, deployment of this one was not envisaged in the recent past. Lt. General William J. Evans, an Air Force R&D official, stated on March 26, 1974; "this is an effort that we feel is necessary and it is part of the technology base and technology options that we think we should have on the shelf, depending on what the enemy does. *We are not proposing that we put this additional yield into our Minuteman III force* but we are saying that it is prudent to develop a Mark 12-A." Italics added. Senate, *Fiscal Year 1975, Part 6,* p. 2926.

[74] *Congressional Record,* May 26, 1976, p. S 8054.

[75] John W. Finney, "Arms Budget Rise Is Sought by Ford," *The New York Times,* April 27, 1976; also see George C. Wilson, "Ford Decision on Missiles Stirs Debate," *Washington Post,* May 6, 1976. Although the Pentagon denies that the MK-12A is a first-strike weapon, the Air Force concedes that the new warhead, coupled with the scheduled accuracy improvements, "will provide increased confidence in our ability to execute a limited hard target attack against selected hardened Soviet targets should the need arise." Senate, *Fiscal Year 1976 and July–September 1976, Part 4,* p. 2061.

curement of MK-12A. After noting that the original FY1977 budget request did not contain these items because of the exercise of "deliberate restraint" by the United States, J. W. Plummer, undersecretary of the Air Force, stated:

> We hoped for commensurate restraint on the part of the Soviet Union, and we also hoped for consummation of a SALT II agreement in 1976. . . . Regrettably . . . we must . . . take positive action for two reasons—first, the Soviet Union is clearly proceeding to develop and deploy four advanced ICBMs and two new SLBMs; and second, because we have had more time to note the pace of SALT negotiations.[76]

Thus, by implication, the MK-12A and increased Minuteman III production are linked together both as psychological and contingency bargaining chips.

But they are qualitatively different. Procuring MK-12A is a major decision for a new weapon. The procurement decision was to be made in the fall of 1977. It is a weapon with impressive counterforce potential. Senator Cranston questioned the request for MK-12A, which appeared,

> to be a rather offhanded and hasty decision. . . . To produce the Mark-12A is a major change in our deployment position. This is the first production buy of a major counter-force weapon—one that could be used for a limited first strike against hardened targets in the Soviet Union. A major production decision on our first counter-force weapon should not be made under political pressure and should not be piggy-backed onto another weapons system buy.[77]

The Department of Defense answered this charge by suggesting that the MK-12 was no longer in production and that the MK-12A would, hence, be needed for the sixty new Minuteman III's. But Deputy Secretary Ellsworth added: "The MK-12A is also a potential warhead for the M-X and Trident II missiles."[78] Given the usual inclinations of the military, the long-range mission postulated for the MK-12A, and the fact that testing for the MK-12A and another MX warhead was accelerated to beat the March 1, 1976, date beyond which underground tests above a certain yield were banned,[79] it is difficult to resist the conclusion that the MK-12A, much more than the increased Minuteman III production, is likely to be a building block—a fixture in the American arsenal of the 1980s. By coupling a bargaining chip rationale for the sixty Minuteman III's *and* the MK-12A, the Pentagon seemed to make both dependent on the slow pace of SALT and the ongoing Soviet missile programs. The contingency chip rationale for MK-12A may be fragile indeed, as it is a counterforce warhead which complements the recent doctrinal pronouncements of the Pentagon.

---

[76] *Congressional Record*, May 26, 1976, p. S 8053.
[77] Ibid., p. S 8054.
[78] Ibid., p. S 8056.
[79] Henry Simmons, "Report on the National Scene: Strategic Arms—Worries and Cold Comfort," *Astronautics and Aeronautics*, April 1976, p. 8.

MARV

The bargaining chip potentialities of our newest technological breakthrough have yet to be determined. This may be the case because the SALT negotiators have still to address themselves to the problem of qualitative improvements and guidance accuracies of strategic missiles. When and if they do, MARV may turn out to be the most difficult bargaining chip of them all.

The maneuverable reentry vehicle (MARV) is defined by a recent Library of Congress study as "a ballistic missile warhead or decoy whose accuracy is improved by terminal guidance mechanisms."[80] There are, however, two types of MARV's. One (e.g., Navy MK-500) is an evader MARV designed to overcome ballistic missile defenses. The other is a high-accuracy MARV with a counterforce mission.[81] The former follows an erratic pattern to confuse ballistic missile defense radars. The latter may have the capability to achieve an accuracy of a 100-*foot* CEP. As Senator Humphrey put it: "These re-entry vehicles could have a 99 percent or better probability of destroying ICBM's in hardened sites."[82]

As a result of this accuracy, MARV may be used by the military as justification for *mobile* land-based ICBM's. This is so because whatever uncertainty may exist about the capability of MK-12A and current MMIII's to destroy Soviet ICBM's, there is no such uncertainty about MARV. When projected for Soviet ICBM's, MARV will similarly threaten United States silos. Based on calculations of Congressman Robert L. Leggett (D-Calif.), both sides can have an anti-ICBM first strike with MARV's by around 1990 (the United States will actually acquire it, according to Leggett, in the mid-1980s).

According to Congressman Downey (D-N. Y.), the first flight tests of high-accuracy, terminally guided MARV's are to occur in 1978 or 1979.[83] But tests of evader MARVs are going forward, and these tests, according to Congressman Leggett, can be confused over time with those of the terminally guided, high-accuracy MARV. Leggett makes the crucial point—as valid for MARV as it was for MIRV:

> The Soviets know that the United States will not have a high accuracy MARV for perhaps 3 or 4 years, so it is important that this year or next year or perhaps both that *we not do any further testing of these vehicles lest we lose this as a*

---

[80] U. S. Senate, *United States/Soviet Military Balance*, p. 63.

[81] For a brief DOD statement on MARV, see U. S. House of Representatives, Committee on International Relations, *The Vladivostok Accord: Implications to U. S. Security, Arms Control, and World Peace: Hearings before the Subcommittee on International Security and Scientific Affairs*, 94th Cong., 1st sess., 1975, p. 138 (hereafter cited as House, *Vladivostok Accord*).

[82] *Congressional Record*, June 6, 1975, p. S 9934. See also Congressman Downey's (D-N. Y.) statement that with MARV providing an accuracy of some 0.02 mile "even a tiny 40 kiloton . . . weapon has a kill probability of well over 99%. Moreover, MARV can achieve this level of accuracy in a submarine-launched missile as well as an ICBM." House, *Vladivostok Accord*, p. 33. MARV, additionally, may be "[retrofitted] into both ICBM's and SLBM's." Carter, "Nuclear Strategy and Nuclear Weapons," p. 25.

[83] House, *Vladivostok Accord*, p. 34.

bargaining chip in SALT, and you can lose it as a bargaining chip in SALT because unlike ABMs it is not verifiable.[84]

This, then, is a special kind of bargaining chip. If it frightens the Soviets—if they want to control it—it remains useful as a bargaining lever only *until it is tested,* for beyond that point verification by unilateral means becomes virtually impossible. To the extent that MARV is a bargaining chip, it is presumably a psychological one. There is no evidence that the United States has made it a contingency chip for SALT II. Conceivably, it could be a contingency chip which demonstrates United States' capacity to move forward with dramatic qualitative improvements. But Leggett's caveat must be repeated: once MARV is tested, there is little chance it can function as any kind of bargaining chip.

As Herbert Scoville put it in 1975: "MIRVs are a clear-cut case of where weapons, which were bought as bargaining chips, have decreased our security and skyrocketed our defense costs. Secretary Kissinger admitted that he wishes he 'had thought through the implications of the MIRVed world more fully in 1969 and 1970.'"[85] It is time *now* to think through the consequences of the *MARVed* world. It is not clear that the administration is doing this. In his FY1977 statements, Dr. Currie noted that an advanced evader MARV would be tested before 1980 and that examination was continuing of "the technology of terminal fixing and we expect to fly in the intermediate future a terminally guided re-entry vehicle."[86] To the extent that MARV can serve as a bargaining chip, it must be used now, before further flight testing even of the evader MARV. For, like MIRV, once tested, MARV will not—cannot—be bargained away.

Conclusion

How important was our bargaining chip strategy in bringing about the SALT I agreement? A review of this strategy suggests that it served to complicate negotiations by raising arms competition to higher levels, often levels more difficult to control. Critics argue that our insistence upon going forward with Safeguard resulted only in a treaty which authorized a larger ABM system for the Soviet Union than they had before the negotiations started; and that use of MIRV as a bargaining chip resulted only in its not being covered by SALT I due to Soviet fears of technological inferiority and a desire to develop their own

[84] Ibid., p. 18. Italics added. Congressman Downey agrees: "A MARV ban would be effective, and it is feasible as long as we get it signed before the first terminal MARV test." Ibid., p. 34. For a pro-MARV view, see the testimony of John M. Deutch, ibid., especially pp. 103–104.

[85] Ibid., p. 68.

[86] Senate, *Fiscal Year 1977, Part 4,* p. 2104. For diverging views on the impact of improved accuracy on the strategic balance, see the testimony of Congressman Leggett, House, *Vladivostok Accord,* pp. 8–20; Kosta Tsipis, "The Accuracy of Strategic Missiles," *Scientific American,* 233 (July 1975), 14–23; and Thomas A. Brown, "Missile Accuracy and Strategic Lethality," *Survival,* XVIII (March–April 1976), 52–59. The latter is a critique of Leggett and Tsipis.

MIRV. Critics are convinced that weapons initially justified as bargaining chips soon become building blocks—weapons systems which become permanent parts of the arsenal. As Senator Kennedy (D-Mass.) has put it, "a bargaining chip is good so long as it is not played. Once played, its only effect is to raise the stakes."[87]

The bargaining chip approach may, according to another critical perspective, heighten the sensitivities of the superpowers to incremental advantages in arms competition obliging them to match each step with corresponding measures. In that sense the bargaining chip strategy may undermine the essential parity which is the basis for mutual concessions and fruitful negotiations. Students of Soviet behavior such as Marshall Shulman argued in 1972 that "if now we continue to follow the logic of the bargaining chip tactic and [try] to widen our techno-logical advantage, we shall in fact be undermining the basis of present and future SALT agreements."[88] In a similar fashion Samuel B. Payne has concluded in his study of Soviet attitudes toward SALT that the Russians will not negoti-ate from a perceived position of inferiority.[89]

Others argue that the bargaining chip can be used for domestic political purposes to salvage a weapons program in trouble with Congress. Such use may leave a legacy of superfluous and often expensive arms programs which frequent-ly develop their own constituencies and become, therefore, difficult to remove. The critics then see the bargaining chip ironically turning arms talks against themselves and making them a stimulant to the arms race.

The argument also is made that the bargaining chip is only a theoretical construct, incapable of practical application. There are few historical precedents, particularly in the cold war, of political decision makers testing and developing

[87] Senate, *SALT Agreements,* p. 252.

[88] Ibid., p. 140.

[89] Samuel B. Payne, Jr., "The Soviet Debate on Strategic Arms Limitations: 1969–72," *Soviet Studies,* XXVIII (January 1975), 27–45. Soviet behavior prior to entering the SALT talks may be instructive in this regard. Between the original date for the beginning of SALT (fall 1968) and its actual beginning in November 1969, the Soviets acquired 375 more ICBM's and SLBM's, at which point they stopped construction, having exceeded the 1054 ICBM's the United States had maintained since 1967. It is possible that knowing they were catching up with the American lead in ICBM's, the Soviets could approach the talks with more confidence. Bargaining chip policies may produce a similar set of policies in the Soviet Union. Former SALT negotiator Raymond L. Garthoff has suggested that the Soviet Union is currently match-ing some of our more recent bargaining chips. Garthoff observes: "There is strong basis to conclude that the Soviet military leadership sees their current programs to build up the SLBM force, and above all, to replace part of SS-11 and SS-9 with MIRVed SS-19's and SS-18's (and perhaps to produce a strategic bomber as well) as necessary and prudent actions in order to preserve parity by matching the already programmed building of U. S. Minuteman III, Posei-don, Trident and B-1 strategic forces." In "SALT and the Soviet Military," *Problems of Com-munism,* XXIV (January–February 1975), 30–32. For trends in the Soviet and American ar-senals see International Institute for Strategic Studies, *The Military Balance, 1975–76* (Lon-don, 1975), p. 73.

successfully new weapons systems only to see them removed in an arms control agreement. Jack Ruina sees an inevitable political contradiction in the concept: "It is hard to think of an arms program that simultaneously is good enough to worry an opponent and bad enough for the military to be willing to give it up in negotiations."[90]

Bargaining chip rationales appear to vary for each weapons system according to circumstances, as one type of chip often dissolves into another. With MIRV, for instance, what originated in part as a domestic chip evolved into a psychological chip, was briefly presented as a specific chip, and eventually became a building block.

The inconsistent and at times elusive use of the concept by government officials forces the conclusion that no carefully developed set of bargaining chip policies as yet exists. If such policies do exist, many important participants in the policy-making process lack an understanding of what they are. The civilian leadership, as the conflicting testimony makes apparent, has not communicated to the military any sense of what is meant by a bargaining chip. To develop a weapon without seeing a place for it in the arsenal is a concept that the military, as in the case of MIRV and the cruise missile, finds difficult to comprehend. Possibly bargaining chips can serve a useful function so long as they remain only as *potential* threats. Leslie Gelb and Anthony Lake argued this position after the signing of SALT I: "Of course the President needs bargaining chips. But new weapons systems do not actually have to be deployed in order to give him bargaining power. This power derives from the American potential to deploy, not actual deployment."[91] In other words, a bargaining chip can exist in the form of research and development, avoiding the costs of deployment and reducing its chances of becoming a building block. "The threat of deployment," Paul Warnke has argued, "might energize diplomacy but the fact of deployment would defeat it."[92] This approach attempts to fit Jack Ruina's description of a "good" bargaining chip, i.e., one that could be "particularly irritating or threatening to the other side without being so attractive to [ourselves] that it could not be curtailed."[93]

Senator Brooke (R.-Mass.), for one, does not find this argument persuasive. In arguing for an amendment to prohibit counterforce research and development, Brooke told the Senate that research and development programs were "notoriously bad bargaining incentives because they are ambiguous signals of U. S.

[90] Jack Ruina, "SALT in a MAD World," *The New York Times Magazine*, June 30, 1974, p. 48.

[91] Quoted in *Congressional Record*, July 27, 1972, p. 25701.

[92] Quoted in Frye, *A Responsible Congress*, p. 36.

[93] J. P. Ruina, "U. S. and Soviet Strategic Arsenals," in Mason Willrich and John B. Rhinelander (eds.), *SALT: The Moscow Agreements and Beyond* (New York, 1974), p. 42. A similar view was taken by fourteen Republican congressmen who stated in 1973 that "maintaining a strong R&D program would not only act as an effective bargaining ploy, but could also result in material savings in defense expenditures," *Congressional Record*, March 19, 1973, p. S 5104.

intent," and could cause "an already suspicious and hostile adversary to redouble their efforts."[94]

This confusion may be symptomatic of a larger confusion over strategic doctrine. What may be a bargaining chip for some may be an effective new counterforce weapon for others. MARV may be illustrative of just this type of paradox. Adherents to the assured destruction doctrine may find it quite dangerous to use a potentially counterforce weapon such as MARV as a bargaining chip.

If a commitment to assured destruction were to be made, then, conceivably, a bargaining chip policy could be fashioned. Such a policy might involve acts of deliberate restraint on weapons research, development, testing, or acquisition—transforming the bargaining chip into a peace initiative.[95] Weapons that complicate verification (cruise) or are destabilizing (MARV) would be withheld from the testing phase, signaling our interest in a stable deterrence pending agreement to control such weapons.

One current suggestion for controlling MARV may be illustrative of how bargaining chip policies could be transformed. Senator Hubert Humphrey (D-Minn.) in 1975 introduced an amendment which would have banned MARV testing unless the president certified its necessity under certain conditions. The Humphrey amendment would have allowed R&D on MARV while prohibiting testing. Senator Frank Moss (D-Utah) interpreted it as "a signal to [the Soviets] that we have no desire to escalate the arms race."[96]

Bargaining chips that enhance trust, signal a desire not to let technology get out of hand, and are kept clear of projected force postures, may, in the final analysis, be the only ones we should play.*

[94] *Congressional Record*, June 10, 1974, p. 10202.

[95] For several works that discuss reversing the arms race by exercising restraint, see; David V. Edwards, *Creating a New World Politics: From Conflict to Cooperation* (New York, 1973), especially pp. 123–126; Amitai Etzioni, "The Kennedy Experiment," in his *Studies in Social Change* (New York, 1966), chap. 4; and Charles E. Osgood, *An Alternative to War or Surrender* (Urbana, Ill., 1962).

[96] *Congressional Record*, June 6, 1975, pp. S 9933–9936.

* This article is a revision of a paper presented at the 1976 Annual Meeting of the American Political Science Association in Chicago.

Tactical Nuclear Weapons
and Deterrence in Europe

The deterrence of Soviet aggression in Europe has been a cornerstone of American policy for thirty years. It was undoubtedly World War II
and specifically the reality of Soviet troops as far west as the Elbe that created
the peculiar "mind set" in American foreign-policy makers that envisions the
Russians straining desperately at the leash waiting for the opportune time to
"continue" the conquest of Europe. In this view, only the stalwart forward defenses of NATO coupled with the ever-alert SAC have prevented the powerful
bear from crashing through to the English Channel and possibly beyond. Given
such a heavy burden for NATO it is no wonder American policy makers become glassy eyed as the alliance proves unable, throughout twenty-eight years,
to bring its forces and its doctrines into some kind of congruence that would
make sense to the world, or at least to ourselves. In vain have we struggled
through all those years to provide the right mix of technology, manpower, and
doctrine to make NATO rational.[1] This article argues that of all the frantic and

[1] There is someting to be said for the position that much of what happens in politics is not
rational. Some would argue that the force levels and weapons employed in Europe are the result
of many pressures and various forms of internal political bargaining rather than of some rational strategy. While such a position has merit it is also true that when a NATO commander
appears before congressional committees and justifies additional expenditures for improving
weapons systems he does so by marshaling arguments perceived to be rational by congressmen.
If we can demonstrate that those arguments are not so rational after all, it becomes more difficult, regardless of other pressures, for Congress to act on the basis of them. Even if "rational-

PHILIP W. DYER is an associate professor of political science at the University of Nebraska-
Lincoln. He has published articles in the *Political Science Quarterly, Journal of Thought, Polity,*
and other scholarly journals.

Political Science Quarterly   Volume 92   Number 2   Summer 1977   277 irrational things done in the name of deterring the Soviets in Europe, the most dangerous and wasteful has been the emplacement of tactical nuclear weapons on European soil.

THE POLITICAL SETTING FOR DETERRENCE

In an effort to see these weapons and their role in NATO in a different light we shall first consider the problem of deterrence in Europe generally, and then focus on the alleged roles of tactical nuclear weapons in that deterrence. It is very difficult to see under what combat conditions, especially in Europe, these weapons would ever be employed.[2] Here the task is to determine if perhaps some deterrent role can be found for the weapons despite the difficulty of envisioning a combat role.

Perhaps the best way to begin answering the question of what stops the Soviet Union from invading Western Europe tomorrow is to ask what stops NATO from invading Eastern Europe tomorrow? It is not enough simply to say that we are peace loving or we do not have any desire to invade, because those are simply expressions of intentions that are difficult to validate. The Russians might well say the same thing about their own intentions, but we naturally do not believe them. As military analysts frequently point out, not only are intentions difficult to assess but they also can change rapidly and therefore should not form the basis of one's policy.[3] Our intentions aside, it might not be too simplistic to argue that essentially what deters us, or any nation, from launching a war is the result of some form of cost-benefit calculation however rudimentary, crude, and imprecise that calculation might be.

Eastern Europe—unlike the Middle East, for example—has few natural resources that the West needs. Therefore the primary benefits would have to be the people, their strategic position, and their industrial base, especially in East Germany. But how, precisely, would the people and the industrial base help us? Even assuming we could occupy the area with a minimum of troops, how could we profit from such an occupation? Our economy does not particularly need what Eastern Europe produces and it is difficult to see what else we would stand to gain except a little better strategic position vis-à-vis the Soviet Union. Thus just

---

ity" is only a façade behind which other motivations hide it is useful to destroy the façade wherever possible and perhaps thus get closer to whatever is hiding behind it.

[2] Philip W. Dyer, "Will Tactical Nuclear Weapons Ever Be Used?" *Political Science Quarterly*, 88, no. 2 (June 1973), 214–229.

[3] Here is one presentation out of the many that could be selected supporting this common position: "First, let me say a few words about the threat in Europe, that is, the capabilities of the potential enemy. . . . I am not speaking of enemy intentions, for planning can be based on intentions only when one knows what they are. . . . Intentions can and do change overnight, whereas it takes years to develop and refine military capabilities." General Lyman Lemnitzer, "From the American Point of View," in Lord St. Oswald (ed.), *The Soviet Threat to Europe* (London, 1969), pp. 21–33. Also see the discussion in Thomas C. Schelling, *Arms and Influence* (New Haven, Conn., 1966), p. 35.

considering the problem from the benefit side we can see that there is not much to be gained even if we could seize that area tomorrow without a fight.

However, when costs are calculated the idea becomes clearly absurd. The immediate and direct cost would be, undoubtedly, a large-scale conventional war with the Warsaw Pact army that would represent a considerable expenditure of lives and money. That cost in itself when weighed against the marginal value of the prize to us is probably enough to deter NATO from undertaking such an adventure. However, an even far greater cost lurks down that road since the world's two nuclear superpowers would be involved in an armed conflict over an area of the world that at least one of them apparently considers vital to its own security. Obviously, then, into the calculation must go at least the possibility that such a war might end in a thermonuclear exchange between the United States and the Soviet Union. Thus, we have a marginal benefit overbalanced by a substantial real cost coupled with the possibility of a catastrophic potential cost all of which results in the decision that it would be foolish from our perspective to engage in such an undertaking.

From the Soviet perspective, an invasion of Western Europe by the Red army would entail a similar cost-benefit analysis. Like Eastern Europe, Western Europe is not richly endowed with natural resources, so the gain there, too, would be primarily the people, the industrial base, a superior level of technology, and possibly an improved strategic setting. How, precisely, would the Soviet Union be strengthened by occupying such a large territory as Western Europe? Since it is naive to imagine that the local population would be friendly, it would be necessary for the Soviets to field a rather substantial army of occupation. Puppet governments might well be used, of course, but the experiences of Hungary and Czechoslovakia have shown the Soviets that puppet governments are not always reliable and certainly do not eliminate the need for large military forces to be stationed in a country.

Although the USSR is a superpower it is not Superman. The only way in which Russia is a superpower compared to Western Europe is in its possession of an awesome strategic thermonuclear strike capability. Otherwise, it is a country of approximately 250 million people with a GNP of approximately $650 billion. Western Europe, even without Great Britain, is composed of more than 270 million people with a combined GNP in excess of $800 billion. The Russians occupying such a region conjures up a vision of one whale trying to swallow another. In the occupation of Western Europe nuclear weapons are not especially relevant, so that two roughly equal entities are to be considered. Here the experience of France in the nineteenth century and Germany in the twentieth, both of whom enjoy a more favorable geographic location, might be useful in showing the difficult and short-lived nature of any modern attempt to occupy all of Europe.

Even if the Russians were willing to field and maintain indefinitely a huge army of occupation, there are several other considerations that they would have to weigh as they attempted to figure out the benefit to them of seizing Western Europe. One problem whose magnitude has become obvious in recent years is the question of energy. The Soviet Union is roughly self-sufficient in oil, at least for the present, but it certainly does not have the resources to slake Europe's enormous thirst for that mineral. Would Middle Eastern oil flow to a Soviet-occupied West Europe in its present quantities? That would depend, among other things, on what the United States chose to do. Assuming that a Soviet rush to the English Channel would have overrun NATO and 250,000 American troops (the costs will be considered later) America might well use its naval forces to reduce the flow of oil. An occupied Western Europe without sufficient oil could turn out to be more of a liability than a benefit to the USSR.

Another equally serious matter is for the Soviets to determine specifically how they would benefit from such an occupation even if the problems of the army and energy were solved. Are Western products to be confiscated and sent directly to the Soviet Union so tht each Soviet citizen will drive a Volkswagen, Fiat, or Renault? Are the economies of that whole area to be combined into one super common market? Are machine tools and factories to be disassembled and shipped to the Soviet Union as they were after World War II? (The army of occupation would have to be increased.) Does the Soviet Union really need such "benefits"? How does the substantial economic strength of East Germany presently help the Soviets? If the Russians need Western products so badly why have they not confiscated East German goods and shipped them eastward? Would the Russians be strengthened internationally? Would all future military calculations have to assume that the armies of Western Europe must be added to Soviet forces when put in the balance? But if Europe had been overrun what future war would involve armies in that area? Would it not be a question of the two thermonuclear powers eyeing each other across the Atlantic? In such a confrontation how does the occupation of Western Europe strengthen the Russians? Would the Soviet nuclear threat be so appreciably enhanced by the seizure of the French *force de frappe* (if that had not already been employed) that Russia's position vis-à-vis the United States would become noticeably improved? These questions are not easy to answer but hopefully they at least suggest that from the Soviet perspective the seizure and occupation of Western Europe might not produce benefits of such a clear and enticing nature as to make that adventure worthwhile even if the costs were negligible. However, the costs are not insignificant and it is to them that we shall now turn.

What are the tangible direct and potential future costs of a Soviet drive to the Channel? Unquestionably such an undertaking would at least cause a conventional war of substantial proportions. On the first day of hostilities the Warsaw Pact would have 576,000 troops (339,000 Soviet) deployed against 660,000 NATO troops (200,000 American). Within thirty days the figures might be 1,067,000 Warsaw Pact (677,000 Russians) against 1,045,000 NATO (285,000 American); while sixty days after the invasion the figures would not have changed significantly—1,241,000 Warsaw Pact (842,000 Russians) against

1,105,000 NATO (345,000 Americans).[4] It should be noted that because of their wide geographic distribution not all of the NATO troops would necessarily be engaged against the enemy. In any event if one wanted to question the reliability of Eastern European forces in a clear war of aggression against the West the Soviet Union would, indeed, be outnumbered by NATO forces fighting for the defense of their own homeland. The first real cost the Soviets would face, then, would be a substantial conventional war that they could not be guaranteed of winning. A second possible cost, as with the earlier example, derives from the fact that the world's two nuclear superpowers would be shooting at each other in an area of the world that one of them, at least, has indicated is of crucial importance to its own security. Thus, just as with a NATO invasion of Eastern Europe here, too, there would be a reasonable chance that the hostilities might culminate in a thermonuclear exchange. The Soviets, therefore, would be faced with the real direct cost of a large conventional war in Europe and with the possibility of a catastrophic thermonuclear war. These two costs, one actual and one potential, weighed against the doubtful benefits described earlier help to show why there has been no war in Europe to date.[5] But if deterrence in Europe is a function of doubtful benefits, real conventional costs, and potential thermonuclear strategic costs, then how do the tactical nuclear weapons presently stationed in Europe fit into this deterrence picture? In a word, they do not; and it is to a consideration of this peculiar weapons system and its alleged roles in deterrence that we shall now turn.

THE WEAPONS AND THEIR PROPOSED ROLES

Before discussing the proposed roles of the tactical nuclear weapons stationed in Europe it is necessary first to bring the reader up to date on the weapons themselves. The ground-launched weapons consist primarily of artillery and surface-to-surface rockets and missiles. The artillery includes the 155 millimeter and 8 inch howitzers of both the towed and self-propelled variety. These are standard artillery weapons organic to any American division-size unit, as well as to artillery units at higher levels. The nuclear shells for these weapons have been engineered to fit the conventional artillery piece without modification, thus making all 600 or so of these weapons presently in Europe nuclear-capable. The

---

[4] These figures came from Jeffrey Record, *U. S. Nuclear Weapons in Europe: Sources and Alternatives* (Washington, D. C., 1974), p. 17.

[5] To those who would object that such a simplistic cost-benefit calculus does not allow sufficient room for ideological considerations that may be crucial in understanding Soviet behavior, I would respond that neither Soviet actions since the end of World War II nor their rhetoric, especially in the twentieth and twenty-second Party Congresses, convinces me that they have such "a passion for souls" that ideological convictions about world dominant messianic communism play any significant role in their calculations.

range of the weapons is from point blank (not advised with a nuclear round) to approximately 17,000 meters and the yield varies from less than one kiloton (kt) to more than 10 kt.

The second category of ground-launched weapons are the rockets and missiles including the Honest John and the Sergeant; their replacement, the Lance; and the longer-range Pershing; as well as the Nike-Hercules which is primarily an air defense weapon.[6] The Lance and the Pershing have ranges from 5000 meters to almost 80 miles and 110 miles to 450 miles, respectively, with yields of 1–100 kt and 60–400 kt. In addition there are atomic demolitions of various sizes about which not much is known.[7]

The tactical air capability greatly increases both the range and yield of atomic weapons available to the Supreme Allied Commander Europe (SACEUR). The two principal weapons are the Air Force's F-4 and F-111 which have respective strike radii of 800 and 1700 miles and are each able to carry bombs that vary from .1 kt to 1 *megaton*.[8] Thus, at least in theory, the Soviet ports of Murmansk and Odessa could disappear under a 1 million ton TNT-equivalent mushroom cloud and yet from our perspective the war would still be a tactical nuclear one. It is precisely because of the ranges and yields of these weapons that there is no probable war in Europe when the weapons would ever be used.[9]

What deterrent roles do observers see for such an impressive array of weaponry? Probably the least frequently used rationale is that the weapons deter the Russians from using their own tactical nuclear weapons. One reason this argument is not made often is that the Russians are believed to have a conventional military advantage in Europe that obviates their need to use the weapons. Also, if they had decided that Western Europe was worth taking (despite the great costs discussed above) there would be little sense in their destroying what they had set out to conquer. Further, the Russians developed their weapons after ours and even now the yields of their weapons (most exceed 20 kt) as well as their doctrine, which emphasizes mass employment of nuclear weapons, seem to indicate that the planned Russian use of the weapons is not conducive to the seizure of an intact Western Europe.[10] Thus it would appear that the Soviets would probably not use these weapons first if they had set out to overrun Western

---

[6] Even our allies have agreed to buy the Lance according to *The New York Times*, June 7, 1973, p. 7.

[7] Performance characteristics of these weapons differ somewhat from source to source. To avoid possible criticism the author has used only data from the public domain even if it is somewhat inconsistent. For example, see Record, *U. S. Nuclear Weapons*, pp. 20–25; *The Defense Monitor*, 4, no. 2 (February 1975), 5; and U. S. Congress, Joint Committee on Atomic Energy, *Hearings Before the Subcommittee on Military Applications*, 93d Congress, 1st Sess., May 22 and June 29, 1973, part 1, p. 9. (Hereafter cited as *Hearings*.)

[8] For comparison it is well to keep in mind that the Hiroshima and Nagasaki bombs yielded approximately 14 kt.

[9] See note 2, above.

[10] For a recent discussion of Soviet doctrine see A. A. Sidorenko, *The Offensive (A Soviet View)* (Washington, D. C., 1973).

Europe. Therefore few Western strategies seriously suggest that the primary role for our tactical nuclear weapons is to deter the Soviets from using theirs.

The deterrent role most frequently cited for these weapons is to inhibit the Russians from launching that large-scale conventional invasion that NATO might otherwise be unable to contain. The precise role to be played by our tactical nuclear weapons takes one of three different forms in this view and it is well to consider each form separately and carefully because they are often presented with such glib ease that they sometimes escape examination. The first possibility, which is still expressed from time to time, apparently envisions a unilateral use of these weapons by a NATO that is then able to stop the onslaught.[11] The questions that arise are not only how realistic is the assumption that the Russians will not use their nuclear weapons, but also how willingly will the West Europeans agree to our use of these weapons knowing that Soviet doctrine and weapons could make quite a mess out of Europe? Oddly, analysts often argue as if the difficult decision is the Russian one of whether they ought to retaliate, with nuclear weapons, whereas it seems that the really awesome decision would be the one to *initiate* this form of war.[12]

The second variation of this argument recognizes that the Soviets may well use their weapons and then admits that it is not known at this time whether the use of these weapons helps the attacker or defender. However, this argument then suggests that when the Russians recognize that we are serious about defending Western Europe, they will discover that the war will cost them more than they had originally calculated and will probably call it off without having accomplished their goals.[13] The hope is that the actual and potential escalation in the level of violence will deter the Russians. What is frequently overlooked, of course, is that much of the additional violence will be directed against the

---

[11] A recent restatement of this curious position that may have made sense twenty years ago can be found in Wynfred Joshua, *Nuclear Weapons and the Atlantic Alliance* (New York, 1973), pp. 53–54. Dennis Gorley believes that even Richard Nixon envisioned NATO's first use of these weapons but does not indicate whether the former president also saw their use as unilateral. See Dennis Gorley, "NATO's Tactical Nuclear Option: Past, Present and Future," *Military Review*, 53, no. 9 (September 1973), 3. The following statement of this position is revealing: "In the event of a conventional attack which cannot be held by conventional means, tactical weapons would be used by the West in very limited numbers. . . . *What happens next is not quite so clear and is believed to be still under study* in the NPG [Nuclear Planning Group of NATO]." (Italics added.) Bernard Burrows, *The Security of Western Europe* (London, 1972), p. 64.

[12] Consider, for instance, this very curious wording: "In response [to NATO's use of nuclear weapons] the Soviet Union could, of course, *consider escalation.*" (Italics added.) Is it the Soviet Union that would be escalating the war or the West which had first introduced the weapons? See Wynfred Joshua, "A Strategy for the West: An American View," in Richard B. Foster, Andrew Beaufre, and Wynfred Joshua (eds.), *Strategy for the West: American Allied Relations in Transition* (New York, 1973), p. 102.

[13] Two, among many, examples of this argument are: Albert Legault and George Lindsey, *The Dynamics of the Nuclear Balance* (Ithaca, N. Y., 1974), p. 142; and General Andrew J. Goodpaster in *Hearings*, part 2, pp. 55–56.

peoples of Europe and if the war continues for any length of time Europe may find itself in the same position as the unfortunate Vietnamese town of several years ago which was destroyed in order to be saved. As we shall see in the discussion below there are far less traumatic ways to indicate to the Russians that the level of violence may spiral upward.

The final variation in this series of supposed deterrent roles sees our deployment of these weapons as an indication to the Soviets that we are willing to cross the nuclear threshold in defending Europe—thus raising the possibility of Armegeddon. It is odd how often such a view is presented today,[14] odd because one of the strong arguments originally presented in defense of these weapons was that they would offer an alternative to massive retaliation by giving us other viable options short of holocaust for the defense of Europe. Now, later analysts seem to be suggesting that the weapons are primarily an indication of our willingness to resort to strategic thermonuclear bombing of the USSR in order to protect Europe. Several problems emerge from this apparent reversal of our earlier position. If the purpose of battlefield atomic weapons is essentially to demonstrate our willingness to go the final mile do we need 7000 weapons to do that? The second, and possibly even more serious, problem is precisely how does the firing of a 155 mm atomic shell signal to the Russians that the next step may be up to SAC? Wouldn't it be more reasonable to assume that since we have so many of the weapons, and since we have developed the concept of limited nuclear war to such a fine point, the use of tactical nuclear weapons signals nothing other than that we are using tactical nuclear weapons? Finally, if our intent is, indeed, to show our willingness to go all the way, why be unnecessarily vague about it? The best way, it would seem, to truly show our intention to employ strategic bombardment is to fire a strategic missile. Surely rung number 26 on Herman Kahn's ladder makes more sense, if that is our true intention.[15] It may not necessarily be true that we want to defend Europe with a thermonuclear exchange but if we do, there are far more effective ways to demonstrate this fact to the Russians than by employing tactical nuclear weapons.

Despite the confusion over their deterrent roles, however, according to another theory the weapons themselves are real and tangible and their existence in Europe represents an American commitment that the Europeans themselves do not want to see changed.[16] For want of a better term this perspective should be dubbed the "inflation argument." The crucial question that begs to be answered

14 In addition to the Joshua and Burrows pieces cited in note 11, a few other examples would be Robert Ball, "Rethinking the Defense of Europe," Fortune, February 1973, p. 63; and Record, U. S. Nuclear Weapons, pp. 58–59. Also see The New York Times, December 2, 1973, p. 1.

15 Rung 26 is a "demonstration attack on zone of interior" with a strategic nuclear weapon. Kahn sees at least forty-four different rungs on an imaginary ladder of increasing violence between "ostensible crisis" and "spasm war" or wargasm. See "Escalation as a Strategy" in Henry A. Kissinger (ed.), Problems of National Strategy (New York, 1965), pp. 17–33.

16 Burrows, for instance, believes that these weapons "restore the credibility of the deterrent." The Security of Western Europe, p. 67.

is this: To what, exactly, do these weapons commit America? Possible answers to that question have already been considered and the results were not very satisfying. Usually, though, that question is avoided and the argument remains that we must show the Soviets we are serious about defending Europe and surely one of the most dramatic ways to do this is to put a pile of nuclear weapons over there.

The inflationary nature of this argument is clear to all those who remember that many years ago that same reasoning was used to justify placing American troops in Europe. We had to show the Russians that we were serious about defending our allies and what better way could we do this than by stationing 300,000–400,000 troops on the forward edge? It is probably inevitable in our era that many things lose their value over time. Now apparently 250,000 men are not enough to convince the Russians of our seriousness but they must be augmented by 7000 tactical nuclear weapons. One wonders if in another ten or fifteen years it may not be necessary to position a substantial strategic capability in Western Europe to prove our intentions.

It may well be that many things lose their value through time but it is equally true that some things remain constant and some even increase in value. That America will fight for Western Europe is as well demonstrated today by 250,000 men as it was twenty-five years ago. And it is certainly much more convincingly demonstrated by the soldiers than it is by the atomic weapons for two reasons. One is that the soldiers can neither be destroyed in place nor evacuated—we simply do not have enough airlift capability to remove that many Americans immediately after hostilities begin. The second follows obviously; there is no alternative for the soldiers but to fight or surrender, while battlefield "nukes" do not have to be used at all. The existence of a sizable American troop commitment in NATO, together with the other contributions, of course, guarantees (unlike tactical nuclear weapons which can guarantee nothing) that a Soviet invasion will create a substantial conventional war and raise the possibility of a total war which, as has been suggested before, is more than enough cost to deter the Russians from exploiting the doubtful benefits involved in invading and occupying Europe. Therefore, it would appear that despite the passage of time America's commitment to Europe is still more clearly demonstrated by troops than by an ambiguous weapons system.[17] If, however, "commitment" in this argument means really willingness to defend using all weapons up through nuclear ones then we must refer to what has already been said about more clearly indicating that intent.

As for the last part of this argument, that the Europeans themselves want these weapons to remain and that removing them would be disastrous for European stability, it may well be that this is no issue at all. What the Europeans undoubtedly want is to get under the American nuclear umbrella. Tactical nu-

---

[17] This article will make no attempt to consider the very important question of how many troops are necessary to keep deterrence credible.

clear weapons are the best they have been able to do because that is all that we have clearly offered. Those Europeans who are pleased to see the weapons in Europe, and their numbers may not be large, derive comfort from the fact that the weapons are at least a link to the strategic ones. There are probably very few Europeans who are enthusiastic about tactical nuclear warfare per se no matter how often Americans point out all the good features of that form of insanity.[18] The French have certainly displayed something less than enthusiasm for the idea. At least since 1956 and operation "Carte Blanche," many European observers have clearly realized that for them there may be little or no distinction between tactical and strategic nuclear warfare.[19] Therefore, there may be no substantial European devotion to these particular weapons but there is an eagerness to use America's strategic nuclear umbrella as a deterrent. We do ourselves and our allies a disservice by either being committed to thermonuclear exchange in defense of Europe when we say we are not, or by letting our allies think they may be under the umbrella when actually they may still be in the rain.

The final argument for the deterrent value of these weapons is one that has become more popular in recent years, perhaps as a result of all of the problems that do not disappear. It is the "confusion argument" which suggests that even if all of the objections raised so far are true the weapons still have substantial deterrent impact precisely *because* of the ambiguity surrounding them. This argument is ingenious for making a virtue out of a vice. Especially popular with General Andrew Goodpaster, former SACEUR, but not limited to him, this position essentially argues that since we do not know what we are going to do, the Russians certainly do not and out of this resultant ambiguity a stable deterrent emerges.[20] Another general has worded it this way: "I happen to believe, personally, that an uncertainty in the enemy planner's mind that we might respond with our nuclear artillery or other nuclear weapons creates an uncertainty as to how the war will go, which, I think makes him more deterred, because he cannot control the course of events."[21]

It is probably true that we do not know what we would do if Western Europe were invaded tomorrow. Despite all the position papers and all the labors of NATO's Nuclear Planning Group, the NATO commander of today probably

---

[18] A forceful presentation by a European who expresses grave reservations about these weapons can be found in John L. Holst, "Malaise in Europe: Diagnosis and Prognosis" in Foster, Beaufre, and Joshua, *Strategy for the West*, p. 172. Holst does, however, believe he sees some hope in a new generation of "mini-nukes." Evidence of other European reservations can be seen in *The New York Times*, December 2, 1974, p. 34.

[19] In addition to Holst, see Gordon C. Craig, "NATO and the New German Army," in William W. Kaufmann (ed.), *Military Policy and National Security* (Princeton, N. J., 1956), p. 226.

[20] For two of his presentations of this idea see Andrew J. Goodpaster in *Hearings*, part 2, p. 56, and "The Defense of Europe," *The Royal United Service Institution Journal*, March 1971, p. 36.

[21] Statement by Major General Edward B. Giller, USAF, in *Hearings*, part 1, p. 11.

still suffers from the problem identified by Roger Hilsman seventeen years ago—he is not sure what kind of war he will be called upon to fight.[22] The first use of nuclear weapons, not to mention an entire nuclear war, over the continent of Europe is an event of such awesome and catastrophic magnitude that it is difficult to see Europe's friend, the United States, beginning such a thing. So we can agree with the military planners that we are not sure what we would do.

The second part follows logically. If we are not certain what we are going to do the Russians cannot be certain what we are going to do either. They know relatively confidently that there will be a conventional war of some magnitude and beyond that they, too, can only guess. Now we also know for a fact that there has been no war in Europe for the last thirty years, or if one wants to word it more positively that the Russians have been "deterred" from attacking Europe for the past thirty years.

The flaw in this argument emerges when we causally link our confusion over tactical nuclear weapons specifically to the deterrence of the Russians. There is no way, of course, to prove or disprove empirically that our present confusion deters the Soviets but there are some logical grounds to question that position. Throughout those thirty years of deterrence America's posture has changed from having only a small monopolistic nuclear capability and almost no conventional capacity (1945–1949); to a growing strategic nuclear and conventional capability (1949–1954); to a large strategic nuclear capacity, a substantial conventional capability, and an increasing tactical nuclear capability, but a strategic doctrine that called for massive retaliation (1954–1960); to an overwhelming strategic and tactical nuclear capacity, increasingly matched by the Soviets, a still considerable conventional capacity and a strategic doctrine of flexible response or graduated deterrence (1960–present).[23] Despite (or as some might argue because of) the variety of weapons, forces, and doctrines, throughout that period there was peace in Europe. If we are going to make the claim that the present confused doctrine and weapons system is really deterring the Russians then we have to say that all of the previous doctrines and weapons systems deterred the Russians with equal success. Yet for eight of those years (1945–1953) the Russian army was probably strongest vis-à-vis the West and there were no tactical nuclear weapons in Europe. Thus, one wonders what exactly has changed between 1945–1953 and the present day that requires so much conventional and tactical and strategic nuclear capacity to stop the Russians. The obvious response—that the Russians have so much more tactical and strategic capacity (but not, oddly, more conventional power)—would begin to make Yossarian nervous. It would also be an admission that strength levels in Europe

[22] Hilsman compares it to the German General Staff's nightmare of having to fight a two-front war. The difference is that today's NATO commander may be armed to fight one kind of war and then find he has to fight a different kind. See "NATO: The Developing Strategic Context" in Klaus Knorr (ed.), *NATO and American Security*, (Princeton, N.J., 1959), p. 27.

[23] One might argue with the precise dates of these eras as well as each characterization but those details do not affect the argument.

are simply reactive to those of the other side. If this is true, removing the tactical nuclear weapons might begin to wind levels down for a change. Finally, if confusion does deter, is it confusion over tactical nuclear weapons that deters or confusion over the fact that the war might become total that stops the Russians? The discussion in the first part of this article seems relevant here.

Another question that must be asked is this: If mixed "baskets" of weapons, strategies, and forces, however inconsistent, have been successful in deterring the Soviets must we assume that *each* ingredient in those mixed baskets is a *necessary* one? Must we assume that every new weapon added to the arsenal plays a material role in deterrence? Might not some of them be redundant? And is each particular basket the only one that is sufficient to deter the Soviets? Even a former secretary of defense has indicated that there is no magic surrounding the figure of 7000 for the number of tactical nuclear weapons stationed in Europe.[24] Of course, this writer would go one step further and suggest that there is no magic surrounding the weapons system at all and that it is an *unnecessary* ingredient in the deterrent basket for Europe.

In addition to the faulty causal link between all the components of our ambiguous basket and deterrence there is also some difficulty with the notion that ambiguity is a significant deterrent.[25] The assumption is that the Soviets must develop more contingency plans to account for various NATO options and the more the options, even if ambiguous, the more the Russians refrain from activity.[26] Usually, it is true of course, that an improved or additional capability developed by one's antagonist must be considered but that is not particularly significant unless the capability entails a critical difference. For instance, if the increased complication in Russian plans caused by tactical nuclear weapons is what *actually* deters them then it is well worth our while to introduce ambiguity. But the argument above concerning the period when there were no such weapons in Europe seems to weaken this perspective. If, however, the increase in confusion is a marginal thing that adds only a little greater difficulty to something they have already decided not to do then its value disappears. The doubling of NATO's ground forces would also complicate plans to overrun Europe. But if the Russians are already deterred from that course by the present size of NATO it does not make sense either militarily or financially to double NATO's ground forces. So, too, if they are already deterred by the prospects of

[24] *The New York Times,* April 25, 1974, p. 7.

[25] See the discussion, for example, in Thomas C. Schelling, *The Strategy of Conflict* (New York, 1963), chap. 8.

[26] Statement by Dr. Carl Walske, chairman, Military Liaison Committee to AEC, in *Hearings,* part 2, p. 49. Although the dean of American strategists, Bernard Brodie, has argued that we should not limit our options through psychological paralysis concerning tactical nuclear weapons, much of his discussion centers around the demonstrative value of the weapons. See Bernard Brodie, *Escalation and the Nuclear Option* (Princeton, N. J., 1966), pp. 123–131. However, this article has already indicated that there are serious problems with this role for tactical nuclear weapons.

a large conventional war and a possible thermonuclear one, then adding additional confusion into their calculations is redundant and a waste of resources. Finally, because of the extreme ambiguity concerning the weapons as well as the fact that it is we who would probably have to decide on first use one wonders if they do not really complicate our planning a good deal more than that of the Soviets.

CONCLUSION

Tactical nuclear weapons do not play a sufficiently significant role in the deterrence of Soviet aggression against Europe to justify their expense. With each individual atomic artillery shell costing perhaps $400,000 this weapons system is not cheap.[27] For the kind of resources absorbed by these weapons we must have a greater payoff than the fact that they may have made slightly more complicated Soviet plans for overrunning Europe. The Russians are deterred from invading Europe by a cost-benefit calculation that shows highly ambiguous and doubtful benefits more than offset by the certain cost of a large conventional war and the possible cost of a thermonuclear exchange. Tactical nuclear weapons appear only marginally in that calculation. Additionally their presence in Europe is to our disadvantage insofar as they force the Soviets to consider preemptive tactical nuclear war as a possibly necessary option. Those weapons on Quick Reaction Alert add a destabilizing element to the balance of terror that is not in our best interest.[28] Finally, the security and control of these weapons consumes the equivalent of over one full division of American troops who could be used more profitably in another role.[29] For these reasons, the weapons should be removed from Europe.

---

[27] That figure was used by Senator Stuart Symington in *Hearings*, part 2, p. 101, where the issue under consideration was a proposed $1 billion program to modernize small nuclear weapons.

[28] Former Secretary of Defense James Schlessinger indicated his willingness to remove 250 Pershing missiles from this ready status. *The New York Times*, April 25, 1974, p. 7.

[29] Record, *U. S. Nuclear Weapons*, p. 69.

Oil and the Decline
of Western Power

EDWARD FRIEDLAND
PAUL SEABURY
AARON WILDAVSKY

Oil is energy; energy is money; money is control; control is power. Oil in the wrong hands is money misspent and control corrupted; control corrupted is power abused; power abused is force misused. With oil out of control, force follows. With force out of control, so may be the world.

What does the price of oil signify? An 1100 percent increase? All at once? A little thing, really: a mere 2 percent increase in the cost of commodities, hardly 10 percent of America's wealth in ten years. The enormous increase in the oil price is not a crisis but a catastrophe. It constitutes so large an amount as to cause a qualitative change in world systems. The crisis will not be short, nor limited in effect. The change is systemic. Its success inspires others to emulate it. Other primary-product cartels already are doing so.

EDWARD FRIEDLAND is visiting professor of political science at the University of California, Berkeley. PAUL SEABURY is professor of political science at the Univeristy of California, Berkeley, and the author of a number of books on foreign policy and diplomacy. AARON WILDAVSKY is dean of the Graduate School of Public Policy, University of California, Berkeley, and the author of more than a dozen books on political, social, and economic problems. Professors Freidland, Seabury, and Wildavsky are also the authors of the recently published book, *The Great Detente Disaster: Oil and the Decline of American Foreign Policy.*

Such effects extend from daily personal lives to patterns of relations among nations. They affect the quantity and quality of our lives, our standard of living, and life expectancy. They concern not government alone; they affect citizens. They affect not merely the economy but the polity; not America alone but the entire world; not just how we live but whether we and others will subsequently live.

The systems we refer to are economic and political, international as well as domestic. The elements are connected. By "systemic" we understand that changes in some elements have effects on others; everyone's behavior is altered. The consequences are extensive—felt on a worldwide basis—and intensive—large in amplitude. Since the elements are tightly linked, change in one rapidly reverberates to the rest; when systems themselves become tightly coupled, alterations in one affect the others. These world systems now are growing unstable and unpredictable. Old linkages have been broken, old couplings divorced, without predictable new partners to take their place. Rather than ending in a smooth return to equilibrium, these shocks amplify to extents no one yet fully understands.

We seek to comprehend what is happening, to predict what might happen, and to suggest preventive measures. We dislike what we foresee for ourselves as individuals, for our country, and for most of the rest of the world. Let us start where the oil price increase begins, with the international and national economies.

An immediate consequence of the oil price increase has been mass starvation in poor countries. Foreign exchange is used up purchasing oil. Poor nations now pay more in additional charges for oil than they receive in foreign aid. Oil goes into making and transporting fertilizer. The poor are caught in a double bind: they cannot purchase the fertilizer they need to grow food; the cost of transporting food from other countries has more than doubled. India, central African countries, and many others will be unable to feed many of their people.

An oil rise also fuels inflation in rich countries. The direct costs are not the half of it. An inflationary psychology is spreading. Each economic actor seeks to protect itself by adding a mark-up to every price increase. The result is not, say, to add 10 percent on top of the oil increase but to keep multiplying that mark-up at every step from the supplier of raw materials to the manufacturer, wholesaler, distributor, and retailer. The original 2 percent quickly becomes 3. It then becomes part of the justification by which wages are increased and inflation keeps going. There is still a substantial difference between a single- and a double-digit rate of inflation—the difference between a rate of inflation barely in hand, and one going out of control. But this is not all.

The flow of oil generates an even larger outflow of money from importers to exporters. Importers run up huge debts. For industry this means that less money is available for investment, leading to production, that would soak up available purchasing power. For government, oil debts mean huge balance of payments deficits, which they must finance by selling assets, borrowing, or by monetary manipulations. Their temptation to run the printing presses overtime is as overwhelming as it is ultimately self-defeating. Oil adds to inflation, then, in many ways besides its direct costs. Although oil was not responsible for stoking the fires of inflation in the first place, pouring oil on inflation is about the worst thing that could be done. The problem now is not how inflation got started but how to end it, and anywhere one looks the slippery slope is covered with oil.

Inflation could be fought by recycling oil dollars as investments in productive countries with capital shortages. Unfortunately, this is unlikely to happen. More than money is involved; there are problems of control, of power. Oil exporters will have at their disposal approximately $60 billion a year in liquid capital after having consumed another $40 billion themselves. This sum is small in relation to the total wealth of the oil importers but huge in proportion to the capital available for investment. Fears of foreign control are bound to grow. Capital-deficit nations may welcome oil money in theory but are likely to oppose oil investment in practice. No country wants its media of information, its steel mills, its defense industry, and who knows what else controlled by foreigners, especially foreigners who are suspected of having interests incompatible with those of the host country. The oil cartel is bad enough. And, as inflation worsens, the value of stocks plummets. Who wants to hang out a sign saying "My country for sale, one-third discount"?

Oil money might be welcomed if it brought new industry instead of buying out old. But there are formidable obstacles in the way. Domestic producers are likely to complain about competition. Why should they send money abroad, only to find it financing their commercial foes at home? Just as small business legislation in the United States includes protection against competition with existing businesses, so will legislation be sought against massive foreign competitors. The largest obstacle, however, is likely to be the fears of oil exporters about expropriation. If they are identified as full owners, they risk suffering exactly the same treatment they have meted out to the international oil companies. So they will try to keep a low profile. Their money, however, is so massive it can hardly be kept hidden.

If stationary investments become too tempting a target for interference or expropriation, moving money around is likely to become a preoccupation of oil producers. They will keep large sums on short-term deposits. They will play the currency and commodity markets seeking short-term gains. Inevitably these monetary maneuvers will prove destabilizing. Banks never will know how much they have for how long, or how much they can lend to whom, because their financial picture will keep shifting as money is moved in and out. To prevent constant chaos host nations will try to impose penalties (negative interest rates) on short-term deposits. At the same time, however, the oil exporters will not be prepared to meet the conditions imposed by investors for long-term deposits.

Like any prudent investor, OPEC (Organization of Petroleum Exporting Countries) will want safeguards for its money. It will want to invest in countries with rich and stable economies. Why hold on to currencies subject to rapid depreciation? Hence the "Third World" will be left out because they are poor; various European nations will be turned down because they are becoming unstable. To them that hath will be given, as Matthew said, and them that hath not will lose a further opportunity. Those who need most will get least.

OPEC wants what no other nations have—protection against inflation and guarantees against expropriation. OPEC wants what everyone wants, a secure future as well as an affluent present. OPEC wishes not just a dazzling decade, but a stupendous century. The trouble is not with these understandable desires but with their consequences for the other parties to the transaction.

Compensating oil exporters means condemning importers. It means that importers must accept more, in terms of higher petroleum prices, of the very phenomenon against which they are struggling. It means also that they bear all the costs while OPEC gets the benefits. Having contributed to inflation, OPEC wants to dissociate itself from the consequences of its own acts. That is a good deal if one can get it.

It would be possible, though undesirable, to provide automatic mechanisms for allowing oil prices to rise with those of other basic commodities. But how could OPEC be guaranteed against expropriation? It could get the same kind of paper guarantees from host countries that some of its members already have violated, but these guarantees would be rejected. It could try to recycle its funds through a special international agency. No matter how large a voice OPEC had in this agency, however, nothing could stop member nations from withdrawing individually or collectively if they found this to be to their advantage. The only guarantee against expropriation of foreign assets in theory is control of domestic government in fact. And sovereignty is the last thing governments and their citizens would be willing to give up.

Thus far our focus has been on what OPEC could or might do; now it is time to look at how other nations might be expected to react. They will be torn between the need for OPEC's resources and dislike of the conditions attached to them. They want money, to be sure, but they do not wish to give up control. They cannot exist as short-term depositories and they do not want to give long-term guarantees. As their economies worsen, they will alternately be attracted by the prospect of fresh infusions of capital and repelled by realizing that the cure of foreign control may be worse than the disease of lowered living standards. By themselves how can they alleviate their distress?

Some can try to emulate OPEC. They can, if they are fortunate, use their own commodities to form cartels and drive up prices to match what they must pay OPEC. The United States could do this with food, Jamaica with bauxite for aluminum, Chile might go with copper, and the devil take the hindmost. A few countries might do well, most would do poorly, but not all could even try. If resources were equally distributed around the world, everything might level out, but they are not. The most likely consequence of all this running hard merely to stay in the same place would be internal exhaustion and external disruption of international markets.

The rule of comparative advantage suggests that each country produce the thing at which it is most efficient and import that which would cost more to make at home. No longer. OPEC has taught that every nation must try, even at a financial disadvantage, to produce whatever it can at home so its supplies cannot be disrupted or suddenly spiral in cost. Most nations would be made poorer by being denied the advantages of international trade, but each would better be able to control its own destiny.

Now it should be apparent why we speak of systemic economic change. Domestic economies are converted, insofar as possible, into self-contained and self-sufficient units. International trade declines. After paying for oil, most nations lack the foreign exchange to buy abroad. Afraid to invest abroad for fear of expropriation, they must invest what is left at home for fear that essential supplies will be cut off. Trade partners change rapidly as commodity cartels are formed, fail, re-form, and fail again. The international monetary system cannot withstand the disorderly markets in commodities and the subsequent unpredictably large flows. Flexible exchange rates alter too rapidly and a fixed rate cannot withstand endless rags-to-riches and riches-to-rags. Too much money is being pumped out, not enough flows in. Back to barter. Short-term exchange of commodities is still possible.

Disturbance abroad is matched by consternation within nations. Most are faced with a combination of unemployment, inflation, and capital shortage. Efforts to deal with each of these problems separately aggravate the others. Squeezing future investment capital out of a declining economy leaves less for current employment. Putting people to work by governmental action adds to inflation without increasing productivity. Curbing inflation by withdrawing money from the economy aggravates unemployment and discourages investment. The real meaning of increasing the price of oil eleven times: a large decrease in the standard of living among the oil consumers must be allocated, and for some reason domestic political processes do not seem to be able to come up with widely acceptable means to this regrettable end.

Who, in other words, will pay? That is the question. Will the costs of the oil increase be paid by the rich or the poor, young or old, black or white? Pouring oil on old wounds reinflames the scar tissue. Whatever the central cleavages in a society may be—class in Britain, race in America, language in Ceylon, caste in India—the effects of oil will be to enlarge them.

The ever-closer interdependence between foreign and domestic affairs will lead to more government intervention in the economy and society. If there is a thirty-cents-a-gallon tax on the price of gas or its equivalent in import duties, or if there is rationing and/or restriction of imports, are these domestic or foreign policies? Naturally, they are both. If there is increased investment in atomic energy to assure future supplies, it may affect the health and safety of millions at home as well as constitute a counter to oil manipulations abroad.

Issues that might have been resolved reasonably, had they been confined to domestic interests, may become intractable when foreign elements are introduced. Conservationists and producers will disagree more sharply over strip-mining, oil shale, nuclear power plants, and the like. Developments that used to take decades will be speeded up to years. As the need for energy becomes more desperate, so will the conservationists who fear the ugliness of strip-mining or the thermal pollution of atomic energy or the air pollution of coal. Contradictory demands on government—produce more energy with less damage to the environment at lower cost—will increase. So will conflicts between social services and defense as the income available to both declines. As foreign news becomes less bearable, governments may try to apply more pressure at home. Yet there is no reason to believe that people will become less attached to their life styles or less interested in benefits from expensive spending programs. It will be difficult to reduce defense expenditures because allies and dependents will be poorer and weaker than they were. The United States may be torn between recent memories of Vietnam (no more foreign adventures!) and older recollections of World War II (intervene before it is too late!). The material losses, great as they are, pale before the spiritual turmoil. People cannot understand why they are suddenly being so deprived. They are the same, the country is the same; they are doing the same work; the country has not lost its productive capacity overnight. Why, then, are sacrifices being imposed on them? What, in fact, is the worth of any man's work compared to an instantaneous income transfer of $100 billion a year? Oil-importing people do not deserve to lose their income, and oil exporters do not deserve to gain so much. But OPEC is far away and mostly mysterious. People are more likely to find scapegoats close at hand—domestic oil companies, profiteers (real or imaginary), and, of course, politicians.

If the popularity of politicians depends on how they and their policies are doing in the world, the news is bound to be bad. Demands for help at home and abroad will increase, with fewer resources to pay for them and less likelihood of support being offered in return. The lot of a politician is not likely to be a happy one.

In view of these circumstances—the barest extrapolation from current events—it seems hardly likely that the United States will have to worry about a too-powerful presidency, a legislative dictatorship, judicial tyranny, or any of the other scare slogans of the day. There will be enough blame for everyone. The complaint will be that American political institutions are too weak in comparison to their responsibilities, not too strong in relation to one another.

Yet the United States is in a much better position to navigate than are the smaller ships of state in Japan and Western Europe. United States dependence on imported oil is much less; two-thirds is produced domestically. The opportunities for further finds on its continental shelves and for developing alternate sources of energy—the country has half the world's known coal deposits and vast amounts of oil shale—are much better. Its economy is much larger and its dependence on foreign trade much smaller. The United States is better able to generate internal resources for investment and to ward off external influences. Its domestic market is large enough to allow its economy to function despite decreasing and disrupted international trade. Its agriculture and industry are so productive that demand for them is likely to continue even on a barter basis. Its traditional allies may have a few of these advantages, but none has them all or in the same degree.

Although no one can predict the precise course of events in so many different countries, no one should doubt that they will be bad. Political instability will be the norm. There will be rapid changes in government as each succeeding administration fails to meet insuperable obstacles.

Elections will not be able to decide anything because new governments will be unable to do better than their predecessors. Extremist movements will arise to exploit discontent. Democracy will be in danger. The weaker among United States allies will ask for help but the stronger, taken with their own troubles, will be increasingly disinclined to supply it. So the search will be on for new allies. Charges of selling out to OPEC will mingle with cries of capitulation to capitalists. As the international economic system moves from trade to barter, the international political system will move from its present fragile stability to an unstable equilibrium characterized by successive seismic shocks.

International politics after World War II could be described fairly as a roughly equivalent bipolar system. Both the United States and U.S.S.R. expanded their global influence. The great powers, as they were properly called, reached a series of understandings that avoided armed conflict in a nuclear era. The United States did not intervene in East Berlin, Hungary, and Czechoslovakia when these countries were beset by internal revolts. The Soviet Union backed off from West Berlin and from the emplacement of missiles in Cuba.

The 1960s brought the barest beginnings of multipolarity. Western European nations began to move away from dependence on the United States through the Common Market. Eastern European nations gradually expanded their trade and cultural contacts with the West. The Soviet Union had been thwarted in China. The United States had been vexed in Vietnam. There were stirrings of self-consciousness among Latin American, Asian, and African governments leading to the term "Third World." How have these developments been affected by the oil crisis?

Oil has greased the way for greater consolidation in the Soviet Bloc and for disintegration of the Western alliance. The Soviet Union is an energy exporter; the rest of Eastern Europe—with the exception of Poland, which has coal aplenty—are energy importers. Inevitably the most advanced industrial countries—East Germany, Hungary, and Czechoslovakia—depend most on oil. Of necessity, therefore, the East is less able to trade with the West: it pays more for oil and it depends for supply on the U.S.S.R. The trade of the East with the West is now, in effect, routed through Moscow. Through the same set of circumstances, moreover, Russia is made richer. It can sell its arms and its oil at higher prices. Its economy grows stronger than either its Eastern allies or Western opponents.

Just the opposite occurs in the West. The Common Market can continue only as long as its strongest members, preeminently West Germany, subsidize the weaker ones. Germany still has a foreign trade surplus. But since France and Italy (its largest trading partners) are compelled to inhibit imports, and since Britain, Japan and America have also cut back, this surplus cannot survive. The temptation of each country to export its deficit by monetary means will mount. Competitive devaluations will be difficult to avoid. Cracks in the common cause between Britain and Norway on the one side, which have new sources of oil, and the other countries, which do not, are bound to widen. Fissures developing from the issue of whether it is more feasible to make separate deals with the petroleum potentates (which France favors) or to join in a united consumer front (which America prefers) cannot be easily closed.

The United States does not have oil to burn. And it is denying the necessity to undertake the kind of drastic measures that might enable it to send other forms of energy, such as coal, to the aid of its allies. Below all the rhetoric, at the bottom line, lies the stark fact that the United States cannot help; it can only seem to hinder. When the United States asks for diplomatic support in favor of Israel, or military liaison during armed conflict, it asks the European countries to risk Arab retribution without any prospect of real return. If the name of the game is oil, the United States cannot play.

NATO is a necessity that could fast become a nonentity. The North Atlantic Treaty Organization was a military umbrella under which post-World War II reconstruction took place. Until now any conceivable conflict between guns and butter has been controlled by the fact that it has been unnecessary to choose. The first aid came from the United States through the Marshall Plan and the second from high rates of economic growth. While America maintained its arms and the Soviet threat receded in the background, military expenditures went down and domestic spending (as proportions of Gross National Product) went up. But growth meant there was enough. Now that growth is gone and decline has taken its place, the issue of guns versus butter (we should say oil) can no longer be contained.

Energy is enervating NATO. Each member is poorer than it was. No member wants to bear the burden alone. Arms and oil cannot be bought at the same time. Forced to choose—between a remote and problematic Soviet attack and the certain threat of domestic disruption—NATO nations will choose the immediate and insistent.. Yet they will find it difficult to negotiate mutual arms reductions because their situations differ. NATO soon may become a superior source of quarrels rather than a mediator of disputes. The United States, which already bears a disproportionate burden, will be asked to pick up the slack at a time when its own economy is suffering. A repeat of the dispiriting debacle of the October war—when NATO members took turns denying the United States the use of joint facilities, is only too likely because the situation remains the same: Europe needs energy which America cannot supply.

NATO will not be the last ship of hope to flounder on the shores of the Persian Gulf.

Before the war of October 1973, the Middle East was the area in which the United States and the Soviet Union had not worked out an accommodation, but it was also an area that did not truly engage the vital interests of either side. The United States was joined to Israel by ties of affection, by the affinity of two democratic governments, and by the desire to maintain a dependable ally in the Middle East. The Soviet Union wished to carve out a sphere of influence which would create dependable access to the Mediterranean, deny American hegemony, and give it a greater voice in an area bordering its own. Survival was not at stake for either. But oil has changed all that.

Oil has become the universal dissolvent. Oil has given the United States a vital national interest in Israel. For without Israel, America would have nothing with which to bargain in the Middle East. With Israel, Arab states still have something to gain from the United States, whether it be territorial concessions or limitation on Israeli advances in a new war or adjustments in the status of Jerusalem. The absence of Israel would remove any rationale for restraint.

Why should the Arab states charge any less for oil than they can get? Just because this question is an obvious one, it does not mean that it can be ignored. Wealth opens up new vistas. The more opportunities wealth brings—opportunities not only for the wealth itself but for the power it buys—the more eagerly wealth will be pursued. Within the Arab world the unifying force of enmity to Israel will be replaced by the bonds of limitless booty. Maintaining the unity of OPEC to keep the price high would become more important than anything else precisely were the main distraction—Israel—to be removed from the scene. Israel has been, for America, a sentimental favorite; oil now has made Israel an indispensable irritant without which the oyster of Arab oil price solidarity cannot be pried open.

Nor has oil had an emollient effect on the Soviet Union's interest in the Middle East. Russia's attention has been piqued by the fact that it is getting paid in today's currency for yesterday's military hardware. That attention has been deepened by the profits it makes on its own oil, and by the enhanced control this gives it over the economies of Eastern Europe. The picture of a prostrate West does nothing to lessen the interest. And the prospect of sharing in the $100 billion OPEC income is by itself enough to convert a modest interest into a major one. For as OPEC grows in wealth it will grow in fear, and as it grows in fear the Soviet Union will be close at hand. Indeed, should the United States withdraw from concern with the Middle East, the Soviet Union could turn tutelage into tribute and get paid for its protection.

Why should the United States wish to withdraw? The game is now being played for higher stakes, and it is by no means certain the United States will not be bluffed out. During the October war, when great power stakes were much lower, the Soviet Union threatened to send troops after its allies had attacked America's ally by surprise. Instead of insisting that it was impermissible to introduce armed forces in a place where neither power had used them before, and where direct confrontation would then be possible, the United States insisted that Israel retreat. Would not the Soviet Union's interest in intervention have increased for the next time; would it not expect a weaker response from a weaker America? And would it not be more dangerous to do the unexpected when the stakes have been raised?

Consider the condition of all concerned. Third World countries are sympathetic to the idea of getting higher returns for their resources. Though they suffer, too, from the oil price rise they see no sign of help from the United States. Only OPEC has the resources to help them. Japan and Western Europe are in a similar situation. If they felt that supporting the United States could be successful in overcoming the effects of oil, they might join in. But this is in the realm of supposition. The fact they face is that oil will be embargoed and aid will not be available. Neutrality is the best they can offer. Hence the United States, should it help to defend Israel, will face OPEC, the Arab states, the Third World, and perhaps Western Europe, as well as the Soviet Union. Today the United States convinces itself that it is not primarily a supporter of Israel but is following an even-handed policy toward the Arabs and Israel. But this illusion must evaporate. There is a fundamental contradiction between opposition to OPEC and support for its Arab members in the Middle East. America will have to decide whose side it is on, if only because the Arabs can now exert enough financial leverage, and the Israelis sufficient military force, to make it choose. The choice will not be an easy one.

Miscalculation is the menace. The United States has raised expectations it may not wish to meet under changed circumstances. The Soviet Union has the motivation to move in. Confrontation could become a catastrophe.

Surrender is not the only solution. Driven desperate, the United States, with or without (probably without) support from Western Europe, might attempt to seize oil in Kuwait or Saudi Arabia. Then it would attract support because it had oil. But the dangers are a deterrent, from the small chance of a Soviet response to the likelihood of protracted guerrilla war. A deliberate decision need not be made. The United States could seize upon the next war between Israel and its neighbors to reverse the results of the previous one, encouraging Israel to move into

Libya and itself seizing Abu Dhabi and/or Kuwait. Saudi Arabia is not an impossibility. The likelihood of Soviet intervention would increase, but the Israelis would bear the brunt of military action. These are hardly riskless alternatives. They would be better undertaken, if at all, after the mobilization of American opinion and the support of allies. Still the risks may not seem so rash in comparison with the rapid decline of Western economies, the consequent collapse of their polities, and the decay of their societies. It may seem a pity to let two hundred years of Western civilization go by default.

Is this not scare talk? Oil is not (or need not be) the Archimedes lever of the Western world. After all, this argument continues, the next decade may be difficult but by 1985 most Western nations will have overcome their dependence on oil or obtained their own sources. They will then be poorer than they might have been, but still richer than most men have ever been and than many nations are now. So-called advanced societies cannot be worth much if they cannot take a little adversity. Who said Western standards of living were sacred or that democracy could not be defiled? Change, any change, is good for a wicked world. Let the proud be humbled and the mighty thrown down.

It is hard to tell whether the argument is that the judgment of the oil god is just or that judgment day is still a long way off. Escapism today takes the form of a "Rip Van Winkle effect." It is as if the Western world were to awake after ten years to discover that everything was the same for the surprising superabundance of energy. The destabilizing defects of the decade disappear. This is not goal attainment but wish fulfillment.

Virtue can be a vice; placed too high, virtue can lead to the subjection of the so-called uncivilized; put down too low, it can lead to subjection of the self. Excessive self-confidence is hardly the worry of the West. Loss of self-esteem is more the order of the day. If the West is not preserved, this will most likely be because its people do not believe their culture is worth preserving. Franz Fanon, not Edmund Burke, will be their prophet. Is the West so depraved that the oil of absolution is the only remedy? What is the alternative?

If oil money were flowing from the rich to the poor, evidence of a benevolent hand might be found. If the oil exporters gave evidence of charity, humanity, justice, or any other virtue, their preeminence might be preferable. But no one believes any of these things. They are, in the main, reactionary feudal regimes, or military dictatorships, or royal despotisms. Not one is governed by the consent of its people. Not one is known to deal kindly with critics inside their countries; why should they behave better to outsiders?

If what we fear is as apparent to others as it is to us, why doesn't OPEC recognize its self-interest in limiting convulsions that would ultimately engulf it as well? A disorderly world would not be desirable for Iran, Saudi Arabia, Abu Dhabi, or Kuwait, to mention a few likely losers. Perhaps they have discovered a new principle of international relations—richer is better—and wonder why others try to persuade them that poorer is better. Perhaps they miscalculate. Perhaps they think they can control the consequences of their present policy. They will, however, be wrong. They never had much order to begin with, anyway, and most of their people will not notice the difference. No one asked them what they thought before and no one will ask them now. They did not share in the wealth before and they can still participate in poverty now. The only difference is that if misery loves company, they will be not so alone.

One should never discount dreams, especially dreams of glory. The Shah of Iran dreams of restoring the glories of Persia. The King of Saudi Arabia foresees a Moslem renaissance. Visions of redressing ancient wrongs and modern misdeeds abound. Risks, then, may be worth running for the dreamer. It must be pleasant, after the real and imagined insults of subservience, to rise up and be importuned by finance ministers with outstretched hands and supplicant eyes, to assure these finance ministers sincerely that prices are too high only to watch their Western faces drop when a mere 30 cents-per-barrel increase, less than a penny a gallon, costs them around $4 billion a year. How sweet it must be! The taste lingers. Maybe, after so exquisite a design, the chances of being caught in one's own web are worth taking because the weaving of it is so wonderful.

Oil is working its way through the warp and woof of established relationships. West and East vie to sell arms anywhere and everywhere they can bring a return. Iran is becoming a vast arsenal. Nuclear reactors are being sent from France, with what safeguards no one knows. Money flows to this insurrectionist movement and that established regime. Revolts and repressions may be financed by certain members of OPEC without public knowledge of who is responsible. The lesson (for anyone disposed to challenge OPEC's position) will be that it is best to stay on the safe side. As the European Economic Community declines and NATO falters, fear and foreboding will increase. As governments fall and are replaced by new regimes, who can predict what they will do or where they will go? The old international order will evidently have declined, but it is doubtful whether the new disorder will be less dangerous.

The Russians may abandon detente. If detente means what Secretary of State Kissinger says it does—not cooperation but coexistence, conflict being pursued up to but not at (nuclear) sword point—then the term is merely a new synonym for the cold (instead of hot) war that has existed since shortly after World War II. Maintenance of that tacit understanding has all along required that neither side be tempted irresistibly to take advantage of the other. If the threat of mutual destruction is the immovable object, then the threatened loss of oil may be the irresistible force. Settling for the status quo is one thing; haggling over small advantage is another; giving up great gains is something else altogether.

Since World War II the nuclear powers have exchanged pieces, taken and lost pawns, always avoiding attacking the center. Whether the Soviet Union will rest content to wait and wear down its opponent in the middle game or whether it will be tempted to rush toward checkmate remains to be seen. The fact that changing the rules of the game is now a possibility shows how quickly the last quarter century of systemic stability has been subverted.

How does a stable equilibrium become unstable? A useful metaphor is the dual-control electric blanket with a difference—it can make one cold as well as hot. The system is stable so long as energy flows equally to both parties and the connections between the elements work. Adjusting the controls requires no coordination. He can become cooler and she warmer at will without affecting mutual relationships. Suppose, however, that the wires are crossed. Immediately the system becomes unstable. As he tries to get cooler he makes her too cold, and as she tries to get warmer she makes him too hot. Left unattended, the system goes into an unstable (though symmetrical) equilibrium: the one becomes frozen and the other burns up. Energy just flows in the wrong direction. Coordination is required. Recognizing a mutual interest in accommodation, the two parties find out what is wrong, rewire the elements, and bring their system back into equilibrium.

Let us now make a different assumption: energy is uneven; power is diverted from one to the other. She is able to keep warm but he cannot keep his cool. The system has become asymmetrical. He demands restoration of mutual accommodation but she prefers to keep things as they are or, more accurately, as they are becoming. His last chance, he thinks in his weakened state, is to equalize energy by pulling the plug so they will both have an interest in restoring the one thing on which they might agree—the old equilibrium. She wonders whether increasing the energy drain might not make him too weak to shut the whole system down. Whether this story has a happy ending depends on whether the storyteller prefers the old system, the new system, or no system at all. These are the questions the oil crisis now forces us to answer.

United States Policy toward Southern Africa: Economic and Strategic Constraints

WILLIAM J. FOLTZ

The Angolan civil war of 1975–1976 and the succeeding challenge to white rule in Rhodesia thrust southern Africa into American consciousness to a degree not matched since, perhaps, the Boer War. At the same time the contradictions and the general ineptitude of American foreign policy in southern Africa were revealed as never before. Only a small part of the ineptitude can be put down to "bad luck," an unfortunate guess as to Portugal's staying power in Africa. Rather, one must question why it is that American policy makers chose not only to believe that all the various forms of white rule in southern Africa would last, but to assume as well that American interests would best be served by helping them last. Such questions are not only of historical interest; even more urgently they must be asked about the assumptions on which American policy toward southern Africa continues to be based. Chief among these assumptions is that southern Africa is a part of the world in which the United States has definite "vital interests."

The purpose of this article is to disprove the claim that there are tight economic and strategic constraints on American policy toward southern Africa, especially the supposition that it is possible to identify economic and strategic interests that are clearly "vital" to the United States and to its policy makers. Such interests could be considered vital for two reasons: first, they may be of such real and compelling importance that no prudent policy maker could neglect to take them into account; second, they may be so important either to the electorate at large or to certain politically powerful individuals and institutions

WILLIAM J. FOLTZ is professor of political science at Yale University and associate director of the Yale-Wesleyan Southern Africa Research Project. His writings include *From French West Africa to the Mali Federation* and a forthcoming book on American policy toward southern Africa.

that, without them, the continuity of an administration or its ability to carry out a coherent foreign policy would be jeopardized. Either situation would naturally provide serious constraints on foreign policy toward a particular region of the world. The logical conclusion, then, is that those who make policy are to be faulted not for blindly responding to real economic and security constraints; but for failing to take advantage of the considerable latitude of policy innovation which in fact is available.

Both conservative and radical critics of United States policy toward southern Africa seem to agree that certain fundamental economic and strategic interests derived from the very nature of America's domestic and international situation must underlie this policy. They then disagree on everything else. On the economic side, conservatives lament the absence of "realistic" trade and investment policies, particularly toward Rhodesia and the Republic of South Africa, and decry the weakness of the "bleeding hearts" in the Department of State's African Bureau. Radical critics see the lobbyists of multinational corporations behind every policy change and with varying degrees of enthusiasm trace America's postwar economic preeminence to unsavory profits made from the sweat of oppressed black labor. On strategic questions, conservatives (not necessarily the same as those arguing the economic case) point to the growth of the Soviet fleet or even the building of the TanZam railway as a threat to American survival. While few of their radical opponents go so far as Admiral Gorshkov in seeing the Soviet fleet as a force for peace (most prefer not to see it at all), they agree that a "military-industrial complex" has gotten hold of American policy formulation and warped its African enterprises, so that the military protection of American capitalism overrides any concern with political or social issues. Both sides, finally, agree on the further assumption that these interests are part and parcel of America's own version of capitalism and democracy; they disagree only on whether or not that version should survive.

Economic Factors

The basic economic facts are relatively straightforward and have been ably discussed by others; a brief summary should suffice here.[1] In terms of overall American trade and investment, Africa as a whole continues to be the "least important continent," though some major changes may be taking place. The trade figures show the greatest recent movement: in 1972, Africa provided 2.87 percent of America's imports; in 1974, 6.55 percent. In 1972 Africa took 3.2 percent of American exports; in 1974, 3.74 percent (arms exports not included). Of the $6.6 billion worth of African goods imported into the United States in 1974,

---

[1] Trade figures given are from International Monetary Fund, *Direction of Trade: Annual 1970–74* (Washington, D. C., 1975). A convenient summary is in *Marchés Tropicaux* (November 21, 1975), 3363–3364. Useful discussions include Donald McHenry, *United States Firms in South Africa* (Bloomington, Ind., 1975) and Timothy H. Smith, *The American Corporation in South Africa* (New York, 1970).

about half came from one country, Nigeria. In third and fourth places respectively (behind Algeria), South Africa and Angola accounted for $600 million and $400 million. Southern Africa's total exports to the United States were, then, less than one-third of those coming from Nigeria alone, which ranked seventh in the world, between Mexico and Italy, as a supplier of the American market.

The American export side reveals a different profile. Of America's $3.6 billion exports to Africa, the Republic of South Africa bought about one-third ($1.15 billion), almost as much as the next four clients (Egypt, Algeria, Nigeria, and Morocco) combined. South Africa thus ranked eighteenth, between Israel and Switzerland, as a market for American goods.

The change in these figures over recent years may be as important for our purposes as the absolute position in the latest figures. Between 1969 and 1975 American trade with South Africa tripled to reach $2.16 billion; in the same period trade with the rest of Africa went up sevenfold to $11.6 billion. The turning point emerges as 1973, the year in which total American trade with Nigeria surpassed that with South Africa. The key, of course, is oil, with Nigeria now standing among the principal foreign suppliers of petroleum for the American market, a position which seems unlikely to be challenged in the foreseeable future, and which presumably is of some relevance to American policies toward Africa generally.

Even with Nigeria's decisive replacement of South Africa in American trade relations, the argument can be made that South Africa still is essential as the one major African country with which the United States enjoys a decidedly positive balance of payments. While not totally irrelevant, the argument must be viewed with suspicion for two reasons. First, there is no rational economic principle that says the United States should balance its payments with a particular continent, as opposed, say, to all countries whose names begin with the letters A through F. Second, had the figures gone the other way, with the United States depending on vital South African exports to fuel its industrial machinery, while Nigeria bought our exports, the same economic determinists would probably seize on those facts to explain that we were in a dependent relationship with Pretoria which thus called the tune in our foreign policies.

The following seems to be the only clear generalization one can make from these gross statistics: *to the degree* that foreign policy is conditioned directly by the desire to maintain good relations with countries which are strong economic partners, South African needs and desires should have some influence over United States policy, but that influence should have declined substantially during the 1970s by comparison with that of Nigeria. If this generalization holds, then the degree of influence involved must be so slight as to escape all but the most finely tuned analysis and to have only the most marginal influence on policy making.[2] One must conclude that, from the perspective of overall Amer-

2 One can also argue the converse: to the degree that American economic ties produce foreign

ican economic involvements, the situation is politically permissive. That is to say, within certain very wide limits, foreign policy toward southern Africa can be made without fear of damaging vital American economic interests—unless perhaps both South Africa and Nigeria were to line up strongly on the same side of a vital issue.

Of course one must look behind those aggregate figures to discern probable patterns of influence. Influence need not come directly from the host country; rather it can come indirectly through the American corporation involved or seeking involvement there. American corporate involvement in South Africa and its dependents is clearly of some economic significance, though rather more for South Africa than for the United States. The $1.24 billion of direct American private investment in South Africa in 1973 represented 1.12 percent of United States private investment overseas (yielding 1 percent of foreign earnings), but 17 percent of all foreign investment in South Africa. Some 340 South African firms were American owned, wholly or in significant part, and the American companies involved represented a cross section of the biggest of American big business. Out of the 10 largest American corporations, 9 were included, as were 136 of the *Fortune* top 500. Furthermore, although earnings have diminished somewhat in recent years, they still are noticeably higher than those in other parts of the world. In the manufacturing sector, which accounts for almost half of American investment, earnings in the 1960s averaged 20.2 percent, as opposed to 9.4 percent worldwide.[3]

The very size of the American corporations involved, which should augment their potential influence with the United States government, also means that the South African operations represent a fairly small portion of their total overseas investments and an even smaller part of their combined foreign and domestic operations. South Africa is important, but far from crucial, for these great corporations.[4] In the absence of competing interests and countervailing pressures such as those generated by investments in black African states like Nigeria and Zambia, Chrysler, Ford, Firestone, Cummins Engine, Standard Oil, and IBM, not to mention those who would like to imitate such giants, would certainly try to promote a rapprochement between American and South African

---

policy compliance from America's partners, Nigeria should increasingly have aligned its foreign policies on those of the United States. One can, of course, construct much more complex variants of these propositions by introducing time-lag effects and policy-arena distinctions, but neither generalization looks like a promising statement about a major influence on anybody's foreign policy.

[3] McHenry, *United States Firms.*

[4] Both public and private statements by corporate officers tend to overstate the importance of southern African operations. Public statements usually proceed from an understandable premise of "don't yield an inch or they'll take a yard." Private statements usually are obtained from those corporate officers most directly involved in southern African operations. For those individuals' careers, maintaining the southern African connection may indeed be crucial. Members of large private bureaucracies are no less likely than their public counterparts to confuse the success of their own work group with that of the organization as a whole.

interests. But the competing interests are actively or potentially there for all these corporations, and the countervailing pressures may be there, sooner or later, as well.[5]

Additionally, one must admit the hypothesis that highly particular interests may be effectively represented behind the scenes by a powerful or well-connected person or group. One man in particular, Charles Engelhard, whose name graces many of the gold ingots Americans are now able to buy directly, was often singled out. Engelhard was the last American member of the board of the Anglo-American Corporation and a liberal contributor to political campaigns according to the purest capitalist principles. He was in favor of the winner, whoever he might be. Engelhard was reportedly on good personal terms with Lyndon Johnson (whom he represented at Zambia's independence celebration) but had no difficulty in expressing equal admiration for Johnson's successor in the White House. For all the mystique surrounding Engelhard, however, there is little evidence that he had any major impact on United States policy in southern Africa, though it is quite likely that he did influence minor policy decisions to the advantage of his personal interests. Engelhard died in 1973, and no one has yet been able to step into his shoes.

Kenneth Rush, president of Union Carbide from 1966 to 1969, illustrates another pattern of business influence. He first spent a year in the largely honorific position as member of the Public Advisory Committee on U. S. Trade Policy for Lyndon Johnson; next, Richard Nixon made Rush in succession ambassador to Germany, deputy secretary of defense, deputy secretary of state, and counselor to the president for economic policy; and then Gerald Ford sent him to Paris as ambassador. In his Washington stints Rush was clearly in a position to have a say in American policy toward southern Africa, and doubtless had a particular interest in Rhodesia, from which his former company continued to export chrome to the United States under the so-called Byrd amendment allowing violation of sanctions for the importation of critical minerals. In confirmation testimony, however, Rush specifically denied "discussing, either formally or informally, the subject of chrome with anyone."[6] Although skeptics were not so sure, it would seem almost immaterial whether or not Rush was scrupulous about his conflict of interest. His position was well known, and indeed Nixon chose him because he was the sort of man who would enthusiastically carry out the kind of policy that the president himself favored.

Business has been good in South Africa and there continue to be opportunities for some to make it better, particularly if they can influence American policies.

[5] Several of the largest firms have interests in both Nigeria and South Africa, and others would clearly like to join the list. See Jean Herskovits, "An Overview of American and African Policies in Regard to Southern Africa," *Issue: A Quarterly Journal of Africanist Opinion*, 5, no. 3 (Fall 1975), 58.

[6] See the articles by Bruce J. Oudes, "Clark MacGregor's Vacation: 'Different' Might Be an Understatement," *Africa Report*, 18, no. 1 (January–February 1973) and "Nigeria, Humphrey, and the Chrome Caper," ibid., no. 2 (March–April 1973).

The Fluor Company of California has been actively lobbying, along with the South African government, for the reversal of a twelve-year-old policy denying Export-Import Bank loans to South Africa. On the outcome of their effort may depend a billion dollar contract for the construction of a coal gasification and petroleum production plant. So far the administration has stood firmly by its policy of denying such loans. One must ask why this should be an issue if business influence on American policy is all that weighty. Why has American business not been allowed to go in like their French counterparts, selling anything the South Africans are willing to buy with the explicit collusion of, among other groups, the Ministry of Defense? Surely it is not just the countervailing opposition of those who support the Washington Office on Africa, or of the World Council of Churches, or of the participants in university seminars on southern Africa. All such efforts can hardly be considered to have had a major effect on foreign policy.

Before abandoning economic explanations, we must look with some sophistication at the role of economic interests in setting the tone for the way in which leading Americans think about policy toward southern Africa. Bruce Russett and Elizabeth Hanson have recently completed a major empirical study of business and other elite attitudes toward a range of relevant foreign policy issues.[7] While their inquiry does not deal directly with southern African affairs, it does investigate the broader issues of the way these individuals see the world of which such affairs are a part. The core of their research was a comparison of a set of questionnaires administered to a variety of American elites, including business executives, military officers, Republican and Democratic politicians, labor leaders, civil servants, heads of voluntary organizations, and leaders of the communications media. Their first positive finding, which had "moderate support," contains few surprises:

> Businessmen will be more favorable than other elites toward United States government activities to protect American business interests abroad, and toward the promotion of governments in less developed countries that are well disposed to the activities of foreign investors and maintenance of the free enterprise system; similarly they will be more hostile toward socialist and communist governments in less developed countries.[8]

Two groups in the sample, however, went against the proposition; labor leaders by and large shared business attitudes on these issues, and Republican party officials were decidedly to the right of the businessmen. Something other than economic motivation narrowly construed must be operating.

A second set of questions specifically separated out those executives whose firms do substantial business in less developed countries and compared them

---

[7] Bruce M. Russett and Elizabeth C. Hanson, *Interest and Ideology: The Foreign Policy Beliefs of American Businessman* (San Francisco, 1975). See also Raymond A. Bauer, Ithiel de Sola Pool, and Anthony Dexter, *American Business and Public Policy* (New York, 1963).

[8] Russett and Hanson, *Interest and Ideology*, pp. 95–96.

with domestically oriented business leaders. The former group, as might be expected, were more favorable than their fellows "toward United States government activities to protect American business interests abroad." Surprisingly, however, they were not more favorable toward "the promotion of governments in less developed countries than are well disposed to the activities of foreign investors and maintenance of the free enterprise system." Neither were they "more hostile toward socialist and communist governments in less developed countries than . . . executives from other corporations." In short, with the exception of foreign policy efforts to help the most narrow definition of their corporate goals, the foreign-oriented business executives did not differ from their domestic-oriented counterparts, nor were both groups substantially out of line with the rest of elite opinion.[9]

A third part of the Russett-Hanson study sought to compare the degree of influence on business executives' foreign policy preferences produced by three factors: economic motivations and interests, domestic political ideology, and strategic (military and anticommunist) motivations. Domestic ideology was clearly the most important factor, followed by strategic motivations. "In only a very few instances did economic interests and motivations account for even as much as 2 percent of the variance in foreign policy preference."[10] Strategic motivations, while often powerful, frequently produced contradictory policy preferences, as, for example, during both the Korean and Vietnamese wars when business executives, like others, were divided over whether "communism" had to be stopped then and there, or whether this was "the wrong war, in the wrong place, at the wrong time."

The most consistent finding of the Russett-Hanson study is that political ideology has the most powerful and independent effect on foreign policy preferences of all the variables tested. Specialists in conservative political ideology and practice, exemplified by professional Republican politicians, consistently take the most right-wing position on foreign policy questions of all elite groups. Conservative business leaders tend to agree with them, while more liberal or moderate executives tend to disagree with them *irrespective of their corporate economic interests.*

Let us be quite clear on what this means. It certainly does not mean that most business executives are either raving liberals nor in most of their affairs heedless of their economic interests. It does mean, however, that these economic interests are only very weakly translated into foreign policy preferences, and then through the more powerful intermediaries of political ideology and of geopolitical strategic preferences, each of which has an independent force. And in this, they are not unlike other Americans. If we are to search for the impact of economic interests on American policy toward southern Africa, then, we must expect to find it subordinated to, or at least heavily attenuated by, more broadly held prefer-

---

[9] Ibid., pp. 122–123.
[10] Ibid., p. 249.

ences derived from general political ideology and from shared views of the relationship between such policies and the strategic interests of the United States vis-à-vis Communist powers.

STRATEGIC FACTORS

One strategic concern takes a primarily economic form: the rare minerals that the West buys, principally so far from South Africa, South West Africa, and Rhodesia. In addition to gold and diamonds, these include chrome, ferrochrome, nickel, berrylium, cobalt, and other "vitamin" minerals which go into making high-performance alloys. The arguments over repeal of the Byrd amendment (allowing American corporations to violate sanctions against Rhodesia by importing metals and ores) have produced much conflicting testimony as to just which was how vital for what and to whom.[11] Unfortunately, little of the argument focused on the issue of long-term access to these resources, which presumably should provide the principal serious constraints on the development of foreign policy. Since the United States' strategic stockpiles of these minerals are ample, the long term is indeed the major concern. In thinking about the long term, one historic precedent is unambiguous: so far, at least, no regime anywhere in Africa, of any ideological or dermatological pigmentation, has refused to sell the United States any valuable mineral it produces when offered something like the going international commodity price.

Past performance is, of course, an imperfect guide to the future, and policy makers must think prudentially about keeping open the greatest number of possibilities for access in a troubled area. Should, nevertheless, one be forced to choose sides, the hardheaded choice is not necessarily to cater to those who at present control the most valuable resources; rather, it is to discriminate against those who have the fewest alternative possibilities for disposing of them elsewhere. Of course, the hardheaded businesslike attitude is not necessarily the one that should prevail in this or other foreign policy decisions. But if one is to argue the hardheaded case with regard to access to strategic minerals, one must recognize that it works against automatic support for wobbly white minority regimes. Moderately prudent management of American foreign relations should make it possible to avoid such a clear choice as a desperate means to guarantee the right to purchase strategic minerals. If that is so, the evidence supports the proposition that foreign policy makers in fact have considerable latitude in designing southern African policy, if only they choose to take it.

The withdrawal of British military presence from east and south of Suez and

---

[11] In addition to the extensive congressional testimony, see "Southern Rhodesia: the Question of Economic Sanctions," *Current Foreign Policy*, Department of State Publication 8744, African Series 55 (December 1973), and Edgar Lockwood, "An Inside Look at the Sanctions Campaign," *Issue: A Quarterly Journal of Africanist Opinion*, 4, no. 3 (Fall 1974), 73–75.

the introduction of Cuban troops to Angola have increased the military compo-nent of strategic concerns in Washington as well as in Pretoria. The Republic of South Africa's government tirelessly expounds the argument that the defense of southern Africa and its attendant sea lanes is a crucial component of "the defense of Western civilization." Increasingly, South Africa seeks to bring its message to broad segments of American opinion. Thus, on February 9, 1976, as the out-come of the Angolan war became clear, a South African publicity front published a full-page advertisement in *The New York Times* and other leading newspa-pers. Under the heading "The Free World stands today in greater danger than at any time since the darkest days of World War II . . ." the advertisement ex-tolled South Africa's fight against "Soviet colonisers" in Angola and recalled South Africa's heroic participation in the Korean war. Similarly, the South African Department of Information commissioned and in 1975 distributed widely in America a book entitled *The Communist Strategy,* with prose redolent of vintage J. Edgar Hoover. It was accompanied by a slightly more sophisticated volume, *The Indian Ocean and the Threat to the West,* edited by a British Conservative M.P., whose contents are predictable from the title.[12]

Such propaganda efforts are not particularly important by themselves. Their seeds will germinate only if they fall on fertile ground prepared by a propensity of the general population to believe such arguments, and with specific groups having direct interests at stake. Within the general American population there exists indeed a diffuse propensity to see the Soviet Union, and to a lesser de-gree China, as expansionist threats, particularly in the Third World. Presidential candidates of both parties have sought to capitalize on popular concern that the Soviet Union is getting strategic advantage out of détente at the expense of the United States. When, early in January 1976, Americans and samples from twelve other nations were asked whether or not they expected the "power" of the United States, Russia, and China to increase or decrease in 1976, Americans split 42 to 44 percent over whether or not their own nation's power would increase or de-crease. They felt, however, that Soviet power would increase rather than decrease (63 to 18 percent) and that Chinese power would do the same (65 to 11 percent). Americans expressed these last two opinions more decisively than the citizens of the other twelve nations sampled.[13] It must be emphasized that these are very diffuse attitudes, at many steps remove from any policy issues directly affecting southern Africa. Still, people do volunteer some connection. A 1973 study spon-sored by the Overseas Development Council (ODC) asked a national sample the open-ended question of what Third World countries would do if American aid were suspended. Far and away the top negative answer (20 percent of all

[12] C. F. De Villiers, F. R. Metrowich, and J. A. Du Plessis, *The Communist Strategy* (Pretoria, South Africa, 1975). Patrick Wall (ed.), *The Indian Ocean and the Threat to the West: Four Studies in Global Strategy* (London, 1975).

[13] *The Gallup Opinion Index,* no. 126 (January 1976) and Gallup Poll news release, January 18, 1976.

replies) was that they "would go communist."[14] From this scattered evidence one can conclude at least that there is some disposition to be concerned about strategic cold-war issues and to see them as relevant to areas like southern Africa. At the same time, there is clearly little disposition to go rushing in with American troops, or even with substantial military aid. This latter, however popular it may have been with some parts of Congress, is far and away the most unpopular form of aid among the American public (opposed flatly by 49 percent of the sample in the ODC study, a figure that would be no lower today).[15]

The principal elite interest group with a stake in accentuating the strategic component of American foreign policy is, of course, the military. Compared with business leaders or the population as a whole, military officers consistently favor higher defense spending and demonstrate willingness to use armed intervention as a policy instrument in peripheral areas of the world. Even with this group, however, there are important nuances. For example, in the Russett-Hanson study, military officers are far more inclined to see upheavals in the Third World as occasioned by nationalism than by communist penetration—and on this issue, at least, they adopt a more "liberal" position than politicians of either party or than business or labor leaders.[16] Furthermore, as students of the American military and of Washington bureaucratic politics remind us, the military is hardly a unified group. Getting the Air Force and the Navy to agree on any aspect of a strategic doctrine (except that ground forces should receive lowest priority) requires diplomatic skills and the exercise of raw power of a very high order. Still, while the services and other interest groups within the Department of Defense and some of the intelligence agencies may argue over the relative priorities of expenditures and of favorable arrangements with accommodating foreign governments, when pressed their arguments are likely to be less of the "either/or" variety than of the "both/and"; that is, they will, when pushed, reinforce one another in the hopes of picking up trade-off support for future higher-ranked priorities. Thus, if the Navy wants to get concerned about the safety of the Cape route, the Air Force may eventually be persuaded to go along with such an unpromising distraction in hopes of later Navy enthusiasm for high-performance bombers.

Southern Africa's noneconomic strategic interest for the United States should be considered under at least three quite distinct rubrics, each of which has potentially very different policy ramifications: (1) U. S.-USSR mutual nuclear deterrence; (2) protection of the shipping lanes; (3) competition for political and military influence in southern African countries.

Southern Africa enters the arcane calculus of the Soviet/American balance

[14] Paul A. Laudicina, *World Poverty and Development: A Survey of American Opinion* (Washington, D. C., 1973), p. 39.

[15] Ibid., p. 42. For some roughly comparable 1975 attitudes toward United States military aid, see "U. S. Commitments Should Remain Unchanged in Post-Vietnam Era," *The Gallup Opinion Index*, no. 121 (July 1975), 14–29.

[16] Russett and Hanson, *Interest and Ideology*, p. 71.

of terror principally through the possibility of stationing atomic missile-bearing submarines in the Indian Ocean. That body of water is blessed with a complicated bottom configuration which produces irregular currents and thermal layers capable of baffling listening devices; thus, the Indian Ocean is an attractive place to hide submarines. The escalation of Soviet surface movements along the eastern African littoral began in 1967, the same year in which the deployment of Poseidon submarines brought the central Soviet Union within the range of missiles launched from the Indian Ocean north of the equator. (Soviet port visits have increased from one in 1966 to an average of forty-five in recent years.) Trident I missiles have a range of 4000 miles (putting Moscow in range of a submarine off Zanzibar) and the 1980s generation of Trident III missiles, with a 6000-mile range, would allow a submarine commander to devastate Petropavlovsk by pushing a button while cruising off Beira.[17]

The Soviet Navy is quite aware of such strategic calculus, and Admiral Gorshkov has doubtless used these points to argue for the establishment of the new Soviet surface (and presumably submarine) fleet in the Indian Ocean, with its principally defensive and antisubmarine warfare armament. (Whether or not this surface power actually would serve to catch any of the American submarines is another question.) Following suit, the American Navy, particularly the carrier Navy, has used the presence of the Soviet surface fleet to argue for the stationing of a nuclear carrier task force in the Indian Ocean and, of course, the construction of a major Indian Ocean base in the middle of the water at Diego Garcia.[18] Diego Garcia, as an uninhabited (or more precisely, recently depopulated) archipelago, offers the political attraction of no native population to cause diplomatic fusses. At the same time, it is unlikely to possess the extensive facilities needed to service large numbers of ships in a major extended confrontation, so the newly enlarged service yards at Simonstown on the Cape peninsula might yet get the use the South Africans so ardently covet. Indeed, the presence of Diego Garcia, rather than serving as a substitute for an African continent base, might in time be used as an argument for a mainland backup facility.[19]

Many questions remain to be answered concerning the Indian Ocean's po-

[17] The writings on Indian Ocean strategic questions are voluminous. In addition to the indispensable hardware discussion in *Jane's Weapon Systems 1976* (London, 1976), a neophyte should see J. Bowyer Bell, "Strategic Implications of the Soviet Presence in Somalia," *Orbis*, 19, no. 2 (Summer 1975); A. J. Cottrell and R. M. Burrell, "The Soviet Navy and the Indian Ocean," *Strategic Review*, 2, no. 4 (Fall 1974); David Johnson, "Troubled Waters for the U. S. Navy," *Africa Report*, 20, no. 1 (January–February 1975); and Michael T. Klare, "Superpower Rivalry at Sea," *Foreign Policy*, 21 (Winter 1975–1976).

[18] The U. S. Navy has paid much public attention to Admiral Gorshkov's ideas, including the translation, annotation, publication, and dissemination of a volume of his collected writings. Sergei G. Gorshkov, *Red Star Rising at Sea* (Annapolis, Md., 1974). One wonders if the Soviet Navy has been equally assiduous in spreading the thought of Admiral Zumwalt.

[19] See U. S. House of Representatives, Hearings before the Sub-Committee on the Near East and South Asia of the Committee on Foreign Affairs, 83d Congress, 2d sess., *Proposed Expansion of U. S. Military Facilities in the Indian Ocean* (Washington, D. C., 1974). The testimonies

tential role in nuclear deterrence. For example, since the Indian Ocean lies at a considerable distance from any American submarine base, a Polaris or Trident vessel must spend a substantial percentage of its cruising time just getting to where it can be on station within range of a worthwhile target. At present it seems likely that the United States views the Indian Ocean principally as an open option to be used very occasionally, but with enough flexibility so that the Soviets feel obliged to stretch their antisubmarine warfare resources to patrol a large, distant, and frustrating body of water.[20] Given the financial and po-litical complications of such a strategy, except as a rationale for the navies of both sides to increase their forces, its logic appears as shifting as the Indian Ocean's currents.

The defense of the Cape route, once extolled as necessary for guarding British control of India, has taken on renewed interest now that the Western world has noticed how much it depends on oil. The Cape route is easily linked in the public mind with the Indian Ocean, and the Indian Ocean with strategic access to the oil-producing states of the Arabian Gulf. These linkages must be regarded with some skepticism. Diego Garcia is already 2000 miles away from most of the oil-producing states, and any South African base is so far away that the only quick strike capability would have to come from a sea-launched nuclear mis-sile—not the best way of assuring a continued oil flow. Southern African bases are simply irrelevant to the protection or intimidation of the Gulf states. The Cape shipping route is another matter, but again one must look carefully at what the issues are. There are over 1000 miles of open water south of the Cape of Good Hope; while Antarctic gales increase the hazards of passage far off shore, hostile submarines would still have to be deployed in massive numbers in order to interdict passage of oil. Their activities could, of course, raise the cost of such shipment, particularly to Europe, but serious harassment would quickly be regarded as a *casus belli* by the afflicted nations, thereby transforming the conflict into one which would probably be fought elsewhere. If the Soviet Union were seriously going to interdict shipping from the Persian Gulf, it would do so at the Strait of Hormuz, reachable by airplanes based in the Soviet Union itself, or by ships operating some 6000 miles away from the Cape of Good Hope.

The final strategic concern that affects policy toward southern Africa is that involving the balance of influence between East and West in the southern Af-rican states themselves. This is primarily a political issue, but it has two sep-arate military elements. The first of these, much heralded since the 1975 visit of the American congressmen to Somalia, is the threat that the Soviet Union

---

of Earl C. Ravenel, and Admirals Gene R. La Rocque and Elmo R. Zumwalt, Jr., are particularly relevant.

[20] A concise discussion of such antisubmarine warfare considerations can be found in Geof-frey Kemp, *Nuclear Forces for Medium Powers; Part II and III: Strategic Requirements and Options. Adelphi Papers,* no. 107 (London, 1974), pp. 7–8.

will actually construct major military bases in the southern African area which would be used to augment Soviet strategic military power in opposition to that of the United States. The evidence seems very slight that the Soviets want such bases, even slighter that any countries in the area are prepared to give them such facilities, and slighter yet that such bases would serve any substantial military purpose, except possibly to increase the bureaucratic weight of the Navy within the Soviet military establishment. The existing Soviet military bases in Africa, in Conakry and Berbera are much further north where they bear some relation to European, Mediterranean, and Arabian sea interests, and in any case are small-scale service stations, in no way comparable to American bases like Rota, Subic Bay, or Yokosuka, or even potentially Diego Garcia.[21] One can hardly claim that the Conakry base has in any way interfered with major American interests in Guinea, which have been confined to making sure that Olin Mathiessen and Harvey Aluminum continue to enjoy profitable access to Guinean bauxite. Given the games the two countries have been playing in the Indian Ocean, it would seem that the best way of dissuading the Soviets from wanting to establish any sort of military base in southern Africa is for the United States to make it clear that it is not going to try to beat them to the punch.

The second military aspect is, of course, the use of American military force, through showing the flag and less subtle forms of gunboat diplomacy, to affect the political course of the independent nations of southern Africa. The so-called Nixon Doctrine of 1969 envisages the promotion of what it calls "orderly change" through the combination of military support for "responsible" local powers, and the coercive offshore influence of the U. S. Navy and the Marines. The political background for this doctrine's application in southern Africa was laid in the famous "option II" of the 1969 National Security Council study NSSM 39, which advocated a "tilt" toward the white regimes.[22] The objections to the Nixon Doctrine, particularly as it might be applied in southern Africa where the definition of "responsible powers" is subject to varying interpretation, go beyond the subject of this article. Suffice it to say that simple political means appear to be far and away more cost-effective than any major military presence in the area, and that "disorderly" change in the area is likely to be of far greater concern to the Republic of South Africa than to the United States of America.

Understanding the Political Dimensions

An influential study published in 1969 by the Council on Foreign Relations began its discussion of American policy toward Africa thus: "Through most of American history . . . Africa essentially did not exist as an independent concern

---

21 Klare, "Superpower Rivalry at Sea."

22 The leaked text of NSSM 39 has been published as *The Kissinger Study of Southern Africa*, edited and introduced by Mohamed A. El-Khawas and Barry Cohen, preface by Edgar Lockwood (Westport, Conn., 1976). The authenticity of the text is not seriously disputed.

of foreign policy. . . . Militarily, economically, and politically, Africa in American governmental policy was only an adjunct to relationships with Europe."[23] Despite sporadic flurries of interest during the Kennedy and Johnson years, one must conclude that this historic pattern has remained dominant, particularly in the political domain. American policy in southern Africa in particular has proceeded in the absence of any accepted political analysis of southern African issues on their own merits or as they directly relate to American political interests independent of its involvements with the rest of the world. When such analyses have been prepared, as by the Department of State's African Bureau and occasionally by the Central Intelligence Agency, they have been neglected by the secretary of state and the White House, and their future production has been discouraged. Congressional leaders concerned with Africa, such as Congressman Diggs and Senator Clark, have encouraged more independent analysis, but their public and intragovernmental impact has been largely confined to the already committed.

Without such a generally accepted political analysis, American leaders have reacted to southern African events in three different ways: by ideological projection, by denial of political reality, and by treating Africa as an adjunct of more pressing relationships. Consistent with the Russett-Hanson findings, they have reacted overwhelmingly by projecting their domestic political ideology onto Africa. A comparison of Senate voting on four southern African issues between 1971 and 1975 with an index of the conservatism of their overall voting records demonstrates this projection. Of the ninety-two senators for whom sufficient information could be obtained, sixty-one are given scores by the Americans for Constitutional Action (ACA) lying either between 0 and 20 (very liberal) or 80 and 100 (very conservative).[24] The scores are based on their 1974 votes on nineteen issues (none of them dealing with Africa) selected by the ACA as a test of true conservatism/liberalism. The direction of their voting on the southern African issues can be predicted accurately for all but two senators (both known mavericks) on the sole basis of degree of conservatism/liberalism of their ideology as revealed in their votes. Nor is their degree of conservatism merely a reflection of their states' corporate interests: if one looks at the pairs of senators from those eight states in which the two differ by more than 50 points on their ACA rating, the votes split in the predicted direction in fourteen of the sixteen cases. (Interestingly, the two deviants were the more conservative senators from states containing corporations with substantial investments in South Africa who nevertheless voted on the liberal side of the southern African issues.) Recent

23 Waldemar A. Nielsen, *The Great Powers and Africa* (New York, 1969), p. 245.

24 The African votes are reported by the Washington Office on Africa, "Congressional Voting Record on Southern African Issues," Washington, D. C., May 1976. A fifth vote, that on the Mansfield resolution to prohibit the expansion of the Diego Garcia base, was not included as it seemed less clearly a southern African issue than the others. The ACA ratings are from *Congressional Quarterly Weekly Report*, 33 (February 22, 1975), 387–389. No votes in the ACA scale concern any African issue.

presidents have tended politically to treat Africa, if they treated it at all, as an area for vague symbolization of an ideological or domestic policy position. Thus, John Kennedy made his very first appointment that of the ebulliently liberal Soapy Williams as assistant secretary of state for Africa. Lyndon Johnson halted American naval visits to Simonstown after black sailors were denied permission to go ashore, at the time when he was preoccupied with programs for racial equality at home. And Richard Nixon's "southern strategy" could be beautifully symbolized by his barely concealed support for the Byrd amendment and "tilt" toward white rule displayed in option II of NSSM 39. Nor do the majority of concerned constituents seem to behave much differently. The greatest volume of congressional mail on a southern African issue has been generated by groups opposing the repeal of the Byrd amendment. A very high percentage of these letters also include paragraphs on other authentic conservative causes, particularly the retention of the House Un-American Activities Committee and rejection of domestic gun control legislation.[25]

In typical American fashion, this political ideological dimension is scarcely articulated. Irrespective of ideology, Americans display a peculiar tendency to play down long-range political and ideological issues and to prefer to talk in economic and military terms, as if they were somehow more real, hardheaded, and practical. In debates over southern African policy this tendency has often concealed America's own interests and covered up the premises on which much of its policy has been based. This was most startlingly apparent during the Nixon years when the State Department repeatedly articulated the formal fiction that African leaders' overwhelming interest in economic development relegated their concern with political issues like liberation of still-dependent territories and racial justice to peripheral status. In effect, this represented a wishful projection of official American thinking onto the Africans themselves. In November 1974 the then assistant secretary of state for African affairs, Donald Easum, publicly broke with this position by reporting after a southern African tour that "two major issues dominated the thoughts of my hosts. They concerned, first of all, human dignity and racial equality in southern African—and secondly, decolonization and national self-determination."[26] The speech was his swan song, as he was soon replaced in that post by the former ambassador to Chile, an appointment explained as part of Henry Kissinger's campaign to break up State Department area fiefs and to promote a more global political perspective within the department.

For Kissinger the global perspective has meant a subordination of African policy to considerations of America's more pressing relations with the Soviet Union and China, with the Western alliance, and with such priority concerns as the Middle East, Latin America, and residues of involvement in Asia. Ambassadors to Africa complain that they receive detailed instructions from Washing-

[25] Personal communication, Albert Cover, University of Michigan.

[26] Donald B. Easum, "Lusaka Manifesto Revisited," Patterson School of Diplomacy and International Commerce, University of Kentucky, November 26, 1974 (mimeo.).

ton on what to say about the Panama Canal, Palestinian refugees, or democracy in South Korea, but very little about the issues that directly interest the governments to which they are accredited. The costs of such subordination of Africa's own concerns became abundantly apparent in the Angolan war when the secretary of state refused to listen to his own African Bureau's recommendations and reacted entirely as if the issue were a U. S.-USSR confrontation.[27] Consistent with the Nixon doctrine, he backed South African intervention and thereby provided the ultimate justification in most African eyes for the introduction of Cuban troops. Nor did congressional opponents of Kissinger's Angolan policies come to grips with the African dimension of the war. The Congress earned itself Gerald Ford's description of "weak-kneed" not by challenging the political premises of policy, but by invoking symbols of congressional privilege, CIA dirty tricks, and American boys dying in Vietnam.

True to his supremely political nature, Kissinger developed his policy in disregard of the most prominent American economic interest in Angola, that of Gulf Oil. Here was a situation in which a major American multinational firm was pumping 144,000 barrels of oil a day from Cabinda and paying taxes and royalties to the government bank in Luanda. From all reports the relations between Gulf and the Soviet and Cuban-backed Movimento Popular de Libertação (MPLA) were cordial, and Gulf's payments substantially exceeded the amount of money that the United States government was covertly funneling into the MPLA's opponents, the Frente Nacional de Libertação de Angola (FNLA) and the União para la Independência Total de Angola (UNITA). Through direct State Department pressure, Gulf was obliged to suspend operations and to pay its royalties and taxes into a special escrow account. These funds were eventually turned over to the Angolan government and operations resumed, at about one-third the previous level, only after the MPLA's victory was recognized by the world community. In the meantime Angola's MPLA leaders bitterly attacked the State Department as well as Gulf for acceding to the department's pressures, while praising the more cooperative attitudes of other multinational corporations.[28]

CONCLUSION

With no significant domestic constituency and little public concern or understanding, southern Africa is, in political terms, something of a "free-play area"

[27] See, in particular, Kissinger's press conference remarks on Angola, December 23, 1975.

[28] As Robert Keohane has pointed out in "Not 'Innocents Abroad': American Multinational Corporations and the United States Government," *Comparative Politics*, 8, no. 2 (January 1976), 307–320, political manipulation of American multinational corporations, particularly the oil companies, by the U. S. government has been a recurrent feature of American policy in areas of the world where major political interests are deemed to be at stake. While in the long run the government may well find some way of sweetening Gulf's disappointment, we must not loose sight of the fact that the decision to halt production was imposed by State's Kissinger, not by the MPLA's Neto or Gulf's Dorsey.

for American political leaders. Most have reacted passively, as we have seen, in terms of their domestic political ideology. The few who have become more directly involved have in general received neither reprisals nor rewards from their constituents. Kissinger eventually sought to capitalize on this free-play characteristic by sharply reversing the "tilt" in his southern African policy in his Lusaka speech of April 27, 1976, and then following up with his shuttle diplomacy on the Rhodesian issue. Characteristically, Ronald Reagan's attempt in the 1976 primary elections to capitalize on Kissinger's reversal evoked little voter interest in comparison to his jingoistic statements on the Panama Canal, and neither Gerald Ford nor Jimmy Carter was able to turn discussion of southern African policy to his advantage in their televised debate on foreign policy.

In light of the above, one may conclude that within very broad limits, America's vital economic and strategic interests set few serious constraints on the development of policy toward southern Africa. In the absence of such constraints and of general public awareness, overall policy is most likely to be defined broadly (and somewhat irrelevantly) by the symbolic extension of domestic political ideology with the occasional interjection of considerations derived from concerns with the international balance of power between the United States and the Soviet Union. So long as no leader proposes anything approximating direct American military involvement and massive foreign aid expenditures, public opinion is unlikely to react directly to a policy initiative one way or the other. As with most international issues, southern Africa offers the ambitious politician few rewards in the form of votes, and few deprivations either.[29]

Nevertheless, any American administration inclined to accept the view presented above that the most prudent and cost-effective policy to protect American economic and strategic interests would be to work with, rather than against, the indigenous African forces of change, should find such a policy politically possible to implement. While it is beyond the scope of this article to lay out the details, the following general principles ought to underly such a policy.

In the United States, any redirection of policy ought to be carried out with a minimum of fanfare. With little short-term political advantage to be gained, an administration should avoid the sort of rhetorical excess that invites opposition to mobilize on partisan or ideological lines. It is quite possible to carry out major policy initiatives without the drama of a secretary of state publicly flying between secret meetings and inviting reactions to his person and style, as much as to his policy.

In Africa, American policy should express a broad commitment to full political participation for all African populations, but beyond that eschew attempts to dictate specific outcomes. On the one hand this should permit the United States

---

[29] David R. Mayhew, *Congress the Electoral Connection* (New Haven, Conn., 1974), especially the discussion of particularization of benefits and symbolization, pp. 122–138. Personal communication from some of those few politicians actively interested in African matters confirms the specific applicability of the generalization to Africa.

to avoid identification with any specific contending liberation group, as happened with such cost in Angola. Except at great expense, the United States has few direct means of control over outcomes where black groups oppose one another, and cannot hope to compete with the Soviet Union in terms of credit for past support. By a public and private willingness to cooperate with a variety of groups, the United States offers the eventual winner maximum opportunity to avoid dependence on Soviet support. As Kissinger came to appreciate, the "frontline presidents" (of Angola, Botswana, Mozambique, Tanzania, and Zambia) are the natural group through which to coordinate relations with liberation groups. On the other hand, this same broad commitment includes acceptance of the continued presence of white communities, particularly in South Africa.[30]

Those in Africa and in the United States who would support such a redirection of American policy over the long run might usefully concentrate their efforts on building a greater American understanding of African political issues in terms appropriate to the situation, so that public debate can be carried on in something other than cold-war rhetoric leavened with an occasional injunction about the necessity of preventing a "racial bloodbath." It would also make tactical sense to pay some attention to national elections. South Africa's lobbyists have long understood that the best practical way to affect the overall "tilt" of American policy in southern Africa is to affect the balance in the American government between conservative racists and liberal integrationists, irrespective of their interests in southern African questions per se.[31] Their wisdom is borne out in the analysis of congressional voting presented above. Finally, it is advisable, for practical as well as analytic purposes, to avoid blanket attacks on bogeymen like the "military-industrial complex." However soul-satisfying, such attacks not only miss the target, they miss the opportunity to pick up tactically useful allies, including part of the American business community as well as important segments of the military and foreign policy bureaucracies. For once, progressive critics might find it nice to have a Gulf Oil on their side.

---

[30] It should be noted that the 1969 Lusaka Manifesto on Southern Africa, in which thirteen chiefs of state of East and Central Africa laid out their rationale and strategy for ending white rule in southern Africa, explicitly accepts this last point. Since then, no serious black leader in southern Africa has publicly questioned the principle. Paragraph eight of the Manifesto begins: "Our stand towards Southern Africa thus involves a rejection of racialism, not a reversal of the existing racial domination. We believe that all the peoples who have made their homes in the countries of Southern Africa are Africans, regardless of the colour of their skins; and we would oppose a racialist majority government which adopted a philosophy of deliberate and permanent discrimination between its citizens on grounds of racial origin."
The complete text of the manifesto may be found as Appendix Two in Kenneth Grundy, *Confrontation and Accommodation in Southern Africa* (Berkeley, Calif., 1973).
[31] See, for example, "U. S. Democrats and R.S.A.," *South Africa Foundation News*, 2, no. 8 (August 1976).

American Foreign Policy
and the Postwar Italian Left

ALAN A. PLATT
ROBERT LEONARDI

United States policy toward Italy in the post-World War II period has been influenced and in many cases determined by the nature of relations between the United States and the Soviet Union. The superpower confrontation in Europe has had a profound effect on the establishment of the boundaries within which Italian domestic political choices have been (and are still being) made. The United States has not determined policies in Italy but it has exercised substantial influence on Italian domestic politics through its political, economic, and military linkages with Italy. Given Italy's strategic position in the Mediterranean, U.S. policy has been oriented toward three aspects of Italian politics: strengthening the control of centrist forces; maintaining a market-oriented socioeconomic system; and having Italy's foreign policy objectives and military posture shaped within the organizational framework of NATO. For much of the postwar period, the accomplishment of all three of these objectives has been consistent with keeping the Left—the Socialist (PSI) and Communist (PCI) parties—from playing a role in government.

The precise nature of U.S. policy toward the Italian Left can usefully be analyzed by focusing on the three most critical periods in postwar American-Italian relations, periods when basic choices were made in one or more of the sensitive areas cited. The first period covers the years between 1945 and 1948 when Italy's international position and postfascist socioeconomic model for reconstruction were shaped. The second period, from 1960 to 1963, was characterized by the attempt in Italy to create the international and domestic groundwork for permitting the entrance of the Socialist party into a government coalition. Finally, in the years from 1970 to 1976 the center-left experiment

ALAN A. PLATT, formerly lecturer in political science at Stanford University, is on the staff of the United States Arms Control and Disarmament Agency. ROBERT LEONARDI is assistant professor of political science at DePaul University, Chicago.

collapsed and Communist participation in government ceased to be an absurd hypothesis but became instead an ever closer reality.

U.S. Policy in the Era
of Superpower Confrontation, 1945–1948

In the immediate postwar years, when U.S. policy makers turned their attention to Italian politics, they often did not think of Italian political developments solely on their own terms but consciously considered America's position vis-à-vis the Soviet Union. Indeed, several key American officials were explicitly concerned with halting what "they considered 'the Red flood' before it could trickle and flow into Italy (and) Western Europe."[1]

In terms of Italian domestic politics, this concern—reinforcing earlier leanings—manifested itself in early U.S. support for the anticommunist, postwar coalition of conservative and moderate political forces led by the Christian Democrats. In late 1945 and throughout 1946, such support was limited, though observable.

Moreover, by the beginning of 1947 U.S. policy reflected unreserved alarm at the strength of the Left in Italy and elsewhere. In Italy the Left (particularly the PCI) had made substantial gains in the municipal elections of November 1946, in comparison with their showings in the Constituent Assembly elections of June 1946. One of the major problems faced by the Christian Democrats (DC) was that the Communists and Socialists coordinated their actions and policies through a Unity of Action Pact. The DC had no similar understanding with the smaller parties to its right like the Liberals, or with the Republicans to its left. In essence it stood alone as the major representative of moderation in the system. Accordingly, in early January 1947 the United States invited the leader of the DC, Prime Minister DeGasperi, to Washington to receive first-hand information about economic progress in Italy and the seriousness of the Left. From the Italian point of view these talks promised to be of both real and symbolic value: real in that they would likely lead to increased U.S. economic assistance; symbolic in that the talks signified acceptance of postfascist Italy by the major Western power.

In the course of his meetings with President Truman and Secretary of State Byrnes, DeGasperi stressed two themes: Italy's desperate economic plight as a result of the war, and his determination to combat the increase of Communist influence in his government and in the country as a whole. DeGasperi emphasized that to thwart the Communists, Italy needed strong economic and financial support from the United States.

It has been argued that during the January trip no definite agreements were made between the Truman administration and the Italian prime minister.[2] Nevertheless, the ground was set for an attempt by DeGasperi to create a new

[1] John Lukacs, *A History of the Cold War* (Garden City, N.Y.: Doubleday, 1966), p. 80. See also Roberto Faenza and Marco Fini, *Gli americani in Italia* (Milan: Feltrinelli, 1976).

[2] Simon Serfaty, "An International Anomaly: The United States and the Communist Parties

government coalition that would attempt to reduce Communist and Socialist influence in the policy-making process, especially in relation to economic affairs. In the new coalition of Communists, Socialists, and Christian Democrats that was put together on February 2, 1947, the Left was allocated fewer ministries than in the previous government. Of particular significance was the combination of the portfolios of Treasury and Finance (previously headed by a Communist) under Christian Democrat control. Notwithstanding, it was clear that in February 1947 DeGasperi was not yet looking for a full test of strength with the Left.

In subsequent months, U.S. policy toward Italy was explicitly designed to bolster the strength and legitimacy of the new DeGasperi government by extending to Italy substantial economic aid and food relief while at the same time suggesting that the United States would look even more favorably upon a government without the participation of Leftist parties. Thus a process of bargaining was set in motion between Washington and DeGasperi that was soon to bring an end to the tripartite coalition and heavily commit the United States to both the regeneration of the Italian economy and the shaping of domestic politics in Italy.

On May 7, 1947, U.S. Ambassador to Italy James Dunn sent Secretary of State Marshall an analysis of the current Italian situation. The ambassador advanced the thought that "if it is true that the economic position could be substantially improved through political measures, then aid to Italy perhaps should be based upon a *quid pro quo* of necessary changes in political orientation and policies."[3] Six days later DeGasperi dissolved his cabinet, initiating a political crisis that was finally to be resolved with the creation of a government coalition that excluded both the Communist and Socialist parties. However, before undertaking to create a center-right government composed of Christian Democrats, Liberals, and "technicians,"[4] DeGasperi made sure that the United States would back him up with new and substantial economic concessions. Soon thereafter the United States came forward with a number of economic programs in favor of Italy that foreshadowed the Marshall Plan.[5] While these initiatives of 1947 clearly reflected active U.S. concern for Italian domestic affairs and helped to effect change in the DeGasperi government, they were but a prelude to U.S. involvement and, indeed, intervention in the 1948 elections. These elections became the focal point for an almost apocalyptic struggle between "the forces of revolution" and "the forces of restoration."

in France and Italy, 1945–1947," *Studies in Comparative Communism* (Spring-Summer 1975): 123–146.

[3] "Current Economic and Financial Policies of the Italian Government," May 7, 1947, U.S. Department of State, *Foreign Relations of the United States, 1947*, III (Washington, D.C.: Government Printing Office, 1974), p. 901.

[4] Gianni Baget-Bozzo refers to the "technicians" as notabili (notables). See *Il partito cristiano al potere*, I (Florence: Vallecchi, 1974), p. 153–160.

[5] See "Cable from The Ambassador in Italy (Dunn) to the Secretary of State," May 28, 1947, *Foreign Relations*, p. 911.

In January 1947, while Prime Minister DeGasperi was in the United States, the Socialists split into two factions. At the Socialists' National Congress, revisionist members of the party—under the guidance of Giuseppe Saragat— broke with the dominant leadership in protest against the party's Unity of Action Pact with the Communists; and with the financial backing of the United States they created what eventually became known as the Social Democratic Party (PSDI).[6] The large majority of Socialist members, however, remained with the parent party and, led by Pietro Nenni and labor chief Oreste Lizzadri, these elements formed the Italian Socialist Party (PSI).

Following Saragat's secession, the Social Democrats, along with the moderately progressive Republican Party (PRI), moved toward the right and by December 1947 had joined the DeGasperi coalition. The PSI, on the other hand, came under the domination of its left wing and in January 1948 agreed to the formation of a national "Democratic Popular Front," "an electoral alliance between the Communist and Socialist parties who were to present themselves to the electorate as a single party with a single list of candidates."[7]

The creation of the "Front" further polarized Italian domestic politics and the ensuing campaign was an unequivocal struggle between the Left and the forces of anticommunism. Arrayed in opposition to the "Front" was an alignment of Christian Democrats, Social Democrats, and Republicans, although no formal electoral or postelectoral alliance had been concluded among them. In light of the fervently pro-Western stance of the Christian Democrats and their allies, the outspokenly anti-American position of the Front, and the Communist coup in Prague in February 1948, the United States officially undertook a direct anti-Left role in the 1948 elections in Italy. Indeed, during the 1948 parliamentary campaign "America took the gloves off for the first time."[8]

Unlike the situation in 1947 when American involvement in Italian affairs was largely economic and diplomatic in nature, in the 1948 election campaign the United States massively intervened politically in Italian internal affairs. Viewing Italy as a crucial battleground between the United States and the Soviet Union, American officials—with virtual unanimity in both the executive and legislative branches—thought and acted as if the importance of these elections far transcended national boundaries, believing that it was essential to U.S. interests, not to say ultimate survival, for the Christian Democrats and their allies to emerge victorious in the electoral campaign. Testifying before the U.S. Senate Armed Services Committee in the spring of 1948, Secretary of State George Marshall summarized prevailing official views:

In the world in which we live our national security can no longer be effectively weighed and dealt with in terms of the Western Hemisphere. . . . I wish to express . . .

---

[6] Confidential Interview; Faenza and Fini, pp. 208–222.

[7] Giuseppe Mammarella, *Italy After Fascism: A Political History, 1943–1963* (Montreal: Mario Casalini Ltd., 1964), p. 189. See Norman Kogan, *A Political History of Postwar Italy* (New York: Frederick A. Praeger, 1966), pp. 47–53.

[8] *The Economist* (London), April 24, 1948, p. 658.

concern over the accelerated trend in Europe. In the short years since the end of hostilities, this trend has grown from a trickle into a torrent. One by one, the Balkan States, except Greece, lost all semblance of national independence. Then two friendly nations—first Hungary and last week Czechoslovakia—have been forced into complete submission to Communist control. Within one month, the people of Italy, whose Government we had a large part in reconstituting, will hold a national election. . . . The outcome of that election has an importance far beyond local Italian affairs. It will decide not only whether Italy will continue with its restoration into a true democracy. It will foretell whether the disintegration to which I have referred may reach the shores of the Atlantic.[9]

For the U.S. government, the 1948 elections placed into question U.S. national security vis-à-vis communism in the Mediterranean and in all of Europe. In a recently declassified February 10, 1948 report on the U.S. position with respect to Italy, the National Security Council stated U.S. interests and objectives in Italy:

> The basic objective of the United States in Italy is to establish and maintain in that key country conditions favorable to our national security. Current U.S. policies toward Italy include measures intended to preserve Italy as an independent, democratic state, freiendly to the United States, and capable of effective participaticn in the resistance to Communist expansion.[10]

Consequently, before the election the United States utilized virtually every conceivable political and economic link that it had with Italy in an attempt to stop the Democratic Popular Front. First, and most important, the United States continued its large assistance program to Italy but made it clear that all economic aid, including Marshall Plan funds, would be terminated if the Left was successful in the upcoming election.[11] In addition, the United States instituted a number of political measures to aid the DeGasperi government which included intensified pro-DC propaganda activities and encouragement of Americans of Italian extraction to write to their relatives urging them to vote for the Christian Democratic party.[12]

Parallel to these moves designed to bolster the electoral strength of the anticommunist forces in Italy, U.S. policy makers also considered what the American response should be if the Leftist parties rose to power. Three different scenarios were considered: the Left would win only a plurality of the votes and thus enter a government coalition along with some of the moderate parties; the Front would win an absolute majority in the election; or the Left in defeat would stage an armed insurrection to gain control of the government. In the first eventuality,

[9] U.S. Department of State Bulletin, XVIII (March 28, 1948), p. 428.
[10] "The Position of the United States with Respect to Italy (NSC 1/2)" March 5, 1948, Foreign Relations, 1948, III, p. 766.
[11] See C.L. Sulzberger, A Long Row of Candles: Memoirs and Diaries (1934–1953) (New York: Macmillan, 1969), p. 381. L'Unita, March 6, 1948, p. 4.
[12] Kogan, p. 51. See Ernest Rossi, The United States and the 1948 Italian Elections (Ph.D. Diss., University of Pittsburgh, 1964), pp. 240–369.

U.S. policy was to be oriented toward reinforcing moderate elements in Italy by minimizing the effects of Communist participation, continuing efforts to detach the Socialists from the Communists, and strengthening the military position of the United States in the Mediterranean.[13] Italy would still remain within the political, economic, and military boundaries of the Western camp, but it would be carefully supervised by U.S. forces.

If an absolute majority voted for the Leftist slate, U.S. policy foresaw the need for a much more severe stance. On March 9, 1948, the NSC noted that "in the event the Communists obtained domination of the Italian government by legal means, the United States should:

a. Immediately undertake a limited military mobilization and announce this action as a clear indication of determination to oppose Communist aggression in Italy and elsewhere.
b. Further strengthen its military position vis-à-vis the Soviet Union in the Mediterranean.
c. Initiate combined military staff planning with other European selected nations.
d. Provide the anti-Communist Italian underground with financial and military assistance.
e. Oppose Italian membership in the United Nations."[14]

The maneuvers suggested were designed to quarantine Italy from the rest of the countries in the Mediterranean area and Europe. Only if the Left were to attempt an armed insurrection was U.S. policy clearly oriented toward immediate military intervention by U.S. troops to secure the island of Sicily and Sardinia and to "stabilize" the Italian peninsula at the request of the government.[15]

When the 1948 electoral campaign was over and the returns were in, the Christian Democratic Party emerged as the dominant party in Italy with 48.5 percent of the vote and an absolute majority in Parliament. The Front fell almost one million votes short of its combined Communist-Socialist vote for the 1946 Constituent Assembly elections due in large part to the surprising show of strength on the part of the Saragat Socialists who polled 7.1 percent of the vote. The election results, moreover, represented a triumph for the United States which had played such an active role in the course of the election campaign. With a firmly pro-Western Christian Democratic party in power, the United States looked forward to an era of stability in Italian politics, and from 1948 into the '60s, U.S. policy was firmly oriented toward the encouragement

---

[13] "Position of the United States With Respect to Italy in the Light of the Possibility of Communist Participation in the Government by Legal Means (NSC 1/3)," March 8, 1948, *Foreign Relations*, p. 779.
[14] Ibid.
[15] "NSC 1/2," *Foreign Relations*, p. 769.

and support of the DC centrist coalition which included the Republicans, Social Democrats, and Liberals.

Moreover, the U.S. experience during the 1948 Italian election led to the development of fixed principles that were to guide the formulation and conduct of U.S. policy in Italy till the early 1960s: The United States would not passively accept direct Leftist participation in an Italian government coalition as a subordinate or dominant partner because in either case this would be the prelude to a gradual shift of Italy out of the Western bloc and imposition of Soviet influence over a key Mediterranean country; the United States was ready to use a range of political, military, economic, and psychological measures to prevent such an eventuality; the United States would provide various kinds of support to anticommunist forces in Italy to enable them to keep free from Communist domination or influence; the DC was the central focus for the U.S. anticommunist strategy; the U.S. government encouraged anticommunist private individuals to establish contacts with their Italian counterparts; and the Socialists remained beyond the pale and were deemed unacceptable as coalition partners given their ties with the Communists, their pro-Soviet stance, and their opposition to NATO.

THE KENNEDY ADMINISTRATION AND
THE OPENING TO THE LEFT, 1960–1963

The need to find an alternative to this policy became an increasingly important political problem after the 1953 parliamentary elections. What followed between 1953 and 1960 was a period of relative government instability, fueled to a great extent by debate within the DC about which alternative (leftist or rightist) to follow. The Social Democrats, Republicans, and leftwing factions of the DC came out in support of a suggestion put forward by PSI leader Nenni in 1953 of an opening of the government to the Socialists, that is, a DC-PSI coalition. Earlier in 1953 the PSI had begun to withdraw from the Communist orbit. This process was accelerated by the events of 1956 in Hungary which altered the Socialists' views of the Soviet Union and the Western Alliance. Nevertheless, Nenni's initial suggestion that the DC-centrist coalition be replaced by an "opening to the left" (apertura a sinistra) was strongly opposed by a majority of the Christian Democratic party, the Liberals, business groups, the Church, and the U.S. government. These forces feared that the Socialists would serve as a Trojan horse within the government for the Communists and doubted very seriously the sincerity of the PSI's change of heart on international issues. Despite these misgivings, in the late 1950s and early '60s, momentum slowly built up inside Italy behind the apertura. Leaders like Fanfani and LaPira began to turn opinion around within the DC, the Liberals became increasingly estranged from the other centrist parties, the Church under the new leadership of Pope John XXIII gradually softened its anti-PSI stance, and some parts of the business community increased their dealings with the Socialists.[16] However, before 1961 there was no public sign of change in the anti-Socialist position of the United States.

The first impetus for a change in the U.S. government's total opposition to the Socialists came during the early months of the new Kennedy administration as part of a general re-evaluation of U.S. foreign policy. In early March 1961, President Kennedy sent the New Frontier's Ambassador-at-Large, W. Averell Harriman, to Rome on a goodwill and fact-finding mission. During his three days in Rome Harriman met with a number of Italian public and private figures who explained to him the need for a new kind of government coalition, namely, the *apertura a sinistra*, that could effectively meet the pressing problems of the country. For his part, Harriman continually stressed the Kennedy administration's willingness to rethink past policies and its strong commitment to economic and social change around the world. Harriman came away from his visit to Rome convinced that effective economic and social reforms in Italy were impossible without bringing the Socialists into the government coalition. He also concluded that U.S. support for the Socialists would likely take the PSI out of the PCI's orbit, hence weakening—and perhaps isolating—the Communists. Harriman has subsequently noted that "a change in American policy was not a liberal question (in 1961), it was the sensible thing to do."[17]

Upon his return to Washington, Harriman argued for an openly sympathetic U.S. policy toward the center-left prospect in Italy and on March 30, 1961 he briefed President Kennedy and his national security adviser, McGeorge Bundy, on the need for a change in American policy. Harriman's suggestions were in line with the views of Kennedy's special assistant, Arthur Schlesinger, Jr. Both Harriman and Schlesinger advised the president in the spring of 1961 to offer a formal invitation to Premier Amintore Fanfani to visit Washington.

For Arthur Schlesinger and other members of the administration, the Fanfani visit (scheduled for June 12–14) provided an obvious opportunity to signal a new departure in American policy toward Italy. Schlesinger knew that in preparation for these talks various senior officials in Washington would have to review the whole gamut of issues of common concern to Fanfani and President Kennedy. Schlesinger envisaged this review—and the subsequent Fanfani-Kennedy talks themselves—as the vehicles for bringing about a change in U.S. policy.

Consequently, in late May 1961 Schlesinger actively mobilized allies who would help to allay possible opposition to a change in U.S. policy toward the Socialists. In contrast to the late 1940s, few congressmen or domestic interest groups in early 1961 were actively concerned about Italian domestic politics or the *apertura* issue.[18] Thus Schlesinger's lobbying in favor of the

---

[16] See Giuseppe Tamburrano, *Storia e cronaca del centro sinistra* (Milan: Feltrinelli, 1971), pp. 27–113.

[17] Interview with W. Averell Harriman, March 4, 1971.

[18] Interview with Murray Frank, July 12, 1972. Interview with Arthur Schlesinger, Jr., October 22, 1970.

330 The Making of American Foreign and Domestic Policy

center-left was concentrated on the political and administrative organs involved in the formulation of U.S. policy toward Italy. Within the White House Schlesinger was successful in convincing Robert Komer, Mediterranean specialist of the National Security Council Staff, and his chief, McGeorge Bundy, of the wisdom of his efforts to change U.S. policy toward Italy.

At the various agencies Schlesinger got in touch with Under Secretary Chester Bowles at the State Department; William Bundy of the Office of International Security Affairs at the Defense Department; Deputy Director for Intelligence, Robert Amory, Jr., and European Analyst, Dana Durand, at the Central Intelligence Agency (CIA); Secretary Arthur Goldberg at the Labor Department; and Edward R. Murrow, Director of the United States Information Agency.

In addition to consulting these potential supporters, Schlesinger got in touch with the known opponents of change in the U.S. position on the *apertura* question—the Bureau of European Affairs (EUR) at the State Department— in hopes of persuading EUR to change U.S. policy toward Italy. In late May he invited Foreign Service officer William Blue, Director of the Office of Western European Affairs, and William Knight, the Italian Desk Officer, to the White House for a meeting.

Both Blue and Knight had had some previous experience in Italian affairs. Blue had served in Naples during and immediately after the war and Knight had been posted to the U.S. Embassy in Rome from 1947 to 1951 and had then served as the Italian Desk Officer from 1951 to 1955. Both men argued that the formation of a center-left coalition in Italy in 1961 would be premature and dangerous. Echoing the views of Deputy Chief of Mission Outerbridge Horsey, and clearly reflecting the Embassy's reporting from Rome, Blue and Knight said that allowing the Socialists in the government would pose great risks for the United States, given that the Socialists might cause the Italian government to withdraw from NATO and the European Community and to nationalize a host of Italian industries, including perhaps some U.S. subsidiaries.[19] Both men felt that if the Socialists were to enter the governing majority, their entry should be gradual and should result solely from Italian political maneuvering and not from any U.S. encouragement.[20]

In response Schlesinger attempted to convince Blue and Knight that they were mistaken in their judgments about the positions the Socialists favored and the effect of Socialist participation in the government on Italian policy. Schlesinger argued that Socialist participation in the government would isolate the PCI on the extreme left of the political spectrum and would bring to the Italian government the progressive leadership it needed to meet long-neglected economic and social problems. Schlesinger observed that if the United States continued to pursue past policy, it would dangerously polarize Italian politics by driving the PSI into the PCI's orbit and would forestall any

[19] Interview with William Blue, April 12, 1971.
[20] Ibid. Interview with William Knight, October 22, 1971.

meaningful reform in Italy. Finally, Schlesinger noted that the formation of a center-left government would not bring Italy to a neutralist position but, on the contrary, would likely make Italy a "more effective supporter of the foreign policy of the Kennedy Administration in Europe and elsewhere (e.g., in Latin America)."[21] In the end, neither side was able to convince the other. Blue and Knight left the White House certain that Schlesinger was naive, inexperienced, and badly informed about Italian politics. Schlesinger, on the other hand, was convinced that the Italian Desk in 1961 was manned by "typical" Foreign Service officers—bureaucrats who were inextricably committed to defending the status quo and for whom "risks always outweighed opportunities."[22]

On June 11, 1961 Prime Minister Fanfani arrived in Washington accompanied by Foreign Minister Antonio Segni and several of Segni's top aides. Among the officials they conferred with were: President Kennedy; Secretary Rusk, Under Secretary Ball, and Deputy Assistant Secretary Tyler of the State Department; Secretary of the Treasury Douglas Dillon; Assistant Secretary of Defense for International Security Affairs Paul Nitze; and presidential aides McGeorge Bundy and Arthur Schlesinger. In these talks, many salient international issues were canvassed.

Although "the opening to the left" was not on the formal agenda, President Kennedy raised the issue in private with Prime Minister Fanfani and "formulated a position of sympathy toward the Italian Socialists."[23] In addition, he told Fanfani that "if the Italian Prime Minister thought it a good idea, we (the United States) would watch developments with sympathy."[24]

In light of President Kennedy's personal expression of sympathy for the *apertura* during the Fanfani visit, Arthur Schlesinger assumed that subsequent American policy—as formulated and implemented by the State Department— would be sympathetic to the formation of a center-left coalition in Italy. However, he was mistaken. When the Bureau of European Affairs at the State Department and the Embassy in Rome learned of President Kennedy's private comments to Fanfani, they were convinced that Kennedy's sympathy—if such sympathy had actually been expressed—represented the private talk of one politician to another and nothing more. They did not believe that "President Kennedy had any particular views on the question one way or the other" or that "he had made a decision to change U.S. policy toward Italy."[25] In the absence of a directive from Secretary Rusk, neither EUR nor the Embassy was inclined to act as if there had been an official change in U.S. policy.[26]

Unable to convince the "working levels" of the State Department of the

[21] Interview with Arthur Schlesinger, Jr., October 22, 1970.
[22] Ibid.
[23] Ibid. Interview with McGeorge Bundy, May 18, 1971.
[24] Arthur Schlesinger, *A Thousand Days* (Boston; Houghton Mifflin, 1965), p. 878.
[25] Confidential Interview.
[26] Interviews with Outerbridge Horsey, March 2, 1971 and Foy Kohler, February 2, 1971.

importance of President Kennedy's private comments to Prime Minister Fanfani, Schlesinger then tried to persuade the President to communicate directly with Secretary Rusk. Fearing that there might be high political costs in a direct confrontation with the State Department, Kennedy was unwilling to take the risk over what he considered to be a relatively minor issue. Hence the president refused to take Schlesinger's advice to intervene with Secretary Rusk or, for that matter, to concern himself actively with the *apertura* issue.[27]

What Schlesinger wanted to do was to change the tone and substance of U.S. policy in such a way as to indicate to the top-ranking Italian leaders that the U.S. government was sympathetic to the formation of a center-left coalition, provided the Italians themselves decided upon such a development. For Schlesinger believed, rightly or wrongly, that:

> Italian officials were so deeply persuaded about U.S. opposition to the *apertura* by a dozen years of conditioning . . . that it was necessary to take steps to convey the impression that the United States would not interpose any obstacle or veto if the Italians wanted it ('the opening') . . .[28]

In an effort to change that policy, Schlesinger decided to go around, rather than through, EUR and the Embassy. With the tacit consent of President Kennedy and McGeorge Bundy, he tried to convey to Italian leaders in the fall of 1961 a changed U.S. policy toward the center-left. He began by traveling to Rome in September where, without the knowledge of the Embassy, he met with Pietro Nenni, head of the Socialists, Ugo LaMalfa, chief of the Republicans, and Giusseppe Saragat, leader of the Social Democrats. In subsequent talks with Italian leaders traveling in the United States, Schlesinger made the same points, frequently expressing fervent sympathy for the *apertura* movement. He also attempted to convey to Italian officials a changed American policy toward the "opening to the left" through correspondence on White House stationery.[29] Finally, Schlesinger used such personal friends as Senator Hubert Humphrey, Deputy Assistant Secretary of State for International Organizational Affairs Richard Gardner (currently U.S. Ambassador to Italy), and CIA senior analyst Dana Durand to convey word of a new U.S. policy.

Neither the Italian Desk nor the Embassy was pleased by the efforts of Schlesinger and his allies to win acceptance for the *apertura* movement. Both the Desk and the Embassy felt that Italy was not Schlesinger's legitimate field of responsibility, particularly since he was unable to obtain a mandate from the president to encourage "the opening to the left." They also felt he and his friends were acting in "an unauthorized, unprincipled, and amateurish"

---

[27] Interview with McGeorge Bundy, May 18, 1971.

[28] Interview with Arthur Schlesinger, Jr., November 17, 1971.

[29] See Mauro Lucentini, "Le carte di Kennedy," *Il Mondo*, September 6, 1970, pp. 4–5. It should be noted that Schlesinger has since denied writing letters to Italian politicians on White House stationery regarding the *apertura*. Interview October 22, 1970.

manner in Italy and that their activities had a "disruptive" effect on the operations of the Embassy and on U.S. policy.[30]

In the State Department it was reasoned that it would be counter-productive in the long run and damaging to America's interest if "we became associated (with), or in fact, really pushed for the development of the center-left."[31] As former Ambassador Reinhardt has explained:

> It was anybody's guess as to whether a coalition of this character could hold together, and if the United States had become committed, in one way, and the subsequent developments had pulled this thing apart, it's quite apparent . . . that the U.S. would have lost considerably. Furthermore, there was another element in this development . . . And that was this: that a coalition of this kind would only be put together as a result of very intense bargaining on the part of the two parties. If we had actually pushed one way or the other we would have assumed a direct responsibility, (a) for the success or failure of the establishment of such a coalition, and (b) for the nature of the policies that would subsequently follow.[32]

In an attempt to stop Schlesinger's pro-*apertura* activities, several members of the State Department and the Embassy in Rome undertook a vigorous campaign to reach the top decision makers in the White House. For example, between September and December 1961, Deputy Chief of Mission Horsey personally went to Washington and tried to: convince senior State Department officials of the dangers in allowing the Socialists to enter the government coalition; get the 1961 National Intelligence Estimate for Italy rewritten; and "educate" Schlesinger in depth about Italy. All of these efforts failed to change Schlesinger's views.

In late November 1961, as change in the Italian governing coalition became increasingly likely, a meeting was held at the Embassy in Rome to discuss the *apertura* movement and its consequences for American foreign policy. At the meeting Military Attaché Vernon Walters forcefully advocated the use of U.S. troops to prevent the PSI from entering the government coalition. Walters's argument was supported by key members of the CIA station in Rome. However, it should be noted that the CIA was not unanimous in support of a hard line toward the PSI. The agency was, in fact, split on the issue as was much of the U.S. government. Though several CIA operatives in Rome advocated military action, the key European analysts in Washington were favorable to the center-left. Conflicting attitudes between Washington and Rome and within single agencies permitted moderates to prevail at the November meeting, and a consensus emerged according to which the Embassy would assume a "hands-off" policy if the PSI entered the govern-

---

[30] G. Frederick Reinhardt, Recorded Interview by Richard O'Connor, November 1966, John F. Kennedy Library, 6. Interviews with William Blue, April 12, 1971 and Outerbridge Horsey, March 2, 1971.

[31] Reinhardt, p. 7.

[32] Ibid., p. 4.

ment.[33] Thereafter, the possibility of U.S. intervention just before or after the consummation of an "opening to the left" was excluded from serious consideration.

In short, by the end of 1961 the various bureaucratic elements within the U.S. government had acquiesced in the prospect of Socialists entering an Italian government coalition. Undeniably, it was the initiative taken by Italian political leaders which brought the center-left experiment to fruition, but it seems that the efforts of some U.S. officials helped to accelerate the entry of the Socialists into the government and, at a minimum, differences within the U.S. government over the Socialists dissuaded the United States from trying to exercise a veto power against the *apertura*. Although the U.S. government adopted a somewhat changed policy toward the PSI during the Kennedy administration, it did not alter its view of the Communists. On the contrary, the acceptance of the Socialists was seen by many U.S. officials as an integral part, and even a refinement, of an American anticommunist strategy in Italy. Thus the center-left experiment was to be subsequently judged by many in relation to its effectiveness in reducing the strength of the Communist party in Italian affairs.

U.S. Policy and the PCI, 1970–1976

With the creation of the first Aldo Moro government on December 4, 1963, the center-left alternative achieved full take-off and acceptance among a wide variety of political circles in the United States and Italy. A virtually unanimous consensus had been reached within the U.S. government on the positive nature of the center-left. The anti-PSI forces in the Embassy in Rome and in the State Department were neutralized or shifted to other areas of concern. Symptomatic of these changes was the official establishment of ties between the U.S. government and the PSI. In 1962–63 four top-ranking Socialists visited the United States as guests of the government; PSI leader Nenni was received by Ambassador Reinhardt; and John Kennedy, during his visit to Italy between June 30 and July 2, 1963, unequivocally conveyed U.S. backing for the *apertura* experiment in his conversations with leading government officials.

Though the tragic events of November 22, 1963 unexpectedly elevated Lyndon B. Johnson to the presidency, U.S. policy toward Italy remained unchanged. The position established by John Kennedy and his advisers on the "opening to the left" was carried forward through the Johnson years. Indeed, it could be argued that until 1968 U.S. policy toward Italy did not change as it did toward other countries, such as Vietnam, the Dominican Republic, and Greece where the main problem was the collapse of the moderate forces on which U.S. postwar policies had been based. Italy, by contrast,

---

[33] Confidential Interview.

seemed rather reassuring. The DC had not collapsed in the 1963 parliamentary elections as a result of the *apertura*; the PSI maintained its acceptance of NATO and its relations with the PCI remained strained;[34] and by October 1966 moves toward the creation of a unified Socialist party (PSU) had been consummated.[35]

It was not until 1969 that enthusiasm for the center-left really began to wane in parts of the U.S. government. The reasons for disenchantment are easy to find. The Italian parliamentary elections in 1968 showed that the PSU was incapable of transforming itself into an alternative bloc for leftist votes. Running on separate tickets in 1963, the two components of the Italian Socialist movement gained 19.9 percent of the vote. Five years later, after unification, the PSU was able to maintain only 14.5 percent of its previous electoral base from which it was supposed to challenge the Communists. A good portion of that loss went to the PSIUP (Italian Socialist Party for Proletarian Unity) which broke off from the PSI in 1964 in opposition to the center-left. In contrast to the PSU, the PCI continued to make steady gains. In 1963 the PCI received 25.3 percent of the vote, and in 1968, 26.9 percent. Even more disconcerting was the amount of bickering that continued to lacerate the internal workings of the PSU. Not unexpectedly, the Unified Socialists split again into two parties in July 1969. Persistent divisions within the PSU had rendered it less effective than anticipated in its dealings with the DC and in pushing for socioeconomic reforms. The response to this failure took the form of a wave of student and worker protest strikes and demonstrations that culminated in the "hot autumn" of 1969.

In many ways 1969 represents a watershed in the evolution of Italian politics. It was in that year that possible Communist participation in the government began to assume an explicit form and name—Ciriaco De Mita's "constitutional pact" (working out common agreements on policy) with the PCI. It was also a year when events taking place abroad would soon have an effect on the development of Italian affairs and on the position taken by the United States in response to those developments. Most important, it was the year that Richard M. Nixon became president; Graham Martin was soon thereafter appointed Ambassador to Italy.

Before arriving in Italy, Martin had served as U.S. Ambassador to Thailand (from 1963 to 1967) during the militarization of the country as part of the Vietnam build-up. The Italian assignment came as the result of a shrewdly cultivated friendship with Richard Nixon who, during Martin's ambassadorship, made several trips to Thailand. Robert Anson writes that Martin treated private citizen Nixon with "a deference normally reserved for a Chief of State," and when Nixon became president he saw to it that the State Department did "something for Graham Martin."[36] Martin's tour in Italy lasted

[34] The PSI, however, maintained its working relationship with the PCI in many cities and provinces in the Red Belt regions.

[35] Tamburrano argues that the PSU was an example of a "unification at the top," p. 321.

[36] Robert S. Anson, "The Last of the American Caesars," *New Times*, July 10, 1975, p. 22.

until April 1973 when President Nixon personally picked him to head the Embassy in Saigon. He was the last U.S. Ambassador to South Vietnam.

During Martin's years in Italy, there was little in the Italian or American press that distinguished his tour from those of his predecessors. Little attention was given in the media to the role played by the ambassador or other officials in the formulation of U.S. policy toward Italy, and it was only hinted sporadically that the U.S. government had a continuing program of involvement in internal Italian affairs. For example, in 1971 rumors appeared in the American press that the U.S. government had undertaken to finance the Christian Democrats and other anticommunist parties in preparation for the parliamentary elections expected in 1973. However, the Italian government denied any such interference. The official position was that the United States was solely interested in the continuity of Italy's foreign policy as formulated by the center-left coalition.[37] And it was not until publication in 1976 of the report of the House Select Committee on Intelligence, "The Pike Report," that the extent of U.S. efforts under Martin to aid the noncommunist parties became fully known. The Pike Report revealed that the U.S. government had allocated approximately $10 million to the 1972 parliamentary elections. The request cited the need to reduce interparty conflict and to demonstrate U.S. solidarity with the goals championed by the Italian anticommunist parties.[38]

This kind of aid program was not, in fact, an innovation instituted by Graham Martin. In the previous two decades, approximately $65 million had been allocated to various Italian political parties, organizations, and individuals by the U.S. government. However, what did change under Ambassador Martin was the choice of recipients and the way the money was allocated. In previous years the primary, if not exclusive, foci of U.S. financial assistance were the democratic centrist parties, especially the DC, and the financial arrangements between the Embassy and the recipients were handled by the CIA station in Rome. Martin undertook personally to control decisions of who was to receive money and how it was to be distributed. More important, Martin extended financial support to Italian political groups and individuals on the far right of the political spectrum (that is, to forces close to the neofascist Italian Social Movement, MSI).[39]

The basic motive for Martin's innovative dispersal program was an anticommunist fear. As one observer has noted, "he [Martin] went to Italy with a great anxiety, if not fear, of the worldwide Communist conspiracy."[40] This fear of communism inevitably colored Martin's evaluation of Italian political developments and specific policy recommendations. An example of his bias appears in the February 12, 1971 Annual Report of the Rome Embassy to the State Department, which was drafted by Deputy Chief of Mission Wells

---

[37] See *The New York Times*, February 27, 1971.
[38] See "The CIA Report the President Doesn't Want You to Read," *The Village Voice*, February 16, 1976, pp. 36–38.
[39] Ibid. Confidential Interview.
[40] Anson, p. 21.

Stabler and approved and signed by the Ambassador. In the Report Martin declared that the United States had a crucial stake in the upcoming parliamentary elections. He asserted that the United States had a vast, and sometimes overlooked, reservoir of goodwill and influence at its command, and to use this influence to the fullest, it had to show its solidarity with "certain domestic political forces." One of the justifications offered for this policy was the fear of a broad leftist coalition that could win a resounding victory. Martin felt that "there was too much at stake in preparation for the election campaign for the U.S. to remain detached." He saw the priorities for U.S. intervention in aid of the anticommunist parties in the following order: provision of political encouragement, financial support, and then active help. The latter contingency policy was formulated in such a way that even a military intervention in Italian politics, including a coup d'état, would be conceivable if all other efforts to block the PCI from coming to power failed.[41]

Taken in this perspective, the revelation in the Pike Report of Martin's transfer of $800,000 to a rightist "local intelligence official" (namely, Vito Miceli, head of Italy's Defense Intelligence Service, SID) to conduct a "propaganda effort" fits with the ambassador's overall view of communism and Italian affairs. This new departure in funding, however, disturbed the CIA station chief in Rome and many bureaucrats in Washington concerned with U.S. policy toward Italy. For it constituted a deviation from normal American policy: the ambassador was personally in charge of the operation (which meant that covert funding, if discovered, could tarnish all other operations connected with the Embassy); the U.S. government was undertaking to finance a noted right-wing sympathizer with close ties to the neofascists, a development which would inevitably identify the United States with the far right of the Italian political spectrum; and the U.S. government might be drawn into domestic events in Italy from which there would be no easy exit.[42]

Not surprisingly, considerable tension arose between Martin and bureaucratic elements in both the State Department and CIA over the new U.S. covert funding policy. The following exchange of views reported in a cable from the Rome CIA chief of station to Washington illustrates that Martin had his own ideas about proper U.S. policy toward Italy and wanted to run his own show. Unlike many officials in Washington and Rome, he was more interested in the long run than in the short-term benefits of the project to finance Miceli:

> Chief of Station: Do you really care if his (Miceli's) efforts are successful or not?
>
> Graham Martin: Yes, I do, but not a helluva lot. The important thing is to demonstrate solidarity for the long pull.[43]

And Martin cared enough about demonstrating this "solidarity" that at one

---

[41] Confidential Interview.
[42] Confidential Interview.
[43] *The Village Voice*, p. 39.

point he threatened to have the Embassy Marine guards carry off the CIA station chief over the disposition of the black money.[44]

To Martin and to his successor, John Volpe (1973–76), demonstrating "solidarity for the long pull" meant, in essence, the establishment of a series of contacts and policy measures that would serve as the building blocks for a closer relationship between the United States and staunchly anticommunist, rightist elements within Italy. Both Martin and Volpe believed that only these elements were vigorous enough to prevent the entry of the communists into a governing coalition. Accordingly, both ambassadors endeavored to test alternatives to U.S. policy in support of Christian Democracy in an effort to stem the increase of Communist electoral strength and to shore up the Right. Both failed, in part because bureaucratic elements in the State Department and CIA opposed their ideas and helped to ensure the futility of their efforts.[45]

Major causes of this failure were the ephemeral nature of right-wing support in Italy and the lack of qualified individuals and institutions upon which to build a rightist alternative. In addition, foreign multinational corporations, which had complemented U.S. support for the Christian Democrats in the past, were not inclined to engage in any substantial funding of the Right. In short, the Right in Italy, although the focus of much of Martin's and Volpe's anticommunist attention, lacked both political and economic clout from 1969 to 1976 and proved incapable of halting the gains of the Communists.[46]

CONCLUSION

The key question for U.S. policy makers in 1978 is not whether the Communists will enter the Italian government, for in March of this year they joined the governing parliamentary coalition. The issue is what should U.S. policy be toward a full consummation of the *compromesso storico* (historic compromise between the DC and PCI), through which the PCI would gain control of key cabinet posts and ministries. It is clear that the U.S. government, for both internal and external reasons, no longer has the margin of maneuver to prevent such a governing coalition in Italy, or elsewhere in Europe, by using force. As Victor Zorza perceptively noted in 1974, 'The Soviet Union can afford to invade its allies. The U.S. cannot, and will not, and must therefore find other ways of dealing with the problem of the growth of Communist forces within the western democracies."[47] If Zorza's observation continues to pertain to the Italian situation—and we believe that

[44] See Roger Morris, *Uncertain Greatness: Henry Kissinger and American Foreign Policy* (New York: Harper & Row, 1977), p. 277.

[45] Confidential Interview.

[46] For a discussion of the MSI's electoral fortunes in the 1970s, see Robert Leonardi, 'The Smaller Parties in the 1976 Italian Elections" in Howard Penniman (ed.), *Italy at the Polls* (Washington, D.C.: American Enterprise Institute, 1978), forthcoming.

[47] *The New York Times*, November 5, 1974.

it does—than the U.S. government must re-examine past policy toward Italy to see what lessons can be learned from U.S. attitudes toward the Italian Left during the postwar period.

The analysis presented in this paper leads to at least three major conclusions. U.S. policy toward the Left in Italy—in the current instance toward the PCI—will likely be framed in the overall context of U.S. policy toward the Soviet Union. Many on the Right in both Italy and the United States argue that the recent gains of the PCI are a direct consequence of the Nixon-Ford-Kissinger and now Carter policy of détente between the United States and the Soviet Union. The influence of détente on Italian electoral politics is undoubtedly more complicated than the Right would suggest. But it is likely that future U.S.-Soviet relations will affect U.S. policies toward Italian politics. If, for example, the relationship between the two superpowers should cool, one can expect the United States to adopt a harder line toward the PCI. However, if détente with the Soviet Union continues, at a minimum pressures will build on American policy makers to treat the PCI much as it treats the other major parties in Italy.[48]

A few people within the U.S. government will play determinative roles in shaping future policy toward the Left in Italy, a policy which will most likely have considerable effect on the course of Italian domestic political developments. As we have shown in the preceding analysis, during certain critical periods in Italian postwar history political leaders in Italy have been highly sensitive to official U.S. views about Italian politics. Indeed, for most of the postwar period the United States has influenced the composition of the Italian governing coalition. Whether the United States will be able to exercise such a high degree of influence over the possible consummation of the *compromesso storico* is questionable. But it is likely, given the continuing dependence of the Italian economy on outside economic assistance,[49] that Italian officials will remain extremely sensitive to the attitudes, words, and actions of the U.S. president, the secretary of state, the ambassador in Rome, and the White House staff on the matter of direct Communist entry into the Italian government.

If the president of the United States decides to change U.S. policy toward the Left in Italy, he will likely encounter stubborn resistance from those parts of the government bureaucracy most concerned with Italy. Postwar policy toward Italian politics is a history of bureaucratic resistance to policy changes, particularly in the absence of overt presidential involvement. In the early 1960s presidential assistant Arthur Schlesinger, Jr. tried to shift U.S. policy to a more sympathetic stance toward the PSI only to be resisted by the State Department and the Embassy in Rome.

Again in the early 1970s Ambassador Graham Martin met with similar resistance when he attempted to institute innovative covert funding practices

[48] Confidential Interview.
[49] See Suzanne Berger, "Italy On the Threshold or the Brink?" in David Landes (ed.), *Western Europe: The Trials of Partnership* (Lexington, Mass.: Lexington Books, 1977), pp. 209–236.

in Rome. Only in 1947–48 when the Truman administration shifted to a policy of massive, overt opposition to the Communists did a new policy toward Italy have virtually unanimous support within the U.S. government. And it should be emphasized that in this instance President Truman personally played an active role in enunciating and carrying out the new policy, while neither Kennedy nor Nixon opted to involve himself directly in bureaucratic squabbling or to support new policy initiatives.

At present the Carter administration appears to favor a two-pronged policy toward the PCI: no encouragement whatsoever of the impression that the United States is indifferent to the growth of Italian Communist forces or favorably disposed to the prospect of Communist entry into the government;[50] no overt interference in Italy's internal affairs either through CIA payments to anticommunist elements or through threats to punish the Italian people should they choose to bring the Communists directly into the government.[51] The second part of this policy represents a noteworthy departure from past American practice in Italy. And if President Carter is seriously committed to renouncing U.S. interference in Italian politics, he would be well advised to explain this policy in the most unambiguous terms to the U.S. government bureaucracy and the American people. For only by doing so will he be able to avoid the kind of bureaucratic "drag" and intra-Executive sniping that have characterized U.S. policy initiatives toward Italian politics during earlier eras of the postwar period.*

[50] See "U.S. Statement on Italy, January 12, 1978," *The New York Times*, January 13, 1978.

[51] See "Interview with the President" by David Dimbly et. al., May 2, 1977 (The White House: Office of the White House Press Secretary), pp. 10–11. "Interview with Zbigniew Brzezinski," *Congressional Record*, October 26, 1977, pp. E. 6592–6594; and Interview with U.S. Ambassador Richard Gardner, *Corriere della Sera*, November 15, 1977.

* The views expressed in this paper are the authors' and do not represent the views of any organization or institution.

PART IV
Domestic Policy Issues

The Great Society Did Succeed

SAR A. LEVITAN
ROBERT TAGGART

President Lyndon Johnson's social welfare philosophy captured the imagination of the country in the mid-1960s and spurred it into action after a decade of lethargy. In Johnson's words, "We have the opportunity to move not only toward the rich society and the powerful society, but upward to the Great Society. The Great Society rests on abundance and liberty for all. It demands an end to poverty and racial injustice."[1] Under the banner of the Great Society, there was a dramatic acceleration of governmental efforts to ensure the well-being of all citizens; to equalize opportunity for minorities and the disadvantaged; to eliminate, or at least mitigate, the social, economic, and legal foundations of inequality and deprivation. Congress moved ahead on a vast range of long-debated social welfare measures and pushed on into uncharted seas. In its 1866 days the Johnson administration moved vigorously to implement these new laws and to fully utilize existing authority. The Warren Court aided this dynamism with sweeping, precedent-setting decisions on a number of critical issues. The public supported this activism, giving Lyndon Johnson in 1964 the largest plurality in history, his Democratic party an overwhelming majority in

[1] Congressional Quarterly, *Congress and the Nation, 1965–1968* (Washington, D. C., 1969), Vol. II, p. 650.

SAR A. LEVITAN is professor of economics at The George Washington University and director of its Center for Social Policy Studies. ROBERT TAGGART is administrator of the Office of Youth Programs, U.S. Department of Labor. They are the authors of *The Promise of Greatness*.

both Houses of Congress, and his administration high public approval ratings as action got underway.

Yet only eight years after the end of the Johnson administration, the view is widely held that the Great Society failed. The charge is that it exaggerated the capacity of government to change conditions and ineffectively "threw money at problems," overextending the heavy hand of government, pushing the nation too far, too fast, leaving a legacy of inflation, alienation, racial tension and other lingering ills. The repudiation of the Great Society in the late 1960s was based on a tide of analyses alleging to demonstrate the failures of the Johnson administration's domestic endeavors. There was extensive documentation of the "welfare mess." A crisis in medical care was declared and decried. Scandals and high costs in subsidizing housing were exposed, giving support to theoretical arguments about the inherent ineffectiveness of government intervention. Manpower programs, it was claimed, had little lasting impact on employment and earnings of participants. Doubts were cast on the outcomes of education investments. Urban and racial unrest were blamed on civil rights action and community organization. The economic problems of the 1970s were blamed on economic mismanagement during the 1960s.

A Positive Assessment

A careful reexamination of the evidence for the complete spectrum of the 1960s social welfare initiatives suggests that the conventional wisdom of the Great Society's failure is wrong. Our own assessments of the Great Society and its legacy, based on analysis of a vast array of program data, evaluations, and related statistics, challenge the widespread negativism toward governmental social welfare efforts.[2] We contend that the findings provide grounds for a sense of accomplishment and hope.

1. *The goals of the Great Society were realistic, if steadily moving, targets for the improvement of the nation.* By concentrating on the small minority of welfare recipients who are cheaters or who shun work, critics have chipped away at the ambitions of the Great Society, and have suggested that those in need somehow deserve their fate. This view ignores the overwhelming majority of welfare recipients who have no other alternatives, workers who either cannot find employment or are locked into low-wage jobs, and the millions of disenfranchised who are seeking only their constitutionally guaranteed rights. Other less strident critics emphasize the difficulties in changing institutions and socioeconomic patterns. No matter how desirable a change may be, it is likely to have unwanted side effects, and the process itself can be an ordeal. Where opportunities and rewards are distributed unequally and unjustifiably, redistribution will obviously affect the previously chosen people. Improvements cannot be ac-

[2] Specific analyses and studies are cited in Sar A. Levitan and Robert Taggart, *The Promise of Greatness* (Cambridge, Mass., 1976).

complished without effort and sacrifice, and the existence of impediments is not proof of unrealistic or unattainable goals.

2. *The social welfare efforts initiated and accelerated in the 1960s moved the nation toward a more just and equitable society.* The claims that these programs were uselessly "throwing dollars at problems," that government intervention cannot change institutions or individuals, or that problems remain intractable are glib rhetoric. The results of government intervention varied, undesirable spillover effects occurred, and the adopted intervention strategies were sometimes ill designed; but progress was almost always made in the desired direction. The gains of blacks and the poor, the two primary target groups of federal efforts, offer the most striking evidence. Government programs significantly reduced poverty and alleviated its deprivations. Blacks made major advances in education, employment, income, and rights in the 1960s.

3. *The Great Society's social welfare programs were reasonably efficient, and there was frequently no alternative to active intervention.* The government operates in a fishbowl, so that all its mistakes and excesses are laid bare to the public; similar problems in the private sector are hidden away, leaving the impression of greater efficiency. Criticism of programs is part of the process by which needed or desired changes are engineered, and the discovery of failure is part of a continuing process of improvement.

4. *The negative spillovers of social welfare efforts were often overstated and were usually the unavoidable concomitants of the desired changes.* Examples are legion. Medical care programs were blamed for the inflation in medical costs. Busing was heatedly opposed as inconveniencing the many to help the few. In fact, however, medical costs rose largely because demand was increased suddenly while supply could respond only slowly. Inflation is unavoidable when reliance is placed on the price mechanism to expand and redistribute resources. Busing to achieve racial balance involves difficulties but critics have not offered alternatives to integrate the schools. Every program generates problems, but these have usually been manageable.

5. *The benefits of the Great Society programs were more than the sum of their parts, and more than the impact on immediate participants and beneficiaries.* In attacking a specific problem such as unemployment, for instance, there is a whole nexus of variables. On the supply side, consideration must be given to the education and vocational training of the unemployed; their access to jobs, their knowledge of the labor market; and their work attitudes, impediments, and alternatives. On the demand side, the quality and location of jobs must be considered along with their number. Discrimination and hiring standards are also crucial factors. Unemployment might be combated by education and training, better transportation, improved placement services, sticks and carrots to force the unemployed to take jobs, provision of child care, economic development in depressed areas, equal opportunity enforcement, and a variety of other measures. None of these alone is likely to have much impact, but together they

can contribute to change, not only in the labor market, but in all those dimensions of life so intimately related to work.

6. *There is no reason to fear that modest steps which are positive and constructive in alleviating age-old problems will in some way unleash uncontrollable forces or will undermine the broader welfare of the body politic.* Only dedicated pessimists and gainsayers can doubt our capacity to achieve substantial improvements. And there is no reason to abandon the aim of providing a minimal level of support for all who remain in need. Progress has been meaningful; it can and must continue. As we enter our third century as a nation, we must reevaluate the recent, as well as distant, past to get a realistic understanding of our limitations but also a greater confidence in our potential. We have the power, if we have the will, to forge a greater society and to promote the general welfare.

Evaluating the Record

Many critics of the Great Society have focused on the least successful attempts at social improvement with their attendant horror stories. There is an opposite temptation to concentrate on and generalize from the areas of accomplishment. The only valid approach is to consider the successes and failures over the entire range of social welfare activities.

Income Support

The expansion of income transfers during the 1965–1975 decade has been criticized from many angles. Aid to Families with Dependent Children—usually called "welfare"—drew the brunt of criticism. Supplemental Security Income—the reformed system of aid for the aged, blind, and disabled—then came under fire, as did unemployment compensation. Even the previously sacrosanct social security program was questioned. In reality, the Great Society had less impact on the transfer system than on any other social welfare dimension. To blame it for the "welfare mess" or for the problems of the social security system is to ignore the complicated factors involved; to associate it with the vast expansion in unemployment compensation in the 1970s or with the difficulties of public assistance for the aged, blind, and disabled is an anachronism. Nonetheless, a major thrust of the Great Society was to provide for the needy. If the programs that attempt to do this are ineffective, then the Great Society's vision must be faulted. Is the transfer system indeed a mess?

Doubts about the soundness of the social security program are, if not groundless, certainly exaggerated. During the 1965–1975 decade benefits were raised substantially in real terms, and the system matured to the point where coverage of workers and benefits to the elderly became nearly universal. The redistributive features of the programs were expanded but social security remained a good insurance buy for most workers.

The system remains secure. Declining birth rates mean fewer workers per beneficiary in the future and may require increased revenues. But this problem is more than a quarter century away, during which time productivity gains should provide the wherewithal for the needed transfers. Government contributions from general revenues are a likely possibility to finance the redistributive aspects of the system. And as a result of past improvements, benefits now meet basic needs and will not have to be raised in real terms as rapidly as in the past.

The veterans' pension and compensation system is an important complement to social security. As World War II veterans age, the proportion of needy veterans receiving benefits not carrying the stigma of welfare will rise.

Unemployment compensation grew at an incredible pace during the recession of the mid-1970s. Benefits and coverage extensions financed out of general revenues increased the transfer, as opposed to the insurance, features of the program. While it helps many nonpoor, unemployment compensation has evolved into a form of aid for the working poor who are frequently subjected to forced idleness but who are shortchanged by the welfare system.

Public assistance benefits for the aged, blind, and disabled were markedly improved over the last decade as the growth of social security and private pensions held down the case load and made reform possible. The Supplemental Security Income program that combined these categorical efforts established a federal floor under benefits and reduced geographic eligibility differences.

Aid to Families with Dependent Children has been the center of controversy. The tripling of caseloads and the quadrupling of costs between 1965 and 1972 was alarming to some, as was the subsequent failure to achieve welfare reform. In retrospect, however, the process was neither incomprehensible nor inimical. AFDC benefits were raised substantially to provide most recipients, in combination with in-kind aid, a standard of living approaching the poverty threshold. With liberalized eligibility rules and more attractive benefits, most low-income female-headed families were covered by the welfare umbrella in the early 1970s. Once this had occurred, the momentum of growth slowed.

The welfare explosion did have side effects. No doubt some recipients chose welfare over work as benefits rose above potential earnings. In part, welfare freed mothers from low-paid drudgery to take care of their families. Moreover, the difficulties of placing even the most employable and motivated recipients in jobs paying adequate wages suggested the limited options for the majority of clients. As benefits stabilized in the 1970s, the increase in real wages promised to reduce the attractiveness of welfare to unskilled workers.

The welfare system's bias against families with a male head offered some inducement for nonmarriage or desertion. In cases where AFDC provided a higher or steadier income than male family heads could earn, the costs of broken families had to be balanced against the benefits of improved living standards. The stabilization of real benefits and the rise in real wages should, over time, diminish the inducement to break up homes.

The income support system, including social security, veterans' programs, unemployment insurance, workman's compensation, public assistance for the aged, blind, and disabled, AFDC, and near-cash programs such as food stamps, is incredibly complex. Yet "messiness" is inevitable where needs are multifaceted and where goals clash. Concentrating aid on female-headed families yields high target efficiency, since these families have the most severe needs and fewest options, but undesirable results are unavoidable. High marginal tax rates may discourage work, but they also tend to keep down costs and to help the most needy. Benefits may be too high in some areas and too low in others, but on the average they are close to poverty levels and geographic differentials are declining. Most families receiving multiple benefits have severe or special needs.

The income maintenance system is thus functioning reasonably well. The developments that seemed chaotic and dysfunctional have created a system within sight of assuring at least a poverty threshold standard of living for all citizens through a combination of cash and in-kind aid.

Health Care

The Great Society went far toward eliminating the main concern of the aged and a major problem of the poor—health care. Medicare and Medicaid have generally fulfilled President Johnson's promise of assuring the "availability of and accessibility to the best health care for all Americans regardless of age, geography or economic status."[3]

Medicare experienced early difficulties in striving for a balance between assuring adequate services and avoiding overutilization. Problems were associated most frequently with innovations. For instance, extended care was initiated as an alternative to longer hospital stays but became a subsidy for nursing home care until corrective measures were taken. Overly long hospital stays were shortened through a variety of utilization review methods. Perhaps to quell fears that government intervention would mean government control, Medicare may have displayed excessive generosity in considering the desires of doctors and other vested interests. After problems emerged, however, steps were taken to cut the fat from the system.

Medicaid remains an object of much criticism because of its rapid and unexpected growth. The scapegoats were overutilization and inefficiency, but quite clearly the basic cause was the explosion of AFDC. By the early 1970s the momentum of growth had already subsided as the eligible universe was reached and measures were taken to discourage overutilization and waste. Being tied to AFDC, Medicaid shared the geographic inequalities of that system, with even greater disparities resulting from the extension of aid to the medically indigent not on welfare in only some of the states. Yet these inequities were reduced over the years as more open-handed states cut back on frills while the tight-fisted ones became more generous.

3 Congressional Quarterly, *Congress and the Nation*, p. 665.

Medicare and Medicaid contributed to the rapid inflation of health care prices in the late 1960s. But supply did expand and reallocation occurred. The price rises pinched middle-income families and those at the margin of eligibility, and significant inequities were created, providing cogent arguments for a more comprehensive health care system. But with limited resources, those most in need (as defined by individual states) are generally being helped. Attempts to blame Medicare and Medicaid for the alleged (and very questionably documented) failure of our health care system are misplaced and even critics must admit these programs' effectiveness in performing their basic missions.

Housing

Low-income housing programs provide obvious benefits to participants. Subsidies reduce the strain on limited budgets, and the shelter is far superior to what participants could otherwise afford. The long waiting lists and low vacancy rates argue that poor people value these programs, notwithstanding the drawbacks associated with project housing.

There are secondary benefits. Publicly assisted units have helped to suburbanize low-income minority families. The courts have used these subsidy programs as a lever for countering residential segregation. Other lesser accomplishments of the programs include increasing the stability and long-term economic status of some families, organizing and delivering services using housing as the nexus, and experimenting with new industrialized construction methods.

Most significantly, however, the housing programs have built new homes for the poor. Construction yields a tangible, lasting product, permitting some control over location and quality. Building specifically for the needy tends to soften the low-rent and low-cost housing market, rather than waiting for the trickle down of increased production resulting from aid to the more affluent. Housing is as good an investment for the government as it is for private individuals in the present inflationary environment; and in a construction slump, increased assisted housing production can provide a needed stimulus to the economy.

The real issue is not the benefits, but rather the costs. Assistance programs are expensive because they house larger numbers of people who cannot afford to contribute much to their maintenance. Subsidized units are more expensive when they are built in high cost areas or according to high standards, or when they are subject to union wage or minority contracting requirements. The government has been bilked at times like any other buyer, but the exposés of the early 1970s exaggerated the extent of such violations. The new housing programs introduced in 1965 and 1968 needed to be refined and administered more carefully and changes were introduced to correct the abuses. A housing allowance, the panacea of the Nixon administration, is certainly worth considering, but the payoffs of direct production should not be ignored in deciding on the best course.

Education

Learning is difficult to define or measure and the relationship between educational inputs and outputs is uncertain. Hence, there is little conclusive evidence that intensified efforts on behalf of disadvantaged students have improved their cognitive and social development or that educational gains yield long-run benefits.

The limited and very early evaluations of Head Start indicated that statistically significant improvements in achievement were washed out later when students returned to an "unenriched" environment. Evaluations of Follow-Through suggested that the gains could be sustained, and even more optimistically, that the programs improved with experience. Though these conclusions are all very tenuous, early childhood education is a societywide phenomenon. Given the underlying societal premise that school is worthwhile for younger children, it is sound public policy to concentrate resources on those most in need.

The effectiveness of elementary and secondary education programs for the disadvantaged is equally uncertain. Early studies were not encouraging but more recent findings suggest notable successes. This may reflect the fact that the programs have improved. Compensatory education resources were initially diverted for noneducational purposes and for nondisadvantaged students, but tightened controls have reduced waste and misallocation. Until proven otherwise, there is reason for guarded optimism about the current overall impact of the effort.

Federal aid for higher education can stand on its demonstrated merits. The value of the sheepskin has been documented. The test of success is whether resources are concentrated on those most in need, whether their college attendance has increased, and whether they are able to continue until graduation. By these standards, there has been a high measure of success.

Manpower Services

Training, education, counseling, placement, work experience, and other manpower services can improve the attractiveness of disadvantaged workers to employers and can help open doors to better jobs. Evidence suggests that participants improved their wages and job stability. Further, the value of projected future earnings increments exceeded the average cost of the programs. Society's investment in human resources has been profitable.

Institutional vocational training has been most carefully studied, and the findings indicate beneficial effects despite the usually short duration and a frequent absence of linkages to subsequent jobs. On-the-job training has an even greater payoff as measured by benefit/cost studies because the participant is able to earn while learning and usually is guaranteed employment upon completion.

More intensive remedial efforts such as the Job Corps have had mixed success. The Job Corps has not demonstrated that the average street-hardened youth can be rehabilitated by six or nine months of intensive aid in a specially structured center; the program has shown, however, that at least some will seize the opportunity and benefit substantially. The assertion that the disadvantaged are trapped by their backgrounds or by labor market realities is subject to all-important exceptions and modifications. Many can be helped, and even if the improvements are only moderate, on the average, they are well worth the effort as long as better proven options are unavailable.

Civil Rights

One of the primary aims of the Great Society was finally to secure the fundamental rights of blacks. Along with its impressive legislative record, the administration exerted its leverage in the marketplace and its power as a rule setter while the courts expanded the government's responsibilities and prerogatives. The Nixon and Ford administrations were less forceful, some critics argue. Nevertheless, the stalling points such as employment quotas or busing to end de facto segregation were far different from those of the early 1960s when the rights, rather than the corrective measures, were being debated.

The salutary effects of these civil rights advances were not difficult to ascertain. Black registration and voting increased, with a visible payoff in office holding. Equal employment opportunity efforts had little direct effect in the 1960s, but the screws were tightened considerably in the 1970s. De jure school segregation was largely eliminated and busing to achieve racial balance became widespread despite fervent opposition in some cases and repeated efforts in Congress, with administration prodding, to proscribe busing as a weapon in combating segregation. Fair housing machinery provided legal backing for some victims of discrimination, but little leverage to overcome patterns and practices was included in housing acts or administrative decisions.

While attention was focused on racial issues, there were other areas of advancement. At the beginning of the 1960s, recipients or potential recipients of governmental aid were dependent on the whim and caprice of government bureaucracies. Antipoverty legal efforts established the principle of due process under social welfare programs and pressed the notions of equal protection and welfare as a right, chalking up some noteworthy victories in overturning the man-in-the-house and state residency restrictions.

The neighborhood legal services program was a vital tool in combating poverty, establishing new rights through law reform as well as providing traditional legal aid. Suits on behalf of clients against state and local governments got the program into political hot water. However, since the courts decided most cases in favor of the poor, the program was criticized for its effectiveness and not for its shortcomings.

Community Action

Maximum feasible participation—an ill-defined and much maligned goal—was a basic approach of the Great Society. The aim was to give minorities and the poor a degree of organizational power in order to change institutions, to protect their interests, and to design innovative strategies to serve themselves. Community action agencies, model cities, concentrated employment projects, neighborhood health centers, and community development corporations, though no more participatory or democratic than other groups in our society, had the express purpose of representing the needs of the poor. In doing so, it was necessary to step on firmly entrenched toes, and this generated antagonism, as did efforts to bring about institutional change. Friction was an inevitable ingredient in the process, and though new community leaders sometimes made a virtue of antagonizing the establishment, conflict was mainly rhetorical. Community groups initiated a number of innovative approaches and were condemned for the waste and high failure rate implicit in experimentation. Yet many of the seeds bore fruit locally and nationally.

The community-based programs defy rigorous assessment because of their diversity, but the more narrowly focused efforts can be compared with alternative approaches. Neighborhood health centers, for instance, provided care at roughly the same cost as established institutions. The quality of care was equal, but accessibility and amenability were greater. Health centers used paraprofessionals and took other steps to reach out to those in need, increasing the level of usage. Community development corporations were no more successful in establishing viable businesses in poverty areas than other establishment-run efforts, but the CDC's helped organize the neighborhood and generated short-term employment and income for the poor.

Improving the Status of Blacks

As a result of Great Society civil rights and other initiatives, blacks made very substantial gains on a number of fronts during the 1960s. The purchasing power of the average black family rose by half. The ratio of black to white income increased noticeably. The Great Society's efforts were instrumental in generating advancement. But relative black income fell during the 1971 recession and did not recover subsequently.

Earnings were the primary factor in the income gains made by blacks, although income support and in-kind aid also rose. Blacks moved into more prestigious professional, technical, craft, and secretarial jobs previously closed to them. Earnings rose absolutely and relatively as discrimination declined. Sustained tight labor markets, improved education, manpower programs, and equal employment opportunity efforts all played a role.

The improvements in schooling were dramatic and consequential. Black preschoolers were more likely to enroll than whites, largely because of federally financed early education programs. High school completion increased significantly and compensatory programs provided vital resources to the schools where black youths were concentrated. At the college level, absolute and relative enrollment gains were dramatic, the direct result of government aid programs.

Economic and social progress was not without serious drawbacks. Dependency increased, the black family was buffeted, and already high crime rates accelerated. Without minimizing the negative spillover, there is clear proof that blacks were far better off before the advent of the economic slump than a decade earlier. There is a long way to go to equality and progress has been uneven, but advances have been made.

Fighting Poverty

While the war on poverty was not unconditional, it was more than a mere skirmish. The Economic Opportunity Act programs were only one—and not the primary—front in this assault. The Great Society's economic policies, which combined tight labor markets with structural measures such as minimum wages and manpower programs, helped the employable poor. Welfare, social security, and in-kind aid focused on persons with limited labor market attachment.

The number of poor declined sharply in the 1960s then leveled off. The early declines were achieved by raising the income of the working poor, and their place was taken by female heads with little opportunity for self-support. The combination of deteriorating labor markets, declining numbers of working poor, and accelerating family breakups caused poverty to level off despite the fact that the government's antipoverty expenditures continued to rise in the 1970s.

The continuance of poverty does not mean government efforts have been ineffective. In 1971, 43 percent of the otherwise poor were lifted out of poverty by income transfers, compared with 30 percent in 1965. In-kind aid and services going to the poor are not included as income in the poverty measurements, yet they cost more than the cash poverty deficit. If victory in the war on poverty means providing the minimal standard of living, then the war has very nearly been won, though some battles remain to be fought.

Achieving Full Employment

The economic setting is a crucial determinant of social welfare policy. The Great Society's expanding efforts could be afforded, despite the drain of the Vietnam war, because of the healthy growth dividend. Manpower development, equal employment opportunity, and economic development efforts worked best in a tight labor market. Inflation and rising unemployment in the 1970s increased needs and at the same time reduced society's ability to pay. A fundamental question is whether economic growth and full employment can be achieved through governmental action.

It is ironic that in the economically troubled 1970s the successes of the 1960s were quickly forgotten and even condemned. The Johnson administration placed highest priority on achieving rapid growth and low unemployment. It succeeded, and prices rose slowly (at least by mid-1970s standards). The Nixon and Ford administrations acted on the premise that added joblessness was necessary to combat inflation and to provide a foundation for measured growth. Unemployment rose precipitously and growth declined, but prices continued to rise rapidly. Common sense would suggest that something was being done right in the 1960s, which was not in the 1970s, and prudence would caution against accepting the claims of policy makers and economists anxious to pass the buck for their own dismal record. Common sense would also question the effectiveness of the strategy of combating inflation by increasing unemployment.

The charge that the Great Society's excesses were the primary cause of the mid-1970s economic difficulties does not square with the facts. Needed restraint was not exercised during the last few years of the Johnson administration and inflationary pressures built up. It is entirely possible that the end-of-the-decade recession could have been moderated or even avoided with more timely action. The Nixon game plan was to let the recession run its course and clamp down on spending. But as the 1972 elections approached, a choice was made to spur the economy. Excessive stimulation and the decontrol of wages and prices led to inflation. The international oil and food crises then continued to push up prices while a combination of governmental restraint and international recession dramatically increased unemployment. The Great Society might be blamed for contributing to the 1969–1971 slump, but subsequent policies have missed the mark far more and, together with international events, must bear the blame for the deepening malaise.

The theoretical basis for shifting blame has always been suspect, suggesting a sophisticated witch hunt more than sound analysis. Apologists for the 1970s recessions have argued that there is a natural rate of unemployment. Demographic changes in the labor market have allegedly raised the potential equilibrium so that unemployment of 5 percent or higher must be accepted. Pushing the aggregate rate below this level in the 1960s, it is claimed, set off a price explosion. The statistical evidence for these assertions is rather shaky at best, and it certainly cannot justify the massive joblessness that prevailed in the mid-1970s. To dismiss structural measures such as manpower training, public employment, and economic development as if the public policy trade-offs were set in concrete is merely to ensure that they will be. The Great Society's structural programs were not of a scale to change things dramatically, but they were certainly steps forward.

Defeatism about reducing unemployment goes back to the 1950s when similar arguments led to a lengthy period of stagnation. The Great Society demonstrated that a tight labor market could be achieved and maintained for many years. The nation has paid dearly for continuing to ignore this lesson.

Redistributing Income

The money income shares of the highest and lowest quintiles are not much different now than at the outset of the Johnson administration. The aim of the Great Society was not a large-scale redistribution of income, but rather the opening of opportunities for those at the end of the line so that they could gradually pull themselves up. Meanwhile it attempted to provide minimal income, goods, and services for all citizens. From 1960 to 1973, total government social welfare spending rose by 5 percentage points of GNP and needs-based aid by less than 2 percentage points. This was certainly a modest effort at redistribution through direct transfers. The subsequent recession lowered GNP while raising transfers, but the lower income quintiles lost ground relatively because they were hardest hit by the loss of jobs.

Offsetting the recession-related increase in inequality, federal taxes have become more progressive, leaving the poor a larger proportion of income. The continuing expansion of payroll taxes has been detrimental to the working poor, but the burden was alleviated by raising the tax base more than the tax rate and by altering the benefit formula to make it more redistributive. Tight labor markets are unquestionably the most effective redistributive mechanism. Low unemployment in the 1960s, combined with boosts in the minimum wage, helped those at the end of the labor queue. Conversely, the subsequent recession hurt them most.

Much was made in the late 1960s of the squeeze on middle-income families. The culprit was the slowed growth of real earnings and not redistribution of income. During the Great Society, the gains of the poor were achieved by reducing the share of the rich, but the rich were still better off in absolute terms as aggregate GNP grew rapidly. The Nixon administration claimed to champion the forgotten Americans, but its tax and transfer policies did little to improve their status.

THE CANONS OF GAINSAYERS

A combination of shifting fashions among opinion makers and limited analysis of the facts seems to be responsible for the attacks on the Great Society not only by its opponents, but also by many of its former champions and even its beneficiaries. To assess the effectiveness and value of diverse and complex social welfare endeavors, a judgmental framework is needed. Determinations of statistical significance begin with the articulation of an hypothesis. Using some standard of proof, the evidence may then be tested to ascertain whether contradictions are too frequent to allow acceptance. In assessing performance, one hypothesis would be that a program works, demanding contrary evidence of failure. The converse would be to assume failure and require proof of effectiveness. Different results can be obtained from these different hypotheses when measurements are imprecise and proof equivocal. If clear evidence of success is demanded to discount an assumption of failure, then a positive verdict is unlikely; while if absolute failure must be demonstrated to alter the assumption of success, a more positive judgment is inevitable.

What is the most reasonable hypothesis? A primary consideration must be the danger of drawing the wrong conclusion. Almost all social welfare efforts provide benefits to those who would be worse off without them—extra nutrients, a roof that does not leak, more cash, or preventive health care. To conclude that these goods and services are unnecessary, less important than others which could have been acquired with the same funds, or ineffectively delivered, runs the risk of seriously affecting the welfare of recipients if conclusions are wrong. It may also become the basis for retrenchment or counterproductive change. In evaluating social welfare efforts, the small monetary costs to each citizen must be weighted against the possibly severe losses to particular individuals in need. In considering programs with altruistic goals, the compassionate approach is to assume success until failure is reasonably demonstrated. Critics have frequently stressed economy over compassion.

Questionable Standards

Besides basing judgments on negative hypotheses, critics have applied a number of other questionable standards supportive of their gainsaying. One sure way to support a negative case is to measure the real against the ideal. In support of revenue sharing, for instance, the ideal of a politically accountable and locally adaptable decentralized and decategorized system was compared with the realities of categorical federally run efforts with their inherent administrative complexities. Yet where revenue sharing was tried, it did not significantly alter either adaptability or accountability, while the loss of federal control had some negative consequences.

New and experimental efforts will usually come up wanting when compared to long-standing programs. Most Great Society endeavors got underway in 1965 or later, yet their failure was being trumpeted by the late 1960s on the basis of evidence drawn from the first few years of operation. A longer time period encompassing the evolution of the more successful approaches, the retrenchment of the less successful, as well as the implementation of needed reforms, is required to get an adequate perspective.

Secondary and nonquantifiable goals were frequently ignored, biasing judgments against multipurpose programs. The Great Society efforts usually had multiple aims: to deliver goods and services but also to achieve institutional change, to maximize help for the disadvantaged, and to improve the status of minorities. These were not usually as efficient as programs whose sole purpose was service delivery, but they had more positive spillovers.

While the positive secondary effects of programs frequently were ignored, the negative secondary effects were often in the spotlight. Opponents and threatened interests were quick to seize on incidents of gross failure. Side effects were sometimes taken as proof of failure even when these were part and parcel of achieving the primary aims. For instance, programs redistributing resources by paying for the needs of the poor were blamed for raising prices, while efforts to supply goods and services directly were blamed for competing with alternative sources of supply which had demonstrably failed to provide for the same clients.

Critics applied contradictory standards to social welfare activities. Opponents railed against large or mounting costs as if these inherently demonstrated failure or else stressed the inefficiencies and exaggerated potential savings. Critics of the opposite persuasion focused on what was not being done—target groups who were not being served and benefits which were not adequate to meet minimal standards. The result was a discordant critical chorus of complaints against excessive spending and demands for expanded aid.

Dynamic processes often were ignored in the focus on the problems of the day. Few approaches are right for all seasons and many Great Society initiatives were dependent on rapid economic growth and low unemployment, becoming less effective in subsequent slack labor markets. Some approaches suitable in the early stages of development were inappropriate or unnecessary later. For example, categorical programs staked out new areas and after expansion set the stage for comprehensive reform. These reforms were pushed by emphasizing previous failures when, in fact, they were only feasible because of the successes in building up a foundation through categorical efforts.

Critics tended to use the tools and perspectives of economists, examining the equity and efficiency of existing arrangements, focusing on the pluses and minuses at the margin and implicitly accepting the status quo. Such emphases and methods, presumed to be purely objective and completely rational, were inherently biased. One of the most frequent charges against the Great Society's social welfare programs was their inequity. Geographic disparities and uneven treatment of client groups were inherent in building a system from the ground up. Variations in living conditions and values permitted only gradual standardization. Analysts frequently assumed that inequalities were necessarily inequitable and reprehensible, when in fact they stemmed from a decentralized approach to determining what was equitable.

Great Society programs were also criticized for inefficiencies. If a program aims to change institutions, to experiment with new approaches, or to let a hundred flowers bloom, then it is bound to be inefficient. Change is not an efficient process.

During the Great Society, social analysts and humanists balanced the views of the economists. The latter triumphed in the subsequent years (despite their dismal record in their own area of expertise) because they provided apparent rigorousness and raised the hard-nosed questions consistent with the Nixon and Ford administration philosophies. The result was a deemphasis of nonquantifiable ends, of social and economic change, and of dynamic rather than static analysis.

An Example of Negative Thinking

The critical fallacies are perhaps best illustrated in the critique of the income support system. The performance of welfare programs tended to be measured against an idealized comprehensive system devoid of inequities or inefficiencies, a system in which all those in need would be given cash aid without work disincentives and without any negative spillovers on family stability. Advocates of guaranteed income schemes tended to brush aside fundamental questions of work disincentives, the role of in-kind aid, the difficulties of altering disparities, and many other critical issues. The existing system was contrasted with and found deficient relative to an alternative which was unrealistic and unattainable, as the difficulties of reforming aid for the aged, blind, and disabled demonstrated.

Critics usually ignored constructive processes in their efforts to find fault with the welfare system. Over time, variations among areas were significantly reduced, standards were raised to near the poverty level, and most of the defined universe of need was reached, yet there was little recognition of these achievements in the debate over the welfare mess.

Critics overemphasized the negative spillovers on work and the family. As welfare standards approached or exceeded wages available to potential clients, some chose to stop or reduce work. While some left the labor market, the supply of workers was still excessive and unemployment rates for the unskilled remained at high levels. Although paid labor may have been reduced, it is still a presumption in our society that children are better off with a mother's care and supervision.

The income support programs have been judged by contradictory standards, criticized simultaneously for costing too much and doing too little. Conservative critics focused on in-kind and cash packages which exceeded prevailing wages in some states. Liberal critics focused on the benefits in other states which fell below subsistence levels. These groups joined hands briefly under the banner of welfare reform when conservatives were convinced that the extension of benefits to male heads was the only way to check the growth of AFDC. When the costs became apparent and growth slowed on its own account, there was a parting of company.

The influence of economists was predominant in the welfare reform debate. The work disincentives issue was argued in terms of trade-offs between lower marginal tax rates, income guarantees, and costs, glossing over the evidence that the 1967 changes which made work more profitable for those on welfare had resulted in almost no increase in work and that training and employment programs for mothers on AFDC accomplished little because jobs were not available. Focusing on the margin where work and welfare overlap, broader realities such as expanding help to increasing numbers of needy and consequent slowing growth were ignored.

Beyond the Welfare State

The "big gun" of critics, wheeled out to shore up weak arguments or when all else fails, is the specter of an all-consuming welfare state. However affluent, the nation cannot afford a continuous expansion of social welfare efforts at the rate of the previous decade. The extrapolation of the 1965–1975 trends led the critics to the inevitable conclusion that the rising welfare expenditures would lead the government to tax employed workers to the poorhouse in order to support idlers. But is such expansion ineluctable or needed?

The social welfare explosion during the previous decade resulted from rapidly rising benefit levels and expanded eligibility. There were millions of deprived persons who qualified for aid. Once they had been helped, the growth momentum slowed. By the mid-1970s, public assistance was reaching almost all the low-income aged, blind, and disabled, as well as most needy female-headed families. Health programs also treated most of the indigent. The food stamp program expanded rapidly to serve an increasing share of the eligible population once standards were liberalized in the early 1970s. After this rapid saturation process, the pressure for expansion eased. There was a distinct leveling off in 1973 and 1974.

Spending accelerated thereafter not because of expanding responsibilities and commitments, but rather because of the severe economic troubles. The combination of rapid inflation and the highest unemployment since the Great Depression forced millions to rely on their social insurance and swelled the number qualifying on the basis of need for in-kind and cash aid. There were no new initiatives on the order of Medicare and Medicaid, assisted housing construction, the war on poverty, or even an old-fashioned WPA-type program. Social welfare expenditures grew because social problems intensified, not because policy makers were openhanded. Real social welfare spending will in all likelihood recede or at least stabilize when the economy recovers.

Once a minimally adequate social welfare system is established, many of the problems which seem so insurmountable dissipate. As in any building process, most of the spillovers occur during early construction and these have already occurred. Many female family heads and disabled males withdrew from the labor force when offered alternative income options, and other low-income families split when welfare provided support for female-headed units. But once welfare levels stabilized in real terms and began to decline relative to earnings, caseload growth slowed and the impact upon work and family diminished. Over the long run, rising real earnings and stable or slowly growing welfare standards will increase the attractiveness of work and stable families.

Once a package of aid is provided that guarantees an income above the poverty threshold, improvements in the system should prove easier. Welfare reform floundered in the early 1970s because the costs of establishing an adequate minimum were too great and because some reformers were seeking retrenchment rather than improvement. Eliminating allegedly ineffective approaches proved difficult when their termination would have left former beneficiaries in greater deprivation. Once everyone in need is guaranteed a minimum, it will be easier to substitute one form of aid for another and to concentrate on program performance and effectiveness rather than on dividing too few loaves among the multitudes.

Work disincentives have been a continuing concern, but the problem cannot be attacked until a comprehensive system is in place. Aid to low-income male-headed families, even if packaged so as to maximize work incentives, will still leave some of the less motivated the means to avoid work. If unemployables are provided adequate support, some employables will find ways to qualify. But once the shock effects have been weathered, it will be possible to start improving work incentives without pushing down on the help offered to those who cannot work and to minimize the number of nonworkers by making available attractive jobs.

The choice between public or private provision of goods and services can be more easily resolved once the specter of deprivation is eliminated. As long as welfare standards are inadequate, social insurance programs are pressed into service as transfer mechanisms. Once everyone is above poverty thresholds, the scale and scope of transfer payments can be decided on relative merits rather than on the basis of pressing needs. Similarly the issue of relative versus absolute poverty standards can be addressed directly once a minimum is secured.

Each step we take forward makes the next one easier, while also opening new vistas and opportunities. As President Johnson put it, "The Great Society, is not a safe harbor, a resting place, a final objective, a finished work. It is a challenge constantly renewed, beckoning us toward a destiny where the meaning of our lives matches the marvelous products of our labors."[4]

Liberalism Upside Down:
The Inversion of the
New Deal Order

EVERETT CARLL LADD, JR.

A new class-ideology alignment has taken form over the past decade as part of the transformation of political conflict and hence of the American party system. Since the mid-1960s, there has been an inversion of the relationship of class to electoral choice from that prevailing in the New Deal era. Broadly interpreted, the New Deal experience sustained the proposition that liberal programs and candidates would find their greatest measure of support among lower-class voters and that conservatives would be strongest within the high socioeconomic strata. Now, in many although not all instances, groups at the top are more supportive of positions deemed liberal and more Democratic than those at the bottom. We also see some evidence of an emergent curvilinear pattern, with the top more Democratic than the middle but the middle less Democratic than the bottom.

Table 1 reviews the "classic" pattern of class voting as it persisted throughout the New Deal era and into the early 1960s. What had been well established as the "traditional" configuration held neatly for the several sets of groups represented in this table and indeed for all of the various socioeconomic groupings which we can locate with survey data. For example, 38 percent of whites of high socioeconomic status (SES) voted for Democratic nominee John Kennedy in 1960, compared to 53 percent for Kennedy among middle SES whites, and 61 percent of low SES white voters. By 1968, the relationship had changed

EVERETT CARLL LADD, JR., is professor of political science and director of the Social Science Data Center at the University of Connecticut. He is the author of numerous books and articles on American politics including *American Political Parties: Social Change and Political Response* and *Ideology in America*. This article draws upon and extends a line of anlysis from his latest book (with Charles D. Hadley), *Transformations of the American Party System*.

markedly. For the most part, the top gave the higher measure of backing to the relatively more liberal Democratic nominee than did the bottom. Humphrey was supported by 50 percent of high status whites under thirty years of age, but by only 39 percent of their middle SES age mates and by just 32 percent of young, low status electors. The newly emergent conformation was even clearer in 1972, when the somewhat distorting factor of the Wallace candidacy was removed. Among whites—for blacks continued to constitute a "deviating" case of voters disproportionately in the lower socioeconomic strata but overwhelmingly Democratic—those with college training were more Democratic than those who had not attended college; persons in the professional and managerial stratum were more Democratic than the semiskilled and unskilled work force; and so on. McGovern was backed by 45 percent of the college-educated young, but by only 30 percent of their age mates who had not entered the groves of academe. Comparing 1948 and 1972, we see a reversal of quite extraordinary proportions.

Table 1 also suggests, somewhat lightly, the emergence of a curvilinear relationship between class and support for relatively more liberal as opposed to more conservative candidates. McGovern was weakest within the middle strata: among whites holding positions as skilled workers; among women of middle socioeconomic status; among young people holding positions as skilled manual

TABLE 1

Democratic Percentage of the Presidential Ballots,
White Voters by Socioeconomic Position, 1948 – 1972

	1948	1960	1968	1972
All				
High SES*	30%	38%	36%	32%
Middle SES**	43	53	39	26
Low SES***	57	61	38	32
Women				
High SES	29	35	42	34
Middle SES	42	52	40	25
Low SES	61	60	39	33
Under 30 years of age				
High SES	31	42	50	46
Middle SES	47	49	39	32
Low SES	64	52	32	36
College educated	36	45	47	45
Noncollege	56	49	33	30

SOURCE: Data are from the following AIPO surveys: for *1948,* #430, 431, 432, 433; *1960,* #635, 636, 637, 638; *1968,* #769, 770, 771, 773; *1972,* #857, 858, 859, 860.
    * High SES includes persons having upper white collar and managerial occupations who have had college training.
    ** Middle SES includes persons having lower white collar or skilled manual occupations.
    *** Low SES includes persons having semiskilled and unskilled occupations, service workers, and farm laborers.

workers. On the whole, McGovern's strength was greatest among those of high status, lowest within the ranks of the middling strata, and somewhat higher again in the lower reaches of the socioeconomic distribution.

Some qualification is in order. While a massive transformation of the relationship of class in voting has obviously occurred, the old pattern has not been obliterated everywhere. If blacks are included, the lower socioeconomic strata still appear more Democratic than the higher cohorts. Even within the white population, some distributions from the 1968 and 1972 presidential contests show the top more Republican than the bottom—although in all cases by a margin markedly reduced from that of the New Deal era. The proportion of professional and managerial whites backing McGovern was 3 percentage points lower than that of blue-collar whites. However, comparing professionals alone (excluding businessmen) to manual workers, we find the former 4 percentage points more Democratic than the latter—the first time since the availability of survey data that this inversion has occurred. And for the first time in the span for which we have survey materials, the college educated in 1972 gave the Democratic nominee a higher percentage of their vote than did the noncollege population. So while there are some exceptions, depending upon how the high and low status publics are defined, an inversion of the New Deal relationship has indeed occurred.

Even though this inversion is most notable in presidential voting, the general *direction* of the shift is evident at other levels as well. In Table 2, we compare the congressional vote of the several socioeconomic strata for the elections of 1948, 1960, 1968, and 1972. The weakening of traditional class voting can be seen clearly, especially among young voters. In 1947, just 36 percent of high status voters under thirty cast their ballots for Democratic congressional candidates, as against 66 percent of their low status age mates—a margin of 30 percentage points between these two groups. By 1968, the direction was the same —with those of low status more Democratic than their high status counterparts —but the margin had shrunk to just 8 points. In 1972, even the direction had shifted, as 60 percent of the high status young, 53 percent of their age mates of middle status, and only 51 percent of those of low status, cast ballots for Democratic congressional contenders.

For some observers, the 1974 balloting showed the evanescent character of the forces that had contributed to inversion.[1] Yes, issues arose in the 1960s which divided the populace along new lines, different from those of the New Deal years, and thereby scrambled the old class-party relationships. But the conflict of the 1960s lacked staying power, according to this view, and it has faded as quickly as it once arrived. By 1974, issues running coincident with the basic line of cleavage of the New Deal party system had reasserted themselves:

[1] See, for example, James L. Sundquist, "Hardly a Two-Party System," *The Nation* (December 7, 1974), 582–586. Sundquist believes the 1974 electoral results support an argument he had developed previously in *Dynamics of the Party System* (Washington, D. C., 1973), that the New Deal alignment remains essentially intact.

TABLE 2

Democratic Percentage of the Congressional Ballots,
White Voters by Socioeconomic Position, 1948–1972

	1948	1960	1968	1972
All				
High SES	33%	46%	42%	48%
Middle SES	49	60	51	49
Low SES	63	66	55	54
Women				
High SES	35	41	42	48
Middle SES	49	57	49	45
Low SES	64	64	55	56
Under 30 years of age				
High SES	36	49	46	60
Middle SES	54	54	51	53
Low SES	66	59	54	51
College educated	42	51	46	55
Noncollege	60	55	52	53

SOURCE: Data are from the following AIPO surveys: for *1948*, #430, 431, 432, 433; *1960*, #635, 636, 637, 638; *1968*, #769, 770, 771, 772; *1972*, #857, 858, 859, 860.

as soon as Vietnam, race questions, and the social issue gave way to class questions and issues of governmental intervention in the economy, the existing party system [that of the New Deal] took on meaning once again. In 1974, the questions were whether people were going to have jobs, whether their wages would keep pace with the prices in the grocery story, whether oil company projects were too high, who was going to bear the brunt of inflation and of taxes. These aroused class feelings. . . . Sensing that they were threatened, people of traditional Democratic leanings turned instinctively to *their* party. . . .[2]

This argument contains a large element of truth—and a fundamental flaw. It fails, in the first instance, to account for what actually happened in the 1974 voting. Examining the data in Table 3, we see that the Democrats *did* do exceptionally well among low status voters. Working-class whites, who had deserted McGovern (although not the congressional Democrats) in 1972, overwhelmingly endorsed Democratic candidates for House and Senate, and those running for lower offices, in 1974. Economic worries, together with a Watergate reaction, did in fact submerge the social and cultural issues that were so prominent between 1964 and 1972.[3] Even in this time of economic woe, however, when the economic dimension of conflict loomed larger than it had in the preceding years, there was no return to the class-party relationship of the 1930s and 1940s, even to that which persisted into the early 1960s. The Democrats

[2] Sundquist, "Hardly a Two-Party System," p. 385.
[3] Gallup has provided survey confirmation of this. See *The Gallup Opinion Index*, 113 (November 1974), especially pp. 1–2, 29–31.

did not do as well among whites of high socioeconomic status in 1974 as among low status whites but, considering the circumstances, they came remarkably close.

The contrast between the 1974 vote distributions and those of 1964—the great congressional landslide a decade earlier—is sharp. The Democrats did no better among middle to lower status voters in 1974 than in 1964, in fact they did not do quite as well, but they bettered their performance markedly within the high status cohorts. While conditions in both elections evoked memories of the New Deal—some said Goldwater wanted to repeal it, and some felt we were entering anew in 1974 the situation that precipitated it—there was no reappearance of class voting in the more recent of the two contests. The "distance" between high and low status voters, immense in 1964, was modest a decade later. Indeed, where noncollege whites under thirty years of age were 18 percentage points more Democratic than their college age mates in the former election, there was no difference at all between the vote of these two groups in 1974.

Nothing in the above commentary offers any comfort to the Republicans. They were badly—almost identically, in the overall percentages—beaten in the 1964 and 1974 congressional contests. The 1974 results actually seem a bit more gloomy for the GOP, since the party lost even its old base among high status voters, a base which had remained relatively secure in the general Goldwater rout. It is essential to note that the Republicans lost *differently* in 1974 than during the New Deal era. The "old New Deal coalitions" were not put back together in the 1974 balloting. Indeed, the only thing that 1934 (or 1964) and

TABLE 3

*Democratic Percentage of the Congressional Ballots,
White Voters by Socioeconomic Position, 1964 and 1974*

	1964	1974
All		
High SES	48%	57%
Middle SES	65	62
Low SES	74	67
Women		
High SES	44	60
Middle SES	64	61
Low SES	74	68
Under 30 years of age		
High SES	50	66
Middle SES	70	68
Low SES	74	73
College educated	53	69
Noncollege	71	69

SOURCE: Data are from the following AIPO surveys: for *1964,* #697, 699, 701, 702; *1974,* #915, 916.

1974 appear to have in common is that Democratic congressional candidates trounced their Republican opponents on each occasion. Can anyone seriously describe a contest in which Democrats secured the support of two-thirds of young college-trained, professional and managerial white voters as a "New Deal type" election?

We have here a basic element in the disruption of the New Deal alignment. In the party system that Franklin Roosevelt built, the top had been decisively more Republican than the bottom. A structure of class voting was erected, remained intact, and became "natural." It was natural in the context of the social group composition and political agenda of the industrial state. It is in no sense natural in postindustrial America. Among its other dimensions, the contemporary party system transformation comprises an inversion of the old class relationship in voting, an inversion first evident at the presidential level but likely to penetrate the entire range of electoral contests where broad policy issues can intrude. The performance of liberal—often but not always Democratic—candidates at the top of the socioeconomic ladder increasingly is approaching, and even surpassing, that at the bottom.

REPUBLICAN WEAKNESS AT THE TOP

The coin, one side of which is proportionally increased backing for liberal, and thereby often Democratic, candidates among the upper social strata in the United States, has a second surface. Support for conservative, often Republican candidacies within the higher status groups has markedly declined.

Before the New Deal, the Republicans were the party of the American "establishment," although that term was not applied then to the dominant business interests. Even during the New Deal period, the GOP remained the establishment party, in the sense that it held the loyalties of disproportionate numbers of people among those groups who controlled major social institutions, notably the economy. With entry into the postindustrial era, however, two related developments have eroded this Republican position. The *composition* of the establishment has changed with the ascendancy of new political classes, principally of a broad professional stratum—or with substantial overlap and a somewhat different perspective, a massive new intelligentsia. Apart from this altered composition, the ideological proclivity of large segments of the establishment has experienced a major shift.

The Republicans' hold on that loose array of groups and interests which might be said to exercise disproportionate influence in the society has slipped. The intellectual community has grown in numbers and importance. But the Republican position has grown weaker, not stronger, within it. There has been, we know, a long-standing tendency of intellectuals generally to be critics, and of American intellectuals to be socially critical from a liberal perspective.[4] So the

[4] For extensive analysis of this subject, see by Everett Carll Ladd, Jr., and S. M. Lipset, *The Divided Academy: Professors and Politics* (New York, 1976).

GOP, as the more conservative party, has long had good reason not to expect the intellectual community to be one of its strongholds. Still, intellectuals are a variegated group, and they are for the most part among the advantaged rather than disadvantaged segments of the populace. During the New Deal era, there was substantial Republican support within the intellectual stratum. Over the last two decades, this support has declined. In 1948, for example, college faculty were only 6 percentage points less Republican than the electorate generally. The 1972 Republican professorial vote, however, was 18 percentage points below the Republican vote within the electorate at large.[5]

Data on the politics of college students show a similar progression. S. M. Lipset has noted that Harvard University students, generally more liberal and Democratic than their counterparts at other campuses around the country, were solidly Republican in presidential preference up until the 1960s. The respectable straw polls conducted by the *Harvard Crimson* indicated that Thomas Dewey was the choice of 56 percent of the Harvard student body in 1948, while just 25 percent favored Truman. In 1952 and 1956, Adlai Stevenson demonstrated considerable appeal in Harvard Yard, but he still ran behind Eisenhower in the universitywide student balloting. It was not until 1960 that a Democratic presidential nominee was recorded as the choice of a majority of Harvard students, when the *Crimson's* straw poll found Kennedy securing about three-fifths of the student vote. In the elections of 1964, 1968, and 1972 the Harvard student body, so solidly Republican during the New Deal when Harvard alumnus Franklin D. Roosevelt was the popular Democratic standard-bearer, supported the Democratic presidential nominees by overwhelming margins.[6] Harvard is certainly part of the American intellectual establishment—a training ground for so many of the top leaders of government, business, science, the arts, and culture. Throughout the New Deal, its student body was Republican. By the 1970s, Harvard students have become strongly Democratic.

While the absolute distributions are different from campus to campus, the student population of the 1930s and 1940s had been generally Republican, following the normal class distributions of the time: groups of higher socioeconomic status tended to be Republican, and college students were drawn largely from the middle and upper middle classes. During the Eisenhower years, too, students were solidly Republican in presidential politics, supporting Eisenhower by

[5] For further data and explanation of faculty voting, see Everett Carll Ladd, Jr., and S. M. Lipset, *Academics, Politics and the 1972 Election* (Washington, D. C., 1973), chaps. 3 and 4. See, too, by the same authors, *The Divided Academy*, chap. 9.

[6] For a discussion of the Harvard student straw vote historically, see S. M. Lipset, "Political Controversies at Harvard," in Lipset and David Riesman, *Education and Politics at Harvard* (New York, 1975), chap. 8. There have been changes in the social group composition of the Harvard student body since World War II, of course, but these are not sufficient to account for the partisan shift. The representation of blacks has increased, but blacks remain less than 10 percent of Harvard students. The proportion Jewish is about the same now as in 1948. Harvard students are still an enormously privileged group, in terms of social background, compared to the public at large.

much greater margins than did the general public.[7] By the late 1960s, however, the national college student population was decisively Democratic—or, more precisely, heavily anti-Republican, since large numbers of students were self-described independents consistently voting against Republican presidential nominees. Gallup found a marked drop in Republican allegiance among students continuing during the late 1960s and early 1970s. In 1966, 26 percent of college students described themselves as Republicans, 35 percent as Democrats, and 39 percent as independents; by 1970, Republican identifiers in the student population had declined to 18 percent, compared to 30 percent self-described Democrats, and a massive 52 percent independents; and in 1974, the Republican proportion was at an all time low of 14 percent, as against 37 percent Democratic, and 49 percent in the independent category.[8] Among graduate students, an almost unbelievably low proportion of 9 percent identified with the GOP, while 43 percent thought of themselves as Democrats, and 48 percent as independents.[9] A 1972 CBS election day survey found 54 percent of students in the eighteen to twenty-four age category voting for McGovern, 16 points higher than the proportion among the public at large.[10] Gallup reported in October 1972 that 68 percent of graduate students planned to vote for McGovern, compared to just 31 percent for Republican incumbent Richard Nixon.[11]

These current distributions are really quite extraordinary. Not only are college students an important component of the intelligentsia, but from their ranks will come the bulk of the leadership of the principal institutions in the United States. When only 14 percent of all students and just 9 percent of graduate students profess an affinity for the Republican party, the extent of the latter's decline—and even more, the scope of its potential decline—among the principal political classes becomes evident.

The position of the GOP is even bleaker than these data suggest. Among students at major colleges and universities, Republican electorate support falls below that within the general student population. For both faculty and students, the most prestigious and influential—and most affluent—sectors are the most solidly Democratic.[12]

What we have noted for students and faculty and other segments of the intellectual community applies in all essential regards to the higher and ascendant socioeconomic strata in the United States generally. Data on partisan identification and congressional vote from the New Deal through to the present demon-

---

[7] For supporting data, see S. M. Lipset and Everett Carll Ladd, Jr., "College Generations: From the 1930's to the 1960's," *The Public Interest*, no. 25 (Fall 1971), 105–109.

[8] *The Gallup Opinion Index*, no. 109 (July 1974), 15.

[9] Ibid.

[10] CBS News Election Day Survey, data made available to the Social Science Data Center, University of Connecticut, courtesy of CBS News.

[11] *The Gallup Opinion Index*, no. 88 (October 1972), 3.

[12] For supporting data and analysis, see Ladd and Lipset, *The Divided Academy*, chaps. 5 and 9.

strate clearly the dramatic decline of Republican backing among the higher status cohorts.

In Figures 1 and 2, we compare the Democratic and Republican proportions of party self-identification and congressional vote throughout the New Deal era and into the contemporary period, for three groups of high socioeconomic status, all of which have expanded greatly as the society has moved into postindustrialism. The college educated, people employed in professional occupations, and young whites of high socioeconomic status—defined as the college educated employed in professional and managerial positions—are not the only representations of the high socioeconomic strata and the intelligentsia which we could make, but they faithfully illustrate developments occurring in the larger stratum.

One basic fact comes through with absolute clarity from the data presented in these two figures: groups of high socioeconomic status were solidly Republican throughout the New Deal era; sometime in the late 1950s and early 1960s there was a pronounced move toward the Democrats. In 1964, for the first time, Democrats outnumbered Republicans (in terms of self-identification) throughout many high SES cohorts, and majorities of these groups backed Democratic congressional candidates. While there was some temporary falling off in Democratic support among these groups immediately after 1964, the overall secular progression has not been interrupted. Substantial portions of the high socio-

FIGURE 1

Percentage Point Difference (+, More Democratic; - , More Republican) in the Party Self-identification of Selected Social Groups, 1940–1974

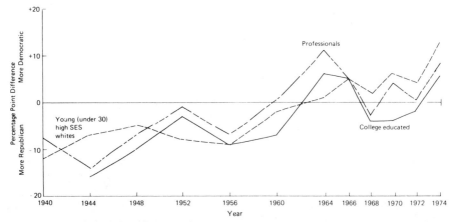

SOURCE: Data are from the following year AIPO surveys: for *1940,* #208, 209; *1944,* #328, 329; *1948,* #430, 431, 432, 433; *1952,* #506, 507, 508, 509; *1956,* #572, 573, 574, 576, *1960,* #635, 636, 637, 638; *1964,* #697, 699, 701, 702; *1966,* #724, 729, 737; *1968,* #769, 770, 771, 773; *1970,* #814, 815, 816, 817; *1972,* #857, 858, 859, 860; *1974,* #889, 897, 899, 903, 906.

FIGURE 2

Percentage Point Difference (+, More Democratic; –, More Republican) in the Congressional Voting of Selected Social Groups, 1940–1974

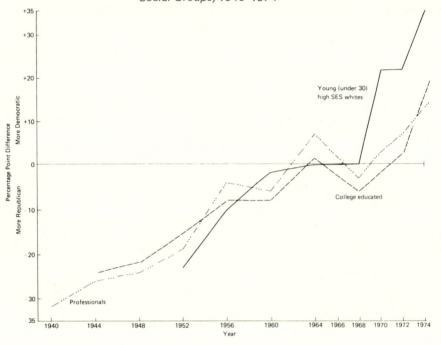

SOURCE: Data are from the following AIPO surveys: for *1940,* #208, 209; *1944,* #328, 329; *1948,* #430, 431, 432, 433; *1952,* #506, 507, 508, 509; *1956,* #572, 573, 574, 576; *1960,* #635, 636, 637, 638; *1964,* #697, 699, 701, 702; *1966,* #724, 729, 737; *1968,* #769, 770, 771, 773; *1970,* #814, 815, 816, 817; *1972,* #857, 858, 859, 860; *1974,* #889, 897, 899, 903, 906.

economic strata in the United States are consistently displaying absolute Democratic majorities in both self-identification and congressional balloting.[13]

Particularly ominous for the long-run prospects of the GOP is the disaffection of young high status whites. During the New Deal era, this group was solidly, indeed massively, Republican. By the mid-1970s, it has become solidly, massively Democratic. These voters will grow older, of course, and perhaps become relatively more conservative, swinging somewhat toward the Republicans, apart from what happens as a result of changing issues and changing party positions. But Figures 1 and 2 make clear that we are dealing with a long-term secular shift, not simply an artifact of Watergate. The Republicans have lost their

[13] Not all high SES groups show Democratic majorities, of course. People in the very highest income groups—over $25,000 a year—and business executives, still display Republican majorities, although the extent of the GOP advantage has been reduced even here.

grip on the American establishment, most notably among young men and women of relative privilege.[14]

The partisan changes thus far described have their origins within broader social and political transformations. Three interrelated arguments form the explanation: (1) The composition of the several broad social classes or strata has changed, and so has their social and political character. (2) The thrusts and meanings of liberalism (and, of course, conservatism) have been altered. (3) Because of this, the high SES cohorts (as now composed) are much more liberal (as now defined) than were their counterparts of times past. Indeed, they often act as the primary sustainers of what now commonly passes as liberalism. This is evident in candidate and party support, as noted, but can be seen as well in stands on issues.

Let us look first to class composition. Enterpreneurial business has largely passed from the scene. It is no longer a major interest collectivity. Managerial business remains an important stratum. But it experiences peculiar fracturings which could not have been contemplated in earlier periods. Increasingly large segments of the broad new upper middle classes, of the professional and managerial community—primarily those at once the most affluent and secure and most closely associated with advanced technology—cease to function as defenders of business values. More to the point, they cease to think of themselves as "business" in the historic sense. They become incorporated into a rising "new class," the intelligentsia, responding to intellectual values and orientations rather than those traditionally associated with business.[15] At the same time,

[14] Some commentators have insisted that the inversion of the New Deal class-idology relationship carried with it great opportunities for the Republican party, along with the problems noted above. No one has advanced this argument more persistently and forcefully than conservative journalist Kevin P. Phillips. Large segments of the old working class have in the post-World War II years become middle class and supportive of conservative positions—although not of old-style business conservatism. As the GOP lost ground in an increasingly liberal establishment, it could have more than compensated for its losses by inroads into the massive new bourgeoisie. The populism of the New Deal had a conservative establishment to attack and was directed to the support of liberal programs and policies. The populism of the late 1960s and 1970s, confronting instead a liberal establishment, has led to neoconservative policy responses. But the Republicans have blown this "ideological opportunity of a generation." They have lost ground at the top and have failed to gain in the middle. Phillips, "The Future of American Politics," *National Review*, 24 (December 22, 1972), 1398. See as well his *Mediacracy: American Parties and Politics in the Communications Age* (Garden City, N. Y., 1975). My own views on why the GOP has failed to achieve any widespread, persistent advance as a result of the inversion cannot be covered within the limits of the present article.

[15] Public opinion analyst Louis Harris has drawn upon his survey data in developing one aspect of this argument. Noting that in postindustrial America, "at the key executive level, more people [are] employed in professional than in line executive capacities," he stresses the finding that "the one quality that divided most professionals from line executives in business organizations was that professionals felt much more beholden to their outside discipline—

parts of the business community, especially those linked to newer enterprises and the top managers, continue to promote business values and reflect relative conservatism.

The intelligentsia, dramatically enlarged, operates as a distinctive social and political class of postindustrial America. It expresses powerful commonalities. Its members are generally secure in their affluence. More importantly, they share contact with intellectual activity—which does not mean, of course, that they participate in high culture or advanced intellectual pursuits—through that extraordinary nexus of 2500 colleges, 8.8 million college students, 600,000 professors, 900,000 artists, authors, and editors. They are linked by a communications network of unparalleled scope and pervasiveness, an instrument of technology (e.g., television) and wealth and intellectual sophistication.[16]

When we identify upper status groups in the contemporary United States—whether in terms of high educational attainment, the holding of "professional or managerial" occupations, high income, or any combination of such variables—we are not locating primarily a "business class" in the 1930s sense. The upper strata have expanded, become more diverse, assumed a new social coloration.

At the same time, "working class" has taken on a quite different social and political character than it held in the 1930s. Most members of the urban working class were economic "have nots" in the 1930s, who either experienced immediate economic privation or operated with precious little margin over subsistence needs. As such, they supported government-directed changes in the economic order. And the trade union movement, which gathered momentum in the 1930s, organized this "have not" working class and served as one of the principal new claimants for economic betterment and security and influence. These objectives were in large measure attained though governmental intervention and economic growth. The unionized labor force has moved up the socioeconomic ladder. For this group, the victory over economic privation has been won. Producing a wonderfully American semantic contradiction, this segment of the *working class* has become (lower) *middle class...*

The head of the American labor movement, AFL-CIO president George Meany, has spoken insightfully to the transfiguration of labor's place in the postindustrial era. In a 1969 interview with *The New York Times*, Meany was willing to accept both "middle class" and "conservative" as descriptions of the membership of the labor movement.

---

whether it be systems engineering, teaching, scientific research, or other professional ties—than to the particular company or institution they worked for." *The Anguish of Change* (New York, 1973), p. 45.

[16] College training, an experience shared by more than 35 million Americans, defines the outer boundaries of the intelligentsia. I use *intelligentsia* to include those persons whose background and vocation associates them directly in the application of trained intelligence. It includes, that is, not only intellectuals—people involved in the creation of new ideas, new knowledge, new cultural forms—but also that larger community whose training gives them some facility in handling abstract ideas, or whose work requires them to manipulate ideas rather than things.

Labor, to some extent, has become middle class. When you have no property, you don't have anything, you have nothing to lose by these radical actions. But when you become a person who has a home and has property, to some extent you become conservative. And I would say to that extent, labor has become conservative.[17]

A working class that is middle class and conservative—that is a distinctive feature of the contemporary social structure.

The Meanings and the Objectives of Liberalism

Americans have imposed one more obstacle in the path of intelligent public discourse of political matters by an insistence upon using *liberal* and *conservative* with several different meanings. First, the entire United States political tradition is described, quite appropriately, as liberal. This usage brings to mind Louis Hartz's great book, *The Liberal Tradition in America.* Liberalism here is a body of ideas associated historically with the emergent middle classes of the seventeenth and eighteenth centuries. It stands in opposition to classical conservatism—the defense, again historically, of aristocratic norms, values, and institutions. In the New Deal era, liberalism came into common usage with a quite different meaning.[18] Liberals were those who favored a major expansion of intervention by the state, the shift of responsibility for guiding the society from the private (chiefly business) sphere to the public sector. State intervention was on behalf of new beneficiary groups, notably the industrial working class. In this context, conservatives were those who continued to hold to the desirability of the old "business nationalism," those who opposed the New Deal state.

Now, *liberal* and *conservative* are receiving other applications. We are told, for instance, that Senator Henry Jackson is of the "conservative wing" of the Democratic party—although Jackson's liberal credentials are impeccable in both the classical and the New Deal senses of the term. Lewis Coser, Irving Howe, and their associates write of "the new conservatives," in whose intellectual ranks they place such as Nathan Glazer, Norman Podhoretz, and Daniel Patrick Moynihan.[19] They recognize explicitly that the perspective in question does not resemble business conservatism. The new conservatives are not New Deal conservatives. Rather, they are New Deal liberals who have come to emphasize a "limits of politics" approach as a result of being seared by public failures of the past decade. Although there is a good bit of disagreement at the level of specifics, there is fairly widespread agreement on a general usage of *conservatism* which encompasses people who, while remaining faithful to New Deal liberal

[17] "Excerpts from Interview with Meany on Status of Labor Movement," *The New York Times,* August 31, 1969.

[18] Samuel H. Beer, "Liberalism and the National Idea," *The Public Interest* (Fall 1966), 70–82.

[19] Lewis A. Coser and Irving Howe (eds.), *The New Conservatives: A Critique from the Left* (New York, 1974).

tenets, draw back from certain contemporary facets of social change and extensions of the idea of equality.

All of the basic understandings of *liberal* and *conservative*, of course, revolve around equality. The latter concept historically has received varying interpretations, has been taken to require different public policies. The "beneficiary groups" have thus changed, and so have the "contributory groups." Liberals are in some sense partisans of the idea of equality, but the idea has been taken to mean different things and so the liberal ranks have shifted.

Much of the working class has become *bourgeois* and behaves as the bourgeoisie has historically—anxious to protect a status achieved at considerable effort and often tenuously held. The thirst for change which characterized this stratum in the New Deal era has been quenched by the affluence of the last three decades. Many of the current pressures for equalitarian change, moreover, ask for sacrifices from the lower social strata. In contrast to the 1930s, when policy innovation often involved efforts by the working class to strengthen its position vis-à-vis the business strata, some of the most tension-laden areas where equalitarian change has been sought over the past decade have found the white working class (or lower middle class) and the black underclass confronting each other. More secure in their position, less threatened by such quests for societal transformation, typically residing some distance from the "front," the upper social strata have come easily to a more change-supportive posture.

The equalitarianism of the New Deal tended to be majoritarian in terms of its targeted beneficiaries. The contemporary variety is minoritarian, and often asks more of the middle-to-lower strata than of the top.

The dominant concerns or objectives of equalitarianism have shifted. Representative of the current emphasis are the busing of school children to achieve higher measures of racial integration, a rejection of the "equality of opportunity" definition of the egalitarian society with stress instead on "equality of result," and heightened concern over extensions of civil liberties, notably the rights of the accused. The beneficiaries of such commitments on the whole are quite different from those of New Deal equalitarianism.

Even in the area of domestic social spending, lower-middle income cohorts have moved in striking fashion toward contributor status; at the same time, the relative contributor burden of upper income groups has expanded more modestly. Public expenditures for health, education, and welfare have grown at an extraordinary rate over the past two decades—from $49.9 billion in 1953 to $410.5 billion in 1975, an increase of over 800 percent in current dollars and just under 400 percent in dollars of constant (1975) purchasing power. (Over the same span, military expenditures jumped 240 percent in current dollars and just about held even in constant dollars.) This major growth in domestic spending has been sustained in part by increases in the effective tax rate. And for those families earning incomes around the national median, the rise has been much steeper than for upper-middle and upper income families. Those at the median experienced a *doubling* of the proportion of their income going to taxes between 1953 and 1975, compared to a *50 percent* increase among families with incomes two to four times the median.[20] Families earning four times the median in 1953—about $20,000—paid 20.2 percent of their income in taxes, while those at the median paid 11.8 percent; twenty-two years later median income families were taxed 22.7 percent of their income, while the rate for those earning four times as much had climbed more slowly, to 29.5 percent.

Trying to sum up the meaning of these data, David Broder commented that it is "no wonder there is a tax revolt in this country."[21] It might be more appropriate to draw the following conclusion: no wonder there is an inversion of the New Deal class order. The top does not pay a much higher share of its income in taxes than does the lower middle, even though it has much more of a cushion, and the burden of an expanding role for the state has in one sense been borne disproportionately by the lower-middle cohorts.

Social policies may be described as liberal on grounds that they employ the state for objectives widely perceived as equalitarian. But the equalitarian thrust may in fact be modest, and what there is of it may not be majoritarian in terms of beneficiaries. Furthermore, such policies need not make any special demands on privileged minorities. If they are modestly equalitarian and at the same time define contributors as the many rather than the few, they may come to be perceived by a large segment of the upper strata as "good buys"—that is, supportive of values, such as basic system stability, which the upper status cohorts can appreciate, at a reasonable price.

Liberalism in the mid-1970s has a different mix of beneficiaries and contributors than it did in the 1930s. Its programmatic thrusts have changed. This is another part of the explanation for the inversion of the New Deal class order, but again it is incomplete. A strict self-interest calculus is useful. It is important to recognize that high status Americans, as a group, have a greater "interest" in liberalism than did their counterparts four decades earlier. There are other dimensions, however, which the self-interest calculus does not capture. The most important element involves the role, and the measure of autonomy, of ideology. The political beliefs and orientations people hold are not simply products of their most proximate interests.

In the contemporary setting, the more prosperous strata are in fact frequently the most demanding and sustaining of social and cultural change, rather than the most resistant to such changes. The crude Marxist model suggests just the opposite, of course—that real conflict is economic, between the rich and the poor, with the rich generally satisfied and the poor at least intermittently dissatisfied and producing demands for change. But in an affluent society, with classical economic tensions muted, a new set of relationships and precipitants is introduced. Just as much of the working class has come to think like a bour-

[20] Advisory Commission on Intergovernmental Relations, *Significant Features of Fiscal Federalism—1976 Edition*, Part I (Washington, D. C., 1976).

[21] David S. Broder, "The Shift in Spending and Taxes," *Washington Post*, August 4, 1976.

geoisie, so substantial numbers of higher SES Americans have been brought into the intelligentsia. As such, they share in at least some of the critical, change-demanding orientations long associated with intellectual life.

One of the first to write with some precision about this phenomenon—of Marx being stood on his head by the new cleavages, of the blanketing of old tensions, the rise of the white working class to middle-class standing, the detachment of much of the upper middle class from traditional business concerns and their incorporation into the intelligentsia—was the sociologist C. Wright Mills. Fifteen years ago, Mills made light of "some New Left writers" who clung fiercely to the notion of the working class "as *the* historic agency" of social change, labeling their fixation upon workers "a legacy from Victorian Marxism."[22] Under some historical conditions, to be sure, industrial workers have operated as "a-class-for-themselves," and have served as the decisive instrument for change. But such conditions were not present in the United States. Instead the intelligentsia was emerging as the primary lever.

Entry into the contemporary era involves the placing of a wide range of new issues on the political agenda. In particular, there are important shifts occurring with the introduction of new value configurations. An affluent, much more highly educated, more leisured public casts off many of the older norms and standards of behavior. The survey work conducted by Daniel Yankelovich and his associate offers a more precise indication of the rapid circulation of new moral norms including more liberal sexual attitudes, a weakening of automatic respect for established authority structures, a decline of "old fashioned" patriotism; changing orientations toward work, marriage, and family, and the relative importance of material achievement in defining success; and a heightened concern with individual self-fulfillment and expression.[23] Not surprisingly, since the transition to the new social setting and the new value configurations is very recent, conflict arises as some sectors sustain while others oppose the emergent value structure. In this conflict pattern, age and socioeconomic position are the most important differentiating variables. The young, less socialized into the value structures of the old order, become for better or worse more receptive to the new; and within each age cohort, higher SES groups, more exposed to bodies of ideas encouraging change and experimentation and inclining to the perspective that the old is often unnecessarily narrow and restrictive, give a larger measure of backing for the new life styles and mores than their counterparts of lower socioeconomic status.

In general, support for elements loosely grouped under "new life styles and values" has become incorporated in the new liberalism. And it has come much

---

[22] C. Wright Mills, "The New Left," in a collection of Mill's essays, *Power, Politics, and People*, edited by Irving Louis Horowitz (New York, 1963), p. 256. The piece was first published in the *New Left Review* (September–October 1960).

[23] Daniel Yankelovich, *The New Morality* (New York, 1974).

more from the higher than from the lower social classes. Has there been any
period in which the culturally avant-garde has been a lower class or petit bourgeois phenomenon? Cultural experimentation by the upper classes is not new.
The size of the upper classes *is* new, as is the boldness of their assault on older
values and life styles. A broad array of issues now dominate the political agenda
around which the upper social groups are "naturally" more change supporting
than the lower middle and working classes.

There is another, quite different, ideological component of the inversion. It
has become progressively easier for groups of high socioeconomic status to support policies of the kind described above because the old ideological objections
to intervention by the state have been so greatly weakened. The upper classes
of the New Deal years opposed the interventionist programs of the Roosevelt
administration not only because they saw threats to their ascendancy and economic costs in the programs but also because they *believed* that private solutions
were intrinsically preferable to public ones. Philosophical disagreements over
the proper scope of government were deep and widespread.

The American establishments have long since abandoned this view. While
some people still oppose the prevailing levels of governmental intervention as a
matter of principle, Lowi was broadly correct when he argued that "statesmen
simply no longer disagree about whether government should be involved. . . .
Once the principle of positive government in an indeterminable but expanding
political sphere was established, criteria arising out of the very issue of principle
itself became irrelevant."[24]

During the New Deal era, it was possible to distinguish people who thought
of themselves as liberals from those who described themselves as conservatives
rather sharply by their attitudes on the size and scope of government. In 1964,
"the size of government issue split the population along classical liberal/con-
servative lines."[25] That year, 25 percent of the liberals said government was
too big, the position also held by a massive 71 percent of the conservatives. In
1968, continuing to follow views on this issue through University of Michigan
Election Study data, Nie and Andersen found that the direction of the relationship remained the same but its strength had begun to decline. By 1972, there was
no longer any difference between liberals and conservatives as to the size of
government, with 57 percent of the former and 60 percent of the latter taking
the position that government was "too big." This is not to suggest that self-
described liberals and conservatives took the same view on the range of public
issues. In fact, policy differences proved exceptionally sharp. But mass publics
along with the "statesmen" to whom Lowi referred are no longer divided in any
coherent ideological fashion on the question of the size and scope of government.

[24] Theodore Lowi, *The End of Liberalism* (New York, 1969), pp. 67, 57.
[25] Norman H. Nie with Kristi Andersen, "Mass Belief Systems Revisited: Political Change
and Attitude Structure," *The Journal of Politics*, 36 (August 1974), 556.

THE SCOPE OF THE INVERSION

An examination of survey data reveals the extent to which high socioeconomic groups in the United States now stand "to the left" of the middle to low status cohorts, and the broad policy range over which this applies. However "high socioeconomic status" is defined, members of the category appear more socially critical, more supportive of cultural change, more inclined to extensions of the idea of equality than the lower strata. This relationship is clear and unambiguous among whites. Black Americans are an exception—disproportionately in the lower socioeconomic strata and at the same time very highly supportive of change. The long history of discriminatory treatment to which blacks have been subjected readily explains their generalized aversion to the status quo and their generalized commitment to extending equality. All of the following survey distributions are for the white population only, in order to bring into sharper focus the inversion which has occurred there but which is not yet widely evident in the black community.

In the 1930s, 1940s, and 1950s, high SES cohorts in the United States were more conservative in a rather consistent fashion than the middle and low status groups. The former were more inclined to describe themselves as conservatives and to reject parties and causes labeled "liberal"; they were generally more opposed to programs associated with New Deal liberalism. The high strata were more internationalist than the middle and low cohorts, and they displayed a somewhat greater sensitivity to civil liberties causes, but on the whole their relative conservatism was clear.[26] This normal New Deal configuration involving policy stance carried over into the early 1960s. For example, in 1964 Gallup asked his national sample which way they would like to see public policy move: "go more to the Left . . . or go more to the Right."[27] Of professionals, 42 percent picked "Left," the position of 59 percent of blue-collar workers. Of those employed in professional and managerial jobs and college educated, 33 percent said "go more to the Left," as against 55 percent of unskilled workers. In the civil rights area, high status whites had begun by 1964 to show somewhat greater sympathy with black demands than low SES whites, but even here the differences were not large. The question of whether blacks should stop demonstrations "now that they have made their point," for example, found professionals and trade unionists taking almost identical positions.[28] As recently as 1966, questions like the legitimacy of employing the death penalty for persons convicted of murder yielded minimal differences among whites by social and economic status: 40 percent of professionals and 46 percent of the college edu-

---

[26] For further data on the policy orientations of Americans by their socioeconomic position, see Everett Ladd and Charles Hadley, *Political Parties and Political Issues: Patterns in Differentiation Since the New Deal* (Beverly Hills, Calif., 1973).

[27] AIPO Survey No. 702, November 18, 1964.

[28] AIPO Survey No. 699, October 6, 1964.

cated, compared to 41 percent of blue-collar workers and 41 percent of unskilled workers indicated they favored the death penalty.[29]

Over the last ten years, however, a shift of considerable magnitude has occurred. It has been as rapid a break from the past as it has been extensive. In most policy areas, whites in the higher socioeconomic status categories have become decisively more liberal than the middle and lower cohorts. There are exceptions in economic policy, but even these are being reduced and removed.

The symbol *liberal* is much more in favor at the top than at the bottom. In 1970, 35 percent of whites in professional and managerial jobs described themselves as liberals, the position of just 18 percent of unskilled workers.[30] In the spring of 1975 the National Opinion Research Center found 41 percent of college graduates calling themselves liberals, compared to 35 percent of those with some college, 21 percent of high school graduates, and 22 percent of persons with less than a high school education.[31] Yankelovich has reported that 25 percent of Americans with incomes over $25,000 a year (1974) accept the designation liberal, as against 18 percent of those earning $5000 or less.[32]

On questions involving race relations it is much the same. In 1968, Gallup found 64 percent of professionals in favor of "open housing" legislation, compared to 37 percent of skilled workers and 32 percent of whites in semiskilled or unskilled manual labor positions.[33] Busing to achieve school integration was endorsed in 1975 by only a distinct minority of Americans, but the proportion was nearly twice as high for college graduates as for the grade school educated.[34] At the time, 28 percent of those with less than high school education, but only 19 percent of college graduates, argued that the country was spending too much to improve the condition of black Americans.

Other, "newer" extensions of equality find much more sustenance among upper status groups. In 1972, 62 percent of professionals, in contrast to 41 percent of manual workers, expressed support for the position that men and women should have an equal role "in running business, industry and government."[35] The idea that there is "too much concern with equality" was rejected strongly in 1974 by 25 percent of those earning $25,000 or more a year but by only 16 percent of persons with incomes under $5000; by 28 percent of the college educated but by just 15 percent of the grade school educated.[36]

Matters involving cultural change and new life styles, which have crowded into the agenda over the past decade, show some of the largest differences be-

[29] AIPO Survey No. 729, May 17, 1966.
[30] AIPO Survey No. 815, October 7, 1970.
[31] NORC General Social Survey, 1975.
[32] Yankelovich, Skelly, and White, Survey No. 8400, March 1974.
[33] AIPO Survey No. 769, September 24, 1968.
[34] NORC General Social Survey, 1975.
[35] University of Michigan, Center for Political Studies (CPS), 1972 Election Survey.
[36] Yankelovich, Skelly, and White, Survey No. 8400, March 1974.

tween the top and the bottom. The argument that abortion "is morally wrong and should not be legally permitted" was rejected without reservation by 69 percent of college-educated Americans in 1974, compared to 41 percent of high school graduates and 27 percent of persons with less than a high school education.[37] Of respondents from families with annual incomes of $5000 or less, 66 percent strongly agreed that the government should "crack down more on pornography," a position taken by only 18 percent in the $25,000 and higher cohort.[38] About half of the poorest Americans, in contrast to just one-third of the richest, strongly believe that too much permissiveness is hurting the United States badly.[39]

Even in domestic economic policy, there has been movement toward an inversion of the old class relationships, although it has not moved as far as in the social and cultural arenas—for the rather obvious reason that people of middle to low socioeconomic status in many instances remain beneficiaries of ameliorative economic legislation. In 1972, 46 percent of professionals indicated they favored increasing the tax rates for people with high incomes, while a slightly higher 48 percent of blue-collar workers took this position.[40] In the spring of 1973, 67 percent of professionals and a slightly smaller 64 percent of blue-collar workers asserted that the country was spending too little "on improving and protecting the nation's health."[41] Also, 51 percent of manual workers and a higher 59 percent of professionals argued that we are spending too little on programs to solve the problems of the big cities.[42] The argument has been made that too many dollars that should go for social welfare programs have been channeled into the defense budget. But the 1972 CPS study and the 1974 and 1975 NORC surveys show the high SES cohorts more in favor of cutting the military budget than their low SES counterparts, though the former remain generally more internationalist.[43]

Among grade school trained Americans, 74 percent, as against just 66 percent of college graduates, profess strongly that "the right to private property is sacred."[44] And 29 percent of our poorest citizens, but only 18 percent of our richest, think that "in the past 25 years, the county has moved dangerously close to socialism."[45] The proportion among the grade school educated who favor more governmental regulation of business is exactly the same as it is among the college educated.[46] It is hard to find much of the working-class awareness and

---

[37] Ibid.
[38] Ibid.
[39] Ibid.
[40] CPS 1972 Election Survey.
[41] NORC General Social Survey, 1973.
[42] Ibid.
[43] CPS 1972 Election Survey; and NORC General Social Surveys, 1974, 1975.
[44] Yankelovich, Skelly, and White, Survey No. 8400, March 1974.
[45] Ibid.
[46] Ibid.

marked antipathy for business which characterized distributions in New Deal years.

Political opinions are complex things. Rather modest changes in question wording can shift responses significantly. Exceptions can surely be found to the pattern outlined above. But the growing conservatism of lower class whites vis-à-vis the upper social strata is shown clearly in scores of recent surveys.

CONCLUSIONS

Over the last decade, a decisive inversion has taken place in the relationship established during the New Deal of class to sociopolitical commitments. The high social strata now consistently provide a greater measure of support for liberal programs and candidacies than do the lower strata. This is no temporary phenomenon. No return to the New Deal pattern should be expected. The sources of the inversion lie buried deeply within broad transformations of the society and its political conflict. An understanding of the inversion yields more general insights into the character of contemporary politics.

What we now call liberalism frequently makes the old New Deal majority contributors rather than beneficiaries. Lower-status whites more often feel threatened than encouraged by current extensions of equalitarianism. There has been a significant *embourgeoisement* of the working class. The high socioeconomic cohorts, which had such a distinctive business coloration in the 1930s (and earlier), have changed their social and political character—notably through the growth of the professional stratum. Such developments are central to the inversion described herein.

Nothing in the above requires that the Democrats always find more support at the top than at the bottom. The relationship is between class *and ideology*. The top is more supportive of the new liberalism than is the bottom, and more inclined to the Democrats only when and to the extent that they are perceived as the partisan instrument of the new liberalism.

POSTSCRIPT

Can the inversion described above be seen in the 1976 balloting and, to the extent that it cannot, why not?

First it should be emphasized that the inverted relationship between class and ideology remains essentially unchanged. Various measures of opinion taken in the course of the 1976 campaign show high-status groups giving more backing than low-status cohorts to programs and policies associated with the contemporary statement of liberalism. And the former continue to show much more positive feeling than do the latter for the symbol *liberal*. To cite one illustration, a national poll conducted by NBC News in mid-September found 40 percent of respondents with advanced degrees calling themselves liberals, compared to 35 percent of those with undergraduate training, and just 22 percent and 23 percent respectively among the high school and the grade school educated.[47]

The effects of this relationship were sharply evident in the 1976 Democrat presidential nomination contest. Throughout the primaries, it was a case of the more liberal the contender, the greater the proportion of his overall support drawn from among people of high socioeconomic status. For example, the NBC News survey of Massachusetts Democratic primary voters found that "two candidates—Harris and Udall—seem to be competing at the liberal end of the party spectrum. Both men appeal to upper socioeconomic status voters in the suburbs."[48] Bayh and Shriver occupied intermediate positions, in terms of the perceived extent of their liberalism and the education-occupation-income status of their supporters. Jackson, Carter, and Wallace did best among lower-status Democrats. Other NBC News polls and those of *The New York Times*/CBS News located similar distributions over the winter–spring 1976 primary season.[49]

Various national surveys confirm these state-by-state findings adding, of course, a measure of overall precision. For example, the April 1976 study of Yankelovich, Skelly, and White shows the most prominent Democratic contenders thus arrayed by the self-defined liberalism or conservatism of their supporters (among Democrats and independents): Udall, who had the highest proportion of liberal and the smallest percent of conservative backers; Humphrey; Jackson; Carter; and Wallace, whose backers were decidedly the most likely to think of themselves as conservatives.[50] (The differences in the Humphrey, Jackson, and Carter voter profiles, it should be noted, are modest.) And the candidate array by the socioeconomic status of their adherents is largely the same. Thus 35 percent of the Udall people were from families where the head of household held a professional or executive position, compared to 26 percent of Carter's backers and 14 percent of Wallace's. An extraordinary 50 percent of those favoring Udall claimed to have completed at least three years of college, the status of 26 percent in the Jackson camp, 25 percent of those supporting Humphrey and Carter, and only 11 percent of the Wallace loyalists.

Much of the commentary immediately following the 1976 general election, however, carried an emphasis quite different from that of this article. It was as-

[47] NBC News, National Poll #55, September 16–18, 1976.
[48] NBC News, "The Election Newsletter," February 11, 1976.
[49] For reports on these surveys documenting the above conclusion, see Robert Reinhold, "Poll Finds Voters Judging '76 Rivals on Personality," *The New York Times*, February 13, 1976, pp. 1, 30; R. W. Apple, Jr., "New Political Universe," *The New York Times*, March 3, 1976, pp. 1, 17; Maurice Carroll, "Jackson Won in New York by Narrowly Based Voting," *The New York Times*, April 8, 1976, p. 30; and Robert Reinhold, "Poll Links Udall Strength to Low Vote in Michigan," *The New York Times*, May 20, 1976, pp. 1, 29.
[50] These data were made available by Yankelovich, Skelly, and White, and the author wishes to express his appreciation to Ruth Clark, vice-president of that organization. Democrats and independents in the April 1976 survey were asked: "If you had to make a choice among Jackson, Carter, Udall, Wallace and Humphrey as the Democratic candidate for the Presidency, whom would you choose?"

serted that Jimmy Carter's victory resulted from a restoration of "the old New Deal coalition"—most notably in a return of the older pattern of class voting. This argument contains a large element of truth—but it has been substantially overstated.

The differences generally in voting patterns between 1976 and, for instance, 1936 are massive. The South was a cornerstone of the New Deal Democratic majority and the region gave the 1976 Democratic nominee his core support. But an exceptional shift has occurred in the underlying structure. During the New Deal era as earlier, blacks were largely disenfranchised in the South and the region voted Democratic because an overwhelming majority of whites were so inclined. In 1976, even with a moderate white Georgian as the party's standard bearer, white southerners appear to have cast a majority of their votes for the Republican nominee.[51] The region went Democratic, then, because relatively recently enfranchised southern blacks returned a heavy Democratic majority.

During the New Deal years, Catholics were heavily and consistently Democratic, in keeping with a pattern of partisan loyalties stretching back to the age of Jackson. In 1976, however, Catholics split their vote evenly between Ford and Carter.[52] Protestants and Catholics voted almost identically in the 1976 presidential balloting—the first time in the period for which we have reliable survey data, and probably the first time in United States history that Catholics have not been notably more Democratic than Protestants.

Even on the matter of class voting, 1976 was hardly a typical New Deal election. According to the NBC election day survey, college students—still a relatively privileged group in social background—continued their recent Democratic ways. The national election day survey conducted by the Associated Press indicates that a large majority of college-educated Americans voted for Democratic House of Representatives nominees. Fifty-six percent of those with advanced degrees backed Democratic congressional candidates. While persons with a high school education or less were more heavily Democratic than the college-educated groups, the differences, according to the AP survey, were modest, on the order of 6 percentage points. The CBS election day survey found higher-income Americans (with family incomes of $20,000 a year and more) dividing 51–49, Republican and Democratic, in the 1976 congressional balloting. This is hardly the New Deal pattern. The movement toward an inversion noted in voting for U.S. House

[51] The *Times*/CBS News election day poll reported a Ford majority among white southerners. Working with these data, with data from the Associated Press election day poll, and with actual aggregate voting data from each southern state, I have concluded that Carter received a majority of the white vote only in Georgia, Arkansas, and Tennessee, among the eleven states of the old Confederacy.

[52] The various national surveys do not agree exactly on the distribution of the vote of Catholics. According to the Harris survey conducted just before the election (October 29–31), for example, Catholics broke 50–50. The *Times*/CBS News election day survey shows Carter with 54 percent of the Catholic vote. The Associated Press survey also indicates Carter won 54 percent of the Catholic vote. All of the major national surveys agree that the distribution was very close.

of Representatives candidates for the elections of the late 1960s and early 1970s was not reversed in 1976.

At the presidential vote level, there *was* a somewhat different pattern in 1976 than we saw in 1968 and 1972—and one more in keeping with the early 1960s. There was a fairly steady increase in the Ford proportion with movement up the socioeconomic ladder, however SES is measured. But any suggestion that class voting was as distinct in the 1976 presidential contest as in those of the New Deal years is, quite simply, wrong. There were clearer differences between high- and low-status voters in 1976 than in 1972 or 1968, but the high- and low-status groups were much less differentiated in 1976 than in the 1936–1948 period.

Louis Harris found, for example, that grade school-educated whites were about 14 percentage points more Democratic in 1976 than were their college-trained counterparts. Whites from families earning less than $5,000 a year were approximately 16 points more for Carter than were whites with family incomes of $15,000 and higher per year. Data made available from the election day "intercept" polls of the *Times*/CBS News and NBC News show similar distributions. In the 1930s and 1940s, by way of contrast, high- and low-status whites were separated by between 30 and 40 percentage points in presidential preference. Robert Reinhold, reporting on the *Times*/CBS News survey, noted a related facet of the secular diminution of class voting when he observed that "Mr. Carter succeeded in eating into groups that normally tend to vote Republican. For example, he did better among professional and managerial people than any Democrat in the last quarter century except Lyndon Johnson."[53] Actually, it could be extended to the last half century.

The 1976 Democratic presidential nominee over his long campaign attempted quite successfully to muffle the various social and cultural issues which have been transforming the meaning of liberalism. He did not seek to mobilize—indeed, he sought to avoid mobilizing—a distinctively New Liberal coalition. After eight years in the presidential wilderness and especially because of their overwhelming 1972 defeat, the Democrats generally were willing to follow Carter's lead and sheathed ideological knives in the interests of appeals at once more diffuse and more traditional in their economic emphases. So the 1976 balloting showed some backing away from the inversions of 1968 and 1972. But the relationship described involves, basically, *class* and *ideology*, and the 1976 political experience does not indicate any reversal of the long-term inversion this article has sought to treat.

[53] Robert Reinhold, "Carter Victory Laid to Democrats Back in Fold, Plus Independents," *The New York Times*, November 4, 1976, p. 25.

Monitoring the Block Grant Program
for Community Development

RICHARD P. NATHAN
PAUL R. DOMMEL
SARAH F. LIEBSCHUTZ
MILTON D. MORRIS

By and large, the social science community has not devoted much effort to implementation studies of major new federal programs. Longitudinal research on what happens to new laws once they are enacted requires not only a major investment of time, but, for a nation as large as the United States, a network of researchers equipped to tackle the multiple aspects of program impact. Once a new program is enacted, the tendency among social scientists has been to turn their attention to the next hot issue, rather than to conduct research on how well any given piece of policy fulfills its intended purposes.

This article reports on the highlights of an ongoing monitoring study by the Brookings Institution of the new block grant program for community development (CDBG). The Housing and Community Development Act which established this program was enacted August 22, 1974, as Public Law 93-383. The act authorized $8.4 billion to be distributed by the Department of Housing and Urban Development in the form of broad, flexible payments made by the federal government to qualifying local governments. The CDBG program took seven previ-

RICHARD P. NATHAN is a senior fellow and MILTON D. MORRIS is a research associate at the Brookings Institution. PAUL R. DOMMEL, associate professor of political science at Holy Cross College in Worcester, Massachusetts, and SARAH F. LIEBSCHUTZ, associate professor of political science at the State University of New York at Brockport, are consultants to Brookings. The four authors are participants in the Brookings Institution monitoring study of the community development block grant programs, of which Richard Nathan is the project director.

ously established federal assistance programs—urban renewal, model cities, water and sewer facilities, open spaces, neighborhood facilities, rehabilitation loans, and public facility loans—and combined them into a single new grant program.

FRAMEWORK OF THE LAW

Although CDBG funds are less restrictive as to their use than were the individual program funds, there are legislatively established substantive and procedural requirements. An application is required from each participating city and urban county,[1] including so-called entitlement cities which receive a formula allocation under the new system. Each application must contain a three-year community development plan, an annual community development program statement, and what the act calls a "Housing Assistance Plan" (HAP). "National goals" and permissible uses for funds, although quite broad, are outlined in the act. Public hearings and citizen participation are required. Priority must be given to activities that benefit families with low or moderate incomes.

Within this framework, an application can be disapproved by HUD only if the intended uses are, in the language of the act, "plainly inappropriate" to meet the stated needs and objectives or if the facts presented or the stated needs and objectives are "plainly inconsistent" with the known facts. If such disapproval is not made within seventy-five days of submission, the application is automatically approved.

THE MONITORING STUDY

The Brookings monitoring study, being conducted under a HUD research contract, contemplates two rounds of field research, each covering one year of experience under the new program. There are sixty-two jurisdictions in the sample, selected as a representative group of thirty central cities, twelve "satellite" metropolitan cities (not central cities) with populations above 50,000, ten urban counties, and ten nonmetropolitan jurisdictions. The sample represents 8.1 percent of all central cities in the program, 7.9 percent of all "satellite" cities, and 13.7 percent of urban counties. Sample jurisdictions are evenly distributed on a regional basis. They range in population from 9600 (Alma, Mich.) to New York City. In dollar terms, the sample accounts for 22.7 percent of all CDBG funds allocated in the first year of the program.

The study, like the parallel Brookings monitoring study of the general revenue

---

[1] An urban county is a county within an SMSA that (1) is authorized under state law to undertake community development and housing assistance activities in its unincorporated areas, and (2) has a total population of 200,000 or more, excluding the population of metropolitan cities within its borders and communities that specifically choose to be excluded from the urban county for CDBG purposes.

sharing program,[2] covers three main areas: (1) the uses and beneficiaries of CDBG funds; (2) the allocation of CDBG funds by generalist officials of local governments; and (3) the impact of the federal distribution formula.

First-Year Findings

The following points summarize the findings for the first year of the Brookings monitoring study of the CDBG.

1. The basic idea of the block grant appears to be working to the extent that its proponents sought to combine two principal elements—an emphasis on capital expenditures for community development and features to promote greater flexibility for recipient governments in determining their communities' needs and priorities.

2. Capital spending clearly predominated in the first-year allocations of CDBG funds. This involved a combination of new capital spending (in large measure for relatively short-term purposes) and the continuation of preexisting and long-range urban renewal projects.

3. Attempts were made by many jurisdictions to use block grant funds as leverage to secure private funds as well as other public funds. The leveraging effects that can be observed, however, are not large and are characterized by implementation delays. Housing rehabilitation is the largest functional area for combined public-private activities undertaken with CDBG funds.

4. Generalist officials, particularly chief executives, have played prominent roles in community development decision making, both on procedural and substantive matters. Their roles tend to be much more important under the block grant program than they were under the preexisting federal grant programs for community development, which in the case of urban renewal and model cities generally were administered by quasi-autonomous or independent local agencies or authorities.

5. Citizen participation, contrary to what some observers anticipated, has been a very significant feature of the program's implementation in the first year, especially in those cases in which local officials demonstrated a strong positive attitude toward these activities.

6. The CDBG program did not significantly contribute to the legislative objective of encouraging "spatial deconcentration" of housing for lower-income persons. In almost all of the sample sites, associates reported that local officials did not consider this objective in preparing their applications, and furthermore that the related requirements for a Housing Assistance Plan were not emphasized or consistently enforced.

7. A similar situation was found to apply to the "A-95" requirement for metropolitan planning and coordination, a clearance system closely related (or at

[2] The second volume on the Brookings monitor study on the general revenue sharing program has just been published: Richard P. Nathan, Charles F. Adams, Jr., and Associates, *Revenue Sharing: The Second Round* (Washington, D. C., 1977).

least potentially so) to the "spatial deconcentration" objective in the law.
Pro forma sign offs predominated under the A-95 requirement.
8. In relative terms the allocation system favors small and suburban jurisdictions; it disadvantages older and distressed central cities.

While our study generally avoids recommendations for program changes, we do suggest specific changes in the allocation system and show how they would affect major units entitled to CDBG funds. Two major types of changes, discussed later, are considered, a "dual formula" for the basic allocation system and supplemental CDBG grants, or "bonus" grants, for needy cities.

The Uses and Beneficiaries of CDBG Funds

Beyond the broad goals of developing "viable urban communities . . . , and a suitable environment . . . , principally for persons of low and moderate income . . . ," the Housing and Community Development Act of 1974 mandates no single most desirable usage of community development block grant funds, nor does it specify what combination of activities the funds should support. Within the broad parameters of the act, applicants and recipients have latitude to determine and implement their own programs for community development.

At this point, we can look at some specific examples of the impacts of the grants, first in two large cities.

In *Boston, Massachusetts* (population 641,000), the focus of the first year of the CDBG program was on neighborhood stabilization. The city received $32.1 million. Boston has high unemployment, a high property tax rate, and a recently reduced borrowing rating; it also faces a projected loss under the full CDBG formula. The city allocated a large portion of its grant to capital projects outside the former model cities and urban renewal areas. According to the field research associate, "There was an explicit desire on the part of the mayor's office to provide some visible artifact in each neighborhood of the allocation of these funds—street lights, parks, sidewalks, community facilities, trees." A spreading effect is reflected not only in spending for public facilities and improvements, which totaled about $6 million, but also for the $7.25 million housing rehabilitation program. Housing rehabilitation was carried out in neighborhoods throughout the city. Boston utilized a citizen participation strategy for CDBG focused on its eighteen "Little City Halls." The associate reported that in a mayoral election year this spreading effect for benefits could have been predicted. According to the associate, "The block grant budget presented an opportunity for the mayor to exercise his discretion and to distribute money his way rather than HUD's."

Pittsburgh, Pennsylvania (population 520,089), which received $16.4 million under CDBG in 1975, had extensive experience under the previous "categorical" grants, particularly in the urban renewal and model cities programs. Even before the advent of the block grant program, the city was in the process of phasing out these two programs, which officials viewed as "too expensive." According to the field research associate, city leaders, strongly committed to fiscal conservatism and the maintenance of a budgetary surplus, showed "a willingness to undertake only those programs of a capital nature that can be completed within a short period of time, and impose only the minimal and necessary operating cost to the city." The emphasis was on capital improvements rather than new facilities. With CDBG funds, improvements were made to existing recreational centers, playgrounds, swimming pools, and senior citizens' centers. No new facilities that could lead either to a long-term financial commitment or to continuing operating costs were included in the block grant applications. No new operations were undertaken with block grant funds. The underlying concern in the allocation of funds was twofold: (1) to avoid expanding programs beyond what could be accomplished entirely with CDBG funds so that, in the event the federal grant was suddenly withdrawn, the city would not be burdened with the cost of such programs; and (2) to prevent the further decline of good residential areas which were excluded under the old categorical grant programs.

Urban counties also receive grants under the block grant program for community development. In *Orange County, California* (population 1,420,386), the block grant had an especially important impact.

The Orange County administration had in recent years sought a more prominent role in coordinating the development activities of both incorporated cities and unincorporated areas. The CDBG program was found to have contributed to an increased role for county government. The county's administrative staff, especially the planning department, had been increasingly concerned about growth problems and limited opportunities to influence how incorporated cities respond to these problems. In the view of the field research associate, the CDBG program "for the first time gave county planners the opportunity to have leverage over the cities to force integrated planning and attention to the needs of the county's low- and moderate-income population." The county received $1.4 million for 1975.

Although Orange County qualified as an urban county with only the population of its unincorporated areas, the county government encouraged participation by the incorporated cities in a joint application. Responsibility for negotiating with the cities and preparing the county's application was assigned to the county planning department. A staff team from the department spent many weeks explaining the program to city officials and negotiating for their participation. The associate reported that "initially, many of the cities were reluctant to get involved in an application for federal funds, particularly HUD funds, which connote such things as 'integrated housing' and 'economic mixing.'" Ultimately, however, all seventeen cities with populations under 50,000 joined the county in the first-year application.

For its part, the county promised that in addition to passing on funds to the participating cities, it would undertake its own projects in unincorporated areas adjacent to participating cities. "It provided technical assistance to the cities needing it, and generally encouraged expenditures on activities likely to benefit low- and moderate-income groups."

Small cities, too, can receive block grants for community development, on a discretionary basis. For such units, the new program tends to operate in much the same manner as the earlier categorical programs. A good illustration of this is *Casa Grande, Arizona* (population 11,000).

Casa Grande's application for discretionary funds (it received $235,000 in 1975) was tailored to meet HUD area office demands. Although the city had hoped to be awarded aid for property acquisition and parks, the application was modified to include only capital spending for housing rehabilitation, which accounted for three-fourths of the first-year grant. According to the field research associate, "For all intents and purposes, the finally approved version of the application was perceived by the local officials to be categorical. The funds were new, to be spent for a limited purpose in accordance with federal directives and regulations. Although forms and procedures may be different, I can't see any meaningful difference between the process Casa Grande has gone through and any other categorical grant request. I know that it is the way local officials perceived the process." Although local officials would have preferred to share the benefits of this grant with all residents in need of housing assistance, HUD required the selection of a specific target area.

Under any law, the impact of federal funds on recipient governments is a central problem in the analysis of a grant program. Under a broad-gauged program, it is especially complex. Several questions necessarily arise. What differences do CDBG funds make in the expenditure and revenue decisions of recipient jurisdictions? How does federal assistance affect particular functions and programs? What is its impact on the economy of recipient communities and on different income groups?

Fiscal and Programmatic Effects

In analyzing fiscal effects, the field research associates were asked to answer a difficult question: What did CDBG funds enable recipient governments to do that they would not otherwise have done? An important aim of this analysis has been to identify how and to what extent CDBG funds have been used to pay for activities that would otherwise have been undertaken and paid for from other revenue sources. These so-called substitution effects occur under all types of fiscal subventions. The associates classified fiscal effects as new spending, program maintenance, and substitution effects, and the three categories were subdivided and defined as follows:

1. New spending effects

   a. New capital spending. Spending for capital projects or the purchase of equipment that, without block grant funds, would either not have occurred at all or would have occurred at least one year later.

   b. New or expanded operations. Operating expenditures initiated or expanded with block grant funds.

2. Program maintenance effects

   a. Community development program continuation. Allocating CDBG funds to ongoing programs formerly funded by grants now included in the CDBG program.

b. Continuation of noncommunity development federally aided programs. Allocating CDBG funds to ongoing programs formerly funded by grants not related to community development that, without block grant funds, would now be cut back or eliminated.

c. Other program maintenances. Allocating CDBG funds to ongoing programs formerly not federally assisted which without CDBG funds would now be cut back or eliminated.

3. Substitution effects

a. Increased fund balances. Allocating CDBG funds to ongoing programs, with the net effect of increasing fund balances.

b. Avoidance of borrowing. Substituting CDBG funds for borrowing that would have been undertaken in the absence of CDBG funds.

c. Tax stabilization. Using CDBG funds to finance existing programs, in order to avoid a tax increase that otherwise would have been necessary and approved.

d. Tax reduction. Using block grant funds to finance ongoing programs, in order to keep up the jurisdiction's own resources and thereby permit a reduction in the tax rate.

In contrast to general revenue sharing, new spending and program maintenance are far more prominent fiscal effects of the block grant program than are substitution effects. For the sample as a whole (sixty jurisdictions are included here), more than 53 percent of the first-year allocations were for new spending purposes, almost 32 percent were for program maintenance, and only 7 percent were for substitution effects. New capital spending and community development program continuation are the two largest fiscal effects for all types of recipients as shown in Table 1.

New capital spending was the biggest single net effect. In the fifty-five sample units that allocated funds for new capital purposes, spending for public facilities (for example, centers for health, recreation, and community activities) and for housing rehabilitation (both loans and grants) accounted for two-thirds of total new capital allocations. Fifteen percent was devoted to spending for public improvements (streets, sidewalks, and sewers) and 12 percent for property acquisition.

Looking at the new capital spending data in the aggregate, it is necessary to ask whether and to what extent these uses resemble the kinds of capital projects undertaken by the previous programs. Two general observations can be made. First, a focus on conservation and rehabilitation, rather than on land acquisition and new construction, emerges. Second, the location of these new capital uses indicates a distinct shift away from the typically more concentrated geographical pattern of the urban renewal program. These two findings are interrelated. The net result is that new capital spending under the CDBG programs tends to have a geographical *spreading effect*, particularly evident in plans for "neighborhood conservation programs."

TABLE 1

Net Fiscal Effects of CDBG Allocations in the Sample Jurisdictions,
by Type of Recipients,[a] in Mean Percentage Indices[b]

Fiscal Effect	Metropolitan Jurisdictions			Nonmetro-politan Juris-dictions	All Juris-dictions
	Central Cities	Satellite Cities	Urban Counties		
New spending	49.1%	52.9%	44.9%	74.0%	53.3%
New capital	34.8	33.3	27.2	57.9	37.1
New or expanded operations	14.3	19.6	17.7	16.1	16.2
Program maintenance	44.0	25.1	17.3	19.3	31.9
Community development program continuation	42.1	11.3	16.3	17.8	27.9
Noncommunity development federally aided program continuation	1.1	.2	1.0	c	.7
Other program continuation	.8	13.6	0.0	1.5	3.3
Substitution	3.4	16.7	5.9	4.3	6.6
Increased fund balances	2.4	5.3	2.5	0.0	2.6
Avoidance of borrowing	.7	10.0	3.1	4.2	3.5
Tax stabilization	.3	1.5	.3	.1	.5
Tax reduction	c	0.0	0.0	0.0	c
Other	c	0.0	1.5	0.0	.3
Unallocated	3.5	5.3	30.4	2.4	7.9

SOURCE: Field research data.

[a] For purposes of this table, the sample includes twenty-nine central cities, twelve satellite cities, ten urban counties, and nine nonmetropolitan jurisdictions. Two jurisdictions in the sample (Florence and Columbia, S. C.) are not represented because data from them were not available at the time this table was prepared.

[b] The mean percentage indices of fiscal effects are unweighted; that is, they are not weighted to reflect different population sizes of sample units.

[c] Mean percent index less than .1.

Income-Group Effects

There is a second and more difficult question for analysts of government programs: *Who benefits?* The block grant title of the Housing and Community Development Act of 1974 has something to say about who should benefit. It states that the program should give "maximum feasible priority to activities which will benefit low and moderate-income families or aid in the prevention of slums and blight." This wording, including the qualifying second phrase, however, is less precise than the provision in the Senate bill, removed in conference, which would have limited to 20 percent the proportion of program expenditures "not intended to be of direct and significant benefits to families of low and moderate income or areas which are blighted or deteriorating." Despite the language of the act calling for priority to expenditures on lower-income groups, CDBG applications may in fact be approved if the applicant certifies that "other activities (aside from those targeted on low- and moderate-income families) are required to meet other community development needs having a particular urgency." There is, then, a general intent of Congress concerning low- and moderate-income groups, but in keeping with the flexibility goal of the block grant program, the legislation is neither specific nor mandatory on this point.

Methodological problems in analyzing the income group benefits involved definitions of lower- and moderate-income persons and assessing the nature of benefits to them. Low income is defined as less than 50 percent of the median income of the SMSA; moderate income is 50–80 percent. A relatively narrow concept of benefits was adopted, concentrating on *direct and immediate or near-term* benefits. Table 2 presents first-year and tentative data on the impact of the uses of CDBG funds on different income groups within the sample jurisdictions, as assessed by the field research associates. For the sample cities, low- and moderate-income groups emerged as the beneficiaries of a majority of the first-year CDBG allocations on an unweighted mean basis. Almost 52 percent of all program benefits were assigned to these two groups, as shown in Table 2.

The figure in Table 2 of 28.7 percent of direct program benefits to low-income families and individuals, of course, needs to be considered in the context of the categorical grants. Of these earlier amounts, 25.4 percent was allocated for the

TABLE 2

Income-group Incidence Data for Fifty Sample Jurisdictions by Unweighted Mean Percentage

Income-group Categories	Mean Percentage
Low-income families and individuals	28.7
Moderate-income families and individuals	23.2
Other income groups	
Communitywide/nonincome specific	25.4
Not allocable on this basis	12.8
Number of jurisdictions	50[a]

SOURCE: Field research data.

[a] Central cities, satellite cities, and nonmetropolitan jurisdictions only. Urban counties are excluded; income-incidence data were not available for Columbia and Florence, S.C., when this table was prepared. Although neighborhoods (usually census tracts) were used for this analysis, associates in some cases identified projects as directly benefiting lower-income persons even though they were not in high-concentration poverty areas. If half or more of the benefits were for lower- or moderate-income persons, a project was included in whichever group applied. In most cases, the 50 percent rule was not needed; projects for lower- and moderate-income persons were mainly for their benefit. To emphasize that this is a difficult assessment task, associates were asked to summarize the income- group incidence findings in 5 percentage point intervals. In combining the data, however, we have used more specific summary percentages in this table.

model cities program, 64.9 percent for urban renewal (which sometimes did and often did not benefit the poor), and 9.7 percent for the other programs.

These on-the-scene benefit assessments by our associates are, to restate, direct near-term benefits. The point is often made—and often defensible—that secondary and perhaps longer-term benefits to lower-income groups are of major importance. In many ways, this is the essential question for analysis. In a number of communities there was open debate about the merits of direct investments in the poorest areas versus what are considered transitional or salvageable neighborhoods. In a long-term context, these transitional neighborhoods may be the areas into which the poor might move in the future.

It is in a way reassuring that a similar debate has been conducted at the national level and in the academic literature: that is, should the nation's strategy for dealing with the often poorly defined "urban crisis" emphasize the physical and social development of the most seriously distressed urban areas or concentrate instead on neighborhood conservation? In keeping with the decentralization purposes of CDBG, this debate can be said to be shifting from the national to the local level.

Although low- and moderate-income groups are the main direct beneficiaries of first-year allocations, they do not benefit uniformly among all types of jurisdictions. The average proportions of benefits were 60 percent for the low- and moderate-income groups in central cities, 53 percent in nonmetropolitan units, and 29 percent in satellite cities. Three factors appear to explain these variations: (1) the size of the poverty population, (2) a jurisdiction's experience under the model cities program, and (3) the nature and effectiveness of citizen groups. Thus we can make the following general conclusions:

1. The higher the poverty rate of a given jurisdiction, the higher the proportion of direct program benefits allocated for lower-income persons
2. Jursidictions with model cities experience allocated higher proportions of direct program benefits to low- and moderate-income groups than those without model cities experience
3. Where effective citizens' groups are organized around demands relating to low- and moderate-income concerns and where public officials are sympathetic to these demands, benefits tended to be higher than in communities where this is not the case

Overall Impact

Putting together the data on uses and net effects with that on income incidence, it is possible to generalize about strategies and patterns in the allocation of first-year CDBG funds. *Far and away the predominant approach to community development under the block grant program in its first year of operation involved a neighborhood conservation and growth strategy designed primarily to prevent urban blight.* Several groups of sample units come under this approach. We distinguish between old and new target areas; the former refers to areas which were targets for the model cities program or for urban renewal, the latter to lower-income areas which were not included under the categorical programs.

Of the fifty cases in Table 2, there were none which we classified as having a decidedly redistributive pattern in their use of CDBG funds—that is, of involving a shift away from lower-income target areas under the categorical programs to moderate- or upper-income areas. As stipulated in the law, the plans for the sample units tended to emphasize low- and moderate-income groups and areas; the main exceptions were communitywide development projects, which in many cases were justified because their principal long-term beneficiaries would be low- and moderate-income persons. In only three cases (Auburn and Bangor, Maine, and Sioux City, Iowa) did recipient jurisdictions use most of their CDBG funds to complete ongoing downtown renewal projects. These cases come the closest to being redistributive.

Auburn, Maine (population 24,151), for example, had no model cities experience and a poverty population of 10.9 percent; it allocated 80 percent of its first-year block grant to complete its downtown urban renewal project. A citizen advisory committee indicated interest in a new inner-city development project along with citywide public improvements. However, the city manager and a city planner decided instead, partly as a result of conversations with the HUD area office, that it was in the city's best interest to complete the Great Falls urban renewal project. Fear of jeopardizing prior city investments and of possible legal complications concerning the payment of urban renewal notes were major factors in reaching this decision. Alternative funding choices initially proposed by the citizen advisory committee for the CDBG program were not explored once the decision to continue the urban renewal project had been made.

Twenty-seven sample cities were classified as having a defined neighborhood conservation and growth strategy, concentrating on identified target areas, as shown in Table 3. In seven of these cases, the bulk of first-year CDBG funds was

TABLE 3

Strategies and Patterns in the First-year Use of CDBG Funds for Fifty Cities, Brookings Monitoring Study, January 1977

	Numbers of Jurisdictions Strategy of Community Development			
Geography of Allocations	Completion of Urban Renewal	Defined Neighborhood Conservation	Generalized Neighborhood Conservation	Citywide
Existing target areas only	3	—	—	—
Existing and new target areas	—	20	13	—
New target areas only	—	7	1	—
No target areas	—	—	—	6

SOURCE: Field research data.

allocated for old target areas. In the rest, new target areas received more than half of the first-year allocations.

St. Louis was one of the cities classified as having a defined neighborhood conservation and growth strategy in which a majority of first-year CDBG allocations were made in old target areas. According to the associate, the rest was used in relation to "a new housing strategy to save what could be preserved, revive some areas, and in others eliminate deteriorated housing."

Among the cities with a defined neighborhood strategy which allocated more than half of their CDBG funds in the first year for new target areas, two examples are of particular interest. For Cleveland, the associate specifically mentioned a "triage philosophy" focused on "salvageable" neighborhoods. In Houston, the associate reported that the framers of the first-year application envisioned that CDBG funds for housing rehabilitation would be supplemented in the target neighborhoods by locally generated funds earmarked for neighborhood public improvements—streets, lighting, and sewerage.

Fourteen cities were classified in the first year as having adopted a generalized, as opposed to a defined, neighborhood approach. Low- and moderate-income neighborhoods were stressed, but the definition of the areas involved tended to be less clear. For example, in Denver, it was noted by the associate that all council districts received some CDBG funds. Most funds were spent in the model cities area, "the rest on a concentrated basis in selected neighborhoods throughout the city." Likewise, in Newark, New Jersey, the associate noted "a wider distribution" of funds under CDBG with supportive service programs "geared for citywide impact." Philadelphia is also in this group. Here the associate reported that CDBG funds were used "citywide, but on a neighborhood-centered basis." In a similar vein, the associate for Huntington Beach, California, reported that there was a "concentration of projects in low- and moderate-income areas," along with projects for public facilities with citywide benefits.

Six sample units, all of them relatively small, were classified as having used the bulk of their CDBG funds on a citywide basis. Two are nonmetropolitan discretionary units. The remaining four are satellite cities eligible for formula allocations. In the latter group, for example, Greece, New York, used its CDBG funds for drainage projects. Cleveland Heights, according to the associate, specifically avoided the designation of a target area, believing that "such a designation would result in a negative label being applied to the area involved."

As these various strategies come into clearer view, they suggest important questions for the second stage of the research; current plans call for the collection of additional field data on how target areas are defined and selected, as well as data on who benefits from these selections.

The Allocations of CDBG Funds by Generalist Officials of Local Governments

Federal grant programs are more than fund transfers. They are, in varying degrees, transfers of power. While the political consequences of grant programs have long been apparent, they are often not taken into account in designing federal grants-in-aid. In the CDBG program, however, they were explicitly considered. The program was deliberately designed to bring about certain political consequences. These are usually referred to under the designation, "decentralization," involving the participation of both generalist officials of local government and private citizens. Who, then, decides on the allocation of these funds?

First, local government officials have become more influential in policy making for community development than was the case prior to CDBG. Local chief executives and other generalist officials of the executive branch have been the principal actors. This applies both to the procedural and substantive aspects of the CDBG program. There was significant involvement by local legislatures in nearly half of the sample units in the first year of the CDBG program.

Second, the role of specialists was commensurately downgraded, with some specialized urban renewal and model cities agencies playing no role at all. In a few cases, where staff members of specialized agencies became key CDBG decision makers, they were absorbed into other agencies of city government.

Third, the CDBG program has prompted administrative reorganization which in a number of cases has been conducive to more comprehensive planning and policy development at the local level. Planners generally have benefited in this context.

Fourth, by placing general-purpose local government in charge of decision making, the block grant program has stimulated a more competitive policy-making process in many jurisdictions. This increased competition, involving chief executives, legislators, and specialists, becomes even more apparent when we take into account the involvement of various citizens' organizations. In this connection, one should note that benefits which may result from comprehensive policy making may be dissipated by the more competitive political process under the block grant programs.

Fifth, local governments went well beyond the minimum legal requirements in encouraging and providing for citizen participation. The field data indicate that the level of citizen participation was substantial in most sample jurisdictions. Minority groups (both blacks and Hispanic) were heavily represented. Another important characteristic of the element of citizen participation was its tendency to be on a broader basis in the community, involving more groups and areas, as compared to the old target areas, for example, under the model cities program. This can be seen as *a political spreading effect,* parallel to the spreading of the programmatic effects and benefits noted earlier.

Impact of Citizen Participation

The fifth point, above, leads directly to the issue of whether, and in what way, citizen participation influenced the decisions and policies reflected in applications for CDBG funds. In the first-year CDBG application process, citizens made their views known in various ways—some of them formal and public and thus available for examination by researchers, but others in an informal setting, making it impossible to identify or evaluate the impact of citizens on decision making. Moreover, what occurs in the citizen participation process is not a simple, one-way transmission of ideas from citizens to the appropriate officials; rather, it is a much more complex interaction in which local officials can in many ways shape the kinds of demands made by citizens.

With these points in view, we tried to ascertain how and to what extent citizen participation influenced the preparation of CDBG applications. In addition, we examined the impact of specific major participating organizations. To deal with the first issue, we relied on summary assessments made by the field associates after they had completed their reports on the first-year application process. They were asked whether the following statement applied: "Citizen participation was influential in terms of the final outcomes contained in the CDBG applications." The associates were instructed to rank their responses according to whether the statement applied in their jurisdictions without qualification, whether it applied to a limited extent, or whether it did not apply. In eighteen jurisdictions citizen participation was judged not to have been influential; in twenty-six jurisdictions it was judged influential to a limited extent; and in eighteen jurisdictions it was rated as influential.

For a closer look at the influence of citizen participation in the application process, the research focused on the eight major participating groups. Data for these groups according to the extent of their influence on the CDBG applications in the sample jurisdictions is shown in Table 4.

Three groups stand out by a significant margin as being most influential— neighborhood groups, senior citizens, and model cities organizations. The case of senior citizens is particularly interesting in that they were identified as among the most influential in twenty jurisdictions although they were among the most active in only twelve of these jurisdictions.

TABLE 4

Community Group Involvement in the CDBG Application Process

Organizations or Groups	Jurisdictions Rated: "Among the Most Active"	Jurisdictions Rated: "Among the Most Influential"
Neighborhood groups	36	28
Senior citizens' groups	32	20
Model cities groups	22	11
Housing groups	11	5
League of Women Voters	12	2
Civic organizations	15	2
Areawide/citywide minority organizations	21	—
Religious groups	6	—

SOURCE: Field research data.

TABLE 5

Type of Citizen Participation Structure, by Extent of Citizen Influence[a]

| | Extent of Citizen Influence | | |
Type of Citizen Participation Structure	Influential	Moderately Influential	Not Influential
Public hearings only	2	4	7
Public hearings and neighborhood meetings	10	5	2
Citizens' advisory committees and public hearings	1	11	7
Citizens' advisory committees, public hearings, and neighborhood meetings	5	5	2

SOURCE: Field research data.
[a]One jurisdiction, Hennepin County, did not offer citizen participation at the country level.

It is also worth noting that although citywide/areawide minority organizations ranked fourth among the most active groups, with an "active participation" rating in twenty-one jurisdictions, in no jurisdictions were they judged to be among the most influential.

A number of different organizational approaches were taken to citizen participation under the CDBG program. When we began the study, we expected to find citizen participation more influential in jurisdictions where citizens' advisory committees were used, because they were organized, generally experienced, and had the potential for continued working involvement. Table 5 shows, however, that this was not the case. The format that was associated most often with significant influence was public hearings plus neighborhood meetings. Ten of the nineteen cases in this category showed influential citizen participation. The lowest incidence of influential participation was among the thirteen jurisdictions with public hearings only. In five of these, citizen participation was influential or moderately influential. The experience of jurisdictions with citizens' advisory committees and public hearings was surprising: among the seventeen in this category, ten had moderately influential participation; in only one case—Minneapolis—was participation judged influential.

The factor that appeared to have been the strongest determinant of whether citizens effectively contributed to the CDBG application was the amount of importance attached to citizen participation by local officials. Table 6 shows that of the twenty-three jurisdictions where public officials were reported to have viewed such participation as being very important, fifteen had influential citizen participation while only one was not influential. (The table shows the associates' assessments of citizens' influence in relation to the importance assigned to citizen participation by local officials.)

The analysis of the field data, then, leads us to the conclusion that the attitude of local officials, and not so much the procedures set up for citizen participation, was the key factor in determining whether or not citizens' views were reflected significantly in the block grant application. This finding tends to support the

TABLE 6

Local Officials' Views and the Influence of the Citizen
Participation Process—Summary Statements

Importance of Citizen Participation in CDBG Application Process: Local Officials' Views	Influence of Citizen Participation Process			
	Not Influential	Somewhat Influential	Influential	Total
Not important	11	1	—	12
Moderately important	6	17	4	27
Very important	1	7	15	23
Total	18	25	19	62

SOURCE: Field research data.

view of the program's framers that a prescribed format for participation would not particularly strengthen the citizen participation process under the CDBG program. A second finding is that overall there was a lack of any clear relationship between the activity level of citizen participation and its influence. Of course, all of the findings and conclusions in this report pertain only to the first program year, and may change as the program progresses.

THE IMPACT OF THE FEDERAL DISTRIBUTION FORMULA

Formulas, often at the center of domestic policy making, are designed to give preference—whether stated or unstated—to certain kinds of jurisdictions or conditions. Analytically, a distribution formula has two components: (1) the eligibility element—who may participate in the program; and (2) the allocation process—how much money goes to the eligibles. For the CDBG program, nearly all general-purpose units of state and local government (meaning any city, county, town, township, parish, or village) are eligible to compete for CDBG funds, but only a relatively small percentage are actually *entitled* to funding. There are two forms of entitlement.

1. A *formula entitlement* is a sum earmarked for a particular community on the basis of the three formula criteria: population, overcrowded housing, and poverty (weighted twice). This amount is not available to any other community unless the entitlement community does not use the money. Formula entitlements go to all central cities in metropolitan areas; certain eligible urban counties, towns, and townships; and all municipalities other than central cities that have populations of 50,000 or more.

2. A *hold-harmless entitlement* essentially guarantees communities as much funding during each of the first three years of the new program as the annual average of what they had received under the categorical grant programs during the five-year period from 1968–1972. After the third year, in all situations, the excess of hold-harmless amount over the formula entitlement is to be phased out by thirds. Thus, by the sixth year, all central cities, other metropolitan cities

with populations over 50,000, and urban counties would receive their actual CDBG formula amounts. There would no longer be hold-harmless funds and all hold-harmless communities not entitled to formula funding would be eligible only for discretionary funds as discussed below.

The following was the breakdown of the 1342 jurisdictions with formula or hold-harmless entitlements for fiscal year 1975:

Metropolitan cities with formula entitlement	
Central cities	365
Noncentral cities	156
Urban counties	73
Hold-harmless communities	
Metropolitan	299
Nonmetropolitan	449

In addition to the formula and hold-harmless funds, the act also provides *discretionary grants* for distribution to smaller communities (population under 50,000) within metropolitan areas. These smaller communities compete against others within a given metropolitan area. Communities outside of metropolitan areas have a separate discretionary fund for which they can compete.

Comparing the New and the Old

A central question of the distributional analysis under the CDBG program concerns the relative advantage or disadvantage to communities under the block grant system as compared with the situation in previous years under the folded-in categorical grant-in-aid programs.

In the early years of the program the ultimate distributional effects of the block grant formula are obscured because of the operation of the hold-harmless provisions. The distributional implications of the CDBG program can be seen in their entirety by projecting to fiscal year 1980, when the formula would be fully implemented, assuming for the moment that the law is continued in its present form beyond 1977.

In this analysis, confined to the fifty states and the District of Columbia, comparisons are made between funding levels under the categorical programs, represented by the 1968–1972 hold-harmless base period, and a projected 1980 allocation. The projected funding level used for fiscal 1980 is $2.95 billion, the amount authorized in the original legislation for the CDBG program for fiscal years 1976 and 1977. Comparisons are made both in total dollar terms and on the basis of per capita indexes expressed as a percentage of the national mean.[3]

---

[3] For purposes of this analysis, the number and mix of eligible recipients is held constant. In reality, the number will increase with the addition of new central and satellite cities and urban counties.

TABLE 7

Categorical or Folded-in Grant Distribution by Region Compared with Projected Formula Allocation of CDBG Funds in Fiscal 1980: Levels of Overcrowded Housing and Poverty

Region[a]	Folded-in (millions of dollars) (1)	Percent of Total (2)	Formula[b] (millions of dollars) (3)	Percent of Total (4)	Change in Share (percent) (5)	Folded-in per Capita Index (6)	Formula per Capita Index (7)	Per Capita Index Change (8)	OVH Index (9)	Poverty Index (10)
U. S. total	2088	100	2790	100	—	100	100	—	100	100
New England	206	9.9	130	4.7	-5.2	170	80	-90	84	65
Middle Atlantic	475	22.7	486	17.4	-5.3	124	95	-29	84	77
East North Central	332	15.9	480	17.2	+1.3	80	87	+7	88	72
West North Central	161	7.7	188	6.7	-1.0	96	84	+12	92	98
South Atlantic	314	15.0	460	16.5	+1.5	99	109	+10	111	129
East South Central	125	6.0	221	7.9	+1.9	95	126	+31	124	178
West South Central	170	8.2	345	12.4	+4.2	86	130	+44	135	155
Mountain	75	3.6	110	3.9	+.3	88	96	+8	113	101
Pacific	230	11.0	370	13.3	+2.3	84	101	+17	98	80

SOURCES: The folded-in grant allocations and the indices were calculated directly from hold-harmless determinations and data elements used by the Department of Housing and Urban Development in making first-year CDBG allocations. The fiscal 1980 allocations were computed by applying the first-year data on objective needs to a projected fiscal 1980 appropriation.

a Regional divisions used by the U. S. Bureau of the Census are: New England—Maine, New Hampshire, Vermont, Massachusetts, Rhode Island, Connecticut; Middle Atlantic—New York, New Jersey, Pennsylvania: East North Central—Ohio, Indiana, Illinois, Michigan, Wisconsin; West North Central—Minnesota, Iowa, Missouri, North Dakota, South Dakota, Nebraska, Kansas: South Atlantic—Delaware, Maryland, the District of Columbia, Virginia, West Virginia, North Carolina, South Carolina, Georgia, Florida: East South Central—Kentucky, Tennessee, Alabama, Mississippi; West South Central—Arkansas, Louisiana, Oklahoma, Texas: Mountain—Montana, Idaho, Wyoming, Colorado, New Mexico, Arizona, Utah, Nevada; Pacific—Washington, Oregon, California, Alaska, Hawaii.

b The SMSA discretionary fund allocations, incorporated into the formula amounts, are approximations. They do not take into account the population, poverty, and overcrowded housing of hold-harmless communities that will be added to SMSA discretionary areas. Thus the allocated discretionary amounts may change somewhat. The allocated discretionary dollar figures are based on data balances for years 1 to 3.

Regional Patterns

Regionally, the New England and Middle Atlantic states were most "advantaged" in the distribution of funds under the previous programs. In fact, these two areas were the only ones in which per capita grants under the categorical programs exceeded the national average of communities receiving funds. The per capita grant in New England was 70 percent above the national mean; the Pacific region, by contrast, had a per capita grant 16 percent below the national average. (See column 6 of Table 7.)

Under full formula funding the most significant gains are made by the sixteen states of the three southern regions—South Atlantic, East South Central, and West South Central. Their per capita index figures go up substantially while the New England, Middle Atlantic, and West North Central states show sharp declines. (See columns 6 and 7.) In terms of shares, which is the more significant way to view the altered distributional patterns, the New England and the Middle Atlantic regions, those with the greatest per capita declines, have a reduction in their collective share from 32.6 percent under the previous grants to 22.1 percent of the CDBG total. The three southern regions, however, increase their share from 29.2 to 36.8 percent of the total (columns 2 and 4).

The shift in shares is the net result of previous funding levels under the categorical programs and the poverty and overcrowded housing factors, as shown in columns 9 and 10.

Metropolitan Distribution Patterns

During the 1968–1972 base-year period ,the nation's metropolitan areas received 87.4 percent of the funds distributed under the seven urban grants folded into the CDBG program.

Under full formula funding the metropolitan allocation increases from $1.825 billion under the previous programs to $2.24 billion in 1980. However, this results entirely from the increase in the total amount of funding provided. The proportion of CDBG funds going to metropolitan areas declines by 7.4 percentage points because of an 80–20 metropolitan–nonmetropolitan split of the law.

Metropolitan Share. Although metropolitan areas as a whole would receive more money in 1980 under the law as originally passed, the principal beneficiaries within SMSA's are small communities, eligible for discretionary funds. (See Table 8.) The most striking point is that the nearly 600 formula entitlement areas (central and satellite cities and urban counties) collectively would receive less under the formula in 1980 than they had received annually under the previous programs in the hold-harmless base period, declining from $1.659 to $1.612 billion. The share of total funds going to these formula entitlement communities declines from 79.5 to 54.6 percent.

Small Community Shares Combined. As a class, small communities gain sig-

TABLE 8

Categorical or Folded-in Grant Distributions Compared with Projected 1980 Allocation of CDBG Funds within Metropolitan Areas

Recipient Metropolitan Area, by Type	Number	Folded-in (millions of dollars)	Percent of Total	Formula (millions of dollars)	Percent of Total
Metropolitan areas					
Central cities	362	1498	71.8	1182	42.2
Satellite cities	152	94	4.5	140	5.0
Urban counties	73	67	3.2	290	10.3
Rest of SMSA's[a]		166	7.9	628	22.5

SOURCE: The folded-in grant allocations and the indices were calculated directly from hold-harmless determinations and data elements used by the Department of Housing and Urban Development in making first-year CDBG allocations. The fiscal 1980 allocations were computed by applying the first-year data on objective needs to a projected fiscal 1980 appropriation.

[a] Places under 50,000 population that receive discretionary grants.

nificantly under the CDBG program as projected. Combining the metropolitan and nonmetropolitan allocations, communities under 50,000 would receive $1.18 billion in fiscal year 1980.[4] This means that 42 percent of total CDBG funds in that year would be allocated to these small communities on a discretionary basis. Under the categorical grants, 22 percent of the funds went to these small communities. If we assume that all of the $290 million projected to be received by urban counties in 1980 will be spent in small communities, the allocation for small communities would be $1.45 billion, *or 52 percent of the total.*

Furthermore, if the $60 million allocated to central cities under 50,000 is included, the total increases to $1.53 billion, or nearly 55 percent of the entire appropriation.

Finally, if one considers a small city to be under 100,000 population, then approximately $1.8 billion or about two-thirds of the total funds are projected to go to small cities in the sixth year of this program.

Central City Allocations. The principal recipients collectively under the earlier grants were the central cities. This was to be expected under programs focused on reducing urban blight and providing social services. This central city advantage under the categorical programs is shown by the fact that central cities received nearly 72 percent of all funds (see Table 8.) Under the formula system, however, central cities as a group lose both in absolute and relative terms.

The 1980 projections indicate central city losses in the aggregate of more than $300 million, with their share of total funds declining from 71.8 to 42.2 percent. The central cities are the only jurisdictional types within metropolitan

---

[4] This does not include central cities with a population under 50,000.

areas to lose funds under the formula allocation system compared to the hold-harmless base.

Analysis of central cities shows important regional differences; losses are not experienced in all sections of the country. Generally, central cities in the East North Central, East and West South Central, Mountain, and Pacific regions show a per capita gain under the formula system. However, the central cities of the New England, Middle Atlantic, West North Central, and South Atlantic regions show a per capita decline, with the greatest aggregate losses among the central cities being in the New England and West North Central regions. For New England, the decline is particularly sharp, its per capita index dropping from 204 to 87 (mean per capita equals 100) and going from the highest to the lowest per capita allocation. Central cities in the South Atlantic region also experience a collective loss relative to previous funding, but the central cities of that region, unlike those of New England, remain well above the per capita mean under the formula because of their high incidence of overcrowded housing and poverty.

Among the three regions in the northeast quadrant (New England, Middle Atlantic, East North Central), the area that contains many of the nation's oldest and most distressed central cities, only one region—the Middle Atlantic—has a central city formula allocation above the national mean. This is the result of the major gain to New York City under the formula in relation to its relatively low (in per capita terms) hold-harmless base.

Formula Changes

As awareness of these full and ultimate effects of the CDBG formula increased, so did the strength of our conclusion that it needed to be revised to give greater weight to the needs of older, declining cities. A number of proposed formula modifications emerged as the third and final year of the initial appropriation approached (fiscal 1977), including the idea of a dual-formula as presented in the Brookings analysis.

In considering formula changes, we begin by looking at the original formula factors. We generally accept the need for a population factor, even though it contributes materially to the spreading effect of the CDBG program. If a city with a population of over 50,000 had no overcrowded housing and no poverty (and there are some satellite cities for which this is nearly the case), that city would still receive an entitlement based on population.

The case for the poverty factor, however, is more complicated. The CDBG program is not customarily seen as a means of eliminating poverty, although it is aimed at alleviating the conditions of physical blight that accompany urban poverty. Viewed from the local level, poverty-impacted communities tend to spend a higher proportion of their budget on services for the poor while deriving relatively fewer tax dollars from this group. Hence, the poverty factor can be said to serve as a proxy for both physical and fiscal need.

The overcrowded housing criterion is, in our view, the most questionable of the three formula factors. The extent of poverty and overcrowded housing are closely associated (with a correlation coefficient of .6411). Thus, the overcrowded housing factor has the effect of further weighting the poverty factor, further contributing to the regional imbalance of the original formula.

What is missing from the formula is a measure of physical need to serve as an indicator of the physical condition of a community and its facilities—streets, curbs, sewers, schools, housing, etc. The best available statistical indicator for this purpose is census data on the amount of housing stock built prior to 1939. (Because of the low level of housing construction during the 1930s, the pre-1939 housing figure can to a significant extent be viewed as a pre-1930 figure.) Not all housing built before 1939 is deteriorated or deteriorating, but, based on our analysis, the age of housing appears to be linked to the rehabiliation needs of urban communities and to the physical development purposes of the CDBG program.

The Dual-Formula Approach

Among the alternative formulas tested, the one that seemed most feasible as a *basic approach* to formula change is referred to in our analysis as a "dual-formula."[5] It retains the formula in the original law and at the same time adds a new formula of population, poverty, and pre-1939 housing (weighted twice). The second formula, as can be seen, simply replaces the overcrowded housing factor with pre-1939 housing, which, as discussed, is an indicator of the physical dimension of urban need. Each formula entitlement area receives CDBG funds according to whichever formula yields the highest amount in its particular case. This means that the total entitlement allocation under the two formulas increases to approximately $1.88 billion.[6] There is then an important residual effect—the metropolitan discretionary fund is automatically reduced, in this instance to $360 million, or to about 16 percent of the total metropolitan allocation.

In testing this approach, it seems that the three southern regions and the Mountain and Pacific areas would continue to be better off under the existing formula; the Northeast and North Central regions, however, would gain under the dual formula. This pattern is evidenced by the number of entitlement communities falling under each formula. Of 512 central and satellite cities, 241 communities, primarily from the southern and western states, would receive their allocations under the existing formula while 271 would benefit from the alternative age-related formula. Of these 271 communities gaining, 218 are in the Northeast and North Central regions.

Under the dual-formula approach, the nation's central cities increase their

---

[5] See Chapter 6 of Richard P. Nathan et al., *Block Grants for Community Development* (Washington, D. C., 1977) for the eight other formula alternatives tested.

[6] For purposes of these calculations, we have assumed total funding of $2.95 billion in the year in which full formula funding goes into effect—i.e., the hold-harmless feature in the law, as scheduled, is completely phased out.

share of the metropolitan funds by nearly 10 percentage points from a 52.8 percent share under the present system to 62.2 percent (see Table 9).

Supplemental Funds for Needy Cities

There is a second set of formula issues yet to be considered. Once a program exists for distributing money for community development on a broad basis, as a practical political matter, there would appear to be a much better opportunity than would otherwise be the case to concentrate some amount of additional funds on the cities with the most acute development needs. One such option studied in our research is a formula add-on limited to the neediest cities. The Carter administration in its budget revisions for fiscal year 1978 proposed an add-on, although not a formula add-on. It proposed that $400 million be added to be allocated by the secretary of HUD on a discretionary basis according to urban needs and the related development potential of the cities applying. There are obviously many positions that can be taken on the issue of whether and to what degree supplemental CDBG funds should be distributed on an automatic or formula basis, including the possibility of a full formula allocation or less precise approach involving a statistical "test of admission," on which basis the secretary of HUD could then make grants to eligible "needy cities" on a discretionary basis. Our approach as tested in the first-year research program, was to concentrate on a full-formula system for distributing supplemental funds, allocating $500 million to demonstrate the way in which formulas could be devised for this purpose. The formula for our supplemental funding approach is presented in detail in the Appendix to this article.

Using supplemental funding on a needs-tested basis would also provide an opportunity to take into account other important characteristics of urban distress. Population change is stressed in this process; it is used twice in the allocation of supplemental CDBG funds. Among CDBG entitlement cities there are important

TABLE 9

Comparison of Allocations to Metropolitan Areas Under the Existing CDBG Formula with the Dual-Formula Alternative (Projected Fiscal Year 1980)

Community Type	CDBG Percent Total	Dual-Formula Percent of Total
Central cities	52.8	62.2
Satellite cities	6.3	7.5
Urban counties	12.9	14.3
SMSA discretionary	28.0	16.0

SOURCE: Calculated from data used by the U. S. Department of Housing and Urban Development in making first-year CDBG allocations. Data on pre-1939 housing are from *1970 Census of Housing, Detailed Housing Characteristics*, Series HC (1) B, Tables 35, 43, and 62. Township housing data are from *1970 Census of Population and Housing, Census Tracts*, Series PHC (1), Table H–2.

socioeconomic distinctions between the 150 cities losing population and the 356 cities that gained population between 1960–1970 as shown in Table 10.

Overall, the income of blacks is about 60 percent that of whites; CDBG entitlement cities with declining populations tend to have much higher proportions of blacks and of lower-income persons. The declining cities also have lower median housing values than the growing cities.

While these data are significant, they reflect the situation at a given point in time. Examining the rate of change of two important resource factors, income and housing values, it can be seen that between 1960 and 1970 per capita income increased almost 5 percent faster in the growing cities (column 4, Table 10) than in the declining cities; home values increased nearly 6 percent faster (column 6) in the growing CDBG cities.

In sum, distressed cities are characterized by old age, an increasing concentration of the socially and economically disadvantaged, and population decline (or slow growth). The dual formula described earlier covers two of these aspects of distress: poverty and community age. The system for distributing CDBG supplemental funds uses all three factors.

We would stress that in respect to both the dual formula and the supplement, our discussion presents what to us are reasonably feasible and straightforward *examples* of types of formula changes. We regard the allocation system as a framework of movable parts, the positions of which depend upon the nature and degree of the distributional shift desired. The formula for a $500 million supplement is one among an unlimited number of ways in which a further skewing to deal with "urban need" could be achieved.

These formula ideas are intended as illustrative of the ways in which the present law could be changed. Our basic approach has been that the law provides a framework of movable parts which can be modified in ways that achieve different people's objectives as to how urban needs should be met. To us, the most important points are the dual formula and the provision of supplemental CDBG funds for "needy" cities. Both the Ford and Carter administrations in 1977 rec-

TABLE 10

Important Characteristics and Rates of Change during 1960–1970 for CDBG Cities, Grouped by Population Gains or Losses

Group	Percent Population Change (1)	Average Percent Black 1970 (2)	Per Capita Income 1970 (dollars) (3)	Percent Income Change 1960–1970 (4)	Median House Value 1970 (thousands of dollars) (5)	Percent Value Change 1960–1970 (6)
150 losers	−6.7	17.3	3062	57.0	15.9	32.5
356 gainers	20.5	10.2	3354	61.7	18.8	38.2

SOURCE: Population, income, and housing data from U. S. Bureau of the Census, *County and City Data Books, 1962 and 1972*, Table 6.

ommended a version of the dual formula, in both cases with a stronger urban focus than that of the dual formula originally developed as part of the Brookings monitoring study of the block grant program. The principal reasons for the stronger urban focus of these proposals is that instead of using population as one of the three factors (along with pre-1939 housing and poverty), they use population *change*, thus giving recognition to population decline or slow growth in the basic formula.[7] HUD Secretary Patricia Roberts Harris also presented a proposal to the Congress for supplemental CDBG funds. Unlike the suggestion for a formula-based supplement presented in this article, the Harris proposal is in the form of discretionary funds for so-called "Action grants" for special projects*.

APPENDIX

The following two-step procedure was devised to determine both eligibility for supplemental funding and the amount the eligible jurisdictions would receive.

Step 1. Constructing an Eligibility Index

The first step is the determination of eligibility. We confine eligibility to metropolitan cities. The following equation is used to scale the needs of metropolitan cities.

$$\text{Eligibility index} = \frac{(\text{percent of pre-1939 housing}) \times (\text{percent of poverty})}{100 + \text{rate of population change}}$$

Such an eligibility index number was determined for all formula entitlement metropolitan cities.

Then, assuming that the eligibility threshold is set at the mean, 196 cities qualify, of which 122 (62 percent) are below 100,000 population, 177 are central cities, and the rest (19) are satellite cities. Regionally, the Northeast and North Central states have 121 cities that qualify—61.8 percent of the total.

Step 2. Calculating Individual Allocations

The second step is the calculation of individual allocations for the eligible cities. We use a formula equally weighting population, poverty, and pre-1939

[7] The Ford proposal has the strongest urban focus of the three, as it uses population *decline;* the Carter version uses population *decline or below average growth;* the original Brookings version uses *straight* population.

* The material presented reflects the findings and interpretations of the authors, not the views of the trustees, officers, or other staff members of the Brookings Institution. The research is being performed under a contract with the U. S. Department of Housing and Urban Development. The first report on this study, on which this article is based, is Nathan et al., *Block Grants for Community Development.*

housing and derive a coefficient for each eligible city to be applied against the total fund of $500 million. However, before applying these coefficients, they were adjusted for two other purposes.

Population Decline Adjustment. For the 196 eligible cities, the average population change was -2.1 percent between 1960 and 1970. A rate of population change ratio is calculated:

$$\frac{\text{Population}}{\text{change ratio}} = \frac{100 + \text{rate of change for individual city}}{100 + \text{mean rate of change for participants (i.e., 97.9)}}$$

Then the allocation share is determined as follows:

$$\frac{\text{allocation}}{\text{share}} = \frac{\text{coefficient number}}{\text{population change ratio}}$$

Scaling Adjustment. To increase this spread (make it more redistributive) and reduce the "notch" problem (i.e., for the 197th city) a further formula adjustment is used to scale the final allocations. This is done by multiplying the allocation share by an "eligibility adjustment factor," which is the ratio of an individual city's index to the mean index of the eligible cities.

$$\frac{\text{Scaling}}{\text{adjustment factor}} = \frac{\text{individual city eligibility index}}{\text{mean eligibility index of eligible cities}}$$

Thus the final allocation is determined:

$$\frac{\text{Individual}}{\text{supplement}} = \left(\frac{\text{allocation}}{\text{coefficient}} \div \frac{\text{population}}{\text{change ratio}} \right) \times \frac{\text{scaling adjust-}}{\text{ment factor}} \times \$500 \text{ million}$$

Applying this approach to the 196 cities, East St. Louis (the top city) receives $42.48 per capita; Seattle (the bottom city), $5.64 per capita.

The Causes of New York City's Fiscal Crisis

CONGRESSIONAL BUDGET OFFICE

New York City's current budget problems have been pre-cipitated by its inability to borrow money in the municipal bond market. Since March [1975], when New York was last able to sell notes on its own behalf, a series of stopgap measures have been used. . . . First the city was advanced some $800 million in state aid that it was scheduled to receive after the start of the fiscal year in July. Next on June 10, the state established the Municipal Assistance Corporation (MAC) to serve as an interim borrowing agency for the city, in order to transform much of New York's short-term debt into long-term obligations. Origi-nally, MAC was authorized to borrow $3 billion, an amount sufficient to tide the city over until October. It was hoped that by this time the city would be in a position to reenter the bond market on its own.

While new city securities were unmarketable, it was anticipated that MAC bonds would be viewed differently by investors: first, because they were being issued by an agency of the state and carried with them the "moral obligation" of the state to meet any shortfall in debt

This article is adapted from a report issued to members of Congress in October by the CONGRESSIONAL BUDGET OFFICE (CBO). The *Quarterly* has chosen to publish it because it is a compact, authoritative, and nonpartisan analysis of the causes of New York City's fiscal problems. The authors of the report were Robert D. Reischauer, Peter K. Clark, and Peggy L. Cuciti. The CBO was established in February 1975 to provide Congress with independent analysis of policies affecting the budget and the economy and to provide general staff support for the new congressional budget processes mandated by the Congressional Budget and Impoundment Control Act of 1974.

services;[1] second, because the revenues from the city's sales and stock transfer taxes were to be diverted directly to the corporation to cover its debt service costs; and finally, because the city was directed to reform its financial practices and balance its budget under a new, state-approved accounting system.

In spite of these assurances, MAC immediately encountered difficulty borrowing for the city. Although MAC's first issue bore unprecedented tax-exempt interest rates of up to 9.5 percent, it could be marketed only with difficulty, even after a number of banks and insurance companies agreed to buy two-thirds of the total. When these bonds were freed from the sales price restrictions placed on them by the underwriting syndicate, they immediately plummeted in value, confirming a lack of investor interest in MAC bonds. In August MAC was able to borrow less than half of its planned offering, even though the new issue carried interest rates of up to 11 percent.

As August wore on, the New York clearinghouse banks that usually market New York City offerings became more reluctant to underwrite new MAC issues because these institutions were experiencing increasing difficulties reselling the bonds they already held to other investors. They found themselves holding more city obligations than they considered to be prudent banking practice. Thus in September MAC found itself in the situation that had faced the city in April—unable to find a syndicate that would underwrite its borrowing.

The next stopgap measure was the Financial Emergency Act, which was approved by a special session of the state legislature and signed by the governor on September 9. This legislation was part of a plan to provide the city with roughly $2.3 billion—enough to meet its cash requirements through early December, by which time it is hoped the other elements of the plan will allow the city to reenter the bond market on its own. The key element in the plan is the Emergency Financial Control Board which is dominated by state appointees and charged with administering the city's finances. By late October this board must approve a three-year financial plan that includes transition to a truly balanced budget by fiscal year 1978, a reduction in short-term city borrowing, the removal of expense items from the capital budget, and a growth in controllable spending (all but welfare, pensions and debt service) of not more than 2 percent per year. The board is also given the responsibility for estimating the city's revenues and keeping spending within

---

[1] A "moral obligation" requires the governor to include in his proposed state budget funds sufficient to cover any shortfall in debt service. This does not legally bind the legislature to appropriate these funds as would be the case of shortfalls associated with securities backed by the state's "full faith and credit."

these revenue limits; reviewing and approving major contracts; approving all city borrowing; extending, if necessary, the pay freeze on city employees through fiscal year 1977; and dispersing city revenues, but only after it is satisfied that the expenditures are consistent with the three-year fiscal plan. The powers of the board extend to the city's semi-independent agencies which provide elementary and secondary education, higher education, hospital, and other services.

As with MAC, the emergency assistance plan ran into difficulties soon after it was put into effect, giving rise to concerns that this stopgap measure might not be sufficient to keep the city solvent even until December. Banks, insurance corporations, and private investors have not agreed to buy the full $406 million in MAC bonds that the plan calls upon them to purchase. Some of the city and state pension funds, which are legislated to supply $755 million of the $2.3 billion total, have balked at investing in MAC bonds. The state pension funds have obtained a New York State Court of Appeals ruling, which states that, despite the provisions of the Financial Emergency Act, they cannot be required by legislation to purchase MAC bonds. Finally, the state, which has agreed to loan the city $750 million, has encountered increasing difficulty in borrowing.

Although these notes were backed by the "full faith and credit" of the state, the state was forced to pay 8.7 percent on the first notes issued to aid the city. Next, Standard and Poor's, which rates the risk associated with various municipal bonds, warned that, if the state extended more assistance to New York City than that called for in the emergency plan, it would be compromising its fiscal integrity and jeopardizing its high credit rating. Finally, Moody's Investors Service, another organization that rates bonds, withdrew its rating from the state's Housing Finance Agency, effectively squeezing this agency out of the municipal bond market and leaving it dependent upon the state for capital.

Moody's also lowered its rating of New York state and city securities. . . .

The City's Need to Borrow

While most state and local governments borrow money, many can postpone issuing bonds or notes for a few months or even for an entire year if conditions in the municipal bond market appear to be adverse. However, New York City's situation makes such a delay impossible. In fiscal year 1976, the city's anticipated borrowing requirements are approximately $8 billion. This borrowing has three different purposes.

Capital Projects

First, like almost all state and local governments, New York City borrows to finance capital projects. Generally long-term bonds are issued to pay for the construction of schools, public buildings, highways, sewers, and similar projects. The accepted rationale for financing such facilities with long-term debt is that all of the taxpayers who will benefit from such long-lived facilities should pay for them, and such payments should be made in installments during the facility's usable life span. As of June 1, 1975, New York City had $9.4 billion outstanding in long-term debt, the great bulk of which was backed by the city's "full faith and credit" through a first lien on tax revenues. A small portion of the debt was offset by money deposited in sinking funds. This debt represents roughly 6 percent of the nation's total long-term municipal debt.

Short-term bond anticipation notes are used by some states and local governments to support the construction phase of a project or to avoid borrowing in the long-term market when interest rates are abnormally high. New York has depended heavily upon issuing such notes, $1.6 billion of which it had outstanding on June 30, 1975. Frequently the city has made little or no effort to substitute long-term borrowing for such bond anticipation notes, preferring instead to "roll over" or refund these obligations periodically. This has made New York particularly dependent upon continued access to short-term credit markets.

While long- and short-term borrowing for capital projects is accepted practice, there is evidence that in recent years New York has misused such borrowing authority by placing approximately $700 million worth of items, which appropriately belonged in its operating budget, into the capital budget. This was one of the "gimmicks" the city used to present a "balanced" operating budget.

According to the city's budget, it planned to issue roughly $2 billion in new obligations to support capital projects and to "roll over" between $1.2 and $1.8 billion in bond anticipation notes in fiscal year 1976. If the city were unable to borrow for these purposes, its large capital improvement and construction program would eventually grind to a halt, causing a general deterioration of the city's stock of public buildings and facilities and exacerbating unemployment in the construction industry. Possibly of more immediate significance would be the necessary termination of the operating budget items that have been hidden in the capital budget.

Expenditure and Revenue Flows

The second purpose for which New York borrows is to match its income flow to its expenditure pattern. Spending occurs at a fairly regular pace throughout the year, driven by payrolls and welfare payments that must be met bimonthly or monthly and by the steady purchase of the goods and services required to keep city programs operating. Revenues, on the other hand, come in at more infrequent intervals. For example, property taxes are collected quarterly, state and federal aid may be paid quarterly or even annually. Lacking large unencumbered cash balances, New York, like some other states and municipalities, issues tax and revenue anticipation notes to tide itself over until the taxes or other revenues are obtained. If it operated in a prudent fashion, New York could be expected to require approximately $1.5 billion in short-term debt in fiscal year 1976 for "legitimate" revenue anticipation purposes ("legitimate" in the sense that these notes could be repaid by revenues collected during the fiscal year). Without access to such borrowing, the city would have to reshape its expenditure pattern to that of its receipts or to build up cash balances sufficient to tide itself over periods of low revenue inflow.

Short-Term Notes for Deficit Financing

The final purpose for which New York City needs to borrow in fiscal year 1976 is to "roll over" or refund $2.6 billion in outstanding short-term notes and to finance this year's $726 million projected current account deficit. The $2.6 billion represents the accumulation of the past decade's operating deficits which have been financed each year primarily by issuing more revenue and tax anticipation notes than could be covered through actual revenue collections. The existence of this large short-term debt and the magnitude of the current deficit mean that New York must borrow every month or so regardless of how unattractive market conditions may be to "roll over" the part of its short-term debt coming due and to finance its monthly shortfall between current revenues and expenditures. The only alternative would be to repay the principal and interest due out of current revenues. The impracticality of this approach can readily be seen by the fact that it would absorb roughly half of the city's annual tax revenues, leaving little to support essential public services.

New York City had $5.3 billion of short-term notes—29 percent of the national total—outstanding on June 1, 1975. Had the market not closed for the city, New York could have been expected to issue between 27 and 33 percent of 1975's total short-term municipal notes.

To summarize, New York's borrowing needs in fiscal year 1976 total some $8 billion. Had a crisis of confidence not emerged, the city would have issued $2 billion in long-term securities and sought an additional $6 billion in the short-term market. Instead, the market effectively closed to New York City in April. MAC, first on its own and then with the assistance of the state, has stepped in to borrow for the city. The strategy behind this intervention is to substitute long-term securities for short-term notes, thus providing the city with an opportunity to reform its fiscal practices and accumulate surpluses sufficient to repay its past deficit-related debts.

CAUSES OF THE PROBLEM

A variety of factors have contributed to New York's current fiscal problems. It is useful to distinguish the short-term factors that are responsible for precipitating the immediate crisis from those longer-term trends that have contributed to the city's deteriorating fiscal position.

Short-Term Factors

The immediate crisis stems from a loss of investor confidence in the credit worthiness of the city. To some extent the sudden shift in the attitudes of investors toward the city's ability to meet its obligations must be attributed to psychological factors for surely the city's long-run economic outlook, which is what determines its ability to pay off its debts, cannot be much different today than it was one or two years ago.

Any discussion of the factors that affect the psychological attitudes of investors must be speculative. It is possible that investor confidence was eroded by the public debate and confrontation politics that took place between the mayor, the city controller, and the governor over the city's fiscal year 1976 budget. It is also probable that the temporary default of the New York State's Urban Development Corporation and the memories of the Penn Central, Lockheed, and Franklin National Bank collapses have made investors increasingly skittish. Any hint of financial instability may send them scampering away. Investor uncertainty becomes a self-feeding process, for the fewer the number of persons willing to lend the city money, the greater the probability of default and the greater therefore the uncertainty, and indeed, the risk.

However, it would be wrong to attribute all of the loss of investor confidence in New York to psychological factors. Objective market conditions should be considered as well. As Table I indicates, 1975 has proven to be an extremely heavy year for municipal borrowing. Therefore, New York has been forced to compete for funds with many other state and local governments with far sounder fiscal conditions as well as with the large borrowing requirements of the federal government. While the volume of issues has grown, the recession probably has diminished the desire and ability of banks, corporations, and individuals to buy tax-exempt bonds. This has clearly been the case with commercial banks;

TABLE 1

Volume of Municipal Borrowing (1967–1975)
(Amounts are par values in millions of dollars)

Year	Long-Term	Short-Term	Total
1967	14,300	8,000	22,300
1968	16,300	8,600	24,900
1969	11,700	11,700	23,400
1970	18,888	17,811	35,999
1971	25,006	26,259	51,265
1972	23,748	24,705	49,018
1973	23,957	24,705	48,662
1974	24,317	29,543	53,860
1975[a]	30,124	33,932	64,056

Source: Securities Industry Association, *Municipal Market Developments.*
[a]Annual rate based on January–June volume.

during the first quarter of 1975 they dropped out of the municipal bond market almost entirely (see Table 2).

With respect to individuals, it has been suggested that interest rates on municipal offerings have to be raised significantly to entice new buyers into the market. Such buyers must be drawn primarily from middle-income groups which benefit less from the tax-exempt status of municipal bond interest and are less capable of purchasing municipal bonds because these securities generally are available only in large denominations. Furthermore, the market for New York City securities is concentrated largely in New York State where the interest is exempt from not

TABLE 2

Annual Net Changes in Holdings of Municipal Securities
by Major Holder Groups (1970–1975)
(Amounts are par values in billions of dollars)

Holder	1970	1971	1972	1973	1974	1975[a] First Quarter	Second Quarter
Commercial banks	10.7	12.6	7.2	5.7	5.5	−2.7	6.9
Households	−.8	−.2	1.0	4.3	10.0	13.9	9.3
All other[b]	1.3	5.2	6.2	3.7	1.9	2.9	4.5
Total	11.2	17.6	14.4	13.7	17.4	14.0	20.7

Source: Unpublished flow of funds data from the Board of Governors of the Federal Reserve System (Processed: August 19, 1975).
[a]Annual rate.
[b]This includes corporate business, state and local general funds, mutual savings banks, insurance companies, state and local government retirement funds, and brokers and dealers.

only federal but also state and local taxes. This market may be close to saturated by the large quantities of state and city securities outstanding. To broaden the market to nonstate residents would require interest rates sufficiently high to compensate for the fact that non-New York holders would have to pay state income taxes on the interest earned from their New York City securities.

The recession is a second short-term condition that has contributed to New York City's problems. Compared to other local governments, New York's revenue system is highly responsive to economic conditions because it relies heavily on cyclically sensitive sales and income taxes rather than on the more stable property tax. While property taxes accounted for 62 percent of the total revenues raised by the local governments serving metropolitan areas in fiscal year 1972–73, they accounted for only 43 percent of revenues raised by New York.

The recession's impact on New York's sales tax base is illustrated in Table 3. Despite a 9.3 percent increase in consumer prices in the year ending June 30, 1975, the volume of taxable sales in the city rose by only 1.7 percent. In New York even the property tax has proven to be unreliable. Delinquencies have risen rapidly from 4.2 percent of collections in fiscal year 1970 to 7.2 percent currently.

The recession has caused high unemployment and stationary incomes which have increased the city's expenditure requirements as well as undercut its expected revenue growth. Not only have the numbers of families eligible for welfare programs increased (see Table 3), but it is also likely that the demand for other city services, such as hospitals, has been boosted by the recession because fewer city residents are able to afford the costs of the alternative private institutions.

The severe inflation of recent years has also had a negative effect on the fiscal position of New York. While in the long run, inflation may increase the value of the local tax base sufficiently to compensate for the decreased purchasing power of the tax dollar, in the short run, expenditure levels tend to be more responsive to inflationary pressures. This imbalance stems from the nature of property tax administration, for it is very difficult to reassess property rapidly enough to keep pace with the continually inflating market values of real estate.

Moreover, the situation is exacerbated by the long time period that transpires between the date at which the property tax levy is set and the dates on which the tax payments are due. In recent years a considerable amount of unanticipated inflation has occurred during these periods. It should be noted that New York's situation with respect to inflation may be better than that of other large cities, because of New York's heavy reliance on sales and income tax receipts which do respond quickly and automatically to price hikes and inflation-induced salary increases.

TABLE 3

Measures of the Recession's Impact on New York City

Year		Unemployment Rate[1]	Welfare[a] Recipients[2]	Sales Tax[a] Base[3]
1970		4.8	101.5	78.1
1971		6.7	109.5	81.5
1972		7.0	112.9	NA
1973		6.0	106.4	91.9
1974		7.2	101.4	96.7
1974	June	6.9	100.0	100.0
	July	7.3	100.2	100.4
	Aug.	6.8	99.3	100.2
	Sept.	7.3	100.5	99.1
	Oct.	7.2	101.3	99.8
	Nov.	7.4	101.3	99.6
	Dec.	8.5	102.4	100.4
1975	Jan.	10.3	102.8	101.0
	Feb.	10.2	102.5	101.0
	Mar.	11.0	103.1	101.7
	April	10.8	104.3	102.0
	May	10.9	104.3	101.9
	June	11.7	105.0	101.7
	July	12.0		
	Aug.	11.0		

Sources: 1. New York State, Department of Labor.
2. New York State Department of Social Services.
3. Annual figures from New York State Department of Taxation and Finance. Monthly figures from Municipal Assistance Corporation.

[a] Indexes use June 1974 as the base period (Sales Tax Base 100 = $1.6 billion; Welfare Recipients 100 = 949,000). Sales Tax Base is equal to the total value of sales subject to taxation. Index is based on a twelve-month moving average to eliminate seasonal effects.

The Welfare index includes recipients under the AFDC and home relief programs.

Long-Term Factors

The longer-term roots of New York's fiscal problem are both complex and difficult for the city to change. In part they represent the same forces that have buffeted the other large central cities of the northeast and north-central states. These cities have been called upon to assimilate a new wave of rural migrants into the industrial economy just when the industries offering employment opportunities are shifting their bases of operation out of the cities.

As a result of the immigration from the South, the out-migration to the suburbs, and the natural aging of the existing population, those more heavily dependent on city services—the poor, the uneducated, the aged, the non-English speaking—comprise an ever-increasing segment of the

TABLE 4

Change in Jobs and Population in New York City

Year	Total Jobs[1] (in Thous.)	Index[a]	Private Sector[2] Jobs (in Thous.)	Index[a]	Population[3] (in Thous.)	Index[a]
1960	3,538.4	94.5	3,130.2	98.4	7,782.0	98.6
1970	3,744.8	100.0	3,182.0	100.0	7,895.6	100.0
1971	3,609.4	96.4	3,040.2	95.5	7,886.6	99.9
1972	3,563.1	95.1	2,998.6	94.2	7,847.1	99.4
1973	3,538.4	94.5	2,964.0	93.1	7,664.4	97.1
1974	3,458.4	92.4	2,877.7	90.4	7,567.1	95.8
1975[b]	3,375.8	90.1	2,802.6	88.1	NA	NA

Sources: 1. 2. Bureau of Labor Statistics.
               3. Bureau of the Census.

[a] Data indexed using 1970 as base year.
[b] January–June 1975.

city's population. For example, between 1950 and 1970 the fraction of the city's population over sixty-five years of age has gone from 8.0 to 12.1 percent while the proportion of the city's families with incomes below the nation's median income level has risen from 36 to 49 percent.

The city's tax base has failed to grow as rapidly as its revenue requirements. This situation can be attributed to shifts in the location of economic activity as well as to the continued suburbanization of middle- and upper-income groups. Many industries are leaving the Northeast altogether while others find it more profitable to operate in the suburbs

TABLE 5

The New York City Tax Burden

Fiscal Year	Personal Income ($ Billions)	Taxes[a] ($ Billions)	Taxes as Percent of Personal Income
1963–64	27	2.013	7.6
1964–65	28	2.193	7.9
1965–66	29	2.152	7.3
1966–67	31	2.410	7.7
1967–68	34	2.626	7.8
1968–69	37	2.802	7.6
1969–70	39	2.958	7.5
1970–71	41	3.178	7.7
1971–72	43	3.736	8.7
1972–73	45	4.017	8.9
1973–74	48	4.506	9.4
1974–75	50	5.111	10.2

Source: New York City Finance Administration.

[a] Excludes fees and charges, stock transfer taxes and nonresident income taxes.

or on the fringes of the metropolitan area. While its population has remained relatively constant, New York has lost jobs at a rapid rate over the last five years (see Table 4).

The city can exert little influence over either the population shifts or the tax base trends. Together they have produced a steady increase in city tax levels which has, in turn, probably affected the types of persons and businesses willing to remain in or move into the city (see Table 5).

An additional factor that has contributed materially to the city's fiscal problems is the manner in which the responsibility for providing welfare and health-care services has been divided in New York State. New York is one of only twenty-one states that requires its local governments (e.g., counties) to contribute to the support of cash assistance for the aid to families with dependent children program (AFDC) or to Medicaid payments. Of these twenty-one states, the local share is the highest in New York, where it amounts to almost one quarter of the total or half of the nonfederal share (see Table 6).

TABLE 6

Fraction of AFDC Cash Assistance and Medicaid Payments Borne by Local Governments (Fiscal Year 1974)

State[a]	Percent
New York	23.0
Minnesota	21.8
Wyoming	18.5
California	14.5
Kansas	11.3
Colorado	9.4
Nebraska	8.8
Nevada	8.3
N. Carolina	8.3
Indiana	6.9
New Jersey	6.5
Iowa	4.8
N. Dakota	4.6
Maryland	4.2
Montana	2.8
Virginia	0.6
Utah	0.6
Louisiana	0.2
Oregon	0.1
New Hampshire	b
Mississippi	b

Source: Department of Health, Education and Welfare, "State Expenditures for Public Assistance Programs."

[a]States not listed do not require any local contribution.
[b]Less than 0.1 percent.

While county governments in New York also must bear half of the cost of the Home Relief Program, New York State's relatively generous general assistance program, this division of responsibility does not differ from the pattern that prevails in the rest of the nation. All told, New York City's welfare-related expenditures amount to some $3.5 billion, or approximately one-third of its current spending. One billion dollars of this must be raised by the city. If the city constituted just part of a large county—as is true of Los Angeles, Newark, and all but a handful of the large cities located in the twenty-one states requiring local welfare contributions—the costs of supporting the city's income-security programs would be shared by some suburban jurisdictions. However, being a city-county, New York must bear the cost alone.

New York's long tradition of providing enriched levels of public services also has contributed to its current fiscal difficulties. The more obvious services in which New York far outdistances most other local governments include the city university system, the municipal hospital system, the low- and middle-income housing programs, and the extensive public transportation network. For many years there seemed little doubt that the city's wealth was sufficient to support its chosen level of services. However, in recent years it has proved difficult politically to reduce services in line with the city's declining relative fiscal ability to afford them or to raise taxes and fees.

Finally, one cannot ignore the city's questionable accounting procedures and loose fiscal management in relation to the current crisis. These procedures masked the fact the New York officials were failing to make the difficult choices that were required if the city's expense budget was to be truly balanced as required by law.[2] The fault does not rest with the city alone. Many of the "gimmicks" which allowed the budget to appear balanced were tolerated or even suggested by state officials and were certainly not secrets to the banking community. These "gimmicks" produced small deficits which were allowed to accumulate and grow, producing a problem of large and unmanageable proportions.

Is New York Unique?

Are New York's problems simply of a larger magnitude or are they qualitatively different from those of other major cities? Much of the public discussion suggests that New York is very different from other

2 "Annual budget and financial reports are filed with the Division of Municipal Affairs in the office of the State Comptroller. Budgets are reviewed in substance and legality. . . . Deficit financing is not recognized in the operation of units of Local Government in New York State and can only be legally validated by legisltive en-

cities, that it has an abnormally large welfare population, an unusually large and well-paid public labor force and has expenditure patterns that are significantly higher than other cities. At the same time, there is the belief that the fiscal crisis being visited upon New York soon will afflict other cities. Generally neither of those contradictory sets of impressions is valid.

In recent decades New York has been buffeted by the same socioeconomic forces that have affected other large, older urban centers and has responded to these pressures in a fashion similar to that of other cities. According to most measures, New York's situation is far from the worst in the nation. One composite index of central city disadvantages shows New York in better shape than Newark, Baltimore, and Chicago as well as eight other large urban centers not included in Table 7 (see column 1). A smaller fraction of New York's population receives welfare than is the case in Philadelphia, Baltimore, Newark, or Boston (see Table 7, column 2).

Comparisons of the expenditure and employment patterns of New York City with those of other large municipal governments indicate that New York is far out of line with other jurisdictions (see Table 7, columns 3a and 4a). Yet this is a misleading conclusion which stems from the fact that New York City provides services that in other areas may be supplied by a county government, a school district, or another specialized government. If one compares the New York employment and spending patterns with those of *all* of the local governments providing services to the residents of other large cities, New York appears to be less extraordinary (see Table 7, columns 3b and 4b). While its per capita expenditure and public employment levels are above those of any other major city area, some of the differences with respect to such cities as Boston and Philadelphia can be explained by the fact that welfare is a state function in Massachusetts and Pennsylvania. While New York also spends a great deal more than other cities on higher education, hospitals, and mass transportation, its expenditure on the services commonly provided by municipalities is not out of line with those of other large cities (see Table 7, columns 3c and 4c). With respect to the salaries paid public employees, New York is generous but not the most generous of large cities (see Table 7, column 5). Considering that New York's cost of living—as measured by the Bureau of Labor Statistics (BLS) intermediate family budget—is higher than all but that of Boston, its wages are not particularly out of line (see Table 7, column 6).

actment." Advisory Commission on Intergovernmental Relations, *City Financial Emergency*, Washington, D. C., 1973, p. 168.

TABLE 7

New York City Compared to Other Large Central Cities

City	(1) Index of Central City Dis-advantage	(2) Fraction of Population Receiving Welfare Pay-ments*	(3) Per Capita Expenditures 1972–1973			(4) Local Government Employment Per 10,000 Population 1974		
			(a) City Govern-ment	(b) (c) All Local Governments* Serving Central County		(a) City Govern-ment	(b) (c) All Local Governments* Serving Central County	
				Total	CMF‡		Total	CMF‡
New York City†	211	12.4	$1,224	$1,286	$435	517.1	528.2	263.7
Boston	198	16.9	858	756	441	378.0	465.0	249.2
Chicago	245	11.1	267	600	383	140.0	352.5	250.1
Newark	422	14.4	692	827	449	391.1	421.5	304.6
Los Angeles	105	8.0	242	759	408	162.2	401.1	256.0
Philadelphia†	205	16.2	415	653	395	163.8	414.5	301.5
San Francisco†	105	9.1	751	1,073	488	312.5	488.3	244.4
New Orleans†	168	11.4	241	431	260	177.3	357.7	271.3
St. Louis†	231	15.8	310	610	360	241.9	424.6	227.8
Denver†	143	7.2	473	721	375	237.0	410.5	280.9
Baltimore†	256	16.3	806	814	470	434.1	434.1	312.5
Detroit	210	11.1	357	650	396	194.8	354.3	258.6

*Central county.

†Boundaries of the city are coterminous with those of the central county.

‡Common Municipal Functions (CMF) include elementary and secondary education, highways, police, fire, sanitation, parks, general control and financial administration.

Sources:
1. Richard Nathan "The Record of the New Federalism: What It Means for the Nation's Cities" (Washington, D.C., 1974).
2. Department of Health, Education and Welfare, Recipients of Public Assistance Money Payments and Amounts of Such Payments by Program, State, and County. February 1975 DHEW Pub. No. (SRS) 76-03105 NCSS Report A-8 (2/75). Includes AFDC and general assistance recipients.

However, it should be noted that what little reliable evidence there is seems to indicate that New York City provides its employees with considerably more in the way of fringe benefits—pensions, health insurance, etc.—than is offered the employees of other large cities.

While New York's situation in many ways does not differ markedly from that of other large central cities, some of its problems are clearly not shared with other cities. First there is New York's debt situation. On a per capita basis the city has far more debt outstanding than do the local

New York City Compared to Other Large Central Cities (Cont'd.)

(5) Public Employee Average Salaries 1974**				(6) Cost of BLS's Inter-mediate Family Budget (Index 1974)	(7) Debt Outstanding Per Capita 1972–73*	
(a) Teacher	(b) Police	(c) Fire	(d) Sanitation		(a) Total	(b) Short-Term
$17,018	$14,666	$16,964	$15,924	116	$1,676	$352
13,938	14,352	13,844	10,666	117	1,385	334
17,409	14,146	15,525	11,956	103	733	169
13,720	13,282	13,282	8,473	116	616	112
13,058	15,833	21,180	13,168	98	650	14
12,800	14,354	13,869	13,337	103	1,015	101
14,855	15,529	17,765	13,023	106	1,225	151
8,715	10,746	10,645	4,170	NA	770	39
14,894	11,748	13,185	9,593	97	731	49
13,505	12,907	14,198	10,258	95	786	52
10,488	10,098	10,980	8,126	100	609	45
18,836	15,636	16,107	13,814	100	658	63

**Estimated from October 1974 payroll per full-time equivalent worker per function. To the extent possible, census estimates for teachers have been adjusted to reflect whether payment is on a ten- or twelve-month basis.

Sources: (Cont'd.)
3a.   U.S. Bureau of the Census, "City Government Finances in 1972–73," GF73, No. 4.
3b., d., 7. U. S. Bureau of the Census, "Local Government Finances in Selected Metropolitan Areas and Large Counties 1972–73," No. 6.
4., 5.   U.S. Bureau of the Census, "Local Government Employment in Selected Metropolitan Areas and Large Counties 1974," GE74, No. 3.
6.   Bureau of Labor Statistics, "Autumn 1974 Urban Family Budgets and Comparative Indexes for Selected Urban Areas" (4-9-75).

governments providing services in the other central city areas (see Table 7, column 7). This is particularly true of short-term debt in which New York stands alone in its needs continually to enter the market to "roll over" large quantities of notes. Second, New York, as far as can be told, has been the only major city that has chronically run a large current operating deficit in both good and bad economic years. Finally, as was mentioned previously, New York revenues and expenditures are much more sensitive to the ups and downs of the business cycle. . . .

Conclusion

The focus of this paper has been largely on the immediate crisis facing New York City. . . . However, the crisis will only be delayed temporarily unless the underlying causes of the city's fiscal difficulties are addressed. While it may be comforting to believe that these problems can be handled by the city alone, this probably is not the case. Certainly efficient management, strict accounting procedures, and the introduction of new technology can help, but such measures alone will not balance New York's budget and pay off a substantial portion of its accumulated short-term debt. Substantial service cutbacks and tax increases will be required to accomplish these objectives. Yet such actions will make the city a less attractive place in which to live and probably will hasten the exodus of middle- and upper-income families and commercial and industrial establishments. This, in turn, will undercut the city's ability to support even a reduced level of services.

Given these forces, it is probable that the underlying problems facing New York, as well as a number of other large, aging cities, can be dealt with effectively only by the states or by the federal government. Unless one is willing to consider policies that would redistribute the low-income populations among other jurisdictions, or would redraw city boundaries so as to encompass suburban areas, or that would radically equalize income, the main alternative left for addressing the city's problems is to relieve the city of some major portions of its current fiscal responsibility. As has been mentioned previously, New York City's situation would be aided immensely if the state or the federal government assumed the burden now borne by the city for welfare and related services to the poor.

School Desegregation
and White Flight

CHRISTINE H. ROSSELL

White flight from cities has been a much discussed phenomenon in the last decade. Despite widespread speculation over which policies aggravate this trend and which slow it down, there has been little systematic research as to its causes and consequences. Nevertheless, administrators and politicians often claim that school desegregation, perhaps one of the most controversial policies of the last decade, is counterproductive because it acclerates white flight. The most recent proponent of this theory is James Coleman, best known for *Equal Educational Opportunity*, often called the "Coleman Report."[1] He has stated that "The extremely strong reactions of individual whites in moving their children out of large districts engaged in massive and rapid desegregation suggests that in the long run the policies that have been pursued will defeat the purpose of increasing overall contact among races

[1] The earlier work on which Coleman built his reputation is a massive study showing that school desegregation raises the achievement scores of black students: James S. Coleman et al., *Equality of Educational Opportunity*, (Washington, D.C., 1966). The latest work in which he claims school desegregation increases white flight is James S. Coleman, Sara D. Kelly, and John Moore, "Recent Trends in School Integration," paper presented at the annual meeting of the American Educational Research Association, Washington, D.C., April 2, 1975; James S. Coleman, Sara D. Kelly, and John Moore, "Trends in School Segregation, 1968–73," Urban Institute Working Paper, August 1975.

CHRISTINE H. ROSSELL is an assistant professor of political science at Boston University. She is the author of several articles and papers on school desegregation and its impact, and is currently conducting a study of a school desegregation in 113 cities, funded by the National Institute of Education.

in schools."[2] The mass media has tended to disseminate statements such as these with little attempt to ascertain their accuracy, despite the mounting criticism within academic circles of Coleman's methods and findings.

The data in this article show that school desegregation has little or no effect on white flight. Even in the two high desegregation school districts that had significant white flight, it is minimal (about a 3 percentage point increase over the previous trend) and temporary. By the third year after desegregation, white flight stabilizes to a rate lower than the predesegregation period in these districts. For all "high desegregation" school districts the rate of decline is lower by the third year after desegregation than any year prior to desegregation. Furthermore, if a school district does have any negligible white flight it typically comes before the opening of school in the first year of the major plan, and rarely after that. Desegregation under court order does not increase white flight, nor does massive desegregation in large school districts. In short, this study contradicts Coleman's recent assertions regarding the deleterious effect of school desegregation on white flight, and demonstrates the fundamental error in his measurement of that phenomenon.

METHODOLOGY AND PRIOR RESEARCH

In conducting public policy research, it is important that one's methodology be appropriate to the phenomenon being studied. While on the face of it, a longitudinal design seems the most appropriate method of determining the impact of a policy, certain kinds of longitudinal designs can be extremely misleading. For example, just looking at the white enrollment before and after school desegregation—a technique often used by newspapers, local school officials, and desegregation opponents—obscures the fact that while there may be a loss of whites incurred after school desegregation, it is usually no greater than losses incurred in previous years. Thus, this type of design does not uncover patterns of white out-migration that developed long before the school issue was litigated. Longer longitudinal designs of the type used by Coleman can be misleading if there is no attempt to fix the point of school desegregation policy implementation, and changes in school racial mixtures are simply compared to changes in percentage white enrollment. This technique, while seemingly more sophisticated than a before and after design, also errs in confusing the covariation of two secular demographic

---

[2] Coleman, Kelly, and Moore, "Recent Trends in School Integration," pp. 21–22.

trends (white flight from cities and ghetto expansion into white school attendance zones) with a causal relationship between white flight and governmentally or court-imposed desegregation policy.

Probably the most appropriate methodology for analyzing public policy impact is a time series quasi-experimental design. None of the previous analysts of school desegregation and white flight has used this design. This may be due to unfamiliarity with it, or to an unwillingness or inability to spend the necessary time and money collecting data over time. The particular quasi-experimental design used here is the interrupted multiple times series quasi-experiment with a nonequivalent control group, developed by Campbell and Stanley.[3] It is characterized by (1) periodic measurement on some variable (e.g., percentage white enrollment) obtained at equally spaced points in time; (2) the "introduction" of a quasi-experimental variable (e.g., school desegregation) somewhere into the series; and (3) a control group, which has not received the quasi-experimental variable against which the experimental groups can be compared. In this article, then, the effect of school desegregation on white flight will be analyzed as a time series quasi-experiment. (A more detailed explanation of the methodology is presented in Appendix 1.)

The small amount of academic research on school desegregation and white flight has, with the exception of Coleman's work, tended to show no relationship between the two phenomena. Clotfelter found no statistically significant relationship between school desegregation and white flight when a number of demographic and economic variables were controlled for, although his measures of school desegregation is a dichotomous variable not easily generalizable, and his longitudinal analysis only involves two points in time. Reynolds Farley, using a measure of school integration similar to Coleman's in that it does not measure actual policy, but using more sophisticated statistical controls, found integration has no discernible effect, on the average, on the rate of white flight.[4]

A research design prepared by the Rand Corporation for the U.S. Commission on Civil Rights analyzes the change in the percentage white students in the Washington, D.C., public schools over a twenty-three-

---

[3] Donald T. Campbell and Julian Stanley, *Experimental and Quasi-Experimental Designs for Research* (Chicago, 1963), pp. 47–48.

[4] Charles Clotfelter, "The Detroit Decision and White Flight," *Journal of Legal Studies*, forthcoming; Reynolds Farley, "School Integration and White Flight," paper presented at the Brookings Symposium on School Desegregation and White Flight, Washington, D.C., August 15, 1975.

year period. The analysis shows school desegregation (open enrollment after the 1954 Supreme Court decision) to have had a minimal effect in increasing the flight of whites to the suburbs. However, since open enrollment typically involves very few students, it is difficult to generalize from this finding to that of mandatory busing.[5]

One of the most promising studies of school desegregation and white flight is summarized in a recent issue of *Integrated Education*. The study was conducted in eight desegregated school districts in Florida in 1973. Only 3.6 percent of the parents interviewed rejected school desegregation by withdrawing their children from their assigned schools. The authors conclude that if a low annual rate of aggregate white flight is a prime criterion for evaluating progress, then school desegregation in these districts should be rated at least a qualified success.[6] The findings of most studies then, despite differing methodologies, is that the effect of school desegregation on white flight is negligible when compared to other factors that cause relocation of whites.

CONDUCT OF THE STUDY

Sample and Data Collection

In this analysis aggregate data are used to describe a sample of eighty-six northern cities and their school districts. This represents the northern sample of a larger study of both northern and southern school districts (yet to be analyzed) and is biased in favor of medium and large cities/school districts.[7]

Defining School Desegregation

Most research, including Coleman's, defines "school desegregation" as any situation where there happens to be a significant number of black

---

[5] Robert L. Crain et al., *Design for a National Longitudinal Study of School Desegregation*, Vol. II., *Research Design and Procedures* (Santa Monica, Calif., September 1974), p. 79.

[6] Everett Cataldo, Micheal Giles, Deborah Athos, and Douglas Gatlin, "Desegregation and White Flight," *Integrated Education* (January 1975), pp. 3–5. The compliance/rejection status of their respondents was determined from official school records. Compliers were defined as those parents who had a child attending public school in both 1971–1972 and 1972–1973. Rejecters were those who has a child in public school in 1971–1972, but transferred the child to private school in 1972–1973. The eight county school districts were Dade, Palm Beach, Duval, Leon, Jefferson, Escambia, Manatee, and Lee.

[7] All but two of the eighty-six school districts in this study have the same name

and white children in the same school at the same point in time.[8] The problem with this definition is that it obscures the reason for the integrated situation. For a good many schools in the United States, integration is, thus, unstable and temporary. Actual governmental or court implemented school desegregation, on the other hand, is not the result of ghetto expansion into an attendance zone (also called "ecological succession") and is, not surprisingly, characterized by different patterns.

This study attempts to overcome the limitations of measures of school desegregation commonly used in the past, by defining "school desegregation" as the reassignment of black or white students by a local governmental body or court for the purposes of school integration.[9] Data were collected by means of a mail questionnaire that listed the biracial schools (defined as a minimum of 10 percent black and 10 percent white)[10] in a

---

and virtually the same boundaries as the city. The decision to desegregate in every case involves interaction between the city and school officials and citizens of both legal entities. The result is that for most practical purposes the distinction between city and school district is almost nonexistent.

[8] Coleman, et al., "Recent Trends in School Integration"; U.S. Commission on Civil Rights, *Racial Isolation in the Public Schools*, 2 vols. (Washington, D.C., 1967); Thomas Dye, "Urban School Segregation, A Comparative Analysis," *Urban Affairs Quarterly*, 4 (December 1968), 141–165, the last two using a measure of the percentage of black students in predominantly black schools. Reynolds Farley and Alma F. Taeuber, "Racial Segregation in the Public Schools," *American Journal of Sociology*, 79 (January 1974), 888–890, and Farley, "School Integration and White Flight," both using an index of dissimilarity adapted from the Taeuber Index of residential segregation. Another recent study uses a measure of the change in the proportion of minority students attending "ethnically balanced" schools from 1966 to 1971: Eldon L. Wegner and Jane R. Mercer, "Dynamics of the Desegregation Process: Politics, Policies, and Community Characteristics as Factors in Change," in Frederick M. Wirt (ed.), *The Polity of the School* (Lexington, Mass., 1975), pp. 123–143.

[9] Studies using other measures have been: Donald R. Matthews and James W. Prothro, "Stateways versus Folkways: Critical Factors in Southern Reactions to *Brown* v. *Board of Education*," in Gottfried Dietze (ed.), *Essays on the American Constitution* (Englewood Cliffs, N.J., 1964); James W. Prothro, "Stateways versus Folkways Revisited: An Error in Prediction," *Journal of Politics*, 34 (May 1972), 352–364; Robert L. Crain, Morton Inger, Gerald McWhorter, and James J. Vanecko, *The Politics of School Desegregation* (New York, 1969), all using a dichotomous variable: did desegregate —or did not desegregate. David J. Kirby, T. Robert Harris, and Robert L. Crain, *Political Strategies in Northern School Desegregation* (Lexington, Mass., 1973) used a qualitative measure of the characteristics of the desegregation plan.

[10] Other minorities, such as Asian-Americans, Spanish surname, and Indian have been excluded from the computation of this measure because the concern of this study is with the political pressures and responses to the segregation of blacks from whites. Nonblack minorities simply do not exert the same kinds of pressures nor arouse the same fears as blacks. Indeed, even in many western school districts where their proportions are larger than in other regions, nonblack minorities have often sided

district and asked administrators to indicate the reason for their bi-racialness and the approximate date of any action taken to adjust racial balance.[11] The measures of school desegregation policy were computed as follows: the number of black and white students in a school in the year in which an action was taken was subtracted from the number in the same school during the preceding year. The difference was attributed to administrative action if it increased racial integration. The number of black and white students reassigned in this way in each school was totaled for the school district. This was then standardized by converting the raw number of blacks and whites reassigned into the percentage of the total school district black population that was reassigned and the percentage of the total school district white population "reverse inte-grated" (sent to predominantly black or formerly black schools). These figures, (percentage blacks and percentage whites reassigned) were added together to comprise an index measuring school desegregation for each year from 1963–1964 through 1972–1973.[12]

Further policy classification was unnecessary because the percentage of black and white students reassigned proved to be highly related to the type of action. Mandatory busing results in the highest percentage of students reassigned, while voluntary busing never amounts to more than a small percentage of students reassigned.[13] Furthermore, a straightfor-ward quantitative measure avoids the problems of semantics encoun-tered with inflammatory policy issues.

The effect of school desegregation on white flight is measured by the percentage white enrolled in public schools for as many years before

---

with the white majority against desegregation. Therefore, desegregation plans have tended to be overwhelmingly focused on integrating blacks into white schools.

[11] Racial composition data were obtained from the U. S. Department of Health, Education, and Welfare, *Directory of Public Elementary and Secondary Schools in Se-lected Districts,* Fall 1970, Enrollment and Staff by Racial/Ethnic Groups (Washing-ton, D.C., 1971). There are also volumes for Fall 1967, Fall 1968, and unpublished data for the odd years since 1967. Data for desegregation claimed in earlier years was obtained from published records of the school districts themselves. A more detailed explanation of this measure can be found in Christine H. Rossell and Robert L. Crain, *Evaluating School Desegregation Plans Statistically* (Baltimore, Md., 1973), pp. 4–11; or Kirby, Harris, and Crain, "Measuring School Desegregation," *Political Strategies in Northern School Desegregation,* chap. 12.

[12] The two measures were combined because they are highly correlated (.80) and there is so little reassignment of whites to black or formerly black schools.

[13] The relationship between the percentage of a plan which is mandatory and the percentage of students reassigned is .94 for white students and .77 for black students using gamma.

and after the major school desegregation plan as data are available, with 1972–1973 being the last year of the study. Data of percentage white were obtained from HEW statistics from fall 1967 to fall 1972. For periods earlier than that, data were collected by writing to each school district in the sample. Only about 61 percent had such data (in a few school districts it was illegal to keep it).

FINDINGS

The change in percentage white students in each of the eighty-six northern school districts before and after their major desegregation plan is presented in Appendix 2.[12] The index of the percentage of black students reassigned added to the percentage of white students reassigned in the largest desegregation action is presented in column 1. The change in the percentage white each year before the major desegregation plan is given in columns 3 through 9. The change in the percentage in each year beginning with the major plan is presented in colums 11 through 18. School desegregation actions taken in addition to the major action are indicated by asterisks next to the change in the percentage white for that school year. For example, Pasadena's major desegregation plan reassigned 98.48 percent of the black and white students in 1970. The opening of school in the first year of the plan saw an increase in the average annual decline in percentage white of about 2 percentage points. In the fall of 1972, as indicated by the asterisk in column 13, Pasadena implemented more school desegregation. By this time, however, the decline in the percentage white is close to the trend exhibited prior to the major desegregation plan. The additional action brought their total desegregation, presented in column 22, up to 100.8.[15]

The first figure in column 17 is the result of the single-Mood test, while

[14] Data on the actual percentage white in each school district for these years can be obtained by writing the author.

[15] Since the index represents the percentage of black students reassigned to white schools, and the percentage of white students reassigned to black or formerly black schools, the index could go as high as 200 percent. However, reassigning 100 percent of each race is not efficient. The most efficient reassignment in a perfectly segregated system is 50 percent of each race which equals an index of 100. Because school districts also have political and social considerations, they tend to avoid reassigning whites to black or formerly black schools, and thus the index usually reflects the percentage of black students reassigned to white schools. Pasadena is one of the few school districts that reassigned a large proportion of white students to black or formerly black schools. Either they did more reassignment than was efficient, or there is some measurement error in the index.

the second figure is the result of the double-Mood test, both explained in Appendix 1. (When N.S.—not significant—is reported, it means that the change in percentage white after desegregation is probably no greater than fluctuations that occurred before desegregation.) The figures reported for Pasadena indicate that a decline of 4.2 in 1970 (column 11) is large enough to be the result of school desegregation, rather than simply being random fluctuation. The second figure indicates that the change in percentage white when the whole postdesegregation period is examined is again large enough to be the result of school desegregation.

Column 20 shows the average change in percentage white from year to year in the predesegregation period, and column 21 shows the average change in percentage white from year to year in the postdesegregation period. While in general there is greater white flight after desegregation than before, it stabilizes by the third year after school desegregation (column 13) to a rate similar to that of the predesegregation period.

Pontiac, the second school district shown in Appendix 2, also has a significant increase in white flight after their major school desegregation plan. However, the decline stabilizes by the second year so that the rate is lower than any year before the desegregation. Both Pontiac and Pasadena desegregation plans were court ordered, but as we shall see, of the eleven court-ordered school districts, they are the only two that had a significant increase in white flight.

The remarkable characteristic of these data is that, of the top ten school districts that implemented a high degree of school desegregation, only two showed any significant increase in white flight. Furthermore, there is some indication that other factors probably contributed to white flight in Pasadena.[16] Further research on Pontiac may turn up additional factors here as well. These ten "high desegregation" school districts include one of the few school districts in the entire sample to ever have an increase in their percentage white. By the third and fourth year after their 1968 desegregation plan, the percentage white in the Berkeley school district actually increased by .2 percent and .9 percent respectively.

The next group of school districts, those implementing an intermediate degree of school desegregation, have not a single case of any school

---

[16] Wirt points out that although Pasadena's white (Anglo) student population declined after school desegregation, two districts in the San Gabriel Valley (the hot, smoggy valley in which Pasadena is located) that did not desegregate lost even more whites than Pasadena. Frederick M. Wirt, "Understanding the Reality of Desegregation," (unpublished paper, Berkeley, Calif., June 21, 1972).

district exhibiting significant white flight after their major desegregation plan. In the third group of school districts, those that reassigned
less than 5 percent of their black and white students in their major plan,
one had less decline than would have been expected from the previous
trend (South Bend, Indiana), and three others had a significant increase
in white flight. However, the three exhibiting white flight implemented
so little desegregation that the relationship to school desegregation
should be treated with suspicion. As indicated in Appendix 1, the control group (those implementing no school desegregation) was assigned
a "treatment point" of 1968. In other words, changes in percentage
white before 1968 are compared to changes after 1968. This point comes
after the 1968 summer riots and is also when a good number of school
districts desegregated. In this way, it was hoped that possible secular
trends could be isolated. Unfortunately, the control group suffers from
poor record keeping (in some cases because it was illegal to keep such
data). However, of those school districts that had pre-1967 data, two
show a significant increase in white flight after the summer of 1968.
Other school districts show a large increase from the previous year,
but without the pre-1967 data it is impossible to tell if this is a change
in the trend. At the very least, it is useful to compare these data to
those of the desegregating school districts.

In order to summarize the data, the school districts are divided into
five groups: court ordered; high desegregation (greater than 20 percent); medium desegregation (5-20 percent); low desegregation (less
than 5 percent); and the control group. The average for each group
for four years before and four years after their major plan is presented in Table 1 and represented graphically in Figure 1. As Table 1
indicates, none of the various desegregating groups shows any
significant white flight, although the highest desegregation group
shows a negligible increase of about 1 percentage point from the
previous trend.[17] The important phenomenon here is that any loss of
whites occurs *before* school opens in the first year of the plan. After
that, white flight stabilizes to a rate slightly better than the predesegregation period. Therefore, white flight, if it occurs at all, occurs
not from the problems experienced during the first year of desegregation, but from the fear of problems. In other words, if whites leave, it is

[17] The school districts were also grouped according to their total desegregation,
rather than their largest action. This made little difference in the trend for each
group, although the highest desegregating group showed even less change in white
flight, after school desegregation.

FIGURE 1

*Change in Percentage White for Four Desegregation Groups
and a Control Group (0 Desegregation)*

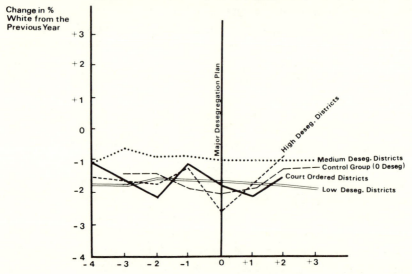

School Years Before and After Desegregation

typically not because they participated in the plan and did not like it, but because they refused to participate at all. Apparently, whites who did participate in the first year of the plan did not leave after that. This has enormous policy implications because it means administrators should concentrate their efforts on eliminating fear and controversy *before* the plan is implemented.

The findings of this study thus support the proposition that school desegregation does not cause significant white flight, and tend to disprove Coleman's thesis. Furthermore, although Coleman has maintained that "in an area such as school desegregation . . . the courts are probably the worst instrument of social policy,"[18] Figure 1 and Table 1 show no significant increase in white flight in northern school districts that desegregated under court order.

Table 2 shows the change in percentage white before and after school desegregation, controlling for degree of desegregation and city size. Within each desegregating group and the control group, the larger cities show no greater white flight than the medium and small cities, and none is significant. Although Coleman has maintained that the greatest white

[18] Coleman et al., "Recent Trends in School Integration," p. 21.

TABLE 1: Change in Percentage White for Four Desegregation Groups and a Control Group

Group	Change in % White.								Signif. Level	Average Pre-series	Average Post-series
	−4 Years	−3 Years	−2 Years	−1 Years	0 Years	1 Years	2 Years	3 Years			
Court ordered	−1.1	−1.8	−2.2	−1.0	−1.8	−2.1	−1.4		N.S.	−1.5	−1.8
High desegregation (> 20%)	−1.5	−1.8	−1.8	−1.2	−2.4	−1.8	−.8		N.S.	−1.5	−1.7
Medium desegregation (5–20%)	−1.1	−.7	−.9	−.9	−1.0	−1.0	−1.0		N.S.	−.9	−1.0
Low desegregation (< 5%)	−1.8	−1.8	−1.4	−1.5	−1.6	−1.6	−1.5	−1.7	N.S.	−1.6	−1.6
Control group (0)		−1.5	−1.5	−1.9	−2.2	−1.8	−1.3	−1.2	N.S.	−1.2	−1.6

TABLE 2: Change in Percentage White for Four Desegregation Groups and a Control Group Controlling for City Size

Group	−4 Years	−3 Years	−2 Years	−1 Years	0 Years	1 Years	2 Years	3 Years	Signif. Level	Average Pre-series	Average Post-series
Large cities (> 500,000)											
High desg.	−1.3	−.7	−2.8	−.4	−2.3	−2.3	−1.4		N.S.	−1.0	−2.0
Med. desg.	−4.0	−1.0	−1.1	−.9	−1.1	−1.1			a	−1.8	−1.1
Low desg.		−1.5	−1.7	−3.6	−.8	−.9	−.4		N.S.	−2.3	−.7
Control	−2.1	−1.3	−1.3	−1.9	−1.7	−1.6			N.S.	−1.6	−1.7
Med. cities (100,000–500,000)											
High desg.	−1.3	−1.6	.3	−1.3	−2.0	−1.8	−2.2	−.8	N.S.	−1.1	−1.7
Med. desg.	−.8	−1.3	−.6	−1.2	−1.2	−2.1	−1.1	−1.1	N.S.	−1.0	−1.4
Low desg.	−1.3	−2.5	−1.8	−1.3	−1.3	−1.6	−1.4	−1.3	N.S.	−1.7	−1.4
Control		−1.0	−2.0	−2.1	−2.4	−1.8	−1.3	−1.3	N.S.	−1.7	−1.7
Small cities (< 100,000)											
High desg.	−2.2	−3.3	−4.8	−1.8	−3.6	−1.2	−1.1		N.S.	−3.0	−1.9
Med. desg.	−.2	−.7	−1.2	−.2	−.9	−.3	−.9		N.S.	−.6	−.7
Low desg.			.6	−.5	−.7	−1.5	−1.5		a	−.6	−1.2
Control					−2.2	−1.9	−1.6	−1.2	a	a	−1.7

aUnable to compute.

flight is in "large districts engaged in massive and rapid desegrega-tion,"[19] the two large school districts, San Francisco and Denver, that engaged in such massive and rapid desegregation show no significant white flight. Nor do most of the other large school districts that imple-mented lesser degrees of school desegregation (Seattle; Milwaukee; Kansas City, Mo.; Indianapolis; Baltimore; Philadelphia; Los Angeles; and Chi-cago). Thus the data of the present study contradict almost every claim Coleman has made regarding school desegregation and white flight.[20]

IMPLICATIONS

It appears that, although Coleman has claimed in television appearances and newspaper interviews that he is conducting research on school de-segregation policy, this is not precisely what he is doing. Indeed, there is no evidence that he knows what school desegregation policy has been implemented in the school districts he is studying. A *New York Times* research study of Coleman's twenty cities—in which key officials in each were questioned by telephone—could find no court-ordered deseg-regation in any of the cities during the 1968–1970 period he studied, despite Coleman's assertion that such desegregation was causing massive white flight. Court suits were pending in many cities, but desegregation was limited to a few modest open-enrollment plans, used mainly by blacks. If there was "massive and rapid" desegregation as Coleman said, it could not have been due to court-ordered remedies.[21] Since there has been no massive and rapid desegregation in the South without a court order, there is not much evidence of any kind of rapid and massive desegregation in his sample. In fact, in the same *New York Times* article, Coleman conceded he was "quite wrong" to have called the change in segregation "massive."[22]

The fact is that Coleman is studying changes in school racial mix-tures, not school desegregation policy, and while he briefly acknowl-

[19] Ibid.

[20] In the later paper, "Trends in School Segregation, 1968–73," Coleman acknowl-edges that the estimated loss in northern cities which have undergone desegregation is less than in the southern ones, but this did not stop him from filing another court affidavit on September 2, 1975, in Boston on behalf of antibusing groups, pre-dicting that school desegregation will increase white flight in Boston. In general, while the second paper is much more reasonable in the conclusions it draws, Coleman's pub-lic statements have not reflected this.

[21] Robert Reinhold, "Report of Failure of Busing Conceded by Author to Exceed Scientific Data," *The New York Times*, July 11, 1975.

[22] Ibid.

edges the difference in his later paper, "Trends in School Segregation, 1968–73," he continues to draw conclusions and policy recommendations that use the term, "school desegregation."[23] The clearest indication that he does not understand the difference can be seen in Coleman's affadavit in *Morgan et al. v. Kerrigan et al.* Nos. 75–1184; 75–1194; 75–1197; 75–1212, filed in the U.S. Court of Appeals for the 1st Circuit (September 3, 1975) on behalf of the Boston Home and School Association, an antibusing group in Boston. In this affadavit, he predicts that full-scale desegregation will increase the number of whites leaving the city, and that the exodus will be caused by the citywide scope of the desegregation plan and its impact at the elementary school level.[24] However, his prediction is based on his prior research in which he only measures changes in racial mixtures through a statistical measure of the proportion of blacks and whites attending school with the opposite race, and therefore does not distinguish between ghetto expansion into a white attendance zone (ecological succession) and an actual governmental policy resulting in the same thing—integration. As mentioned earlier, in the case of ecological succession, the integration will be temporary and the eventual resegregation will look like white flight resulting from "school desegregation policy." This confusion of two different phenomena means that, in most cases, Coleman's prediction is invalid for governmental or court-ordered school desegregation policy.[25]

Furthermore, in a careful review of the issues and policy implications of white-flight research, Orfield points out that even if one were to accept both the validity of Coleman's method of analysis and the maxi-

---

[23] Coleman et al., "Trends in School Integration, 1968–73."

[24] In an analysis of Boston's Phase I and Phase II desegregation plans (fall 1974 and fall 1975) recently completed by the author and included in Appendix 3, the percentage white in Boston public schools declined by five percentage points after Phase I. This represents an increase of only 3 percentage points from the average rate of white flight prior to Phase I. Furthermore, even with many white students still boycotting, the rate of white flight has declined during Phase II to a rate lower than that experienced after Phase I.

[25] Coleman also measures loss in white enrollment in a way that may tend to exaggerate white flight in some cities. He compares the raw figures on white enrollment in one year to the raw figures on white enrollment in the previous year and then claims white flight if the latter is lower than the former. Yet one can easily predict cases where due to job layoffs, factory closings, etc., both whites and blacks leave a city at a faster rate than before, but blacks leave at a higher rate. Although this would result in the percentage black decreasing and the percentage white increasing, Coleman would still call this white flight, even though it might more properly be called "black flight." In the final analysis, the most important variable for policy purposes is the percentage white, not the number white.

mum force of his results, his study suggests only that the initiation of desegregation in a city with a 50 percent black enrollment will produce an additional loss of 5.5 percent of the white students. This "flight" is significantly less than the same school system can expect to lose for other reasons in a normal year. In short, it seems that Coleman himself has not followed his research to its logical conclusion—that at worst, his model predicts desegregation of a 50 percent black school system would bring the schools to their ultimate ghetto status only about a year sooner than otherwise projected.[26] Therefore, an even greater problem than the inappropriate methodology used by Coleman is his apparent unwillingness to accept the policy implications of his own research.

CONCLUSIONS

This study has demonstrated that school desegregation causes little or no significant white flight, even when it is court ordered and implemented in large cities. Despite the popularity of the claim, researchers and analysts familiar with the white-flight phenomenon in cities should have been able to predict that the effect of school desegregation would be minimal compared to other, more important, forces such as increasing crime and public fears of violence, rapid movement of jobs to suburban facilities, much greater housing construction in the suburbs than in the cities, decline in the actual level of some central city services, major urban riots, and deteriorating city schools and declining achievement scores. These and other factors have contributed to the suburbanization of middle-class families who tend to be predominantly, although not exclusively, white.[27]

While almost all school districts (with the exception of Berkeley, California) are still experiencing white flight, it is quite encouraging that by the second and third year after desegregation, the school districts engaging in massive and rapid desegregation have a rate of white flight that is lower than their rate in the predesegregation period and lower than that of any other group, including those that did not implement

---

[26] Gary Orfield, "White Flight Research: Its Importance, Perplexities, and Possible Policy Implication," Brookings Institution paper, September 1975.

[27] Orfield points out that middle-class black families are also fleeing cities whenever they are allowed to buy suburban housing. Moreover, among black families who retain central city residence, there are substantial numbers who have fled to private schools. In Washington, D.C., for example, the suburbs experienced a 61 percent increase in black population in the first four years of the 1970s, and among the blacks who remained in the city, about 10,000 are using private schools. Ibid., pp. 8–9.

any desegregation at all. This is a heartening phenomenon and may mean that school desegregation, and the educational innovation that typically accompanies it when it is city wide, could impede the increasing ghettoization of American cities. While a good number of researchers and citizens maintain that the only way to avoid the problem of white flight and accomplish stable integration is to integrate housing, the findings of this study suggest that the process could in fact be the reverse. As Orfield points out, it would be extremely difficult to implement stable housing integration involving a large number of blacks, without a framework of area-wide integrated schools.[28] Once blacks begin to move into a particular area, that area tends to become increasingly more black unless new white families move in to replace those who leave in the normal process of residential mobility. Under the existing laissez-faire system, however, there is absolutely no incentive for a white family to move into a neighborhood with a substantial number of black neighbors because, based on past experience, the neighborhood school will in all probability become predominantly black in the future. Even those who would accept integration will very seldom allow their child to be in an all-black school. Therefore, without a desegregation plan, the white family often does not perceive a choice between an integrated and an all-white school, but only between an all-white school and one that is almost certain to become virtually all black. The only way to break this cycle of expectations is to assure families that the schools will be integrated wherever they move in the city, and they will not become overwhelmingly black anywhere. This assurance, which can only be supported by a city-wide school desegregation plan, could stem the flight of whites to the suburbs in search of schools that will not become all black in the near future.

Serious recommendations about school desegregation policy should be based on an analysis of policy alternatives that might lessen the incentives for the departure of the middle class in all cities, and even provide some encouragement for their return. It is not enough to simply say white flight is not increased by school desegregation. We need to know how to stop flight altogether. Perhaps the most important step to be taken next in the research described here is to determine how Berkeley was able to increase its white percentage, and why Pasadena and Pontiac experienced a brief significant white flight after school desegregation and other school districts did not. In addition, it is necessary to understand the mechanisms operating in school desegregation that account for the fact that, if any white flight occurs, it typically occurs

[28] Ibid., pp. 15–18.

before school opens in the first year of the plan, and rarely after, and why there is a decline in the rate of white flight by the second and third year 'after the major plan is implemented. Closer study of the best and worst cases, and of the intricacies of the patterns observed, might well suggest procedures and policies that can help avoid any initial loss of enrollment, and perhaps stop the loss of whites altogether from central cities.*

APPENDIX 1 : METHODOLOGY

Because this study is comparative and school desegregation occurs at different times for different school districts, a modification had to be made in the interrupted multiple times series quasi-experimental design. The treatment point is usually a fixed point or year for all cases in quasi-experimental designs. Unfortunately for the neatness of the design, some school districts take two and occasionally three years to complete their desegregation plans. However, one action is usually much larger than any of the others and that was the point chosen for those taking multiple actions. Change is then analyzed for as many years before and after the major desegregation plan as data are available (ending in 1972–1973), although for some school districts this will mean the first point in the series is 1963 and for others it is 1967. However, most school districts desegregated in 1968, with the next largest groups desegregating in 1969 and 1970 respectively. For the control group—those that did not desegregate at all—1968 is used as the "treatment" point because it is the year in which the largest number of districts desegregated, and it is a year in which a good deal of disruption and change occurred in this country. Therefore, 1968 marks a turning point used to isolate possible short- or long-term systematic trends.

Measuring Discontinuity: Tests of Significance

The question of whether the occurrence of an event under study had an effect on the variables being measured cannot be solved simply by visual

---

* This is a revision of a paper, "The Political and Social Impact of School Desegregation," presented at the American Political Science Convention, September 1975. The APSA paper was a preliminary report of a study of the social and political impact of school desegregation in 113 northern and southern school districts from 1963–1973. The study analyzes the effect of school desegregation on voting patterns, racial composition of school boards, white flight, residential integration, community organizational participation, attendance, suspensions, expulsions, racial composition and integration of teaching staff, student organizations, and athletic teams. Steve Cohen

inspection of plots of data. A test of significance must be applied to estimate whether or not an observed change exceeds the limits of what is expected on the basis of chance fluctuations.

Two tests of significance, the single-Mood and double-Mood tests, are used in the interrupted time series. Each of these tests is based on a calculation of the difference between expected and observed values of points or distributions (or expected and expected values in the case of the double-Mood test), where expected values are based on an extrapolation of the regression line. The two tests, plus an additional one, are described in Joyce Sween and Donald T. Campbell, "The Interrupted Time Series as Quasi-Experiment: Three Tests of Significance" (Evanston, Ill., 1965, mimeographed). (The computer program that utilizes these tests is distributed by the Northwestern University Computing Center as NUC 0049 Timex.)

The first test, the single-Mood test (Alexander Mood, *Introduction to the Theory of Statistics*, New York, 1950, pp. 297–298), is a t-test using a simple least-squares line-fitting technique where the slope of the line is used to "predict" the first value occurring after the quasi-experiment. The standard error is based on pretest variance only. The single-Mood test is appropriate for testing hypotheses regarding the immediate effect of an event.

The double-Mood test extends the logic of the single-Mood test to include both a prechange linear fit as well as a postchange linear fit (see Mood, *Introduction to the Theory of Statistics*, pp. 350–358; and Walker and J. Lev, *Statistical Inference*, New York, 1953, pp. 390–400). The comparison is between two predictions by these two estimates of a hypothetical value lying midway between the last prechange and the first postchange point. The standard error is based on the entire series variance.

An underlying assumption of these tests is that there is no autocorrelation (correlation of errors). Since it rarely happens that errors are uncorrelated in longitudinal studies, Sween and Campbell have determined through Montecarlo simulation the degree of adjustment necessary in the significance level at which one should reject the null hypothesis for various levels of autocorrelation (Sween and Campbell, "The Interrupted Time Series," pp. 11–17).

---

adapted the quasi-experimental computer program to the IBM 360 at Boston University and completed all the computer runs.

APPENDIX 2: CHANGE IN PERCENTAGE WHITE FROM THE PREVIOUS SCHOOL YEAR COMPUTED FOR EACH YEAR BEFORE AND AFTER SCHOOL DESEGREGATION

School District	(1) % Students Re-assigned	(2) Court Ordered	(3) −7 Years	(4) −6 Years	(5) −5 Years	(6) −4 Years	(7) −3 Years	(8) −2 Years	(9) −1 Year	(10) Major Plan Date	(11) +0 Years	(12) +1 Year	(13) +2 Years	(14) +3 Years	(15) +4 Years	(16) +5 Years	(17) +6 Years	(18) +7 Years	(19) Signif. Level	(20) Average Pre-series	(21) Average Post-series	(22) Total Deseg.
Pasadena, Calif.	98.48	yes		−2.7	−1.5	−1.9	−2.1	−2.0	−2.4	1970	−4.2	−4.5	−2.5*						.01,.05	−1.2	−3.7	100.80
Pontiac, Mich.	83.47	yes		−1.3	−1.0	−3.0	−3.1*	−1.7	−2.4*	1971	−5.4	−.4							.02,.02	−2.1	−2.9	87.09
Berkeley, Calif.	57.72			*		−2.2*	−2.2	.7	.7	1968	−2.2	−.6	−.8	.2	.9				N.S.	−.9	−.3	66.32
Wichita, Kans.	44.36				−.8*	−.4	−.4*	−1.0*	−1.0*	1971	−1.3	−1.4							N.S.	−.7	−1.4	56.63
San Francisco, Calif.	42.49	yes			−2.9	−1.2	0	−4.1	−.2	1971	−3.0	−2.1*							N.S.	−1.7	−2.6	46.58
Ft. Wayne, Ind.	34.60				−.4	−.5	−1.6	.2	−1.1	1971	−.8	−1.0							N.S.	−.7	−.9	34.00
Waukegan, Ill. (el.Schl's)	31.72	yes				−1.3	−3.5	−7.8	−1.1	1968	−1.8	−1.9	−1.0	−1.9					N.S.	−3.4	−1.5	31.72
Denver, Colo.	24.64	yes				−1.3	−1.4	−1.5	−.6	1969	−1.5	−2.4*	−2.0*	−1.7*	−1.0				N.S.	−1.2	−1.8	29.77
Providence, R.I.	24.10							.7	−.6*	1967	−1.5	−2.0	−.2*	−1.0	−1.7*	−1.0	−1.5		a	a	−.9	36.00
Riverside, Calif.	21.40						−.6*	0		1966	−1.5	−1.2*	−.2*						N.S.	−1.1	−1.1	38.20
Las Vegas, Nev.	19.24	yes		−.1*	−2.2	.3	−.6*	−.6*	−.3*	1972	−1.5								a	−.2	−.8	30.05
Evansville, Ind.	15.77	yes			−2.2	.3	−.1	1.2*	0	1972	−.8								a	−.8	−.7	29.57
Muncie, Ind.	15.10					.3	−.9	−2.6	1.9	1972	−.7								a	−.1	−.3	15.10
Stamford, Conn.	13.20				−2.6	−1.3*	−.8	−1.8*	−1.8	1970	−1.5	−.9	−.7						N.S.	−1.7	−1.3	21.42
Niagara Falls, N.Y.	11.76						*	−.4*	−.6	1970	−1.3	−.5	−.3*						N.S.	−.5	−.8	30.26
Sacramento, Calif.	11.10	yes						*	−1.3	1966	−.2	1.2	−.3*	−1.0	−1.1				a	−1.3	−.5	19.98
Oklahoma City, Okla.	10.82	yes						−2.2	−1.1	1968	−1.6	−4.9		−.4	−1.6				N.S.	−1.7	−1.9	11.50
Saginaw, Mich.	9.60	yes				−2.6	−.5	−.6	−2.3	1972	−2.2								a	−1.5	−2.2	9.60
Grand Rapids, Mich.	9.40								−3.7*	1968									a	a	−1.6	10.16
Springfield, Mass.	9.10					−1.8	−1.8	−.6	−.5	1968	−3.1	−1.9	−.8	−1.8	−2.2*	−.8	−1.1		N.S.	−1.6	−2.0	23.05
Ann Arbor, Mich.	9.00							.9*		1965	−1.3	−.1	−2.2	−2.0*	−.6	−.4		−1.2*	a	−.5	−.9	15.48
Lexington, Ky.	8.91									1967	−.1	−.1		−.4*	−.3				a	a	−.2	9.66
Baltimore, Md.	7.92			−6.2	−1.5	−4.0	−1.0	−1.1	−.9	1971	−1.1	−1.1	0						N.S.	−2.5	−1.1	7.92
Tulsa, Okla.	7.83	yes		−.1	−.2	−.4	−4.8	−.1	−.6*	1971	−.5*	−1.9*	−1.0*	−1.1*					N.S.	−1.0	−1.2	14.36
Peoria, Ill.	7.83									1968	−.8	−.9*	−.9*						N.S.	a	−1.0	15.86
Cambridge, Mass.	7.30	−.6			−.1	−1.8	0	−1.2	−.9	1972	−.9	2.0							N.S.	−.7	.6	7.30
Lansing, Mich.	7.18	0		−.1	−.2	−.6	−1.1	−2.2*	1969		−.7	−1.8*	−1.4	−2.1*					N.S.	−1.0	−1.5	22.54

APPENDIX 2: CHANGE IN PERCENTAGE WHITE FROM THE PREVIOUS
SCHOOL YEAR COMPUTED FOR EACH YEAR BEFORE AND AFTER SCHOOL DESEGRATION (CONT.)

School District	(1) % Students assigned	(2) Court Ordered	(3) −7 Years	(4) −6 Years	(5) −5 Years	(6) −4 Years	(7) −3 Years	(8) −2 Years	(9) −1 Year	(10) Major Plan Date	(11) +0 Years	(12) +1 Year	(13) +2 Years	(14) +3 Years	(15) +4 Years	(16) +5 Years	(17) +6 Years	(18) +7 Years	(19) Signif. Level	(20) Pre-series	(21) Post-series	(22) Total Deseg.
Racine, Wisc.	6.80							−1.1*	−.4*	1967	−.5	−.4	−.7*	−.8	−.1	−.9			N.S.	−.8	−.6	12.30
Tacoma, Wash.	6.50							−.7	−.3	1968	−1.4*	−.6*	−.9	−.9*	−.1				N.S.	−.6	−.8	9.44
San Bernardino, Calif.	5.10						−.9*	−.1	−.7	1970	−.8	−1.3	−.5						N.S.	−.6	−.9	7.10
Minneapolis, Minn.	4.90			−.6			−1.0*	−1.3	−1.0*	1971	−1.5	−1.3							N.S.	−1.0	−1.4	11.16
Waterbury, Conn.	4.80				−1.5	−1.5		−2.4	−1.3	1970	−.9	−1.7	−.5						N.S.	−1.9	−1.0	4.80
Rochester, N.Y.	4.30			−2.4	−2.5	−1.6	−3.0	−2.8	−2.4*	1971	−3.3	−3.1							N.S.	−2.4	−3.2	5.16
Seattle, Wash.	4.14			−1.1*	−1.5	−.6	−.8*	−.9	−1.6	1971	−1.5	−1.1							N.S.	−1.1	−1.3	10.25
Dayton, Ohio	3.20		−1.0						−.6	1969	−1.1	−1.4*	−2.0	−2.0					a	−.6	−1.6	3.96
Buffalo, N.Y.	3.20									1967	−2.5	−4.0*	−1.3*	−1.3*	−1.2	−2.2			a	a	−2.1	5.79
Warren, Ohio	2.80								−.5	1969	−.7	−.3	−.5	−.9					a	−.5	−.6	2.80
St. Paul, Minn.	2.57									1965		*			−1.0	−.5	.7	−.5	a	a	−1.3	6.77
South Bend, Ind.	2.50									1970	0	*	−.9						N.S.,.05	−1.2	.7	3.80
Rockford, Ill.	2.40							−1.3	−1.0	1969	.9	−1.3	−.6	−1.1		(less decline than expected)			a	.7	−.5	2.40
Flint, Mich.	2.39						−3.5	−1.5*	−2.0	1971	−2.9	−1.7*							N.S.	−2.3	−2.3	3.69
Syracuse, N.Y.	2.20						−2.6	−1.4	−1.7*	1967	−1.9	−1.8*	−1.7	−2.0	−1.7	−2.0*			N.S.	−1.9	−1.9	3.65
Colorado Springs, Colo.	2.10							.4*	−.3	1971	−.1	−.2							a	.1	−.1	2.30
Indianapolis, Ind.	2.02	yes			−1.3	−1.0	−.2	−1.6	−1.7	1970	−2.6	−1.9*	−1.7*	−3.0*	−2.9*	−3.3*	−2.3*		N.S.	−1.1	−2.4	3.06
New York, N.Y.	1.76				−2.0	−1.9	−1.8	−.3	−.5*	1964	−1.7	−2.9*	−2.0*	−.4	−.8	−.8*		−1.4	−1.3,.02,N.S.	−1.9	−.8	7.67
Pittsburgh, Pa.	1.44							−.3	−4.3	1968	−1.7	−.5*	−.5*	−.2					N.S.,.02	−.4	−.4	3.18
Toledo, Ohio	1.20							−.6*	.7	1969	−.5*	.2	−1.0*						a	−.5	−.5	1.37
Waterloo, Iowa	1.91							−.6*	−.4	1971	−.6	−.4							a	−.5	−1.8	2.25
Gary, Ind.	1.30							−.3	−2.5	1967	−1.9	−2.2							a	a	−1.9	1.64
Milwaukee, Wisc.	1.10				−.3	−.9		−1.0		1972	−2.2	−1.9							a	−1.4	−2.2	2.02
Louisville, Ky.	.83								0*	1972	−.1	−1.5	−.3	−.6					a	−1.9	−.4	.83
Des Moines, Iowa	.82						.2*		0*	1969	−1.6	−1.5							a	0	−1.6	1.10
Los Angeles, Calif.	.66							−1.5	−1.8*	1971	−3.7			−4.2	−4.3*	−4.4			a	−1.0	−3.8	1.56
E. St. Louis, Ill.	.29							−2.7*	−1.6	1967	−1.8	−2.5*	−1.9	−2.3*	−1.2*				N.S.	−2.1	−1.9	.73
Kansas City, Mo.	.26					−2.4	−1.9	−1.9	−1.9	1969	−1.9	−2.8	−2.0*	−.2	−.4				N.S.	−2.5	−1.8	.44
Detroit, Mich.	.25					−4.5	−1.8	−1.2	−2.0	1967	−5.6	−2.0*	−.5	−.2	−1.8*	−1.3			N.S.,.01	−1.6	−1.3	.26
San Diego, Calif.	.19							−1.4	−4.9	1967	−3.7	−1.6*	−1.5*	−2.0	−1.8*				N.S.,.01	−1.6	−2.1	.19
Chicago, Ill.	.17						−1.4	−1.4	−1.1	1968	−.1								N.S.	−2.5	−.1	.46
Philadelphia, Pa.	.02		−2.0	−3.0		−3.3		−.9	−1.1	1972	−1.8								a	−1.8		.02
Hartford, Conn.	.01			−3.0	−1.0		−3.8	−3.7	−2.5	1968	−3.6								N.S.	−3.3	−3.2	.01

APPENDIX 2: CHANGE IN PERCENTAGE WHITE FROM THE PREVIOUS SCHOOL YEAR COMPUTED FOR EACH YEAR BEFORE AND AFTER SCHOOL DESEGRATION (CONT.)

School District	(1) % Students Re-assigned	(2) Court Ordered	(3) −7 Years	(4) −6 Years	(5) −5 Years	(6) −4 Years	(7) −3 Years	(8) −2 Years	(9) −1 Year	(10) Major Plan Date	(11) +0 Years	(12) +1 Year	(13) +2 Years	(14) +3 Years	(15) +4 Years	(16) +5 Years	(17) +6 Years	(18) +7 Years	(19) Signif. Level	(20) Average Pre-series	(21) Average Post-series	(22) Total Deseg.
Control Group:																						
Akron, Ohio	0						−1.0	−1.0	−1.0	—	−1.0	−.7	−.9	−.5	−1.1				a	−1.0	−.8	0
Albany, N.Y.	0								−3.1	—	−1.8	−2.2	−1.1	−2.1	−1.1				a	−3.1	−1.7	0
Albuquerque, N.M.	0									—		−1.3	−.3	−.5	−.4					a	−.6	0
Boston, Mass.	0									—										a		0
Camden, N.J.	0						−1.4	−.3	−1.5	—	−3.9	−2.5	−1.9	−2.6	−1.9				.05, .01	−1.0	−2.6	0
Charleston, W. Va.	0									—	−4.4	−2.7	−2.3	−2.8	−1.8				a	a	−2.8	0
Cleveland, Ohio	0									—	.1	−.2	0	−.1	.1				a	a	−.0	0
E. Orange, N.J.	0									—	.2	−1.2	−1.0	.1	−.3				a	a	−.4	0
Erie, Pa.	0									—	−4.7	−3.9	−3.2	−3.4	−2.6				a	a	−3.6	0
Hamilton, Ohio	0									—	−.3	−.7	−.6	−.2	−.9				a	a	−.5	0
Jersey City, N.J.	0									—	−.2	−.2	.3	−.2	−.2				a	a	−.1	0
Kansas City, Kans.	0									—	−3.9	−2.1	−2.9	−1.0	−2.0				a	a	−2.4	0
Lima, Ohio	0									—	−3.3	−1.6	−.9	−2.0	−1.7				a	a	−1.9	0
Omaha, Neb.	0									—	−1.3	−1.5	−.5	−1.4	.6				a	a	−.8	0
Newark, N.J.	0									—	−1.3	−.6	−.1	−.5	−.6				a	a	−.6	0
Santa Monica, Calif.	0							−3.0	−2.2	—	−2.7	−2.9	−.9	−2.0					N.S.	−2.6	−2.1	0
Trenton, N.J.	0									—	.1	−.6	−2.1	−.6	−.9				a	a	−.8	0
Utica, N.Y.	0									—	−4.1	−2.2	−1.9	−1.8	−.9				a	a	−2.2	0
Washington, D.C.	0			−2.3	−1.9	−1.8	−1.4	−1.5	—	−1.3	−.6	−.7	−1.4	−.5				N.S.	−1.8	−.9	0	
Portland, Oreg.	0						−.6	−.3	−.2	—	−2.1	−.9	−.5	−.6	−.4				.02, .01	−.4	−.8	0
Passaic, N.J.	0									—	−2.5	−.9	−.6	−.9	−1.1				a	a	−1.2	0
Paterson, N.J.	0									—	−7.8	−2.6	−3.7	−3.4	−2.4				a	a	−4.0	0
Phoenix, Ariz.	0									—	−3.8	−3.1	−3.9	−2.3	−1.5				a	a	−2.9	0
Wilmington, Del.	0									—	−1.4	−1.1	−1.1	−1.2	0				a	a	−.7	0
Youngstown, Ohio	0						−3.0	−2.3	−3.4	—	−3.9	−7.1	−3.9	−1.3	−1.8				N.S.	−2.9	−3.6	0
Springfield, Ill.	0									—	−.5	−1.1	−.5	−1.0					a	a	−1.1	0

* Additional desegregation implemented.
N.S. = not significant.
a = unable to compute.

APPENDIX 3: BOSTON'S PHASE I AND PHASE II DESEGREGATION
(1974 AND 1975)

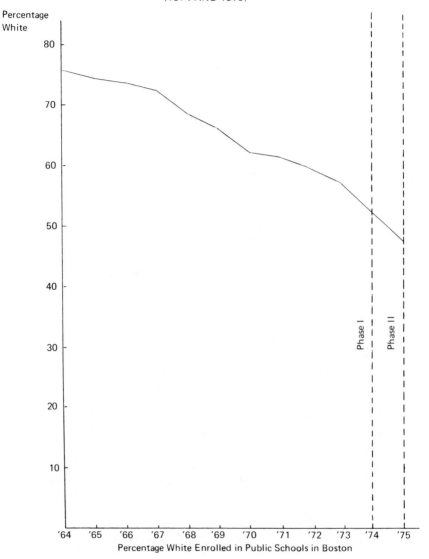

Percentage White Enrolled in Public Schools in Boston

The Politics of Exclusionary Zoning in Suburbia

MICHAEL N. DANIELSON

With growing awareness of the impact of suburban policies on metropolitan settlement patterns in recent years has come increasing criticism of local land-use and housing practices. One major civil rights group, the National Committee Against Discrimination in Housing, has concluded that "there can be no effective progress in halting the trend toward predominantly black cities surrounded by almost entirely white suburbs . . . [u]ntil local governments have been deprived of the power to exclude subsidized housing and to manipulate zoning and other controls to screen out families on the basis of income and, implicitly, of race. . . ."[1] At the same time, the National Association for the Advancement of Colored People was calling the suburbs "the new civil rights battleground" and urging blacks "to do battle out in the townships and villages to lower zoning barriers and thereby create new opportunities for Negroes seeking housing closer to today's jobs at prices they can afford to pay. . . ."[2]

Similar views have been expressed by a wide variety of urban interests. Residential developers have attacked "selfish and exclusionary zoning barriers" and urged that a way "be found to get away from the constrictive home-rule aspects

---

[1] See Joseph P. Fried, *Housing Crisis U.S.A.* (New York, 1971), pp. 50–51.

[2] See Geoffrey Sheilds and L. Sanford Spector, "Opening Up the Suburbs: Notes on a Movement for Social Change," *Yale Review of Law and Social Action*, II (Summer 1972), 305.

MICHAEL N. DANIELSON is professor of politics and public affairs at Princeton University. He is the author of *Federal-Metropolitan Politics and the Commuter Crisis*, coauthor of *One Nation, So Many Governments*, and editor of *Metropolitan Politics*. He has recently completed a study of *The Politics of Exclusion*.

of the legislation that supports and protects these restrictions."[3] Editorials in metropolitan newspapers warned "the entrenched, well-to-do suburbanites" that they must recognize "that one-half of the nation cannot afford to build barriers of any sort against the other half—whether it be the barrier of racial discrimination or the practical barrier of long and time-consuming commuting."[4] And housing experts condemn an "arrangement that benefits the wealthy and the middle class at the expense of loading large costs onto the very poor" as "a gross injustice that cries out for correction."[5]

REACTION IN THE SUBURBS

To most of this clamor, the average suburbanite and the typical suburban office holder turn a deaf ear. Few of those who demand changes in local policies live within particular suburban jurisdictions in sufficient numbers to have a significant impact on local opinion or the actions of local officials. Lower-income and minority families which would benefit from relaxed suburban barriers are kept out of most communities by the high cost of housing and exclusionary policies motivated by racial prejudice, the fear of crime, fiscal and environmental considerations, and the desire to preserve community character. As a result, neither victims of exclusion nor local supporters of open housing usually can aggregate sufficient political strength to secure much influence or representation on local councils and planning boards, particularly in the smaller and more homogeneous suburban jurisdictions.

The negative response of local political systems to calls for change also reflects the satisfaction of most suburbanites with the existing system of housing and land-use control. Relatively few residents of the suburbs see housing for less affluent groups as a major problem. Only 10 percent of those questioned in a survey in New York's Westchester County in 1972 expressed dissatisfaction with their present housing. Drugs, property taxes, crime, education, pollution, the problems of the elderly, and mass transportation were all listed as more important matters for state and local governments than broadened housing opportunities (see Table 1).

In addition, few suburbanites are willing to acknowledge the role of suburban exclusion in fostering and maintaining an economically and racially separated society. Instead, most emphatically reject the notion that the "suburban sanctuary of the middle class has been created at the expense of the urban poor by compelling them to live in areas of concentrated poverty."[6] Nor are many suburban dwellers prepared to accept any responsibility for the city, its residents,

[3] Stewart M. Hutt, counsel, New Jersey Builders Association, quoted in Richard J. H. Johnston, "Low-Income Housing Exclusions in U. S. Assailed," *The New York Times*, November 7, 1969.

[4] "People, Jobs and Housing," editorial, *Washington Post*, July 6, 1971.

[5] Anthony Downs, *Opening Up the Suburbs: An Urban Strategy for America* (New Haven, Conn., 1973), p. 11.

[6] Ibid., p. 166.

TABLE 1

*Perceptions of State and Local Governmental Priorities
by Residents of Westchester County, N. Y.*

	All Residents	Upper and Middle Income Residents	Moderate and Lower Income Residents
		(Percent listing problem as important)	
Drugs	47	44	51
Property taxes	46	48	43
Crime	31	30	31
Education	27	28	27
Air and water pollution	25	25	24
Help for senior citizens	25	20	34
Mass transportation	21	24	15
Low and moderate income housing	14	13	16
Middle income housing	10	8	14
Race relations	8	9	7
New jobs	8	9	7
Roads and highways	7	8	6
Planning and zoning	7	8	7
Recreation	7	9	4

SOURCE: Oliver Quayle and Company, "A Survey of Attitudes Toward Government Assisted Moderate and Low Income Housing in Westchester County,"Study #1546 (Bronxville, N.Y., December 1972), p. 21.

and their housing problems. A suburban mayor in the Cleveland area feels "the public housing people are just looking for a lot of land for Cleveland's problems which Cleveland isn't willing to take care of."[7] Outside St. Louis, a key official rejects suburban involvement in "the problems of the unfortunate people in the city."[8]

Given local autonomy, the nature and attitudes of suburban constituencies, the benefits that residents of the suburbs derive from exclusionary policies, and the dependence of local governments on property taxes, the suburban political system provides few incentives for its components to act in anything but their self-interest. Speaking of the costs associated with subsidized housing, a suburban mayor emphasizes that "appeals to the good nature and selflessness of the suburban official or the suburban voter will be pointless if the economic cards are stacked the wrong way."[9] As a result of these political realities, most suburbs

[7] Mayor Robert Lawthur, Lakewood, Ohio, quoted in Roldo Bartimole, "A Close Look: Cleveland," *City*, V (January–February 1971), 45.

[8] Supervisor Lawrence K. Roos, St. Louis County, Mo., quoted in Robert Adams, "Suburbs Feel No Debt to City," *St. Louis Post-Dispatch*, July 23, 1971.

[9] Supervisor John F. McAlevey, Ramapo, N. Y., quoted in Richard Reeves, "Counterattack by Cities," *The New York Times*, March 8, 1971; reprinted as "Counterattack by the Cities," in Louis H. Masotti and Jeffrey K. Hadden (eds.), *Suburbia in Transition* (New York, 1974), p. 242.

successfully resist pressures at the local level for major changes in their housing and zoning policies, particularly when the aim is the expansion of housing opportunities for lower-income and minority groups.

VARIATIONS AMONG SUBURBS

Resistance, however, is not a universal suburban reaction to demands that local housing barriers be lowered. Large suburban jurisdictions with heterogeneous populations tend to be more responsive to pressures for change than smaller-scale and relatively homogeneous suburbs. Opinion is less monolithic in these suburbs; and political leaders are less constrained by dominant constituency interests. In addition, minorities are more visible, their collective voices louder, and their interests more easily aggregated in larger jurisdictions. Big suburbs, particularly suburban county governments in major metropolitan areas, also are more likely to employ planning and housing professionals. These officials examine housing needs and development trends on a communitywide and metropolitan basis; and their professional training and personal values prompt concern about the problems of lower-income and minority groups. All of these factors lead to greater recognition of housing problems by political leaders in suburban jurisdictions such as Nassau County in New York, which had 1.4 million residents in 1970. "There is no excuse for a generally affluent suburban community, where 90 percent of the people enjoy good housing," Nassau's elected executive told the county legislature in 1969, "to permit the other 10 percent to live in conditions which rival some of the worst slums in the nation."[10] Two large suburban counties in the Washington area, Fairfax and Montgomery, have been among the most active suburban governments in seeking to develop and implement plans designed to broaden housing opportunities for their diversifying populations. On the other hand, many large suburbs such as Oyster Bay in New York and Baltimore County have steadfastly resisted efforts to ease local housing restrictions.

Here and there, affluent suburbs with troubled social consciences seek to diversify their populations. In Princeton, a university community amidst the suburbs of central New Jersey with a penchant for both liberal causes and exclusionary zoning, the local planning board warned in 1973 that "Princeton will become a one-class, upper-income community [unless] positive steps are taken to halt the trend." Arguing that "the health and vitality of the community depend on a diversity of people of different cultural backgrounds, ages, incomes, and interests," the local planners recommended that almost half of the new housing construction in the community during the 1970s and 1980s be earmarked for families presently priced out of the local housing market.[11] Concern in Summit,

[10] County Executive Eugene H. Nickerson, quoted in Roy R. Silver, "Nickerson Urges Housing for Poor," *The New York Times*, January 12, 1969.

[11] See Craig E. Polhemus, "Princeton Is Encouraging Low-Income Housing," *The New York Times*, July 22, 1973.

an upper-income suburb of 25,000 in northern New Jersey, over housing conditions for local blacks led to community sponsorship of 90 units of low-rent garden apartments in 1968. Across the continent in Palo Alto, similar constituency concerns spurred the local government in 1972 to approve the construction of 740 units of mixed-income housing.

Local officials with strongly held views about the social responsibilities of their communities also can make a difference. A successful campaign for a limited number of units of subsidized housing in Ramapo in New York's Rockland County was led by the community's mayor, a self-styled "believe[r] in public housing from way back" who was "willing to absorb 500 units to make the point that public housing isn't the horrible thing that most of the recent expatriates from New York City think it is."[12]

Another factor motivating suburban leaders to advocate some relaxation of zoning barriers is the fear of losing local autonomy. In the view of a council member in an exclusive Connecticut suburb, "local zoning restrictions must be eased not only for social reasons, but because if this does not happen, then sooner or later our local autonomy or choice will be taken away by the State Legislature."[13]

For most suburbanites, however, perhaps the only persuasive argument for relaxing exclusionary barriers is the housing needs of local residents. In the Westchester County survey, 78 percent agreed with the statement: "I tend to favor more moderate and low income housing in Westchester so that public servants such as teachers, firemen, and policemen can live in the communities they serve"; while 70 percent supported "more subsidized low and moderate income housing in Westchester to enable our young people to stay here instead of being forced to live elsewhere."[14] Support for subsidized housing was heavily conditioned on its availabilty to members of the local community. While 83 percent were favorable if first priority was given to "people now living in this town . . . and second priority to people now working here," 76 percent were opposed if no priorities were assigned on the basis of where the occupants lived or worked.[15]

Concern over the housing needs of local public employees was the principal factor underlying the enactment of legislation in Fairfax and Montgomery Counties designed to spur the construction of lower-cost housing by private developers. The Fairfax Board of Supervisors approved a series of ordinances in 1971 requiring that 6 percent of the housing in most developments of fifty or more units be priced below $20,000, and that 9 percent be priced between $20,000 and $25,000,

[12] Supervisor McAlevey, Ramapo, N. Y., quoted in Alan S. Oser, "Innovator in Suburbs Under Fire," *The New York Times*, March 28, 1971.

[13] Town Selectman Henrietta Rogers, New Canaan, Conn., quoted in "New Canaan Aide Questions Zoning," *The New York Times*, March 7, 1971.

[14] Oliver Quayle and Company, "A Survey of Attitudes Toward Government Assisted Moderate and Low Income Housing in Westchester County," Study # 1546 (Bronxville, N. Y., December 1972), p. 74.

[15] Ibid., p. 63.

provided that federal subsidies were available. A similar plan was adopted by the Montgomery County Council in 1973. A group of ministers organized as the Coalition for Housing Action led the campaign in Fairfax, and placed heavy emphasis on the needs of county employees, 90 percent of whom earned less than $12,000 a year in 1971. Supporters of the new law in Montgomery also stressed the needs of employees, pointing to the requirement that county police officers making $12,000 a year were required to live within a jurisdiction where an annual income of $25,000 was needed to purchase a new home in 1973. In both counties, backing for the housing plans came primarily from public employees. Typical was the view of the Fairfax County Police Association which emphasized that "most of our police officers, in order to buy a home, must go out into Prince William and Loudoun Counties. We feel they should be able to buy housing here."[16]

In most suburbs, however, concern over local housing needs is not automatically translated into broadened housing opportunities. The fact that "our own cops, firemen and teachers can't buy houses in Westport"[17] led the Planning and Zoning Commission of the affluent Connecticut suburb to approve a change in local zoning in 1973 to permit the construction of 400 apartments in scattered sites, with 60 of the units priced within the range of town employees and others with moderate incomes. Within a month, vehement opposition to apartments from residents prompted the forty-member representative town meeting to overturn unanimously the proposed apartment ordinance. In Bergen County in northern New Jersey, 1600 residents of a community signed petitions that helped kill a garden-apartment proposal despite concerns such as those expressed by one local resident: "My daughter will be getting married in a few years and I'd like to see her remain here. A nice little development wouldn't hurt anyone. Give our kids a chance. It's unfair. We had our chance to move out here."[18]

Opposition to improving housing opportunities for local residents stems from many of the basic considerations that fuel the politics of exclusion—dislike of apartments, the bad image of subsidized housing, fear of community change, worries about property values, and concern over local services and taxes. Another important factor is the suspicion of suburbanites that priority for local residents cannot be maintained if the barriers to the construction of lower-cost housing are lowered. As the mayor of one of New Jersey's largest suburbs notes: "We'd welcome lower-cost housing for our youth and elderly. But there's no guarantee we could keep it for them. And given the choice, we just won't do it."[19]

---

[16] Charles Boswell, president, Fairfax County Police Association, quoted in Monroe W. Karmin, "Forced Integration? Not in Fairfax," *Wall Street Journal*, September 29, 1971.

[17] See Franklin Whitehouse, "Westport Warms to Apartments," *The New York Times*, May 24, 1970.

[18] See Richard Reeves, "Land Is Prize in Battle for Control of Suburbs," *The New York Times*, August 17, 1971; reprinted as "The Battle Over Land," in Massotti and Hadden, *Suburbia in Transition*, p. 308.

[19] Mayor Newton Miller, Wayne, N. J., quoted in Jack Rosenthal, "Suburbs Abandoning De-

Variations among suburbs also reflect the inherent difficulty of achieving general policy changes in a decentralized polity through political action at the grass roots. Extraordinary political resources, a highly decentralized base of support, or a widely perceived need for action resulting from a crisis are requred to produce similar policy changes in large numbers of local governments. When the units are small and numerous, as is the case with suburbs in most of the larger metropolitan areas, the prospects for securing general policy changes through grass-roots efforts are reduced further. At best, such efforts are likely to result in occasional victories and piecemeal change in local policies.

LOCAL ARENAS AND LOCAL INTERESTS

Because of the obstacles to broad-based action at the grass roots, the suburban political arena primarily attracts those with local interests and narrow objectives. Groups whose interests transcend a particular locality tend to focus their energies on the states, the national government, or the courts, where successful efforts frequently result in policy changes which affect large numbers of local jurisdictions, rather than only a single unit as is the case with victories at the grass roots.

Efforts to change suburban housing and land-use policies have followed this general pattern quite closely. Among open-housing groups, challenges at the grass roots have come primarily from locally oriented interests, such as fair-housing committees, neighborhood stabilization groups, civic and civil rights organizations, and community-based developers of low-cost housing. Typically, these interests have limited objectives and capabilities. They tend to focus on housing conditions in their particular community and the needs of local residents. More often than not, their activities are confined to a single jurisdiction. Thus, a suburban fair-housing committee seeks to expand housing opportunities for middle-income blacks within its community, while a local civil rights group campaigns for municipal approval of a housing project for lower-income families.

As suburban housing restrictions attracted increasing attention in the late 1960s, national civil rights and religious groups, labor unions, foundations, and public-interest organizations were drawn to the issue. The growing involvement of these broader-based interests played a major role in both increasing the visibility of suburban housing restrictions and forcing judges, federal administrators, and other public officials at all levels of government to address the problem. Unlike local groups, these broader interests devoted little of their energy to persuading individual suburban governments to change their housing and land-use policies. Their common objective was policy changes which would improve the access of lower-income and minority groups to housing in large numbers of suburban jurisdictions rather than in a particular community. Thus, even when dealing "with local cases or problems," as Sheilds and Spector emphasize, the

---

pendence on City," *The New York Times,* August 16, 1971; reprinted as "Toward Suburban Independence," in Masotti and Hadden, *Suburbia in Transition,* p. 302.

national open-housing interests "seek situations which will have importance nationally."[20]

These objectives have led the American Civil Liberties Union, the Lawyers' Committee for Civil Rights under Law, the NAACP Legal Defense and Education Fund, and the National Housing and Economic Development Law Project to focus almost exclusively on court actions designed to overturn restrictive suburban housing and land-use policies. Other national groups, such as the Leadership Conference on Civil Rights, the Center for National Policy Review, and the Housing Opportunities Council of Metropolitan Washington, have concentrated on lobbying for changes in federal policies. Coordination, and the collection and dissemination of information concerning suburban housing problems have been the primary activities of another set of groups, including the National Urban Coalition, the Exclusionary Land-Uses Practices Clearing House, and the National Job-Linked Housing Center.[21]

Not all national open-housing interests, however, eschew involvement at the local level. Much of the energy of the National Committee Against Discrimination in Housing (NCDH) since its creation in 1950 has been devoted to the organization of fair-housing groups at the grass roots and efforts to secure local fair-housing legislation. Other national organizations with local affiliates also are active at the suburban grass roots. A number of the NAACP's 1700 branches have been involved with housing issues in particular suburbs. Local affiliates of the American Jewish Committee and the Urban League also have engaged in grass-roots activities designed to broaden housing opportunities in the suburbs.

Among the national organizations interested in opening the suburbs, probably the most active at the local level has been the League of Women Voters (LWV). The league is more decentralized than the other major open-housing groups as well as being the only one with a substantial political base in suburbia. A federation of 1250 chapters with a largely white, upper-income suburban membership of 170,000, the league places considerable emphasis on local autonomy and grass-roots action. In the early 1970s, over 100 of its chapters were engaged in efforts "to educate their communities to the goal of a free choice of a decent home in a decent environment for every family."[22] In the process, LWV chapters pressed for the creation of local housing authorities, supported the construction of low-income housing, participated in the organization of nonprofit development corporations to sponsor subsidized housing, fought local discriminatory practices, endorsed zoning reform, and backed metropolitan "fair-share" plans for the allocation of subsidized housing among suburban jurisdictions.

Despite the importance of local activities for groups such as the NAACP, the

[20] Sheilds and Spector, "Opening Up the Suburbs," p. 305.

[21] For an informative review of the activities of these and other national open-housing organizations, see ibid., pp. 301–305.

[22] League of Women Voters Education Fund, "Suburban Zoning, The New Frontier" (Washington, D. C.), p. 3.

NCDH, and the LWV, none concentrates all its efforts on grass-roots activities. The national headquarters of the NAACP has been involved in challenging suburban zoning in the courts, lobbying for open housing in Washington, and conducting educational efforts aimed at reducing suburban hostility to residential integration. NCDH has become increasingly committed to suburban housing activities that transcend particular localities, including litigation, lobbying in Congress and administrative agencies, and research and technical assistance. Even the highly decentralized League of Women Voters is engaged in court action through its national litigation office.

Given the orientation of the broader-based open-housing interests, the primary burden for action at the suburban grass roots falls on local groups, be they purely local or affiliated with national organizations. Among these organizations, substantial differences exist in size, resources, and constituency base. Their objectives, programs, priorities, vitality, visibility, and effectiveness also vary considerably. In general, diversity reduces the incidence of cooperation and cohesion among open-housing interests within a particular community or suburban area. Collective action also is impeded by the fragmentation of local government in suburbia, since supporters of open housing typically are scattered among a variety of local jurisdictions. And the combination of group diversity and dispersed constituency support handicaps efforts to change local housing policies in the hostile political climate of the typical suburban jurisdiction.

Among the various open-housing interests in the suburbs, fair-housing groups are the most common. A substantial majority of the more than 2000 local fair-housing committees in the United States have been organized in suburban areas. Their goal is the elimination of racial discrimination in the sale and rental of housing; and they have taken the lead in pressing for the enactment of fair-housing ordinances and local human-relations commissions in the suburbs. Most suburban fair-housing groups lack professional staff, have a membership composed largely of upper-income whites, and devote much of their energy to finding housing for blacks who can afford to live in the suburbs, often on a highly individualized basis.

Exceptions to this general pattern are the handful of fair-housing groups which have full-time staff, a substantial membership base, and other resources which enable them to pursue more ambitious and systematic programs. For example, the Mid-Peninsula Citizens for Fair Housing in the San Francisco area tests compliance with local fair-housing laws, investigates complaints of racial discrimination, undertakes legal actions against discriminatory housing practices, seeks to educate local officials and the suburban housing industry about their legal obligations to ensure equal housing opportunities, and campaigns more generally for open housing. Elsewhere, larger and more sophisticated fair-housing groups operate housing information centers and comprehensive housing-listing services, provide counseling services for families seeking homes in the suburbs, and undertake "carefully planned and conducted testing operations for the purpose of filing complaints with state human rights agencies and with HUD and the Department of Justice."[23]

Despite the increasing sophistication and capability of some fair-housing groups, most continue to focus their resources on discriminatory practices affecting the access of blacks to the existing housing stock in suburbia. Relatively few local groups followed in the footsteps of the national fair-housing organization, NCDH, which in the 1970s placed more and more emphasis on increasing the supply of lower-cost housing in the suburbs and removing zoning and other local barriers which reinforce segregated residential patterns. Typical of the attitude of local groups is that of the Fair Housing Congress of Southern California, which sees so much illegal discrimination in the existing housing market that its leaders are reluctant to divert their scarce resources to other activities.

Another local open-housing interest with a limited perspective on the suburban housing problem is the neighborhood stabilization movement. Neighborhood stabilization groups were organized in the 1960s in a number of city and suburban areas undergoing racial transformation. Their primary concern has been existing housing conditions, and the creation of stable racially integrated neighborhoods. Most of these groups and their umbrella organization, the National Neighbors, "have recognized that to stabilize any one neighborhood, it is essential to assure an open housing market and general mobility."[24] These groups, however, tend to be preoccupied with their pressing local problems; and few have the time or resources to get very involved in broader issues such as the production of suburban housing or the removal of local barriers to the outward movement of lower-income and minority families. Moreover, most of the stabilization groups are active in communities undergoing racial transformation, which typically are the result rather than the cause of suburban exclusion.

Direct challenges of suburban zoning and housing policies usually come from more amorphous local groupings. Campaigns for subsidized housing and zoning reform have been launched by local coalitions of civil rights, civic, and religious groups. Similar groupings have organized nonprofit housing corporations in the suburbs. In Princeton, New Jersey, for example, the local chapter of the League of Women Voters and other community groups formed Princeton Community Housing to build subsidized housing. Nonprofit housing corporations which have sought to build in the suburbs also have been created by labor unions in the case of the Region Nine United Automobile Workers Housing Corporation in Mahwah, New Jersey; religious groups as with the Park Heights Corporation in Black Jack in the St. Louis area and the Interfaith Housing Corporation in the Boston region; and minority-group organizations such as the Colored People's Civic and Political Organization in Lackawanna outside Buffalo and the Southern Alameda Spanish Speaking Organization in suburban Union City in the San Francisco Bay area.

[23] George Schermer, "Strategy, Tactics, and Organization for the Fair Housing Movement," (Washington, D. C., January 16, 1973), p. 2.

[24] Ibid., p. 3.

More often than not, these efforts are limited to a single local jurisdiction. When the groups involved also are locally based, there tends to be a heavy emphasis on local needs. Local groups and coalitions seeking eased zoning, the creation of a local housing authority, or permission for a nonprofit housing corporation to build suburban housing typically stress the community's responsibilities to its own residents rather than its obligations to lower-income and minority families in general. Suburban open-housing interests are especially likely to ignore or downplay the housing needs of inner-city blacks.

Even when suburban open-housing groups have a broader perspective, political realities often narrow their focus. The ministers who launched the campaign for zoning reform in Fairfax County initially were drawn to the issue by concern over the plight of blacks unable to find housing outside the District of Columbia. As the campaign developed, however, the search for support led the Coalition for Housing Action to an increasing emphasis on local housing needs, and especially the housing problems of teachers, policemen, and other local-government employees. The leaders of the campaign justified the shift on pragmatic grounds. They also argued that increasing the stock of lower-cost housing in Fairfax would inevitably benefit inner-city blacks. "When you open up a community economically," insisted Rev. Gerald Hopkins, a minister, "you open it up racially."[25] But this objective of zoning reform rarely was voiced during the drive for political support among the overwhelmingly white population of Fairfax County.

Opening the Suburbs through Confrontation

Concern for local sensibilities, priorities, and political feasibility has not been a conspicuous feature of the activities of the Suburban Action Institute (SAI), a public-interest organization founded in 1969 by Paul Davidoff, a planner and attorney, and Neil Gold, a former staff member of NCDH. Based in Westchester County, Suburban Action has directly challenged local zoning in a lengthening list of communities in the New York area. Unlike most local open-housing groups in the suburbs, SAI has emphasized the need "to open the suburbs for all, in particular for the non-affluent and non-white."[26] Suburban Action's stress on bringing blacks and the poor to affluent suburbs, its insistence on far-reaching changes in local housing and land-use policies, its lack of a constituency in the communities it has challenged, and the abrasive and publicity-oriented style of its founders have made SAI the most controversial of all the open-housing interests active at the suburban grass roots. The organization's style is best appreciated in the words of Paul Davidoff, its chief spokesman:

> Suburban populations . . . have employed the power of the state to protect their own very selfish desire to create a community that is amenable to themselves,

---

[25] Quoted in Karmin, "Forced Integration? Not in Fairfax."

[26] Paul Davidoff, "A Lake Is Backdrop for Debate on Suburban Integration Plan: Pro," *The New York Times*, November 4, 1973.

but to prohibit the large mass of the population from sharing in those amenities. They have not bought the land, but instead have done the cheap and nasty thing of employing the police power to protect their own interest in the land and to exclude the largest part of the population. . . . We think this is terribly abusive, terribly inappropriate for a group which is politically not inclined to argue the case for increased government control.[27]

Suburban Action's perspective on housing in the suburbs has been broader than that of most local open-housing groups. SAI stresses the linkages between the plight of the older cities and suburban policies which restrict access to housing and jobs. For Davidoff, "decent housing means reasonable access to employment, good education, recreation and environment . . . the key to these is locational choice."[28] In broadening locational choices, and in particular in creating "new opportunities for linking suburban jobs to unemployed and underemployed residents of slums and ghettos," SAI sees the contemporary problem in the suburbs "as larger and more complex than the fair housing issue of the fifties and sixties . . . [when] no changes were necessary in the allocation of land resources."[29] Solution of this problem, in SAI's view, required fundamental changes in the suburban land-use control system, heavy emphasis on the production of housing for lower-income and minority groups in the suburbs, and public policies which ensure that low-cost housing is dispersed throughout the metropolis.

To accomplish these objectives, Suburban Action has engaged in a wide range of activities. Research has been undertaken on a variety of suburban housing and land-use issues. Efforts have been made to educate and raise the consciousness of suburbanites, large suburban employers, and opinion leaders. Local zoning ordinances and housing policies have been criticized in a variety of local forums and the media, with the "focus on rich people's communities, especially those with rich liberals as residents."[30] Corporate decisions to locate offices and plants in suburban areas which exclude moderately priced housing developments also have come under fire, with SAI filing complaints with the Equal Employment Opportunities Commission and other federal agencies in an effort to check corporate moves to exclusionary suburbs. Litigation was another important element to Suburban Action's program. By 1974, it had filed suits against exclusionary zoning in dozens of suburbs in the New York area. SAI also has gone to court to block the federal government from making sewer and recreation grants to an exclusionary suburb in Westchester County, to prevent the construction of an

[27] Quoted in Jerome Aumente, "Domestic Land Reform," *City*, V (January–February 1971), 56.

[28] "A Lake Is Backdrop for Debate on Suburban Integration Plan: Pro."

[29] Suburban Action Institute, "Statement of Purpose" (Tarrytown, N. Y., September 1973), pp. 2–3.

[30] Neil Gold, Suburban Action Institute, see National Urban Coalition, Clearinghouse on Exclusionary Land Use Policies, "Report: Seventh Conference on Exclusionary Land Use Policies" (Washington, D. C., June 24, 1971), p. 18.

Internal Revenue Service processing center in a community on Long Island with strict housing controls, and to force the construction of low-cost housing on the site of a former military base in Nassau County.

Of most importance to local government, and certainly the most controversial of Suburban Action's activities, have been the organization's efforts to build housing in suburbs with restrictive land-use controls. Typically, SAI has quietly secured options on land, often in conjunction with private developers. Then plans have been prepared for a large-scale mixed-income housing development which could not be implemented without changes in local zoning. Finally, a well-publicized announcement of the plan is accompanied by a threat to seek relief in the courts if local approval is not forthcoming. In 1973, for example, SAI declared that it was ready to develop housing for 8000 people on 253 acres adjacent to Candlewood Lake in New Fairfield, Connecticut. In explaining how the plan would be implemented in the face of local hostility, Neil Gold indicated that Suburban Action probably would have to go to court, and expressed confidence "that the courts will sustain our right to build a mixed income racially integrated community on Candlewood Lake."[31]

Suburban Action unveiled similar plans for a number of other suburbs in the early 1970s. Most ambitious was a scheme for a $150 million planned community on 720 acres in Mahwah in northern New Jersey. If built the project would almost triple Mahwah's 1970 population of 10,000. Of the 6000 housing units in the proposed new community, 2400 were to be priced for families with annual incomes under $10,000, with the remainder within reach of those with incomes of less than $20,000 a year. In this case, litigation preceded the housing proposal, as SAI challenged restrictive zoning in Mahwah and three neighboring suburbs in the courts a few months before its plans for 'Ramapo Mountain" were announced. For Readington, a rural area strategically located in the path of suburbanization in New Jersey's Hunterdon County, SAI sought to have 230 acres rezoned from single-family homes on lots of one and three-quarter acres to permit the construction of 2000 apartments. In Western Suffolk County on Long Island, Suburban Action wanted to build as many as 6000 housing units on 400 or more acres. And an 850-unit complex has been designed for a site in Fairfax County in Virginia.

The coupling of local development plans with court action reflected the concern of SAI's leadership that litigation alone would do little to broaden housing opportunities for lower-income families in the suburbs. Unless open-housing groups were prepared to construct housing when suburban land became available, Suburban Action was convinced that private builders and affluent families will be the prime beneficiaries of successful litigation against zoning. To provide home-building capability, SAI created Garden Cities Development Corporation to handle the preparation of development plans, land acquisition, and construction. Although

---

[31] Quoted in Michael Knight, "New Fairfield Zone Board Bars Candlewood Lake Development," *The New York Times*, October 12, 1973.

Garden Cities was "geared up [and] ready to move" in 1974,[32] the development corporation had yet to construct a single unit of housing in any of its proposed new communities.

In fact, except for stimulating a flock of lawsuits, nowhere had the politics of confrontation borne fruit for SAI. Instead, the proposals of Suburban Action and Garden Cities encountered fierce local resistance in most instances, and outright rejection at the hands of local zoning boards. Three-fourths of the adults in New Fairfield, a community of 8000, signed petitions against the SAI plan for Candlewood Lake; and the local zoning board unanimously rejected the project. In another Connecticut suburb where SAI took an option on eleven acres for the purpose of building 160 units of federally subsidized housing, the mayor told the press that "everyone I've spoken to is wholeheartedly opposed to the project"; and the local planning board refused to rezone the land in question.[33] A local official in Suffolk County insisted that "they are going to have to abide by our zoning ordinances" and predicted " an uphill fight all the way" if SAI persisted with its planned 6000 housing units on Long Island.[34] Nor was local support forthcoming in Mahwah, whose mayor indicated that "the town and the country are fed up with loudmouths and radicals seeking to divide us and destroy everything we love and have worked for."[35] The planning board in Mahwah refused to consider SAI's request for rezoning, citing a moratorium it had imposed on rezoning pending revision of the local master plan, a revision prompted in part by the fact that the existing master plan had permitted planned-unit development in the area selected by Suburban Action for "Ramapo Mountain."

In all of these suburbs, SAI's motives in seeking changes in local housing and land-use policies have been attacked. "What are they going to get out of it?" is a question constantly asked by suburbanites in communities confronted by SAI.[36] Fueling these questions is the involvement of Suburban Action and Garden Cities with private developers and landowners. SAI was accused by a prominent resident of Candlewood Lake of playing "the part of a destroyer" by paving the way for the "big land speculators" who are "cheering every time Suburban Action Institute brings another suit in another court."[37] Suspicions about SAI's arrangements with private developers, as well as complaints about its efforts to influence local legislation, have prompted suburban foes to seek a federal investigation of

[32] Neil Gold, Garden Cities Development Corporation, quoted in Ernest Dickinson, "Activists in Suburbs Under Fire as Landlords," *The New York Times*, March 24, 1974.

[33] First Selectman Joseph L. McLinden, Ridgefield, Conn., quoted in Jonathan Kandell, "Ridgefield Faces a Housing Battle," *The New York Times*, August 6, 1972.

[34] Supervisor Charles W. Barraud, Jr., Brookhaven, N. Y., quoted in David A. Andelman, "Suffolk Is Facing Zone Challenge," *The New York Times*, February 28, 1973.

[35] Mayor Lawrence Nyland, Mahwah, N. J., quoted in Jan Rubin, "Nyland Blasts Tactics of SAI," *Ridgewood Herald News* (New Jersey), May 4, 1972.

[36] See Richard Zimmerman, "The Open Housing Activists: One Goal, Different Styles," *Sunday Record* (Bergen County, N. J.), June 18, 1972.

[37] Malcolm Cowley, "A Lake Is Backdrop for Debate on Suburban Integration Plan: Con," *The New York Times*, November 4, 1973.

the organization's tax-exempt status. Suburban Action also has been called "a racist organization" which "uses black Americans as pawns and patsies in its effort to upset the zoning laws." According to this critic, SAI has no real concern with the housing problems of inner-city blacks and Puerto Ricans, most of whom could not afford to live in the developments proposed by Suburban Action and Garden Cities. Instead, the plight of lower-income blacks is "a means by which Suburban Action Institute can wheedle money from foundations and instill a feeling of guilt in middle-class white liberals."[38]

To counter local opposition, Suburban Action's founders hoped to build "a local base of support" among "the Suburban church; builders and housing developers; some groups within the fair housing movement; and suburban employers of low and moderately skilled workers."[39] Little backing for SAI, however, came from any of these groups. Other open-housing interests in the suburbs found Suburban Action's aggressive style counterproductive. They feared that their own quieter and more locally oriented efforts would be jeopardized by the backlash from local confrontations with SAI. In addition, Suburban Action has, in the view of its founders, "run up against strong opposition" because of its insistence "that local housing groups begin to demand housing not only to meet the needs of local residents, but also to meet the needs of the region's population."[40]

While winning Suburban Action few allies in the suburbs or within the open-housing fraternity, public attention has helped SAI secure funds from social-action oriented foundations such as the Field Foundation, the Ford Foundation, the Dr. and Mrs. Martin Peretz Foundation, the Florence and John Schumann Foundation, the Stern Foundation, and the Taconic Foundation. In fact, most of the major victories of Suburban Action's politics of confrontation were won in the board rooms of foundations rather than in suburban town halls. While these successes enabled Suburban Action to make some headway with two of its prime aims—"to document social and economic discrimination [and] focus public attention on it"—the unequal odds posed by the local political arena to the advocates of open housing in the suburbs have thwarted SAI's professed central purpose of developing "strategies that can lever significant change."[41]

The Lack of a Suburban Constituency for Open Housing

Regardless of their approach, open-housing groups in the suburbs have failed to mobilize significant constituency support. This failure has resulted primarily from the desire of most suburbanites to maintain existing local housing and land-

---

[38] Ibid.

[39] Paul Davidoff, Linda Davidoff, and Neil Newton Gold, "Suburban Action: Advocate Planning for an Open Society," *Journal of the American Institute of Planners*, XXXVI (January 1970), 21.

[40] Ibid., p. 17.

[41] Suburban Action Institute, "Statement of Purpose," p. 1.

use policies rather than from the organizational, strategic, and tactical weakness of open-housing interests in the suburbs. To be sure, an approach such as Suburban Action's which emphasizes large-scale change and suburban responsibilities for the urban poor is much less likely to appeal to residents of the suburbs than efforts which seek small additions to the local housing stock to meet the needs of those who live and work in the local community. Even when campaigns are focused on local needs, however, widespread support rarely is forthcoming.

Among the various components of the suburban population, lower-income suburbanites clearly have the most to gain from an expansion of the supply of moderately priced housing. These residents, however, are hardly a cohesive force in suburban politics. Large numbers of suburbanites with modest incomes have little stake in increasing housing opportunities. Many are homeowners who perceive a substantial interest in the suburban status quo. Others are satisfied with their existing housing. Even more are fearful that relaxed housing and land-use controls will bring blacks into their neighborhoods. These racial fears are played on with considerable success by opponents of open housing in the suburbs. Awareness of these fears also leads advocates of change to deemphasize or ignore the needs of blacks in their efforts to mobilize the support of lower-income whites in suburbia.

Those lower-income suburbanites who are dissatisfied with existing housing conditions commonly lack influence in most suburban political arenas. In the suburbs as elsewhere, individuals with modest incomes tend to be less interested and involved in politics than those with higher incomes. They tend to be poorly informed, to fail to perceive their stake in local public policies, and to lack the time, resources, skills, and organizational capabilities to promote and defend their interests effectively. Further limiting the influence of lower-income groups is the small scale of most suburbs, which makes it difficult for minority interests to overcome their political weaknesses by the strength of numbers, as is possible in larger jurisdictions.

Because they often possess a strong organizational base, public employees have been more active on housing issues than other lower-income suburbanites. Local public employees played an important part in the campaigns for zoning reform in Fairfax and Montgomery Counties. Teachers, firemen, and other local civil servants were mobilized in Greenwich, Connecticut, during the mid-1960s to support rezoning so that they could realize the "dream of owning a moderately priced house in their hometown."[42] Such efforts have been limited, however. Socioeconomic differentiation and the small scale of most suburbs means that many local employees do not live in the same jurisdiction in which they work. As a result, local employees and other less affluent residents of the suburbs have neither flocked to the banners of the open-housing movement nor otherwise or-

[42] See William Borders, "New Faces in Greenwich," *The New York Times*, March 7, 1967. The campaign was organized by Lewis S. Rosensteil, a large landowner, who offered to sell half-acre plots to local employees for under $1000 if Greenwich would rezone his holdings to permit more intensive development. Nothing came of the effort.

ganized effectively to press for changes in local housing policies in most of suburbia.

Black residents of the suburbs also have provided little support for the open-housing movement at the grass roots. Since many blacks in the suburbs have relatively modest incomes, the same factors which limit the involvement of lower-income whites in local politics restrict black participation. Further constraining the political capabilities of suburban blacks on the housing issue is their concentration in a handful of jurisdictions and their almost complete exclusion from the more exclusionary suburbs. In addition, blacks who have made the move to attractive suburban areas often are as hostile to open-housing policies as whites. Frequently with good reason, middle-class blacks fear that their neighborhoods will be the prime targets for subsidized housing and the resettlement of lower-income blacks should suburban housing barriers be lowered. Opposition from homeowners caused local officials in North Hempstead on Long Island to drop plans for the construction of single-family public-housing units in a black neighborhood. In Manhasset, also on Long Island, middle-class blacks organized as the Great Neck Civic Association fought the location of a $10-million public-housing project adjacent to their homes, contending that it would concentrate minority housing.

Among the remaining groups in suburbia, most of the support for open housing comes from backers of liberal causes at the upper end of the income and education scales. Upper-income suburbanites troubled by the socioeconomic separation of the metropolis provide most of the backing for the efforts of fair-housing organizations, chapters of the League of Women Voters, affiliates of the American Jewish Committee, and other groups promoting open housing at the grass roots in suburbia. They also constitute most of the audience for educational efforts in the suburbs. Of the "up to 2000 people" who attended suburban meetings of the Regional Plan Association dealing with housing issues in the New York area, most according to the planning association were "people with college educations and substantial incomes."[43]

While building support among upper-income suburbanites is hardly a waste of time—witness the fierce opposition in New Fairfield to Suburban Action's plan for Candlewood Lake—affluent liberals in the suburbs do not provide a sufficient constituency base for open-housing action in most communities. In the typical metropolitan area, such individuals constitute a significant proportion of the population in only a handful of suburbs. Where concerned suburbanites are concentrated, local governments often are more willing to seek to diversify their populations than is generally the case. Even when successful, however, the impact of these efforts is inherently limited by the small number of jurisdictions involved. Also restricting the amount of lower-cost housing that is feasible within these suburbs is local concern about higher taxes, fears of possible change in com-

[43] C. McKim Norton, Regional Plan Association, see National Urban Coalition, Clearinghouse on Exclusionary Land Use Policies, "Report: Sixth Conference on Exclusionary Land Use Policies" (New York, April 15, 1971), p. 6.

munity character, and the high price of land in wealthier suburban areas. Whatever housing results often falls short of the needs of local residents, to say nothing of a particular suburb's "fair share" of the housing needs in the metropolis as a whole. It is probably true that "communities with the attitude of Summit are in a ratio of one to several hundred," as NCDH noted in praising the New Jersey suburb for its plans to provide low-cost housing for local blacks.[44] But the ninety units planned for Summit would accommodate only less than a quarter of the families with housing problems in the affluent suburb. And four years after the plan was announced, only forty of the units had been constructed, with progress on the remainder stalled by siting controversies.

[44] National Committee Against Discriminations in Housing, *Jobs and Housing: An Interim Report* (New York, March 1970), p. 63.

Index

257, 261, 262, 263, 264, 266,
268-72
Munich agreement, 238
Municipal Assistance Corporation (MAC),
411, 412, 415
Murrow, Edward, R., 330
Muskie, Edmund, 68, 137, 159, 168
Mutual Balanced Force Reduction, 227

Nader, Ralph, 123
Nathan, Richard P., 385-410
National Aeronautics and Space Adminis-
tration (NASA), 183, 184
National Association for the Advancement
of Colored People, 448, 455, 456
Legal Defense and Education Fund, 455
National Committee Against Discrimination
in Housing, 448, 455, 456, 457, 458,
465
National Court of Appeals, 205
National Emergencies Act (1976), 127,
130, 137, 140
National Housing and Economic Develop-
ment-Law Project, 455
National Job-Linked Housing Center, 455
National Opinion Research Center, 379
National Security Agency, 66
National Security Council (NSC), 102,
104-5, 108-9, 113, 121, 252, 257,
316, 326, 327, 330
National Urban Coalition, 455
Nebraska Press Case, 216
Nelson, Gaylord, 159
Nenni, Pietro, 325, 328, 332, 334
Neustadt, Richard E., 101-10, 112-14,
248
New Deal, 31, 35, 76, 81, 87, 122,
246
inversion of, 361-84
New Frontier, 76
Newhouse, John, 260, 261
Nie, Norman, 236
Niebuhr, Reinhold, 23, 26
Nigeria, 306, 307

Nike-Hercules missile, 282
New York City (N.Y.), 405, 452, 459
fiscal crisis of, 411-26
Nixon, Richard Milhouse, 113, 115-17,
120, 122, 125-27
administration of, 130, 140, 141,
165, 175, 189, 232, 239, 241,
248, 249, 254-56, 258-60, 264,
308, 335, 339, 340, 348, 351,
354
as chief executive, 96, 98, 99,
103-8, 113, 115-17, 120,
122, 125-28
as congressman, 57
as lawyer, 57
personality and character of, 51-66,
69-75
as Vice President, 57-58
Nixon Doctrine, 316, 319
North Atlantic Treaty Organization
(NATO), 247, 277-81, 283, 285,
286, 288, 298-99, 302, 322, 328,
330, 335
Nuclear Planning Group (NATO), 286
Nuclear Test Ban Treaty, 89
Nuclear weapons, 253, 314
tactical, 277-89

Office of Drug Abuse Policy, 108
Office of Economic Opportunity,
(OEO) 117
Office of Management and Budget
(OMB), 91, 102, 103, 106, 109,
117-18, 121, 128, 135, 136, 178,
180
Office of Science and Technology
(OST), 104
Office of Science and Technology Policy
(OSTP), 104
Office of Telecommunications Policy
(OTCP), 108
Office of Western European Affairs, 330